Africa and the Future of International Criminal Justice

"This is a vital, important contribution to the literature on international criminal justice in Africa. Although the subject is often reduced to simplistic assessments in some public discourse, this collection of essays demonstrates the complexity both of the landscape and of the responses to impunity on the continent. In some sense, Africa is the primordial laboratory for international criminal justice. To understand it, this book is essential reading."
William Schabas, Professor of international law, Middlesex University, Professor of international criminal law and human rights, Leiden University, Emeritus Professor of human rights, National University of Ireland Galway

"In this book, Professor Nmehielle, a leading voice on Africa and international criminal justice, has edited one of the most insightful contributions to the contentious subject of Africa and international criminal justice. The book leaves nothing to imagination, and lays bare the heated debates of Africa's current entanglement with international criminal tribunals. It is a work that will become a reference point for people thinking and working on the subject."
Makau Mutua, Dean, SUNY Distinguished Professor, Floyd H. & Hilda L. Hurst Faculty Scholar, SUNY Buffalo Law School, State University of New York

"Recent discussions on international criminal law and justice in Africa have tended to focus on narrow contentious aspects of the relationship between Africa and the International Criminal Court. The essays presented in this volume offer a timely reminder of the wider range of issues implicated in this debate and the broader compass through which this subject must be examined. While these contributions specifically interrogate issues central to a proper understanding of international criminal justice in Africa today, the relevance of these discussions goes beyond the African continent. In this book Professor Nmehielle has assembled a fine collection of thoughtful and critical contributions which should be of interest to scholars, practitioners and policy-makers in Africa and elsewhere, and to those with more than a passing interest in international criminal justice."
Tiyanjana Maluwa, H. Laddie Montague Chair in Law, Penn State Dickinson School of Law, Director, School of International Affairs, Pennsylvania State University

"In recent years, the indictment of African leaders by the International Criminal Court (ICC) has ignited considerable debates in Africa and beyond, raising profound questions about the place of new international norms on state behavior. Is the ICC a new tool of imperialists to humiliate and subjugate Africa or is it a mechanism that seeks to punish and deter egregious human rights violations that prevail across the continent? Are the new instruments of international legality too blunt or judicious in addressing the magnitude of the problem? This book seeks comprehensive answers to these questions through wide-ranging analytical and policy prisms. Vincent Nmehielle has assembled competent scholars and practitioners to lend insights into one of the most contentious issues in contemporary international law and politics. The fifteen chapters are a wealth of knowledge on the causes of ICC intervention, African and global perspectives on international criminal justice, and ways of ending the protracted stalemate about the ICC's role in Africa. This book makes a significant contribution to debates that are merely in their formative stages."
Gilbert Khadiagala, The Jan Smuts Professor and Head of Department of International Relations, University of the Witwatersrand, Johannesburg

"The future disposition of the international criminal law order will ironically be determined by how Africa embraces its dual role as a subject and object of international criminal justice. Professor Nmehielle's excellent collection of essays examine this tenuous dichotomy and locates the imperial and counter-imperial dimensions of international criminal justice without surrendering the vital accommodative elasticity required of African states, regional organizations and civil society to combat impunity and fortify the rule of law and democracy. This cutting-edge book is essential reading for students, scholars and policy-makers interested in the internationalization of justice."
Jeremy I. Levitt, JD, Ph.D., Associate Dean for International Programs, Distinguished Professor of International Law and Director, Center for International Law and Justice, Florida A&M University College of Law

Africa and the Future of International Criminal Justice

Vincent O. Nmehielle (Ed.)

With my profound respect to
a veteran of
international law

eleven
international publishing

Published, sold and distributed by Eleven International Publishing
P.O. Box 85576
2508 CG The Hague
The Netherlands
Tel.: +31 70 33 070 33
Fax: +31 70 33 070 30
e-mail: sales@budh.nl
www.elevenpub.com

Sold and distributed in USA and Canada
International Specialized Book Services
920 NE 58th Avenue, Suite 300
Portland, OR 97213-3786, USA
Tel: 1-800-944-6190 (toll-free)
Fax: +1 503 280-8832
orders@isbs.com
www.isbs.com

Eleven International Publishing is an imprint of Boom uitgevers Den Haag.

ISBN 978-94-90947-62-0

Printed in The Netherlands

To all victims of mass atrocities in Africa who continue to yearn for true justice, peace and good governance from their leaders

Table of Contents

Foreword

Among mechanisms of international criminal justice, the International Criminal Court (ICC) is arguably the most controversial of any of the building blocks of contemporary architecture of global governance. Founded in terms of the Rome Statute in 2002, ten years on seems a naturally propitious moment to take stock of the place and work of the ICC in fostering international criminal justice and accountability through the critical eyes of academics. Heralding the compilation of this book on Africa and the Future of International Criminal Justice was an international conference the University of the Witwatersrand School of Law was honored to host in 2010. Scholars interested in human rights and humanitarian law, and the evolving international criminal law and justice, took critical reflections at this newest addition to the panoply of the comity of nation's instruments of global governance. Their seminal insights are published in this book, thus, contributing to wider discourse among scholars far and wide on an institution whose long-term significance can only be matched by controversies surrounding its workings. And yet to an ordinary citizen who, for decades, has lived in the shadow of capricious atrocities perpetrated by rulers and left with limited or no recourse at all to domestic courts of justice for redress, the ICC must be god-sent and long overdue.

This book will be useful to students, scholars, policymakers and practitioners of international law, human rights and humanitarian law. It will in no small measure become handy to international relations practitioners within governments and to Non-Governmental Organizations plying their trade in these areas. It enables readers to understand the historical context of the founding of the ICC and examines its operations, criticisms that have been leveled against this institution and counters some of the common-place claims against the ICC.

The book sets the scene by discussing the ICC's kindred international humanitarian tribunals such as the International Criminal Tribunal for Rwanda (ICTR) and the Special Court for Sierra Leone (SCSL). This is a useful bench-marking effort that helps to place the ICC in a broader perspective. Readers will find the discourse on the present stand-off between the African Union (AU) and the ICC especially riveting given that many of the signatories and parties to the Rome Statute are member states of the AU. Clearly disconcerting for Africa is the fact that some of the countries who refer cases to the ICC through the UN Security Council have placed themselves beyond the Court's jurisdiction. The case in point is that of the USA which not only declined to subscribe the Statute of Rome but has signed scores of bilateral treaties with other nations exempting possible US suspects who may find themselves in those countries from being handed over to the ICC. The concern also is that the ICC is not accountable to regional bodies, nor does it take their sensitivities into consideration in the pursuit of its work. While these realities hold far-reaching international implications in terms of the Court's perceived impartiality and legitimacy as an organ that treats atrocity crimes equally, there can be little doubt of its welcome impact in humanizing the uses of political power.

Governments in whose jurisdictions alleged atrocity crimes have been committed will find wise counsel in the book. The contributors to this volume explore and draw useful attention to the ample scope within the provisions of Statute of Rome for crimes of this nature being tried within the domestic courts. Thus, for those who charge that the ICC trumps sovereignty, the ball is in the court of affected countries to demonstrate that they can act against impunity and atrocities.

The broad scope of issues presented in the book makes it a compelling read for many interested in the emerging field of international criminal justice, human rights, humanitarian law and the developing international law. I positively recommend the book and I am certain many will find it useful in the search for answers to many questions of research interest.

Prof. Nqosa L Mahao
Dean, Faculty of Commerce, Law and Management
University of the Witwatersrand University, Johannesburg, South Africa.

Abbreviations

ACC	African Criminal Court
ACHPR	African Charter of Human and Peoples' Rights
ACJHR	African Court of Justice and Human Rights
AfCHPR	African Union Charter of Human and People's Right
AFRC	Armed Forces Revolutionary Council
ANC	African National Congress
APC	All People's Congress
AU	African Union
AUHLIP	African Union High Level Implementation Panel
AUHPD	African Union High Level Panel for Darfur
AUPD	African Union High-Level Panel on Darfur
AUPD	African Union Panel on Darfur
BiH	Bosnia Herzegovina
CAR	Central African Republic
CDF	Civil Defence Force
CICC	Coalition for the International Criminal Court
CNDP	National Congress for the Defence of the People
CPA	Comprehensive Peace Agreement
DRC	Democratic Republic of the Congo
DOMAC	Domestic Criminal Procedures In Mas Atrocities Cases
ECCC	Extraordinary Chambers in the Courts of Cambodia
ECOMOG	Economic Community of West African States Monitoring Group
ECOWAS	Economic Community of West African States
EDA	Excess Defense Article
EDA	Excess Defense Articles
EU	European Union
FARDC	Armed Forces of the Democratic Republic of Congo
FDLR	Democratic Liberation Forces of Rwanda
FDLR	Forces démocratiques de libération du Rwanda
FLN	National Liberation Front
FMF	Foreign Military Financing

GoS	Government of Sudan
HRW	Human Rights Watch
ICC	International Criminal Court
ICCPR	International Covenant on Civil and Political Rights
ICJ	International Court of Justice
ICTR	International Criminal Tribunal for Rwanda
ICTY	International Criminal Tribunal for Yugoslavia
ILC	International Law Commission
ILR	International Law Reports
IMET	International Military Education and Training
IMT	International Military Tribunal
LRA	Lord's Resistance Army
MLC	Mouvement de Libération du Congo Central African Republic
MONUC	Supported by the United Nations Organization Mission in the
MONUSCO	United Nations Organization Stabilization Mission in the DRC
NATO	North Atlantic Treaty Organization
NFPL	National Patriotic Front of Liberia
NPRC	National Provisional Ruling Council
NRA/M	National Resistance Army/Movement
OAU	Organization of African Unity
OCHA	Office of the Coordinator of Humanitarian Affairs
OPCW	Organization for the Prohibition of Chemical Weapons
OTP	Office of The Prosecutor
PALU	Pan African Lawyers Union
PCIJ	Permanent Court of International Justice
RDF	Rwandese Defence Forces
RPA	Rwandese Patriotic Army
RPF	Rwanda Patriotic Front
RUFP	Revolution United Front Party
SADC	Southern Africa Development Community
SCSL	Special Court for Sierra Leone
SLA	Sudan Liberation Army
SLPP	Sierra Leone People's Party
SLTRC	Sierra Leone Truth and Reconciliation Commission
SPLM/A	Sudan People's Liberation Movement/Army

TRC	Truth and Reconciliation Commission
UDHR	Universal Declaration of Human Rights
UHRC	Ugandan Human Rights Commission
UNGA	United Nations General Assembly
UNSC	United Nations Security Council
UPDF	United People's Defence Force
VRWG	Victims' Rights Working Group
WVS	Witness and Victims Section

Contributors

Jessie Chella is a PhD Candidate with Bond University in Australia. She was recently admitted to the International Criminal Court's List of Assistants to Counsel for Defense and Victims. She has interned with the International Criminal Tribunal for the Former Yugoslavia in The Netherlands, and her work experience also includes various legal and administrative roles undertaken in Australia and Zimbabwe. She received a LLM (Research), PostGrad Dip Leg Prac and LLB from Bond University.

David Chuter worked for more than thirty years in two governments, international organizations and universities think-tanks, mainly on international security questions. His last post was as Special Adviser to the Policy Director of the French Ministry of Defense. He took early retirement at the end of 2008, and is now an independent author, consultant, lecturer and translator based in Paris. During his official career he was responsible for a number of international policy and operational issues, including, from 1997-2001, war crimes in the Balkans and elsewhere. He is the author of four books, of which the most recent are *War Crimes* (2003), and *Governing and Managing the Defense Sector* (2011). He is currently Senior Research Fellow, Centre for Security Sector Management, Cranfield University, UK, and Lecturer, *Fondation nationale des Sciences politiques,* Paris.

Janine N. Clark is a lecturer in the Politics Department at the University of Sheffield, UK. She also taught at the Queen's University of Belfast and at the University of York, and has held two Postdoctoral Fellowships in the International Politics Department at Aberystwyth University. Her research interests include transitional justice and the relationship between criminal trials and inter-ethnic reconciliation; war crimes; ethnic conflict and post-conflict societies, particularly in the former Yugoslavia and the African Great Lakes. Recent work includes: 'Fieldwork and its Ethical Challenges: Reflections from Research in Bosnia', *Human Rights Quarterly* (forthcoming, August 2012); 'The ICTY and Reconciliation in Croatia: A Case Study of Vukovar', *Journal of International Criminal Justice* (forthcoming, July 2012); 'Reflections on Trust and Reconciliation: A Case-Study of a Central Bosnian Village', *International Journal of Human Rights,* 16:2 (January 2012), pp. 239-256; and 'Youth Violence in South Africa: The Case for a Restorative Justice Response', *Contemporary Justice Review*, 15:1 (March 2012), pp. 77-95.

Eric Colvin is Professor of Law at the University of the South Pacific, Fiji. Professor Colvin was educated in England and Canada: BA (Hons) (Oxford), MA (Reading),

LLM (Toronto), PhD (Cambridge). He taught at several universities in Scotland and Canada before moving to Bond University in Australia, where he was Dean (1995-2000). He has written on issues in jurisprudence and Canadian constitutional law as well as the criminal law of Canada, Australia and the South Pacific Island Nations. His publications have often been cited by the Supreme Court of Canada.

Ntombizozuko Dyani (Zozo) is a senior lecturer at the School of Law of the University of the Witwatersrand, South Africa. She holds both LL.B and LL.M degrees from the University of the Western Cape in South Africa. She has recently submitted her thesis for SJD in international law entitled 'Sexual violence during armed conflict in Africa and the African Union's right to humanitarian intervention' at the University of Wisconsin-Madison. She was recently a visiting scholar at the Global Legal Studies Center, the University of Wisconsin-Madison Law School from 1 July-31 December 2011, and was also a recipient of the Carnegie Sandwich Fellowship Grant to work towards finalising her SJD thesis in 2011. She is a former intern (Legal Researcher) in the Chambers Section at the United Nations International Criminal Tribunal for Rwanda (ITCR) clerked for the former Chief Justice Ngcobo of the Constitutional Court of South Africa. Her research interests are in international law, specifically humanitarian law, human rights law, criminal law as well as the South African Bill of Rights particularly rights of women and children. She publishes in these areas in both local and international peer reviewed journals. She currently lectures international human rights law, public international law, and constitutional law to both undergraduate and graduate students.

Sigall Horovitz is currently completing a PhD in Law (specializing in Transitional Justice) at the Hebrew University of Jerusalem. She also heads the Transitional Justice Project of the Hebrew University's Minerva Center for Human Rights. Sigall's PhD research is titled 'the Contribution of International Criminal Courts to National Reconciliation in Africa'. It focuses on the effectiveness of the International Criminal Tribunal for Rwanda (ICTR) and the Special Court for Sierra Leone (SCSL). In particular, it assesses whether and how effective these courts were in achieving their goal of promoting national reconciliation in their target countries. Previously, Sigall worked for three years as a legal adviser to the President of the International Criminal Tribunal for Rwanda (ICTR) in Arusha, Tanzania, and served for a year with the Office of the Prosecutor at the Special Court for Sierra Leone. Sigall completed her LLM (with honors) at Columbia University in 2003.

Pacifique Manirakiza is an Associate Professor at the Faculty of Law (Common Law Section), University of Ottawa. Professor Manirakiza joined the Faculty of Law in 2004 where he teaches Canadian criminal law and international criminal law. He has also been a member of, and a faculty advisor to the Editorial Board of the Ottawa Law Review. Before coming to the University of Ottawa, he held positions at the University of Burundi and at Hope University in Kenya. In summer 2011, Prof. Manirakiza was a visiting Professor at Université Martin Luther King and Hope Africa University in Burundi. Manirakiza also participated as legal adviser in Burundi's peace negotiations held in Arusha (Tanzania) between 1998 and 2000. He was a member of a Defense team at the International Criminal Tribunal for Rwanda between 2000 and 2004 where he previously served as a legal intern. In July 2011, he was elected a member of the African Commission on Human and People's Rights for a four-year term. In that capacity, he is the Chairperson of the newly established Working Group on Extractive Industries, Environment and Human Rights Violations.

Caroline Nalule is an advocate of the High Court of Uganda. She holds a Masters Degree in International Human Rights and Humanitarian Law from Lund University and the Raoul Wallenberg Institute for Human Rights and Humanitarian Law. She also holds a Post-Graduate Diploma in Legal Practice from the Law Development Centre, Kampala; and a Bachelor of Laws Degree from Makerere University, Kampala. She has worked as a legal researcher for private legal practitioners as well as in the Court of Appeal of Uganda. She worked as the head of the legal department of an investment and legal consultancy firm before she joined the Uganda Human Rights Commission, where she served in various capacities in the Directorate of Research, Education and Training and was later appointed Director of Complaints, Investigations and Legal Services. Presently, she is the regional coordinator of the Africa Office (based in Accra, Ghana) of the Commonwealth Human Rights Initiative (CHRI), an international, non-partisan, non-governmental organization, mandated to work for the *practical* realization of human rights of the people of the Commonwealth. Her areas of interest and expertise are human rights law and advocacy; social justice, criminal law and transitional justice, good governance, democracy and constitutionalism.

Mba C. Nmaju obtained his undergraduate law degree in Obafemi Awolowo University, Ile-Ife Nigeria. He was called to the Nigerian Bar in 2003. While in private practice in Nigeria, he was inducted as a Chartered Mediator and Conciliator. He obtained his LLM and PhD degrees from Queen Mary University of London. His PhD thesis was titled 'Multiple Forums and the Implementation of International Criminal Law: Issues of Fragmentation and Divergence in The Development of the Law'. It was an inquiry into whether the differences in the enforcement of international criminal justice by states indicate a fractured system; or a form of coherence that is analogous to the system of Public International Law. He has taught at Queen Mary university of London and London SouthBank University. He is currently working as a Legal Advisor/Consultant at Cleveland & Co Solicitors. His major teaching and research interest is in public international law, Africana studies, conflict resolution, international humanitarian law, international criminal law and diplomatic law.

Vincent O. Nmehielle has over 21 years of professional and academic experience. He is currently the Head of the Wits Programme in Law, Justice and Development in Africa at the University of the Witwatersrand (Wits) School of Law, Johannesburg, South Africa where he has taught since February 2002. He is a Barrister and Solicitor of the Supreme Court of Nigeria. Nmehielle held the Bram Fischer Chair in Human Rights Law at Wits Law School from 2002-2004. He was a Professorial Lecturer in Law at the Oxford University and George Washington University Human Rights Program in 2003 and 2004. From 2005-2008 Nmehielle served as the Principal Defender of the United Nations-Backed Special Court for Sierra Leone in Freetown, Sierra Leone. He returned to Wits in June 2008. He holds a Bachelor of Laws degree from the Rivers State University of Science & Technology, Port Harcourt, Nigeria; a Master of Laws degree in International Law from the University of Notre Dame, in the USA; and a Doctor of Juridical Science Degree in International & Comparative Law from the George Washington University in Washington, DC. Nmehielle's professional, academic and research interest is in the theme area of Law, Governance, Justice and Development in Africa.

James Nyawo is a doctoral candidate at the Middlesex University in the UK. His research focuses on the implementation of international criminal justice in Africa, especially the work of the International Criminal Court (ICC) and its exclusive focus on African states. He has extensive experience in working with refugees and internally displaced persons in Africa's conflict and post-conflict zones including Angola, Uganda, Sudan and South Sudan. James is interested in transitional justice, humanitarian policy issues and conflict resolution mechanisms in Africa.

Godwin Odo is a Program Officer with the MacArthur Foundation's Africa Office in Abuja, Nigeria. He is responsible for grantmaking in the human rights and international justice program in Africa. Mr. Odo holds an LL.M in International Human Rights Law from the University of Essex, a Barrister-at-Law degree from the Nigerian Law School, and an undergraduate law degree from the University of Nigeria. He is qualified as a solicitor and advocate of the Supreme Court of Nigeria. His research interests include the African regional human rights system, International justice, globalization, civil society and the right to health.

Rachel Odoi-Musoke is currently a Technical Advisor with the Justice Law and Order Sector (JLOS) in Uganda where she is primarily responsible for managing reforms in land and commercial justice. In addition she worked as Technical Advisor for Transitional Justice during the formation of the JLOS transitional justice programme and the formation of the International Crimes Division and related structures. Ms. Odoi-Musoke is currently coordinating the work of the Justice Law and Order Sector Transitional Justice Working Group and its sub-committees. She is an enrolled Advocate of the Courts of Judicature of Uganda and she holds a Bachelor of Laws (Honours) from Makerere University Kampala, a Diploma in Legal Practice from the Law Development Centre, Kampala Uganda and a Master of Laws from the University of the Witwatersrand. Her areas of specialties are Company law, Human Rights, International law and policy and legislative reform. Ms. Odoi-Musoke previously worked as a Principal Legal Officer in the Uganda Law Reform Commission, in charge of research and law reform and as a Regional Human Rights Officer for the Uganda Human Rights Commission. She has also worked as national coordinator for Greenwatch (U) Ltd environmental rights NGO and practiced as an Advocate in Uganda.

Lutz Oette is counsel at REDRESS where he leads the project for criminal law reform in Sudan, and a lecturer in international human rights law at the School of Oriental and African Studies (SOAS), London. He has worked and published extensively on human rights protection, justice and the role of law in the context of repression, conflict and transition.

Henry J. Richardson III is a Professor of Law at Beasley School of Law, Temple University, Philadelphia, USA where he has been a Faculty member since 1981. He is a distinguished and leading international law scholar with a special interest in Africa. He obtained his A.B. from Antioch College in 1963. Upon graduating from Yale Law School in 1966, Professor Richardson became International Legal Adviser to the government of Malawi shortly after its independence for more than two years, where he advised on inherited treaties and a range of southern African international legal negotiations and questions. Thereafter, he returned to the US to become Faculty Africanist at Law and to earn an LLM at University of California at Los Angeles (1971) with a focus on international law and development in Africa. He was active in several anti-apartheid groups relative to international law. From 1977-1979, he served on the National Security Council Staff in charge of African Policy and United Nations issues in President Carter's administration. Professor Richardson was subsequently a Senior Foreign Policy Adviser to the Congressional Black Caucus and an Attorney in the Office of General Counsel of the Department of Defense. In 2008 Professor Richardson published *The Origins of African American Interests in International Law*. He is a member of the Council on Foreign Relations, a past vice president and honorary vice president of the American Society of International Law, and a founding member of both the National Conference of Black Lawyers and the Project on the Advancement of African-Americans in International Law.

ACKNOWLEDGEMENTS

The road to producing this book has been a very long one. However, it is with profound gratitude that I express my thanks to many organizations and individuals through whose invaluable assistance and support the publication of this volume was made possible. Firstly, I am eternally grateful to our funders who believed in the young Wits Programme in Law, Justice and Development in Africa and on the need for a debate on the theme of this book, and generously funded the international conference on which this book is based – the Open Society Foundation for South Africa (OFSA), particularly, the Executive Director, Dr. Zohra Dawood and her former Programme Director for Human Rights and Governance, Mr. Glen Mpani; the Open Society Initiative for Southern Africa (OSISA) – with special thanks to the Law Programme Manager, Ms. Louise Olivier and her colleagues; and the MacArthur Foundation – with particular thanks to Mary Page, Director, Human Rights and International Justice Programme, Ms. Brandee Buttler, former Programme Officer, Human Rights and International Justice and Godwin Odo, Esq., Programme Officer in the MacArthur Africa office; and finally, the University of the Witwatersrand, Johannesburg and the School of Law of the University for their support in not just providing some seed funds through SPARC but in also providing the venue for the conference and other logistical support.

Secondly, I most sincerely thank the authors who contributed to this volume for not only vigorously participating in the conference but also for taking time to write their chapters, to revise and update them in order to incorporate current events, taking into account the time between the conference and the finalization of the book as required by the peer review process. Their resolve to intellectually engage in the debate on Africa and international criminal justice enriches this volume. Also I would like to specially mention and profusely thank some African senior citizens who gave up their time and busy schedules to attend the conference and played some key roles at the conference: His Excellency, Mr. Adama Dieng, Assistant Secretary-General of the United Nations and Registrar of the International Criminal Tribunal for Rwanda; Honourable Justice Sandile Ngcobo, former Chief Justice of the Republic of South Africa; Honourable Justice Lovemore G. Munlo, Chief Justice of the Republic of Malawi; Honourable J.T. Radebe, MP, Honourable Minster of Justice & Constitutional Development of the Republic of South Africa, represented by the Honourable Deputy Minister, Mr. Andries Nel, MP; Honourable Judge Daniel Nsereko, Judge of the Special Tribunal for Lebanon and former Presiding Judge of the Appeals Chamber of the International Criminal Court; Mrs. Fatou Bensouda, Prosecutor Elect and Deputy Prosecutor of the International Criminal Court; Professor Shadrack

Gutto, Professor of African Renaissance Studies, University of South Africa, Pretoria and former Director of the Centre for African Renaissance Studies; and a Diaspora African and representative of the Africa Interest Group of the American Society of International Law, Professor Jeanne M. Woods, Henry F. Bonura, Jr. Distinguished Professor of Law, Loyola University College of Law, New Orleans, Louisiana, USA. Similarly, I am grateful to the other numerous participants in the conference that space will not allow me to mention in this acknowledgement for their strong participation and very useful insights on the various themes covered at the conference.

Thirdly, I am forever indebted to our panel of eminent peer reviewers who gave of their valuable time to critique and proffer useful comments and feedback to the authors on their various contributions. Without these scholars and professionals, this volume would not be what it is. In this regard, my profound thanks go to Dr. Babafemi Akinrinade, Assistant Professor, Fairhaven College of Interdisciplinary Studies, Western Washington University, Bellingham, Washington State, USA; Professor Michelo Hansungule, Professor of Human Rights Law, Center for Human Rights, University of Pretoria, South Africa; Charles Jalloh, Assistant Professor of Law, University of Pittsburgh School of Law, Pennsylvania, USA; Dr. Kolawole Olaniyan, Legal Advisor, Amnesty International, International Secretariat, London, United Kingdom; Dr. Ben Simon Okolo, Post-Doctoral Fellow, United Nations University, Tokyo, Japan; Professor Oladejo J. Olowu, Research Professor of Law, Faculty of Law, Northwest University, Mafikeng Campus, South Africa; Enyinna Nwauche, Associate Professor of Law, Faculty of Law, Rivers State University of Science & Technology, Port Harcourt, Nigeria and Director, Centre for African Legal Studies, Port Harcourt, Nigeria; and Professor Ron Slye, Professor of Law, Seattle University School of Law, Seattle, Washington, USA and Commissioner in the Kenyan Truth and Reconciliation Commission, Nairobi, Kenya.

Fourthly, I will like to offer my special and undiluted thanks to my academic colleagues at the Wits Programme in Law, Justice and Development in Africa in the School of Law for their immense support before, during and after the conference and for holding the fort during my unplanned but forced absence: Sanele Sibanda, Mtendeweka Mhango, Ms. Ntombizozuko Dyani, and Professor Jonathan E. Klaaren – the current Dean and Head of Wits School of Law. I will also like to thank the administrative support staff in the School of Law that worked tirelessly to make the conference a success – Mrs. Asma Ooni, Mrs. Marion Flynn and Mrs Moshina Cassim. Many thanks to the following doctoral students at Wits – John-Mark Iyi, Kingsley Orievulu, Paradzai Garufu, and a master's student Ms. Yolanda Chekera for their editorial assistance during the process of producing this volume. They worked tirelessly on cite-checking, ensuring proper referencing, re-reading and proof-reading revised submissions.

Fifthly, I am grateful to the publisher, Ms. Selma Hoedt of Eleven International Publishing for agreeing to publish this volume. I am hoping that this is the beginning of a mutually beneficial academic publication relationship with Africa. Let me also use this opportunity to thank the Oxford University Press, the United Kingdom for the permission it granted to republish the contribution *Peace, Justice and the International Criminal Court: Limitations and Possibilities* by Janine Clark, which though was presented at the conference, was thereafter published in the Journal of International Criminal Justice, Vol. 9, No 3 (July 2011), pp. 521-545.

Finally, I will not forget my wife and eternal mate, Nkechi Obisie-Nmehielle and our beloved five children for believing in me and standing by me during one of the most difficult periods of my personal and professional life at the University of the Witwatersrand.

Above all, my everlasting thanks go to the Lord God Almighty, the maker of heaven and earth and who rules and reigns in the affairs of men and women.

Vincent O. Nmehielle
Johannesburg, February 2012

1 Introduction

Africa and International Criminal Justice: Issues and Contentions

Vincent O. Nmehielle

1.1 Africa-Related International Criminal Justice Activities

Within the last twenty years Africa has witnessed a series of activities in the domain of international criminal justice arising from brutal conflicts in African states. Some of these states include Rwanda,[1] Sierra Leone,[2] Liberia,[3] Uganda,[4] the Sudan,[5] the Democratic

---

1 1994 witnessed a brutal war in Rwanda that unleashed untold genocide on mainly the Tutsi population of Rwanda which led to the death of about 800,000 people. The aftermath of the genocide was the International Criminal Tribunal for Rwanda (ICTR) that was specifically set up to bring about some accountability for the heinous international crimes. For further detaifls on the Rwandan genocide, see Rwanda: The Preventable Genocide, Report of an International Panel of Eminent Personalities to Investigate the 1994 Genocide in Rwanda and the Surrounding Events, established by the Secretary-General of the Organization of African Unity in 1998 (Report on file with this author). The Report is also available at <www.africa-union.org/official_documents/reports/report_rowanda_genocide.pdf> (last accessed December 29, 2011).

2 Sierra Leone was engulfed by a decade-long and brutal war that lasted from 1991 to 2002. The effects of the war are still felt today as the country makes strides to recover from the devastating war that represented one of the worst forms of egregious violations of human rights and international humanitarian law as well the commission of atrocity crimes. Again, an international tribunal, the Special Court for Sierra Leone (SCSL) was established as an accountability mechanism for atrocities committed during the war. See generally, Adekeye Adebajo, Building Peace In West Africa, Liberia, Sierra Leone and Guinea-Bissau (2002) and Thelma Ekiyor, *Reflecting on the Sierra Leone Truth and Reconciliation Commission: A Peacebuilding Perspective, in* Peace Versus Justice: The Dilemma of Transitional Justice in Africa 153-170 (Chandra Lekha Siriam & Suresh Pillay eds., 2009).

3 Liberia descended into civil war from 1989 to 2003. The war was also very brutal and led to untold loss of lives of innocent victims of the war that represented struggles between "big men." On the Liberian conflict, see generally, Jeremy Levitt, The Evolution of Deadly Conflict in Liberia: From 'Paternaltarianism' To State Collapse (2005).

4 Uganda's Idi Amin was notorious for brutal human rights violations. His fall led to a struggle that brought President Yoweri Museveni to power through a rebellious resistance in 1986. Yet Uganda continues to face brutal internal conflicts as represented by the Lord's Resistance Army (LRA) led by Joseph Kony whose deadly activities affect countries like Central African Republic and South Sudan. Issues arising from this brutal Ugandan conflict are before the International Criminal Court (ICC).

5 South Sudan fought a long historical war of liberation against Khartoum and only recently became Africa's and the world's newest independent nation. The Darfur conflict in the Sudan continues to rage and represents another brutal African war that has consumed innocent victims in their thousands in what various organizations have labeled as genocide. See Vincent O. Nmehielle, *Preventing and Responding to Atrocity Crimes in Africa: Interrogating the African Response in Darfur*, 1 African Journal of Legal Studies 209-224 (2011). Yet again, issues from Darfur are before the ICC.

Republic of Congo (DRC),[6] Central African Republic,[7] Kenya,[8] and most recently Ivory Coast[9] and Libya.[10] These activities were exemplified by the establishment of the United Nations International Criminal Tribunal for Rwanda (ICTR) in 1994[11] to try the alleged perpetrators of the 1994 Rwanda genocide; the United Nations-Backed Special Court for Sierra Leone (SCSL) in 2002[12] to try those that "bear the greatest responsibility"[13] for the atrocities that were committed in Sierra Leone's decade-long civil war; the proposed and long-awaited trial in Senegal, under a special African Union-backed regime, of Hissene Habre, the former President of Chad[14] for crimes against humanity committed during his reign as president of Chad; the botched debate about a Special Court or Tribunal for Kenya to deal with the aftermath of Kenya's 2007/2008 brutal free-for-all post-election violence, and the various cases before the International Criminal Court (ICC) originating from Africa.

Within the realm of the politics of international criminal accountability, the indictment of Charles Taylor in 2003, the then Head of State of Liberia, for atrocities allegedly committed during the Sierra Leone conflict drew a lot of sentiments and raised serious concerns for

6 The history of the DRC is one of the pains of war. From the assassination of its first Prime Minister Patrice Lumumba, the fall of its brutal dictator, Mobutu Seseseko, to the coming of the Kabilas, it has been a tale of human misery. The death of Mobutu saw a free-for-all war that was fuelled by greed for natural resources which subjugated innocent civilians, mainly women and children, to untold violations and abuses resulting in an ICC case and investigations. For more on the DRC see generally, GERARD PRUNIER, AFRICA'S WORLD WAR: CONGO, RWANDAN GENOCIDE, AND THE MAKING OF A CONTINENTAL CATASTROPHE (2008) and Mika Vehnämäki, *Diamonds and War Lords: The Geography of War in the Democratic Republic of Congo and Sierra Leone*, 11(1) NORDIC JOURNAL OF AFRICAN STUDIES 48-74 (2002).

7 The Central African Republic was also not spared of conflicts that were complicated by the involvement of elements from the DRC as well as Uganda's LRA. Though Jean Pierre Bemba is from the DRC he is currently facing charges at the ICC for crimes allegedly committed in Central African Republic.

8 Kenya experienced its most deadly episode of violent conflict since independence during the electoral disturbances of 2007/2008 in which innocent citizens were slaughtered by supporters of different political camps that contested the presidential election of 2007. Flowing from that conflict, the ICC indicted six high-ranking officials, three each from the two camps in what became the case against the "Kenya Six" or the "Ocampo Six".

9 The latest in Ivory Coast's series of conflicts was that of 2010/2011 after the presidential election run-off which incumbent President Laurent Gbagbo lost but refused to hand over power to Alassane Quatara. The renewed conflict involved mass atrocities which have now led to the indictment of former president Gbagbo by the ICC.

10 Libya's war is the most recent African conflict that began on the heels of the "Arab Spring" which started in Tunisia in early 2011. The conflict led to a brutal war that took the life of Libya's former leader, Muammar Gaddafi and resulted in the referral of the conflict situation by the United Nations Security Council to the ICC.

11 ICTR was established by the United Nations Security Council (UNSC) under Resolution 955 of 1994 to prosecute the perpetrators of the Rwandan genocide of 1994.

12 The then President of Sierra Leone, Tejan Kabbah wrote a letter to the United Nations requesting it to establish the SCSL to prosecute the rebel group – the Revolutionary United Front that he believed was responsible for the atrocities in Sierra Leone during its deadly conflict. See Letter from Tejan Kabbah, President of Sierra Leone, to Kofi Annan, UN Secretary-General (12 June 2000), U.N. Doc. S/2000/786, August 10 , 2000.

13 See Art. 1 of the Statute of the Special Court of Sierra Leone.

14 See Decision on the Hissene Habre Case and the African Union, Assembly/AU/Dec.103 (VI) of January 2006, which established a Committee of Eminent African Jurists to study the situation regarding the case and make recommendations to the AU. See also AU Decision of July 2006, Assembly/AU/Dec.127 (VII) that mandated Senegal to put processes in place and try Hissene Habre on behalf of the African Union.

regional peace and stability in West Africa in general and Liberia in particular. The Taylor's indictment was the first time a sitting African Head of State was charged and being put through an international criminal justice and accountability process. The timing for unsealing the Taylor indictment by the SCSL Prosecutor was criticized as insensitive to the Liberian peace process that was being negotiated in Accra, Ghana within the period.[15] The subsequent surrender of former president Taylor three years later by Nigeria, his country of negotiated voluntary exile after the peace negotiations in Accra, and his subsequent arrest and transfer to the Special Court for Sierra Leone for trial added to the apprehension of a breakdown in African relations and solidarity and perceived threat to regional peace and security. Former president Taylor's eventual transfer to The Hague, the Netherlands for trial rather than in Freetown, Sierra Leone further divided opinions as to whether there was another agenda other than ensuring justice for the victims of the alleged war crimes and crimes against humanity said to have been committed by Mr Taylor and his lieutenants.

Most, if not all rule of law-minded individuals, scholars, practitioners and human rights activists around the word would agree that the coming into force ten years ago in 2002 of the Rome Statute that established the ICC was the height of the creation of an international criminal justice mechanism of global character and reach. Despite the global significance of the creation of the ICC, there is an African peculiarity to it. One aspect of this African peculiarity of the birth of the ICC is the overwhelming support that African states gave to the creation of the ICC at a time when it was very clear that the incessant conflicts and grievous violations of human rights in many African states needed to be dealt with in a more accountable manner. Another aspect of the African peculiarity of the birth of ICC is the enthusiasm displayed by African states in ratifying the Rome Statue of the ICC in that Africa stands as the regional block with the most ratification of the Rome Statute.[16] More importantly, the African peculiarity of the ICC is emphasized by the fact that all the present cases in the ICC for which indictments have been issued have solely African accused persons.[17] It is no secret that this situation has fuelled the perception among many

15 See Abdul R. Lamin, *Charles Taylor, the Special Court and International Politics, in* PEACE VERSUS JUSTICE: THE DILEMMA OF TRANSITIONAL JUSTICE IN AFRICA, *supra* note 2, 248 at 256.

16 As of October 2011, 33 African States had joined the Rome Statute Regime. Cape Verde is the most recent to join on 11 October 2011.

17 These are fourteen cases from seven "situations" in the following African countries: ***Uganda*** *(The Prosecutor v. Joseph Kony, Vincent Otti, Okot Odhiambo and Dominic Ongwen)*; the ***DRC*** (*The Prosecutor v. Thomas Lubanga Dyilo*; *The Prosecutor v. Bosco Ntaganda*; *The Prosecutor v. Germain Katanga and Mathieu Ngudjolo Chui*; and *The Prosecutor v. Callixte Mbarushimana*); ***Darfur, Sudan*** (*The Prosecutor v. Ahmad Muhammad Harun ("Ahmad Harun") and Ali Muhammad Ali Abd-Al-Rahman ("Ali Kushayb")*; *The Prosecutor v. Omar Hassan Ahmad Al Bashir*; *The Prosecutor v. Bahar Idriss Abu Garda*; and *The Prosecutor v. Abdallah Banda Abakaer Nourain and Saleh Mohammed Jerbo Jamus*); ***Central African Republic*** (*The Prosecutor v. Jean-Pierre Bemba Gombo*); ***Kenya*** (*The Prosecutor v. William Samoei Ruto, Henry Kiprono Kosgey and Joshua Arap Sang* and *The Prosecutor v. Francis Kirimi Muthaura, Uhuru Muigai Kenyatta and Mohammed Hussein Ali*); *Libya* (The Prosecutor v. *Muammar Mohammed Abu Minyar Gaddafi, Saif Al-Islam Gaddafi and Abdullah Al-Senussi*); and ***Côte d'Ivoire*** (*The Prosecutor v. Laurent Gbagbo)* See ICC, *Situation and Cases* <www.icc-cpi.int/Menus/ICC/Situations+and+Cases/> (Last accessed January 3, 2012).

people, particularly Africans, rightly or wrongly, that the ICC is targeting Africans and that Africans are being used as the ICC's guinea pigs.[18] In this regard, the indictment in 2009 of Omar Al Bashir, the President of Sudan, for atrocities in Darfur further fuelled this perception and appeared to have created a sense of speculative fear as to whom the next African head of state to be "humiliated" would be under an agenda said to be perpetrated against Africa by the West.[19] Since the Al Bashir indictment, a number of other prominent African leaders have been indicted by the ICC – the six Kenyan political leaders (the famous Ocampo six),[20] Laurent Gbagbo, the former president of Ivory Coast,[21] and most recently, the late Muammar Gaddafi, former leader of Libya.[22]

1.2 The Relevance of a Debate on Africa and International Criminal Justice

The scenario painted in the preceding section clearly demonstrates a situation in which there is strong recognition of the difficult position that Africa as a continent has been – a situation in which brutal conflicts and egregious violations of human rights have dehumanized the ordinary African individual and groups of individuals or communities, as members of the nation state without much accountability. Yet there is agreement that impunity in the commission of mass atrocities and flagrant violations of human rights in Africa as in other parts of the world cannot be allowed to continue to go unpunished. Thus, the generally recent emphases on international criminal justice, as exemplified by the establishment of ad hoc international criminal tribunals and special courts in general and the ICC, as a permanent international court with criminal jurisdiction in particular, is a phenomenon that is geared toward ensuring the existence in this sphere, of accountability that had generally been lacking in the world. However, there are strong arguments, vociferous debates and disagreements from various quarters such as academics, politicians, diplomats and even activists on the implementation of the accountability mechanisms and the legalities of the actions taken in that regard.

An examination of Africa's place in the future of international criminal justice is therefore quite timely for a number of reasons. Firstly, the reality of the effect of brutal conflicts, the commission of mass atrocities and egregious violations of human rights in Africa as a continent over the years is not contestable. Secondly, the African Union (AU), successor to the

18 See *ICC Accused of 'Exclusively' Targeting Africans* (an interview credited to Jean Ping, Chairperson of the African Union Commission) Mail & Guardian Online April 20, 2011. Available at <http://mg.co.za/article/2011-04-20-icc-accused-of-exclusively-targeting-africans> (Last accessed December 14, 2011).

19 *Id.*

20 See *supra* note 17.

21 *Id.*

22 *Id.*

liberation-minded Organization of African Unity (OAU), taking the long history of brutal conflicts on the continent as well as the associated egregious violations of human rights into account, has normatively rejected the commission of these crimes with impunity. This means that the continued commission of these crimes will have to be properly dealt with one way or another and not just left unattended to. Thirdly, the large representation of African regional contributions and support for the processes leading to the adoption of the Rome Statute coupled with the large African regional ratification of the Rome Statute is a testimony to Africa's relevance to the new phenomenon of emphasized international criminal justice accountability for atrocity crimes. Fourthly, the incontrovertible fact that currently, all accused persons undergoing trial in the ICC, the permanent international court with criminal jurisdiction are Africans, makes it all the more important to assume that Africa as a region affects the future of international criminal justice as is presently being played out. Finally, the mix of high-level political considerations in international criminal justice as exemplified by the AU's strong position on indictments against sitting African heads of States relative to the high politics of the United Nations Security Council (UNSC) on referral of cases to the ICC has serious implications for current day international criminal justice mechanisms and processes.

It is against the background of the issues and contentions highlighted above that this book, which is based on an international conference with the same theme as its title, organized under the auspices of the Wits Programme in Law, Justice and Development in Africa in July 2010 in collaboration with the Africa Interest Group of the American Society of International Law, is being produced as an edited work. Even though the time between July 2010 when the conference on this work was organized and 2012 that this book is being published is a fairly long time, the contributions in this book are up to date. Each contributor to the volume took time to update his or her contribution to incorporate current events relative to the individual topics dealt with.

1.3 Questions and Issues Addressed in this Volume

This book interrogates a number of the issues implicated in the background-setting sections above whether based on perception or reality, in terms of what international criminal justice portends for Africa and vice versa. A number of vitally important and resonating questions are addressed by various contributors to the volume to the following effect: how has Africa's experience with international criminal justice mechanisms affected the behaviour of African states? To what extent are perceptions of Africa's witch-hunt beclouding the need for justice arising from the victimization of innocent civilians largely made up of women and children in conflicts engineered by power mongers and brokers in Africa? Are there external political agendas that are failing the needed universal credibility of international criminal justice mechanisms? Does Africa object to international criminal justice, having vociferously supported the birth of the ICC? If so, does Africa have any alternative mechanism for satisfactorily dealing with justice for gross violations of international humanitarian law and the perpetration of violent conflicts in the region that gives rise to the clamour for justice? To what extent can Africa implement the complementarity requirement of the Rome Statute as a commitment to ensuring justice for egregious crimes committed on the continent as defined in the Rome Statute and for which a large number of its component states have accepted obligations? What are the limits of the ICC's impact as an international criminal justice mechanism in Africa? Many other such questions are dealt with in evaluating the future of international criminal justice as a process and as a mechanism that has Africa as a prominent participant in it whether that participation is done willingly or otherwise.

The book is divided into five parts that deal with the various themes covered in the volume. In addition to the introductory and concluding chapters, the book is made up of fifteen chapters. Part I (chapter 2-3) deals with the impact of the first two international criminal justice mechanisms that were established in Africa – the ICTR and the SCSL relative to dealing with impunity and issues associated with accountability for atrocity crimes. The central questions here are: to what extent have these two accountability mechanisms impacted on impunity and gross human rights violations in Africa? How effective have these institutions been in achieving their mandates? What legacies would they leave behind in Africa in general and the countries where they operate in particular? In this regard, in chapter 2, Sigall Horovitz examines 'The Impact of the ICTR and the SCSL on Impunity in Rwanda and Sierra Leone.' She argues that by their nature, international accountability mechanisms such as the ICTR and the SCSL have limited mandates and resources that constrain them from dealing with large numbers of cases of mass atrocity, thus limiting their impact in truly curtailing impunity in states that have suffered such mass atrocity. She points out that, for international courts to meaningfully impact the reduction of impunity in domestic settings; there must be domestic-related mechanisms that would complement the work of such international courts. It is on this premise that she evaluates both the ICTR and the SCSL, which though are still in operation, have gone quite far into completing their mandates.

In chapter 3, Mba Chidi Nmaju's 'From Protracted Conflict to Sustained Peace in Sierra Leone: the Contributions of the Special Court for Sierra Leone and the Sierra Leone Truth and Reconciliation Commission (SLTRC)' examines the part that the SCSL and the SLTRC played in the promotion of peace and security in Sierra Leone as well as in advancing the rule of law in the country. Nmaju argues that both institutions contributed to sustained peace in Sierra Leone despite their different mandates. He posits that it may be a viable way of dealing with conflicts and mass atrocity if there is a model of combing restorative and retributive mechanisms as was the case in Sierra Leone.

Part II (chapter 4-7) considers the debate on Africa and the ICC relative to whether there are any genuine concerns on the criticism that have trailed the work of the ICC on the continent. Questions interrogated in this part include what grievances Africa has against the ICC; whether Africa is withdrawing its massive support for the ICC; whether there is a conspiracy against Africa in the exercise of the ICC's mandate; how real the perception is that the ICC is using Africa as guinea pig; whether Africa is protecting impunity for mass atrocities and gross or egregious violations of human rights; and how Africa can ensure continuous support for the ICC to exercise its mandate on the continent.

Henry J. Richardson III opens discussions on this part in chapter 4 with 'African Grievances and the International Criminal Court: Issues of African Equity under International Criminal Law' in which he argues that the debate about the relationship between the ICC and Africa should not be confined to just treaty obligations but one that also addresses African equity in global issues. He contends that there are three dilemmas inherent in the debate – one that centers on "the principle of necessary self-help for subordinated peoples"; another that revolves around Africa's ability under the African Union to take decisions on how it wants to deal with issues of international criminal accountability of its subjects; and a final dilemma that borders on normative assumptions and authority to make decisions regarding immunity and amnesty.

James Nyawo offers a 'Historical Narrative of Mass Atrocities and Justice in Africa: Implications for the implementation of International Criminal Justice' in chapter 5. He traces Africa's experience with slavery and colonialism that resulted in untold mass atrocities that were not accounted for. Thus, he wonders whether "historical injustices" such as the Herero genocide in colonial Namibia, King Leopold's atrocities in the Congo Free State as well as the French atrocities in the Algerian war of independence, among others, are playing in the minds of African leaders in their recent, very vociferous objections to the implementation of international criminal justice under the ICC mechanism. He, however, argues that the issue is about ending impunity, which Africa must be seen to show leadership in, notwithstanding the perceived imbalance in the power relations battle between Africa and its former colonial oppressors.

In chapter 6, David Chuter's provocative piece 'The International Criminal Court: A Place for Africans or Africans in their Place?' exposes the high-level political considerations inherent in international criminal justice. He argues that because of this high politics, the ICC would only be able to proceed "against small, poor, friendless states, especially in Africa." To conclude part II, Ntombozuko Dyani in chapter 7 boldly asks the question 'Is the International Criminal Court Targeting Africa?' In answering this question, Ms. Dyani reflects on various heads of the debate, ranging from the jurisdiction of the court, the duty to prosecute, issues of immunity of heads of state and amnesty, among others. She emphasizes that the issue is not about whether Africa is being targeted by the ICC or not but about whether serious crimes were not committed, or being committed for which the ICC is endowed with jurisdiction to deal with. She argues that the only way that African states would not feel targeted by the ICC is for them to ensure the existence of domestic measures that give effect to their obligations to prosecute perpetrators of atrocity crimes within the rubric of the complementarity principle of the Rome Statute.

Part III (chapter 8-9) deals with the principle of complementarity under the Rome Statute relative to the importance of its implementation and impact on domestic rule of law and justice in Africa. The central issue implicated here is whether Africa, having massively supported and accepted the ICC as a permanent international criminal justice mechanism of last resort as a regional block, is maximizing the benefits of the complementarity principle of the Rome Statute. Accordingly, the question remains, should Africa not direct its attention to the ability of its domestic systems to deal with atrocity crimes?

This part begins with chapter 8 in which Vincent O. Nmehielle looks at the need for Africa to emphasize complementarity in 'Taking Credible Ownership of Justice for Atrocity Crimes in Africa: The African Union and the Complementarity Principle of the Rome Statute.' Nmehielle reiterates the point that the Rome Statute makes the ICC a court of last resort, giving primary jurisdiction to the domestic justice system. He argues that this gives Africa the most important singular opportunity to take ownership of the justice process in dealing with atrocity crimes in the continent, and that this ownership must be credible in the spirit of a determination to end impunity within the injunctions of the Constitutive Act of the African Union and the obligations undertaken by African member States of the Rome Statute. Thus, the future of international criminal justice in Africa is in the hands of African States if only they take the domestic measures necessary to fully implement and benefit from the complementarity principle of the Rome Statute. The chapter underscores the point that it is not just enough to cry foul at the skewed nature of international criminal prosecutions (despite this reality), but that Africa must find a way of effectively dealing with the seeming daily occurrence of atrocity crimes in its various territories. The African Union must therefore lead the way in taking credible ownership of justice for atrocity crimes in Africa by prevailing on its member states to put in place domestic accountability measures.

Caroline Nalule and Rachel Odoi-Musoke in chapter 9 discuss the complementarity principle relative to Uganda's attempt to take domestic measures for atrocity crimes in 'The Complementarity Principle of the Rome Statute Put to the Test: Uganda's Experience'. The chapter examines the steps taken by the Ugandan Government to demonstrate not only its willingness but also its ability to investigate and prosecute crimes under the Rome Statute. The authors argue that although the Rome Statute was domesticated in Uganda and steps were taken and are still being taken, Uganda is not necessarily in a position to efficiently prosecute the indicted Lord Resistance Army (LRA) leaders that are sought by the ICC. They argue that more needs to be done in terms of bringing all the relevant existing legislations in conformity with the Rome Statute; building the capacity of all institutions to deal with international crimes; and finding appropriate domestic solutions to the various complex issues that the LRA conflict has generated. The authors are not convinced that Uganda's efforts thus far can be considered sufficient to bring the complementarity principle into play such that should the issue arise, the ICC would be satisfied to have the case initially brought before it transferred back to be tried under the Uganda's justice system.

Part IV (chapter 10-11) considers the limitations of the ICC mechanism in the quest to achieve peace and justice in Africa. In 'Peace, Justice and the International Criminal Court: Limitations and Possibilities' – chapter 10, Janine Clark engages the age-long debate on the relationship between peace and justice relative to the ICC. She argues that the ICC is neither "an obstacle to," nor "an instrument of peace." Thus, she offers "a more nuanced, exploratory analysis focused on both the Court's limitations and possibilities as a tool of justice and peace." She stresses that justice entails far more than simply retribution, and underscoring the point that the relationship between criminal trials and peace remains empirically under-researched. She contends that the ICC can potentially contribute to peace but only as part of a comprehensive approach to justice that is deeper and thicker than criminal trials alone.

In chapter 11 Eric Colvin and Jessie Chella interrogate the legitimacy of international criminal justice in Africa based on the limitations in international justice mechanisms like the ICC in dealing with other aspects of international crimes committed in Africa in 'Multinational Corporate Complicity: A Challenge for International Criminal Justice in Africa'. The authors observe that allegations have been raised with respect to the complicity of multinational corporations in the commission of international crimes in parts of Africa; "yet, international criminal law does not currently recognize corporate criminal liability in any form." They point out that the result is one where attention is focused solely on the responsibility of African perpetrators of crimes to the neglect of the potential responsibility of multinational corporations contributing to these crimes. The authors argue that the recognition of the central role of corporations in modern commerce, and of the potential for criminal conduct to occur in the course of corporate operations, has led to radical changes to the nature and scope of corporate criminal liability in many domestic jurisdictions. They contend that the challenge for international criminal justice is to respond to these developments and that meeting this challenge has particular significance for the legitimacy of international criminal justice in Africa as represented by the ICC process.

Part V (chapter 12-14) takes up the issue whether in dealing with impunity, there are any African international criminal justice alternatives – against the background of the perception that Africa is now rejecting or objecting to the ICC as a permanent international criminal justice mechanism. In this regard, the question as to feasibility and practicability of the call for an African criminal justice mechanism to deal with African situations is examined. This part commences with Godwin Odo's 'At the Crossroads: Deconstructing the Challenges of International Justice and the Fight Against Impunity in Africa' piece in chapter 12 in which he examines the rationale and validity of arguments and views of both proponents and opponents of the assertion that international justice, reflected particularly through the International Criminal Court is unduly biased against Africa. Odo reviews the African Union resolutions on the abuse of the principle of universal jurisdiction; the ICC indictment of the President of Sudan; the possibility of conferring criminal jurisdiction on the African Court on Human and Peoples' Rights; and the trial of Hissene Habre by Senegal, on behalf of the African Union. He argues that the move to confer criminal jurisdiction on the African Human Rights Court is suspect and will create an impunity gap on the continent given the timing of the proposal, the earlier rejection of the proposal by the AU itself, and the abysmally low rate of ratification and domestication of Africa's own treaties by member states, particularly the Protocol on the Establishment of an African Court on Human and Peoples' Rights. Odo, however, argues that the ICC could have managed the indictment of President Omar Al-Bashir of Sudan better, taking into consideration its timing and implications for on-going AU-led peace initiatives. He calls for genuine dialogue and better collaboration between the African Union and the ICC to ensure an effective fight against impunity in Africa.

Lutz Oette in chapter 13 examines the utility of regional mechanisms in trying to find solutions to the challenges inherent in international criminal justice in 'The African Union High-Level Panel on Darfur: a Precedent for Regional Solutions to Challenges Facing International Criminal Justice?' He reasons that the African Union High-Level Panel on Darfur (AUPD) constitutes an important African Union led approach to the conceptual and institutional challenges facing international criminal justice in Africa. He argued that the AUPD's broad consultations in Sudan opened space for public debates and enabled it to map out a contextual approach towards justice, reconciliation and peace in Darfur and the whole of Sudan. He, however, points out that the process-oriented nature of the AUDP risks politicization in the implementation phase that may weaken if not undermine altogether the potency of its recommendations. Nevertheless, Dr. Oette argues that AUPD-style interventions can be a valuable tool and will likely be most effective if pursued as part of a broader regional approach that develops the legal and institutional framework needed to strengthen the capacity of national and regional bodies in ensuring international criminal justice.

In concluding Part V Pacifique Manirakiza makes 'The Case for an African Criminal Court to Prosecute International Crimes Committed in Africa' in chapter 14. He reasons that the status quo has been that the international criminal justice system stands on two pillars: international criminal courts, whether *ad hoc* or permanent and national courts but that the regional level has not yet been explored. This is in spite of the existence of regional institutions tasked with the objectives of mainly promoting continental political and economic interests. The author argues there is a place for an African Criminal Court to prosecute crimes committed in Africa in addition to national and international criminal mechanisms aiming at combating impunity. He contends that this should be the case particularly because the commission of international crimes has been identified and listed as an internal threat to common African security. Thus, a regional court would help the AU achieve its goals and missions in terms of promoting human rights and security in Africa.

Finally Vincent O. Nmehielle's 'Conclusion: Ensuring a Balanced Future for International Criminal Justice in Africa' in chapter 15 distils out the germane contentions and insights in the volume. He positions the debate in terms of the prospects for the future, which should be the mutual relevance of Africa to contemporary international justice systems and mechanisms such as the ICC and vice versa.

This volume makes a meaningful contribution to knowledge on the interaction between Africa as a continent and a political entity that is represented by institutions such as the AU and contemporary international criminal justice systems. The book presents a balanced rather than a one-way approach to the debate. It speaks truth to both mass atrocities that have reigned in Africa and the need to confront them as well as the unhealthy politics of international justice that appears to victimize the very mechanism that is designed to provide some redress to the innocent victims of egregious violations of human rights and mass atrocities.

Part I
From Rwanda to Sierra Leone

The Impact of the United Nations International Criminal Tribunal for Rwanda and the Special Court for Sierra Leone on Impunity in Africa

2 The Impact of the International Criminal Tribunal For Rwanda and the Special Court for Sierra Leone on Impunity in Rwanda and Sierra Leone

Sigall Horovitz

2.1 Introduction

From April 7 to July 18, 1994, about a million people were slaughtered in Rwanda in what has been considered the fastest genocide in history. Most victims were Tutsi civilians, who were often tortured and raped before being killed, mostly by Hutus. Meanwhile, across the continent, the West African state of Sierra Leone was in the midst of a decade-long civil war. Rebels and pro-government forces murdered and amputated civilians, brutally raped women, and forced children to fight. These unspeakable atrocities compelled the international community to respond by establishing the International Criminal Tribunal for Rwanda ("ICTR" or "Tribunal") in November 1994, and the Special Court for Sierra Leone ("SCSL" or "Court") in January 2002. By trying and punishing the individuals who committed these atrocities, the international community sought to send a message that impunity cannot be tolerated for such acts and the rule of law must prevail.[1]

But was this message received in Rwanda and Sierra Leone? Such an assessment can be difficult to make, especially in light of the relatively short time that has elapsed since the atrocities and their international prosecution, precluding any significant findings about the recurrence of similar violence over time or levels of norm compliance in the relevant countries. In view of this challenge, this chapter seeks to make this assessment through

1 These international courts also have other goals which will not be addressed in this chapter, such as to contribute to national reconciliation processes in their target countries.

identifying a more "tangible" domestic impact of the ICTR and SCSL: their impact on domestic atrocity-related proceedings in Rwanda and Sierra Leone.[2]

The chapter's point of departure is that domestic accountability processes are necessary in order to effectively fight impunity and advance the rule of law in the aftermath of mass atrocities, even when an international criminal court becomes involved. This is because the limited mandates and resources of international courts allow them to prosecute only a small fraction of the perpetrators in each mass atrocity case. For example, the ICTR prosecuted so far around seventy defendants and the SCSL only ten. Both courts are about to conclude their activities. Such a small number of prosecutions, even if targeting top level perpetrators, may undermine the ability of these international courts to reduce impunity and improve the rule of law in Rwanda and Sierra Leone, unless their trials are complemented by genuine and fair national prosecutions (or other effective accountability processes). Thus, the position of this chapter is that international courts increase their chance to reduce impunity in their target countries when they encourage domestic atrocity-related proceedings in these countries.

It is stressed, however, that the ICTR and SCSL were not designed to proactively encourage national trials. Even when the UN Security Council adopted a resolution urging the ICTR to complete its work and to that end refer cases to national jurisdictions, it did not provide it with clear guidelines or resources to collaborate with Rwandan courts.[3] In the case of the SCSL, although its "hybrid" structure was expected to contribute to the strengthening of Sierra Leone's justice system, the Court lacked the mandate and resources to create links with the national judiciary. In addition, by refraining from challenging the national amnesty regime, the SCSL precluded itself *a priori* from encouraging domestic prosecutions of the wartime atrocities. However, as shown below, the ICTR and SCSL still had some impact on national atrocity-related prosecutions in their target countries, or at least on the relevant domestic norms and capacities that are required for handling such proceedings. By identifying elements of this impact, I hope to deepen our understanding of whether and how these international courts contributed to reducing impunity and improving the rule of law in Rwanda and Sierra Leone.

---

2 The present chapter was presented at an international conference titled "Africa and the Future of International Criminal Justice" at the University of the Witwatersrand, Johannesburg, on July 14-16, 2010. The research leading to this chapter has received funding from the European Union's Seventh Framework Programme under grant agreement no. 217589 (Impact of International Criminal Procedures on Domestic Criminal Procedures in Mass Atrocity Cases (DOMAC)). The research was conducted from mid-2008 to mid-2010, and the chapter therefore does not refer to subsequent developments.

3 UNSC Res 1503 (August 28, 2003), UN Doc. S/RES/1503, (hereinafter: "UNSC Res 1503").

In particular, this chapter will identify the impact of the ICTR and SCSL in Rwanda and Sierra Leone in the following four areas: (1) rates of and trends in domestic prosecutions of atrocity crimes; (2) the domestic application of international norms in atrocity-related proceedings; (3) domestic sentencing practices in relation to atrocity crimes; and (4) national capacity to handle domestic atrocity-related proceedings. These four areas of focus were chosen as indicators of whether the ICTR and SCSL have encouraged domestic accountability processes in their target countries. It is stressed that the impact of international criminal courts on national justice systems can extend beyond atrocity cases, especially when the international courts encourage the development of domestic norms and institutions that affect all criminal cases. To promote a better appreciation of the overall impact of the ICTR and SCSL on impunity and the rule of law in their target countries, areas where their domestic impact extends beyond atrocity-related proceedings will also be emphasized.

Sections 2.2 and 2.3 focus on the cases of Rwanda and Sierra Leone, respectively, while section 2.3 presents some concluding remarks. But before proceeding, a brief comment on methodology is warranted. Interactions between international courts and national judiciaries are not always documented. Furthermore, judicial decisions in Rwanda and Sierra Leone are often unpublished. These factors made it hard to identify the domestic impact of the ICTR and SCSL. To overcome these methodological difficulties, I interviewed over fifty professionals affiliated with the ICTR, the SCSL, or the national justice systems of Rwanda and Sierra Leone. The interviewees were selected based on their seniority and knowledge of the relevant justice systems. They included top judicial policy makers and prominent lawyers at the international and national levels, as well as experts who contribute to the development of the relevant national judiciaries. Since many of the interviewees did not want the information they provided to be attributed to them, they are referred to in generic terms such as "a senior Sierra Leonean official", or "an ICTR judge". The interviewees were asked open-ended questions which allowed them to describe in detail the interactions between the international and national judicial responses to the atrocities, and the effects of these interactions on the domestic level. Thus the interviews provided important information on which this chapter is partly based. Additional sources of information included UN and NGO documents, international and national jurisprudence, academic articles, news reports, etc.

My own professional background is also relevant. Between the years 2003 and 2010, I served in legal positions both at the ICTR and SCSL. This first-hand knowledge of the work of these courts and the ways in which they interact with domestic jurisdictions, guided my choice of interviewees and questions, and helped me understand the answers.

2.2 The ICTR and Rwanda

2.2.1 Background to Domestic Response to the Atrocities

Before addressing the impact of the ICTR on the Rwandan justice system, it is important to note Rwanda's own remarkable judicial response to the atrocities. Immediately after the genocide, the Rwandan government arrested masses of suspected genocide perpetrators. In 1996, it started prosecuting them in national courts under a newly enacted law criminalizing genocide and crimes against humanity ("Genocide Law of 1996").[4] When conventional criminal justice proved too slow, Rwanda established community-based "gacaca" courts.[5] By mid 2006, gacaca courts took over the vast majority of the country's genocide-related cases, leaving to the ordinary (conventional) courts only cases involving the gravest crimes and the most senior suspects.[6] As of the time of writing, gacaca courts have prosecuted about a million genocide-related cases (including cases concerning property offences).[7] Ordinary courts, it is estimated, handled slightly over 10,000 genocide cases.[8]

4 Organic Law No. 08/96 of 30/8/1996 on the Organization of Prosecutions for Offences constituting the Crime of Genocide or Crimes against Humanity committed since 1 October, 1990 [Rwanda] (hereinafter: "Genocide Law of 1996"). The term "organic law" in Rwanda refers to laws that are normatively superior to regular laws, secondary only to the Constitution.

5 Organic Law No. 40/2000 of 26/01/2001 Setting up Gacaca Jurisdictions and Organizing Prosecutions for Offences Constituting the Crime of Genocide or Crimes Against Humanity Committed between 1 October, 1990 and 31 December, 1994 [Rwanda] (hereinafter: "Gacaca Law of 2001"). This law was later replaced by Organic Law No. 16/2004 of 19/6/2004 Establishing the Organization, Competence and Functioning of Gacaca Courts Charged with Prosecuting and Trying the Perpetrators of the Crime of Genocide and other Crimes Against Humanity, Committed between October 1, 1990 and December 31, 1994 [Rwanda] (hereinafter: "Gacaca Law of 2004").

6 The Genocide Law of 1996, *supra* note 4, classified genocide-related crimes into four categories, depending on the level of the perpetrator and gravity of the crime. Category I included the most serious crimes and offenders, which continued to be sent to ordinary courts even after the gacaca courts were established. For a more detailed discussion of the classification of genocide crimes in Rwanda see footnote 48 below and accompanying text.

7 Gacaca courts started their "data-collection" activities in mid-2002. Their trials started in March 2005, initially in 752 "pilot" locations but from July 2006 gacaca trials were held in over 9,000 locations throughout Rwanda. As of March 2010, about a million people have been judged. *See* Hirondelle News, *Gacaca Closure Postponed One More Time* (March 31, 2010) <www.hirondellenews.com/content/view/13340/332/> (Accessed May 16, 2010).

8 Bert Ingelaere, *The Gacaca courts in Rwanda, in* Traditional Justice and Reconciliation After Violent Conflict 45 (International IDEA, Luc Huyse & Mark Salter eds., 2008). ("The classical justice system [in Rwanda] dealt with 10,026 [genocide related] cases between 1997 and 2004"). Prof. Schabas also estimated that around 10,000 cases were dealt with by the end of 2004. *See* William A. Schabas, *Genocide Trials and Gacaca Courts*, 3 Journal of International Criminal Justice 879, 888 (2005) (hereinafter "Schabas, Genocide Trials"). According to Human Rights Watch, 62 persons were tried by ordinary courts in Rwanda in 2005, 73 persons were tried in 2006, 83 persons were tried in 2007, and 4 persons were tried in the first quarter of 2008. *See* Human Rights Watch, *Law and Reality: Progress in Judicial Reform in Rwanda*, 25 July, 2008, (hereinafter: "HRW, Law and Reality"); Annex 1 at 101-102 (referring to statistics compiled by the "Republic of Rwanda, Supreme Court, 'Raporo y'urwego rw'ubucamanza 2006' and other tables provided by the Inspectorate of Courts"). After March 2008, very few genocide trials were heard in ordinary courts.

However, both gacaca and ordinary courts in Rwanda have been internationally criticized for failing to meet minimum fair trial standards and meting "victor's justice" against Hutus while Tutsis enjoy impunity.[9] Whether or not these claims are justified, identifying the ICTR's impact on Rwandan judicial proceeding can help us understand the extent and nature of its contribution to accountability and rule of law in Rwanda. The remainder of this section focuses on the impact of the ICTR on atrocity proceedings before Rwandan ordinary criminal courts, and not gacaca courts.

2.3 ICTR Impact on Prosecution Rates and Trends

2.3.1 *Genocide Prosecutions*

Rwanda's ambitious attempt to prosecute all genocide perpetrators was a result of the strong political will of its post-genocide governments to establish accountability for the genocide. Rwandan officials and lawyers stressed that the ICTR did not play a role in encouraging national prosecutions of genocide perpetrators.[10] Nonetheless, even if the ICTR had little or no impact on *rates* of genocide trials in Rwanda, it had some influence on certain *trends* in Rwandan atrocity-related proceedings. For example, in 2005, when the ICTR Prosecutor transferred dossiers (investigation files) to the Prosecutor General of Rwanda, he ultimately encouraged Rwandan ordinary courts to (re-)engage in prosecuting high or mid level genocide suspects.[11] A senior ICTR official stressed that this transfer of evidence also encouraged Rwanda to start seeking the extradition of genocide suspects from third states, as all of the suspects whose dossiers were transferred from the ICTR resided outside Rwanda.[12]

---

9 See, *e.g.*, Human Rights Watch, World Report 2009: Events Of 2008. (hereinafter: "HRW 2009 World Report"); Amnesty International, Report 2009: The State of the World's Human Rights. (hereinafter: "AI 2009 World Report"); Amnesty International, *Rwanda: Gacaca: A Question of Justice* (December 17, 2002) (hereinafter: "AI, Gacaca: A Question of Justice"). On the claim that Rwanda practices victor's justice see, *e.g.*, Nicholas A. Jones, The Courts of Genocide: Politics and the Rule of Law In Rwanda And Arusha 100 (2010). It is also noted that European courts and the ICTR have refused to extradite or transfer genocide suspects to Rwanda partly on the basis that fair trials are unavailable in Rwanda. See, *e.g.*, Decision by the High Court of England and Wales in *Brown (aka Vincent Bajinja) et al. v. Government of Rwanda et al.* [2009] EWHC 770 Admin, Judgment, April 8, 2009 (denying extradition to Rwanda and referring, in para. 47, to other European court decisions which denied extradition of genocide suspects to Rwanda). However, this trend may be changing as both the ICTR and European courts have recently approved the referral of genocide cases to Rwanda.

10 Interview notes with author.

11 In 2005, the Prosecutor of the ICTR transferred to the Rwandan authorities about 35 dossiers (investigation files) of suspects who were investigated but never indicted by the ICTR. See Letter from Hassan B. Jallow, Chief Prosecutor, ICTR, to Kenneth Roth, Executive Director, Human Rights Watch, 2 (June 22, 2009) <hrw.org/sites/default/files/related_material/2009_06_Rwanda_Jallow_Response.pdf> (Accessed August 21, 2009) (hereinafter "Letter from ICTR Prosecutor to HRW"). Since these suspects have not been formally charged by the Tribunal, it was within the Prosecutor's discretion to transfer their dossiers to Rwanda, without requiring the ICTR judges' authorization.

12 Interview notes with author.

Even when one of these dossiers concerned "revenge crimes" allegedly committed by four officers of the Tutsi-dominated Rwandan Patriotic Front ("RPF"), Rwanda took the matter seriously and prosecuted RPF members for crimes committed against Hutu civilians in 1994.[13] This domestic prosecution of RPF crimes, which in my view constitutes an important impact of the ICTR on Rwanda, is discussed in the following paragraphs.

2.3.2 War Crimes Prosecutions

As opposed to genocide and crimes against humanity, war crimes do not fall under the jurisdiction of gacaca courts. Thus, soldiers and militia members affiliated with the previous Hutu-dominated regime are not prosecuted in Rwanda for war crimes. However, they are tried for the "greater" crime of genocide. But what about offences committed by combatants who opposed the former regime, which do not amount to genocide but may qualify as war crimes?[14] These cases fall under the jurisdiction of Rwanda's military courts. Indeed, several dozen members of the RPF, who fought against former government forces, were tried in military courts for crimes related to the war.[15]

---

13 Letter from ICTR Prosecutor to HRW, *supra* note 11 at 2.

14 In July 1994, the UN appointed a Commission of Experts to investigate the events between April 6 and July 15, 1994 in Rwanda. The report of the Commission concludes that both sides to the armed conflict in Rwanda perpetrated war crimes and crimes against humanity between April 6, 1994 and July 15, 1994. Regarding the crime of genocide, the Commission only found evidence that Hutus committed this crime. See Preliminary Report of the Independent Commission of Experts (29 September 1994), annexed to Letter dated 1 October 1994 from the Secretary-General addressed to the President of the Security Council (4 October 1994) U.N. Doc. S/1994/1125, paras. 146-148. According to Human Rights Watch, "the United Nations estimated that between 25,000 and 45,000 persons were killed by RPF soldiers in 1994". See HRW 2009 WORLD REPORT, *supra* note 9. However, these figures do not appear in the above report of the UN-appointed Commission of Experts.

15 In June 2009, Rwanda's Minister of Justice stated that a total of 42 RPF soldiers were prosecuted in Rwanda as of April 2007 for crimes perpetrated in connection with the war. See Official website of the Republic of Rwanda, Ministry of Justice, 'RPF Never Ignored to Punish Soldiers Guilty of War Crimes' <www.minijust.gov.rw/spip.php?article133> (Accessed July 26, 2009) (hereinafter: "RPF Never Ignored War Crimes"). Referring to this statement, the ICTR Prosecutor added that "of these 42 RPF soldiers on this list, 19 were actually prosecuted for offences committed in 1994 falling within the jurisdiction of the ICTR with the rest being prosecuted for offences committed post-1994 against civilians suspected of being genocidaires. Of the 19 soldiers, 12 were convicted and sentenced to various terms of imprisonment, 5 were acquitted and the remaining two cases did not proceed due to the absence of the accused persons". See Letter from ICTR Prosecutor to HRW, *supra* note 11. However, Human Rights Watch provided slightly different statistics. See HRW, Law and Reality, *supra* note 8 at 4. ("According to government statistics, only 32 soldiers have been brought to trial for crimes committed against civilians in 1994, with 14 found guilty and given light sentences"). For details about each of the trials, including names of defendants and the sentences they received, see HRW, Law and Reality *supra* note 8, Annex 2, at 103-109.

In this area, the ICTR may have had a more discernible impact on Rwandan proceedings than in the area of genocide trials: In 2008 the ICTR Prosecutor deferred to Rwanda a case concerning four RPF officers suspected of committing war-crimes in Rwanda in 1994, including executing thirteen catholic priests in the Kabgayi Cathedral. The allegations were investigated by the ICTR but the four were eventually not indicted by the Tribunal. By defering to Rwanda the jurisdiction over the RPF officers, the ICTR Prosecutor encouraged Rwanda to prosecute them: They were eventually tried before a military court in Kigali in June 2008 for war-crimes charges. The trial, referred to as the "Kabgayi Trial", was the first war-crimes prosecution in Rwanda, as previous prosecutions of RPF crimes in Rwanda concerned ordinary (although war-related) crimes. Several interviewees noted that Rwanda would not have held the Kabgayi Trial had it not been for the ICTR's involvement.[16]

The Kabgayi Trial was held in public. The defendants included Brigadier General Gumisiriza and three junior officers. Gumisiriza and one of the junior officers were acquitted, while the two remaining officers, who admitted to having shot the victims, were convicted and sentenced to five years of imprisonment. Representatives of the ICTR Prosecutor who monitored the Kabgayi Trial reported that it complied with fair trial standards.[17] However, Human Rights Watch complained about the short proceedings and light sentences, and called the trial "a political whitewash".[18] The Rwandan Justice Minister responded that a "five years sentence is not a small punishment for a person who admitted to have committed the crime."[19] Human Rights Watch also criticized the Rwandan government for prosecuting the four officers only because the ICTR prepared a case against them, and complained that neither Rwanda nor the ICTR anticipate further prosecutions of RPF members.[20]

Nonetheless, in the author's view, a national war-crimes trial against RPF officers (including a high ranking commander) is a significant event, even if it was exceptional and conducted only to prevent ICTR trials of RPF officers. Besides, the threat of international

16 Interview notes with author. One interviewee suggested that the referral of this case by the ICTR Prosecutor to Rwanda was motivated by political considerations. In particular, according to the interviewee, the ICTR sought to mitigate the international criticism that it has been pursuing "selective" or "victor's" justice.

17 Letter from ICTR Prosecutor to HRW, *supra* note 11 at 2-3.

18 Human Rights Watch, *Rwanda: Tribunal Risks Supporting Victor's Justice* (1 June 2009) <www.hrw.org/en/news/2009/06/01/rwanda-tribunal-risks-supporting-victor-s-justice> (Accessed December 23, 2009). It is noted that the ICTR Prosecutor wrote to the Executive Director of Human Rights Watch that "[a]lthough you admit to HRW monitoring the trial, you have not, seven months since the verdict, brought to my attention any evidence to support your allegation that the trial 'proved to be a political whitewash and a miscarriage of justice'". See Letter from ICTR Prosecutor to HRW, *supra* note 11 at 2-3.

19 RPF Never Ignored War Crimes, *supra* note 15.

20 HRW 2009 World Report, *supra* note 9.

trials is a legitimate means by which international courts can encourage national trials. After all, the principle of complementarity enshined in the Rome Statute of the International Criminal Court ("ICC") encourages states to prosecute their own atrocities in order to avoid being subjected to proceedings before the ICC.[21]

2.4 ICTR Normative Impact

2.4.1 *ICTR's Referral Procedure and Rwanda's Transfer Law*

Although the ICTR was created in 1994 as an ad hoc tribunal, the Security Council established a deadline for its activities only nine years later, through its Resolutions 1503 (2003) and 1534 (2004).[22] These resolutions define what is known as the ICTR's "completion strategy". In particular, they request the ICTR to complete its investigations by 2004, first-instance trials by 2008, and all work by 2010.[23] The resolutions also request the ICTR to submit a progress report to the Security Council every six months. Until then, explained a senior ICTR official, the Tribunal operated with no real strategy or time limit in mind.[24]

To enhance compliance with the newly imposed deadlines, Security Council Resolution 1503 urged the ICTR to transfer cases involving mid and low level accused to "competent national jurisdictions, as appropriate, including Rwanda".[25] Consequently, Rule 11*bis* of the ICTR Rules of Procedure and Evidence was amended in 2004 to allow the referral of cases from the ICTR to national jurisdictions, including to states "in whose territory the crime was committed".[26] The amended ICTR Rule 11*bis* provides that "[i]n determining whether to refer the case … the Trial Chamber shall satisfy itself that the accused will receive a fair trial in the courts of the State concerned and that the death penalty will not be imposed or carried out".[27]

Rwanda wanted to receive cases from the ICTR.[28] In 2007, it adopted Organic Law No. 11/2007 to regulate cases transferred from the ICTR or third states ("Transfer Law").[29] The Transfer Law implemented domestically many of the ICTR's due process standards, requiring their application in cases transferred to Rwanda from the ICTR or third states.[30]

21 Whether this kind of pressure is an effective means of encouraging domestic trials is a separate question.

22 S.C. Res. 1503, *supra* note 3; S.C. Res. 1534 (26 March 2004); U.N. Doc. S/RES/1534.

23 These resolutions also apply to the International Criminal Tribunal for the Former Yugoslavia (ICTY). They were adopted in light of the increasing donor fatigue associated with the ICTY and ICTR. The deadline for the completion of the ICTR's first instance trials was since extended twice by the Security Council (in 2008 and 2009), and is currently set at December 2010. See S.C. Res. 1878 (7 July 2009), U.N. Doc. S/RES/1878.

24 Interview notes with author.

25 S.C. Res. 1503 *supra* note 3.

26 ICTR Rules of Procedure and Evidence, Rule 11 *bis* (A) (i).

27 ICTR Rules of Procedure and Evidence, Rule 11 *bis* (C).

Since no cases have been transferred to Rwanda from the ICTR or third states, as of the time of writing, the Transfer Law has not yet been applied.[31] Nonetheless, it is significant that the ICTR (thanks to its referral procedure) has encouraged Rwanda to improve the due process norms provided by its domestic laws.

Interestingly, Rwanda was not required by ICTR Rule 11*bis* to adopt the Transfer Law, but it wanted to send a clear message that defendants transferred from abroad will receive a fair trial in Rwanda. The Transfer Law also went an extra length by providing that ICTR evidence and established facts would be admissible in Rwandan proceedings.[32] The application of these provisions could significantly increase the ICTR's impact on Rwandan case law. Moreover, the Transfer Law encourages cooperation between Rwanda and the ICTR. Thus, it allows the ICTR to provide technical assistance to Rwandan courts and to monitor the trials, and regulates the remand of cases to the ICTR upon a revocation of the referral order.[33] These provisions, if applied, can also enhance the ICTR's domestic impact in particular on due process standards.

The ICTR's referral procedure also encouraged Rwanda to amend some of its sentencing laws to meet the requirements set by the ICTR for referring cases. These important Rwandan legal developments are discussed below in connection with the ICTR's sentencing impact.

28 Hirondelle News, *Rwanda Wants to Detain Defendants, to Try Them and to Possess the Archives* (December 11, 2007) <www.hirondellenews.com/content/view/5466/92/> (Accessed May 16, 2010) ("...'the position of the Rwandan government is that the most possible cases must be transferred to Rwandan courts for trial', stated Joseph Nsengimana. 'Having cooperated with the ICTR, Rwanda should not be subordinated to other national systems', he said. According to him, the transfer of cases to Kigali 'will reinforce the policy of the government in the organization of the reconciliation, which is central to the mandate of the ICTR'. Joseph Nsengimana estimated that 'there should not be any doubt about the will of Rwanda to take the cases of the tribunal and to supervise the sentences imposed by the tribunal'..."). Also see Institute for War & Peace Reporting, *Rwandan Tribunal Under Pressure to Wind Up* (January 29, 2007) <www.iwpr.net/report-news/rwandan-tribunal-under-pressure-wind> (Accessed May 16, 2010). "Rwanda's UN representative Joseph Nsengimana told the Security Council that although there was still a lack of capacity in the national judicial system, he thought it was time for Rwanda to 'regain full national ownership of the process of administration of justice for crimes committed during the genocide'. Nsengimana added that the Rwandan government has been working with the tribunal to prepare for the transfers."

29 Organic Law No. 11/2007 of 16 March 2007 Concerning Transfer of Cases to the Republic of Rwanda from the ICTR and from Other States [Rwanda] (hereinafter: "Transfer Law").

30 Transfer Law *supra* note 29, Arts. 13-17. While the Transfer Law does not adopt all of the ICTR's due process norms, it covers the most important ones such as those concerning the rights of an accused.

31 It is noted that after this chapter was finalized, the ICTR Appeals Chamber approved the referral of a case to Rwanda. See Appeals Chamber decision *Jean Uwinkindi v. Prosecutor* Case No. ICTR-01-75-AR11bis (Decision on Uwinkindi's Appeal against the Referral of his Case to Rwanda and Related Motions) (December 16, 2011) upholding the Trial Chamber's decision in *Prosecutor v. Jean Uwinkindi* Case No. ICTR-2001-75R11bis (Decision on Prosecutor's Request for Referral to the republic of Rwanda) Rule 11bis of the Rules of Procedure and Evidence, (June 28, 2011).

32 Transfer Law, *supra* note 29, Arts. 7-12.

33 Transfer Law, *supra* note 29, Arts. 18-20.

2.4.2 Other International Norms in Rwanda

The above legal developments in Rwanda were clearly encouraged by the ICTR's referral procedure. But there were additional post-genocide legal developments in Rwanda which at first glance could seem attributable to the ICTR. For example, Rwandan law, similarly to the ICTR Statute, defines genocide according to the definition provided in the 1948 Genocide Convention,[34] and recognizes the principle of command responsibility in relation to international crimes.[35] In addition, the Rwandan Constitution of 2003 and Code of Criminal Procedure as amended in 2004, explicitly safeguard certain due process guarantees which are also provided in the ICTR Rules, for example the right of the accused to legal counsel.[36]

However, there is no evidence that Rwanda was influenced by ICTR norms when it adopted the definition of genocide, the principle of command responsibility, or the above procedural norms. Two prominent Rwandan legal experts recalled that Rwandan officials consulted many international law experts in connection with country's legal reforms of 2004, including ICTR staff members.[37] But the reforms were ultimately inspired by international instruments such as the Universal Declaration on Human Rights ("UDHR") and the International Covenant on Civil and Political Rights ("ICCPR"), and not necessarily by ICTR norm.[38] Indeed, a logical explanation for the similarities between certain Rwandan and ICTR norms is that they were both inspired by the same international instruments, such as the 1948 Genocide Convention, the UDHR and the ICCPR, as well as by international customary norms, for example in the case of command responsibility.[39]

---

34 Rwanda's Genocide Law of 1996, *supra* note 4; Gacaca Law of 2001, *supra* note 5 and Gacaca Law of 2004, *supra* note 5, essentially adopt the Genocide Convention's definition for genocide.

35 Gacaca Law of 2004, *supra* note 5, Art. 53. Also see Law No. 33*bis*/2003 of 06/09/2003 Repressing the Crime of Genocide, Crimes Against Humanity and War Crimes [Rwanda], Art. 18. In this context, see ICTR decision in *Prosecutor v. Hategekimana*, Case No. ICTR-00-55B, Decision on the Prosecution's Appeal Against Decision on Referral Under Rule 11*bis*, December 4, 2008 (hereinafter: "*Hategekimana* Appeals Decision of 4 December 2008"), para. 12 ("the Appeals Chamber is satisfied that command responsibility is recognized under Rwandan law, in particular the *Gacaca* Law and the Organic Law No. 33*bis*/2003, and that the Trial Chamber therefore erred in assuming that Rwandan law does not recognize command responsibility").

36 Constitution of the Republic of Rwanda, May 26, 2003 <www.mod.gov.rw/?Constitution-of-the-Republic-of> (Accessed December 16, 2009) (hereinafter: "Rwandan Constitution of 2003"), Arts. 10-44. Also see Law no. 13/2004 of 17/5/2004 concerning the Code of Criminal Procedure, published in the Official Journal of 30 July 2004 [Rwanda], Arts. 64, 89, 96 (granting defendants the rights to legal counsel and to be brought before a judge following their arrest).

37 Interview notes with author.

38 Interview notes with author.

39 Indeed, the Rwandan Constitution reaffirms Rwanda's adherence to the 1948 Genocide Convention, UDHR and ICCPR. See Rwandan Constitution of 2003, *supra* note 36, preamble, para. 9. The principle of command responsibility is a well-established norm of customary international law. See *e.g. Prosecutor v. Delalić et al.*, Case No. ICTY-96-21-T, Trial Judgment (November 16, 1998), paras. 333, 734.

Nonetheless, the fact that Rwanda consulted ICTR members at the time may suggest that it considered ICTR norms to be a possible source of inspiration for national laws. In addition, Rwanda's increased awareness of international norms may (at least partly) be attributable to the work of the ICTR. In any event, further research in this area could perhaps reveal stronger links between the ICTR and the above legal developments in Rwanda.

2.4.3 Domestic Application of ICTR Jurisprudence

As far as the manner in which international norms (substantive or procedural) are applied and interpreted by Rwandan courts, interviews suggested that the ICTR's jurisprudence had little (if any) impact.[40] A senior Rwandan prosecutor explained that Rwandan courts do not need to resort to certain doctrines followed by the ICTR, such as command responsibility and joint criminal enterprise, because they mostly deal with perpetrators who directly committed the crimes, and can easily access witnesses and evidence that connect the suspects to the crimes. A Rwandan Supreme Court judge added that Rwanda follows the civil law system, where little reference is made to case-law or precedents and thus the ICTR jurisprudence is not referenced.[41] This was also confirmed by a senior ICTR prosecutor. However, the prosecutor suggested that this could change as the ICTR is exposing Rwandans to its jurisprudence through training activities, outreach programs, and the distribution of CD-ROMs containing ICTR decisions and judgments.[42] Indeed, a Rwandan attorney noted that he anticipates a wider use in Rwanda of the ICTR's jurisprudence in the next few years.[43]

A foreign legal expert based in Rwanda rejected the argument that there are no references to ICTR jurisprudence in Rwandan cases because Rwanda follows the civil law system. He stressed that European courts which follow the civil law system often refer to decisions of higher courts. In his opinion, there are no references to ICTR jurisprudence because of the lack of experienced lawyers and the low level of legal education in Rwanda.[44] Another foreign legal expert based in Rwanda suggested that Rwandans may not be aware that they can refer to the ICTR in domestic trials.[45] However, this last opinion is not convincing as Rwandan judges have been referring to foreign judgments in constitutional cases.[46]

40 Interview notes with author.
41 Interview notes with author. But the judge added that Rwandan judges are beginning to see the importance of comparative law, and in some constitutional cases have been referring to South African jurisprudence.
42 Interview notes with author.
43 Interview notes with author.
44 Interview notes with author.
45 Interview notes with author.
46 See *supra* note 41.

Finally, it should be noted that most genocide-related judgments in Rwanda focus mostly on factual rather than legal matters.[47] This may provide another explanation as to why ICTR norms had such a limited impact on Rwandan case law.

2.5 ICTR SENTENCING IMPACT

2.5.1 *Abolition of the Death Penalty*

The Genocide Law of 1996 classified genocide-related crimes into four categories, depending on the level of the perpetrator and gravity of the crime, with Category I including the most serious crimes and offenders, followed by Categories II, III and IV.[48] The law also provided that Category I convicts were "liable to the death penalty".[49]

It is recalled that in 2004, Rule 11*bis* of the ICTR Rules was amended to allow the referral of cases to national jurisdictions. According to this rule, a condition for referring a case to a national jurisdiction is that the accused will not receive capital punishment in that jurisdiction. In 2007, shortly before the ICTR judges were requested for the first time to refer a case to Rwandan courts, Rwanda abolished the death penalty.[50] Most interviewees considered that the ICTR encouraged Rwanda to abolish the death penalty, by prohibiting the application of such penalty in transferred cases.[51] This is despite the fact that ICTR Rule 11*bis* does not require the receiving state to abolish altogether the death penalty but only to refrain from applying it to transferred cases.

---

47 Schabas, Genocide Trials, *supra* note 8 at 889. Interestingly, there was some indications that references were made by a Rwandan court to facts (but not norms) established by the ICTR: A senior Rwandan prosecutor noted that during the Rwandan trial against former Rwandan Justice Minister Agnes Ntamabyariro, references were made to factual findings made by the ICTR about meetings where Ntamabyariro was present with Justin Mugenzi (who is accused before the ICTR). Interview notes with author.

48 Genocide Law of 1996, *supra* note 4, Art. 2. Category I included: (i) "the planners, organizers, instigators, supervisors and leaders of the crime of genocide or of a crime against humanity", (ii) individuals "in positions of authority" who committed or encouraged these crimes, (iii) "notorious murderers" who committed the crimes with particular zeal or malice, and (iv) "persons who committed acts [of] sexual torture". Category II covered persons who committed murder or violent crimes resulting in death and did not fall within Category I. Category III offenders included those who committed serious crimes against the person. Finally, Category IV covered property offenders. These categories were modified later in the Gacaca Law of 2001, *supra* note 5 and the Gacaca Law of 2004, *supra* note 5.

49 Genocide Law of 1996, *supra* note 4, Art. 14. The law's sentencing guidelines were modified later in the Gacaca Law of 2001, *supra* note 5 and the Gacaca Law of 2004, *supra* note 5.

50 Organic Law No. 31/2007 of 25 July 2007 Relating to the Abolition of the Death Penalty [Rwanda]. Rwanda not only abolished the death penalty, but also ratified the Second Optional Protocol to the ICCPR regarding the abolition of the death penalty.

51 Interview notes with author.

It is noted that before 2007 the death penalty applied in Rwanda not only to Category I genocide crimes but also to ordinary crimes such as murder. According to a foreign legal expert based in Rwanda, the Rwandan government obtained public support for the abolition of the death penalty by stressing that there were as many as 500 or 600 people on death row in Rwanda. The population agreed that it was too inhumane for the president to sign the deaths of that many people. Still, noted the expert, victims' groups in Rwanda criticize the abolition of the death penalty.[52] A Rwandan lawyer insisted that the abolition of the death penalty was only partly attributable to the ICTR, as Rwandans have been ready for years to abolish this penalty. He noted that domestic pressure to abolish the death penalty started building up after a public execution in Rwanda of 22 genocide convicts, in 1998, which was perceived negatively by the population.[53] Indeed, this was the last time the death penalty was applied in Rwanda, although this punishment was abolished only nine years later.[54]

2.5.2 *Exclusion of Life Sentence in Isolation*

When the death penalty was abolished in Rwanda in 2007, life sentence in isolation replaced it as Rwanda's maximum punishment. In 2008, the ICTR judges denied five requests to refer cases to Rwanda.[55] One of their bases for denying the requested referrals was that the penalty of life imprisonment in isolation, which could be imposed in Rwanda in cases transferred from the ICTR, amounts to cruel and inhuman treatment and therefore breaches international norms.[56]

52 Interview notes with author. In this context it is interesting that a senior ICTR official recalled a conversation he had several years ago with Rwanda's President Kagame, where the latter indicated that he was not opposed to abolishing the death penalty, but needed time to consult with the people of Rwanda about taking such a step. At the time, there was still a lot of emotion in the country, and a decision by the President to abolish the death penalty may not have been supported by the local population. Interview notes with author. Amnesty International reported that 682 genocide perpetrators were on death row by mid-2002. See AI, Gacaca: A Question of Justice *supra* note 9 at 17 (referring to statistics by Liprodhor).

53 Interview notes with author. The lawyer placed this event in 1997, but he seems to have been referring to the public execution of 22 genocide convicts which took place in Rwanda on April 24, 1998. See *Rwanda executes genocide convicts*, (BBC News April 24, 1998) <http://news.bbc.co.uk/2/hi/africa/82960.stm> (Accessed December 12, 2009). Also see Amnesty International, *Rwanda: 22 People, executed on 24 April*, AI Index: AFR 47/15/98, April 27, 1998.

54 For a discussion on Rwanda's inclination toward abolishing the death penalty irrespective of the ICTR's impact see Audrey Boctor, *The Abolition of the Death Penalty in Rwanda*, 10 Human Rights Review 99, 105 (2009).

55 *Prosecutor v. Munyakazi*, Case No. ICTR-97-36, Decision on the Prosecution's Appeal Against Decision on Referral Under Rule 11 *bis*, 8 October 2008 (hereinafter: "*Munyakazi* Appeals Decision of October 8, 2008"); *Prosecutor v. Kanyarukiga*, Case No. ICTR-2002-78, Decision on the Prosecution's Appeal Against Decision on Referral Under Rule 11 *bis*, October 30, 2008 (hereinafter: "*Kanyarukiga* Appeals Decision of October 30, 2008"); *Hategekimana* Appeals Decision of 4 December 2008, *supra* note 35; *Prosecutor v. Gatete*, Case No. ICTR-2000-61, Decision on Prosecutor's Request for Referral to the Republic of Rwanda (Trial Chamber), November 17, 2008 (no appeal was filed); *Prosecutor v. Kayishema*, Case No. ICTR-01-67, Decision on Prosecutor's Request for Referral of Case to the Republic of Rwanda (Trial Chamber), December 16, 2008 (no appeal was filed).

56 See *e.g. Kanyarukiga* Appeals Decision of October 30, 2008, *supra* note 55 at para. 15.

In December 2008, Rwanda excluded the penalty of life sentence in isolation from cases transferred from the ICTR and third states, and in April 2010, its parliament expunged this penalty from Rwandan law altogether.[57] According to interviews, the discussions in Rwanda about abolishing the penalty were encouraged by the ICTR's refusal to refer cases, and Rwanda's will to receive cases from the ICTR in the future.[58]

2.5.3 *Plea Bargains and Acquittals*

As noted above, the Genocide Law of 1996 imposed the death penalty on those convicted for Category I genocide crimes. The law also provided sentencing guidelines in relation to the other categories: It set life imprisonment as the maximum penalty for Category II crimes, applied the sentencing standards of the Rwandan Penal Code to Category III crimes, and subjected Category IV crimes to civil damages only.[59] Importantly, the law offered significant sentence reductions to Category II and Category III defendants who confessed.[60] Statistics published by Amnesty International indicate that sentences imposed by Rwandan ordinary court in genocide cases became more lenient each year since these trials started taking place in early 1997 and until 2002.[61] The acquittal rate in these cases, according to Amnesty International, almost tripled itself from 1997 (8.9%) to 2002

57 Organic Law No. 66/2008 of 21/11/2008, amending Organic Law No. 31/2007 of 25/07/2007 Relating to the Abolition of the Death Penalty [Rwanda] (excluding the penalty of life imprisonment in isolation from applying to cases transferred from the ICTR and third states); Edwin Musoni, *Parliament Expunges Solitary Confinement* (Allafrica News, April 3, 2010) <http://allafrica.com/stories/201004050423.html> (Accessed May 2, 2010); noting that the Rwandan parliament has approved the abolition of life imprisonment in isolation.

58 Interview notes with author.

59 Genocide Law of 1996, *supra* note 4, Art. 14. The law's sentencing guidelines were modified later in the Gacaca Law of 2001 and the Gacaca Law of 2004, see *supra* note 5. For the types of crimes that fell within each category, see *supra* note 48.

60 Category II convicts who confessed before their trial started could receive sentences of between 7 and 11 years in prison, instead of the maximum life imprisonment. If they confessed during their trial, they could receive between 12 and 15 years imprisonment. Category III convicts could have their sentence reduced by two thirds if they confessed before their trial started, or by half if they confessed during their trial. Sentence reductions were not allowed in Category I cases, where the death penalty applied. See Genocide Law of 1996, *supra* note 4, Arts. 15-16. These provisions were modified later in the Gacaca Law of 2001 *supra* note 5 and the Gacaca Law of 2004, *supra* note 5.

61 AI, Gacaca: A Question of Justice, *supra* note 9 at 17 (referencing statistics by Liprodhor). The report explains that between early 1997 and mid-2002, Rwandan ordinary courts completed genocide trials concerning 7,181 defendants. It provides an annual breakdown of the sentences imposed in these genocide cases and identifies the following trends: (i) a gradual decline in the percentage of death penalties (from 30.8% in 1997 to only 3.4% in 2002); (ii) a gradual decline in the percentage of life imprisonments (from 32.4 to 20.5%); (iii) an increase in fixed prison terms (from 27.7 to 47.2%); (iv) the acquittal rate almost tripled itself (from 8.9 to 24.8%). Thus, there was an annual decline in the percentage of death penalties and life sentences against an annual increase in the percentage of fixed prison terms.

(24.8%).[62] Sentencing statistics relating to post-2002 genocide cases in Rwandan ordinary courts were difficult to find but it is likely that these trends did not change.[63]

Could the sentencing trends in Rwanda genocide cases have somehow been affected by the ICTR's sentencing practices? Scholar Mark Drumbl provides two possible explanations for the graduals movement towards more lenient sentences in Rwandan genocide cases: first, the perpetrators prosecuted in earlier trials were more notorious than those prosecuted later, and second, recourse to guilty pleas became more popular with time.[64] Indeed, by law, confessions in genocide cases in Rwanda almost automatically lead to sentence reductions.[65] At first glance the confession procedure in Rwandan genocide cases may seem similar to the plea bargaining practices of the ICTR, in the sense that the convict's sentence is reduced in return for a confession. However, in Rwanda, sentence reductions are prescribed by law and automatically follow valid confessions, while the ICTR employs a conventional plea practice, characteristic to common law systems, where the sentence reduction is negotiated. In addition, it seems unlikely that the ICTR encouraged the use of guilty pleas in Rwanda, because the confession procedure was introduced in Rwanda for its own domestic reasons – mainly to reduce the burden on the national prisons. According to a prominent Rwandan lawyer, the introduction of this practice in Rwanda was not an impact of the ICTR but rather a more general influence of international law.[66] Or, we can accept Drumbl's second explanation for the gradual leniency of sentences, namely, that the perpetrators prosecuted in the earlier trials were more notorious than those prosecuted later.[67]

---

62 *Id.*

63 With regard to acquittal rates, it is noted that in a 2008 decision, the ICTR noted that "The acquittal rate in Rwanda in genocide cases is considerable. Many accused of Hutus origin have been acquitted by the ordinary courts, including cases where convictions are overturned on appeal." The supporting footnote stated that "The Chamber does not take a position on the exact percentage of acquittals, which may differ according to whether not only the ordinary courts but also Gacaca proceedings are included in the calculation. It simply observes that the acquittal rate is considerable. Of ten cases reported in Volume VII (2004-2005) of *Recueil de jurisprudence contentieux du genocide* (*supra* note 28 above), five involved an acquittal of some type. In *The Prosecutor v. Yussuf Munyakazi*, Counsel for the Republic of Rwanda referred to an acquittal rate in his country of "close to 40 per cent" (T. 24 April 2007 p. 31, see also pp. 37, 38)." See *Prosecutor v. Kanyarukiga*, Case No. ICTR-2002-78, Decision on Request for Referral to the Republic of Rwanda, June 6, 2008, at para. 37.

64 However, Drumbl stressed that Amnesty International did not provide information about the factors the domestic courts consider in sentencing. See Mark A. Drumbl, Atrocity, Punishment and International Law 16 (2007) (hereafter "Drumbl, Atrocity and Punishment") As noted above *supra* note 4, the Genocide Law of 1996 imposed the death penalty in relation to Category I crimes. In relation to Categories II and III it also provided sentencing guidelines but allowed the judges a certain amount of discretion.

65 The Rwandan Genocide Law of 1996, *supra* note 4, as well as the Gacaca Laws of 2001 and 2004, *supra* note 5, offer reduced sentences to defendants who confess to and apologize for having perpetrated genocide-related crimes.

66 Interview notes with author.

67 See Drumbl, Atrocity and Punishment *supra* note 64.

Focusing specifically on acquittal rates, it is noted that, as of May 2010, the ICTR acquitted eight out of 39 accused suggesting a 20.5% acquittal rate.[68] According to Amnesty International, the acquittal rate in genocide cases before Rwandan ordinary courts in 2002 was 24.8%.[69] There are indications that the same or a higher acquittal rate characterized genocide cases in subsequent years.[70] Thus, the acquittal rate in genocide cases both at the ICTR and in Rwandan ordinary courts is over 20%.[71] But despite this similarity, there is no evidence that the ICTR had any impact on Rwandan courts in this regard.

2.6 ICTR Capacity Impact

Another important result of the ICTR's referral procedure is that since its adoption, the Tribunal has been carrying out various activities in Rwanda aimed at enhancing local capacity to handle transferred cases. This is done mainly through the Tribunal's Prosecution but also through its Registry and Chambers. These activities, as well as other means by which the ICTR has affected Rwandan judicial capacity, are discussed in the following paragraphs.

2.6.1 Training Activities and Consultations

It is recalled that Security Council Resolution 1503 of August 2003 urged the ICTR to transfer cases to "national jurisdictions... including Rwanda". To this end, the resolution called on the international community "to assist national jurisdictions... in improving their capacity".[72] According to senior ICTR officials, Resolution 1503 was understood by

68 These figures relate to accused that had final judgments in their case and to genocide-related cases and *not* to any contempt of court cases.

69 AI, *Gacaca: A Question of Justice*, *supra* note 9 at 17 (referencing statistics by Liprodhor).

70 *Prosecutor v. Kanyarukiga*, Case No. ICTR-2002-78, Decision on Request for Referral to the Republic of Rwanda, June 6, 2008, para. 37. The ICTR Trial Chamber noted that "[t]he acquittal rate in Rwanda in genocide cases is considerable. Many accused of Hutus origin have been acquitted by the ordinary courts, including cases where convictions are overturned on appeal." The supporting footnote stated that "[t]he Chamber does not take a position on the exact percentage of acquittals, which may differ according to whether not only the ordinary courts but also Gacaca proceedings are included in the calculation. It simply observes that the acquittal rate is considerable. Often, cases reported in Volume VII (2004-2005) of *Recueil de jurisprudence contentieux du genocide* ... five involved an acquittal of some type. In *The Prosecutor v. Yussuf Munyakazi*, Counsel for the Republic of Rwanda referred to an acquittal rate in his country of 'close to 40 per cent'..."

71 As of May 2010, the ICTR acquitted eight accused out of 39 accused that had final judgments in their case, suggesting a 20.5% acquittal rate (these figures relate to genocide-related cases and *not* to any contempt of court cases). In Rwandan ordinary courts, the acquittal rate in genocide cases was 24.8%, at least as of mid-2002, see *supra* note 69 and accompanying text. I will assume this remained the rate afterwards, as statistics pertaining to subsequent years are lacking (see *supra* note 70 above and accompanying text).

72 UNSC Res 1503, *supra* note 3. The resolution also noted "that the strengthening of national judicial systems is crucially important to the rule of law in general and to the implementation of the ICTY and ICTR Completion Strategies in particular".

Tribunal officials as mandating the ICTR for the first time to engage in capacity building in Rwanda.[73] Rwandan and ICTR officials explained that since 2006, the Tribunal's Prosecution has been training Rwandan prosecutors and investigators in areas such as investigation techniques, crime analysis, evidence management and storage, international criminal law, trial advocacy, and indictment drafting.[74] These trainings are mainly funded by the European Union ("EU").[75] Some of them (but not all) are intended to facilitate the transfer of cases to Rwanda.[76]

Two members of the ICTR Prosecution regarded a training session which concerned indictment drafting as particularly successful.[77] One of them mentioned that several months after this training, the Rwandan prosecution authorities introduced a new format for their standard indictment, inspired by the ICTR training.[78] He added that the Rwandans asked for this training because they wanted to improve their system and not for the sake of receiving ICTR cases.[79] A senior Rwandan official confirmed that as a result of the ICTR training on indictment drafting, many local prosecutors in Rwanda have improved their capacity. He generally considered the ICTR training activities in Rwanda to be useful, explaining that they are usually planned jointly by the ICTR and Rwandan officials, and constitute one of several resources the Rwandans are using for their ambitious capacity

73 Interview notes with author. Before 2003, the ICTR did not generally engage in capacity development in Rwanda. However, it carried out outreach activities in Rwanda earlier, mainly through its documentation centers, the first of which was established in Kigali in 2000. Outreach activities can contribute to national capacity: for example, if lawyers and law students learn about the ICTR's work and norms through its outreach activities, this in turn will enhance their capacity as legal professionals.

74 Interview notes with author.

75 Also, other capacity-building activities of the Tribunal are funded outside its regular budget. Senior ICTR officials spoke about the financial challenges faced by the Tribunal in connection with its capacity-building efforts in Rwanda. Even after Security Council Resolution 1503 was adopted in 2003, the UN refused to fund the Tribunal's capacity-building initiatives. Consequently, the ICTR established a voluntary Trust Fund by appealing to donors, mostly the EU and European countries, but also the US and some African countries, to finance its capacity-building activities in Rwanda. The EU is a major contributor to the ICTR Trust Fund, and it also provides direct funding to some of the ICTR's capacity-building projects in Rwanda. Interview notes with author.

76 A senior ICTR official explained that eventually the ICTR and Rwanda managed to build a relationship which allows capacity building projects to take place even when they are not related to the referral of cases to Rwanda. Interview notes with author.

77 Interview notes with author. The interviewees explained that the training was held in April 2008, conducted through four sessions of three days each, and given to a total of 150 local prosecutors. Its aim was to improve prosecutorial practices. The training was requested by the Rwandan Prosecutor General, who wanted to improve the format of the indictments used throughout Rwanda. Until then, Rwanda has been using an old model for its indictments, which contained only a summary of the charges, without informing the accused of his rights. The Rwandan Prosecutor General wanted the indictments to inform defendants of their rights and better inform them of the accusations.

78 Interview notes with author. The interviewee explained that this new standard format is now required under the internal instructions of the Rwandan prosecution authorities. Copy of new indictment format with author.

79 Interview notes with author.

building program.[80] There is no empirical evidence that these trainings directly strengthened the Rwandan justice system, but if they encouraged local prosecutors to include in their indictments more details about the charges, they may have contributed to improving the rights of defendants in Rwanda.

The Tribunal's Registry and Chambers also engage in capacity building in Rwanda, explained ICTR members, particularly by holding seminars and training sessions for Rwandan judges and defense lawyers. So far, the ICTR trained about 50 Rwandan defense lawyers on key aspects of international criminal law and procedure, and plans to train about 200 more defense lawyers once it secures the necessary funding. The ICTR official stressed that the main sponsor for these activities is the EU. Depending on the availability of funds, the ICTR will implement additional capacity building programs.[81] A prominent Rwandan judge recalled that in 2007 he attended an ICTR seminar on criminal procedure.[82] It was also noted in interviews that ICTR staff periodically lecture to Rwandan law students, as well as provide them with books and assistance in setting up libraries.[83]

The ICTR official explained that from about mid 2006, Tribunal representatives have been meeting their Rwandan counterparts to discuss and design possible capacity building programs.[84] A senior Rwandan official confirmed that Rwandan judges, prosecutors, and defense attorneys plan activities together with ICTR members.[85] Both an ICTR official and a Rwandan Supreme Court Judge indicated that ICTR training sessions for Rwandan court reporters are currently being considered.[86] Moreover, Tribunal officials mentioned that an "attachment program" is being planned, possibility funded by the EU, under which Rwandan professionals will be seconded to certain sections of the ICTR for three-month terms.[87]

Another area which the ICTR is currently assisting Rwanda to develop is the area of witness protection. It is recalled that in 2008 the ICTR denied five requests to transfer cases

80 Interview notes with author. However, he added that the ICTR as an institution has not contributed to the development of judicial capacity in Rwanda. Rather, such contribution was achieved through sporadic initiatives undertaken by certain ICTR leaders as a result of their personalities and not because of an institutional obligation imposed on the Tribunal.

81 Interview notes with author.

82 Interview notes with author.

83 Interview notes with author.

84 Interview notes with author. A senior ICTR official explained that when Rwanda complained that the Tribunal was not helping it enough, the ICTR decided to give more visibility to its activities in Rwanda and established a team to coordinate these activities vis-à-vis Rwanda.

85 Interview notes with author.

86 Interview notes with author.

87 Interview notes with author.

to Rwanda.[88] The ICTR's refusal to transfer cases was based on two grounds: the unavailability of fair trials in Rwanda and a penalty structure which violates international law.[89] The latter ground was discussed earlier, in connection with the ICTR's sentencing impact. The former ground is based on the Appeals Chamber's finding that the defendants may be unable to obtain witnesses to testify on their behalf in Rwanda, because such witnesses may fear being harassed, subjected to gacaca trials, or charged with the crime of "genocide ideology".[90] Senior ICTR prosecutors explained that they have subsequently continued to collaborate with the Rwandan authorities in order to address the weaknesses identified by the Tribunal's judges, with the intention of eventually applying again for the transfer of cases to Rwanda.[91] Thus, noted one ICTR official, Tribunal and Rwandan officials are together considering ways to improve Rwanda's witness protection scheme. One issue under discussion is whether the ICTR should be allowed to provide protection measures to defense witnesses who reside outside Rwanda and are reluctant to come to Rwanda to testify in national trials.[92] As part of this capacity building program, a three-day workshop on witness protection issues was given by ICTR officials to Rwandans, in November 2009 in Arusha.[93] The program's main aim was to move the current witness protection system in Rwanda out of the prosecutor's office, to be administered by an objective body so that it could be trusted by defense witnesses. Another aim of the program was to generally improve the protective measures available to witnesses in Rwanda.

88 See *supra* note 55. It is stressed that when this chapter was finalized, these five were the only referral requests made by the ICTR Prosecutor. At a later stage, however, three additional requests were made. In December 2011, the ICTR approved the first referral of a case to Rwanda. See *supra* note 31.

89 *Id.*

90 See, *e.g.*, *Munyakazi* Appeals Decision of October 8, 2008, *supra* note 55 at para. 37; *Kanyarukiga* Appeals Decision of October 30, 2008, *supra* note 55 at para. 26. The ICTR judges also added that many of the potential defence witnesses live abroad and will refuse altogether to enter Rwanda for these reasons. See *Munyakazi* Appeals Decision of October 8, 2008, *supra* note 55 at para. 40; *Kanyarukiga* Appeals Decision of October 30, 2008, *supra* note 55 at para. 31. Moreover, the ICTR judges suggested that the witness protection scheme in Rwanda is underfunded and understaffed, and that "the availability of video-link facilities is not a completely satisfactory solution with respect to the testimony of witnesses residing outside Rwanda". See *Munyakazi* Appeals Decision of October 8, 2008, *supra* note 55, para. 38; *Kanyarukiga* Appeals Decision of October 30, 2008, *supra* note 55 at para. 33. Charges of "genocide ideology" could be made under a Rwandan law from 2007, which imposes a sentence of 10 to 25 years' imprisonment for manifesting "genocidal ideology". According to Amnesty International, the law's terms are "vague and ambiguous", and it "could potentially stifle freedom of expression, and restrict the ability of the accused to put forward a defence in criminal trials". See AI 2009 WORLD REPORT, *supra* note 9.

91 Interview notes with author. Rwanda as well, has called the ICTR to refer cases to its national courts. See Hirondelle News, *Kigali Reiterates Its Requests to Try ICTR Cases* (June 5, 2009) <http://allafrica.com/stories/200906230906.html> (Accessed June 24, 2009).

92 Interview notes with author.

93 ICTR Press Release (November 16, 2009) <www.ictr.org/ENGLISH/PRESSREL/2009/623.htm> (Accessed February 22, 2010).

The above mentioned ICTR activities, it must be stressed, can improve Rwanda's judicial capacity to handle not only atrocity cases but also any other criminal cases.

2.6.2 *Employment of Rwandans by the ICTR*

The ICTR has also been contributing to Rwanda's judicial capacity by employing Rwandans since 2003.[94] ICTR officials stressed that Rwandans are also involved in the Tribunal as interns and legal researchers.[95] An ICTR judge recalled that the Tribunal, in its early years, employed Rwandans only as translators. However, at a later stage, the ICTR adopted a policy of including Rwandans in other sections, such as the Witness and Victims Support Section, the Protocol Unit, the Outreach Program, and the Prosecution. In addition, every ICTR Defense team has Rwandan investigators.[96] The judge stressed that in 1996-1997 it would have been impossible to let a Tutsi attorney cross examine a Hutu witness (or vice versa), but this has changed over time and today the ICTR Prosecution employs several Hutu and Tutsi lawyers.[97] A senior ICTR prosecutor noted that Rwandans serve in the Prosecution as trial attorneys and "associate investigators".[98] Still, two senior Rwandan officials criticized the ICTR for not employing Rwandan prosecutors and investigators before 2003, and for not including Rwandan judges until today.[99]

A senior ICTR official considered that the Tribunal cannot involve Rwandan judges because they may not be (or may not be perceived to be) objective.[100] According to an ICTR

94 This assumes that these Rwandans eventually return to Rwanda with the knowledge they gained at the ICTR. Two Rwandans, who are currently employed by the ICTR, indicated in interviews that they plan to return to Rwanda once the Tribunals winds up. One of them explained that he wanted to teach at a Rwandan university, or become a prosecutor in Rwanda. He stressed that working at the Tribunal has enhanced his knowledge of international law and his understanding of the crimes which were committed in Rwanda. It also developed his ability to be objective and think independently. These skills, he believed, would make him a good prosecutor in Rwanda. Interview notes with author.

95 Interview notes with author. Further, a Rwandan law professor noted that each year since about 2003, six or seven Rwandan law students engage as legal researchers at the ICTR for periods of two months. These students consequently develop an interest in international criminal law and the ICTR. Interview notes with author.

96 Interview notes with author.

97 Interview notes with author. A Rwandan working at the ICTR also confirmed that the ICTR did not want to employ Rwandans in the past, based on its belief that the animosity between Hutus and Tutsis would influence the quality of their work and jeopardize their objectivity. Interview notes with author.

98 Interview notes with author. The prosecutor explained that the associate investigators were qualified attorneys back in Rwanda. At the ICTR they assist with crime analysis. Their fluency in Kinyarwanda is highly valued in light of the limited language resources at the Tribunal's Prosecution, a section which has to deal with a lot of material in Kinyarwanda. These employees could return to the local system to work, which will be a way of transferring skills to Rwanda. However, some of them may end up being employed by other international tribunals.

99 Interview notes with author.

100 Interview notes with author.

judge, the bitterness and lack of trust across the ethnic divide in Rwanda in 1994 made it impossible for the Tribunal to engage Rwandan judges in its early years. But even later and until today such tension makes it problematic for the ICTR to employ Rwandan judges.[101]

2.6.3 *Infrastructural Development*

The ICTR Statute provides for the possibility that the sentences imposed by the Tribunal be served in Rwanda.[102] According to a senior Rwandan official, prison facilities in Rwanda were improved in view of the possibility that the ICTR will transfer its convicts to serve their sentences in Rwanda. He added that the improvements were financed by the Netherlands, not by ICTR.[103] An ICTR official confirmed that thanks to Dutch support, Rwanda has been able to build a prison conforming to international standards. In this light, the ICTR Registrar signed an agreement on the enforcement of sentences with Rwanda.f However, as of the time of writing, no ICTR prisoner had been transferred to Rwanda. The Tribunal official explained that the ICTR must be convinced that Rwanda can guarantee the safety of its prisoners before it transfers them to Rwanda.[104]

Another ICTR official noted that, in addition to improving prison facilities to meet the Tribunal's standards, Rwanda also developed a chamber that could host ICTR proceedings in its Supreme Court. This was done in anticipation that ICTR judges would hold trial sessions in Rwanda, a possibility provided by the ICTR Rules but which never materialized.[105]

---

101 Interview notes with author.

102 ICTR Statute, Art. 26.

103 Interview notes with author. The Rwandan official suggested that this is in contrast to the situation in the other African countries with which the ICTR has concluded agreements on enforcement of sentences, including Mali and Benin, which are getting capacity support from the ICTR, including for prison infrastructure development.

104 Interview notes with author. According to a Rwandan official, the provision on sentence enforcements in Art. 26 of the ICTR Statute is very unequivocal in stating that "sentences shall be served in Rwanda". Indeed, it continues with the words "or elsewhere", but the preference for Rwanda is demonstrated by the choice of the word "shall" as opposed to "will" or "may". He expressed frustration that notwithstanding this provision, as of the time of the interview, no prisoners were transferred by the ICTR to Rwanda, even after an agreement on the enforcement of ICTR sentences in Rwanda came to force in November 2008. He added that such an agreement was not required by the ICTR Statute, and thus ICTR prisoners could have been transferred to Rwanda even before November 2008. Interview notes with author.

105 Interview notes with author. The ICTR official noted that this court renovation project started as early as 1997, and was eventually completed years later with EU funding. Also see <www.delrwa.ec.europa.eu/en/whatsnew/Cour-Minijust-en.pdf> (Accessed July 7, 2009, noting that the EU provided funds since 2005 for refurbishing Rwanda's Supreme Court, but there is nothing in this item suggesting that this had any relation to the ICTR).

2.6.4 *Final Remarks on Capacity Building*

In light of ongoing capacity building activities by the ICTR in Rwanda, it may be premature to conclude to what extent the Tribunal has contributed to Rwanda's judicial capacity. But it can still be argued that had the ICTR started its capacity building activities in Rwanda at an earlier period, its domestic impact would have been greater by the time of writing these lines. While the length of time the Tribunal has been engaged in capacity building activities in Rwanda is only one out of several factors that can increase its impact on Rwanda, it is nonetheless an important one for several reasons: First, given the anticipated closure of the ICTR, capacity building activities starting in 2000 would have lasted more than double the duration of those that commenced in 2007. Had the training started earlier, not only would they have influenced more issues and people, but they may have also been able to benefit from a greater "improvement curve" due to more lessons learned over a longer period of time. Moreover, given the state of the Rwandan justice system in the immediate aftermath of the genocide, Rwanda would have benefited much more from judicial capacity building activities in those years than in any other period. Further, the willingness of the Tribunal's mandate-providers and supporters to fund or otherwise assist such activities may have eroded over time, both because of the ICTR's expected closure and Rwanda's reduced need for capacity building.

However, interviews revealed mixed opinions on whether the ICTR should have engaged earlier in capacity building activities in Rwanda. One senior Tribunal official expressed his personal view that the ICTR should have engaged in capacity building since its inception, but explained that some Tribunal officials discouraged such an approach at the time. Further, the Rwandan authorities did not cooperate with the Tribunal in those years, and Rwanda's civil society was too weak to generate the cooperation needed for capacity building.[106] Another senior ICTR official explained that the emotional turmoil and tension in Rwanda in the immediate aftermath of the genocide would have made it difficult for the ICTR to engage in capacity building activities at the time.[107]

Rwandans also expressed mixed views about this matter, but were generally more inclined than ICTR officials to accept that the ICTR's capacity building activities in Rwanda could have started earlier. A Rwanda lawyer suggested that the ICTR could have started its capacity building activities in Rwanda around the year 2000, once the Rwandan justice system was sufficiently developed to allow ICTR involvement.[108] A Rwandan Supreme Court

106 Interview notes with author.
107 Interview notes with author.
108 Interview notes with author.

judge understood that the ICTR was reluctant to engage in capacity building in Rwanda before 2003 because it wanted to appear objective, neutral, and independent from Rwanda. But he did not justify this reluctance.[109] Another prominent Rwandan judge added that the ICTR could not have engaged in capacity building activities in Rwanda before 2003 due to its own "teething problems".[110]

2.7 The SCSL and Sierra Leone

2.7.1 *Background to Domestic Response to the Atrocities*

In sharp contrast to Rwanda's judicial response to the genocide, Sierra Leonean national courts hardly prosecuted any of the war's atrocities. In fact, such proceedings were prevented by a blanket amnesty provided in the Lomé Peace Agreement of July 1999 ("Lomé Amnesty").[111] The Lomé Amnesty exempts perpetrators from prosecution by national courts for atrocities pre-dating the peace agreement. In lieu of such prosecutions, the peace agreement called for the creation of the Truth and Reconciliation Commission ("TRC").[112] While truth commissions can establish some degree of accountability through providing a historical account of the atrocities and associating them with certain groups and individuals, it remains questionable whether the TRC contributed to the eradication of impunity in Sierra Leone.[113] Eventually, as discussed in further detail below, Sierra Leonean courts tried only 88 low level suspects for relatively minor war-related crimes committed in 2000 (whereas the war's worst atrocities were committed before July 1999). Still, a showing that the SCSL somehow affected Sierra Leonean accountability processes can enhance our understanding of whether and how the Court contributed to reducing impunity and improving the rule of law in Sierra Leone. The remainder of this section focuses on the SCSL's impact on atrocity proceedings before Sierra Leonean criminal courts, and not the TRC.

109 Interview notes with author.

110 Interview notes with author.

111 Peace Agreement between the Government of Sierra Leone and the Revolutionary United Front of Sierra Leone (Lomé, July 7, 1999) <www.sierra-leone.org/Loméaccord.html> (Accessed May 30, 2009), Art. IX.

112 *Ibid*, Art. XXVI (1).

113 In October 2004, the TRC submitted its final report to the government. See Final Report of the Sierra Leone Truth and Reconciliation Commission (October 2004) <www.trcsierraleone.org> (Accessed December 20, 2009) (hereinafter: "TRC Report"). Its recommendations included increasing the protection of human rights, strengthening democracy and the rule of law, improving good governance, abolishing the death penalty, repealing laws that criminalize seditious libel, increasing the transparency of the mining industry, and establishing a reparations fund for war victims. Over four years later, both Amnesty International and Human Rights Watch criticized the Government for its slow progress in implementing the TRC recommendations. See HRW 2009 World Report, *supra* note 9; AI 2009 World Report, *supra* note 9.

2.8 SCSL IMPACT ON PROSECUTION RATES AND TRENDS

It is noted at the outset that the potential of the SCSL to influence domestic proceedings in Sierra Leone was *a priori* limited as domestic proceedings (at least for pre-Lomé crimes) were prevented by the Lomé Amnesty. The creators of the SCSL did not consider it their task to encourage national trials in Sierra Leone, and accordingly, did not mandate the Court to achieve this aim. Indeed, as shown below, the SCSL did not so far encourage the initiation – or even discussions about the initiation – of Sierra Leonean proceedings addressing pre-Lomé atrocities. A senior SCSL official considered that it is better not to have national trials if the local system cannot offer fundamental guarantees. Even if international standards of justice are provided by law, national trials should only be held if these standards are applied in practice, including protection to victims and witnesses. In Sierra Leone, added the Court official, there are concerns of fairness towards the accused and witnesses, and it may take time until fair trials are possible. However, the same official noted that the creators of international courts should bear in mind that the international cases may eventually have to be handed over to national courts. They should therefore plan in advance how to ensure that national courts are ready to receive such cases.[114]

On May 27, 2008, the Rules of Procedure and Evidence of the SCSL were amended to allow the Court to transfer cases to national courts, but the SCSL Prosecution never requested (or indicated that it would request) the Court's judges to refer cases to Sierra Leonean courts. Such a referral request, or an indication that one was being contemplated, could have encouraged national discussions about the need to abolish or restrict the Lomé Amnesty to enable Sierra Leonean courts to prosecute crimes addressed by the SCSL. However, in contrast to the parallel ICTR rule on case referrals, the relevant SCSL rule does not allow the Court to monitor or recall cases after having transferred them to national courts. This, combined with the lack of fair and efficient criminal proceedings in Sierra Leone, militated against such a request by the SCSL Prosecution. It is noted in this context that, according to a Sierra Leone Supreme Court judge, national discussions about prosecuting post-Lomé crimes never took place in Sierra Leone.[115]

In one of its earliest decisions, the SCSL Appeals Chamber ruled that the Lomé Amnesty was inapplicable to cases before international courts or national courts applying universal jurisdiction.[116] But the decision did not address the issue of the amnesty's applicability to cases before the national courts of Sierra Leone, perhaps because this issue was not raised before the SCSL

114 Interview notes with author.
115 Interview notes with author.
116 *Prosecutor v. Morris Kallon*, Brima Bazzy Kamara, SCSL-2004-15-AR72 (E), SCSL-2004-16-AR72(E), Decision on Challenge to Jurisdiction: Lomé Accord Amnesty, March 13, 2004.

judges, or because they did not consider it within their interest or authority to encourage national prosecutions. Still, had the SCSL staff wanted to encourage national discussions about abolishing or restricting the Lomé Amnesty, its outreach or capacity building initiatives could have included a public discussion about the status of blanket amnesties under international law and the above Appeals Chamber's decision (even if it did not specifically address the issue of the amnesty's applicability to national cases). Such public activities could have been especially effective given the lack of local reactions to the SCSL's amnesty decision.

The SCSL fell short of encouraging national prosecutions in Sierra Leone not only regarding pre-Lomé atrocities, but also regarding post-Lomé atrocities (which are not covered by the amnesty). In fact, a Sierra Leonean lawyer suggested that the SCSL may have encouraged national courts to remain inactive about one of the main *post-Lomé* atrocities: the abduction of 500 UN peacekeepers. The local lawyer considered that this event was not subject to national criminal proceedings in Sierra Leone because it was addressed by the SCSL.[117] Legally speaking, the two court systems can address the same event so long as each system deals with different defendants. Thus, since the SCSL only pursued the highest leaders of the crimes, the national courts could have prosecuted the mid-level commanders (and foot-soldiers) involved in the abduction. But if the lawyer is right, the handling of this event by the SCSL discouraged national courts from addressing it.

2.9 SCSL Normative Impact

2.9.1 Substantive/Procedural Norms

The SCSL is authorized by its Statute to prosecute certain Sierra Leonean domestic crimes, and, when amending or adopting SCSL Rules, be guided by domestic criminal procedures.[118] However, the Court refrained from resorting to domestic norms. A SCSL judge considered that the Court thus missed an important opportunity to interpret and develop national law, as well as to promote a public debate on whether Sierra Leonean courts can prosecute certain atrocities.[119] According to two senior members of the SCSL, who are

117 Interview notes with author. It is noted that only the top-level perpetrators are prosecuted by the SCSL while the mid and low level perpetrators who were involved in the abduction were never prosecuted.

118 SCSL Statute, Arts. 5 and 14(2).

119 Interview notes with author. Another senior member of the SCSL suggested that the Court's first Prosecutor refrained from charging the accused with national crimes because he assumed that the Lomé Amnesty would require the SCSL judges to cancel the charges. At the same time, however, the interviewee noted that it would have been useful to have charged some of the SCSL's defendants for the domestic crime of setting fire to property (under Art. 5 of the SCSL Statute), as eventually their burning acts became un-punishable. Interview notes with author.

familiar with the Sierra Leonean justice system, the SCSL has not been able to encourage the national system to improve procedural or substantive criminal norms.[120]

An examination of domestic atrocity-related trials, which took place in Sierra Leone after the establishment of the SCSL, further suggests that the SCSL had no normative impact on national criminal proceedings. In 2005 and 2006, the High Court in Freetown held two trials against a total of 88 individuals for war-related crimes which were perpetrated after the Lomé Peace Agreement (and therefore not covered by the Lomé Amnesty).[121] Both trials concerned low level perpetrators,[122] who were accused of relatively minor crimes committed in connection with insular incidents of hostilities. All 88 accused were charged with multiple domestic crimes, as international crimes are not covered by Sierra Leonean law.

The first trial concerned the shooting of demonstrators on May 8, 2000, where at least 20 people were killed. The 57 defendants were members of the political party of the Revolutionary United Front ("RUF"), the rebel faction that started Sierra Leone's civil war when it attacked the country from Liberia in 1991. They were charged with 81 counts of murder, conspiracy to commit murder, and shooting with intent to murder.[123] The judgment was rendered in April 2006.[124] Of the 57 defendants, only ten were convicted.[125] But before their appeal was heard, they were released as a political gesture by the President of Sierra Leone, Ahmad Tejan Kabbah of the Sierra Leone People's Party ("SLPP"). The exact reasons for their release are unknown. A Canadian lawyer who provided pro bono assistance to the defendant suggested that there was no political will to continue the trial. Another defense lawyer who was involved in this case suggested that the defendants were "unceremoniously released when the former ruling government wanted to use them to disrupt the 2007 general elections".[126]

The second trial concerned the abduction by rebels of 11 British soldiers near Freetown on August 8, 2000. The 31 defendants were members of the West Side Boys ("WSB"), a splinter group of the rebel faction Armed Forces Revolutionary Council ("AFRC") which was

120 Interview notes with author.

121 A valuable source of information about these trials was Clare da Silva, a Canadian lawyer who provided pro bono assistance over a number of years to the defendants.

122 The high level perpetrators who were arrested by the national authorities in 2000 were either transferred for trial to the SCSL (*e.g.* Foday Sankoh), or released before the national trials commenced (*e.g.* Mike Lamin).

123 The political party of the RUF was the Revolutionary United Front Party ("RUFP").

124 The accused were all arrested between May and November 2000. The case was committed to the High Court in Freetown on May 29, 2002. The trial started on June 7, 2005 and the hearings lasted until December 2005.

125 They were convicted of 15 counts of conspiracy to commit murder and received a sentence of ten years for each count to be served concurrently.

126 Interview notes with author.

involved in Sierra Leone's civil war.[127] The WSB members were charged with 31 counts of conspiracy to commit murder, robbery with violence, wounding with intent, and wounding. The High Court rendered its judgment on April 5, 2006, convicting seven of the 31 defendants.[128] All seven have appealed within the prescribed time-limit, but are still detained at the time of writing (four years later), waiting for their appeal to be considered.[129] In addition to this miscarriage of justice, other due process violations were common throughout the proceedings.[130] The first trial was also rife with due process violations.[131]

It may also be useful to examine a third national trial in Sierra Leone, which concerned a 2003 armed attack committed by elements of the AFRC on a military installation outside Freetown.[132] The attack took place after the official end of the war, and was regarded as a coup attempt by the ruling party at the time, the SLPP. It accordingly involved treason charges. But the trial can still teach us something about the quality of war-related domestic proceedings in Sierra Leone because, even if it did not concern atrocities against civilians, it addressed political violence similar to that which prevailed during the war (*i.e.* a rebel faction that fought the government during the civil war is now attacking the same government). The trial judgment was rendered by the High Court in Freetown on December 20, 2004. Of the 15 defendants, ten received the death penalty, one was sentenced to ten years of imprisonment, and four were acquitted. The SLPP was still in power when the trial

127 The AFRC was created by officers who left the army in 1997 and joined the RUF in fighting against government forces.

128 They were convicted of ten counts of conspiracy to commit murder, and sentenced to ten years for each count to be served concurrently, starting from the date of conviction (six years after the accused were arrested and four years after their case was committed to the High Court).

129 According to Clare da Silva, there seems to be little political interest in moving this trial forward.

130 Clare da Silva explained that while the arrests were made in 2000, and the case committed to the High Court in Freetown on May 29, 2002, charges were not made known to the accused until several years later. Also see OCHA, *Humanitarian Situation Report on Sierra Leone* (July 2004) <www.reliefweb.int/rw/rwb.nsf/db900sid/EVIU-63HJ45?OpenDocument> (Accessed May 30, 2009) ("On 21 July an incident occurred within the Pademba Road Prison in central Freetown, involving 33 former-West Side Boys. The insurgents have been held in the Prison for over two years without charge and were scheduled to appear in court. At the last minute, they were notified by the High Court that their case had once again been postponed indefinitely and thus should not appear in court. Upon receiving the message the indictees became highly agitated and started yelling that they 'must go to court today'. This situation led the prison authorities to contact the [Sierra Leone Police] who subsequently deployed anti-riot elements at the Prison location.").

131 It was stressed by Clare da Silva that the accused first received legal representation around the time the trial started in June 2005, about five years after they were arrested in 2000. Also, the sentences were to start from the date in which the case was committed to the High Court (two years after the accused were arrested).

132 Johnny Paul Koroma, the former leader of the AFRC, was arrested by the national authorities in connection with this event, but escaped two months before he was indicted by the SCSL (for wartime atrocities). The author obtained information about this case from Clare da Silva, who provided pro-bono assistance to the accused in this case. See also, Amnesty International, Sierra Leone: Amnesty International expresses dismay at 10 death sentences for treason (December 21, 2004) <www.amnesty.org/en/library/asset/AFR51/009/2004/en/dom-AFR510092004en.html> (Accessed May 30, 2009) (hereinafter: "AI Expresses Dismay").

judgment was issued. A Canadian lawyer who assisted the defense criticized the fairness of the proceedings. She also noted that the court convicted individuals who were merely present at the crime scene but had no other links to the crimes.[133] In addition, the imposition of the death penalty only weeks after the TRC recommended its abolition attracted criticism.[134]

Four years after the High Court's judgment, the Sierra Leonean Court of Appeals overturned the convictions, revoked the death penalties, and acquitted all the defendants. A senior SCSL official noted that although the acquittal was considered in Sierra Leone as a victory of justice, it was based on a technical detail, namely, the lack of corroboration of an accomplice's testimony.[135] It is noted that by the time the appeals judgment was rendered, Sierra Leone's ruling party was the All People's Congress ("APC"), which replaced the SLPP after winning the 2007 elections.[136] Since the APC had some affiliation to the AFRC, the appellate court may have been influenced by political pressure to issue an acquittal.[137] Regardless of whether it was justice or politics, there is nothing indicating that the SCSL had any impact on the proceedings in this case.[138]

According to a Sierra Leonean lawyer, some of the defense attorneys in the above national cases were also involved with the SCSL. However, no references to SCSL norms were made during the national proceedings. The lawyer explained that referring to SCSL norms in national trials would have been useless, as the bench would not have applied such provisions.[139] This is unfortunate, in my view, as perhaps some of the due process violations would have been avoided if SCSL procedural norms had been more influential in domestic proceedings.

133 Clare da Silva, *Will Justice Prevail?* (June 4, 2007) <www.guardian.co.uk/commentisfree/2007/jun/04/will-justiceprevail> (Accessed May 30, 2009).

134 *Id.* See also, AI Expresses Dismay, *supra* note 132.

135 Interview notes with author.

136 On August 11, 2007, Sierra Leone held nation-wide presidential and parliamentary elections, which were considered internationally as credible and peaceful. The APC, the opposition party since 1992, won a parliamentary majority taking 59 of 112 seats, while the previously ruling SLPP took 43 seats. Ernest Bai Koroma of the APC was elected as Sierra Leone's president. This outcome reportedly "marked a smooth democratic transition from one government to the other". See The Human Rights Commission of Sierra Leone, "First Annual Report on the State of Human Rights in Sierra Leone 2007" (March 2008). Copy with author.

137 For example, the APC chief presidential bodyguard is former AFRC combatant Idriss Kamara (nicknamed "Leather Boots"). It is noted that the APC party was previously in opposition to the SLPP government, and it was the latter which requested the creation of the SCSL.

138 In addition, criminal proceedings were initiated in recent years against former RUF spokesman Omrie Golley. He was arrested in 2006, when the SLPP was in power, and charged with an attempted coup. Golley was in pre-trial detention for 22 months, at which stage the charges against him were dropped and he was released by the current APC government. Similar to the acquittal of ten soldiers on death row, the dropping of the treason charges against Omrie Golley could be a result of either improved justice standards or political pressure. Either way, nothing indicates that this development is attributable to the SCSL.

139 Interview notes with author.

2.9.2 *Jurisprudential Impact*

The Sierra Leonean lawyer explained that in addition to lacking references to SCSL norms, domestic proceedings in Sierra Leone also lack references to SCSL case-law. He suggested that the development of criminal law in Sierra Leone is generally discouraged, and national courts do not normally rely on new jurisprudence, especially when it relates to human rights issues. He added that national judges and lawyers lack knowledge of SCSL jurisprudence.[140] As for certain doctrines followed by the SCSL, such as command responsibility and joint criminal enterprise, the local lawyer noted that there was no need to apply them in the above national cases as they concerned the direct conduct of the accused.[141]

2.9.3 *Possible Future Impact*

Sierra Leone's national law currently does not cover international crimes. The SCSL has not made any formal attempts to encourage Sierra Leone to criminalize international crimes, but at least two of its prosecutors (including a Sierra Leonean national) have been lobbying the Sierra Leonean government to domestically implement the Rome Statute.[142] If their advocacy efforts prove successful, and international criminal law norms are consequently internalized into Sierra Leonean law, such norm internalization could be regarded as an impact of the SCSL on Sierra Leone's justice system.[143] But interviewees explained that even if Sierra Leone implements the Rome Statute domestically, the implementing legislation would not apply to atrocities committed during the country's civil war of 1991-2002 as it could only have a prospective effect.[144] Still, the introduction of such a domestic law would have an important general effect on the national justice system, and signal that Sierra Leone no longer tolerates impunity for atrocities.[145]

140 Interview notes with author.

141 Interview notes with author.

142 Interview notes with author. It is noted that Sierra Leone has ratified the Rome Statute. However, as Sierra Leone is a dualist country, the Rome Statute must be incorporated into its national law before it can be applied domestically.

143 While this internalization is encouraged not by the SCSL directly but rather by its staff members acting in their personal capacity, it could still be considered an SCSL impact because it was made possible by the Court's presence in Sierra Leone. Further, one of the advocates of this norm internalization is a Sierra Leonean, whose increased awareness to the importance of domesticating international criminal norms may have stemmed from his work at the SCSL.

144 Interview notes with author.

145 However, as of the time of writing, it is too early to tell whether the advocacy efforts of the SCSL prosecutors will succeed.

2.10 SCSL Sentencing Impact

The maximum sentence in Sierra Leone is the death penalty, which was last applied in 1998 in connection with treason charges.[146] The SCSL, consistent with international law, cannot impose the death penalty. It has so far imposed sentences ranging from 15 to 52 years imprisonment. Sentences issued by the Sierra Leonean courts in the above-mentioned atrocity-related national trials were much lower. One reason for this difference could be that the crimes addressed by the national courts were of lesser gravity than those addressed by the SCSL. But still, a senior government official in Sierra Leone considered that the sentences imposed at the SCSL were too high even for the atrocities it addressed.[147] This is particularly interesting considering that in Sierra Leone the death sentence is applicable by law to ordinary crimes such as murder (even if it has not been applied in practice since 1998).

It is recalled that the High Court in Freetown convicted and sentenced to death ten persons in 2004, in connection with the 2003 coup attempt. Following this ruling, Amnesty International lobbied for the abolition of the death penalty in Sierra Leone by calling for "an end to the discrepancy [in sentencing practices] between national courts and the Special Court for Sierra Leone".[148] Thus, the SCSL sentencing norms are used by human rights groups in their efforts to advocate for the abolition of the death penalty in Sierra Leone. However, aside from "allowing" its sentencing norms to be used in this manner, the SCSL has not been actively encouraging Sierra Leone to abolish the death penalty. A Sierra Leonean human rights activist explained that the SCSL has also refrained from encouraging national actors to advocate for the death penalty's abolition.[149]

As discussed above, the death sentences imposed by the High Court of Freetown were reversed on appeal in 2008. A subsequent news article reported that it was "the first successful appeal against a death penalty... opening the possibility of an eventual end to capital punishment [in Sierra Leone]".[150] However, despite this expression of hope, and the TRC's recommendation in 2004 that the death penalty be abolished,[151] capital punishment still exists

146 In October 1998, 24 persons were publicly executed after a military court convicted and sentenced them to death for treason charges. Although death sentences were imposed in Sierra Leone after this trial, none were actually executed. As of the end of 2008, Amnesty International reported that 13 persons were on death row. See AI 2009 World Report, *supra* note 9. Human Rights Watch reported that 12 individuals were on death row in early 2009. See HRW 2009 World Report, *supra* note 9.

147 Interview notes with author.

148 AI Expresses Dismay, *supra* note 132.

149 Interview notes with author.

150 Mohamed Fofanah, *Death Penalty – Sierra Leone: Successful Appeal Strengthens Case For Abolition*, IPS News, Freetown, December 12, 2008) <http://ipsnews.net/news.asp?idnews=45088> (Accessed May 30, 2009).

151 TRC Report, *supra* note 113, Vol. 2, Ch. 3, para. 54.

in Sierra Leone. Amnesty International reported that attempts made in August 2008 by civil society groups to pressure the Sierra Leonean Constitutional Review Commission to abolish the death penalty were unsuccessful, and that Sierra Leone abstained, in December 2008, on a UN General Assembly resolution calling for a worldwide moratorium on executions.[152]

While the SCSL did not have an impact thus far on Sierra Leone's sentencing norms, it may still have such an impact in the future, if, for example, activists will persuade the government to abolish the death penalty by stressing the discrepancies between the SCSL penalty norms and local standards.

2.11 SCSL Capacity Impact

As the SCSL's mandate comes to its end, it is increasingly becoming engaged in capacity building initiatives in Sierra Leone.[153] Some of these initiatives are motivated by the Court's desire to leave behind a legacy.[154] Others are inspired by the Sierra Leonean members of the SCSL who want to see their national system improve. There are also capacity building activities that have resulted from the Court's need to ensure the long term fulfillment of its ongoing residual obligations. Thus, for example, the SCSL has recently become involved in helping Sierra Leone establish a national witness protection program. This and other SCSL activities that can strengthen the judicial capacity of Sierra Leone are discussed in the following paragraphs. It is stressed that while these activities do not necessarily focus on enabling national prosecutions of the war's atrocities, they are important in that they can help enhance Sierra Leone's capacity to handle complex criminal proceedings, thereby strengthening the national criminal system as a whole.

2.11.1 National Witness Protection Scheme

As noted above, the SCSL has recently become involved in supporting the establishment of a national witness protection program in Sierra Leone. According to a SCSL official, this two year program is led by the SCSL Witness and Victims Section ("WVS") and funded

152 AI 2009 World Report, *supra* note 9.

153 Thus, the SCSL President reported to the UN Security Council in 2007 that "[t]he Court was continuing to transfer expertise to Sierra Leoneans through a number of programmes, including training on courtroom interpretation, witness protection and detention standards." See Security Council, Department of Public Information (News and Media Division), Special Court for Sierra Leone Faces Funding Crisis, as Charles Taylor Trial Gets Underway; Security Council Told Today in Briefing by Court's Senior Officials, U.N. Doc. SC/9037 (June 8, 2007).

154 *Id.* (the SCSL President stating that "It should come as no surprise that, as the Court approaches the end of its mandate, legacy issues are one of its top most priorities").

by the Oak Foundation. WVS has already provided the Government with a layout of the infrastructural requirements, personnel needs, a tentative budget, and draft legislation. It is also preparing for the program's implementation process, including holding training sessions for the Sierra Leone Police with trainers from a UK police force.[155] According to the SCSL official, the Government is receptive to the Court's suggestions, and Sierra Leone's President and other senior officials agree that there is a need for a national witness protection program.

Another SCSL official explained that the national interest in a witness protection plan was a result of the SCSL's presence and process. Sierra Leoneans requested the SCSL to encourage their local authorities to set up a witness protection system on the national level.[156] According to yet another SCSL official, a national witness protection scheme would allow the Sierra Leonean authorities to deal better with ordinary criminal cases, as today even basic contact with witnesses is lacking.[157] It is noted that an official of the Sierra Leonean judiciary, who was generally critical of the SCSL, referred with satisfaction to the SCSL's intention to establish a national witness protection program.[158]

2.11.2 Other Training Activities and Consultations

A top SCSL official noted that in late 2008 the Court has embarked on about 20 different training programs for Sierra Leoneans, from teaching the anti-corruption commission how to use "insider witnesses" in their proceedings, to holding a course on defensive driving given by the SCSL's transport unit. Any skill which exists in the SCSL is being transferred to relevant Sierra Leoneans. The SCSL plans to continue on this path until it winds up, he added.[159] According to other SCSL members, a Legacy Working Group has been established within the Court, in which national institutions participate. The group's primary aim is to ensure skill transfer to the national level. The SCSL has assessed the needs of national institutions, such as prisons, police, and the Attorney General's office. It is now training the personnel in these institutions in the needed areas. The Court is also training investigators of the national Human Rights Commission and Anti-Corruption

155 Interview notes with author. Also see SCSL Press Release, November 5, 2009 <www.sc-sl.org/LinkClick.aspx?fileticket=kJu0OgoLU2E%3d&tabid=53> (Accessed December 3, 2009) (referring to a one-month training program given by the SCSL to local officers with the assistance of UK trainers).

156 Interview notes with author. The official added that since such activities were not budgeted for in advance, the SCSL had to fund-raise for this initiative.

157 Interview notes with author.

158 Interview notes with author.

159 Interview notes with author.

Commission, as well as court reporters.[160] Additional capacity building initiatives of the SCSL in Sierra Leone, explained a Court official, include conducting seminars about international humanitarian law at the law school of Foray Bay College and at the local Bar School. This is done every year or two.[161]

Moreover, a SCSL staff member mentioned that the Court is encouraging the establishment of a public defense office at the national level, which would select and assign duty counsel, and which would largely rely on the local bar association.[162] A senior Sierra Leonean official confirmed that the government has been encouraged by the SCSL to create a national public defender's office.[163]

SCSL officials have also focused on developing a legal and institutional framework to prosecute future international crimes: As noted above, SCSL officials are promoting the domestic implementation of the Rome Statute.[164] In addition, a SCSL official indicated that there are discussions within the SCSL about encouraging the establishment of a war crimes office under Sierra Leone's Ministry of Justice.[165] It is also noted that the SCSL intends to leave behind its physical building for local use.

2.11.3 *Employment of Sierra Leoneans by the SCSL*

The SCSL's reliance on national staff has a strong capacity building component. It could ensure that once the Court completes its work, Sierra Leone will be left with professionals capable of supporting a rule of law society. More than half of the SCSL's staff members are Sierra Leoneans. While many of them are in non-professional posts, such as drivers, security guards and cleaners, others are placed in senior professional positions. In addition, both the Defense and Prosecution recruit young Sierra Leonean lawyers as "Junior Professional Consultants",[166] and there is an internship program for Sierra Leoneans at the SCSL. Further, Sierra Leonean police officers and investigators are seconded to the

---

160 Interview notes with author.

161 Interview notes with author.

162 Interview notes with author.

163 Interview notes with author.

164 Interview notes with author.

165 The official explained that while there is no political will to hold national cases for past atrocities, such a war crimes office may be useful in future cases of atrocities. Interview notes with author.

166 A Sierra Leonean lawyer, who was involved with the SCSL, explained that the Defence teams at the SCSL were initially hesitant to employ Sierra Leoneans. However, when the Registry allocated resources for this purpose (out of a special EU fund) the Defence teams began recruiting young Sierra Leonean lawyers as "Junior Professional Consultants". This was done to build domestic capacity, but also to reinforce the Defence teams. From 2007, the lawyer added, the Prosecution also began admitting national lawyers as Junior Professional Consultants. Interview notes with author.

SCSL for 90 day periods, sensitizing them to complex criminal investigations and evidence handling techniques.[167]

Two senior SCSL officials explained that by employing nationals, the Court exposes them to international standards of trial conduct, including with regard to evidence management and court administration, and that this will eventually bring knowledge and expertise into the Sierra Leonean system.[168] Also a SCSL judge considered that by employing nationals, the SCSL creates an important impact on national capacity.[169] However, SCSL officials also stressed that there is a risk that nationals working at the SCSL would not return to the national system after the Court winds up, preferring instead to seek international jobs. For example, it is unlikely that the Sierra Leonean judges at the SCSL will later serve with the Sierra Leonean judiciary. From this perspective, the Court may be depleting national capacity instead of improving it.[170]

Moreover, a Sierra Leonean lawyer indicated that too few local lawyers were involved in the SCSL's process to be able to influence national criminal proceedings. When several local lawyers tried to participate in criminal proceedings before national courts in a manner influenced by their previous practice before the SCSL, their approach was too foreign for their local colleagues to accept. In his view, had more national lawyers been involved in the work of the SCSL, a more significant local impact would have resulted.[171] Another interviewee, a Sierra Leonean human rights activist, also suggested that some Sierra Leoneans who had worked at the SCSL and subsequently returned to the national judiciary, did not eventually use the skills they acquired at the SCSL to improve processes at the national level.[172]

2.11.4 Final Remarks on Capacity Building

The SCSL's geographical location, combined with the institutional support it receives from the Government of Sierra Leone, provide it with an excellent opportunity to engage in

167 See INTERNATIONAL CENTER FOR TRANSITIONAL JUSTICE, PROSECUTIONS CASE STUDIES SERIES: THE SPECIAL COURT FOR SIERRA LEONE UNDER SCRUTINY (Tom Perriello & Marieke Wierda, March 2006). "Some human rights observers have expressed concern privately about police involvement [with the SCSL], given the negative track record of the police during the conflict, but in general the officers conducted themselves well and generated no complaints. Two of the officers who spent extended time working with the [SCSL Office of the Prosecution] have returned to top positions in the police, one as the third-highest ranking member of the office and another as director for the Eastern District." The report also highlights that Sierra Leonean police officers have been working as investigators at the SCSL since it became operative, and were responsible for the arrests of five of its indictees within a matter of hours in March 2003.

168 Interview notes with author.

169 Interview notes with author.

170 Interview notes with author.

171 Interview notes with author.

172 Interview notes with author.

local capacity building initiatives. However, while most interviewees agreed that the SCSL should contribute to capacity building in Sierra Leone, they expressed mixed views on whether the Court is in fact achieving this aim.[173] An official of the Sierra Leonean judiciary, who was generally very critical about the SCSL, did not consider that the Court has significantly contributed to national capacity.[174] When asked about a recent training the SCSL has given to national court reporters, the official complained that only a limited number of nationals were trained, and that the training was too short to be significant.[175] The local judiciary official was also critical about the SCSL's intention to leave behind the court-house building to the national judiciary, noting that the national system does not have the available means to maintain the building.[176]

Moreover, a SCSL judge expressed uncertainty as to the willingness of Sierra Leone's national judges to learn from the experience of the SCSL.[177] Another SCSL judge, who tried once to interest the former Chief Justice of Sierra Leone in establishing a liaison between national and SCSL judges, explained that there was little interest among both judiciaries.[178] According to a senior SCSL official, the Court had unsuccessfully attempted to hold training sessions in cooperation with the local bar association.[179] Such formal or informal liaisons, including training sessions involving both international and local legal professionals, could have helped increase the SCSL's impact on domestic capacity to handle war related prosecutions. However, according to SCSL officials, the Court is expected to increase its capacity building activities as it winds up its work.[180] Therefore, it may be premature to draw conclusions about the Court's contribution to capacity building in Sierra Leone, because its

2.12 Conclusion

International courts can only prosecute a handful of perpetrators in each mass atrocity case. Therefore, to effectively fight impunity in their target states, the international community should adopt a comprehensive approach which promotes the parallel utilization

173 Interview notes with author.
174 Interview notes with author.
175 Interview notes with author.
176 Interview notes with author.
177 Interview notes with author.
178 Interview notes with author.
179 Interview notes with author.
180 Interview notes with author. It should also be noted that any capacity building activities undertaken by the SCSL were not mandated by the Court's creators and were therefore not budgeted for in advance. This forces the Court's staff to continuously raise funds to finance capacity building initiatives. It also means that such initiatives are designed according to their personal vision, and not as part of an organized comprehensive plan aimed at enhancing national capacity (and willingness) to try perpetrators of war-related crimes.

of international and national accountability processes. While such a comprehensive approach can (and should) be implemented through a variety of means, one way to encourage fair and genuine national accountability processes is to ensure that the relevant international court has a positive impact on domestic procedures. It is also important that the international and national processes complement rather than compete with each other. An international court is set up when the national justice system is struggling to rebuild what was destroyed as a consequence of the mass atrocities. At that stage, the international court is well placed to support national courts and in particular encourage them to prosecute the atrocities in parallel to its own trials. A calibrated effort to prosecute all perpetrators (or at least the high and mid level ones), by utilizing in parallel national and international courts, will ensure that norms and procedures developed in international courts will be applied domestically where needed.

Furthermore, international courts have more resources to attract leading world experts on international criminal law. If the national and international systems work together, the contribution of these experts (for example in the area of norm development), would be more likely to permeate into the national level. In such an environment the international court will become more relevant and acceptable on the local level, inevitably enhancing its ability to promote accountability in the relevant society. As noted above, the impact of international criminal courts on national justice systems can be linked specifically to (the quantity and quality of) domestic atrocity-related proceedings, or more broadly relate to the national criminal justice system as a whole. The position of this chapter is that both types of impact are avenues through which international criminal courts can reduce impunity and improve the rule of law in their target countries.

Focusing on the ICTR and SCSL, this chapter has identified the influences of these international courts on judicial procedures in their target countries. As shown above, the SCSL's impact on the Sierra Leonean justice system was relatively limited. This suggests, according to the point of view of this chapter, that the Court's contribution so far to reducing impunity and improving the rule of law in Sierra Leone was also limited. Indeed, Sierra Leone's national amnesty regime limited the potential impact that the SCSL could have had on domestic atrocity-related proceedings, but the Court could have tried to encourage national prosecutions by sending a clearer message on the domestic level that international law is developing in the direction of prohibiting such blanket amnesties from covering international crimes, even in national courts. It could have also tried to create better links with national judicial institutions, even informally, for example, through its current or former Sierra Leonean staff members. In addition, by steering away from applying domestic law, the SCSL missed an opportunity to contribute to national normative developments. Thus, even years after the Court's establishment, it has not managed to encourage accountability for past atrocities in Sierra Leone. Nonetheless, the SCSL did (and still does) have a certain degree of impact on national capacity to handle criminal proceedings in Sierra Leone.

In Rwanda, where mass domestic prosecutions address the atrocities, the ICTR may not need to encourage national trials in order to reduce impunity and improve the rule of law. Rather, it could play a role in helping Rwanda improve the quality of the national accountability procedures. It is recalled that the Rwandan justice system has been internationally criticized for being unfair and imposing victor's justice. If the critics are correct, then accountability may not be achieved in Rwanda until the quality of domestic justice is improved. But even if the critics are wrong, and Rwanda's justice system does offer fair trials and treats citizens equally, their criticism can still undermine the struggle to achieve accountability for the atrocities. This is because the mere perception of the international community that Rwanda's domestic justice system is unfair will prevent third states from extraditing to Rwanda the many perpetrators who still live freely outside Rwanda. As most of them will not be prosecuted in their countries of residence, due to lack of political will or judicial jurisdiction, the attainment of accountability for Rwanda's atrocities can be adversely affected. Thus, even if the critics are wrong, by helping or motivating Rwanda to further strengthen its judiciary, the ICTR could encourage more favourable international perceptions about Rwandan justice and thereby increase its own contribution to accountability and rule of law in Rwanda.

A senior Rwandan prosecutor considered that if the UN Security Council wanted the ICTR to have an impact on national trials in Rwanda, it should have opted for a model of an international court that was more complementary to national proceedings.[181] However, research shows that other existing models of international courts were not necessarily more successful in encouraging national trials. For example, the ICC, even though its jurisdiction is complementary to national courts, has thus far not been able to encourage national atrocity-related prosecutions in its target states.[182] Also the SCSL, as demonstrated above, despite having jurisdiction over domestic crimes and including national judges, did not encourage national atrocity-related proceedings in Sierra Leone.

181 Interview notes with author.

182 Sigall Horovitz, Uganda: Interaction Between International and National Responses to the Mass Atrocities (DOMAC Report, forthcoming); Sigall Horovitz, DR Congo: Interaction between International and National Responses to the Mass Atrocities (DOMAC Report, forthcoming); Sigall Horovitz, Sudan: Interaction between International and National Responses to the Mass Atrocities' (DOMAC Report, forthcoming). However, there is evidence that the ICC has had some success in encouraging domestic atrocity-related proceedings in Colombia, where the ICC has not commenced investigations as of the time of writing, but indicated that it might do so. See, *e.g.*, Alejandro Chehtman, The Impact of the ICC on Colombia: Positive Complementarity on Trial (DOMAC Report, forthcoming).

By contrast, as this chapter demonstrates, the ICTR has managed to encourage significant normative and capacity developments in Rwanda, include strengthening due process guarantees, improving capacities to handle atrocity proceedings, and promoting the abolition of the death penalty and life imprisonment in isolation. The ICTR also motivated the improvement of Rwandan prison facilities and, importantly, encouraged a national war-crimes trial involving RPF defendants. The Tribunal managed to generate many of these domestic effects by introducing a procedure for referring cases to national jurisdictions. Domestic influences of the ICTR were also enabled by its proactive Prosecutor, who co-operated with the Rwandan authorities by sharing evidence against suspects who had not yet been indicted by the ICTR.[183] Significantly, Rwanda's own approach was also crucial in this regard. Many of the ICTR's domestic influences were enabled by Rwanda's policy of accountability for past atrocities. Further, Rwanda's judicial authorities, by repeatedly making adjustments to meet the ICTR's requirements for transferring cases and evidence, despite the challenges facing a justice system being (re-)built almost from scratch, played a significant role in enabling ICTR domestic influences. These conditions, which were lacking in Sierra Leone, may explain variations in the respective domestic influences of the ICTR and SCSL. But the position of Sierra Leone was clear from the time the SCSL was established. Thus, as suggested above, to more effectively contribute to accountability and rule of law in Sierra Leone, the SCSL should have made greater efforts to influence the national justice system.

It is stressed that the domestic impact of the ICTR and SCSL may need to be re-assessed later, given that both courts are still engaged in capacity building activities as they prepare for closure. However, I hope that by identifying their domestic impact to date, this chapter has enriched our understanding of whether and how these international courts have contributed so far to reducing impunity and improving the rule of law in Rwanda and Sierra Leone.

183 It is noted that, in addition, the ICTR Statute's provisions on prisoner transfers have led to domestic influences.

3 From Protracted Conflict to Sustained Peace in Sierra Leone

The Contribution of the Special Court for Sierra Leone and the Sierra Leone Truth and Reconciliation Commission

Mba Chidi Nmaju

3.1 Introduction

Almost a decade after the brutal civil war in Sierra Leone, the country has found stability and peace. The conflict had for a decade appeared intractable and protracted. The several unsuccessful peace deals demonstrate the intractability of the conflict. As a result, it became protracted. Fighting continued for almost 10 years. In addition, it was a complex yet brutal conflict that involved several parties. There were high expectations that the Lomé Peace Agreement would finally usher in prolonged peace and stability. The Truth and Reconciliation Commission (TRC) was established pursuant to the agreement. Despite these measures, the Lomé peace process was abandoned when fighting resumed. The Special Court for Sierra Leone (SCSL) was thereafter established when peace was temporarily restored to Sierra Leone through the efforts of Nigeria and subsequently, ECOMOG intervention. However, the stability of the country was still uncertain at that time.

After several attempts, peace finally returned to Sierra Leone in 2002. This time the peace translated to a relatively prolonged stability. Since then, the TRC has concluded its operations and issued a three volume report. Along with that, the SCSL is in the process of completing its work. There are indications the two institutions have helped in sustaining peace. The available data from the country and the two institutions can fairly indicate the extent of their contribution, if any, to sustaining the peace. In fact, there may be some lessons from the experience of Sierra Leone. There may have been a synergy or conflict in the relationship between the two institutions and as a result the extent to which they collectively or separately facilitated the stability in Sierra Leone may be important for policy makers in other post-conflict societies.

This chapter is in three parts. The first part largely describes the factors that led to the complex, brutal and long civil war. Additionally, it explains how these factors made peace difficult to attain. It traces the advent of a restorative mechanism (TRC) to promote reconciliation and peace; as well as a retributive mechanism (which was added later). The second and third parts examine the extent the two institutions contributed to Sierra Leone's prolonged stability. While the second part reviews the ways the institutions promoted peace and security, the third part investigates their contributions to the rule of law in the advancement of Sierra Leone's legal system.

3.2 An Overview of the Socio-Economic and Political Background to the Conflicts in Sierra Leone

A review of the historical background to the crisis in Sierra Leone is essential to appreciate the impact of the TRC and SCSL. The socio-economic context of the country influenced the conflict, the peace processes and the institutions set up after the conflict. Several factors led to the conflict which was fought with severe brutality. The victims were mainly civilians, most of who were amputated, tortured and raped by the combatants.

Sierra Leone was set up for political and civil disorder by decades of political exploitation. The exploitation led to the breakdown of political, social and economic structure. It culminated in the general distrust that ordinary Sierra Leoneans had for the government led by the All People's Congress (APC). Michael Foray aptly describes the effect on the society:

> In the process of perpetuating and enriching itself, the APC . . . subverted the rule of law, undermined the public institutions, popularized and institutionalized a culture of violence and corruption. The civil service and the judiciary were heavily corrupted, the army and the police were politicized and the economy was radically criminalized and destroyed. In short, the whole fabric of the society was completely shredded.[1]

The consequence of the APC government's policies was the widespread feeling of injustice and unhappiness.

The rebel incursions into Sierra Leone from Liberia, on March 23, 1991, started what turned out to be a long drawn out civil war. The conflict was unlike other African conflicts.

1 Michael Foray, *Peace by Other Means: The Missing Link in DDR Programmes*, in Bound to Cooperate: Conflict, Peace and People in Sierra Leone, 99, 101 (Anatole Ayissi & Robin-Edwards Poulton eds., 2000).

It was not rooted in the traditional antagonisms of religious strife, tribal tensions and hatred between the factions.[2] However, the conflict was similar to other African conflicts to the extent that it was traceable to competition for political and economic resources. The combined effect of corruption and other political factors permeated the social fabrics of the society. In effect, it galvanized the Revolutionary United Front (RUF) into war and diluted the loyalties of government soldiers during the war and thus prolonging the war.

The consequences of the corrupt environment created and sustained by the Sierra Leonean government may have led to the war. In 1970 Siaka Stevens succeeded in entrenching a single-party system of government and a culture of patronage.[3] The one-party system bred a policy of consolidating control by putting resources under the direction of a few party members.[4] Those state officials often used the power to enrich themselves and their associates.[5] There was no mechanism for accountability within the political and legal system. The existing legal mechanisms were either inefficient or inadequate.[6] Therefore, corruption was centralized in the hands of a few party henchmen. The resulting patronage accelerated the disintegration of the Sierra Leonean society and subsequently led to state collapse.[7] It is safe to suggest that the APC rule destroyed democratic accountability within the society.[8]

It has been argued that the APC government's strategy of exclusion and the pervasive official corruption effectively damaged "the enterprise of the people and their will to be governed."[9] For instance, despite the high unemployment rate in the country, state officials lived in affluence.[10] The legitimate efforts of ordinary citizens to earn a living were often limited by the system of patronage which benefited only the cronies of the party (APC). The public discontent was often exhibited by university students who organized rallies

---

2 *Id.* at 99; see also, Alfred B. Zack-Williams, *The Political Economy of Civil War*, 20 Third World Quarterly 148 (1999).

3 Jimmy D. Kandeh, *Ransoming the State: Elite Origins of Subaltern Terror in Sierra Leone*, 26 Review of African Political Economy 349, 350-352 (1999).

4 *Id.*; Joe A.D. Alie, *A Price for Peace? Justice and Reconciliation in Post-War Sierra Leone, in* Bound to Cooperate: Conflict, Peace and People in Sierra Leone, *supra* note 1 at 19-20.

5 Kandeh, *supra* note 3, at 351.

6 There was no transparency and accountability in the system of governance under the APC. The courts and the legal system were inadequately funded and inefficient. Government officials implicated in corruption scandals were not prosecuted under the APC regime. Steven's successor, Joseph Momoh attempted to bring responsibility to the government by setting up some accountability institutions such as 'State of Economic Emergency' and 'Operation Clean Slate' but his efforts failed due to weak political will to tackle the deep problem of corruption. See Alie, *supra* note 4, at 29; David Keen, Conflict & Collusion in Sierra Leone, 33 (2005); Zack-Williams, *supra* note 2, at 146; Kandeh, *supra* note 3, at 92.

7 Kandeh, *supra* note 3, at 20.

8 Zack-Williams, *supra* note 2, at 143.

9 *Id.* at 144.

10 Alie, *supra* note 4, at 29-33.

and protests against the socio-economic situation.[11] It was not uncommon for the APC government to violently break up the rallies.[12] The increase in unemployment and corruption boosted the business of illegal mining of diamonds.[13] The surge in the social and political restiveness of ordinary Sierra Leoneans contributed to the atmosphere which the RUF capitalized on.[14] Rural communities and farmers were marginalized and exploited. Those who opposed the corrupt policies of the government were sidelined and their communities neglected, while those who cooperated with the government were rewarded.[15]

The economic problems of the country exacerbated the tension in the society. Three major factors contributed to the economic predicament. The first factor was the effect of the 1980s collapse of the price of coffee. Second, there was a reduction in state resources due to the continued illegal mining of diamonds. Consequently, the country's debt to the International Monetary Fund (IMF) became financially strenuous. There was a gradual paucity of resources to finance the governance of the country.[16] President Momoh, eventually declared a State of Economic Emergency in 1987. This gave the government wide powers to tackle corruption, gold and diamond smuggling and other economic challenges.[17] However, the measure did little to solve the economic problems. The climax of the economic collapse came when the country could not keep up with the repayment obligations on its debts.[18] Thereupon, the IMF cancelled its 1990 agreement with Sierra Leone.[19]

The government oversaw a system which was exclusionary and corrupt. It was unable to tackle corruption, pay its workers' salaries and provide employment for the increasing number of restless youths. Peaceful marches by students opposing the regime's policies were often violently dispersed and their leaders expelled.[20] Some commentators suggest

---

11 Ismail Rashid, *Student Radicals, Lumpen Youth, and the Origins of Revolutionary Groups in Sierra Leone, 1977-1996*, *in* Between Democracy and Terror: The Sierra Leone Civil War 75-78 (Ibrahim Abdullah ed., 2004).

12 Zack-Williams, *supra* note 2, at 145; Yusuf Bangura, Understanding the Political and Cultural Dynamics of the Sierra Leone War: A Critique of Paul Richard's Fighting for the Rain Forest 29 (Dakar Senegal, African Development CODESRIA, 2000).

13 Zack-Williams, *supra* note 2, at 145.

14 *Id.*

15 *Id.* at 145; Gerald H. Smith, *The Dichotomy of Politics and Corruption in a Neopatrimonial State: Evidence From Sierra Leone 1968-1993*, 21 Issue: A Journal of Opinion 58 (1997)

16 Zack-Williams, *supra* note 2 at 145.

17 *Id.* at 146.

18 *Id.*

19 *Id.*

20 Kandeh, *supra* note 3, at 358-362; Lansana Gberie, A Dirty War in West Africa: The R.U.F and the Destruction of Sierra Leone 44-52 (2005); Ibrahim Abdullah & Patrick Muana, *The Revolutionary United Front of Sierra Leone: A Revolt of the Lumpen Proletariat*, *in* African Guerrillas 172, 174-176 (Christopher Clapham ed., 1998).

that the student leaders expelled in 1978 may have led the birth of the RUF.[21] The system of patronage and centralization excluded the rural communities. Therefore at the outset of the war, the rebels were able to attack the country and strengthen their positions in the rural areas bordering Liberia.

The Sierra Leone crisis was a result of political inefficiency. Its economy collapsed under the weight of corruption, inefficient government and illegal mining of its natural resources. The economy was underdeveloped and the state was unable to utilize its abundant natural resources for development.[22] The factors that led to the Sierra Leone civil war have their roots in the unjust socio-economic and political structures.

3.3 A BRUTAL CIVIL WAR

The civil war that began with the RUF grew to involve other parties. More so, it was fought with so much brutality to the extent that international crimes were committed. This section explores the nature of the civil war.

> The atrocities of the civil war began with the RUF terror campaign against civilians in the areas they over-ran or raided. At the outset of the war, the chiefs and elders of communities were the victims of the rebels' criminal attacks.[23] The attack on chiefs was indicative of the rebels' anger against the system of patronage which enriched the elders at the expense of ordinary citizens. But the crimes became more rampant as the war progressed. The rebels in desperation began committing crimes against the civilian population after the Civil Defense Forces (CDF) commenced activities to protect their communities.[24] Most of the rebels were unemployed school-leavers and expelled students who were angry with the system.[25] They extended the crimes to ordinary civilians when they believed the civilians supported or complied with the system. For instance after the 1996 elections the rebels crudely amputated hands and limbs of civilians in the territories they captured after the elections.[26]

21 GBERIE, *supra*, at 44-60; Ibrahim Abdullah, *Bush Path to Destruction: The Origin and Character of the Revolutionary United Front/Sierra Leone*, 36 JOURNAL OF MODERN AFRICAN STUDIES. 203, 207-217 (1998); Alie, *supra* note 4, at 31-32.

22 KEEN, *supra* note 6, at 9.

23 PAUL RICHARDS, FIGHTING FOR THE RAIN FOREST: WAR, YOUTH AND RESOURCES IN SIERRA LEONE 8 (2004).

24 GBERIE, *supra* note 20, at 14 & 15.

25 Richard Fanthorpe, *Neither Citizen Nor Subject? Lumpen Agency and the Legacy of Native Administration in Sierra Leone,* 100 AFRICAN AFFAIRS 363 (2001).

26 Abdullah & Muana, *supra* note 20, at 190.

The level of atrocities perpetrated against civilians by the rebels, the Sierra Leone army and the CDF illustrate the lack of awareness of the criminality of their actions. The RUF (like Charles Taylor's National Patriotic Front of Liberia [NPFL]) continued the brutality and the forceful recruitment of child soldiers throughout the conflict.[27] The RUF used a strategy of terror, initially against community leaders, to express their anger with the system. The other parties to the conflict also committed atrocities against civilians. The Sierra Leone Army (SLA) raided villages and often colluded with the rebels. The soldiers who turned rebels later in the conflict (for instance the Westside boys) were as vicious against civilians as the rebels. The CDF and the Economic Community of West African States Monitoring Group (ECOMOG) were also accused of committing atrocities against civilians. All the parties tortured and killed their prisoners. With the exception of the Economic Community of West African States (ECOWAS) Military Monitoring group (ECOMOG, all the parties conscripted children as soldiers. The rebels, CDF and SLA were poorly trained in the laws of war. Most of the combatants were youths with no idea of the legal limits to warfare. The CDF were a group of illiterate hunters who were forced into combat to defend their communities from the rebels and SLA fighters.[28] As a consequence, they were unaware of the international rules restricting the conduct of armed conflicts.

The APC regime's use of violence to terrorize opponents and dominate elections may have contributed to the rampant use of terror during the war. According to Paul Richards, the rebels' use of violence against civilians was intended to terrorize their victims and the country.[29] The APC had consistently used terror to dominate the politics of the country for two decades. In the opinion of a commentator, violence was central to Sierra Leone politics.[30] He noted further that "among what distinguished the AFRC/RUF from its elite antecedents was its transformation of violence into a tool of criminal extraction."[31] The APC used violence to maintain their official hold on power and also alienate ordinary citizens. Similarly, the atrocities of the RUF quickly alienated the same ordinary people they wanted to set free.[32] The rebel group employed these tactics of terror by perpetrating gross human rights atrocities against innocent civilians.[33] The RUF leaders brought back the old APC strategy of using terror to subdue communities (especially those within the diamond-rich areas).[34]

27 RICHARDS, *supra* note 23, at 5.

28 MARIANE C. FERME, THE UNDERNEATH OF THINGS: VIOLENCE, HISTORY AND THE EVERYDAY IN SIERRA LEONE, 27 (2001).

29 RICHARDS, *supra* note 23, at xvi.

30 Kandeh, *supra* note 3, at 358.

31 *Id.*

32 GBERIE, *supra* note 20.

33 Fanthorpe, *supra* note 25.

34 KEEN, *supra* note 6, at 243.

3.4 The Road to Peace and Institutions of Accountability

The Sierra Leone civil war was a complicated conflict and peace was difficult to attain. There are several reasons for the difficulty in resolving the civil war. For instance, the complicated war was the consequence of an upsurge in the involvement of differently motivated warring factions. The peace process was difficult because of the multiplicity of parties some of whom were not even invited to the negotiations. In addition, the intransigence of the parties especially the rebels, contributed to the delay in attaining peace and stability.

3.4.1 *Numerous Warring Parties*

The war was complicated by the involvement of many factions which in turn complicated the peace process. There were both internal and external groups actively involved in the conflict. The various external groups fighting in Sierra Leone were doing so on behalf of the Sierra Leonean Government. The Executive Outcomes, a South African-based mercenary group, was contracted by the government (National Provisional Ruling Council [NPRC] regime) to help fight the rebels.[35] They were engaged to replace the *Gurkhars* who withdrew from the conflict.[36] The Economic Community of West African States had a monitoring group (ECOMOG) involved in a peace enforcement role in Sierra Leone but they too later became one of the factions defending the government and Freetown. The other external forces fought alongside ECOMOG or the rebels who were a key internal faction.

There were initially two parties to the war but the Sierra Leone Army became divided when a group of soldiers (*sobels*) turned against the government.[37] Most of the rural communities were constantly under fear of attacks from the rebels and *sobels*. They started vigilante groups in a bid to protect their communities. Some communities transformed their hunting groups to Civil Defense Forces and they eventually became a faction led by Chief Sam Hinga Norman.[38] Their success against the rebels and *sobels* led to tensions with the army. The army became increasingly wary of the CDF when President Kabbah treated them as the *de facto* army of the country. The CDF were responsible (with the foreign fighters – Executive Outcomes and ECOMOG peacekeepers) for keeping Sierra Leone from being over-run by the rebel/*sobel* partnership.

---

35 A. Abraham, *Dancing with the Chameleon: Sierra Leone and the Elusive Quest for Peace*, 19 Journal of Contemporary African Studies 205 (2001).

36 *Id.*

37 The soldiers who were at the battle front often colluded with rebels to loot rural communities. They were to later form a rebel faction known as the West Side Boys; see Keen, *supra* note 6, at 222.

38 Mariane C. Ferme & Danny Hoffman, *Hunter Militias and the International Human Rights Discourse in Sierra Leone and Beyond*, 50 Africa Today 73, 75 (2004).

Sierra Leone was controlled by several governments and there were times there was no government during the ten-year period. After the Abidjan Peace Accord, the army faction ousted the Kabbah government in a coup in collaboration with the rebels.[39] The implementation of the Abidjan Accord was therefore set aside. The country was ungoverned and essentially a collapsed state during the period.[40] There was chaos and disorder throughout the country. The Armed Forces Revolutionary (AFRC) was unhappy with the Abidjan peace deal as well as the role of the *Kamajors* (CDF) in the Kabbah government further complicating the situation.[41]

3.4.2 *Complicated Conflict with a Convoluted Peace Process*

From the outset of the war several peace initiatives were unsuccessful. When the NPRC came to power in 1992, they claimed the RUF were influenced by Charles Taylor and that peace in Sierra Leone was linked to peace in Liberia.[42] Thereafter they requested the assistance of the United Nations (UN) to bring the rebels to the negotiating table.[43] The rebels eventually consented to the first direct peace negotiations with the government of Sierra Leone. The talks were not concluded by the time the newly elected government of Ahmed Tejan Kabbah came to power. The parties failed to reach an agreement although there were signs of progress from the negotiations. In April 1996, the Kabbah government reopened the peace talks despite the rebels' refusal to participate in the elections and their attempt to derail it.[44] The two parties eventually reached an agreement and signed the Abidjan Peace Accord in November 1996.[45] The agreement was a victory of some sorts for the rebels because it accommodated most of their demands.[46]

The RUF did not comply with the terms of the Accord despite having most of their demands met.[47] While the government set up a Commission for the Consolidation of Peace as contained in the agreement, the RUF continued their attacks on rural communities.[48] The rebels also reneged on the agreed membership representation for the Neutral Monitoring

39 Abraham, *supra* note 35.

40 Chris Allen, *Warfare, Endemic Violence & State Collapse in Africa*, 26 REVIEW OF AFRICAN POLITICAL ECONOMY 367 (1999).

41 Abraham, *supra* note 35, at 206; GBERIE, *supra* note 20, at 151.

42 Abubakar Kagbo, *The Long Road to Peace: 1991-1997, in* BOUND TO COOPERATE: CONFLICT, PEACE AND PEOPLE IN SIERRA LEONE, *supra* note 1, at 37.

43 *Id.*

44 JOHN L. HIRSCH, SIERRA LEONE: DIAMONDS AND THE STRUGGLE FOR DEMOCRACY 35-51 (2001).

45 *Id.* at 53; Kagbo, *supra* note 42, at 39.

46 Abraham, *supra* note 35, at 206.

47 *Id.*

48 Kagbo, *supra* note 42, at 39.

Group.[49] Furthermore, Sankoh refused to name his nominees to the Demobilization and Resettlement Committee which was responsible for disarmament. He also became critical of the UN peacekeeping observers.[50] An unsuccessful internal coup, within the RUF, to remove Sankoh complicated things even further.[51] Some RUF officers were unhappy with Sankoh's attempt to disregard the Abidjan peace deal and continue with the war.[52] The leader of the revolt against Sankoh pledged to work with Kabbah. However the coup failed when Captain Philip Palmer, the leader of the revolt, was arrested by Sam Bokarie the RUF battlefield commander.[53]

The peace efforts suffered further setbacks when a faction of the army overthrew the democratically elected President in May 1997. The coup plotters invited the RUF to join their government and formed the Armed Forces Revolutionary Council (AFRC) with Major Johnny Paul Koroma as the leader.[54] The new rulers were condemned by the international community. Thus, the country was far from attaining peace. The coup plotters gave poor welfare of soldiers and the Kabbah government's failure to consolidate peace as reasons for the coup.[55] The AFRC were largely made up of *sobels* who were unhappy at the prominent role of the CDF under the Kabbah government.[56] The CDF, with Executive Outcomes (EO), had been successful in repelling the rebels. They also prevented *sobels* and rebels from looting their communities. When the contract of the South African based private security company (Executive Outcomes) was terminated, the company notified the government of the possible threat of military coup.[57] The CDF were less equipped to prevent the coup which was staged by *sobels* in collaboration with the RUF rebels. A more robust approach was needed to restore the peace progress made by Kabbah's government.

ECOMOG accepted Kabbah's request to reverse the coup. It succeeded in negotiating an agreement with the AFRC to reinstall the democratically elected government within six months. However, ECOMOG eventually had to use military force to retake Freetown. It, thereafter, reinstalled President Kabbah to power. This was after the AFRC was unwilling to implement the terms of an agreement with ECOWAS. The defeated AFRC/RUF alliance retreated into the rural communities and continued the war. The army component of the AFRC remobilized as a rebel faction (the Westside Boys) in the increasingly complicated civil war.

49 *Id.*
50 Abraham, *supra* note 35, at 207.
51 *Id.*
52 *Id.*
53 *Id.*
54 Kagbo, *supra* note 42, at 40.
55 Abraham, *supra* note 35, at 208.
56 Lansana Gberie, *The 25 May Coup d'état in Sierra Leone: A Lumpen Revolt?*, *in* Between Democracy and Terror: The Sierra Leone Civil War 144, 151 (Ibrahim Abdullah ed., 2004).
57 Abraham, *supra* note 35, at 207.

3.4.3 Peace Through Judicial and Quasi-Judicial Bodies

The several attempts at peace finally culminated in an agreement which had a reasonable possibility of succeeding. The country was in dire need of peace after the May 1999 rebel attack on Freetown. The United States became involved in the peace negotiation and coerced President Ahmed Tejan Kabbah to sign the Lomé Peace Agreement on July 7, 1999.[58] Sankoh was reluctant to enter into a peace agreement without any amnesty provision for him and his fighters. To appease him, Article IX of the Agreement granted "an absolute and free pardon"[59] to all combatants and collaborators for their actions prior to the agreement. Nevertheless, the UN observer at the meeting made a reservation that the amnesty would not cover violations of international criminal law. Eager to ensure accountability for the atrocities committed in the conflict, the parties to the Agreement consented to the establishment of a Truth and Reconciliation Commission (otherwise the Commission or TRC).[60]

After several failed peace initiatives, the international community was eager to see an effective ceasefire agreement in Sierra Leone. The Lomé Accord was designed to achieve lasting peace by accommodating the RUF's inconsistencies. The rebels had changed their demands several times in the course of the conflict.[61] Yet the agreement was packaged to pacify them in exchange for lasting peace.[62] The agreement provided for power-sharing between the democratically elected government and the RUF in addition to the amnesty. The negotiators believed a Truth and Reconciliation Commission was the method of accountability that would best reflect the amnesty as well as guarantee peace. A tribunal was deemed inappropriate at that stage of the peace process in order to preserve the fragile peace.

3.4.4 The Truth and Reconciliation Commission

The TRC was established to start operations within 90 days of the signing of the Lomé Agreement. Its final report and recommendations were to be expected within a year of operations. It was to provide a forum for the victims and perpetrators to tell their story, address impunity and break the cycle of violence in the country. This was a

58 KEEN, *supra* note 6, at 251.
59 *See* The Lomé Accord, available at <www.sierra-leone.org/lomeaccord.html> (Accessed November 21, 2011).
60 *Id.* Art. 26(1).
61 Abraham, *supra* note 35, at 212.
62 Alie, *supra* note 4, at 170.

tough mandate to carry out in a fragile period in Sierra Leone. The United Nations' Office of the High Commissioner for Human Rights endeavoured to get the TRC operating within weeks of the Agreement.[63] But it was not until February 2000 that the Sierra Leone Parliament passed the implementing Legislation for the Commission.[64] The TRC was set up in difficult circumstances despite the serious responsibilities it was endowed with.

The TRC had the task of reconciling the country. It was to investigate and report on the causes, extent and nature of the atrocities committed in the civil war as well as promote reconciliation.[65] Some reconciliation and healing was expected through its process of giving victims the opportunity to tell their stories. It was hoped that by doing so, they would experience some sort of catharsis. Nevertheless, there was a delay in the commencement of the TRC's operations due to other underlying problems with the Lomé Accord.

The choice of the TRC was motivated by the goal of achieving lasting peace which had eluded the country several times. The negotiators appeared oblivious of the obstacles to implementing the Agreement. The Agreement was problematic as a result of its selectivity. The negotiators did not consider the complicated context of the civil war. The other factions, especially the rebel soldiers of the AFRC faction, were unhappy to be neglected in the peace negotiations.[66] The Lomé Accord broke down eventually when the RUF renewed fighting after kidnapping some UN peacekeepers.

The establishment and operation of the TRC was delayed in May 2000 when the RUF violated the peace agreement. The TRC was finally set up in March 2002 with an interim Secretariat and was officially inaugurated in July of the same year.[67] It had a mix of international and national commissioners. Despite some early setbacks and its later friction with the Special Court, the TRC submitted its multi-volume report to the President on October 5, 2004.[68] Its activities lasted for about eight months and were carried out in two phases: the statement-taking phase and the hearings phase.[69] Its effect on the society and whether it achieved its objective will be considered subsequently.

---

63 Beth Dougherty, *Searching for Answers: Sierra Leone's Truth and Reconciliation Commission* 8 African Studies Quarterly 39, 41 (2004).

64 Truth and Reconciliation Commission Act, (2000) (Sierra Leone).

65 *Id.* pt III.

66 Keen, *supra* note 6, at 255.

67 Dougherty, *supra* note 63.

68 Williams A. Schabas, *A Synergistic Relationship: The Sierra Leone Truth and Reconciliation Commission and The Special Court*, 15 Criminal Law Forum 3 (2004).

69 *Id.*

3.5 A SPECIAL COURT FOR SIERRA LEONE

The measure of security was the result of an increased involvement of the international community. Additionally, a different method of accountability (retributive rather than restorative) was created. The events following the Lomé Agreement gave the Sierra Leonean Government the reason for a stronger method of accountability. The success of the Agreement would have resulted in the impunity for crimes committed during the war. As mentioned earlier, the rebels were granted amnesty from prosecutions for atrocities committed before 1999 but in May of 2000 they renewed the fighting.[70] The actions of the rebels, who abducted UN peacekeepers and attempted to overrun Freetown, resulted in a two-year delay in the TRC starting its work. Their action was the main reason for the government's rethink on the issue of amnesty. It also led to the establishment of the Special Court for Sierra Leone.[71]

The Court was created after the Sierra Leonean Government requested for assistance from the international community. Though it was eager to sustain the peace, it was also determined to ensure that perpetrators of the numerous brutal crimes were held responsible. The UN Security Council (UNSC) in response to the request passed Resolution 1315 in August 2000.[72] The Resolution recognized the efforts of the Sierra Leonean Government to promote the rule of Law and reconcile the country by establishing the TRC. The Resolution further stated that a system of justice and accountability for the international crimes would end impunity and contribute to the maintenance of peace.[73] Resolution 1315 was similar to Resolutions 827 and 955 which set up the International Criminal Tribunals for Yugoslavia (ICTY) and Rwanda (ICTR) respectively, except that it did not provide the legal basis for the Special Court.[74] Rather the Council decided to create an independent treaty-based court.

The Council requested the UN Secretary General to negotiate an agreement with the Sierra Leone government with the objective of creating an independent court.[75] During the negotiations the Sierra Leone government agreed with the UN that the amnesty provisions

---

70 Sarah Williams, *Amnesties in International Law: The Experience of the Special Court for Sierra Leone*, 5 HUMAN RIGHTS LAW REVIEW 271, 274 (2005); Abdul Tejan-Cole, *The Special Court for Sierra Leone: Conceptual Concerns and Alternatives*, 1 AFRICAN HUMAN RIGHTS LAW JOURNAL 107 (2001); WILLIAM A. SCHABAS, THE UN INTERNATIONAL CRIMINAL TRIBUNALS: THE FORMER YUGOSLAVIA, RWANDA AND SIERRA LEONE, 34 (2006).

71 *Id.*; Dougherty, *supra* note 63.

72 UN Security Council Resolution 1315 (2000).

73 *Id.*

74 Robert Cryer, *A "Special Court" For Sierra Leone*, 50 INTERNATIONAL AND COMPARATIVE LAW QUARTERLY 435, 436 (2001).

75 UN Security Council Resolution 1315, *supra* note 72, para. 1.

of the Lomé Accord would not preclude prosecution before the new court.[76] The Secretary General on October 4, 2000 presented its Report to the Security Council.[77] The Report included the draft Statute of the Court and a draft agreement with the Sierra Leone government. A hybrid court was finally established in January 2002 following months of negotiations and amendments.[78] The domestic legislation implementing the agreement was enacted by the Sierra Leone Parliament in April 2002.[79] Its Judges were appointed and sworn into office in December 2002. It became fully operational after that date.[80]

The Security Council's choice of a hybrid model in Sierra Leone was motivated by financial expediency. The Council, already bogged down with funding the ICTR and ICTY, did not want the financial burden of operating the court to be on the UN.[81] For instance, the cost of running the court for its first year was estimated to be around US$ 22 million while the ICTY and ICTR had an annual budget of US$ 90 million each.[82] The UN did not want to have the additional burden of funding an expensive court on its budget. Therefore it was logical to create a court that had a similar purpose as the ad hoc tribunals. Howbeit, unlike the ICTY and ICTR, the Court was set up to be funded by voluntary contributions from donor countries.[83] The funding structure is similar to that of the ICC. The financial responsibility of the ICC is borne by the parties to the Rome Statute[84] while the ICTR and ICTY as organs of the UN are covered by the UN budget. The hybrid nature was to correspond with the financial arrangement as a *sui generis* court created by an agreement between the UN and Sierra Leone.

The Court was to apply both international law and Sierra Leonean law as part of its hybrid system.[85] The Court's jurisdiction had to reflect both Sierra Leonean law[86] and

76 United Nations Security Council, Report of the Secretary General on the Establishment of a Special Court for Sierra Leone, (October 4, 2000), [hereinafter "Report of the Secretary General"] available at <http://daccess-dds-ny.un.org/doc/UNDOC/GEN/N00/661/77/PDF/N0066177.pdf?OpenElement>; Schabas, *supra* note 68 at 37.

77 Report of the Secretary General, *supra* note 76.

78 Schabas, *supra* note 68, at 38.

79 Special Court Agreement (Ratification) Act, (2002)(Sierra Leone) available at <www.sc-sl.org/LinkClick.aspx?fileticket=3dwfHVBc5VA%3D&>.

80 Schabas, *supra* note 68, at 39.

81 UN Security Council Resolution 1315, *supra* note 72; Report of the Secretary General, *supra* note 76.

82 Report of the Secretary General, *supra* note 76, para. 57-63.

83 Note that from December 23, 2010, the UN General Assembly agreed to the UN Secretary General's request to fund the remaining costs of the Special Court for Sierra Leone out of regular UN-assessed contributions, following a request by the Secretary-General (see UN monthly Forecast on Sierra Leone, March 2011. Available at <www.securitycouncilreport.org/site/c.glKWLeMTIsG/b.6579263/k.1C7B/March_2011brSierra_Leone.htm>. (Last accessed November 21, 2011).

84 Rome Statute of the International Criminal Court, Art. 113-118, July 17, 1998 2187 U.N.T.S 90.

85 Statute of the Special Court for Sierra Leone (SCSL Statute) Art. 1, January 16, 2002, 2178 U. N. T.S 138.

86 *Id.* Art. 5.

international law[87] as a treaty-based institution. The applicable law is both international and Sierra Leone law. The Court's officials, including judges, were appointed by the UN and Sierra Leonean Government.[88] The UNSC envisaged that such a hybrid judicial body located in Freetown and applying both international and Sierra Leone laws, would help re-establish the domestic legal system.

The Court was designed to carry out the task of prosecuting persons "who bear the greatest responsibility for serious violations of international humanitarian law and Sierra Leonean law committed in the territory of Sierra Leone since 30 November 1996 . . ."[89] It was expected to conclude its work within a year of operation.[90] The Court indicted several of those responsible for the atrocities including leaders of the RUF, CDF, and AFRC. As of 2011, it expects to conclude operations by 2012 after the Charles Taylor trial.[91] It was not set up under Chapter 7 of the UN Charter and as a result does not have primacy over the courts of other states except Sierra Leone.[92] Neither the Statute of the SCSL nor the Security Council Resolution imposed an obligation to cooperate on UN member states. Consequently, the Statute of the SCSL provides that crimes committed by peacekeepers during Sierra Leone war were to be prosecuted by their sending states.[93]

3.5.1 Relations between the Special Court and the TRC

The almost frictionless operation of the SCSL and the TRC supports the argument that the different methods of accountability are to complement each other. The two bodies operated side by side, for the short period the TRC was in operation without the expected friction. Though the TRC was established before the SCSL, the two bodies began their activities at about the same time in 2002. They were located in close proximity to each other but operated from two different perspectives of justice. The two bodies largely operated as their creators hoped, by complementing each other with the aim of achieving a common objective.

International criminal tribunals are often established as the key means of accountability in post-conflict societies. However, the distinctive feature of the SCSL post-conflict exercise

87 *Id.* Arts. 2-4.
88 *See* Agreement Between the United Nations and the Government of Sierra Leone on the Establishment of a Special Court for Sierra Leone, Art. 6 (2002).
89 SCSL Statute, *supra* note 85, Art. 1.
90 See Truth and Reconciliation Commission Act, § 5(1).
91 See SCSL, 7[Th] ANNUAL REPORT OF THE PRESIDENT OF THE SCSL, (June 2009-May 2010).
92 SCSL Statute, *supra* note 85, Art. 8.
93 *Id.* Art. 1(2)-(3).

was the parallel existence of the two mechanisms of accountability: the SCSL and TRC.[94] It was not due to careful policy planning that the two institutions were set up to complement each other. Rather it was due to the context of the Sierra Leonean conflict. It was initially a pragmatic step to offer amnesty to the combatants. At that time the fragile situation suggested the choice of a TRC. With the subsequent stability and international assistance, the country could afford to prosecute the worst offenders of international humanitarian law.

The only significant friction between the two bodies highlights the tension between the differences in approach of the institutions. The SCSL and the TRC disagreed over whether the TRC should have access to the testimonies of indicted prisoners before their criminal trials.[95] The Commission's objective of sustaining the peace through restorative justice was based on the testimonies of victims and offenders.[96] Besides, the SCSL was a retributive judicial body with strict evidential rules and procedures.[97] The friction occurred because the TRC had a limited time within which to conclude its activities.[98] It would have been avoided if the TRC was not constrained by its time limitation.[99] It is plausible to believe that the SCSL might have granted the TRC access to individuals detained by it. Alternatively, the SCSL would have wanted to permit access at a time that it would not be prejudicial to the interests of legal justice. It does not appear to be a substantive conflict between the different approaches but was created by their different operational time frames.

3.6 The Contribution of the Two Institutions to Peace

One of the objectives of the TRC was to respond to the needs of victims of the crisis by holding public meetings where perpetrators of crimes and the victims were to give their testimonies.[100] The SCSL on the other hand did not set out its objectives in the Statute which, however, provided for the prosecution of crimes under Sierra Leonean law and

94 William A. Schabas, *The Special Court for Sierra Leone: Testing the Waters: Conjoined Twins of Transitional Justice? The Sierra Leone Truth and Reconciliation Commission and The Special Court* 2 Journal of International Criminal Justice 1082, 1085 (2004).

95 *Prosecutor Against Sam Hinga Norman*, SCSL-2003-08-PT Decision on the Request by the TRC of Sierra Leone to Conduct a Public Hearing With Samuel Hinga Norman, Special Court For Sierra Leone, (October 20, 2003.) The Appeal Chambers refused the appeal by the TRC and Hinga Norman on November 28, 2003.

96 SLTRC, Witness to the Truth: Report of the Sierra Leone Truth and Reconciliation Commission Vols. 1-3 (2004) [hereinafter SLTRC, Witness to the Truth]; see also Truth and Reconciliation Act, Arts. 6-7.

97 SCSL Statute, *supra* note 85, at Art. 14.

98 Neil Boister, *Failing to Get to The Heart of the Matter in Sierra Leone*, 2 Journal of International Criminal Justice 1100, 1101 (2004).

99 The TRC was mandated to produce its report within a year. See Truth and Reconciliation Act, § 5(1).

100 Truth and Reconciliation Commission Act, § 6.

international crimes.[101] It appears both institutions have in some ways supplemented the restoration of Sierra Leone's security and the rule of law.

3.6.1 *The Special Court*

The SCSL has facilitated Sierra Leone's stability in various ways. It has generally assisted in establishing the truth of the events in Sierra Leone and the role of the leaders of the various factions involved in the conflict. The special court in the RUF case issued a subpoena to the former Sierra Leone President, Ahmad Tejan Kabbah to testify before it.[102] The court in the other cases (AFRC, RUF, and AFRC) established the truth of the violations that occurred during the civil war.

The mandate of the SCSL to prosecute only those most responsible for the crimes guided its approach in establishing the truth. The approach differed from that of the TRC. However, both approaches gave room for a comprehensive factual and official report of the war. A combination of the two approaches will positively affect the public order. The restriction on the SCSL's mandate to prosecute only those most responsible for the violations meant that it would clarify the truth from the top. While the TRC, on the other hand would clarify the truth from the lower-ranked fighters and general population. The SCSL sought to clarify the records on the motivations, theories and politics of the war in its greater political and sub-regional contexts.

The SCSL's mandate is restricted to prosecuting the leaders most responsible for the atrocities.[103] It can be argued that the Court destroyed the perceived aura of invincibility of the leaders of the various warring factions. First, it indicted Charles Taylor as a sitting president of Liberia. Mr. Taylor was suspected and subsequently convicted for aiding and abetting the war crimes committed in Sierra Leone by his loyalists (National Patriotic Front of Liberia – NPLF) fighting with the RUF.[104] Mr. Taylor was arrested after renewed fighting in his country forced him out of power. He was then granted asylum in Nigeria and subsequently handed over to the SCSL which proceeded to prosecute him. In addition, the leaders of the other factions including the RUF, AFRC and even the CDF were arrested by the Court. This helped destroy the myth surrounding these leaders. In addition, the years of impunity were destroyed. Consequently it translated to stability and renewed respect for the rule of law.

101 See SCSL Statute, *supra* note 85. Arts. 2-6.

102 See *Prosecutor v. Sesay, Kallon & Gbao*, Written Reasoned Decision on Motion For Issuance of a subpoena To H.E. Dr Ahmad Tejan Kabbah, Former President of the Republic of Sierra Leone, June 30, 2008. Available at <www.sc-sl.org/LinkClick.aspx?fileticket=8ChELQM0gS4%3d&tabid=155>.

103 SCSL Statute, *supra* note 85, Art 1.

104 *Prosecutor v. Charles Ghankay Taylor*, Case Number: SCSL-2003-01-1. Available at <www.sc-sl.org/LinkClick.aspx?fileticket=prr6j5%2Bbmsc%3D>.

There are a few instances of the Court's failure to adequately utilize its capacity to establish or clarify the truth. The Court was acting judiciously as an impartial body when its Trial Chamber refused the Prosecutor's request to amend the charges against the CDF to include sexual crimes.[105] Nevertheless, it missed the opportunity to clarify the truth regarding some allegations against the CDF leaders. It was important for the Court to clarify the extent of the CDF involvement in sexual crimes. The Court ought to have determined whether these were ordinary and random acts of indiscipline or crimes which involved the complicity of the CDF leaders.

Furthermore, the Court's approach would create gaps in the records of the truth for crimes committed during the civil war. There is concern over the small number of indictments issued by the Court.[106] The limited number of those indicted may be due to the Court's focus on the most responsible individuals and the restriction of its temporal jurisdiction to November 30, 1996.[107] The Court did not have comprehensive jurisdiction to establish the truth of the events before November 30, 1996. Under the circumstances, acts committed by mid-level or lower-level fighters were outside its jurisdiction. Accordingly, the truth would not be sufficiently established and recorded by the SCSL. To ensure a comprehensive record, the Court's work should be complemented by the TRC report.

The Court set up an effective outreach programme to explain their work to rural communities and the cities. Public awareness of the Court's work positioned it as an embodiment of public vengeance. The public came to accept the Court's role as the institution responsible for ensuring justice for crimes committed during the war. For this reason, the victims' quest for revenge would be abated. The Court's public awareness efforts were in diverse ways. First, its decisions were made available in the public libraries.[108] In addition, it has ensured that ordinary citizens can follow the trial of President Taylor at The Hague through various means.[109] The importance of outreach programs has been noted as a way

105 See *Prosecutor v. Sam Hinga Norman, Fofana & Kondewa*, SCSL-04-14-PT; Decision on Prosecution's Request for Leave to Amend the Indictment, (May 20, 2004). The Chamber also refused the prosecutions application to appeal the decision; see Majority Decision on the Prosecution's Application for Leave to Amend the Indictment Against Samuel Hinga Norman, Moinina Fofana and Allieu Kondewa, August 2, 2004; available at <www.sc-sl.org/LinkClick.aspx?fileticket=E%2bSYEZIEOfQ%3d&tabid=153>.

106 Human Rights Watch (HRW), Bringing Justice: The Special Court for Sierra Leone Accomplishments, Shortcomings, and Needed Support, 2 (2004).

107 See SCSL Statute, *supra* note 85. Art. 1.

108 Office of the High Commissioner for Human Rights, Maximising the Legacy of the Hybrid Courts 18-19 (2008) ; Human Rights Watch, *supra* note 106, at 35.

109 The court has set up a live video streaming of the Taylor trial on its website <www.sc-sl.org> However, it is doubtful how many ordinary Sierra Leoneans have the facilities to use this free service. On the other hand, the news and video of the trial could easily be broadcast by the news media using the free web video or other means made available by the court or organizations such as the European Union.

of involving the victims and other stakeholders, who otherwise, may not be able to participate in the trials.[110]

The Court has contributed to the security of Sierra Leone through diverse training projects that targeted persons with potential roles in the security of the country. It conducted conflict resolution trainings in Freetown and the provinces as well as Liberia. These focused on training traditional leaders and the youth in the communities.[111] It also trained Sierra Leone security personnel as part of its legacy programme.[112] The legacy project, although started late, has made some impact. It has been argued that the project was an afterthought and not a genuine attempt to contribute to the society's development.[113] Ultimately, notwithstanding its objectives, the Court has in a way contributed to the society though the extent of the impact of such contribution could be questioned.

It is sufficient to assert that the Court has made laudable efforts, (if difficult to access at this point), to contribute to sustainable peace and prevent future conflicts. The trainings (especially for conflict resolution) targeted individuals who played a key role in the conflict (mid-level perpetrators, police, army and youths) and this may eventually contribute to some reconciliation.

The Court appeared to have taken a two-pronged approach in addressing future conflicts. The first was to train the community leaders and others on conflict resolution. The second aimed at the root causes of the ten year war. The court's efforts to tackle the roots of the conflict are illustrated by a proposed initiative to apply for a US$ 165,700 grant from the Peacebuilding fund to establish a Peace Museum on the court's premises where a copy of the court's archives will be deposited. The museum was to be handed over to the Sierra Leone government at the expiration of the court's work.[114] It was recently previewed on April 29, 2011 and will be officially open to the public in 2012.[115] The museum will re-emphasize the essence of peace. It reinforces the work to be carried out by those the court trained in conflict resolution.

---

110 Human Rights Watch, *supra* note 106, at 31.

111 It has been noted that one of the things that triggered the conflict was the corruption of the government and the high unemployment of youths. See Gberie, *supra* note 20; Richards, *supra* note 23.

112 7th Annual report of the President of the SCSL, June 2009-May 2010, *supra* note 91 at 44.

113 Thierry Cruvellier, International Centre For Transitional Justice and Sierra Leone Monitoring Programme, from the Taylor Trial to a Lasting Legacy; Putting the Special Court Model to Test 36 (2009).

114 7th Annual report of the President of the SCSL, June 2009 – May 2010, *supra* note 91, at 48.

115 See Press Release, Special Court for Sierra Leone, Peace Museum Preview Opens at Special Court (April 21, 2011). Available at <www.sc-sl.org/LinkClick.aspx?fileticket=z1NFYg%2BLy2E%3D&tabid=53> (Last accessed May 24, 2011).

3.6.2 *The TRC*

The TRC's activities were aimed at making recommendations to the Sierra Leone government on how to prevent a reoccurrence of the crisis. Its report detailed the history and causes of the conflict. It also listed some of the victims.[116] The TRC report was detailed with testimonies of victims and perpetrators, structural recommendations as well as reparations to the victims.[117]

One of the core mandates of the TRC was creating an impartial historical record of the violations that occurred during the civil war. The mandate is connected to the important objective of preventing a recurrence of violence in the country.[118] The commission's report was an authentic and truthful record of the history of the conflict but it is not exhaustive. The TRC Act restricted the Commissions mandate to the period between 1993 to July 7, 1999 (when the Lomé Accord was signed). This restriction has left a vacuum in establishing the truth of events after that period. The Special Court, whose mandate ought to have made up for this, was purposed on prosecuting the leaders of the various factions for crimes committed after 1996. This leaves out documenting the record of events from the majority of the victims and perpetrators after 1999. The TRC report covered the period after July 1999. It was of the view that its mandate did not restrict it from looking at events beyond 1999.[119]

The TRC sought to provide an impartial account of the civil war despite financial and logistic challenges. Limited financial resources restricted the TRC from extending its operations in the rural communities notwithstanding the requests of community leaders and the prospect of obtaining more of the truth for their records.[120] Furthermore, the internationalization of its members helped allay the fears of Sierra Leoneans that it would suppress certain truths and reveal only those favorable to the government.[121] This led to an increase in the participation of Sierra Leoneans, including ex combatants who committed some of the abuses, their victims and former child soldiers. As noted earlier, the TRC was prevented by the SCSL from exploring more of the truth when the Court precluded its detainees (such as Sam Hinga Norman) from attending the TRC's public hearings.[122] This

116 SLTRC, Witness to the Truth *supra* note 96.
117 *Id.*
118 *Id.* at 24, Truth and Reconciliation Act (2000) (Sierra Leone) Arts. 6(1) & 7(1).
119 Truth and Reconciliation Act Arts. 6(1) & 7(1); see also 1 SLTRC, Witness to the Truth *supra* note 96, at 24.
120 International Centre For Transitional Justice, The Sierra Leone Truth and Reconciliation Commission: Reviewing the First Year, 3 (January 2004).
121 *Id.*
122 *Prosecutor Against Sam Hinga Norman*, SCSL-2003-08-PT Decision on the Request by the TRC of Sierra Leone to Conduct a Public Hearing With Samuel Hinga Norman, Special Court For Sierra Leone, (October 29, 2003). The Appeal Chambers refused the appeal by the TRC and Hinga Norman on November 28, 2003.

turned out to be a lost opportunity to establish the truth. Chief Norman eventually died in custody before the conclusion of his trial. Thereupon the information he was willing to give at the TRC was also not obtained by the court. The TRC would have established more of the truth if it had more resources and time to accomplish this truth seeking task.

The TRC issued a three-volume report that set out a detailed account of the history, nature and government's role in the conflict.[123] The responsibilities of the perpetrators and warring factions were established as well as the sufferings of such victims as women, children and youths. It confirmed that children between 10 and 14 years old were specially targeted for forced recruitment, rape and sexual slavery.[124] It also clarified the role of the government, external players and diamond in the conflict.[125] The TRC also recommended ways to address some of the socio-political failures that led to the war.

One of the TRC's recommendations was the need for a Human Rights Commission to be established to develop a culture of respect in the country. Such a commission would represent ordinary citizens whose rights have been violated. Despite the lack of progress in implementing the recommendations of the TRC, the Human Rights Commission was eventually established in 2004.[126] It is an independent body with the mandate to protect and promote human rights in Sierra Leone.[127] The Human Rights Commission appears to have continued the work of the TRC in the area of promoting human rights. Its first report in 2008 addressed a variety of human rights violations that included police brutality and prolonged detention without charge.[128] An active Human Rights Commission is a useful watchdog that promotes accountability. A Human Rights Commission, in a way, addresses stability through supporting the rule of law.

The operation of the TRC was short lived but it appeared to have laid some of the foundations for a secure society. In fact, though its recommendations have largely been neglected by the government, the emergence of the Human Rights Commission will benefit the promotion of human rights which in turn contributes to the stability of the society.

3.7 Restoring the Rule of Law

The key to sustaining the peace, following an armed conflict, is to complement security concerns with an adequate legal system. An effective legal system helps maintain a balance by ensuring that the rule of law is upheld. Consequently abuses and arbitrary actions are

123 1&3 SLTRC, WITNESS TO THE TRUTH *supra* note 96.
124 *Id*; see especially Vol. 3b at Chapter 4.
125 *Id*.
126 The Human Rights Commission of Sierra Leone Act 9, (2004) (Sierra Leone).
127 Human Rights Commission Act, §7(1).
128 Amnesty International, Amnesty International Annual Report 2011-Sierra Leone, May 13, 2011.

checked in a fragile society where the focus on security could be manipulated to suppress civil rights. The importance of restoring this crucial component of a society's administration is increased by the destruction, during internal conflicts, of the fabrics and structures of the society.[129] The balance of a post-conflict society's security, its law, and order depends on a balanced restoration of both its security and legal system. This symbiotic relationship between these two important aspects of reconstruction creates mutual goals and objectives for the security and legal institutions within the society. Therefore judicial and quasi-judicial institutions established after a conflict would share in the responsibility to restore the legal system and sustain the security of the society. This section evaluates whether the SCSL and TRC have in any way facilitated a stable legal system or respect for the rule of law in Sierra Leone.

3.7.1 The SCSL

The Special Court has contributed to educating and training the Sierra Leone public, professionals and rulers as a way of rebuilding the country's legal system. The court has also used its outreach programs to educate the public on the relevance of justice for war crimes and as such, promoting the stability of the legal order. The Court's outreach department has regional offices throughout Sierra Leone and a head office in Freetown. Its activities include town hall meetings, production and distribution of pamphlets, radio programs, film documentaries; and conducting training seminars.[130] The main focus of the outreach department's efforts is to inform and educate the public on the Rule of law, the court's mandate, decisions and objectives.

The efforts to educate the public may be general but are essential to the restoration of legal order. Since the arrest of Charles Taylor, the court made an effort to ensure that the public is kept abreast of the trial which was transferred to The Hague. It partnered with other organizations[131] to sponsor local media and members of the civil society to The Hague. This was to ensure that the trial was made widely available to the local population.[132] Its activities to educate the public, about the rule of law, have contributed to restoring the legal order. It established the Special Court Interactive Forum (SCIF) to provide a link

129 Christopher P.M. Waters, *Post Conflict Legal Education*, 10 Journal of Conflict & Security Law 101, 101 (2005).

130 SCSL, 4th Annual Report of The President of the SCSL, Jan 2007-May 2007; see also Human Rights Watch, *supra* note 94, at 331.

131 The organizations include BBC World Service Trust, Search for Common Ground and the European Union.

132 SCSL 5th Annual Report of the President of the SCSL June 2007-May 2008; Scott Worden & Emily Wann, United States Institute of Peace (USIP) Briefing: *Special Court For Sierra Leone Briefing: The Taylor Trial and Lessons From Capacity Building and Outreach*, August 2007; available at <www.usip.org/pubs/usipeace_briefings/2007/0821_special_court.html> (Last accessed June 15, 2011).

between the public and the court.[133] The members of the forum include representatives of about 28 local organizations who are to keep the rural communities informed of the court's progress.[134]

The court's notion of promoting the Sierra Leone legal system was extended to Sierra Leoneans who do not ordinarily have any professional relationship with law enforcement. It collaborated with the Sierra Leone judiciary and the Bar Association in establishing the Sierra Leone legal institute to provide information to the society. This was done by permitting ordinary Sierra Leoneans to have uninhibited and free access to legislation and the Supreme Court's decisions. This is fundamentally important in a country where the published laws are not easily available except in the offices of law enforcement professionals. However, it must be noted that the relevance of this important contribution hinges on other factors such as education, and the interest of the educated, especially youths to want to know. The legal information institute will have to be made relevant to Sierra Leoneans in order to attain its aim of promoting a transparent legal system.

The court's outreach to promote the rule of law was directed at the society's leaders. The court has trained local government councilors and local court chairmen on the rule of law, due process, rights of accused persons, international standards of detention and the court's mandate.[135] In recognition of the regional context of the conflict it did not limit the efforts to Sierra Leone leaders. Educative and training outreaches were conducted for Liberian and Guinean leaders. This was a way to promote the respect for the rule of law among leaders in the sub region and to prevent future conflicts.

In addition to the leaders and the educated, the court also promoted respect for the rule of law among ordinary citizens, especially youths. It facilitated the formation of Accountability Now Clubs in the Tertiary Institutions in Sierra Leone as well as Liberia.[136] The court also has an ongoing internship programme that links fresh Sierra Leone graduates and legal associates in the country's law firms.[137] The internship creates the opportunity for young Sierra Leoneans to work with court staff on various aspects of criminal justice.

---

133 Sigall Horovitz, *Transitional Criminal Justice in Sierra Leone*, *in* Transitional Justice in the Twenty-First Century: Beyond Truth Versus Justice 59 (Roht-Arriaza & Javier Mariezcuurena eds., 2006).

134 *Id.*

135 SCSL, 4th Annual Report of the President of the SCSL, *supra* note 123, at 53.

136 As of 2010, the Accountability Now Clubs (ANC) exist in about seven universities in Liberia and 14 in Sierra Leone; see SCSL, 7th Annual Report of the of the President of the SCSL *supra* note 91, at 44.

137 *Id.*

Promoting the rule of law among this demographic group creates an avenue for them to express social or political grievance (through civic pressure group or similar nonviolence activities) rather than resorting to violence as a means of opposition.

The SCSL has contributed to capacity-building efforts aimed at directly engaging with Sierra Leone judicial personnel. Its judges frequently meet with domestic court judges and observed some domestic trials.[138] It began training "Lay Magistrates" (traditional chiefs who engage in adjudication but have little or no formal training) on core aspects of the administration of justice (such as due process and presumption of innocence).[139] It also started the Sierra Leone Rule of Law and Capacity Building Project to train the country's domestic prosecutors, defense attorneys and law enforcement officials.[140] The court set up the country's first legal aid scheme through a project to support indigent citizens accused of crimes.[141]

The court has the capacity to train local experts in the areas of administration of justice, legal representation, case management and adjudication as a result of its hybrid nature. It has also set up internship programs for Sierra Leone students or young lawyers to work in its various units.[142] The Court employs Sierra Leoneans in administrative and professional capacities. About 40% of the professional, non-administrative employees of the Court were made up of persons of Sierra Leonean origin.[143] There are also Sierra Leonean judges on the bench (both in the Trial and Appeal Chambers). Each defense team within the court is required have at least one person experienced in Sierra Leone law, international law and criminal law.[144] The Court's security, investigators and witness protection officers are usually Sierra Leoneans.[145] The Court developed training projects for the local police and investigators to support the Sierra Leone government. It set up a system where police officers are assigned to three month practical training on complex investigations, evidence handling and the strategy and ethic of prosecution.[146] As shown above, the Court has contributed to restoring the legal order through education, trainings and capacity-building.

138 Human Rights Watch, *supra* note 106, at 37.
139 Horovitz, *supra* note 133, at 58, 59.
140 SCSL, 4th Annual Report of the of the President of the SCSL, *supra* note 123, at 42.
141 *Id.*
142 Human Rights Watch, *supra* note 106, at 37.
143 *Id.* at 36.
144 *Id.*
145 *Id.*
146 Tom Perriello & Marieke Wierda, The International Centre for Transitional Justice, *The Special Court for Sierra Leone Under Scrutiny, in* Prosecutions Case Studies, 1, 22 (2006); SCSL, 7th Annual Report of The President of the SCSL *supra* note 91 at 48.

3.7.2 The TRC

The Sierra Leone TRC has played a role in restoring the country's legal order. Its operations lasted for less than two years. Its mandate indicated it was expected to assist in the restoration of the legal order. The TRC's mode of operation gave it the advantage of working closely with ordinary Sierra Leoneans, from the towns to the rural communities. It arguably supplemented the restoration of the legal order through its influence on the society. Also, it took measures to advance the reconciliation of the Sierra Leone society, which also assisted in restoring the legal order. The measures were its outreach, trainings and recommendations to the government on how to prevent a recurrence of the conflict.

The TRC through its outreaches, hearings, and final Report helped Sierra Leoneans understand the law. The TRC report explained its mandate, the law on human rights, international humanitarian law and the rule of law.[147] It went further to create different versions of the report for children and secondary schools. The TRC established the Public Information and Education Unit to keep the public informed of its work.

The TRC may have contributed to restoring the legal order by training Sierra Leoneans with skills which would be transferable to different sectors of the legal system. It had four Sierra Leoneans among its seven commissioners.[148] The Commission ensured that their mostly Sierra Leonean staff was adequately trained to undertake such tasks as statement taking, managing the statements database, researching and investigating the crimes. These skills would be useful for the administration of justice in a depleted legal system.

As noted earlier, the TRC's request for a Human Rights Commission was made a reality in 2004.[149] The human rights commission was intended to have legal powers to support citizens' claim through advocacy and research. After the commission was established, it held hearings on the conduct of the police, army and even the government's social policy on women and children.[150] It can be argued that the commission may help promote the respect for the rule of law through its reports and activities. For instance, it can be a watchdog to check the arbitrary use of power. It is recalled that the decade-long war was partly due to socio-political breakdown. Therefore, the Human rights commission, as an

---

147 1 SLTRC, WITNESS TO THE TRUTH *supra* note 96.

148 *Id.* at 53; see also, Truth and Reconciliation Act, Art. 2(1).

149 2 SLTRC, WITNESS TO THE TRUTH *supra* note 96, at 136; see The Human Rights Commission Act.

150 See Amnesty International, Amnesty International Annual Report 2009. Available at <www.amnesty.org/en/region/sierra-leone/report-2009> (Last accessed June 13, 2011).

offshoot of the TRC has been actively promoting the respect to the rule of law in Sierra Leone.

One of the TRC's recommendations which would directly bear on the legal order was to the judiciary and the government. It recommended that to protect human rights, enforce international humanitarian law and ascertain the rule of law; the judiciary must be independent, impartial and autonomous.[151] An independent and impartial judiciary would be at the core of a society which respects the rule of law.

For all this, it is important to appreciate that the ways the Institutions can assist in restoring the legal order are aimed at re-establishing the rule of law. Their efforts have included creating the political will among the rulers towards reform, as well as increasing the public's awareness and respect for the law. The institutions have performed moderately in assisting the restoration of the legal order in various ways.

3.8 Conclusions

The broken socio-political and economic structures in Sierra Leone led to a brutal war and made peace difficult to sustain. In addition to this, Sierra Leone had several failed peace efforts due to the complexity of the war and the extent of the social problems. The TRC was established to promote reconciliation. Yet it found it impossible to begin operations until the involvement of the international community that also led to the SCSL. Since 2002, there has been relative stability in Sierra Leone. The contributions of the TRC and SCSL were, to some extent, relevant in facilitating the sustained peace. Their efforts towards the public security and the rule of law may appear inconsequential. This chapter illustrates that a closer observation suggests otherwise. Their efforts to educate the public, train leaders, police and professionals as well as the efforts of the human rights commission have saliently contributed to a more secure and stable society.

The above evaluation shows the SCSL has contributed more to the stability of the country than the TRC. This is arguably due to the duration of their operations. The TRC carried out its work for about two years. Yet it made some lasting contributions to the stability of Sierra Leone, including the Human Rights Commission which has arguably continued the TRC's legacy on the rule of law. On the other hand, the SCSL did not start making any meaningful contribution to the country's stability until later in the almost ten years of its existence.

151 2 SLTRC, Witness to the Truth *supra* note 96 at 137, 141-150.

It should be noted that the relationship and operations of the two institutions appear to have worked in tandem to suggest the viability of a joint model of restorative and retributive mechanisms to prevent conflicts. A synergy between the TRC and the SCSL proved an ideal approach in Sierra Leone for peace sustainability. A similar approach was later taken in Rwanda which established the Gacaca courts to supplement conventional judicial bodies. The restorative institutions on their own may not realistically deter crimes. On the other hand, retribution may not foster reconciliation. A combination of the two mechanisms may be a "carrot and stick" approach. Nevertheless, it is a workable framework that should be adopted to resolve other intractable conflicts in Africa.

Part II
Africa and The International Criminal Court

Any Genuine Objections or Just a Disregard for Treaty Obligations

4 AFRICAN GRIEVANCES AND THE INTERNATIONAL CRIMINAL COURT

Issues of African Equity under International Criminal Law

Henry J. Richardson

4.1 INTRODUCTION

The issues we face in this era of globalization and global criminal law are critical for African peoples on the Continent and for peoples of African heritage throughout the world. As a scholar and teacher, I believe that intellectual reflection, around the rule of law in the dominion of justice, has a crucial role in moving African-heritage peoples globally towards freedom from subordination and discrimination, and towards a stronger collective future. Such reflection on law and justice issues can help inform us on the concrete and detailed local issues and dilemmas about decisions that we all must make, and about actions that must follow.

This chapter generally explores such a theme: Issues of Genuine African Objections to the International Criminal Court (ICC), including relative to treaty obligations to that Court. I believe we cannot sufficiently understand Africa's stake in resolving ICC questions without viewing them through a lens wider than that for viewing ICC-related treaty issues. We should approach these issues as questions of equity for African peoples in the global international criminal law process. We must do so because international criminal law, its doctrines, decision making, and consequences are embedded in the dynamic of globalized interdependence in the world community, from which neither Africa nor any other region or state or people can stand apart. We must do so because history is moving towards the spreading of the rule of international law in the world community. The rule of law necessarily includes global decision making about using that law to define and punish criminal behavior, and the question of who controls that decision-making and those definitions. Lastly, we must do so because the modern history and global posture of Africa has been, and continues to be heavily shaped by the struggle for African authority and its legal recognition over global resources and its own people, especially those in Africa. This ongoing struggle against outside authority imposed on African peoples is coupled with continuing subordination narratives under international law. Since criminalization is a familiar form of subordination in any legal system, the African struggle must confront the entwining of subordination with global definitions of criminal behavior under both domestic and international jurisdictions.

The ICC and its current problems are an important part of prescribing and applying international criminal law but they do not constitute the entirety of that global body of law. Indeed, it is distorting to substitute current detailed, narrower legal issues of Africa's relationship to the International Criminal Court for the equally important legal and equitable inquiries on identifying African subordination and resolving issues of African equity in the global international criminal law process.

For example, one such ICC issue involves national and ICC prerogatives and duties under the doctrine of complementarity. Another involves the desirability of further controlling ICC prosecutorial discretion, particularly as implemented through the Prosecutor's own discretion. Yet another raises the global question of whether the ICC was originally intended, or has subsequently been captured by the aim of serving as a prosecutorial tool of Northern Hemispheric states to help subordinate Africa under the rule of international law. These questions, plus others, indicate that allowing the narrow legal issues of African states' relationship under the ICC Statute to the Court to dominate legal discussion about Africa and international criminal law is undesirable. It is undesirable, further, because many of those ICC Statute issues rest on wider legal principles which antedate in international law their drafting into the text of the Statute. Those antecedent principles, for example, the doctrine of exhaustion of local remedies as it underlies ICC issues of complementarity do arise regarding questions of African equity in the global international criminal law process, and they arise along with narrower ICC issues.

Moreover, substituting the latter for the former tends to dilute, or even erase, African global equity issues. It dilutes them in part because it dictates the confining of the African justice inquiry into the narrow spaces of intent, text, and practice of international treaty law regarding the ICC Statute and state obligations. Indeed, treaty law has its large importance for Africa and all of the international community. However the balance of resources and volume of legal, scholarly, and judicial perspectives controlling the interpretation of international treaty law tend to be located among Northern Hemisphere institutions and scholars at the service of those governments and their interests regarding international criminal law.[1] Their interpretations often conflict with those of Africa. Work is being done to equalize this global imbalance more towards African legal decision-making and scholarship, and with some success. But while doing so, care must be taken to advance the framing of African global equity issues in the international criminal law process, and to ensure that ICC Statute issues are interpreted within that global justice framework.

I have thus sketched my approach to the question of African grievances around the International Criminal Court and to clarifying a framework to address and resolve these grievances. I will now move on to explore some of the ICC problems by identifying three policy dilemmas which at present face African leaders, officials, civil society, and African peoples. I will conclude with final reflections and policy recommendations for next steps regarding Africa and the global international criminal law process.

4.2 Three Policy Dilemmas for Africa Regarding International Criminal Law

It is now commonplace that a prominent category of African grievances against the ICC revolve around the Court's arrest warrant against President Bashir of Sudan for Darfur-related crimes. Opposition to this warrant has been expressed by national state governments in Africa, even among many African states which ratified the ICC Statute. More prominent opposition has been notably expressed by two decisions of the African Union Assembly in 2009, which have virtually stated a policy of Continental opposition and non-cooperation regarding the legal validity and enforcement of the Court's warrant.[2] As we know, this opposition policy has not been accepted by all African states, including South

1 See *e.g.*, William Yat Wai Lo, *Soft power, university rankings and knowledge production: distinctions between hegemony and self-determination in higher education*, 47 Comparative Education 209, 209-10 (2011) ("academic resources . . . unequally distributed in . . . contemporary world where prominent higher education institutions in . . . developed world [*i.e.* Anglo-American universities] . . . occupy and control most . . . means and resources of knowledge production, whereas those in . . . developing world can only play . . . role of consumer and follower in . . . global academia . . . an unequal pattern [that] has been further strengthened under . . . impacts of globalization."); Stephen J. Ball, *Big Policies/Small World: an introduction to international perspectives in education policy*, 34 Comparative Education 119, 123 (1998) ("inter-national circulation of ideas" regarding education policy flowing from developed to developing countries, thereby invalidating "local solutions" and requiring scholars from the latter to study in the former in order to obtain credibility from Northern and Southern colleagues).

2 Decision on the Application by the International Criminal Court (ICC) Prosecutor for the Indictment of the President of the Republic of the Sudan, Assembly/AU/Dec.221(XII), February 1-3, 2009; Decision on the Meeting of African States Parties to the Rome Statute of the International Criminal Court (ICC), Assembly/AU/Dec.245(XIII) Rev.1 July 1-3, 2009.

Africa and Botswana.[3] Further, questions have been raised as to the extent of substantive disagreement with the Court among the States voting favorably in the African Union Assembly, as opposed to States' agreement being interpreted more through the operative interpretation of the Assembly rules of procedure.[4]

These Assembly enactments must be analyzed relative to African international legal obligations and prerogatives. They also must be analyzed relative to understanding how Africa should best strike its own balance between its treaty duties under the ICC Statute, and its Continental commitment to prohibit impunity regarding international crimes. Its further commitment to promote democracy, good governance and the rule of law through the African Union, all analyzed through the equitable global treatment of Africa, are essential to frame the ICC issues.

In analyzing these actions – as well as other sources of African grievances regarding the ICC – important policy dilemmas confronting African decision makers must be identified and illuminated, for their roles in arguments for and against African cooperation with the Court. A first such dilemma refers to what I call the principle of necessary self-help for affronted (subordinated) peoples. This refers to the necessity of affronted peoples to mobilize their own resources and responsibility to move on to the next progressive step towards their freedom, irrespective of the injustices imposed by others upon them. It implies the continuing African necessity to meaningfully participate in the global international criminal law process, notwithstanding any injustices from the workings of the International Criminal Court, while still working to reverse those injustices. Here, questions under the doctrine of complementarity arise, along with those about the legal implications of preventing impunity on the African Continent.

A second such dilemma refers to African leaders, lawyers, scholars, and local officials making the best harmonizing decisions between the global authority of the Nuremberg Principles as they have evolved through legal development and subsequent international courts, including the legal definitions in the ICC Statute, and on the other hand, the general African dedication to criminal and reparational accountability in law, custom, communal authority, and prescription of new legal norms. Here, questions about allowable distinctions between prescribed rights and duties under international criminal law and ICC decisions, and their applications by those in authority on local territory are helpful. Here also the question of African regional authority for prosecuting international

3 Government of Botswana Position on AU Summit Regarding ICC, African Press Organization, July 7, 2009; *South Africa Legally Rebuts AU Resolution on Arresting Bashir*, Sudan Tribune, August 3, 2009.

4 David Greenberg, *African Union Declaration Against the ICC Not What It Seems*, Foreign Policy in Focus: Institute For Policy Studies, August 6, 2009.

crimes as superseding global legal authority must be raised, plus issues of Africa and universal jurisdiction, and the question of the Court's equitable exercise of prosecutorial discretion regarding its evident exclusively African list of cases. To explore this dilemma necessarily calls for understanding current well-defined divided perspectives about Africa and strengthening the rule of law, African states' obligations under international criminal law including those towards the ICC, about African civil society groups which generally favor continuing African cooperation with the Court[5] contrasted with many African governments which, at least formally, have called such cooperation into question.

Lastly, a third such dilemma refers to the long-standing question of resolving important international and regional situations, including those producing international crimes, through law and legal accountability, or alternatively, through diplomatic negotiation, trade-offs, and accommodation among the major involved actors and groups in successful transitional peacemaking. This dilemma must be explored in our discussions to ask whether its invocation by African parties hides deeper African grievances about the global international criminal law process. We must ask further about the relation of this dilemma to the authority of universal principles about international crimes, and ask about who has the authority to make the basic choice of law or diplomacy to resolve such situations on the African continent. We must ask finally whether African decisions to resolve this dilemma, in situations involving international crimes, by insisting on approaches resting on negotiation rather than on the application of legal accountability, should be seen as continuing a cloak of legal impunity for prominent leaders. Or should they be seen as innovative approaches which promise better and more just value outcomes in the global international criminal law process, and which can be understood as valued African contributions to that process. Here, of course, further discussion of the Bashir ICC arrest warrant issues is required, with brief reference to the ICC's arrest warrant against Gaddaffi and major states' application of the United Nations Security Council no-fly zone over Libya beginning in early 2011.

Let me now discuss in more detail issues raised under each of these three dilemmas, in turn.

4.3 The First Dilemma

I defined this First Dilemma above as referring to a principle of necessary self-help for affronted (subordinated) peoples. On the global level, life, law, and politics are not always fair, but affronted peoples cannot allow the lack of fairness and justice to paralyze their

5 The Coalition for the International Criminal Court: *Statement Expressing African Civil Society Support for International Justice*, May 2009.

progress towards shaping a just community. Historically, African-heritage peoples have always had to mobilize resources from within ourselves to help ourselves, until principles of justice in the surrounding community caught up to where they were all along supposed to be.[6] And thus it is now necessary for African peoples and governments to continue to meaningfully participate in the global international criminal law process, without being either paralyzed or driven into wrong and unwise actions by any injustices of the ICC.

Part of this African shaping and participation must be through the doctrine of complementarity, not only as it is codified for the authority of the Court under the ICC Statute, but as it refers to the self help competence and duty of African states and peoples to incorporate and enforce international criminal law within their own jurisdictions. It is up to peoples, groups, governments, and scholars in Africa to define the meaning of exhaustion of local remedies, the principle at the core of complementarity. If Africa does not do so, the door will open that much wider for non-African officials, governments, and scholars under international law to do so, and in ways contrary to African interests. So, let us briefly explore the notion of complementarity as it is pertinent for this chapter.

4.3.1 Complementarity, Africa, and International Criminal Law

Complementarity, as already noted, is not only a key principle under the ICC Statute that allocates authority to prosecute between the Court and national states.[7] It is equally a key general principle in the global international criminal law process regarding defining and prosecuting criminal wrongs as legal crimes under international law. Complementarity generally requires that the authority of an appropriate court, for criminal prosecution under international law, vests only after legal or directly implied determinations that the state(s) with citizenship or closest connection to the defendant will not prosecute him or her for that crime.[8] It will not do so for political reasons or because it invoked blocking immunizing interpretations of national law, or it cannot do so because of lack of competent institutions or constitutive procedures, or, of course, some combination of the above.[9]

In Africa, complementarity often bears directly on, as has been noted by many commentators, the delay – or refusal where this can be demonstrated – in most African states which are party to the ICC Statute in enacting their own national laws incorporating

6 Taslim O. Elias, The International Court of Justice and Some Contemporary Problems, 156-163 (1983).

7 Rome Statute of the International Criminal Court, Art. 7, July 17, 1998, UN Doc. A/CONF. 183/9; 37 ILM 1002 (1998); 2187 UNTS 90 (hereinafter Rome Statute).

8 *Id.*

9 *Id.*

complementarity procedures and norms for local prosecutions of international crimes relative to international criminal law, including their treaty obligations to the ICC under its Statute. African civil society groups – singularly and collectively over recent years – have rightly stressed the importance of ending this delay in African national law-making.[10] And the collective fact of this delay has several consequences. One is to render African peoples and cultures more vulnerable to global criticism that Africa rejects or defies international criminal law norms. Such African states, goes the argument, thus support the continuation of impunity of African leaders by refusing to enact the necessary national norms and procedures to prosecute such crimes, while making it more difficult for the ICC to do so.

This criticism contains much inaccuracy. However, African actions creating the opportunities to make it impede Africa's credibility in invoking global equitable principles to specify its own entitlement to equitable treatment and prerogatives in the global international criminal law process. The need to make a demand with "clean hands" is a universal equitable principle under international law.[11] Africa needs to deploy it in the international community to its advantage regarding major injustices directed towards its states and peoples through ICC issues, such as that of selective ICC prosecution as between African offenders and offending leaders and officials in situations featuring Northern Hemisphere states.

But there is an additional level to the question of African states and national law, and the international legal principle of complementarity. As earlier noted, complementarity is a global principle which is reflected through the ICC Statute, but which did not originate with that Statute's text. In part, this global principle rests on the legal doctrine requiring the exhaustion of domestic remedies prior to international authority being exercised, regarding issues arising from that national territory. And we know that the same doctrine requires that the exhaustion of local remedies must be real, and not pretended. Such local proceedings must not be seen as unduly politicized away from general requirements of legal fact-finding and decision making. Nor may they occur in a process where the outcome is foreordained to protect current states' officials and local elites.[12] There is, in other words, a clear global context in international law for the complementarity principle, even as many African detractors ignore its ICC requirement, and focus on making African recognition

10 *Statement by Representatives of African Civil Society and the Legal Profession on the Implications of the African Union's Recent Decisions on Universal Jurisdiction and the Work of the International Criminal Court In Africa*, 3 (June 4, 2009).

11 See, *e.g.*, Bin Cheng, General Principles of Law as Applied by International Courts and Tribunals 156 (1987) (claimant "who asks for redress must present [it]self with clean hands").

12 See, *e.g.*, Ian Brownlie, Principles of Public International Law 18, (5th ed.1998) ("no one can be a judge in his own suit. . .the parties to a case must abstain from any measure capable of exercising prejudicial effect in regard to the execution of the decision to be given") (citation omitted).

of its importance relative to African solutions the equivalent of alleged African support of local impunity and opposition to *any* prosecutions by the ICC.

However, these arguments and equivalences omit a crucial issue in interpreting complementarity in the African context. When African states exercise their national rights to complementarity as a condition for international prosecution through the ICC or otherwise, its "complementary" local legal arrangements to prosecute international crimes on its territory cannot be subjected to colonialist, neo-colonialist, "primitivist", and other such subordinating racial and ideological critiques, as being so "non-legal" in jurisprudence, theory and content, because they are African. African legal arrangements are deemed by those foreign officials who see themselves as controlling the definition of global legal standards – including those of human rights law – to be *per se* ineligible to satisfy the requirements of exhaustion of local and national remedies, and thus the requirements of complementarity under international criminal law.

This *per se* rejection of African customary law, communal and reconciliation jurisprudence and procedures, and limits on individualism to define liability, is a rehash of centuries of old racial and colonialist legal historiography concluding that African law was not "law." The British common law and French codes were invoked as the 'civilized' standards into which African culture and principles of authority had to be forcibly shoved. We know that it has taken the global decolonization movement to provide the platform to reverse such biased jurisprudence, and Africa must now not give up this struggle.

Thus in 1994 the Rwandan government, on the knife-edge still between calming its peoples' fears following its horrific genocide, and the inadequacy of its formal legal system to credibly allocate criminal liability among some fourteen thousand suspected criminal detainees and known genocide participants among the free Rwandan population in any realistic time frame[13] (as of 2001, only about 5,000 trials had taken place, leaving more than 125,000 people in prison awaiting trial)[14] decided on the policy of *gacaca*.[15] Under that application of Rwandan customary law those accused willing to truthfully confess their crimes before their neighbors – except for the most serious perpetrators – and their communities willing to accept their contrite, accurate confessions in turn as a basis for their reconciliation and rehabilitation back into the community, would be discharged from

13 Erin Daly, *Between Punitive and Reconstructive Justice: The Gacaca Courts in Rwanda*, 34 NEW YORK UNIVERSITY JOURNAL OF INTERNATIONAL LAW AND POLICY 355 (2002), 369-370.

14 Chiseche Mibenge, The Netherlands Institute of Human Rights, Address at the Seminar for North-South Aspects of International Justice and the International Criminal Court, Maastricht, The Netherlands: Alternative Forms of Justice: Lessons from Rwanda (April 8, 2005).

15 *Id.*

criminal liability. But even before it was fully implemented, *gacaca* was attacked by all of Rwanda's major aid donors, all Northern Hemisphere governments. Those governments all agreed with the inadequacy of the established Rwandan judiciary and prisons to meet this national crisis. But they had no answer to that crisis – material or jurisprudential – except to sweepingly attack *gacaca* as violating individual due process standards.[16]

However, the local remedy of *gacaca* was the only way forward in Rwanda for these issues at that time and it was a principled, normative way forward under national law. It was not perfect, but it did not represent favoritism for state officials or a cloak for pre-ordained outcomes for the accused. In other words, it represented none of the systemic faults or lack of good faith relative to the international principle of exhaustion of local remedies. It did represent an assertion of African authority of the validity of its own law to allocate liability for genocide and other international crimes within its national jurisdiction in good faith.[17] In doing so, it collided with neo-colonialist interpretations masquerading as narrow claims to due process, where the interpreters' goal was to control the interpretation of African law and standards of fairness to their own policies of fostering more African subordination around the very definition of "what is law".

Such outside reactions to African national good faith policies to national crises are incompatible with Africa's equitable treatment in the global international criminal law process. They frame the necessity that the definition and interpretation of the doctrine of complementarity – both globally and under the ICC Statute – must be a two-way street. Africa must be seen as equal in authority to any other region or group of states to contribute new content and interpretations to the global development of international law, rather than being seen only as a consumer of international legal doctrines and interpretations that are prescribed and applied to Africa by outside processes in which there is no meaningful African influence. This includes ICC and global interpretations of complementarity – both as states decide to prosecute and as they do not prosecute international crimes – that borrow from African legal traditions and jurisprudence, including definitions of what constitutes an effective decision to normatively address international crimes at the national level.

16 See Pernille Ironside, *Rwandan Gacaca: Seeking Alternative Means to Justice, Peace, and Reconciliation*, 15 NEW YORK INTERNATIONAL LAW REVIEW 31, 46-55 (2002) (describing *gacaca's* positive features and causes for concern, the latter including due process issues for both the defendant and the victim); *see also* Jeremy Sarkin, *The Tension Between Justice and Reconciliation in Rwanda: Politics, Human Rights, Due Process, and the Role of the Gacaca Courts in Dealing With Genocide*, JOURNAL OF AFRICAN LAW 143, 164-66 (2001) (contrasting need for expedient trials with due process concerns such as defendant's rights to be represented and appeal).

17 See, *e.g.*, Phil Clark, *Hybridity, Holism, and "Traditional" Justice: The Case of Gacaca in Post-Genocide Rwanda*, 39 GEORGE WASHINGTON INTERNATIONAL LAW REVIEW 765 (2007).

But at the same time, African policies to address international crimes at the domestic level must effectively adapt to produce results within each African state that quash national and local impunity. Borrowing from customary and traditional jurisprudence in this regard must be tested by such revised jurisprudence leading effectively to quashing impunity. This must be the test, because the abuses and damage of impunity being permitted are better known domestically in African jurisdictions (including regionally through AU law)[18] than internationally. This test also is valid because some of the foundations of impunity are entwined with interpretations of customary and traditional jurisprudence about both exercising and putting limits on public authority of high officials.

In understanding complementarity as a two-way street, we might briefly consider the question of African states – which are parties to the ICC Statute – and which self-refer situations of international criminality affecting their territory to the ICC. These self-referred situations are then eligible for ICC prosecution.[19] Recall the foregoing discussion of African states enacting national legislation to meet their obligations of complementarity as required by the Statute, and that of the international interpretation of the legal requirement of complementarity at the national level necessarily and equitably being open to African contributions to international law from its own legal traditions and development. It might be argued that all African states which self-refer situations for prosecution to the ICC, have by doing so, at least in doctrine, resolved the following: (1) struck an acceptable balance in their own laws, policies, and perspectives about their interpretations of their ICC Statute obligations of complementarity, and about the fairness of those interpretations regarding their own national interests relative to the international prosecuting authority of the Court; (2) confirmed that ICC prosecution under such self-reference would not constitute over-reaching or domination by the ICC in that instance regarding their own equity interests under either the Statute or implicitly in the wider global international criminal law process; and (3) generally determined that its national interests were better served – in light of the nature of the situation on its territory – by such self reference to the Court for prosecution than if it had not been done.

---

18 See Constitutive Act of the African Union art. 4(o), July 11, 2000, 2158 U.N.T.S. 3, 37 ("[r]espect for the sanctity of human life, *condemnation and rejection of impunity* and political assassinations, acts of terrorism and subversive activities" guiding principles of African Union) (emphasis added).

19 Rome Statute, *supra* note 7, at Arts. 13(a), 14, 93(10) (Court can obtain jurisdiction with respect to crimes when State Party refers situation to Prosecutor; when State Party makes said referral, it must provide Prosecutor information regarding crimes as available to State Party; upon request of State Party, Court may aid State Party investigate alleged actions constituting international crimes or violations of State Party's domestic law); However, as the ICC intervention at the behest of the Ugandan government shows, a State Party may use the option of self-referral as a means to cover up its own potential crimes against a combating party, while concurrently leveraging their position vis-à-vis the accused (*i.e.* the combating party) in negotiations outside the ICC framework. See Adam Branch, *Uganda's Civil War and the Politics of ICC Intervention*, 21 Ethics and International Affairs 179 (2007).

This argument assumes that the self-referring African state was not coerced by outside parties to refer the situation to the Court, that is, coercion here lying below the threshold of "coercion" as prescribed under the Vienna Convention on the Law of Treaties.[20] It also assumes that the referring African state has, in doing so, declared its willingness to abide by and enforce the Court's holdings and decisions in resolving that situation, and otherwise do nothing that would undermine the Court's authority, absent a discriminatory or otherwise corrupting flaw in that ICC process, or unless the national government acted *ultra vires* its own law in referring the situation.

If we find this proposition credible, it implies that questions of basic fairness and justice between those African states and the work and procedures of the ICC have been resolved pertaining to those States and those cases during their prosecution, trial, and enforcement. It would seem to further imply that the general question of Continental fairness and justice between Africa and the ICC must be shaped, substantially, by actions of individual African states themselves in moving, through concrete decisions, towards or away from the ICC's competence and authority. In this connection, questions of African Continental justice and fairness from the ICC may be additionally examined by whether cases concerning African situations are referred to the Court by the UN Security Council, or opened under the Prosecutor's own initiative under the Statute, as compared to those self-referred by African states.

Self-referral would carry a presumption of perceived ICC fairness, including on issues of prosecutorial discretion, complementarity, universal jurisdiction, and ICC authority to obligate the national government under the Statute. Whereas it might be argued that no such presumption of fairness would attach – without further inquiry – to cases arising in Africa by the Prosecutor's own initiative, or those referred for prosecution by the Security Council. Finally, there is the question of whether the presumption of ICC fairness towards Africa by African states' self-referral of particular territorial situations estops the remainder of African peoples, groups and governments from questioning or concluding a lack of justice towards Africa by the ICC. Many non-African commentators might indeed advance such a notion. However, I believe it does not. First, there are enough constitutive and systemic questions already raised about the Court's capacity over time to do justice towards Africa to dictate resolving these questions through a consistent step by step, case by case approach, through the ICC experiences of individual African states, rather than through broad outside inductive conclusions about what African Continental attitudes about the ICC have been locked in by actions of a few.

20 Vienna Convention on the Law of Treaties, Art. 52, May 23, 1969.

Second, self-reference to the ICC at least gives the African state some control over its interactions and interests with the Court, whereas prosecutorial initiative and reference by the Security Council generally exclude the possibility for African states affected of controlling the exercise of international authority on their territory. Equally, they exclude the possibility of controlling the process of global public normative interpretation of the comparative rightness of the Court's exercise of its authority, versus African state interpretations of its own authority compared to that of the Court. This would seem to especially apply to the prominent question of selective prosecution against Africa generally by the Court.

And third, the question arises of whether in this regard the AU Assembly of Heads of State could, regarding this proposition, step into the shoes of the Continent, regarding a case that was framed under Prosecutorial initiative and advanced by Security Council decision to refuse to defer the Bashir arrest warrant, and resolve the Continental question of the Court's fairness and authority towards Africa. As discussed, the route of this case before the ICC attracts no opening presumption of the fairness of the Court towards Africa, including towards heads of state. But the answer to this question lies well beyond textual interpretation of the relevant provisions of the AU Treaty, particularly since that Treaty itself contains authority to quash impunity and uphold principles of international criminal law.[21] Such an answer must refer to a number of factors, including the Continental acceptance of such a quasi-judicial ruling by the AU Assembly; the record would seem to be mixed, even absent questions about interpreting Assembly procedure around that decision, on the governmental level, and rejectionist on the level of civil society groups throughout the Continent.

A last factor might be one of comparative necessity regarding the Assembly's ruling, asking whether its ruling was necessary to preserve African Continental public order on a scope that only Africa's major regional organization could perceive and encompass. This was the case, for example, in 1964, when the OAU, facing the clear possibility of border wars up and down the Continent in the independence period, balanced the preservation of African public order against the injustices of African colonial boundaries, and ruled that such injustices had to be tolerated for maintaining colonially-drawn national boundaries under the doctrine of *uti posseditis*.[22] That exercise of OAU Continental authority has proved its legitimacy over the decades by generally being observed by African states and peoples. I will return later to the Bashir case in another context.

21 Constitutive Act of the African Union, *supra* note 18, at Art. 4 (guiding principles include: right of AU to authorize intervention in states evidencing presence of war crimes, genocide, and crimes against humanity; respect for democratic principles, human rights, rule of law, good governance, sanctity of human life; condemnation and rejection of impunity, political assassination, terrorism, and subversive activities).

22 Resolutions Adopted by the First Ordinary Session of the Assembly of Heads Of State and Government hheld in Cairo, Uar, from 17 to 21 July 1964, AHG/Res. 16(I) 1964.

4.4 THE SECOND DILEMMA

As stated above, the Second Dilemma refers to African leaders, lawyers, scholars, and local officials making the best harmonizing decisions between the global authority of the Nuremberg Principles as they evolved through legal development and subsequent international courts, including the legal definitions in the ICC Statute, and on the other hand, the general African dedication to criminal, reparational, and reconciliation accountability in law, custom, communal authority, and prescription of new legal norms. In exploring this particular Dilemma, I will briefly discuss issues of equity and Africa in the international community, the global authority of the Nuremberg Principles and African regional authority, applications of international criminal law on African territory regarding the split between governmental and civil society perspectives, the *Yerodia* case regarding *Congo v. Belgium* in the ICJ[23] relative to Africa and universal jurisdiction, and finally ICC prosecutorial discretion and African situations.

4.4.1 Global Equity and African Peoples

The incorporation of equity principles into international law, such as the clean hands doctrine, the principle of unjust enrichment, and the principle of set-off and claim, is undeniable. However, I believe, further, that a related but wider principle of global equity for African peoples in the international community has recently been incorporated into international criminal law.

This principle was framed through former UN Secretary-General Boutros Boutros-Ghali's insistence, regarding the emerging international community policy agreement of bringing into legal existence the ICTY through UN Security Council Chapter VII authority, in 1993, that the formation of such a court would be globally illegitimate if the horror of the Rwandan genocide in Africa was not equally recognized as a crisis for the global rule of law, and an international criminal court for Rwanda was not similarly and immediately established.[24] This indeed occurred in 1994. Thus the global demand that the Nuremberg Tradition be brought forward and applied to a southern European war, and its dissolution of public order, was equalized by the meeting of the parallel demand that the same Nuremberg Tradition be equally recognized as applying to frame international criminal law in Africa, under which genocide and other serious crimes in African territories would be assured to be judged and punished.

23 Arrest Warrant of 1 April 2000 (*Dem. Rep. Congo v. Belg.*), Judgment, 2002 I.C.J. 3.
24 Report of the Secretary-General on Rwanda, U.N. Doc. S/1994/1125 (October 4, 1994).

This recognition of global equity between African and European crimes, and the necessity of equally punishing them under international law, rests on, among other values, the at least formal and facial acknowledgment of the equal humanity of African persons and peoples, potential criminal perpetrators, and potential victims of international crimes. The importance of this recognition is defined by the underbrush of Anglo-European racism, and its methodologies of diminished human worth of each person of color compared to each person of European heritage. Assumptions that "colored peoples'" value individual human life less in their own communities are coupled with enhanced tales of cruelty and mass slaughter in those same communities, which are sometimes covered by academic methodologies of "orientalism".[25] These in turn have been coupled with historic racist precepts against Africans that their existence was rightly symbolic of enslavement by others;[26] that their lives are simply worth less than those of Europeans, and hence can be more easily enslaved and taken, including by European mercenaries, weapons and technology on the African Continent, all in the service of maintaining colonial, neo-colonial and apartheid order over the past generations. So deeply embedded are these discriminatory precepts that it has taken post- colonial international human rights law many years to address these crimes, with only partial effectiveness.

The foregoing is only a sketch of the underbrush through which the notion of common and equal African humanity has had to fight, at least for this bit of facial and formalistic success. As Professor Jeremy Levitt has reminded us, this fight has produced many contributions of African legal scholars and government policy to public international law,[27] including to international criminal law, including to the legal human right of accountability for past crimes affecting the present lives of communities, and to the human right to representative government and to be free from the implied crime of mounting a coup d'état within a state to destroy that right.[28]

In sum, even though there is much more work and struggle to be done here, there is a formal principle of global equity under international criminal law that has been applied to African peoples, perpetrators, and victims, putting Africa on the same plane with Europe. Sometimes, formalistic interpretations of law, where underlying process and enforcement remains weak, can, when invoked and mobilized, be surprisingly rights-protective and

25 See generally, Edward Said, Orientalism (1978).

26 Henry Richardson, III, Origins of African American Interests in International Law 3 (2008).

27 See generally, Africa: Mapping New Boundaries in International Law (Studies in International Law) (Jeremy Levitt ed.) (2008).

28 See generally, Protocol Relating to the Establishment of the Peace and Security Council of the African Union, Arts. 4,7, 15 July 7, 2005. African Charter on Human and Peoples' Rights, June 17, 1981, OAU Doc. CAB/LEG/67/3 rev. 5; 1520 UNTS 217; 21 International Legal Materials 58 (1982).

rights-prescriptive. Here, this principle of global equity regarding Africa must be seen, even if through a formalist lens, as a visible foundation of doctrine for exploring the issues regarding Africa's role in the global international criminal law process.

4.4.2 *The Global Authority of the Nuremberg Principles and African Regional Authority*

I believe the following proposition to be irrefutable: modern international criminal law deriving from the Nuremberg Trials and its Tribunal is now part of the global community constitutive process of authority.[29] As an evolving body of law, it therefore forms part of the constitutive allocation of authority throughout all of Africa – governments and peoples, officials and private persons – in ways that cannot be prevented, disowned, wished away, or serve as grounds for affirmative defenses to those crimes, even if its local enforcement can be temporarily blocked. This proposition therefore is a foundational notion not only of this discussion, but also in understanding the role of Africa in the international criminal law process. The basic principles of international criminal law – including its definitions of crimes – have now traveled around the world, not only through governmental agreement and the works of scholars, but through their internalization in general form in the hearts and definitions of criminality in national populations in most states. Most communities now know the criminality of genocide, torture, rape, systematic brutality of civilians by soldiers, abusive occupations, systematic racism, systematic private murder, and aggressive war, even though the precise legal definitions in some cases lack official agreement, and local enforcement may be problematic.

These notions of criminality have become international factors of local governance, notwithstanding restrictions on constitutional reception clauses about international law. They have entered the bargaining process with dictators and militia leaders in creating transitional peace arrangements. They are manifested among peoples, not usually by court cases, but by unease and protest against official or corporate or group actions, even if such actions cannot be immediately prevented, *e.g.* the United States going to war against Iraq, The Shell Oil Corporation going to war against the Ogoni people.[30] And when we add official and quasi-official African actions of acceptance here such as, votes for General Assembly resolutions incorporating Nuremberg principles, the demand for and general

29 See Ian Brownlie, Principles of Public International Law 299 (6th ed. 2003); Amanda L. Morgan, *U.S. Officials' Vulnerability to "Global Justice": Will Universal Jurisdiction Over War Crimes Make Traveling for Pleasure Less Pleasurable*, 57 Hastings Law Journal 423, 429-434 (2005).

30 See generally J. Oloka-Onyango, *Reinforcing Marginalized Rights in an Age of Globalization: International Mechanisms, Non-State Actors, and the Struggle for Peoples' Rights in Africa*, 18 American University International Law Review 851 (2002-2003).

acceptance of the Rwandan International Criminal Tribunal, the successful global struggle to define apartheid as an international crime,[31] the framing of actions of oppressive officials and governments as crimes against oppressed populations demanding accountability under international law,[32] Africa has clearly accepted the validity and the universal authority of general international criminal law principles and obligations. Again, international criminal law, in its principles, is part of the global constitutive process of authoritative decision making and expectations in the world community, in ways that African national governments cannot prevent, notwithstanding the importance of sovereign acceptance, and notwithstanding the questioning of ICC authority.

Thus, the claims of those, including the AU Assembly, who assert the exclusive sufficiency of regional African authority to define and enforce through regional African courts and other institutions and regional doctrines of basic international criminal law principles,[33] citing flaws in current international institutions of universal jurisdiction, have a significant problem from the beginning. This is particularly the case if their goal is to challenge the universal prescriptive authority of these principles, rather than exploring alternatives in local arrangements to enforce those valid principles in African communities. The latter is not only a valid quest, but in one way or another, has long been a part of the international legal process, again also in Africa.[34] But regional institutions under the UN Charter, especially as they touch international peace and security questions, are constitutively subordinate to the law of the Charter in case of conflict.[35] That subordination is quite probable here, as the law of the Charter encompasses international criminal law, including through the ICC Statute.

It would appear that the AU Assembly, in seeming to invoke the African Court of Human Rights and implicitly other African regional courts, as an alternative in law to the ICC, in the timing and situation in which this was done, is seeking to lay down a policy which can be neither authoritative or effective, but can only pretend that it will be both. This is the case even before we arrive at the conclusions, which have already been well made by African groups and others, that converting the African Court of Human Rights into an international criminal law tribunal would both compromise the necessary and needed

31 International Convention on the Suppression and Punishment of the Crime of Apartheid, Art. I, November 30, 1973, G.A. Res. 3068, 28 U.N. GAOR (No. 50), U.N. Doc.A/9233/Add.1 (1973).

32 *R. v. Evans and others, ex parte Pinochet Ugarte*; *R. v. Bartle and others, ex parte Pinochet Ugarte* (No. 3) House of Lords, 6 BHRC 24.

33 Decision on the Application by the International Criminal Court (ICC) Prosecutor for the Indictment of the President of the Republic of the Sudan, Assembly/AU/Dec.221(XII), February 1-3, 2009.

34 But see Eyal Benvenesti, *Margin of Appreciation, Consensus, and Universal Standards*, 31 NEW YORK UNIVERSITY JOURNAL OF INTERNATIONAL LAW & POLICY 843, 843-844 (1999) (characterizing the doctrine of Margin of Appreciation as conflicting with the idea of Universal Human Rights).

35 U.N. Charter, Art. 53, para. 1. (The Security Council shall, where appropriate, utilize such regional arrangements or agencies for enforcement action under its authority. But no enforcement action shall be taken under regional arrangements or by regional agencies without the authorization of the Security Council).

human rights mission of that Court, plus compromise its authority by forcing it to do what it is not equipped nor sufficiently protected to do.[36]

And lastly, do the AU Assembly decisions here promise, even if somehow largely implemented, to be more effective to fight impunity in Africa than would some form of continuing recognition of ICC authority over international crimes? What would an African doctrine of impunity look like under international law? Would it be heavily defined in new law by governmental and national patterns of practice regarding impunity on the Continent? And would it borrow its different, non-universal regional characteristics of criminal definition and enforcement from the immunities/amnesty side of the impunity equation, or would it borrow them from the accountability and enforcement – under criminal law – of heads-of-state side of the same equation? This matter deserves the gravest reflection, particularly about whether such regionalism is the only way to try to preserve African Continental global dignity and equity during this period.

4.4.3 *The Yerodia Case as a Possible Opening Towards African Regional Authority*

In some quarters, *Yerodia* has come to be interpreted as the firewall in international law between liability, and thus the demise of immunity for ex-heads of state for being prosecuted for international crimes committed during their holding national office (Pinochet), and the continuation of the same immunity from prosecution for sitting heads of state.[37] This firewall is held to exist notwithstanding several doctrinal problems:

1. The previous indictment by the ICTY of Milosevic as the first sitting head of state (and the citation by the Preliminary Tribunal of the ICTY heavily of legal authority, upon Milosevic's challenge to the Court's jurisdiction as by then an ex-head of state, which would have supported the Court's jurisdiction to indeed try a sitting head of state as well as someone formerly in that office).[38]
2. The *Yerodia* facts based on a sitting national (Congo) foreign minister whose personal immunity from Belgian prosecution was held to rest on the international law of diplomatic privileges and immunity.[39] That law comprises a body of doctrine whose

36 *The International Criminal Court bares its teeth*, ECONOMIST, May 12, 2011, available at <www.economist.com/node/18682044> (acknowledging the debate of giving the African Court of Human Rights capacity to hear civil and criminal cases).

37 John Dugard, *Immunity, Human Rights and International Crimes*, JOURNAL OF SOUTH AFRICAN LAW 482, 483-484; *see also* WILLIAM A. SCHABAS, THE U.N. INTERNATIONAL CRIMINAL TRIBUNALS: THE FORMER YUGOSLAVIA, RWANDA AND SIERRA LEONE 57 (2006) (suggesting *Yerodia* established certain international tribunals' right to prosecute former heads of state for crimes such as genocide, with issue of whether same can be said for current heads of state still up for debate).

38 *Prosecutor v. Slobodan Milosevic*, Case No. IT-99-37-PT, Decision on Preliminary Motions (November 8, 2001).

39 Arrest Warrant of 1 April 2000 (*Democratic Republic of the Congo v. Belgium*), 2002 I.C.J. 3, at 21-22 (February 2002).

policies, from the 16th century, aim to protect the survival functioning in host states of isolated ambassadors and embassies of foreign states, as they did their work in the name of and reported back to their national sovereign heads of state. But from only the latter do all responsibility for the lawfulness and effectiveness of national sovereign policies flow.[40]

3. The Court's framing its Opinion to search for a war crimes exception to diplomatic privileges and immunity,[41] whereas Nuremberg and its resulting international law evolved as a body of doctrine *superseding* conflicting international legal immunity at the pinnacle of national state sovereignty, and not as an international legal doctrine of exceptions that privilege lesser doctrines of immunity protecting more minor state officials, *e.g.* Foreign Ministers.
4. The ICJ's admission that Yerodia could be subject to prosecution for international crimes *if* his sponsoring national state waived his diplomatic privileges and immunities as a foreign minister,[42] an admission which contradicts Nuremberg authority by letting the *national state determine* its official's international criminal liability. Whereas Nuremberg law assesses the potential international criminality of all national state officials, from the Head of State on down, and confirms this assessing authority by removing from lower officials the affirmative defense to criminal liability of "superior orders".[43]
5. The admission of the International Court of Justice's majority Opinion that its conclusion that the international law of diplomatic privileges and immunity was subjected to no exceptions for war crimes and crimes against humanity was not based on state practice rejecting such exceptions but on the lack of state practice which confirmed them,[44] a hyper-sovereignty protective holding.

From the above, *Yerodia* is a troubled ICJ decision. It raises questions about whether its precedential authority can bear the weight of interpretation currently placed on it. That *Yerodia* was brought by an ex-colonial metropolitan state – Belgium – against the Foreign Minister for crimes against humanity in its ex-colony – the Congo – itself is cause for concern. The question is inescapable of the responsibility of the brutal policies of Belgium in colonial Congo for present-day international crimes in that troubled territory. It is underscored by the well known and notorious colonial history of Belgian cruelty and a lack

40 Franciszek Przetacznik, *History of the Jurisdictional Immunity of the Diplomatic Agents in English Law*, 7 ANGLO-AMERICAN LAW REVIEW 348 (1978), 349-350.

41 See generally Arrest Warrant of 1 April 2000 (*Dem. Rep. of the Congo v. Belgium*), 2002 I.C.J. 3 (February 2002).

42 *Id.* at 25.

43 Principles of International Law Recognized in the Charter of the Nüremberg Tribunal and in the Judgment of the Tribunal, Arts. 3-4, 1950.

44 Arrest Warrant of 1 April 2000 (*Dem. Rep. of the Congo v. Belgium*), 2002 I.C.J. 3, 24 (February 2002).

of sovereign responsibility towards Congolese Africans, even as compared with the usual coercive and destructive patterns of European colonialism in Africa during the period.[45] The question remains, what is the best policy for international law in addressing Belgium's responsibility?

If the sounding of the Congo crimes under the doctrine of universal jurisdiction is invoked to mitigate Belgium's responsibilities here, we must then decide whether Belgium's being "a good global citizen", by enacting its universal jurisdiction statute to help globally police international crimes, cures in law the effects of its colonial rule. But (a) the US and other countries which brought heavy pressure to force Belgium to greatly trim the reach of its statute;[46] and (b) the Belgium choice to prosecute the *Congo* Foreign Minister (whose crimes are taken here as given), rather than other non-African officials also potentially liable for international crimes, and therefore raising the issue of selective African prosecution by European states, all argue against any legal conclusion mitigating Belgium's colonial responsibility for present war crimes conditions in the Congo.

Yerodia is relevant otherwise to promulgating law to quash a culture of impunity. If African officials, governments, and other officials elsewhere interpret its holding as barring the prosecution of sitting African heads of state and high officials for international crimes, and join such interpretations to other claims of an exclusive African regional authority to define international crimes, they will risk implying their support for the continuation of impunity, and a culture of impunity, on the Continent. They would thus set themselves against Continent-wide policies and commitments, from the AU Assembly decision of July 2009 rejecting the Bashir arrest warrant, through the AU Treaty, through the almost unanimous perspectives of African civil society groups, and through the rejecting of impunity and its damages by millions of non-connected local African people. Such a position would also support the perspectives – rightly or wrongly founded – of non-African governments and observers who see Africa as lacking the political will to use law to reverse a pervasive culture of impunity, and as being unwilling to allow the ICC to provide outside international legal leverage to help facilitate such a reversal, by local law makers, by prosecuting sitting heads of state and officials under its standards of admissibility in its Statute.

Further, adopting such an interpretation of *Yerodia* also carries implications for the question of complementarity. It implies the confirmation of superior state authority in context

45 *See* George Washington Williams to King Leopold II, An Open Letter to his Serene Majesty Leopold II, King of the Belgians and Sovereign of the Independent State of Congo, *in* JOHN HOPE FRANKLIN, GEORGE WASHINGTON WILLIAMS: A BIOGRAPHY 243-254 (1985).

46 Steven R. Ratner, *Belgium's War Crimes Statute: A Postmortem*, 97 AMERICAN JOURNAL OF INTERNATIONAL LAW 888 (2003) 891.

of international criminal facts to Nuremberg law, to shelter with national immunity its own head of state and high officials from Nuremberg-founded prosecution and accountability. In this regard, it unfortunately provides a *soi-disant* legal basis to argue against national complementarity legislation in the thirty African states which have to date ratified the ICC Statute, plus in those states which may do so in the future. Since only a few such African states have adopted this legislation, and since such legislation must necessarily abolish or severely limit national impunity by receiving the outside authority of international criminal law, the negative policy costs on the Continent of interpreting *Yerodia* as the international legal gatekeeper to prosecution, under international criminal law, including as implemented by national statutes, of sitting heads of state and other officials are large and highly undesirable.

Thus, *Yerodia* should be interpreted to greatly restrict its international legal authority. It should be held as restricted to the narrow facts of the case, including its sole applicability to Foreign Ministers under the law of diplomatic privileges and immunities. It should be interpreted as subject to the Nuremberg duty for those crimes on sponsoring states to waive such immunity for their officials. It should be interpreted by recalling that international law lacks a precedential doctrine of *stare decisis* authority, and thus past judicial decisions are only subject to 'due respect'. For the foregoing reasons, the respect due this case holding is low. Further, from the common law should be borrowed and applied here the notion of "distinguishing" a case, to confirm that it should not be seen as part of (mainstream) international legal doctrine.

Accordingly, wide interpretations of *Yerodia* intensify the difficulties of the Second Dilemma. Interpreted as a gateway opinion about the scope and legal rationale of national official immunity from international crimes, *Yerodia* points towards undesirable policies and decision making in Africa about the best policies to harmonize the global authority of Nuremberg – the seat of international criminal law – with the national laws of African states about the liability of officials who commit international crimes. In holding that the law of diplomatic privileges and immunities provides immediate immunity for diplomats against Nuremberg crimes, and that the sponsoring national sovereign state can control Nuremberg immunity against those same officials, *Yerodia* in effect holds that harmonization between Nuremberg law and national sovereign law must proceed largely through the privileging of national authority over international crimes at the expense of Nuremberg authority.

Given the corrosive undermining of international criminal law and the limiting of jurisdictional opportunities to prosecute crimes thereunder, this is a quite undesirable policy direction for this area of international law. It gives more leeway for cultures of impunity by privileging national sovereign government decisions on these questions. It thus removes needed international legal authority at the local level from being available to beleaguered and embattled local prosecutors, legislators and judges, who need that leverage to move against those officials claiming and constructing impunity.

4.4.4 *African Equity Interests and Standards of Prosecutorial Discretion*

African equity interests in prosecutorial discretion exercised under the ICC Statute *cannot be confined* to a strict interpretation of ICC Statute prosecutorial "standards" by which the ICC Prosecutor would be bound. Such 'standards', while important as an issue, cannot solely define the global legitimacy of the ICC as an international law court, including relative to its decisions on African issues.

Such standards cannot solely define ICC legitimacy because of the essential character of prosecutorial discretion,[47] including the following factors:

a) Prosecutorial discretion is essentially *personal* discretion within an institutional framework;
b) With *one* duty regarding such discretion being to apply criminal law to protect the jurisdictional community served by the Court.
c) But there is an equal duty to do contextual and individual justice and equity towards the potentially accused persons, to act equally on all exculpatory possibilities, as the welfare of those persons is tangibly and equitably linked to *their* communities.
d) The balance between b) and c) above must include for prosecutorial decision questions of global equity regarding the power and resource positions of African heritage peoples in the global community – including the comparative likelihood, and the reasoning governing that likelihood, of African peoples being targeted for prosecution, as compared to other national, regional and hemispheric peoples. The legitimacy of the

47 Rome Statute, *supra* note 7, at Art. 17 (defining prosecutor's ability to initiate investigations *propio motu* if it finds there to be a reasonable basis for proceeding with an investigation, based on its analysis of facts – for the collection of which it can call on sources of reliable information – and determination of the seriousness of the crimes alleged, subject to approval of Pre-Trial Chamber); *id.* at arts. 53 (listing general considerations that the prosecutor must take into account when initiating a prosecution, including the existence of a sufficient legal and factual basis that provides a reasonable basis that the alleged crimes have been committed or are being committed, whether issues of complementarity arise, and whether the prosecution would serve the interests of justice); Matthew R. Brubacher, *Prosecutorial Discretion Within the International Criminal Court*, 2 JOURNAL OF INTERNATIONAL CRIMINAL JUSTICE 71, 81-82 (noting "interests of justice" to include the legal status of the conflict and the likely effect prosecution would have on any settlement process); ILIAS BANTEKAS & SUSAN NASH, INTERNATIONAL CRIMINAL LAW 543 (3d ed. 2007) (reasonable basis, complementarity, evaluation of the situation's gravity, and requirement to submit investigations to Pre-Trial Chamber for approval counteract prosecutorial discretion).

exercise of prosecutorial discretion cannot be confined to antedated "standards" of approach and process relative to the ICC decision to prosecute. That legitimacy must be equally defined by assessing, equitably and contextually, the consequential outcomes and effects of the ICC decision to prosecute, both singly and collectively.

e) Personal discretion by the prosecutor (and the relevant ICC reviewing panels) in this process is inevitable and inescapable. Each exercise of it represents a policy decision under international law as the law of the international community. And therefore our inquiry must go to which values and interests of which global actors are permitted to dominate, and which are subordinated, regionally, globally, nationally and locally by prosecutorial decisions and their foreseeable implications. Those answers must interrogate the very fairness of prosecutorial application of the invoked principles of the ICC Statute as they address African situations.

Insofar as the ICC Prosecutor's decisions play an important role in this global process, and given the inevitable importance of non-rule-governed discretion in those decisions, as a partial remedy, all efforts must be made to increase continuing African influence (in its diversity) in the Prosecutor's Office and among its Appellate panels. The recent elevation of Mme. Fatsou Bensouda as ICC Chief Prosecutor should further illuminate the legitimacy of the Court's global selection of situations for prosecution.

The foregoing discussion has only been a sketch of the major issues raised by the Second Dilemma. This Dilemma refers, as noted, to the challenges facing African decision makers in their general administration of international criminal law on the Continent. It refers, more particularly, to African decisions in a steady process that must harmonize the global authority of international criminal law through the Nuremberg Tradition, which includes the authority of the ICC and its Statute on the African Continent, with African legal traditions, principles, and interests in locally applying international criminal law to African situations. And as also earlier noted, these African harmonizing decisions must be understood relative to the equities of Africa's role in the global process of international criminal law. Africa's role must be assessed regarding all pertinent African actors in international criminal law – governments, civil society, traditional authority, and individuals – and not be confined only to government policy making or to ICC holdings. I now turn to the Third Dilemma facing African decision makers.

4.5 The Third Dilemma

This Dilemma refers to African equity issues regarding the UN Security Council, as they affect African participation in the international criminal law process.

Under the ICC Statute, the UN Security Council is given important roles which affect the competence of the Court under law. The Council is permitted to, by decision under its UN Charter Chapter VII authority, formally refer situations to the Court for investigation and potential prosecution.[48] Further, under Article 16 of the Statute, the Council under decision taken through its Chapter VII authority may defer the execution of an ICC arrest warrant for 12 months.[49] This allocation of authority was important to the context and reasoning behind the decision, on July 6, 2009, by the AU Assembly of Heads of State, to refuse to recognize the validity of the ICC arrest warrant against President Bashir of Sudan, and to mandate the same position for all other African states.[50] As cited in its enacting Resolution, the Assembly had petitioned the Security Council to defer the arrest warrant.[51] The Council refused to put the matter on its agenda for discussion, and thus refused to defer the warrant. The Assembly subsequently cited not only the Council's refusal to defer, but the facially dismissive manner of doing so as a principal reason behind its decision to reject the ICC warrant against President Bashir.[52]

The Security Council action regarding the Assembly's petition to defer, as well as the Council's authority to do so on its own decision, irrespective of issues of territorial jurisdiction regarding the accused person, spotlight a major African issue of justice and fairness in the global international criminal law process. This includes the more defined issues of the Council's authority under the ICC Statute as it is exercised towards African persons, states, the AU and other regional organizations.

The Security Council here frames the question of Africa's fair and just treatment in the global international criminal law process because first, the Council has global law prescriptive authority, including functional quasi-judicial authority, binding on all African states through the UN Charter. The trend under the Charter of the Council's interpretation of its authority to prevent and address threats to "international peace and security" has steadily expanded to define major and systemic violations of human rights, especially systemic violations, even if presently contained within national territorial boundaries, as potential threats to international peace and security and therefore within the Council's

48 Rome Statute, *supra* note 7, at Art. 13.

49 *Id.* at Art. 17.

50 Decision on the Meeting of African States Parties to the Rome Statute of the International Criminal Court (ICC), *supra* note 2.

51 Decision on the Application by the International Criminal Court (ICC) Prosecutor for the Indictment of the President of the Republic of the Sudan, Assembly/AU/Dec.221(XII), February 1-3, 2009.

52 Decision on the Meeting of African States Parties to the Rome Statute of the International Criminal Court (ICC), *supra* note 2.

competence.[53] The Council's authority has been exercised over African questions almost since the birth of the UN, from, for example, Rhodesia (UDI), through Namibia,[54] through South African apartheid,[55] through Congo questions,[56] as well as those in Sierra Leone,[57] Liberia,[58] and Kenya,[59] and more recently through Chad[60] and Sudan regarding the Darfur tragedy and the Sudanese civil war.[61] Over the last half century, there are few areas of Africa which have not, at some time, been the subject of Security Council deliberations or decisions. Thus, actions such as the Bashir arrest warrant remain part of the long historical process of Security Council authority exercised on African questions.

This historical process is somewhat magnified by the rise of global perspectives, including as pushed by the United States, viewing the Council as a major international law-prescriber, giving its decisions almost a positivistic command authority over all states through their treaty obligations under the UN Charter. All African states have felt the strong global wind of these perspectives.

Thus here we should recall Professor Shadrack Gutto's perceptive notation in 2005 that Africa's interests in interpreting its relationship to international criminal law and to the Court under the ICC Statute must, in part, pass through the question of reforming the UN Security Council.[62] Professor Gutto is correct, and I will return shortly to Security Council reform and Africa relative to the ICC.

But now, I invite us to expand Professor Gutto's notation to say, additionally, that Africa's interests in international criminal law must also pass through current questions of UN Security Council procedure and politics. It must pass through the Council's two-tier process of decision making comprising bargaining among the five Permanent Members holding each a veto over Council decisions, and then their relations with the ten elected Members, to construct a needed majority of nine votes absent a veto.[63] No African state is

53 S.C. Res. 217, U.N. Doc. S/RES/217 (November 20, 1965).
54 S.C. Res. 385, U.N. Doc. S/RES/385 (January 30, 1976).
55 S.C. Res. 418, U.N. Doc. S/RES/418 (November 4, 1977).
56 S.C. Res. 1565, U.N. Doc. S/RES/1565 (October 1, 2004).
57 S.C. Res. 1508, U.N. Doc. S/RES/1508 (September 19, 2003).
58 S.C. Res. 1509, U.N. Doc. S/RES/1509 (September 19, 2003).
59 S.C. Res. 1450, U.N. Doc. S/RES/1450 (December 13, 2002).
60 S.C. Res. 1778, U.N. Doc. S/RES/1778 (September 25, 2007).
61 S.C. Res. 1706, U.N. Doc. S/RES/1706 (August 31, 2006).
62 Shadrack Gutto, Director, Centre for African Rennaissance Studies, Keynote Address at the Seminar for North-South Aspects of International Justice and the International Criminal Court, Maastricht, The Netherlands: Revisiting the ICC Statute in 2009: Prospects and Pitfalls (April 8, 2005) [hereinafter Gutto Keynote Address].
63 See Jose E. Alvarez, *International Organizations Then and Now*, 100 American Journal of International Law 324 (2006).

a Permanent Member, but one or more African states are always among the elected Members. Depending on the global importance and Northern Hemispheric interests in a given approaching vote, those African states may have varying amounts of leverage within the Council. But they may also be subject to great and even coercive individual pressures by Permanent Members, affecting their overall relations with that Permanent Member relative to a supporting vote of the latter's choosing.

Thus the gulf between US influence and African states' influence in Council deliberations is wide indeed. The question here can sometimes be to what extent does the US control the Security Council, even to the point of corrupting its process. But this is not an absolute proposition, especially when the law-giving authority of the Council clashed with America's inability to get agreement from France and other Permanent Members, and thus get a majority vote to authorize its invasion of Iraq, per Resolution 1441 of 2003. This US failure occurred notwithstanding its tremendous pressures on, *e.g.*, the African state of Mauritius.[64]

Further, in the dynamic of Council decision making, the interesting question arises of to what extent China as a Permanent Member of the Council acts as a guardian, including within Permanent Members' deliberations, of third and fourth world states' interests, including in Africa, as Beijing frequently claims to do. This question has intensified over the past several years because of China's major diplomatic, aid, trade, and investment actions on the Continent, and the receptivity to them – along with problems – by many African governments. Now, regarding the ICC, China's oil and other interests in Sudan and relations with Khartoum only spotlight its role on the Council regarding its refusal to defer the execution of the Bashir arrest warrant, and by the same light, its policy there of supporting the ICC arrest warrant.[65]

Africa generally has long had an interest in acquiring more power and influence in Security Council decisions. We see that the structure of the Council's deliberations prevent African interests from being fairly represented in major Council decisions. This is even true when "fairness" is defined by the minimum due process standard of providing advance notice of decisions, made by others, that bear heavily on the interests of affected parties. Thus, Africa has an equitable interest in the legal interpretation of the authority of the Council, including relative to international criminal law, because of the impact of

64 Henry J. Richardson III, *U.S. Hegemony, Race, and Oil in Deciding United Nations Security Council Resolution 1441 on Iraq*, 17 Temple International & Comparative Law Journal 27, 56 (2003).

65 For an example of China's recent friendly behavior towards Bashir in spite of supporting the ICC arrest warrant, see Stephanie Nebehay, *U.N. Rights Boss Raps China for not Arresting Bashir*, Reuters Africa, June 30, 2011, <http://af.reuters.com/article/worldNews/idAFTRE75T3FO20110630>.

the Council's decisions on African states and peoples, including the impact of decisions about international criminal law. The consistent realization of equitable outcomes from the Council towards African peoples' interests is a continuing struggle, often intense in its north-south value conflicts.

And so the issue becomes that of the Council's treatment of the AU Assembly's petition to defer the Bashir arrest warrant, and whether that treatment was fair to Africa either substantively or procedurally. Since the Security Council appears to have dismissed the Assembly's petition, and given the weight of African Continental concern on this issue and its closeness to Darfur issues including those of African Union peacekeeping, it is difficult to find procedural fairness towards the Assembly's petition, assuming that the petition was an authentic representation of African sovereign perspectives. Any discussion of the substantive fairness of the Council's decision must include a critical question: whether, in a peacemaking situation, demands to apply the rule of law wrongfully displace demands to give normative priority to diplomatic accommodation among the actors and to the accompanying personal immunities of those actors.

This now brings us back to Professor Gutto's proposition that the route to securing Africa's international criminal law interests lies in part through Security Council reform.[66] That question of reform has been before the United Nations for over a decade, and it has flattened into a stalemate. Most agree on the desirability of some kind of Council reform towards it becoming a more globally representative body. Most equally agree that core issue of current Permanent Members giving up their veto or consenting to other states acquiring a veto is currently immovable. Thus proposals for adding more middle and emerging powerful states, without an additional veto, short of a number to make the Council's size paralyzing, is the most frequent narrative, *caveat* to the identity of such states. Nigeria, South Africa, and Brazil are among the candidates mentioned here.[67]

Africa has an interest in Council reform insofar as it redresses the current great imbalance in influence, and ability in deliberations to construct coalitions around key draft resolutions, between Northern and Southern Hemisphere states. Thus in a new dispensation, more than one new African permanent member would be an improvement. However, such changes might not sufficiently address the interests of smaller African states, even as

66 Gutto Keynote Address, *supra* note 64.

67 UTC, *India, Brazil, Germany, Japan Demand Security Council Reform this Year*, South Atlantic News Agency, February 12, 2011. <http://en.mercopress.com/2011/02/12/india-brazil-germany-japan-demand-security-council-reform-this-year>.

they presumably remain eligible for two-year elected Council membership. Such changes may put more emphasis on the centralized Continental authority of the African Union to instruct Council Members, regarding Security Council deliberations involving interests of both larger and smaller African states.

But these approaches to Council reform assume the continuation of the key law-giving authority of the Council in the international community. However, with reform may come efforts by the current Permanent Members and their allies to reinterpret Council authority under the Charter to diminish it in favor of that of, *e.g.*, NATO or some other major regional or extra-UN body. Africa has already seen a similar process in the General Assembly, with the rise of the G-77 and African states' voting prominence on international security and wealth issues, where Assembly authority was, and is pushed to be diminished in favor of that of the Security Council beyond what the UN Charter text provides. On the other hand, third world voting coalitions in the Assembly have become a new route to added global influence on some issues, *e.g.*, to frame legal issues for ICJ Advisory Opinions, in ways that Northern Tier states cannot always prevent, for instance, in the *Israeli Wall* case.[68]

Thus, a reformed Security Council, under current expectations would likely have featured greater African influence in deliberations on an AU petition to put the Bashir arrest warrant on its agenda to discuss voting to defer the warrant. This would be no guarantee of a different outcome, since two-tier intra-Council bargaining with the Permanent veto-holding Members would still be essential to the process. Nor is it predictable that more and larger African States on the Council, even as Permanent Members lacking a veto, would result in unified African positions on key Chapter VII Council issues.

So, all in all, Security Council reform is not a near-term prospect. If it happens, some among several possible configurations of new states and voting arrangements may produce greater numbers of Council outcomes more equitable to African interests. For example, a reformed Council might have at least put on its agenda and seriously discussed a Council deferment of the Bashir arrest warrant, whatever the content of its final decision.

68 See generally, G.A. Res. ES-10/14 U.N. Doc. A/RES/ES-10/14 (December 12, 2003); Ruth Lapidoth, *Should the International Court of Justice Give an Advisory Opinion on Israel's Separation Fence?*, 3 Jerusalem Issue Brief 18 (2004); *Legal Consequences of the Construction of a Wall in the Occupied Palestinian Territory*, Advisory Opinion, 2004 I. C. J. 136, at 158 (July 2004).

4.5.1 *The Substantive (AU) Decision to Reject (at the Head of State Level) the Bashir Arrest Warrant*

Three primary questions challenge any approach to asking about the validity of justifications for such African rejection or acceptance of that warrant:

1. Legitimacy;
2. Rule of Law vs. Diplomacy;
3. ICC Prosecutorial Discretion.

4.5.2 *Legitimacy*

Here I refer to internalized reactions and perspectives of identified audiences about the rectitude – its correctness or its wrongfulness – of an action, program, or public position.[69]

Thanks to African public and scholarly objections on the ICC issues, particularly of discriminatory selective prosecution, and to increased public awareness of European statements of intent supporting such prosecution, the question of the international legitimacy of ICC actions and exercise of its competence has become part of the mainstream global narrative around the Court relative to African issues. A fierce American rejectionist/exceptionalist campaign against the ICC and its citizens coming under ICC jurisdiction, including America's almost 90 infamous 'Article 98' agreements concluded with coercive odors, have all intensified the legitimacy question.[70] So, the question now is, what is the proper priority in international criminal law to assign these legitimacy questions and their resolution? Should legitimacy questions be noted, but then deflected in favor of continuing prior interpretations of law or *realpolitk* asserted as correct? Or, should legitimacy questions modify those legal interpretations towards reinterpretations of ICC authority to remedy the identified illegitimacy?

The audience recognizing that an ICC legitimacy challenge exists is no longer confined to African civil society, organizations and governments. Kenneth Roth, Executive Director of Human Rights Watch, has recently framed the question in terms of the ICC Prosecutor moving towards Kenyan prosecutions on his own initiative under the ICC Statute, while

69 Thomas M. Franck, *Legitimacy in the International System*, 82 American Journal of International Law 705, 725-735 (1988).

70 See William H. Taft IV *et al.*, *U.S. Policy Toward the International Criminal Court: Furthering Positive Engagement*, The American Society of International Law, March 2009 at i-vi, <www.asil.org/files/ASIL-08-DiscPaper2.pdf>.

he has not moved towards prosecuting Euro/Israeli situations under the same authority.[71] Roth finds that this, *inter alia,* confirms the lack of European intention for the ICC to prosecute officials in Europe or America,[72] a perspective even more blatantly recently expressed by a former British foreign minister.

However, having accurately made this finding, Roth frames the issue very restrictively. He does so by rejecting the AU opposition to Bashir's arrest warrant, stating that "just because European victims cannot get international justice is no reason for AU leaders to deny that justice to African victims."[73] Thus Roth immediately assumes the effective justice and legitimacy of the ICC *if and when* it decides to prosecute, and he confines the legitimacy discussion to the denial of benefits to those victims not addressed. But this assumption cannot stand when faced with the integral connection of the validity of the ICC's prosecutor's decisions to the Court's trial decisions. It especially cannot stand when faced with the known and universal duty of prosecutorial discretion to do justice in the contextual situation, by equally identifying justice elements demanding a refusal to prosecute, as well as facts and intentions which frame probable criminality. No court's work can be evaluated – if it has prosecutorial authority – apart from how it exercises that authority.

Here, Roth's position, which purports to prioritize the comparative benefits to classes of victims, makes two further assumptions. First, he assumes the justice equality of European blocking policies under neo-colonialist exceptionalism, to African decisions to forego submitting to the authority of the same Court and law from which Europe demands its exemption. Colonial history all too familiar followed by modern domination/subordination governance strategies towards Africa clearly ensure that the two classes of decisions are quite unequal in their relation to justice and law. And second, Roth's position is a prime example of recognizing that the legitimacy issue infuses the ICC criminal law process relative to Africa, but demanding of Africa that nevertheless the AU (symbolizing here official African decision making on international criminal law questions) must act as if the legitimacy issue does not exist, and thus Africa must refuse to let legitimacy and its equitable and moral compulsion touch prior decisions already made by the ICC.

However on the same issue, America and Europe are permitted to act to block the ICC's prosecutorial competence from their own leaders, officials, and citizens. Such a position is an abuse and exploitation of the history-grounded principle discussed earlier,

71 Rahim Kanani. World Affairs Commentary, An In-Depth Interview with Kenneth Roth, Executive Director of Human Rights Watch, April 12, 2011. <www.rahimkanani.com/2011/04/12/an-in-depth-interview-with-kenneth-roth-executive-director-of-human-rights-watch/>.

72 *Id.*

73 KENNETH ROTH, INTENSIFYING ATTACKS ON HUMAN RIGHTS DEFENDERS, ORGANIZATIONS, AND INSTITUTIONS (2010).

namely, the Principle of Necessary Self-Help for Affronted Peoples, where such people must press onwards towards liberation notwithstanding injustices thrown against them. This is a principle of the necessity of self-reliance and resolve by vulnerable people in a community, as a source of strength. It is not a principle of global legal permission of governments, institutions, and elites who would dominate affronted peoples by taking all or any opportunities to launch injustices their way, especially not under color of the rule of international criminal law.

In the same article regarding the legitimacy question around the ICC, Roth did note that it would be a desirable occurrence, if it happened, for the ICC Prosecutor to move towards prosecuting crimes in non-African situations;[74] desirable, but not determinative of the legitimacy of the Court's actions to date. This notation would seem to particularly refer to opening ICC investigations by the Prosecutor acting on his own discretion and finding a reasonable basis on which to proceed. There are indeed recent additional actions by the ICC Prosecutor in this direction, as I will now set out. Whether they are a promising beginning to resolve – or only a continuation of the problem of – global injustice to Africa from ICC selective prosecution, is an open question.

As of this writing, the ICC has only initiated formal investigations four times, all regarding African situations, and a fifth regarding recent events in Kenya has been added.[75] However, the Office of the Prosecutor (OTP) has commenced 'preliminary analyses' in response to referrals and communications implicating countries in other parts of the world, including the United States,[76] NATO forces,[77] Israel,[78] and both sides of the 2008 conflict in Georgia.[79] None of these preliminary analyses have yet produced formal investigations.

The United States situation involves the war in Iraq. The OTP conducted a preliminary analysis into allegations there of a war of aggression, of genocide, of crimes against

74 *Id.*

75 International Criminal Court website, <www.icc-cpi.int/Menus/ICC/Structure+of+the+Court/Office+of+the+Prosecutor/Comm+and+Ref/>.

76 Letter from Chief Prosecutor of the International Criminal Court, 1 (February 9, 2006) available at: <www.icc-cpi.int/NR/rdonlyres/04D143C8-19FB-466C-AB77->.

77 Louis Charbonneau, *ICC prosecutor eyes possible Afghanistan war crimes*, Reuters, September 9, 2009, <www.reuters.com/article/2009/09/09/us-afghanistan-warcrimes-idUSTRE58871K20090909?sp=true>.

78 Office of the Prosecutor of the International Criminal Court, *Situation in Palestine: Summary of submissions on whether the declaration lodged by the Palestinian National Authority meets statutory requirements,* 3 (May 3, 2010). <www.ice-cpi.int/NR/rdonlyres/D3C77FA6-9DEE-45B1-ACC0-B41706BB41E5/281989/PALESTINE2_2.pdf>.

79 OTP preliminary examination in Georgia: ICC Prosecutor receives Georgian Justice Minister, International Criminal Court, press release, ICC-OTP-20100319-PR507 (March 19, 2010) <www.icc-cpi.int/NR/exeres/AD3A2D6B-A76C-4934-A792-F0C5D7984292.htm>.

humanity, and of particular war crimes regarding the targeting and killing of civilians.[80] For each alleged crime, the OTP decided after preliminary analysis that there was no reasonable basis to go forward to a formal investigation, including no settled definition of aggression, though it would review its decision should new facts and information emerge.[81] The OTP also invoked Article 8(1) of the ICC Statute establishing a gravity threshold for war crimes.[82] It then concluded that the number of potential victims in this case is of a different order than the cases in which the Court has initiated formal investigations, which involved the intentional and large-scale commission of crimes often involving hundreds or thousands of instances and the displacement of millions of people.[83] The situation in Iraq did not meet this gravity threshold.[84]

For the NATO forces situation, in September 2009 the ICC Prosecutor announced he was looking into possible war crimes committed by NATO forces and Afghan nationals on both sides of the struggle in Afghanistan, including allegations of massive attacks, excessive collateral damage, and torture.[85] At present preliminary fact-finding is presumably taking place, following the Prosecutor's indication that a full investigation would be opened if evidence of war crimes within the Court's jurisdiction was found; Afghanistan is a party to the Rome Statute.[86]

Regarding Israel, the OTP is conducting a preliminary analysis into potential crimes committed by Israeli and Palestinian forces in Palestine between December 2008 and January 2009.[87] However there is a dispute whether the Palestinian National Authority's petition of January 2009, under the Statute, to be allowed to accept the Court's jurisdiction has been made by an entity of sufficient sovereign authority to do so. Otherwise, the issue of whether the ICC can take jurisdiction over potential violations in Palestine has been the subject of competing legal briefs by all actors, some of whom the OTP has also met with.[88] The OTP has stated that it will make a decision regarding jurisdictional requirements when it has received and considered all relevant arguments.[89]

80 Letter from Chief Prosecutor of the International Criminal Court, *supra* note 78, at 1, 4-5.

81 *Id.* at 9.

82 *Id.* at 5.

83 *Id.* at 9.

84 *Id.*

85 Louis Charbonneau, *ICC prosecutor eyes possible Afghanistan war crimes*, Reuters, September 9, 2009, <www.reuters.com/article/2009/09/09/us-afghanistan-warcrimes-idUSTRE58871K20090909?sp=true>.

86 *Id.*

87 Office of the Prosecutor of the International Criminal Court, *supra* note 80.

88 *Id.*

89 *Id.* at 4.

Regarding Georgia, the OTP is currently conducting a preliminary analysis of potential crimes committed during the conflict in Georgia in August 2008, by all parties to the conflict. The OTP visited Georgia in November 2008, and planned another fact-finding visit for June 2010.[90]

Thus we return to the prior question: of what significance are these four "preliminary analyses" conducted by the Office of the Prosecutor in situations involving non-African Northern Hemisphere-related allegations of crimes, for evaluating the global equity question of selective prosecution against African situations by the Court? Do these recent Court actions of opening these preliminary analyses cure the equity and legitimacy issues raised by the Court's inaugurating formal investigations exclusively for prosecution in Africa?

I believe the answer must be negative, because none of these preliminary analyses have yet ripened into a full commitment by the Court represented by a formal investigation. However, these analyses do appear to show that the Court has recently grown sensitive to the legitimacy issue of exclusively Southern Hemisphere prosecution. It has done so in the face of Euro-American expressions of 'original intent' that the Court was never intended to prosecute Northern Tier officials and citizens. And it has also done so in the face of widespread international commentary that the Court 'cherry-picked' its first cases as African cases to ensure both the maximum probability of prosecutorial success, and of the absence of Northern Tier official complaints, all towards successfully protecting the inauguration of the Court as a international judicial institution.[91] But, be that as it may, the Court and its Prosecutor have not discharged the legitimacy issue until they have established an ongoing program of formal investigations and prosecutions also of Northern Tier situations and criminals. This is not idealism; it is a minimum equitable requirement of the global rule of international criminal law for the world's most serious crimes.

An important connecting issue arises here: is the OTP's interpretation of the requirements of a crime of sufficient 'gravity' under Article 8(1) and Article 53(1) of the ICC Statute a key barrier to the legitimacy of the Court's actions on selective prosecution? I believe that it is. I have already noted above, regarding the OTP's finding relative to his preliminary analysis in the situation of the United States and Iraq, that the Prosecutor interpreted Article 8(1) as requiring a determination of 'gravity' of the potential crime by determining

---

90 OTP preliminary examination in Georgia: ICC Prosecutor receives Georgian Justice Minister, *supra* note 81.

91 Gadhafi Indictment Hinders Peace: African Union. July 2, 2011, <www.cbc.ca/news/world/story/2011/07/02/world-african-union-gadhafi.html>; see Alexis Arieff, *et al.*, *International Criminal Court Cases in Africa: Status and Policy Issues*, CRS Report for Congress, July 22, 2011.

the comparative numbers of victims in the situation. This interpretation has emerged as a key justification for the Court's current exclusively African formal investigations. But Article 8(1)'s jurisdictional competence for the Court regarding "gravity" refers to *alternate parallel standards, and not to a single standard.* It refers to "war crimes .... committed as part of a plan or policy *or* (emphasis added) as part of a large-scale commission of such crimes."[92]

There is yet no explanation from the Prosecutor as to why he interprets only the second "numbers" standard as the exclusive interpretation of "gravity" under Article 8(1). It may be because it is empirically and administratively easier to do so. But in doing so the OTP prejudicially establishes a critical presumption: that a Northern Tier state or officials' committing war crimes as part of their plan or policy with initial outcomes of fewer victims is less criminal, because the criminal potential of their establishing and realizing such a plan and policy – in its very making by globally powerful interests of such plan and policies – is axiomatically less, even as it produces victims and threatens the rule of law, than such plan or policy which may be made by southern Tier states and leaders which do result in larger initial numbers of victims. It ignores the reality that Northern Tier planning for war crimes is most likely more globally harmful in ways even overtaking absolute numbers of victims, because the resources, military power, and command of value-interests in the world community are significantly greater. *Article 8(1) requires the equal prosecution of both kinds of situations, not the exclusive prosecution of situations of larger numbers of victims.* Both are globally and tragically criminal, recognized as such by the Statute and the Court must so prosecute them. Thus in the Prosecutor's incomplete interpretation of the Statute here, the inequity of the Court's decisions about uniquely African prosecution is sustained, but however, without any permission for us to conclude that the international crimes committed on the African Continent are any less criminal or less worthy of accountability and punishment under international criminal law.

4.6 A Word on Universal vs. Regional Authority of International Criminal Law

Before leaving this discussion, we must note other challenges for Africa on the priority of legitimacy issues relating to the ICC. One challenge is the universal authority of crimes defined under international criminal law, as versus claims that Africa should define and enforce its own definitions of international crimes, and do so exclusively in its own regional courts and institutions. A related challenge is that, given the common formally

92 Rome Statute, *supra* note 7, at Art. 8(1).

stated goal of eradicating impunity on the Continent, what is the intersecting national/international jurisprudence of eradicating impunity which is seen in Africa as a legitimate jurisprudence?

A common thread to both of these challenges, as already discussed, is that it is now impossible for African states, law, institutions and peoples to deny or exclude the universal global authority of international criminal law. However, its local application must have a degree of flexibility about its implementation, but not its principles and duties, regarding local African authority.[93] This proposition refers as much to those norms regarding international criminality that Africa has invited into its legal thinking and processes of authority, such as the criminality of apartheid and norms from Nuremberg, as it does to principles imposed through colonial, neo-colonial, and other dominating legal and intellectual demands from outside of Africa, such as common law notions of crimes to be enforced in favor of those holding state power.

Here, exploring the Thomas Lubanga prosecution can clarify part of the general legitimacy question. As is well known, the ICC investigated and arrested Thomas Lubanga from Ituri District, Eastern Congo, pursuant to the Congo self-referring the situation to the ICC in 2006. The Court charged Lubanga with various crimes concerning the recruitment and using of child soldiers in situations of both international and non-international armed conflict.[94] Subsequently, through defence counsel complaints and Appeals Chambers decisions, the Prosecutor's case and its propriety were questioned on a number of grounds, including prosecutorial refusal to share potentially exculpating evidence with defence counsel, and the sufficiency otherwise for prosecution of the evidence held by the Prosecutor. At the beginning of 2010, an Appeals Chamber found the case too insufficient to go forward, raising the clear possibility of forcing the Court to free Lubanga for him to return to Ituri. His release was, and remains blocked by a Prosecutor's appeal to the Chamber on the evidentiary questions.[95]

My focus here, regarding legitimacy, is the apparent continuing support for Lubanga in Ituri and the Eastern Congo, including for the prospect of his being released by the Court, notwithstanding his arrest and being charged with serious international crimes by the Court for his activities on the ground in that area. It is safe to assume that many people

93 But see Eyal Benvenesti, *Margin of Appreciation, Consensus, and Universal Standards*, 31 NEW YORK UNIVERSITY JOURNAL OF INTERNATIONAL LAW AND POLICY 843, 843-844 (1999).

94 Wairagala Wakabi, *Media buzz on order to release Lubanga*, LUBANGA TRIAL, July 16, 2010, <www.lubangatrial.org/2010/07/16/MEDIA-BUZZ-ON-ORDER-TO-RELEASE-LUBANGA/>.

95 *ICC Suspends Release of DR Congo's Lubanga*, BBCNEWS, July 23, 2010. <www.bbc.co.uk/news/world-africa-10746248>.

in that local District knew or knew of, and had a sense of Lubanga and his activities in a way that would be difficult, if not impossible, to capture in the gathering and assessing of evidence for his trial under ICC rules. Concern has been manifested among the people of that area for Lubanga's welfare.[96] Obviously, in terms of patterns of loyalty, at least for certain groups there, he is one of them.

The question is, what does this continuing loyalty and popularity of Lubanga in his home local district, in the face of the ICC's arrest and charges of his committing serious international crimes, signify regarding the legitimacy of the Court's action, here in this Africa territory? What do such loyalty and popularity mean regarding the Court's authority? Is this a rejection of the Court's authority as comprising any non-Congolese (or non-Ituri) source of authority imposed on those citizens? Is this a rejection of the authority defining the wrongfulness of doctrines framing the international crimes with which Lubanga was charged? Is this a rejection not of defining his acts as some kind of crime, but of some outside 'universal' authority doing so, rather than local 'African' or 'Congo' definitions of criminality and procedure and accountability?

Is this a rejection of the ICC as an institution and of the way it is perceived by people in Ituri to generally operate, including in its treatment of Lubanga? Can the jurisdiction and decisions of the ICC in Africa anywhere be said to be "legitimate" – by global audiences or African audiences – if its actions are opposed, not supported, or not recognized as authority deserving respect in the home territory of the defendant investigated and charged with international crimes? If so, on what grounds for either group of audiences? Likewise, should such a situation as here be invariably fatal to any conclusion of ICC legitimacy because of the refusal of an audience defined as key to accept ICC authority? On the other hand, should any local rejection of ICC legitimacy be interpreted to confirm its global legitimacy? Finally, should we define any such clash of attitudes and authority as being only an initial stage of a continuing process through this period of time of the competing claims – local and universal/local – about authority coming to some different resolution, either favouring one set of claims or another, or producing some third or fourth unanticipated accommodation and basis for resolution?

Conclusive resolution of these questions is beyond the purview of this article. But their importance cannot be ignored. We can note that, significantly, the ICC has perceived their importance as regards the Lubanga case. No less than the ICC President, Mr. Song Sang-Hyun, recently visited Ituri to explain and clarify the Court's work, responsibilities and

96 Helene Michaud, *Iturians Question ICC Head*, International Justice Tribune, December 23, 2009. <www.rnw.nl/international-justice/article/iturians-question-icc-head>.

authority, including as they related to Lubanga in this case, to meet with local residents in a 'town hall' public meeting to address their concerns and hear their voices and questions, including those supporting Lubanga. Reports are that his presence was generally favourably received and appreciated.[97] There were some significant local interventions during his visit. In particular, one questioner asked why the ICC was not prosecuting cases concerning Israel and Europe instead of focusing on Lubanga? The President answered that prosecutions were exclusively left to the Prosecutor's Office.[98] But the question confirms the penetration of the larger African equity problem with the Court into remote African precincts, notwithstanding the work of African NGO's supportive of the Court's jurisdiction. It further indicates that local loyalty interests for a defendant in a particular case need not block local perceptions of the Court's general discriminatory treatment of African peoples as a whole compared to Northern Hemisphere interests.

The jurisprudential issue has its own importance; whether this situation represents a rejection or an attack on the universal authority of international crimes and their defining principles as applied by the ICC, and in doing so, represents a demand that international crimes must be adjudged, enforced, and punished under some "African way" where decisions are made on the Continent? Or, as above, whether we should look at this situation as a dynamic process of opposing claims which in a globally interdependent world is continuing, with potential to produce a different jurisprudential approach and outcome, without, however, doubting the seriousness of each such group of claims?

In this regard, we recall the prior discussion of complementarity and impunity on the African continent.

4.7 The Rule of Law vs. Diplomatic Strategies, Regarding International Criminal Law in Africa and the Bashir and Gaddaffi Arrest Warrants

I want to close this chapter by briefly discussing the connection between global equity to African states and peoples under international criminal law, and a perennial question in the intersection between international relations and international law. This latter question is more urgent regarding the rise of global rights of accountability for oppressed peoples to know what their oppressors have done to them and to hold them accountable.[99] It is the question of whether, in confronting the criminality of heads of state or similar officials of

97 *Id.*

98 *Id.*

99 Jaya Ramji-Nogales, *Designing Bespoke Transitional Justice: A Pluralist Process Approach*, 32 Michigan Journal of International Law 1, 6-24 (2010).

traditional immunity, or present power, or both, in a deadly situation of massive rights and criminal violations, where peacemaking is a primary objective, should international law defining the actions of such leaders as criminal and moving to hold them so accountable, normatively defer to arrangements, bargains, and agreements of negotiation aiming to end the immediate conflict and destruction, even as such agreements and diplomacy aim, in the bargain, to immunize the same leaders from accountability for their international crimes?

This is a perennial question, where normative claims in favor of diplomacy are often pushed by the criminal leaders and their allies, and/or by those actors who have foreign policy, economic, or public order reasons to halt the conflict on whatever terms. The argument is that the application of law and legal accountability would lose these (criminal) leaders' cooperation, and likely bring their retaliation against peacemaking arrangements in the situation, as President Bashir has done against aid workers in Darfur, and as Gaddafi has done in Libya.

4.7.1 Peace, Justice, and Gaddaffi in Libya under UNSC Resolution 1973

We may ask whether in the "peace versus justice" equation, the quest for African global equity relative to international crimes, and relative to asserted African regional authority to prescribe and prosecute such crimes, leads to African interests in privileging the "peace" strategies of that equation, rather than individual legal accountability of African leaders. Such African interests might exist for two categories of reasons: (1) jurisprudential, from the prominence of communal authority, consultative/mediating decision making, and reparational/reconciliation outcomes in African legal traditions; and (2) the privileging of anticolonialism in international legal approaches, as the individual judgments of liability in the latter on the "justice" side of these equations may represent a Northern Tier application of international law to African situations and leaders in inequitable and globally subordinating ways.[100]

Category (2) represents privileging the prevention of these neo-colonial possibilities over the possibilities that upholding Nuremberg Law through ICC authority on the Continent will provide essential leverage to African national lawmakers and prosecutors to roll back the impunity of African leaders. The anti-colonial narrative can, on certain facts, flesh out the origins of local abusive power of some African leaders. But it provides little evidence,

100 See S.C. Res. 1973, U.N. Doc. S/RES/1973 (March 17, 2011). <www.un.org/News/Press/docs/2011/sc10200.doc.htm>. (Nigerian delegate Ogwu stating that foreign occupation was not an option to ensuring peace); Reason Wafawarova, Op-Ed., *Continent in the Crosshairs of Western Extremism,* The Herald – Published by the Government of Zimbabwe, September 8, 2011.

in the international sense invoked above, for constructing doctrines supporting the criminal liability of national African leaders who currently abuse their power and authority to block their accountability.

As of this writing (July 1, 2011), and recalling the Bashir discussion in this article, the Gaddafi question of his being bargained with inducements to leave Libya including immunity from accountability for crimes against humanity, or from his being arrested and prosecuted for the same crimes through the ICC arrest warrant of June 27, 2011, in relation to active African Union mediating policies addressing this situation, all frame the above issues of African global equity, privileging of doctrines, and defining the desirable resolution of the conventional peace versus justice equation.[101]

As this article goes to press, the ICC has announced, on June 27, 2011, the issuance of its arrest warrant for crimes against humanity and other international crimes, against Gaddaffi and several of his top officials. These crimes center on reports and evidence that his regime intentionally used deadly force against unarmed protesting civilians to maintain power, in violation of its responsibility to protect those same civilians.[102] These join with reports of Gaddafi's promises to kill and otherwise eradicate all people opposing his regime, including those who support the Benghazi breakaway rebellion in eastern Libya.[103] Let us recall that these same and similar reports undergirded UNSC Resolution 1973 of 2011, authorizing a no-fly zone and other measures short of military occupation to protect Libyan civilians in this conflict.[104] We further recall that Resolution 1973 formally referred the question of Gaddafi's international criminality to the ICC for investigation, which reference has eventuated in the present arrest warrant.

The Libyan situation creates several analogies to the Bashir situation, as discussed above, regarding African recognition of ICC authority on the Continent. One analogy lies in the role of the African Union in its assessing the desirability of applying ICC arresting and prosecutorial authority to each of these heads of state. The AU in each case has expressed

101 See generally, *Communiqué* of the 265th Meeting of the Peace and Security Council of the African Union regarding Libya. March 10, 2011. <www.au.int/en/dp/ps/sites/default/files/2011_mar_10_psc_265theeting_cotedivoire_communique_en.pdf>. (encouraging the global community to refrain from targeting Gaddafi in the interests of settlement); James M. Lindsay, Op-Ed., *International Arrest Warrant Could Spur Gadhafi to Fight to the Death*, Council on Foreign Relations, May 17, 2011. <www.cfr.org/libya/international-arrest-warrant-could-spur-gadhafi-fight-death/p25013>.

102 Prosecutor's Application for Arrest Warrants Pursuant to Art. 58 of as to Muammar Muhammad Abu Minyar Gaddafi, Saef Al Islam, and Abdullah al-Senussi. No. ICC-01/11, May 16, 2011. <www.icc-cpi.int/iccdocs/doc/doc1073503.pdf>.

103 *Id.*

104 United Nations Security Council, 649th Meeting. March 17, 2011. <www.un.org/News/Press/docs/2011/sc10200.doc.htm>.

opposition to that authority by creating mediating initiatives to bring peace, establish a cease fire, and advocate reform programs, all of which continue the recognition of each leader as a head of state immunized against prosecution.[105] If they remain, they will be obligated to lead/permit national reforms, and if they (especially Gaddafi) depart, they will do so with their international immunity as an enabling bargaining chip, for the good of their people.

These analogies, linked by the role of the AU leadership, raise other significant points. Through Gaddafi's leadership, influence, and political chits from the past decade called in among African Union elites, those elites – not representing all African governments – implicitly confirmed Gaddafi's prior Pan-Africanist claims that he and Libya should be seen and treated as embedded in integral part in Sub-Saharan Africa.[106] These implicit claims arise notwithstanding broad cultural and historic Libyan linkages towards Egypt, Algeria, Tunisia and the Middle East, ties that have long been both perceived and disputed as stemming from a distinct North African Maghreb region. In now being seen to come to Gaddafi's legal assistance in confirming such claims in his hour of maximum need,[107] the AU raises questions about its collective position on impunity of African leaders from legal accountability. In this connection, the AU raises broad skeptical questions about its position regarding the threatened and overthrown leaders of other North African Maghreb countries such as in Egypt, Tunisia, Algeria and Morocco. Simultaneously, its response to Gaddafi re-frames the Continental question of the support African states, peoples, and civil society for the AU position as it implies the negation of ICC authority in Africa.

At this writing, if we compare such issues with the Bashir situation, the responding claims are not as fully clarified. The AU Assembly has not formally spoken to denounce the ICC Gaddafi arrest warrant, and the positions of the thirty African states party to the ICC Statute

105 Communiqué of the 275th meeting of the Peace and Security Council, *African Union*. April 26, 2011. <http://reliefweb.int/sites/reliefweb.int/files/reliefweb_pdf/node-398767.pdf> (enunciating African Union's roadmap for Peace in Libya); *Gadhafi Indictment Hinders Peace*: African Union, July 2, 2011, <www.cbc.ca/news/world/story/2011/07/02/world-african-union-gadhafi.html> (stating that ICC prosecutes only crimes committed in Africa ignoring crimes by Western powers committed in places like Pakistan, Afghanistan, and Iraq).

106 Adejoke Babington-Ashaye, *Regional and Comparative Law: Africa*, 43 International Law 969, 999 (2009); *Libya's Gaddafi says may Pull Africa Investments*, Reuters, January 30, 2008. <http://africa.reuters.com/top/news/usnBAN124642.html> (discussing Gaddafi's desire for federal African government and intimation that he would pull funding from certain initiatives if his calls for greater African unity went unheeded); see also Henry J. Richardson, *The Danger of Oligarchy Within the Pan-Africanist Authority of the African Union*, 13 Transnational Law & Contemporary Problems 255, 268 (2003).

107 *Gadhafi Indictment Hinders Peace*: African Union. July 2, 2011. <www.cbc.ca/news/world/story/2011/07/02/world-african-union-gadhafi.html> (stating that ICC prosecutes only African leaders while ignoring crimes of Western leaders).

remain ambiguous. Outside of AU organizational channels, there has been some indication of African government support for the AU mediating process in Libya,[108] including by strategic silences. But as it did relative to Bashir, Botswana has publicly supported ICC authority regarding Gaddafi,[109] whereas contrary to its Bashir position South Africa has not,[110] and that government has moreover been a leader in the AU mediating process. Some significant NGO's have supported ICC authority here, but, contrary to Bashir, no clear pattern of ICC support has yet emerged among African civil society groups.[111]

However, a second category of AU-Bashir-Gaddaffi linkage issues fall again squarely under the Third Dilemma discussed here. Arguments for privileging bargaining arrangements to induce Gaddafi out of Libya, over those of enforcing his legal accountability for international crimes, had emerged even prior to the formal ICC issuance of the Gaddafi arrest warrant. The Office of the Prosecutor/ICC (OTP) has publicly indicated that it would not withdraw such a warrant.[112] However, some reports from an alleged secret bargaining process have Gaddafi being promised "immunity" upon leaving Libya as part of the "deal". We now must ask, who has the global legal authority to immunize this leader, given credible evidence of crimes and criminal accountability, for crimes attracting universal jurisdiction under international law, and therefore which create obligations on all national states and groups within those states to support and facilitate prosecution? Nuremberg law as customary law, on which sit also in the ICC Statute pertinent definitions of international crimes, takes the issue of the legal competence to immunize in all national jurisdictions clearly beyond the authority of the OTP/ICC. Facially, no one has this authority to immunize Gaddafi, although some may have the power only to create uncertain blocking arrangements against the enforcement of Nuremberg law. Gadaffi's subsequently being killed in Libya does not diminish the validity or current importance of these issues as framed above.

108 *Libya: Zuma Weighs in on NATO bombings*, BUA News June 15, 2011.

109 Khama Dumps Gaddafi, the Voice, February 25, 2011, <www.thevoicebw.com/2011/02/25/khama-dumps-gaddafi/>.

110 *Zuma Weighs in on NATO Bombings*, BUA News (Tshwane), June 15, 2011. <http://allafrica.com/stories/201106150501.html> (President Zuma stated that the NATO bombings and attempts at regime change have been a misuse of UN Resolution 1973, which was meant to protect Libyan civilians).

111 Amnesty International. Org. *Al-Gaddafi Arrest Warrant a Step Toward Justice*. May 16, 2011. <www.amnesty.org/en/news-and-updates/al-gaddafi-arrest-warrant-%E2%80%98-step-towards-justice%E2%80%99-2011-05-16>; Human Rights Watch.Org. *Libya: ICC Prosecutor Names First Suspects*. May 16, 2011. <www.hrw.org/en/news/2011/05/16/libya-icc-prosecutor-names-first-suspects>. E.S. Statement on Chamber of the International Criminal Court. August 3, 2010. <http://igad.int/index.php?option=com_content&view=article&id=234:es-statement-on-chamber-of-the-international-criminal-court&catid=61:statements&Itemid=150> (expressing some support for warrant on part of Amnesty, Human Rights Watch, and Egyptian NGO's but silence from vast majority of NGO's on the continent).

112 AFP, *Gaddafi's Warrant to Stay – Prosecutor*, Times of Malta, July 8, 2011. <www.timesofmalta.com/articles/view/20110708/world/Gaddafi-s-warrant-to-stay-prosecutor.374471>.

This situation frames both the "peace versus justice" conflict, and the indication, *e.g.*, from the 2010 ICC Review Conference, discussed herein, that global expectations are shifting towards privileging international legal authority and accountability for leaders' crimes, over bargaining outcomes excluding law, as creating better outcomes for transitional peacemaking governance. Procedural adjustments of timing coordination between the execution of bargaining arrangements in the supportive relational context of legal accountability, and the enforcement of specific measures of such accountability, appear to be emerging as recommended global policy.

If this trend of expectations continues in the international community, around this perennial question of power and law, it may become more difficult for African states and organizations – even from an African jurisprudential basis preferring mediation and communal accommodation over individual legal accountability for the same acts – to retain the loyalty of their constituencies for policies that attempt to immunize such leaders against international criminality. Otherwise put, the anti-colonialist narrative will be less attractive among African populations as it entails arguments about the necessity of immunity, impunity, and the mythology of the irrelevance of international human rights and international criminal law.

Thus I submit that a primary question here is whether it is in the best African regional interests to foreswear the rule of law and give privilege to diplomatic strategies that overlook criminal violations, in the belief of successful peacemaking. The question is often presented as one of discretionary judgment by "wise persons", resting on eternal wisdom about the "best" way to resolve such a destructive situation, especially involving heads of state and similar military leaders. Such 'wisdom' omits the absurdity of defining such situations as somehow "beyond" the rule of law, and predicting that somehow that imposing a 'non-law' definition is both possible and will produce a better, more durable transitional governmental outcome. Thus the AU Assembly resolution of July 9, 2009, that rejected the Bashir arrest warrant, invoked this "wisdom" while linking it to African traditional values of community negotiation and reconciliation.[113] The implication is that the substance of the perennial rule of law vs. diplomacy question, or 'peace vs. justice' question above is an outside imposition on Africa of both concept and result. I am not so sure.

There is a strong argument that this dilemma may be universal in its origins in the human community and its trade-offs about power, solutions, and continuity of life, particularly when it involves leaders commanding visible military power. The question of whether all

113 Decision on the Meeting of African States Parties to the Rome Statute of the International Criminal Court (ICC), *supra* note 2.

African customary reconciliation strategies are adequate to durably frame such trade-offs under legal authority, under what kinds of adaptation and under what conditions, for 21st century war crimes committed by leaders using coordinated deadly sophisticated state and group strategies with maximum cruelty, is central. More scholarly and policy making attention is needed on this question.

What tribute should law pay to power? I submit that any tribute whereby power is allowed to escape visible legal authority of accountability is both too high, and leads directly back to the grinding African Continental issue of impunity. Notable scholars, such as Professor Jeremy Levitt, are doing valuable work in this regard on the necessity of regional or local African peacemaking arrangements, whether or not brokered by outside organizations, being framed and grounded under available and identified constitutive legal authority in order to be sufficiently durable in the reconstructed community.[114] I submit also that this question is too large to be encompassed by the usual invocations of "realism" aiming to privilege shopworn definitions of power and diplomacy, and privilege any definition of "peace" no matter the value costs imposed on the masses of people involved.

Lastly, during the stocktaking exercise ending the 2010 ICC Review Conference in Kampala, state parties debated the relationship between peace and justice, including as it involved amnesties. Some asserted that while amnesty may have short-term benefits, these benefits are outweighed by the long-term benefits of justice.[115] Others noted that the ICC Prosecutor should be given a measure of flexibility with regard to the time of the issuance of arrest warrants, but this flexibility should not apply to the most serious violations. There was agreement that alternative transitional justice mechanisms should supplement the ICC process.[116] Kenneth Roth, above cited, in closing asserted that the Court has brought about a "paradigm shift" under which the international community can view peace and justice as complementary rather than in tension with one another: it can be difficult to initiate negotiations when there is a possibility of prosecution, but justice should not be viewed as negotiable. States need to both honor and execute ICC arrest warrants.[117] The penultimate word was given to the Chief Mediator on the Ugandan peace negotiations who said that disagreements about the balance of peace and justice are likely to continue.[118]

114 Jeremy Levitt, *Illegal Peace?: An Inquiry Into the Legality of Power Sharing with Warlords and Rebels in Africa*, 27 MICHIGAN JOURNAL OF INTERNATIONAL LAW 495, 506-508 (2006) (discussing the drawbacks of failing to prosecute violators of international law in building peace in African nations).

115 *Stocktaking of International Criminal Justice: Peace and Justice*, International Criminal Court, Press Release, ICC-ASP-20100603-PR536 (June 3, 2010) <www.icc-cpi.int/Menus/ASP/Press+Releases/Press+Releases+2010/Stocktaking+of+international+criminal+justice_+Peace+andjustice.htm>.

116 *Id.*

117 *Id.*

118 *Id.*

4.8 Conclusion

African questions of equity and grievances in the global international criminal law process cannot be encompassed by a sole concentration on African treaty issues under the ICC Statute. Such questions must be understood through a framework linking global issues of African equity with the narrower treaty issues. Such a framework must also facilitate striking a balance from the vantage point of African interests between those two bodies of issues. The process of striking such a balance confronts African decision makers with three policy Dilemmas, the resolution of which helps shape decisions about desirable relationships with ICC authority on particular issues.

The first Dilemma centers on the principle of necessary self-help for subordinated peoples. Resolving it necessarily raises issues about African complementarity under the ICC Statute, and implications about combating legal impunity in African states.

The second Dilemma refers to African decision makers having to make the best harmonizing decisions between the global authority of the Nuremberg Principles and their subsequent legal principles, and Africans' adherence to criminal and reparational accountability in law, custom, communal authority, and prescription of new legal norms. Here, the impossibility of excluding Nuremberg Law from the Continent in favor of exclusive African regional authority to determine international criminal accountability must be confronted, including relative to the African Union and African civil society. Further, the best policies to confront the issue of selective ICC prosecution of African situations must be determined.

A third Dilemma refers to decisions in transitional peacemaking about whether legal accountability should be sacrificed to immunity and amnesty to implement diplomatic negotiated, bargained-for settlements with military wrongdoers. Questions about who has the authority to make such immunity decisions – assuming against doubt that such authority exists somewhere in some body of law – plus whether diplomatic invocations by African parties hide deeper African grievances about international criminal law, must be confronted.

These three Dilemmas demand informed decision making to enable African peoples to establish the most equitable non-subordinated relationship to ICC authority, to determine the correct balances of legitimacy, in the context of Africa's role in the global international criminal law process.

5 Historical Narrative of Mass Atrocities and Injustice in Africa

Implications for the Implementation of International Criminal Justice

James Nyawo

5.1 Introduction

In recent years several African countries and the African Union (AU) have been critical of the International Criminal Court (ICC) and the application of universal jurisdiction, the main criticism of both being that they selectively focus on Africa.[1] The criticism applies mainly to the ICC which has only opened cases against Africans, while universal jurisdiction has been used against individuals and leaders from other regions of the world.[2] Since the ICC was officially inaugurated in 2003 it has opened cases against African individuals from seven African countries, namely Uganda, the Democratic Republic of Congo, the Central African Republic, Sudan, Kenya, Libya and Côte d'Ivoire.

As of December 2011 there were more than 25 African individuals either on the international warrant of arrest list of the ICC, in custody or facing trial at the ICC. The then Deputy Prosecutor of the ICC and now the Prosecuter-Elect Ms Fatou Bensouda, reported that her Office was preparing additional cases with respect to the Democratic Republic of the Congo and Darfur[3] which means that the number of Africans facing justice at the ICC is bound to increase.

---

1 Charles Chernor Jalloh, *Universal Jurisdiction, Universal Prescription? A Preliminary Assessment of the African Union Perspective on Universal Jurisdiction*, 21 (1) Criminal Law Forum 1-65 (2010). (Assessing the allegations that the European Courts are selectively targeting African leaders within their courts and how the African Union has reacted to the selective targeting); Max Du Plessis, The International Criminal Court that Africa wants (2010) (points out several complaints from Africa about the ICC including that it is a hegemonic tool of the west and targeting or discriminating against Africans.

2 Maximo Langer, *The Diplomacy of Universal Jurisdiction: The Political Branches and the Transnational Prosecution of International Crimes*, 105 American Journal of International Law 1, 17 (2010). (His survey of 1,050 universal jurisdiction complaints by nationality of defendants since the Eichmann Trial, there were Chileans, Chinese, Israeli Americans, Germans mainly Nazis also targeted by European countries).

3 William A. Schabas, Progress Report on International Criminal Tribunals, PhD Studies in Human Rights (2011).

The search for possible explanations why Africa has been selectively targeted has attracted the interest of several scholars, international lawyers and African political leaders. Although there is general consensus that Africa has become the main focus of the international criminal justice system, especially the ICC, there is no straightforward explanation for why this should be the case. What is undisputed is that the perceived selective targeting of Africa is damaging the ICC's credibility as a new tool against impunity. Justice Richard Goldstone acknowledges the need for the ICC to balance its investigations and prosecution. He hopes that the Office of the Prosecutor will of its own accord open investigations where there is adequate evidence that international crimes were committed.[4] Furthermore, Goldstone explains that the ICC's focus in Africa is caused by the occurrence of wars and conflicts where international crimes are likely to be committed. He said:

> "It must be recalled that the mandate of the world's only permanent international criminal court is to provide justice for 'victims of unimaginable atrocities that deeply shock the conscience of humanity', many of whom happen to be in Africa. In the face of governments' lack of political will and inadequate legal infrastructure to stem the tide of impunity, the ICC Prosecutor has a duty to target and prosecute the alleged perpetrators involved."[5]

On the contrary, Mahmood Mamdani in his article *The New Humanitarian Order* describes the ICC as a 'Western court to try African crimes against humanity.'[6] He centers his argument on the emerging international norm of the responsibility to protect vulnerable populations which he claims to be monopolized by the United Nations Security Council (UNSC). He argues that although the norm protects the sovereignty of Western states it does not protect the sovereignty of African and Middle Eastern states – the reason being that African and Middle East states are labeled as weak, requiring humanitarian intervention from the powerful and developed states of the West.

President Kagame of Rwanda views the intervention of the ICC in Africa through neocolonial lens. He regards the ICC to be a tool used by the powerful states to control poor countries, and as a manifestation of the return of past injustices such as colonialism and imperialism.[7] He expressed the same views on the exercise of universal jurisdiction by European judges against Africans during his address to the AU Assembly in 2008. In his

---

4 Richard Goldstone, *Does the ICC Target Africa?*, Equality of Arms Review (2009) International Bar Association.

5 *Id.*

6 Mahmood Mamdani, *The New Humanitarian Order*, The Nation, September 10, 2008.

7 AFP. 2009. *Rwanda's Kagame says ICC targeting poor, African countries* July 31, 2008. Available at <http://afp.google.com> (Accessed August 25, 2010).

address he made references to Africa's historical injustices that include the slave trade, colonialism and apartheid before observing that former subjugators were turning themselves into policemen of the world.[8]

The perception that international criminal justice had departed from its original goals and was now being used selectively in a politically motivated manner was also raised by Courtenay Griffiths QC, the lead defense counsel of former President Charles Taylor, at the Special Court for Sierra Leone. As part of his efforts to convince the judges that Charles Taylor's trial was politically motivated, he questioned why the former Libyan leader Mummar Ghadaffi was not standing trial at the Special Court for Sierra Leone when there was evidence that he had been involved in supporting the Revolutionary United Front.[9] This was based on the revelation by the former prosecutor of the Special Court for Sierra Leone, David Crane, that his plans to indict Mummar Ghadaffi were stopped by the United Kingdom government under Prime Minister Tony Blair. According to Crane, the UK government threatened to withhold funding to the Court if it had gone ahead with an indictment of the Libyan leader. It is alleged that the British government did not want Mummar Ghadafi to be indicted because of its economic interests in Libya.[10] This led Courtenay Griffiths to accuse the prosecution of 'turning the lofty ideals of international criminal law by turning this case [Charles Taylor] into a 21st century form of neocolonialism.'[11]

What is intriguing about the criticisms leveled against the exercise of international criminal justice in Africa is that they rarely engage with the judicial aspects of the ICC, reverting instead to the historical injustices which have taken place and imbalances in the North-South power divide. That being said, there are also criticisms against the ICC based on its poor timing and failure to balance the need between peace and justice.[12] However, it is the recurrence of historical injustices in the criticisms of the international criminal justice system which this chapter focuses on, because there is a need to understand the links, if any, between African history and its emerging attitude towards the international criminal justice system.

8 *African Union Refuses Arrest Warrants Against Rwandans*, RWANDA FOCUS, Monday July 7, 2008 <http://focus.rw/wp/2008/07/african-union-refuses-arrest-warrants-against-rwandans/> (Accessed March 20, 2011).

9 *Prosecutor of the Special Court v. Charles Ghankay Taylor 'Transcripts'* (March 9, 2011) at 49389 paras 26-29, at 49390 paras 3-9 (2011).

10 Soraya Kishtwari, *Prosecutor reveals how Britain let Gaddafi off*, THE TIMES, February 25, 2011.

11 *Id. at* 10.

12 See, TIM ALLEN, TRIAL JUSTICE – INTERNATIONAL CRIMINAL COURT AND THE LORD'S RESISTANCE ARMY 85-88 (2008), for how Uganda local leaders and Save the Children UK were worried that the LRA indictment was to negatively impact on the peace process and child protection.

The purpose of this chapter is to attempt to interpret Africa's growing skepticism towards the exercise of international criminal justice on the continent from a historical perspective. It seeks to investigate whether or not the historical atrocities and domination of Africa by European powers have any influence on the region's contemporary approach towards the international criminal justice system, especially the ICC. It will argue that Africa's growing resistance to the involvement of international criminal justice mechanisms could be explained by several historical realities, including the role played by international law in Africa's previous loss of autonomy under colonization and the discriminatory application of law based on 'them' and 'us' which could have sown early seeds of impunity in Africa.

International law played a significant role first in promoting the transatlantic slave trade,[13] then later in the colonization process. The corollary of this historical experience with international law has made African populations and governments want to jealously guard their sovereignty. They seem suspicious that the powerful countries want to continue interfering in their internal affairs, thereby denying them their independence. In addition, the other historical reality is that of atrocities committed with impunity in Africa. Examples include those committed in Congo by King Leopold II and in former German South West Africa, now Namibia, against the Herero people by the Germans where no prosecutions were made. The lack of accountability for past atrocities in Africa can make any attempts to investigate and prosecute Africans by some of these former colonial powers seem hypocritical.

The chapter is divided into four parts; the first being the introduction outlined above which gives the background of the study and its purpose. The second part discusses Africa's early enthusiasm to fight impunity, followed by the third section which outlines how African states became suspicious of the international criminal justice mechanisms, especially the ICC and the exercise of universal jurisdiction by European judges against African governmental officials. The fourth section focuses on the historical injustices, especially atrocities that occurred in Africa. The selected events are the transatlantic slave trade, the Herero genocide, King Leopold II's crimes in Congo, and the Algerian War of Independence. These events illustrate how Africans primarily began to be treated in some ways as objects of European thought and action after they lost their sovereignty to European Powers. The examples also illustrate how the European states that are at the forefront in opening investigations and prosecuting African leaders have themselves a questionable human rights record in Africa.

13 It must be noted that International Law at a later stage helped to stop trans-Atlantic Slave Trade as discussed by Jennifer Jenny S. Martinez, *Antislavery Courts and the Dawn of International Human Rights Law*, 117 Yale Law Journal 550 (2007).

5.2 AFRICA'S EARLY SUPPORT FOR INTERNATIONAL CRIMINAL JUSTICE

The Constitutive Act of the AU is unequivocal on the continent's commitment to end impunity. Some of its guiding principles include the respect for the sanctity of human life, condemnation and rejection of impunity and political assassination, acts of terrorism and subversive activities.[14] The Constitutive Act, Article 4(h) authorizes the AU to intervene in a member state to protect the population from genocide, war crimes and crimes against humanity. According to some commentators on AU institutions, these two principles mark a significant departure by African states from the traditional policy of non-intervention into the domestic affairs of a fellow member state.[15] That said, the AU has been found wanting when it comes to taking decisive action to end impunity or prevent atrocities. Some specific examples include the failure of the AU to raise enough funds to give a timely trial for the former President of Chad, Hissène Habré. This happened against a background where the AU had mandated Senegal to prosecute Habré on behalf of Africa.[16]

On an encouraging note, the AU's efforts to address the justice and accountability issues in Darfur require recognition. The African Union High Level Panel for Darfur (AUHPD) was established by the AU's Peace and Security Council and chaired by the former South African President Thabo Mbeki. Its mandate was to examine the situation in Darfur and to submit recommendations on effective and comprehensive ways to address the issues of accountability and impunity.[17] The AUHPD came up with concrete recommendations. One of their key recommendations on justice and reconciliation was that the government of Sudan should establish a hybrid criminal court as follows:

> A Hybrid Criminal Court which shall exercise original and appellate jurisdiction over individuals who appear to bear particular responsibility for the gravest crimes committed during the conflict in Darfur, and to be constituted by judges of Sudanese and other nationalities[18]

The AU's two main challenges are that at times its best intentions are not adequately funded and that member states do not always comply with its decisions or recommendations. For

14 African Union Constitutive Act (2002) Art. 4(o).

15 Mwanasali Musifiky, *From Non-Interference to Non-Indifference: The Emerging Doctrine of Conflict Prevention in Africa, in* THE AFRICAN UNION AND ITS INSTITUTIONS (John Akokpari, Angela Ndinga-Muvumba & Tim Murithi eds., 2009).

16 African Union, Decision on the Hissène Habre Case Doc. Assembly/AU/12 (XIII) Rev.1. Assembly of the African Union Thirteenth Ordinary Session 1-3 July 2009, 2009, Sirte, Great Socialist People's Libyan Arab Jamahiriya. African Union point number 3 on contributions.

17 THABO MBEKI, QUEST FOR PEACE, JUSTICE AND RECONCILIATION REPORT OF THE AFRICAN UNION HIGH-LEVEL PANEL ON DARFUR (2010).

18 *Id.* at 89.

instance, the government of Sudan rejected its recommendation for the establishment of a hybrid court for Darfur, arguing that such a step was tantamount to ceding its sovereignty. Their decision to reject this recommendation weakens the argument that Africa is being selectively targeted. It was a missed opportunity for Sudan and Africa to demonstrate that it could address impunity in its own backyard and did not require intervention by the ICC.

It is also worth noting that African delegates at the United Nations Diplomatic Conference of Plenipotentiaries on the Establishment of an International Criminal Court in 1998 played a significant and constructive role. During the opening sessions of the Rome Conference, Professor Maluwa, the then Legal Counsel of the Organization of African Unity (OAU) – now the AU – pointed out that Africa was interested in the establishment of a permanent international criminal court because its population had endured violations of its human rights for centuries. He is reported to have said:

> Africa had a particular interest in the establishment of the Court, since its peoples had been the victims of large-scale violations of human rights over the centuries: slavery, wars of colonial conquest and continued acts of war and violence, even in the post-colonial era. The recent genocide in Rwanda was a tragic reminder that such atrocities were not yet over, but had strengthened OAU's determination to support the creation of a permanent, independent court to punish the perpetrators of such acts.[19]

His remarks were echoed by Abdula Mohamed Omar, the Minister for Justice of South Africa, who also spoke on behalf of the Southern Africa Development Community (SADC). He said that the establishment of an international criminal court was a clear sign from the international community to those who commit crimes similar to those experienced in South Africa under apartheid that impunity was no longer an option.[20] It is therefore not surprising that South Africa was part of the group of states that submitted a proposal for apartheid to be included as an element of crime under crimes against humanity.[21]

---

19 United Nations, Official Records Volume II Summary Records of the Plenary Meetings and of the Meetings of the Committee of the Whole 6th Plenary Meeting, A/CONF.183/SR.6. United Nations Diplomatic Conference of Plenipotentiaries on the Establishment of an International Criminal Court, Rome, 15 June-17 July 1998, Rome Italy United Nations p. 104 para. 115.

20 *Id.* at 65 para. 14.

21 The Draft Preparatory Committee on the Establishment of an International Criminal Court has submitted before the Rome Conference had the crime of apartheid as an option under War Crimes, see A/CONF.183/2/Add.1 English at 20. See, United Nations, Report of the Preparatory Committee on the Establishment of an International Criminal Court A/CONF.183/2/Add.1. However, during the proceedings several delegates including South Africa supported the inclusion of apartheid as a crime against humanity and was part of the group that proposed the criminalization of institutionalized racial discrimination. See document A/CONF.183/C.1/L.12.

African support for the ICC went beyond the Rome Conference to the ratification process. Senegal was the first country to ratify the Rome Statute in 1999, and by 2011 Africa had a total of 33 countries that had also ratified it.[22] Several explanations have been put forward to explain Africa's rapid ratification of the Rome Statute. American officials attribute the adaptation of the Rome Statute and its subsequent ratification to 'a strong wave of defiance against the United States….'[23] This view is also shared by some scholars who attended the Rome Conference such as Professor William Schabas.[24]

The other possible explanation, although it is less convincing, is that the rapid ratification of the Rome Statute by African states was due to the fact that the ratification was one of the conditions set by the European Union (EU) for African and Caribbean states under the revised Cotonou Agreement[25] of 2005 to continue receiving financial aid from the EU. It is hard to accept this explanation because approximately 26 African States that ratified the Rome Statute did so in 2002 before the Cotonou Agreement was amended in 2005.

The fact that some African states, resisted immense pressure put on them by the United States (US) to conclude Bilateral Immunity Agreements under Article 98 of the Rome Statute,[26] indicates that perhaps 'bandwagoning for profit' was not the main motive for African support of the ICC. Countries like Kenya, Mali, Namibia, Niger, South Africa and Tanzania had their accounts for International Military Education and Training (IMET), Foreign Military Financing (FMF) and Excess Defense Articles (EDA) frozen for their refusal to sign the Article 98 Agreements with the US.[27] However the US had to change its stance after it realized that cutting aid to some of its allies was affecting the war against terrorism.

Apart from the enthusiasm demonstrated during the Rome Conference, individual African states had shown a similar commitment to end impunity in their own countries. For instance, in 1994 after the genocide in Rwanda, the government requested the United Nations to establish an international tribunal for the sole purpose of prosecuting those

22 See ICC website, <www.icc-cpi.int/Menus/ICC> (Accessed August 22, 2011).

23 See Declassified documents from the United States of America National Intelligence Council available on <www.foia.cia.gov/docs/DOC_0000993739/DOC_0000993739.pdf> (Accessed September 15, 2011)

24 William A. Schabas, An Introduction To The International Criminal Court (3d ed. 2007).

25 Cotonou Agreement is a development and aid framework signed between the EU and 76 African Caribbean Pacific (ACP) countries.

26 Bilateral Immunity Agreement or Art. 98 Agreements were negotiated between the Bush Administration of the United States with several countries to ensure that US nationals operating around the world were immune to the ICC jurisdiction. The agreements were based on Art. 98 of the Rome Statute.

27 Beth Elise Whitaker, *Soft Balancing Among Weak States in Africa*, 86(5) International Affairs 1109 (2010); Congressional Research Service International Criminal Court Cases in Africa: Status and Policy Issues (2011).

who had violated international humanitarian law.[28] In 2000 the president of Sierra Leon, President Kabbah, wrote a letter to the United Nations Secretary General requesting the establishment of an independent court to investigate and prosecute those who violated international humanitarian law during the civil war.[29] The request led to the establishment of a Special Court for Sierra Leone (SCSL)

At the domestic level, Ethiopia and Rwanda are among the few countries that have demonstrated willingness and successfully investigated and prosecuted those responsible for committing international crimes. Other African countries to have attempted to prosecute international crimes include Senegal,[30] the Democratic Republic of the Congo[31] and Uganda.[32] In Ethiopia, the post-Mengistu regime established a Special Prosecutor's Office to investigate and prosecute the Derg members who had committed mass atrocities during its rule of terror between 1974 and 1991. The main charges filed against the Derg suspects include genocide, crimes against humanity and war crimes. It is noteworthy that in Ethiopia the definition of genocide was not a conventional one as it includes political groups, thus extending the scope of protection beyond the four groups – national, ethnic, racial and religious – mentioned in Article II of the Genocide Convention.[33]

In Rwanda the post-genocide government was faced with an enormous task to investigate and prosecute those who had taken part in the genocide. Although Rwanda had ratified the Genocide Convention in 1975 and the Geneva Conventions in 1964, it had not passed the relevant domestic legislation to include the crimes of genocide in its penal code.[34] This

---

28 U.N. Doc. S./RES/955/1994.

29 U.N. Doc. S/2000/786 (2000) Letter sent by the Permanent Representative of Sierra Leone to the United Nations addressed to the President of the Security Council.

30 Senegal has attempted to prosecute the former Chad President Hissiène Habré but has encountered jurisdictional and financial constraints. For Hissiène Habré's trial in Senegal, see K. Neldjingaye, 2011. *The Trial of Hissène Habré in Senegal and its Contribution to the Development of International Criminal Law, in* PROSECUTING INTERNATIONAL CRIMES IN AFRICA (Chacha Murungu & Japhet Biegon eds. 2011); Valentina Spiga, *Non-retroactivity of Criminal Law: A New Chapter in the Hissene Habre Saga,* 9 JOURNAL OF INTERNATIONAL CRIMINAL JUSTICE 5-23 (2011).

31 For trials in the Democratic Republic of Congo, see United Nations, Office of the High Commissioner for Human Rights, Report of the Mapping Exercise Documenting the most Serious Violations of Human Rights and International Humanitarian Law Committed within the Territory of the Democratic Republic of the Congo between March 1993 and June 2003, 394-409 (August 2010).

32 For war crimes trial in Uganda, see Refugee Law Project, *Witness to the trial: Monitoring the Kwoyelo Trial* (2011). Available at <www.refugeelawproject.org/kwoyelo_trial.php:RefugeeLawProject> (Accessed September 23, 2011). For an update, see "*Ugandan LRA rebel Thomas Kwoyelo granted amnesty*," BBC News, September 22, 2011. Available at <www.bbc.co.uk/news/world-africa-15019883> (Accessed September 26, 2011).

33 Convention for the Prevention and Punishment of the Crime of Genocide (December 9, 1948 which came into force on January 12, 1951) 78 U.N.T.S., Art. II.

34 William A. Schabas, *National Courts Finally Begin to Prosecute Genocide the 'Crime of Crimes',* 1(1) JOURNAL OF INTERNATIONAL CRIMINAL JUSTICE 39-63 (2003).

meant that after the genocide the Rwandan government could not prosecute crimes of genocide through its own courts. In response the parliament passed Organic Law 08/96[35] in 1996 and Organic Law 40/2000 in 2000 to incorporate the genocide related crimes into its penal code and to establish the Gacaca Courts respectively. The Gacaca Courts were established to prosecute perpetrators of the crime of genocide and other crimes against humanity committed between October 1, 1990 and December 1994. According to Clark, the aims of the Gacaca Court includes the prosecution of genocide suspects and restoration of the damaged social fabric through courts that combine modern and traditional approaches to justice.[36] Between the establishment of the Gacaca Courts in 2002 and October 2008, a total of 1,127,706 cases were brought, of which 1,123,027 were tried and completed. Only 4,679 cases were still pending trial by the time of writing this chapter.[37]

This section has tried to illustrate the role that Africa has played and continues to play in the fight against impunity. It highlighted the AU's legal framework to protect populations from genocide, crimes against humanity and war crimes and how it attempted to intervene in addressing the justice and accountability issues in Darfur. African delegates also played a constructive role during the Rome Conference where the Rome Statute was negotiated and adopted. The section has also attempted to demonstrate how historical injustices influenced South Africa and other countries to support the proposal for the inclusion of the crime of apartheid in the Rome Statute and Africa's support towards the establishment of the ICC. Beyond the Rome Conference, the majority of African states ratified the Rome Statute and others have already started prosecuting international crimes through their own domestic courts, for instance the Uganda War Crimes Division of the High Court. As discussed in the case of Rwanda, some countries that are supportive of international criminal justice face institutional capacity and financial resource problems which impede them from prosecuting international crimes. The following section will briefly highlight the sources of tension between the African states and the international criminal justice system, especially the ICC.

5.3 Rising Tension and Opposition to the International Criminal Justice System in Africa

The signs of tension between African states and the ICC began to show in July 2008 when the Office of the Prosecutor made an application for an arrest warrant for President Omar

35 *Id.*

36 Phil Clark, The Gacaca Courts, Post-Genocide Justice and Reconciliation in Rwanda Justice Without Lawyers (2010).

37 Wanda National Report to the Human Rights Council Working Group on the Universal Period Review, Tenth Session A/HRC/WG.6/10/RWA/1.

al-Bashir of Sudan. The AU's Peace and Security Council immediately sent a letter to the United Nations Secretary General requesting the United Nations Security Council (UNSC) to defer the process initiated by the ICC Prosecutor in accordance to Article 16 of the Rome Statute. The AU was concerned that the indictment of President Bashir would break the fragile peace process in Darfur. Perhaps this is because the AU had been involved in the peace initiatives in Darfur as early as 2004 and considered the ICC decision to be a spoiler to its initiatives.[38]

The UNSC acknowledged the receipt of the AU request but did not act upon it, and a warrant of arrest was issued against President Bashir on the March 4, 2009. This provoked the AU to step up its criticism of the ICC and its frustration towards the UNSC for not responding to its request.[39] It is possible that the AU interpreted the UNSC's lack of response as a sign of its marginalization from the decision making process on African issues. The lack of response might also have revived the initial concerns that delegates at the Rome Conference had about the involvement of a political institution such the UNSC into judicial matters.[40] This view is shared by a group of African experts who noted that 'the ICC's involvement in Sudan has come to reflect their (African states) central concern about the UN – the skewed nature of power distribution within the UNSC and global politics.'[41]

Apart from Sudan, the ICC's involvement in Kenya and Libya has caused tension with the AU and some African states. Kenya came on the radar of the ICC following the 2008 post-election violence. Kenya is a State Party of the ICC and after the post-election violence it

38 In 2004, the AU co-mediated the ceasefire negotiations which led to the signing of Humanitarian Ceasefire Agreement and a Protocol on Humanitarian Assistance, and agreed to create a team of military observers with a small force to protect them, called the African Union Mission in Sudan (AMIS). See THABO MBEKI, DARFUR THE QUEST FOR PEACE, JUSTICE AND RECONCILIATION (2009).

39 The AU passed several resolutions requesting its member states not to cooperate with the ICC in the arrest of President Bashir, requested African states that are State Parties to the Rome Statute to propose an amendment to Art. 16 of the Rome Statute such that the UN General Assembly could be conferred with powers to act and defer situations in the event of UNSC's failure to act and the AU continued to request the UNSC to respond to its request for deferral. See the following AU Assembly decisions: African Union Decision on the meeting of African States Parties to the Rome Statute of the International Criminal Court, Doc. Assembly/AU/13(XIII) Assembly of the African Union, Thirteenth Ordinary Session 1–3 July 2009; African Union, Decision on the Application by the International Criminal Court Prosecutor for the Indictment of the President of the Republic of The Sudan, Assembly/AU/Dec.221XII, African Union Twelfth Ordinary Session 1-3 February 2009; African Union Decision on the Progress Report of the Commission on the Implementation of Decision Assembly/AU/Dec.270(XIV, on the Second Ministerial Meeting on the Rome Statute of the International Criminal Court Doc. Assembly/AU/10(XV); Assembly of the African Union, Fifteenth Ordinary Session 25–27 July 2010, 2010 Kampala, Uganda Assembly/AU/Dec.296XV).

40 It must be noted that African countries had passed the Ezulwini Consensus in 2005 calling for the democratization of the UNSC. See <www.africa-union.org/News...of.../Ext%20EXCL2%20VII%20Report.doc>.

41 Dapo Akande, Max Du Plessis & Charles C. Jalloh, *Position Paper An African Expert Study on the African Union Concerns about Article 16 of the Rome State of the ICC* (2010).

was encouraged to open its own investigations to hold those responsible for the violence accountable.[42] However, the Kenyan parliamentarians made several attempts and failed to agree on a local tribunal to investigate and prosecute those responsible, and this led the Office of the Prosecutor to successfully apply for authorization to open investigations in Kenya under the principle of *proprio motu*.[43] When the Office of the Prosecutor summoned six top Kenyan politicians including the Minister of Finance, Kenya responded by seeking the AU's support to ask the UNSC to defer the investigations. The AU and Kenyan effort to request the deferral was not successful as the UNSC did not consider the investigations to be a threat to international peace and security.

In addition to seeking a UNSC deferral of the proceedings, the Kenyan government also challenged the admissibility of the cases. It claimed that the government had taken the necessary measures and reforms which included the adoption of a new constitution.[44] This application was not successful because among other things, the cases that the ICC was interested in were not among those that the Government of Kenya had identified for trial. Hence there was a situation of inactivity on the specific cases that the ICC was interested in.

To sum up, it seems the tension between the ICC and African states is more pronounced when high profile government officials are indicted. It is neither the indictment of the Lord's Resistance Army nor of Thomas Lubanga that has triggered claims that the ICC is selectively criminalizing Africa. This can be interpreted as an attempt by African leaders to manipulate international criminal justice to achieve their own ends. What can also be observed is that in both Sudan and Kenya's situations there were missed opportunities to stop or challenge ICC interventions through the hybrid courts or establishing a special tribunal respectively.

Until 2008 the debates on the implementation of international criminal justice in Africa focused mainly on the need to balance peace and justice, and the appropriateness of retributive in comparison to restorative justice[45] and the application of complementarity principle, especially after Uganda's referral. However, the debates took a different direction

42 The power-sharing agreement that was mediated by the former UN Secretary-General Kofi Annan had provided for the coalition government to establish a Special Tribunal to seek accountability against persons bearing the greatest responsibility for crimes committed during post-election violence. However, when the government failed to establish such a Tribunal and the set deadline of August 2009 lapsed, the name of the suspects were handed over to the International Criminal Court. For general information see <www.voanews.com/english/news/a-13-2009-06-11-voa34-68803412.html> (Accessed on December 30, 2011).

43 International Criminal Court, Decision Pursuant to Art. 15 of the Rome Statute on the Authorization of an Investigation into the Situation in the Republic of Kenya Case No. ICC-01/09-19 31-03-2010 1/163 CB PT. (March 31, 2010).

44 International Criminal Court, Application on behalf of the Government of the Republic of Kenya Pursuant to Art. 19 of the ICC Statute (March 31, 2011)

45 Tim Allen, Trial Justice – International Criminal Court and the Lord's Resistance Army (2008).

after the indictment of sitting heads of states and top government officials. The theme of selective targeting of Africa emerged together with the claims that international criminal justice was a tool the European Powers was using to interfere in domestic affairs of African states. This was expressed by Chairperson of the AU Commission, Jean Ping. In 2011, after the African Union Head of States and Government Assembly meeting in Equatorial Guinea where a resolution was passed for African countries not to cooperate with the ICC in the arrest of the Libyan Leader Mummar Ghaddafi, he said:

> We support the fight against impunity, we do not support impunity, we are not even against the Criminal Court……, We are against the way justice is being rendered because … it looks as if this ICC is only interested in trying the Africans….Does this mean that in Pakistan, Afghanistan, Gaza, in Chechnya, there is nothing happening there? ..It is not only in Africa that there are problems. So why no one else except the Africans are being tried and judged by this court?[46]

Similar sentiments on the discriminatory nature of the ICC's targeting process were expressed by some heads of states that were initially supportive of the Court. For instance Senegal was the first country to ratify the Rome Statute in 1999 but in 2008 its President Abdoulaye Wade questioned why the Court was only targeting Africa after the indictment of the Sudanese President Omar al-Bashir, when he said:

> The problem is that today many Africans have the impression that this tribunal is only there to judge Africans and this wasn't my intention when I signed for it. Wherever in the world the people committing genocide are, we should judge them, but not only judge the Africans.[47]

At least the statement by the Chairperson of the AU acknowledges that there are problems in Africa which may require the attention of the ICC, and the main issue is that Africa has been the only geographical region which they have focused on. However, his statement and many others that criticize the ICC's focus on Africa seem to disregard the fact that Africa has complained of being marginalized and the international community has often left Africa to solve its own problems.[48] Some classic examples include the events in

46 *African Union Opposes Warrant for Qaddafi*, (The Associated Press) <www.nytimes.com/2011/07/03/world/africa/03african.html> (Accessed August 25, 2011).

47 Abdoulaye Wade the President of Senegal on the day the warrant of arrest for President Bashir was announced. See *World reaction: Bashir Warrant*, BBC News, March 4, 2009. <http://news.bbc.co.uk/2/hi/africa/7923797.stm> (Accessed June 5, 2009).

48 IFEONU EBERECHI, FROM CONSENT TO SUSPICION: UNDERSTANDING THE AFRICAN UNION'S EMERGING RESISTANCE TO THE ENFORCEMENT OF INTERNATIONAL CRIMINAL JUSTICE IN THE AFRICAN REGION (2009).

Rwanda where the international community failed to take appropriate action to prevent and stop the genocide.

Rwanda has been at the forefront in criticizing the exercise of universal jurisdiction by some European investigative judges against its officials. In 2006 a French investigative judge, Jean-Louis Bruguière, issued international arrest warrants for nine Rwandan government officials for charges related to the shooting of a plane which led to the assassination of President Juvenal Habyarimana of Rwanda and Cyprien Ntaryamira of Burundi together with three French crew.[49] In 2008, Spanish investigative judge Andreu Merelles issued international arrest warrants against forty current or former Rwandan military officials. They were charged with international crimes including genocide, crimes against humanity, war crimes and acts of terrorism committed between 1990 and 2002.[50] The investigations against the Rwandan Officials were initially triggered by the families of the Spaniards who were killed during the period covered by the indictment, although they were expanded to include international crimes committed in the Democratic Republic of Congo by the Rwandan army that are covered under universal jurisdiction.[51]

The Rwandan government reacted to the indictments by rallying African states to oppose their citizens being tried in other countries or by international courts. In May 2008 the Rwandan President Paul Kagame described the indictments as a sign of arrogance by western courts. During an address on the 60th anniversary of the establishment of State of Israel, he said:

> lately, some in the more powerful parts of the world have given themselves the right to extend their national jurisdiction to indict weaker nations'... where does this right come from? Would the reverse apply-such that a judge form a less powerful nations indict those from the more powerful.[52]

In July 2008 during an AU Assembly, President Kagame made several proposals on how Africa was supposed to respond to the abuse of universal jurisdiction by some western countries. During his speech at the Assembly he evoked the anti-colonial rhetoric by making references to historical injustices that Africa faced during the slave trade, colonialism and apartheid. He accused the former subjugators of turning themselves into policemen

49 Jean-Louis Bruguiere, *Issuance of International Arrest Warrants-Ordonnance De Soit-Communique*, Tribunal De Grande Instance De Paris 97.295.2303-0. (ed. 2006).

50 Commentator, *The Spanish Indictment of High-ranking Rwandan Officials*, 6 Journal of International Criminal Justice 1003-1011 (2008).

51 *Id.* at 1004.

52 Hirondelle News. Kagame Announces Once Again "Arrogance" of Western Courts, 2008.

of the world.[53] At the end of the Assembly the African Union adopted a total of eight resolutions, highlighting how the abuse of the principle of universal jurisdiction jeopardizes international law and order and is a violation of the sovereignty of Rwanda.[54]

President Kagame repeated his criticism on the exercise of universal jurisdiction in his speech to the 63rd United Nations General Assembly in New York. He requested that the United Nations ensured that universal jurisdiction was used to serve its original goals of delivering justice and fairness. The same year Tanzania proposed that the scope and application of universal jurisdiction be included on the agenda of the United Nations General Assembly 64th session. Since then the scope and application of universal jurisdiction became one of the key items on the United Nations General Assembly agenda. The Secretary General requested member states to submit their views and experiences on the exercise of universal jurisdiction. Rwanda was among the first few African countries that responded. In its response it emphasized that universal jurisdiction had been abused by French and Spanish judges to settle political scores. It concluded by suggesting the establishment of a system that would allow an aggrieved person to appeal to another judge or tribunal to review the decision of a judge issuing an international warrant.[55]

5.4 Assessing the Tension Between African States and International Criminal Justice

Several assumptions could be drawn from the fact that the tension between Africa and the international criminal justice system, especially the International Criminal Court, intensified only after the indictment of sitting heads of states and top government officials, and not when rebels and leading opposition figures were indicted. One of the assumptions is that it seems African political leaders intend to use international criminal justice for political expediency.[56] They accept the international criminal justice when it serves their own interests against political enemies, and oppose it when it threatens their autonomy and hold on to power. The leaders appear to have adopted a 'them' and 'us' approach in the application of international criminal justice. The approach is similar to the way the

53 African Union Refuses Arrest Warrants Against Rwandans *supra*.

54 African Union Assembly Decision on the Report of the Commission on the Abuse of the Principle of Universal Jurisdiction Doc. Assembly/AU/14 (XI). Assembly of the African Union Eleventh Ordinary Session, June 30-July 1, 2008. For a detailed analysis of the African Union's position on universal jurisdiction, see *Charles Chernor Jalloh, Universal Jurisdiction, Universal Prescription? A Preliminary Assessment of the African Union Perspective on Universal Jurisdiction*, INTERNATIONAL CRIMINAL LAW FORUM (2010).

55 Ministry of Justice, The Republic of Rwanda (2010) Report on information and observations on the scope and application of principle of universal jurisdiction.

57 Williams A. Schabas, *Prosecutorial Discretion v. Judicial Activism at the International Criminal Court,* 6 JOURNAL OF INTERNATIONAL CRIMINAL JUSTICE 731, 751(2008).

international law was used to civilize 'them' under colonial rule.[57] In contemporary debates on international criminal justice the opposition parties and rebels are 'them' and should face justice, whereas the government officials are immune from prosecution.

This selective application of law is not a new phenomenon in African history. In fact the 'them' and 'us' dichotomy in the application of law has a long precedent in history including during pre-colonial and colonial periods. The law appears to have served the interests of the powerful and not the weak. During these periods in history, the colonial powers applied different set of rules and laws in the colonies to those that were applied in their countries of origin. The obvious corollary of the differentiation in the application of law is lack of accountability and impunity for those in position of power. The colonial powers acted in a personalized, arbitrary and unofficial manner against the local populations.[58] The transatlantic slave traders managed to escape with their crimes because there was no law prohibiting it until the late nineteenth century.

The historical lack of consistency in the application of law or quest for justice has been the cause of concern among African leaders, scholars and researchers. Their response strategy has been to try and modify international law wherever possible. One African leader who is critical of the European campaigns for democracy and human rights, President Mugabe of Zimbabwe, made the following remarks to register his frustration on the double standards of the former colonies in their approach to human rights:

> Africa has not called for a Nuremberg trial against the white world which committed heinous crimes against its own humanity. It has not hunted perpetrators of this genocide, many of whom live to this day, nor has it got reparations from those who offended against it. Instead it is Africa which is in the dock, facing trial from the same world that persecuted it for centuries.[59]

It is well-known that President Mugabe and his ruling party's human rights record is very questionable and might well have been the reason that he made these remarks – to ward off any criticism on his human rights record from former colonial powers. However, the remarks could be useful in understanding the perception of some African governments on historical injustices suffered in the continent and the related impunity. In the entire

56 Antony Anghie & B.S. Chimni, *Third World Approaches to International Law and Individual Responsibility in Internal Conflicts,* 2 Chinese Journal Of International Law 77 (2003).
58 Patrick Chabal & Jean-Pascal Daloz, Africa Works - Disorder As Political Instrument (1999).
59 Robert Mugabe, President of Zimbabwe, Address to the 62d Session of the UN General Assembly (September 26, 2007).

speech President Mugabe seems to suggest that since those who perpetrated injustices in Africa benefited from impunity they did not have moral authority to be in the forefront in putting Africans in the 'dock'. Having said that, it is, however, lamentable that President Mugabe's speech does not engage with the plight of victims either under former colonial powers or under post-colonial administrations.

President Mugabe's statement questions the moral authority of former colonial powers to intervene and promote democratic values including justice in Africa when they did not live up to those standards during colonial times. His views are similar to those of President Kagame of Rwanda who pointed out that institutions such as the ICC are tools for controlling the poor countries and that former subjugators have turned to be the world's policeman. In the *Arrest Warrant* case an ad hoc Congolese judge, Mr. Sayeman Bula-Bula, criticized Belgium's claims of being driven by values of democracy and human rights in its issuance of an international arrest warrant for a Congolese government official. He pointed out that Belgium's history is tarnished by human rights violations and undue interference in the internal affairs of sovereign states. Below is part of the remarks in his separate opinion at the International Court of Justice:

> ... Even as the respondent state *(Belgium)* brings its peroration to a glowing close with an invocation of the democracy and human rights which purportedly guided its conduct at the same time it reopens one of the most shameful pages in the history of decolonization. In the 1960s, it appeared to grant the Congo its independence while, with the right hand, it was at the same time virtually ensuring the destabilization of that sovereignty and of the new-born Congolese democracy.[60]

Judging from the speeches of African political leaders, the tension between international criminal justice and African states affirms the continued existence of the legacy of historical injustices especially colonization on Africa's perceptions and views of the international institutions. This was rightly pointed out by Antony Anghie and B.S. Chimni who wrote:

> The experience of colonisation and neo-colonialism has made Third World people acutely sensitive to power relations among states and to the ways in which any proposed international rule or institution will actually effect the distribution of the power between states and peoples.[61]

60 *Arrest Warrant* case (*The Democratic Republic of Congo v. Belgium*) 2002 I.C.J 3 at 107 para. 15 (February 14) (Separate opinion of Judge ad hoc Bula-Bula (translation)).

61 Anghie & Chimni, *supra* note 57 at 78.

Some leaders interpret the exploitation of African resources and political domination by the European imperial powers during colonization as a demonstration of the West's strong and long term interest in Africa's resources.

A combination of African leaders' speeches and their preference to selectively apply international criminal justice systems mainly against their own opponents, points to how they want to maintain their autonomy in handling their domestic affairs. African leaders and their governments appear to be extremely sensitive to any threats towards their autonomy. They view state sovereignty and non-interference as their last line of defence in an international system where power politics appears to influence every facet of international community life.

Furthermore it is argued that at the centre of colonization was the notion that Africans were objects of European thought and action, hence it is understandable that Africans would still be sensitive to any action that appears to undermine their independence and autonomy. This possibly explains why the SADC delegates at the Rome Conference supported proposals that favoured complementarity and respect for independence of the ICC from the United Nations Security Council.[62] They wanted to protect the sovereignty of their states from the ICC. African states' increasing concern with the international criminal justice system and specifically the ICC is that it appears to have become uncontrollable and acting without due caution to their national interests and concerns. Perhaps the ICC's intervention revives the memories of how Africans lost their sovereignty and autonomy during the colonial period.

The decision by the SADC heads of states to suspend the activities of the SADC Tribunal could be a testimony of Africa's approach to international law. The SADC tribunal was suspended in May 2011 at a SADC extraordinary after it passed decisions against Zimbabwe's land reform programme. The tribunal had decided that the land reform programme was a breach of SADC treaty Article 4 which obligates SADC and Member States to act in accordance with the principles of human rights, democracy and rule of law.[63]

In the case *Mike Campbell Pvt and 78 others v. The Republic of Zimbabwe* the SADC Tribunal ruled in favour of the applicant by ordering the Zimbabwean government not to interfere or evict Mike Campbell from his property until the land dispute was finally resolved.[64] President Mugabe responded to the ruling by stating that land issues were

62 Sivu Maqungo, *The Establishment of the International Criminal Court: SADC's Participation in the Negotiations,* 9 AFRICAN SECURITY REVIEW 1, 4 (2000).

63 SADC Treaty Art. 4 (c).

64 *Mike Campbell (PVT) Limited and William Michael Campbell v. Republic of Zimbabwe SADC Tribunal,* Southern African Development Community (SADC) Tribunal Windhoek, Namibia (2007).

Zimbabwean affairs and not SADC affairs.[65] The point here is not to condone the decision to dissolve the court but rather highlight the extent to which some African countries are ready to go in order to defend their independence.

What is sad and fascinating about Africa's history of Western domination and the associated injustices is that some of those who perpetrated them either deny that particular events actually happened or they try to hide it from history.[66] This could be interpreted as double standard especially during an era where truth-telling is encouraged as part of international criminal justice; Africa continues to be side-lined. It is not clear why those responsible for committing atrocities in other parts of the World are ready to acknowledge their mistakes but not when it comes to Africa. There might not be an easy answer to such a question. However it is general knowledge that apologies have been made for some atrocities committed outside of Africa. In 2002 the Pope apologized in Israel for Christian anti-Semitism. The German government together with some German corporations agreed to pay reparations to the Jewish population for the crimes committed during the Second World War. Perhaps one could also make an observation that there is also selectiveness in the way historical injustices are addressed across the globe.

Efforts by African governments to have the transatlantic slave trade declared a crime against humanity or to be acknowledged as part of history did not progress at the World Conference against Racism in 2001.At the same time the campaign by the Herero ethnic group in Namibia for reparations for genocide from the German government and corporations are stalled in the US courts. In addition, the history of atrocities committed by King Leopold II during the rubber boom in the Congo does not even feature in the Brussels Royal Museum of Central Africa, which is considered to be one of the world's biggest museums of Africana.[67] One commentator likened the absence of any reference to the Congolese atrocities in this museum in Brussels as having a huge museum of Jewish art and artifacts in Berlin with no mention of the Holocaust.[68]

65 AFRICA LEGAL AID. 2011. *Is Africa ready for supranational courts?* <www.africalegalaid.com/newsletter:AfricaLegalAid> (Accessed 25 September, 2011).

66 There are reports that when King Leopold II decided to give Congo to the Belgians he told Stinglhamber that 'I will give them my Congo'..... but they will have no right to know what I did there" before he went and destroyed through burning all the records of his operations in Congo. See ADAM HOCHSCHILD 1999. KING LEOPOLD'S GHOST: A STORY OF GREED, TERROR, AND HEROISM IN COLONIAL AFRICA (1999).

67 Adam Hochschild, *Leopold's Congo: A Holocaust We have Yet to Comprehend*, CHRONICLE OF HIGHER EDUCATION 4 (2000).

68 *Id.*

The following section focuses on some of the historical narratives that have not been accounted for in Africa with the purpose of linking them to contemporary debates on the implementation of international criminal justice on the continent. Some of the historical links pertain to the different proposals that were made by African delegates at the Rome Conference. It explores the role that private companies played in the exploitation of African natural resources and the debates on the inclusion of corporate criminal responsibility in the Rome Statute. With regards to the Algerian war, the section seeks to highlight the selective application of law against Africans, and how the French government, which is now among the main champions of international criminal justice in Africa, made legal changes in its judicial system to avoid criminal responsibility for using torture against Algerian liberation movement.

5.5 Historical Injustices and Possible Links to Contemporary Debates on International Criminal Justice in Africa

5.5.1 *The Transatlantic Slave Trade and the Role of Corporations in Human Rights Violations*

The anti-slavery movement of the nineteenth century is considered by some commentators to be a crucial precursor to the contemporary human rights system.[69] Professor Jenny Martinez describes the anti-slavery courts that were established in 1817-1871 through bilateral agreements between Britain and several other countries, to be the first international human rights courts. However, she laments that the literature about the anti-slavery movement is rarely visible in contemporary international human rights and criminal law scholarship.[70] One of the few scholars to have made reference to the anti-slavery movement is Professor Cherif M. Bassiouni who acknowledges the role of the anti-slavery movement in the development of modern international criminal law. He traces the origins of modern international criminal law to the 1815 Congress of Vienna where Russia, the United Kingdom, Portugal and France signed bilateral treaties to abolish slavery.[71] During the lifespan of the anti-slavery courts they heard 600 cases and freed almost 80,000 individuals,[72] which is a very high number of cases in comparison to the modern day's tribunals and courts.

---

69 Jenny S. Martinez, *Anti-Slavery Courts and the Dawn of International Human Rights Law,* 117 Yale Law Journal 550 (2008).

70 *Id.*

71 M. Cherif Bassiouni, *Time Has Come for an International Criminal Court,* 1 Indiana International & Comparative Law Review, 1, 1-44 (1991).

72 It has to be pointed out that the courts were not without their limitations as discussed by Professor Martinez in her article. Some of the weakness included lack of legally trained personal initial lack of support from France and the United States, see *id.* 70 at 603.

However, the human rights narrative is often traced to the post Second World War era instead of the anti-slavery movements. This is attributed to the fact that those who participated and benefitted from the transatlantic slave trade were probably ashamed of their practice, preferring to record a narrative which portrays them positively as the force that defeated Nazi Germany and liberated the Jews from concentration camps. The narrative of liberating the Jews is more appealing compared to one that would expose how the US, France and the United Kingdom profited from the transatlantic slave trade.[73]

It is noteworthy that apart from efforts by private individuals such as William Wilberforce to end the slave trade, Africans were also involved in trying to resist the practice. One example is in the Bakongo Kingdom[74] ruled by King Alfonso, also known as Mvemba Nzinga. In 1526, he wrote a series of letters to the Portuguese King Joao III stating the devastating effect that the slave trade was having in his kingdom.[75] When he failed to convince King Joao to stop Portuguese slave traders from kidnapping his people, King Alfonso sent letters to the Vatican seeking the intervention of the Pope, but to no avail.[76]

In the early 1990s the then Organization of African Unity (now the African Union) with the support of reparationists launched a protracted campaign to get some form of reparation for the slave trade from the West.[77] In 1993, it adopted the Abuja Declaration which made the campaign for reparations a priority for Africa.[78] Some of the main arguments put forward by those who advocate for reparations include that the transatlantic slave trade fast tracked the development of Europe, hence Europe was supposed to appreciate Africa's contribution through the payment of reparations.[79] In 1996 Lord Gifford raised the issue of reparations in the British House of Lords, stating that the transatlantic slave trade had depopulated Africa.[80]

---

73 Martinez, *supra* note 69.

74 Bakongo Kingdom covered the areas which in modern day is part of Angola and parts of Democratic Republic of Congo.

75 In one of the letters quoted by Adam Hochschild the Bakongo King said: "Each day the traders are kidnapping our people…children of this country, sons, of our nobles and vassal, even people of own family…this corruption and depravity are so widespread that our land is entirely depopulated…" Hochschild, *supra* note 66 at 13.

76 *Id.*

77 The 'West' here is a definitional generalization; the specific countries that directly participated in slave trade are Britain, France, Portugal and Holland. See Max Du Plessis, *Historical Injustice and International Law: An Exploratory Discussion of Reparation for Slavery*, 25 Human Rights Quarterly, 624-659 (2003).

78 A Declaration of the first Abuja Pan-African Conference on Reparations for African Enslavement, Colonisation And Neo-Colonisation, sponsored by The Organisation Of African Unity and its Reparations Commission April 27-29, 1993, Abuja, Nigeria.

79 Ali Mazrui, *From Slave ship to Space ship: Africa Between Marginalization and Globalisation,* 2(4) African Studies Quarterly (1999).

80 Hansard, *Slavery: Legacy,* House of Lords of the British Parliament, March 14 <www.arm.arc.co.uk/LordsHansard>.

The reparations debate was a controversial issue at the Durban World Racism Conference in 2001. The United States threatened not to attend the conference had the issue of reparations been put on the agenda. During the conference itself, delegates from Africa and Europe reached a deadlock on the issue.[81] The African group pushed for the recognition of slavery and the slave trade as a crime against humanity, a stance that was rejected by the European delegates out of fear of possible legal liability. However some commentators, such as Max Plessis, cite that there are several counter arguments against Africa's claims for reparations, suggesting that it is more feasible for Africans to consider pursuing reparations from a political and moral standpoint.[82] One of the main arguments against reparations is that the slave trade was not legally prohibited; hence there is no legal basis to claim for reparations. However, such an argument cannot be sustained against the background that the holocaust against the Jews was legally prohibited retroactively and the Germans agreed to pay reparations.

One observation that can be made from the debates surrounding the reparations for the transatlantic slave trade is that power politics have an upper hand in the formation of international law. It is evident that the African delegates and leaders who pushed for the recognition of colonization and the slave trade as crimes against humanity had hoped to modify the substantive content of international criminal law based on their own past experiences. However, this was blocked by the powerful states out of fear of being held accountable for their past crimes.

On the same note, African and Third World delegates at the Rome Conference to establish the ICC had similar experiences of power politics in the law making process. Although the Rome Conference was supposed to be a forum for democratic creation of law, to some extent the conference ended up succumbing to the whims of powerful countries, especially those in the United Nations Security Council. African delegates tried to modify international law to suit their own interests or at least to be a reflection of diversity in the international system without much success. An illustration of Africa's concern about the nature of international criminal law and the justice it delivers was captured in a statement by a Libyan delegate during the Rome Conference below:

> Moreover, it was not acceptable that the Court's jurisdiction should be confined to matters of interest to some States while ignoring different issues of concern to others, in addition to so-called aggression and so-called terrorism, the Court might deal with drug trafficking, insults to religion, violation of humanitarian values, forbidding of religious rites, white slavery, organized

81 Du Plessis, *supra* note 77 at 625.
82 *Id.*

> crime, involvement of children in war, violence and prostitution, economic and financial crimes, aggression against the environment and other threats. Western values and legal systems should not be the only source of international instruments. Other systems were followed by a large proportion of the world's population.[83]

The absence of inclusive substantive law within the Rome Statute led some commentators into questioning the interests that the emerging international criminal justice system protects or serves. Professor J.M Woods questions whether the Rome Statute reflects some form of victor's justice because of the selective nature of the crimes that it codifies.[84] This is because there are many crimes that affect African communities and are linked to the powerful states but were not codified in the Rome Statute. The attempts by African delegates and others from the Third World countries to have criminal responsibility extended to criminal organizations such as those involved in trafficking arms to conflict zones or trading conflict minerals were unsuccessful.[85] This happened despite the fact that the extension of criminal responsibility to legal persons had precedent in the Nuremburg Trials and it was also reflected in the laws of many countries. However, this was not enough to get consensus for the extension of criminal responsibility to private companies and to criminal organizations.

During the Rome Conference Tanzania had supported the proposal to extend criminal responsibility to private companies using the Rwandan Genocide as its justification. The Tanzania delegate pointed out how private companies had played a vital role in providing the logistics for those who committed genocide.[86] The proposal was rejected by the United States, China, Sweden and Singapore who argued that the Statute was based on the principle of individual responsibility. These States's refusal to accept the proposal could be interpreted as fear that codification of arms trafficking would have affected their global markets for selling military hardware.

Although the exact motives behind the rejection to criminalize private companies might be difficult to establish, what is clear is that such an opposition granted impunity to non-state actors especially in the private sector who are directly involved in supporting and

83 See Statement by Mr. Al-Maghur (Libyan Arab Jamahiriya) at the United Nations, Summary Records of the Meetings of the Committee of the Whole 1st Meeting, A/CONF.183/C.1/SR.1. United Nations Diplomatic Conference of Plenipotentiaries on the Establishment of an International Criminal Court, (Rome Italy, 1998) at 101 para. 82.

84 Jeanne M. Woods, *Africa: International War Crimes -Whose Truth? Whose Justice? International War Crimes Conference*, March 3, 2011. Available at <www.Africa.com/stories> (Accessed September 31, 2011).

85 See speeches of the delegates from France and Tanzania, *supra* note 83.

86 See speech by the Tanzania Delegate *id.* at 135 paragraph 52.

funding conflicts in Africa. The rejection technically marginalized the concerns of thousands of victims of small arms across the globe especially in Africa. In this respect the contemporary international criminal justice system failed to take a leaf from the anti-slave trade courts that targeted private companies.

One can only speculate that had the narrative of international human rights and criminal law been traced back to anti-slavery courts where the focus was mainly on non-state actors, especially private companies, perhaps contemporary international criminal law would have had jurisdiction over corporate conduct.[87]

5.5.2 *The Berlin Conference and the Colonization of Africa*

Prior to colonization, pre-colonial African societies had enjoyed independence to manage their affairs and to enter into agreements amongst themselves and also with European emissaries.[88] They were sovereigns and enjoyed absolute and perpetual power over their citizens and subjects. However, the status quo changed drastically following the signing and ratification of the General Act of the Berlin Conference which set out the rules on how European Powers were to acquire territories in Africa.[89] Chapter VI of the Berlin Act stated that the rights of a European Power over land in Africa were to be respected and protected once the power had effective control and authority over such a piece of land.[90] This effectively sanctioned and increased the process of the 'Scramble for Africa' as agents from the European Powers raced to secure treaties and agreements with African kings. In most cases African kings[91] and chiefs did not know how to read and write and were tricked into signing legal agreements that were self-serving for the European Powers.[92] The Berlin Conference transformed the relationship that had existed between pre-colonial African states and European states from a mutual one into effective subjugation and occupation of once autonomous kingdoms and communities.

---

87 Martinez, *supra* note 69.

88 For instance in 1491 Portuguese Priests and Emissaries opened a permanent representative post in the Kingdom of the Kongo.

89 General Act of the Conference of Berlin Concerning the Congo, Berlin Conference (1885). *General Act of the Conference of Berlin Concerning the Congo*, 3 The American Journal of International Law 3, 7-25 (1909).

90 *Id.* Arts. 34 and 35.

91 The Kongo King ManiKongo Nzinga Mbemba Alfonse is one of the kings recorded in history who had the ability to read and write. He is reported to have written letters to the Portuguese King and even to the Pope protesting against the Atlantic Slave Trade. See, Hochschild, *supra* note 67 at 13.

92 Colonial Rule In Africa (Bruce Fetter ed., 1979). A Classical example is the Rudd Concession signed in 1889 between Ndebele King Lobengula and Charles Rudd. The Concession included a clause that granted Cecil John Rhodes full powers over the land of King Lobengula.

On the other hand, the Berlin Act also created obligations for European Powers to respect and protect the rights of natives. This provision was not respected at all. This shall be discussed later in the chapter under the Herero Genocide and King Leopold II's operations in the Congo. Chapter I Article 6 of the General Berlin Act states that:

> All the Powers exercising sovereign rights or influence in the aforesaid territories bind themselves to watch over the preservation of the native tribes, and to care for the improvement of the conditions of their moral and material well-being, and to help in suppressing slavery, and especially the slave trade. They shall, without distinction of creed or nation, protect and favor all religious, scientific or charitable institutions and undertakings created and organized for the above ends, or which aim at instructing the natives and bringing home to them the blessings of civilization.[93]

The history of African colonization and European domination is a fairly recent and short phenomenon. It can be argued that European colonization ended in Africa when South Africa had its first majority elections in 1994. Although colonization ended, it has had far reaching consequences for Africa. One such effect is on how the continent relates to the international community and formulates its foreign policies and interacts with the European and Western powers. The majority of African states' approach towards international law seems to be motivated by the concern to safeguard their autonomy and their sovereignty. As already discussed earlier, the exploitation of African resources during colonization has left many Africans convinced that Europe has long term interests in Africa and they are ready to use any means available to have access to the resources.

In modern debates on the ICC's selective targeting of Africans, the theme of Europe's obsession with African resources is resurfacing as stated by President Kagame. The ICC is viewed as a tool that the European wants to use to maintain their influence in domestic affairs of independent African states just as they did during the colonial period. The situation even becomes more intriguing when former colonizers exercise universal jurisdiction against government officials of their former colonies – for instance, Belgium courts arresting a government official from the Democratic Republic of the Congo. No matter how noble the motives of the Belgium judges could be, the decision to indict an official from a former colony is bound to raise neo-colonial questions.

In addition, since colonization is alleged to have been centered on Africans being the objects of European thought and action and where Africans had lost their sovereign rights,

93 The Berlin Conference, *supra* note 89 Art. 6.

the institutions that appear to threaten the autonomy of African countries are negatively viewed and considered to be an extension of neo-colonization. It appears African governments want to safeguard their independence from any external interference at any cost. This probably explains why the term sovereign equality is very common in the vocabulary of several African leaders, especially when they feel that they are under external pressure such as when issues pertaining to human rights abuses are raised.

Lastly, it is a well-known fact that international law played a significant role in the colonization process of Africa. It was at the Berlin Conference that a treaty was signed for the partitioning of Africa among European Powers and private individuals like King Leopold II of Belgium.[94] After the Conference the Scramble for Africa started where colonial agents such as Henry Stanley and Charles Rudd used trickery to get African kings to sign agreements that they did not understand, only to realize later that they had given away their pieces of land to foreign companies. The mostly illiterate African kings were asked to put an X on the documents to exchange their land for pieces of cloth, alcohol or sugar. Such previous manipulation of law for the benefit of the few by the Europeans could also contribute to the latent suspicions that African states may have on the work of the ICC, especially when it appears to turn a blind eye to historical contexts and heed the demands from African states.

5.5.3 *The Herero Genocide*

Following the signing and the ratification of the General Act of the Conference of Berlin in 1885, Germany increased its presence and influence in German South West Africa. The Germans signed several protection treaties with the Hereros, who were in regular wars with their Nama rivals. The treaties meant that the Hereros ceded some part of their sovereignty. For instance, it granted the control of foreign affairs to the Germans. In return the Germans promised to respect the Herero customs and abstain from any act that would be illegal in their own country.[95]

Around 1887, the Hereros became weary of the Germans' increasing population and disrespect of native culture which included taking liberties with Herero women. The influx of German settlers into Hereroland is linked to a hoax of discovery of gold. The hoax was later linked to Dr Heinrich Ernst Göring, the father of Nazi field Marshall Hermann Göring who was the Imperial Commissioner of German South West Africa at the time.[96] The growing

94 Fetter, *supra* note 92.

95 Thomas Pakenham, The Scamble for Africa 1876-1912, 605 (1996).

96 Jeremy Sarkin & Carly K. Fowler, *Reparations for Historical Human Rights Violations: The International and Historical Dimensions of the Alien Torts Claims Act Genocide Case of the Herero of Namibia*, 9 Human Rights Review 331 at 343 (2008).

mistrust between the Hereros and the German settlers escalated until war broke out between the two sides on January 18, 1904 when the Herero attacked several German garrisons.[97]

The German settlers' response was coordinated by General Lother von Throtha who is famous for issuing a *Vernichtungsbefehl* (extermination order) of the Hereros. Amid opposition from some settlers in German South West Africa and also from Berlin, Lother von Throtha orchestrated a plan to destroy the Hereros as indicated in an extract from his official report to the chief of the army general below:

> The crucial question for me was how to bring the war against the Herero [Nation] to a close ... As I see it, the nation must be destroyed as such ... I ordered the warriors ... to be court -martialled and hanged and all women and children who sought shelter here to be driven back into the sand veld [the Kalahari Desert] .... To accept women and children who are for the most part sick, poses a grave risk to the force, and to feed them is out of the question, For this reason, I deemed it wiser for the entire nation to perish...This is and remains the beginning of a racial struggle...[98]

Trothas' extermination order was effectively executed following the defeat of the Hereros at the battle of Waterberg which was fought in August 1904. The defeated Hereros were forced to flee into the dry deserts of the Kalahari known in Herero language as *Omaheke*. In order to ensure that the Hereros did not have access to water, Trotha poisoned and cordoned off some of the waterholes. He sent troops to pursue survivors deep into inhospitable desert where they died of thirst or poisoned water. The other result of the war was the establishment of concentration camps where the remaining Hereros were kept under very squalid conditions and forced into slave labour. After the war the census in 1911 showed that only 15,000 out of 80,000 Hereros had survived.[99] General Lother von Throtha went to Germany where the Kaiser gave him an Order of Merit.[100]

Since the late 1990s, the Hereros have been seeking reparations from the German government and three German corporations for their role in the crimes committed during the colonial period in German South West Africa. Their determination to seek reparations

97 THOMAS PAKENHAM, *The Kaiser's First War: Berlin and German South West, 18 January 1904 and after*, *in* THE SCRAMBLE FOR AFRICA: 1876-1912, 602-615 (1996).

98 Rachel J. Anderson, *Redressing Colonial Genocide Under International Law: The Hereros' Cause of Action Against Germany*, 93 CALIFORNIA LAW REVIEW 1155 (2005), quoting from HORST DRECHSLER'S, LET US DIE FIGHTING: THE STRUGGLE OF THE HERERO AND NAMA AGAINST GERMAN IMPERIALISM (1884-1915).

99 PAKENHAM, *supra* note 97 at 615.

100 *Id.*

from the German government, the Deutsche Bank and Woermann Line for the atrocities committed during the Herero-German war of 1904-1908 can serve as a classic example of Africa's long struggle for justice for historical injustices.

Initially, the Hereros approached the German government for reparations but their request was denied. In 1998 President Herzog of Germany gave a speech in which he implied that the acts committed during the colonial times were not illegal at the time as there was no law that legally prohibited them. In his speech he also implied that there was no precedent of minority groups seeking reparations.[101] These claims are contestable. First as highlighted earlier, the Berlin Act created an obligation for European powers to protect the natives, and this could be interpreted as international law of the time that prohibited the same acts that were committed against the Herero people. In addition the claims of the German President are not consistent with Germany's practice with regards to its treatment of the Jews in a post-holocaust era. The German government voluntarily accepted to pay compensation to the Jews, even when there was no legislation to justify that the Holocaust victims had rights to reparations.[102] Then the question that could be asked is, if the Germans could volunteer and pay the Jews why would they not do the same for the Herero people? Could this be some form of selective targeting? The Hereros' failure to obtain some form of political and legal redress from the German government prompted them to use the United States courts under the Alien Torts Claims Act[103] to seek compensation from both the German government and the two German Corporations.

The narrative of the Herero genocide raises several points that could be relevant in understanding contemporary debates on international criminal justice systems in Africa. First, the narrative gives a concrete example of Africa's past injustices that were referred to by the former Legal Counsel of the OAU during the Rome Conference. Second, the Herero genocide and many other forms of injustices suffered by the African population are a reminder of how impunity has been chronic in Africa. This contradicts the contemporary impression that chronic impunity is strictly a post-colonial African problem. It shows that impunity can in fact be traced to Africa's early encounter with Western culture.

In addition, any African who is aware of the Herero genocide and the reparations debates that surround it could easily view the selective targeting of Africans by the ICC as history repeating itself, in the sense that Africa has a history of being treated differently from the

101 Sarkin & Fowler *supra* note 96 at 355.

102 Ryan Michael Spitzer, *The African Holocaust: Should Europe pay Reparations to African for Colonisation and Slavery?*, 35 Vanderbilt Journal of Transitional Law 1313 (2002).

103 The Alien Tort Claims Act (ATCA) was adopted in 1789 as part of the Judiciary Act which set up the US federal court system. The Act gives the US district courts original jurisdiction of any civil action by an alien for a tort only, committed in violation of the law of nations or a treaty of the United States.

rest of the world. The fact that Germany volunteered to pay compensation to the Jewish survivors of the holocaust and refused to do the same for the Hereros could be interpreted as double standards.

The other point that could be highlighted from the Herero genocide is the role of private companies in human rights abuses. Although the proposals to include corporate criminal responsibility under the jurisdiction of the ICC were opposed during the Rome Conference, it is clear from the Herero genocide that private companies, or at least their employees and executives, have to be held responsible for either supporting directly or indirectly human rights abuses especially in conflict areas. That being said, since the Rome Conference, there is a growing realization for the need to have a system that would make private companies liable for international crimes. There is increasing demand for the ICC's jurisdiction to be extended to include private multinational companies as noted in an EU external evaluation report on the ICC below:

> It is incumbent upon the members of the European Union to take a proactive role in supporting the extension of the Court's mandate to include forms of individual responsibility for corporate activities, in order to comprehensively reflect the broad and complex dynamics of conflict and atrocity.[104]

The Office of the Prosecutor has indicated, but without elaboration, the possibility of investigating corporate executives and employees for their role in supporting those responsible for atrocities in eastern Congo.[105] It is possible that the ICC could play a vital role in uncovering networks of those who either provide financial assistance or benefit from armies and rebels that are responsible for international crimes by investing any links between finance and conflicts. This might consequently contribute to the reduction of conflicts that are sponsored or supported by private companies.

Lastly, the Herero Genocide could serve as a clear example of the effects of impunity. It can be argued that had the German officials who were responsible for Herero atrocities been held responsible they would not have played a significant role in the holocaust almost 40 years later. However, the failure to reprimand their behavior meant that officials such as Dr Eugen Fischer who oversaw the medical experiments that were conducted on prisoners of war in German South West Africa later became the senior geneticist of the Nazi Regime.[106]

104 See European Union, The Final Report of the European Instrument for Democracy and Human Rights (EIDHR) Evaluation on its Support to the Establishment and Functioning of the ICC-Project No. 2007/146677 – Version 1 (2008).

105 *Id.* at 27.

106 MAMDANI, *supra* note 6, WHEN VICTIMS BECOME KILLERS : COLONIALISM, NATIVISM, AND THE GENOCIDE IN RWANDA, 12 (2002) and see also Anderson, *supra* note 98 at 1155.

5.5.4 King Leopold II and the Congo Free State – Crimes Against Humanity

When King Leopold II proposed to the European Powers that the sovereignty of his private company, International Association of the Congo and later *L'Etat Independent du Congo*, be respected he used humanitarian and philanthropic arguments as his company's primary interest in Central Africa. However, after a few years the brutal nature of King Leopold II's rule emerged both in Europe and the United States. Several reports revealed that there was nothing philanthropic let alone protective of natives about King Leopold's investment in Congo Free State. At first the reports emerged through individual diaries of explorers and missionaries who had missions in the Congo. These were followed by several commissioned investigations that reported on the gruesome and autocratic rule of King Leopold II.

The reports include the Casement Report written by the British Consul of Northern Irish origins, Roger Casement, and letters written by George Washington Williams to the President of the United States of America in 1890. In a letter to the US Secretary of State, George Washington Williams used the term 'crimes against humanity', a term that was used later during the Nuremburg Trials, to describe the treatment of Africans under King Leopold II.[107] In addition, the well-known British author Arthur Conan Doyle published a pamphlet under the heading 'The Crime of the Congo' detailing reports of how the Congo Free State was administered under King Leopard II, and the mistreatment of natives.

The rubber boom that began in the 1890s after John Dunlop invented the inflatable rubber tire used in bicycles and automobiles led King Leopold II to use extreme and diabolical methods to ensure that the natives harvested enough rubber for exports.[108] The demand for rubber intensified the misery of the natives of the Congo under King Leopold II. In order to maximize rubber collection for export, each household was asked to supply a certain quota of rubber on a monthly basis. The order was administered by state agents with the help of *Force Publique*. The *Force Publique* was often reinforced by the local 'savages,' the Capitas, who were reported to be the main perpetrators of many horrible deeds. Some state agents imprisoned women or forced them into prostitution in order to force their men into surrender and work. When villages failed to meet their set target of rubber production, the *Force Publique* were sent to burn and destroys the entire village forcing people deeper into the forest abandoning their children and fields.[109]

107 Arthur Conan Doyle, *The Crime of the Congo* (4 ed., 1909); see also Hochschild, *King Leopold's Ghost: supra* note 66 at 112.

108 Doyle, *supra* note 107.

109 Hochschild, *supra* note 66.

One of the horrible practices used by the *Force Publique* was the mutilation of their victims' hands. *Force Publique* were required to account for each bullet that they used and to do so they had to cut off the hands of all natives that they had killed and take them to the District Commissioner. In 1896, A German newspaper *Kolnische Zeitung* reported from impeccable sources that on one single day 1305 severed hands were turned over to a notorious District Commissioner, León Fievez. In a related event, in a state around the Momboyo River, a state officer is reported having used 6,000 cartridges which meant 6,000 people were killed or mutilated.

The striking element about the crimes committed in Congo by King Leopold II and his private company is that there was very little effort put into holding him accountable. This happened despite the existence of concrete documentation of the abuses. In fact King Leopold II is viewed as a heroic figure in modern day Belgium. At the same time his legacy continues to divide opinion in the Democratic Republic of the Congo.[110] In addition to crimes committed by King Leopold II, the Belgium colonial government continued to seek methods of continuing to maintain their role and position in Congo even after it attained independence in 1960.[111] In 2002, the Belgian Prime Minister implicitly acknowledged the role that was played by some of the Belgian officials in the assassination of the first Congolese Prime Minister Patricia Lumumba immediately after independence.[112]

Since the end of the Cold War Belgium has become one of the main advocates for ending impunity especially through the exercise of universal jurisdiction.[113] It has become the capital of universal jurisdiction[114] although those who are close to Congo's history would find it difficult to reconcile this new image of Belgium with its 'shameful pages in the history of decolonization.'[115] The conviction that Belgian judges have to pursue investigations and open cases against former colonies leaves one wondering whether they are also aware of their historical past and how it could impact their action. The point here is to stress the challenges that former colonizers encounter when they want to champion justice.

110 *DR Congo's Leopold Statue Removed*, BBC News, February 4, 2005, Available at <http://news.bbc.co.uk/2/hi/africa/4235237.stm> (Accessed August 15, 2011).

111 Thomas Turner, *Crimes of the West in Democratic Congo: Reflections on Belgium Acceptance of 'Moral Responsibility' for the Death of Lumumba, in* Genocide War Crimes & the West History and Complicity 231 (Adam Jones ed., 2004).

112 *Id.*

113 Maximo Langer, *The Diplomacy of Universal Jurisdiction: The Political Branches and the Transnational Prosecution of International Crimes*, 105 American Journal of International Law 53 (2010).

114 Jalloh, 2010. Universal Jurisdiction, Universal Prescription? A preliminary Assessment of the African Union Perspective on Universal Jurisdiction. *International Criminal Law Forum.*

115 See footnote 60 for Bula Bula comments.

Professor Jalloh pointed out that the colonial domination between Europe and Africa makes it difficult for former colonizers to take the lead in rendering justice to Africans. [116]

5.5.5 *Criminal Accountability for Algerian Crimes*

The Algerian War of independence fought between the French Colonial government and the National Liberation Front (FLN) was characterized by state sanctioned repression and violence.[117] One of the main strategies used by the French Army and Police against the Algerians suspected of supporting the independence movement was torture. It was relied upon as a weapon of war and by 1958 it was part of France's counterinsurgency training manuals.[118] In addition to torture the French strategies included cruel treatment, enforced disappearances and extra-judicial killings. In 2001, the French Algerian War Veteran General Paul Aussarresses published a book *Service Spéciaux: Algéria,* 1955-1957.[119] In the book General Aussarresses admitted that torture and murder were used against Algerians suspected of working for the liberation movement the National Liberation Front.

However despite credible records of abuses committed by the French Army during the war, and the legal obligations under the Geneva Conventions for the French government to investigate and prosecute those responsible no concrete action was taken by the French government to ensure criminal responsibility. It was only in 1999 that the French Government accepted that there was War between its army and the National Liberation Front in Algeria. The implication of the decision not to recognize the war in Algeria as such, is that the French government absolved itself from the Geneva Conventions obligations especially those that protect Prisoners of War (PoW). This is because the Algerian War of independence had started in 1955 just four years after France ratified the Geneva Conventions which created an obligation for contracting parties to treat Prisoners of War in a respectable manner. By not declaring the operations as "war," this meant the treatment of the captured liberation movement's combatants was outside the protection of international law.

A clear indication that the French government was not ready to hold its armed forces accountable for the human rights abuses in Algeria is evident in how the French judiciary

---

116 Jalloh, 2010. Universal Jurisdiction, Universal Prescription? A preliminary Assessment of the African Union Perspective on Universal Jurisdiction, *International Criminal Law Forum*, 62.

117 Shiva Eftekhari, *France and the Algerian War: From a policy of 'forgetting' to a Framework for Accountability,* 34 Colombian Human Rights Law Review 413 (2003).

118 *Id.*

119 Martin S. Alexander & J.F.V. Keiger (eds. 2002) France and the Algerian War 1954-62; Strategy, Operations and Diplomacy.

continuously changed the definition and applicability of the crimes against humanity. After the Second World War and the Nuremburg Trials the international community realized the London Agreement and Charter had not addressed the issue of statutory limitations of the crimes in domestic law.[120] This meant after several years, it was going to be difficult for some states to use their domestic systems to prosecute the Nazis who were still free. In order to address this problem there was general consensus that the crimes against humanity were made imprescriptible.

In 1964, French Legislature adopted Law 64-1326 declaring the imprescriptibility of crimes against humanity. This step was motivated by the spirit of solidarity with the victims of the Second World War and with the intention that any remaining Nazis would be punished, no matter where they were found.[121] However, approximately nineteen years later in 1983, during the trial of a former Head of Gestapo at Lyon, Klaus Barbie, for crimes against humanity the court decided to redefine the definition of crimes against humanity. The redefinition was somewhat motivated by France's desire to deny accountability of its own atrocities in Algeria as elaborated below.

During Barbie's criminal proceedings his defense lawyer challenged the retroactive application of crimes against humanity. He argued that if his client was to be convicted of crimes against humanity that he committed in France while working for of Nazi Germany by analogy the French soldiers who participated in the Algerian war were also guilty of atrocities that they committed in Algeria.[122] In order to prevent a situation where the French were held criminally accountable for the crimes committed in Algeria, the *Cour de Cassation* which is the highest court of appeal in France decided to redefine crimes against humanity by limiting its application only to crimes committed 'in the name of a state practicing a policy of ideological hegemon.'[123] Since France did not consider itself to have been pursuing a policy of ideological hegemon as Nazi German was, it meant that with this redefinition of crimes against humanity, the French were not to be criminalized for Algerian crimes.

Attempts by the victims of the Algerian war to obtain justice have not been successful even though those responsible for committing murder or torture publicly acknowledge their involvement. The other common legal basis used to deny victims justice was the

120 Leila Sadat Wexler, *The Interpretation of the Nuremburg Principles by the French Court of Cessation: From Touveir to Barbie and Back Again*, 32 COLUMBIA JOURNAL OF TRANSITIONAL LAW 290 (1995).

121 *Id.*

122 Vivian Grosswald Curran, *Politicising the Crime of Humanity: The French Example*, 78(3) NOTRE DAME LAW REVIEW 677 (2003).

123 *Id.*

investigating magistrate's decision to reject claims of crimes against humanity and grade them as war crimes. This is because war crimes were covered by both laws of amnesty and laws of prescription. The single significant trial conducted for the Algerian crimes occurred in 2001 when General Aussaresses was charged with a criminal offense under the 1881 French Press Law for "complicity in the justification of war crimes." The charges were based on the public interviews that he had given and also published accounts of his experiences in Algeria.

The campaign to end impunity for the crimes committed during the Algerian war of independence had started in the late 1950s. However, it was the publication of General 'Paul Aussarresses' *Service Spéciaux: Algéria* book and the willingness of former military officers to publicly talk about the atrocities that added momentum to the campaign. In Algeria, the ruling FLN party has criticized the French authorities for the failure to issue a public apology for the crimes. Bilateral relations between Algeria and France have generally been lukewarm, and it is possible that one of the main causes is the failure of France to publicly address the issue of atrocities committed during the war of independence. For instance, it was only in 1999 that Algeria started to attend the biennial Franco-African Conference which could be an indication for the need for the two states to address their past.

5.6 Conclusion

This chapter has attempted to demonstrate that Africa has experienced atrocities for centuries and that the majority of those who perpetrated them have not been prosecuted or punished, which to some extent refutes the notion that chronic impunity is a new phenomenon in Africa. One of the reasons often given for the absence of criminal accountability has been the absence of a legal framework as discussed under the transatlantic slave trade. However, with regards to atrocities committed after the signing and ratification of the Berlin Act in 1885, it can be argued that Article 6 created an international obligation for the protection of the rights and dignity of native populations. Although there was no individual criminal responsibility under the Berlin Act, the treaty established international law of that time which European Powers were supposed to honor. The fact that there still exists a vibrant movement of African political leadership, scholars and journalists who believe that those past atrocities require some form of accountability demonstrates how important it is for the application of an international criminal justice system to be sensitive to historical injustices in Africa. The history, and brutality, of colonization is very fresh for many Africans. Perhaps it is as fresh as fascism or communism is for many Europeans. It would therefore be naïve to assume that collective memories of colonization have no role in influencing Africans' world view especially as far as truth-seeking through international criminal justice is concerned.

Be the above as it may the chapter has also attempted to situate the current debate on the implementation of international criminal justice in Africa in an historical context. The observations that could be made include that the colonial domination of Africa by European powers makes it hard for judges from France, Belgium or any other former colonial power to attempt to prosecute state officials from their former colonies for two reasons. First is that the former colonial powers committed atrocities with impunity in their former colonies hence their hands are not clean. The second reason is that any interference into the domestic affairs of a former colony is likely to be treated with suspicion and as a sign of neo-colonialism. It feeds in to the assumption that some African countries are satellite/banana republics that major European states are still entitled to run.[124]

An in-depth analysis of the role played by international law during the trans-Atlantic slave trade and a colonization process reveals that it has always been selectively applied or applied to benefit the interests of powerful nations. The Berlin Conference and the resultant Berlin Act did not involve any Africans delegates, even from Liberia or Ethiopia which were independent African states at that stage. The Act legalized the occupation of Africa without any African consent. Furthermore, African illiterate chiefs and kings were made to sign documents (treaties) that they could not read and understand only to discover later that they had given away their land and resources to foreign powers, raising the spectre of fraud, coercion and illegality.

The relations between the colonial powers and the indigenous people were not considered to be part of international law and any attempts to incorporate them as part of international law caused an uneasy feeling among the European Powers including the US. This affected the early conceptualization of international criminal law after the Second World War. For instance when the Allies were defining the crimes against humanity as part of the crime to charge the Nazis with, they made sure that the crime had a nexus to an international conflict. Professor Schabas pointed out that the Allies were uncomfortable with the ramifications of using crimes against humanity for internal conflicts. This is because such a decision would have had implications on how they were treating their own minorities.[125] The influence of power politics in the definitions of international crimes did not end with the Nuremburg trials but continued until the Rome Conference where crimes that were deemed to be sensitive to the interests of the powerful states were either not included (for instance nuclear weapons) or their applicability under the ICC was deferred to a distant future.

The lack of fundamental changes in the power relations between the ICC which is supposed to be a judicial system and the UNSC which is a political institution controlled by

124 Jalloh, *supra* note 54 at 22.

125 Schabas, *supra* note 24. See also Anghie & Chimni, *supra* note 57, 77-103.

five powerful states appears to be one of the sources of the tension between African States and the ICC. This probably explains why the AU has proposed amendments to Article 16 such that the General Assembly which is considered to be more democratic is also given powers to defer cases.[126] The AU adopted a similar approach of trying to shape international criminal law through the General Assembly when it resolved to address the issue of universal jurisdiction through the UNGA Legal Committee.

In general one can say that the more African states feel that power relations between them and former colonial powers or institutions such as the ICC is not leveled, the higher the chances are that they evoke historical injustices to defend their position, which is understandable. Having said that it is important that Africans take leadership and prove that they can play a practical role in ending impunity, especially when it involves heads of states and other powerful people. Such an approach would give African states more control over their affairs and would enable them to reduce to minimum international interventions which are known to have other ulterior motives. Unless such an approached is adopted Africa will continue to be the focus of international criminal justice and continual reference to historical injustices will be interpreted as a sign of Africans not wanting to take responsibility for modern-day atrocities within the continent.

126 Akande, Plessis & Jalloh, *supra* note 1.

6 The ICC

A Place for Africans and Africans in Their Place?

David Chuter

6.1 Introduction

This chapter is concerned with the higher politics of the International Criminal Court (ICC) as it has developed, and as it involves Africa now and in the near future. It is not, except incidentally, concerned with the history and procedures of that organization, nor with its personnel, or the way in which it conducts its business.

The chapter traces the origins of international justice and courts in a tradition of attempting to give a respectable face to political demands for revenge and punishment of those who have offended us. It notes the formidable practical and political difficulties of attempting to conduct fair and honest investigations and trials in such circumstances, and the grave problems the ICC will face in attempting to investigate the activities of western, western-allied or western-protected states, should it attempt to do so. It argues that, for that reason, Africa is likely to be more or less the exclusive customer of the ICC for the foreseeable future, and that the ICC itself is best seen as a kind of Human Rights Theatre, in which representatives of lesser cultures can be ceremonially prosecuted, to show that the western world really cares about human rights violations. Finally, the chapter looks at the likely political consequences of this quasi-exclusive focus of the ICC on Africa.

It should be emphasized at the outset that what follows is not intended as criticism of individuals, whether in governments or in the ICC itself. There have been trenchant criticisms of the ICC and its personnel elsewhere,[1] and I do not intend to add to them now. Rather, I am concerned with those objective political factors which dictate what the ICC is likely to be able to accomplish, irrespective of who is in charge of it, and what the likely political consequences will be.

1 See, for example, Julie Flint & Alex de Waal, *Case Closed: A Prosecutor without Borders*, World Affairs, (Spring 2009).

6.2 Contextualising International Justice in History

Most accounts of the rise of international humanitarian law and of courts and tribunals, come, naturally enough, from those with a human rights background, and they stress, understandably, cumulative attempts to limit "impunity" and to extend the "rule of law." Formally, this is partly true, in the sense that texts of laws, as well as organizations and procedures, have developed and strengthened over time. Likewise, the last generation has seen the rise of courts organized and staffed internationally, and able to try nationals of various different countries.

But the key to understanding the rise of these institutions lies in politics, because without political support, no idea, no matter how brilliant or morally compelling, will ever get implemented. So what are the political preconditions for courts and tribunals to be established, and to function properly? The first and most important point is that effective courts and tribunals are always, in practice, "victors' justice", because they rely for that effectiveness on the ability to conduct investigations, arrest suspects and summon witnesses, all of which depend on control of territory. An example would be the ability of the International Criminal Tribunal for Yugoslavia (ICTY) to conduct investigations in Bosnia after 1995, as opposed to its inability to do so in Croatia for some years thereafter, and of the ICC to conduct investigations in the Democratic Republic of Congo (DRC), as opposed to in Sudan. These are matters of degree, of course, since evidence can be destroyed, suspects protected and witnesses intimidated, even in a benign environment. Nonetheless, the basic requirement remains that the tribunal, and nations or organizations supporting it, have more power than those who may be trying to resist its operations. Conversely, it follows that nations supporting a court or tribunal will generally be powerful enough to prevent investigations being conducted against them, or their interests. Thus, whilst the Serbian government tried to mount trials of western leaders they held responsible for the bombing of civilian targets during the NATO attacks of 1999, they were unable to compel either the accused or western witnesses to appear. All this explains why trials tend to take place after hostilities are over, and when one (or more) faction is no longer strong enough to obstruct the process.

For most of history, organizing trials has not been the favoured method of dealing with an enemy after a war. Depending on the civilization, wholesale extermination, slavery or colonial subjugation were more usual. The first case where some kind of real thought seems to have been given to the fate of a defeated leader is after the abdication of the French Emperor Napoleon Bonaparte in 1814. (It is not an accident that this example comes from Europe: most of those that have helped to shape the development of the law of armed conflict have done so as well.) Napoleon's case is interesting for several reasons.

First, it seems to be the origin of the demonization of a national leader to provide a point of reference for hatred and demands for revenge: a tradition which persists until the present day. Faced with widespread popular sympathy for the ideas of the French Revolution, the British tried to build Napoleon into a pantomime villain and bloodthirsty monster. In parallel, the foreign interpretation of the French Revolution was probably the first systematic use of atrocity propaganda to mobilize popular hatred and revulsion, in this case against democracy and in favour of hereditary monarchy. Indeed, for most of the nineteenth century, the French Revolution, in the hands of popular novelists like Charles Dickens, became a kind of terrible warning against the bloody consequences of any move to a more democratic system of government in Europe. Finally, Napoleon's fate (exile first to the Mediterranean island of Elba, then to distant St. Helena after his unsuccessful attempt to regain power in 1815) was the first time a defeated national leader's future had been considered in this way. The monarchs arrayed against Napoleon would have certainly liked to have him executed, but they were realistic enough to know that this was unpopular politically in France, as well as setting an awkward precedent for themselves. It is not surprising therefore, that legends immediately sprang up that his death in 1821 was due to poison.[2]

In the nineteenth century, European powers fought relatively little among themselves, and devoted much of their energies to carving out colonies. They saw no need to make themselves accountable to anyone for their actions in these colonies, although revolts and uprisings by the natives were put down with some violence, and occasionally a lick of legal varnish. World reaction to the horrors of the Boer War was essentially because the victims – the Afrikaners – were white. Even so, there was no serious suggestion of legal proceedings against the British leaders responsible for the deaths of tens of thousands of women and children.

The beginning of modern thinking and practice about international criminal justice is to be found in the First World War in Europe. In 1914, the British government was confronted with the awkward question of how to sell to a suspicious public the idea of involvement in a potentially dangerous and destructive war against Germany and on the side of France. The British government wanted to stop the Germans dominating Europe and controlling the ports opposite the English coast, but was worried that public opinion would not accept this argument as adequate. As a result, stories of alleged atrocities committed by German troops invading Belgium were taken up, massively exaggerated and fed to an eager mass media. In recent years there has been a tendency to emphasize that some

2 Among the libraries of books devoted to this period, see Max Gallo, Napoleon, Tome 4 L'Immortel De Saint-Helene (2010).

atrocities actually did occur,[3] and they were not entirely invented. This is true, but irrelevant; for the British, the truth of the allegations was unimportant, so long as they could make political use of them.

As the War progressed through four years of mounting horror, political opinion became starkly polarized and ever more extreme. By 1918, the British popular press were howling for revenge against the Germans, (often described as "sub-humans" and unworthy of civilized treatment). Such anger and vengefulness demanded a target of some kind, and so "Hang the Kaiser" became a popular slogan.[4] It might have happened. Public support for hanging (or at least trying) the Kaiser was strong among the victorious powers, and the British Election of 1918 was partly fought on the issue. Conferences of British, French and American officials tried to draw up charges, and political pressure was put on the Netherlands (where the Kaiser had fled) to hand him over. But the Dutch declined to do so, and the idea eventually lapsed. The case is of interest though, because it displays the main characteristics of many later episodes. In the beginning, comes the atrocity propaganda and the cultivation of public opinion, on the basis of stories which may or may not be true. Then there are public demands for revenge, often couched in the vocabulary of justice. Finally, comes the botched realization and the recognition that converting indiscriminate hatred and vengefulness into criminal charges that can be proved beyond a reasonable doubt is not easy. In this case, as has become normal, the guilt of the accused was assumed even before it was obvious what he could be charged with, or even if he could be charged with anything at all. And, as always, the victors did not pause to examine their own conduct: the naval blockade of Germany which helped cause hundreds of thousands of deaths, and continued even after Germany's surrender, was regarded by them as entirely legitimate.

Today's war crimes prosecutors understandably flinch at the mention of the Nuremburg and Tokyo Tribunals, and the ad hoc tribunals and the ICC have certainly conducted themselves better. Yet the cases are interesting because they display essentially the same political dynamic which is behind the ICC. Moral considerations aside, it was obvious to Allied leaders that the Nazi high command could not be left alive after the war. The idea of Hitler taking refuge in Switzerland, for example, was unthinkable. Early suggestions of simply hunting down and killing the Nazi leadership were ultimately abandoned in favour of some kind of judicial process. Obviously the main Nazi leaders would have to be

3 ALAN KRAMER, DYNAMIC OF DESTRUCTION: CULTURE AND MASS KILLING IN THE FIRST WORLD WAR, (2007), discusses these and other episodes.

4 As early as 1917, two American songwriters, James Brockman and James Kendis had written the popular hit *We're Going to Hang the Kaiser.* For Lloyd George and the 1918 election, see for example JAMES PURCELL, LLOYD GEORGE, 74-5 (2006).

executed; they therefore had to be found guilty, which meant that they had to be convicted of something, which meant that charges of some kind had to be brought. Once more, a guilty verdict was taken for granted before the defendants had actually been charged with anything. Framing charges was not easy. Some crimes ("waging an aggressive war") had to be invented for the occasion. Others – such as bombing undefended cities – were withdrawn, out of embarrassment as much as anything else, since the Allies had done far worse. Indeed, Nazi atrocities against the civilian population were not given special priority in the trials, partly because the Allies were uncomfortably aware of the half million German civilians who had died as a result of their bombing raids.

The political leadership probably did not have a great deal of choice. War has a radicalising effect on any population, and six years of brutal conflict had left the British population exhausted and clamouring for revenge. Although the US had not suffered directly from the war at all, its population was at least as radicalized, and in both countries, the political leaderships, the popular media and much public opinion encouraged each other. The Germans – and not just the Nazis – were seen as sub-humans for whom extermination would be too merciful a fate.

Needless to say, the correlation of forces was such that the Allies saw no need to put their own conduct in question, or even to mention it, and there was no one to require them to do so. Not for the first time, and certainly not for the last, the political forces organising the trials regarded themselves as politically and morally superior to the accused, and retrospectively justified in whatever it was that they had done.

The war in the Far East had been a brutally racial one from the beginning, marked by atrocities on both sides.[5] Even before the war, racialist views of the Japanese were widespread in the West, and war propaganda often painted them as animals – monkeys for example – rather than human beings. This, combined with the shock to white cultural superiority of their early victories, created a furious demand for revenge among public and elites alike. The result was the International Military Tribunal for the Far East, set up in Tokyo in 1946. In spite of its name (and the presence of a number of non-US judges) the Tribunal was American in origin, and largely funded and organized by the US. The logic was partly that of Nuremburg – the Japanese leadership had to be destroyed in some fashion – but with a powerful additional need to revenge racial humiliation.[6]

5 John Dower, War without Mercy: Race and Power in the Pacific War (1986).

6 For a recent attempt to partly rehabilitate the trials, see Neil Boister and Robert Cryer, The Tokyo International Military Tribunal: A Reappraisal (2008).

Yet if, as usual, the guilt of the defendants was decided in advance, it remained to convict them of something. The Japanese had destroyed many of their records, and there was little to link the main defendants with any crimes committed against allied forces. The solution was to invent the concept of "crimes against peace," and to charge the defendants with responsibility for such crimes going back to the start of the war in China in 1937. Under the rules of the court, it was not necessary to show that the defendants ordered, or even knew about the crimes: it was alleged instead that they were members of a conspiracy dating back to the 1920s. (Much of the argument depended on an alleged 1927 government document which is widely believed today to be a forgery).[7] In addition, all forms of evidence, including hearsay and even allied propaganda, were allowed to be introduced.

Political reality, however, intervened in one important way to limit the extent of the trials. Whatever the Emperor's personal responsibility for the war (and that is still being debated) it was impossible politically to put him on trial without creating an unprecedented political crisis. Moreover, the US needed Hirohito as a figure to promote stability in a country which few understood, and whose language hardly any Americans spoke. In addition, political imperatives change, and the same figures that were so hated in 1945 soon became valuable, because their nationalism and anti-communism made them useful allies in a country where the prevailing sentiment, after 1945, was pacifist and left-wing. So many were quietly released or pardoned in the years that followed. (Indeed, across the world, all except the highest profile Axis accused had been freed by the mid-1950s, and were often in positions of responsibility once more).

The outcome of the Tokyo trials was a disappointment to most of those involved. Many of the non-American judges expressed severe doubts about the process, and one – Judge Pal from India – eventually disowned it entirely.[8] Much more than at Nuremburg, there was a sense that little existed morally to differentiate the victors conducting the trial from the vanquished in the dock. The awful results of US air attacks on Tokyo were everywhere to be seen around the court as the trials unfolded. But once more, the correlation of political forces, mixed with the unquestioning assumption of moral superiority by the Allies, meant that such questions were not explored.

Other countries tried to deal with the legacy of the war as best they could. After the liberation of France in 1944, the new government under General de Gaulle tried to mount trials of those who had collaborated with the German occupation. Part of the purpose was, as

---

7 The weaknesses of the IMT and its rules of procedure and evidence are well documented in RICHARD H. MINEAR, VICTOR'S JUSTICE: THE TOKYO WAR CRIMES TRIAL (1971).

8 Pal voted for acquittal on all counts. See, among others, Timothy Brook, *The Tokyo Judgment and the Rape of Nanking*, 60 THE JOURNAL OF ASIAN STUDIES, 673-700 (2001).

usual, to get rid of those who still posed a political threat. But it was also to establish the illegitimacy of the collaborationist government, and the legitimacy of the government of de Gaulle, as well as to respond to public anger and the desire for revenge. The eventual outcome was very mixed. Some defendants refused to apologize for anything they had done, claiming they had been defending a legitimate government against communist terrorists. In other cases, government officials admitted signing death warrants for resistance fighters, for example, but claimed that they had used their positions to save many more, and so were really members of the resistance themselves.[9] Most other countries which had been involved in the war, both in Europe and Asia, grappled with variants of the same problem.

The majority of the fighting in the world during the Cold War was related directly or indirectly to the struggle against colonialism and the consequences of it. Here, for the first time, Africans appear as actors. The western struggle to retain its colonies was marked by considerable brutality, and also by the use of legal devices to make agitation for independence a crime. Trial and imprisonment of nationalist leaders was commonplace, and where actual rebellions broke out, they were met with extreme violence, often of a judicial kind. In Kenya, the anti Mau-Mau campaign proceeded through the stages we have already noted: cultivation of public opinion through atrocity propaganda (some based, as usual, on real events), hysterical demands to "do something", followed by a decision to organize trials so that those who needed to disappear could be found guilty of something. Altogether, the British seem to have executed over 1000 alleged Mau-Mau "terrorists" for acts often vaguely defined, on evidence which scarcely stands up to scrutiny.[10] The British showed not the slightest scruple about behaving this way, or about the sadistic torture and casual killings which were a feature of the detention camps into which many alleged criminals were herded. But even the (fairly limited) protests in Britain called only for the policies to be stopped, not for those responsible to be punished. Much the same was true in Algeria, where the French not only tried and executed hundreds of nationalists for various crimes, but also carried out thousands of summary executions.[11] Yet in France, as in Britain, the majority of the population supported almost any policies adopted during the colonial wars, and even the strongest opponents of the Algerian war stopped short of actually demanding trials of those responsible for the killings and the torture. It was other people after all.

---

9 I have said rather more about this episode in David Chuter, Humanity's Soldier: France and International Security 218-25 (1996).

10 David Anderson, Histories of the Hanged: Britain's Dirty War in Kenya and the End of Empire (2005).

11 See an eye-opening memoir by a participant, Philippe Aussaresses, Services Spéciaux, Algérie 1955-1957 (2001).

Indeed, at all stages in the wars of de-colonization, the majority of the population of the colonialist nation supported what their troops were doing. This was true in Kenya and Algeria, and it was also true during the Vietnam War, itself an indirect result of de-colonization. Although large-scale massacres of Vietnamese civilians seem to have been very common, it was only massive media coverage after the accidental discovery of the 1968 My Lai massacre which eventually forced the US Army to put the junior officer responsible – Lt. Calley – on trial. Yet Americans overwhelmingly disapproved of the guilty verdict, and more than half of those subsequently questioned said that the massacre of civilians was justified "if they were communists."[12] Not for the first time, it was political reality, not the absence of suitable institutions, which precluded any further action.

Two important changes were already under way between the end of the decolonization phase, essentially complete by 1980, and the era of courts and tribunals in the 1990s, although each grew in importance between those two dates. The unaccustomed peace in Europe after 1945, and advances there in human rights and social justice, turned the focus of humanitarians in Europe towards the outside world. Much of their energy was initially devoted to anti-colonial campaigns, to opposing the Vietnam War, and to calling for the end of apartheid in South Africa. These campaigns had fewer and fewer targets after 1980, and reached a natural end by about 1990. Political changes in Eastern Europe also meant that human rights concerns there abated somewhat. But naturally the urge to do good in the world did not go away. It had also been mutating for some time. The human rights movement had begun after the Second World War as a way of putting pressure on governments to release those unjustly imprisoned (Amnesty International was founded in 1961). But as the movement grew, and as competition for publicity and resources became increasingly fierce, the focus necessarily changed. Large-scale publicity campaigns and demands for punishment of human rights violators, rather than freedom for the victims, became increasingly common. Human rights groups increasingly harangued governments, demanding that they intervene militarily around the world to prevent such abuses, and kill those responsible for them. Yet it was still hoped that Europe and its ex-colonies would be peaceful: with the end of the Cold War, surely the underlying motor of conflict there had been removed?

The other development was in newsgathering technology, where portable satellite terminals replaced expensive and slow news camera footage. Pictures of atrocities could travel round the world in minutes, presented by journalists who increasingly saw themselves as heroes and moral teachers, instructing governments on their duty. From the mid-1990s, the increasing use of the Internet meant that images and allegations did not even have to

12 HERBET C. KELMAN & V. LEE HAMILTON, CRIMES OF OBEDIENCE: TOWARDS A SOCIAL PSYCHOLOGY OF AUTHORITY AND RESPONSIBILITY 169-179 (1989).

pass through traditional news media – although it also meant that the scope for manipulation and downright lying increased massively.

The first episode when all these elements came together was the fighting in the Former Yugoslavia from 1991-1995. To the consternation and fury of many, nationalist violence erupted in Europe again. Images previously only associated with Africa came to European (and American) TV screens every evening, but the victims were white, and living in a recognisably European environment only a few hundred kilometres from Rome and Vienna. Much of the reporting was exaggerated or misleading – sometimes deliberately so – and the conflict itself took place in a region where the manipulation of outside powers for support had been an art form for well over a century. Well-funded and organized public relations campaigns added to the confusion, and helped to create an angry, if poorly informed, coalition of journalists and human rights groups demanding violent military intervention.

The setting up of an international court – the ICTY – was, at least in part, an accident. Western decision makers were genuinely appalled by the violence on their doorstep, but they were also furious at the skill with which they were being manipulated by the local actors, and their own lack of success in bringing the crisis to an end. Faced with overwhelming demands to "do something" but obviously incapable of fulfilling the militaristic fantasies of human rights groups, they hit on the idea of a court, which would demonstrate that something was being done, and also undermine, or even remove from power, those who were frustrating their efforts. It was established by UN Security Council Resolution 827, in 1993.[13] There was then a precedent, which made it difficult to argue against the creation of the sister Tribunal, for Rwanda, after the events of 1994 in that country.

This was the first time that something resembling really independent judicial criminal organizations had been set up, and the difficulties became apparent immediately. Some practical issues are discussed in the next section, but here I want to emphasize the immediate cultural dissonance which resulted. The primary movers behind the Tribunals (as with the ICC) were human rights lawyers and international lawyers. They thought of law as something basically normative and assertive, and the function of the Tribunals as to punish the guilty. But the prosecutors were from a criminal law background. Their trade required them to prove cases beyond a reasonable doubt, to get their hands on reliable witnesses and compelling evidence, and to decide which charges, if brought, would stand a good chance of success. They were also more interested in conviction than exhaustive

13 The remainder of this chapter is heavily influenced by the author's own personal experience of the issues discussed. See also, David Chuter, War Crimes: Confronting Atrocity in the Modern World, (2003).

historical analysis, and so would often limit the charges brought to those they thought they could prove. In turn, this meant that many incidents, or alleged incidents, were never investigated, or if investigated never charged. Finally, they accepted that a percentage of charges would fail, and that some accused would be released.

They were accompanied by professional investigators, who were well aware that witnesses become confused, forget or invent things, and even lie, especially if money is offered. They were used to demanding standards for collecting and acquiring evidence, and the need to build a case which would stand up in court. On the other hand, they frequently encountered alleged witnesses who had been interviewed in an amateurish fashion by journalists and human rights groups and whose accounts were so contaminated as to be technically useless.

Finally, of course, even accused war criminals were entitled to legal representation, and to defend themselves, although this itself was controversial in some quarters. However, the establishment of the Tribunals was roughly contemporaneous with the triumph of the idea of Victimism in the United States, which spread subsequently to Britain and elsewhere. This doctrine enabled individuals and groups to identify themselves as "victims" of violence or abuse, especially sexual, and to demand compensation and what they described as "justice". Any attempt to question the validity of their testimony, usually procured under hypnosis by psychiatrists committed to their cause, was judged illegitimate because they were, after all, victims. So, for example, lawyers and psychiatrists in the US presented thousands of cases of children allegedly subjected to ritual satanic sexual abuse by organized groups including their parents, and refused to allow the "victims" to be cross-examined. A number of parents and others were actually convicted (normally of mundane offences only) though in general these verdicts were reversed on appeal. Thousands of families were destroyed in the process.[14] There was never any evidence that satanic abuse groups existed, but the media and human rights groups notably failed to question the fantastic allegations, or to provide support to the accused, so frightened were they of being labelled supporters of child abuse. Meanwhile, actual child abuse cases, both sexual and otherwise, went un-investigated for lack of resources.

The read-across to atrocity allegations is obvious enough, and does not need to be laboured here. It is just worth saying that chronologically the satanic panic had died down by the early 1990s, but the cult of the victim, and the fear of questioning what an alleged victim said, remained extremely powerful, and found a new and convenient home in the human rights and war crimes agenda.

---

14 See among other accounts, DEBBIE NATHAN & MICHAEL R. SNEDEKER, SATAN'S ABUSE: RITUAL ABUSE AND THE MAKING OF A MODERN AMERICAN WITCH HUNT (1995).

Inevitably, once allegations of war crimes were looked at by professionals, it emerged that witnesses were indeed sometimes confused, and often contradicted each other, that they gave wrong or misleading testimony, that some were liars, that some had been paid and some threatened. In Arusha, several witnesses had to be discharged after giving highly colourful evidence of things they had not seen, but had heard of from others. In their own culture, the difference between individual knowledge and collective understanding was not so emphasized.

None of this really should have come as any surprise to someone who had been on a jury, let alone someone familiar with the extensive literature which has shown that eyewitness testimony about violent crime is, essentially, useless.[15] But the results, including some acquittals, did come as a severe shock to groups who took it as an article of faith that all of the accused were obviously guilty, and that everyone who claimed to be a victim should be treated as one. In some cases, though, it was less alleged victims who were complaining than the media and Non-Governmental Organizations (NGOs). Quite quickly after the start of the fighting in Bosnia in 1992, for example, NGOs began to charge, and journalists to report, that the Bosnian Serb forces were deliberately committing mass rapes of (usually Muslim) women as some kind of an act of war to destroy Muslim society. There were echoes of the satanic abuse panic, not least in the conspiratorial framework, and the reluctance to allow alleged victims to be interviewed. Other parts of the media and other NGOs naturally felt squeamish about subjecting the claims to any real critical examination, because they did not want to be labelled protectors of rapists. The Yugoslavia Tribunal was sufficiently concerned to devote several years of investigation by an all-female team to the allegations, without turning up any evidence that such a scheme had ever existed. The best informal estimate was that there had been some 10,000 rapes over the three years of the war; a figure that was, sadly, not much higher than the peacetime norm. Individual cases of rape, as well as organized episodes (for example around Foca in Eastern Bosnia) certainly existed, and many were investigated and prosecuted. But the "rape as a weapon of war" meme could not be factually substantiated, although it continues to lead a vigorous life in the media even today.[16]

6.3 The Problem with the International Criminal Court

The collision between the moral impulse to seek punishment of the guilty on behalf of those one had identified as victims on one hand, and the banal processes of criminal

15 See for example Elizabeth E. Loftus, Eyewitness Testimony (1996).

16 See a recent summation of the problem, Amber Peterman, Dara Kay Cohen, Tia Palermo and Amelia Hoover Green, *Rape Reporting During War: Why the Numbers Don't Mean What You Think They Do*, Foreign Affairs (August 2011). For a scholarly demolition of various atrocity statistics, see Sex, Drugs and Body Counts: The Politics of Numbers in Global Crime and Conflict (Peter Andreas and Kelly M. Greenhill eds., 2010).

justice on the other, are a part of the problems of today's ICC, as they were of its predecessors. But there are a series of other ICC problems which relate to the type of organization it is. Some examples are given below. (My concern here is not with the legal status of the ICC, so much as with the sociology of how organizations work.)

Firstly, the ICC is an international treaty organization, rather than a creature of the Security Council. This means that it is analogous to the African Union or the International Telecommunications Union. Membership is voluntary, and can be suspended or even revoked if the state wishes. As with most such organizations, there are obligations, but little ability to police them, and few penalties for non-compliance. In theory, non-compliance with the ad hoc tribunals could have meant being reported to the Security Council, although states or entities supported by the West seldom suffered as a result. Nothing of comparable severity exists in the ICC Statute. Thus, nations are essentially expected to collaborate out of good intentions and respect for treaties they have signed.

In turn, this is because the ICC is an example of a type of international treaty organization where it is assumed that everyone will benefit from membership, and therefore everyone has an incentive to behave. It is like the International Air Transport Association – everyone would be worse off without it. Yet in practice, of course, this is not true, and therein lies one of the organization's main problems. There is, in reality, little practical benefit from becoming a state party other than moral satisfaction. At a minimum, it can involve obligations which are tedious (provision of witnesses, hosting of criminals serving sentences) or potentially awkward (providing documents, arresting indictees). At worst, it can involve handing over elements of one's own leadership to a foreign court, which history has shown to be something between unwise and politically suicidal. Even simple adhesion to the statute implies that the state might lose the right to prosecute those it wishes to, something that even the weakest state will cling to as part of its sovereignty.

So it is not surprising that many of the delegations in Rome in 1998 were nervous and fearful, wondering what it was they would be asked to sign up to this time. The exceptions, of course, were the major western states, apart from the US. These never imagined for a moment that the ICC would ever be used against them, but rather saw the operations of the Court as strengthening their own foreign policy agendas. In this sense, the Court is not so far from the World Trade Organization or the International Monetary Fund. Although in theory its rules and ideology are neutral, in practice it tends to be dominated by a small number of states and to benefit them more, in practice, than the rest of humanity.

The ICC is also an example of an international executive organization set up under a treaty regime. Here, the obvious comparisons are with the International Atomic Energy

Agency, which not only has its own Statute and General Conference but also a link with the Nuclear Non-proliferation Treaty, and the Organization for the Prohibition of Chemical Weapons, the executive arm of the Chemical Weapons Convention. In these cases, as with the ICC, the work of the organization is both technically complex and politically sensitive. The more important the task, the more fundamental are questions of management and expertise within the organization, and the more difficulties arise.

Some of the difficulties are, superficially, banal. In the case of the ICC, there are many excellent judges, prosecutors and investigators around the world, but it will be impossible for them to function unless, in practice, they understand English. The ICC, like many other international organizations, has impeccable multilingual credentials, but field reports, requests to attend meetings, or correspondence with outside governments and the media will overwhelmingly be in English. The seat of the ICC (like the OPCW and the ICTY) is in The Hague, a small, bourgeois, city which is the seat of government (but not the capital) of the Netherlands. Cold and rainy in winter, and mild in summer, its only real industries are government, embassies and international organizations. Government and ordinary people speak English, and sometimes German, but seldom French or any other language. Some understanding of Dutch (a guttural Germanic language spoken nowhere else) is needed to live there on a daily basis. Understandably, the ICTY had difficulty in attracting and retaining a genuinely international cadre of investigators and prosecutors, and even its large Australian contingent complained vocally about the weather.

There are more subtle problems also. The nearest analogy to war crimes investigations is serious transnational organized crime. There are not many countries in the world with experience of investigating and trying such offences. A senior ICTY figure suggested to the author some years ago that there were no more than twelve such states, and, if this number has increased recently, it is probably not by much. Investigators from states without these capacities can never expect to reach senior positions. Likewise, disciplines of criminal and military intelligence analysis, which underpin much of the investigations, are very unevenly represented around the world. Similarly, ICTY judges, even from some western countries, found themselves hopelessly out of their depth with the complexity of political and military factors which impinged on some of the major trials, for which nothing in their experience had prepared them. There is too little collective experience in the ICC to be sure, but there is a good chance that, in practice, Africans will be investigated, analysed, prosecuted and judged predominantly by non-Africans, and not for the first time in history.

These problems exist in part because of the way that war crimes investigations and trials have developed, seeking ever higher and more important targets. The events which give rise to pictures and videos of atrocity, and which cause us to demand revenge and punishment, are by definition relatively small-scale. There is only so much you can show on a screen. But increasingly we have insisted that the *real* criminals be punished; not some anonymous group of militiamen, but the bosses, and the bosses of the bosses. From the time of the ICTY and ICTR Statutes, documents began to talk of those who "planned" "instigated" and "ordered" crimes. Today it is taken for granted that investigations should be launched against senior commanders and even political leaders, in almost every case. But as the level of the target is raised, so the investigation and the trial become exponentially more complex.

Essentially, if someone was not at the scene or did not issue a written order for a crime, then it has to be shown that they were in some way responsible for the crime being committed, or at least did nothing to stop it when they could have done so. This can be a hugely complex endeavour, especially with civilian leaders and irregular military forces. But, from the German Kaiser onwards, we have seen that demands for revenge and punishment tend to cluster around identifiable, high profile figures, and that often moral or legal responsibility is presumed to translate handily into responsibility for criminal acts. This is often not the case.

The complexity of these situations means that a major case, before the ICC, for example, might need to cover a wide range of relatively arcane issues. They could include formal and informal patterns of control within the security forces and between those forces and the government, family, clan, tribal, ethnic, religious and commercial links between actors and their relative importance, ease of communications between main actors, military doctrines, standard and content of training, technical command and control issues, observed patterns of control in the past, written orders, laws and constitutional provisions, whether they reflected reality, records of investigations and trials, if any, as well as all the same factors as they affect second or third nations that might be involved.

Several points need making here. First, with trivial exceptions, these are not legal issues, but technical issues of fact and interpretation, where judges have no special skills. Indeed, they are the kind of subjects that political analysts, anthropologists, historians, journalists and intelligence officers spend decades becoming experts on. Second, it is very hard, if not impossible, to demonstrate any hypothesis on these subjects to a criminal standard of proof. (A century after it finished, there is no sign that one interpretation of the Boer War has been "proved": indeed, it is not clear that this is even possible.) Third, all this is merely background, and does not mean that the guilt of anyone has actually been proved, even if a consensus has been reached on some technical point. So a future trial chamber may decide that even though the President of Country A was at Staff College with the President of Country B and has kept in touch since, and that there are clan links between the two families, there is insufficient evidence that the military support given by A to B in the fighting against the rebels means that the President of A is guilty of any crime committed by the forces of B. Another group of judges, on the same evidence, may decide that there is just enough proof that he is guilty, and condemn him to life imprisonment. A third group of judges, of course, may overturn either verdict.

These problems have become progressively worse as the targets of investigations have become more significant figures. We have seen that, since the days of the Kaiser, it has been normal to demand punishment of those who symbolize countries we dislike, but that it has always been difficult to turn what may in some cases be arguable moral responsibility or political influence into actual criminal charges, unless those charges were invented for the occasion. The most thoroughgoing attempt to charge and convict an acting head of state, and the only complete story (since the individual died in custody) is that of the former Yugoslav President, Slobodan Milosevic. It is a powerful warning of the problems involved.[17]

Milosevic was President first of the Republic of Serbia, and then of the remains of the old Yugoslavia. A former senior Communist Party official, he was elected President in a charged atmosphere where the fate of the Serb minorities in neighbouring Bosnia and Croatia was a sensitive issue. Milosevic's ambition was to be the undisputed political leader of all Serbs, and he faced considerable opposition from hardliners claiming he was selling out his foreign brothers, especially when fighting broke out in the two countries. He appeared to support separatists seeking to join the Serb minorities to Serbia proper, until it became clear that this would be impossible. Milosevic was not a nice man (or he would not have got far in Balkan politics) and there is a respectable argument that his influence on the crisis was at least as malign as anyone else's. But that is very far from saying that there is any proof he had committed criminal offences.

Nonetheless, for the West, he was seen as an obstacle to the final resolution of the Balkans conflict, a skilful politician who taunted western leaders, operated his own agenda, and refused to respect theirs. They were desperate to overthrow him, and replace him with a leader who would work with them. But in the face of a divided opposition, Milosevic continued to win elections, helped by a ruthless political machine. The solution turned out to lie in the southern province of Kosovo, where Serbs were a small minority, and where the majority Albanian community were at odds with Belgrade. A small group of former Maoists, the Kosovar Liberation Army, launched a guerrilla

17 Shortly before this book went to press, former President Charles Taylor of Liberia was found guilty of offences related to the war in Sierra Leone and sentenced to fifty years in prison. Details of the judges' reasoning are not available at the time of writing, but it is already clear that the trial encountered much the same problems as are described in the Milosevic case.

campaign against Belgrade in 1996. As good Maoists, they hoped to mobilize the people by provoking the authorities, after which they hoped that the West would intervene. This strategy broadly worked, and the Serb police overreacted to bombings and shootings by attacking Albanian villages. Several hundred people had died by 1998. The West believed it could use the threat of investigation and prosecution to force concessions from Milosevic – essentially the surrender of Kosovo – which would lead to him being voted out of office.

The campaign went through the various stages we have reviewed. The nasty little insurgency was hyped by the West into a genocidal ethnic cleansing nightmare, and soon NGOs, the media and human rights groups, who had long wanted to get rid of Milosevic, were screaming for him to be prosecuted. After a clumsy NATO bombing campaign in 1999, Kosovo was duly surrendered and Milosevic lost the next election. His political enemies rapidly transferred him to The Hague. That was where the problems started.

There was a reasonably well-established, although rather small, crime-base of atrocities committed by Serb forces in Kosovo during the NATO bombing, and there was a respectable, though not overwhelming, case that Milosevic, as President, either agreed to them or should have stopped them. The majority view is that, had there been a verdict, Milosevic would probably have been found guilty on some of the counts. But the idea of charging him with involvement in atrocities committed by ethnic Serb forces in Bosnia and Croatia had been around for years, and the Tribunal appears to have decided that it had nothing to lose now by bringing charges under those headings. Yet reading the indictments one is struck immediately by the fact that, in effect, he was never charged with anything. It was not actually suggested that he had committed any crimes, rather it was stated, "(T)he Prosecutor does not intend to suggest that the accused physically committed any of the crimes charged personally. "Committed" in this indictment refers to participation in a joint criminal enterprise as a co-perpetrator."[18] It was, in other words, the existence of a "joint criminal enterprise" (effectively a conspiracy), which the Prosecution was trying to demonstrate. If this enterprise could be shown to exist, then Milosevic was vicariously guilty of all of the acts committed by the various members, whether or not he even knew of them.

We will never know whether the judges would have accepted this interesting line of argument (based, as will be apparent, on the methodology of the Tokyo trials), but there are signs that, with the prosecution of Charles Taylor and others, it is becoming the standard

18 *Prosecutor v. Slobodan Milosevic*, IT-02-54-T Amended indictment (Bosnia).

method of attacking national leaders. In many ways, it amounts to a confession of failure; not simply to find evidence, but rather to apply criminal law successfully to high-level strategic political issues. As a result, national leaders who are prosecuted in the future may need, in effect, to have crimes specially designed for them, of which they can then be convicted. The "joint criminal enterprise" argument is very difficult to refute, and the defendant is in a sense required to prove their innocence.

The natural urge to convict an indicted criminal will be accompanied by an equal fear of failure. Acquittals would not be popular, and would lead to accusations of incompetence against the ICC, and demands for resignations of its staff. This is because, in the end, criminal law is only the language in which this debate takes place. The real crimes of national leaders, in the eyes of many, are moral and political, and it is on that basis that vengeance and punishment are sought. Criminal law is only a mechanism, tolerated as long as it produces the right answer. That is why it is acceptable, uniquely in this context, for the guilt of the accused to be assumed before they have been charged with anything, let alone convicted. Their guilt is moral and thus not subject to ordinary rules of criminal evidence. So when the well-known human rights lawyer Geoffrey Robertson claimed that the Hague Tribunal existed to "try those guilty of crimes against humanity in the Former Yugoslavia" his casual dismissal of hundreds of years of the presumption of innocence was not regarded as controversial. He also demanded that Slobodan Milosevic be arrested, at a point where no charges had been laid.[19]

In turn, this has to do with the Judeo-Christian heritage of our traditions of thinking about crime and punishment. What we are really demanding, as we move up the political food chain towards national leaders, is the punishment of sin. And sin, we recall, is a frame of mind, and a moral decision, not the transgression of a set of rules. Virtue consists of doing God's will, even if we do not understand why. Sin is opposing God's will and turning away from obedience, for which we must expect to be punished. Pride (*i.e.* having a different opinion from God) was always the worst sin. This is one reason why it is impossible to imagine any verdict, any punishment, which would have satisfied the mood of apocalyptic hysteria which surrounded the trial of Milosevic.

There will therefore be enormous pressure to indict, and even more to convict, national leaders. If this means doing violence to legal processes, and altering definitions of crime to fit the circumstances (as has happened with genocide, for example), then so be it. Even if it proves possible to mount trials of national leaders, however, such trials require enormous

19 ABC Television broadcast, March 30, 1999. Also The Independent, June 20, 1999.

preparation and huge resources to do properly. In turn, this will only happen if there is a substantial consensus among major players that these indictments and trials are necessary. We have seen that trials in the past have only been possible when there has been an overwhelming correlation of forces in favour. Even the simple Dutch refusal to hand over the Kaiser in 1919 was enough to derail years of planning and preparation. We can take it as read that no major power, treaty signatory or not, will agree to hand its own nationals to the ICC willingly, and that solidarity among major powers will incline them to support each other in such cases. Major powers will also intervene to protect client states or allies, and to obstruct investigations which might reveal embarrassing facts about their own behaviour.

The nations concerned would probably not see such actions as cynical. The great myth of international justice (and I do not use that term unkindly) is that the law is the same for all, and that context makes no difference. But, as we all know, context is everything. Who does what, against whom, and under what circumstances, determines almost entirely what we think of particular episodes. We all make excuses for our own actions, or actions of those we support, even whilst condemning those we dislike. Sometimes, this assumption is revealed almost in passing. Thus, the BBC reported widespread dissatisfaction in Sierra Leone with the prosecution of Hinga Norman, the Kamajor leader during the Civil War, who is "regarded by some in Sierra Leone as a hero for standing up to the rebels who were trying to oust an elected government … his supporters are angry that he is being placed in the same bracket as the rebels."[20] Now logically, whether Norman was a "hero" or not has nothing to do with the issue. But in practice we all believe that "heroes" – or people we support – are entitled to commit crimes where others are not. Likewise, we often have difficulty in imagining that we should be subject to the same rules as everyone else. The author recalls being in Washington at the time of the 1999 NATO attack on Serbia and finding US officials genuinely incredulous that provisions of the ICTY Statute should be thought to apply to them. ("Isn't there something in the Statute that says this doesn't apply to the good guys?" wondered one of them in my presence.) And later it was depressing to see officials from such countries as the US and Israel defending their conduct in the same terms, and sometimes in the same words, that I was used to hearing from the dock in The Hague. The effect of all this is that actually mustering an international consensus to support a prosecution is very difficult, but that obstructing it is relatively easy.

The interference does not have to be overt. The ICC is never going to risk putting itself at odds with even one major power, and may well discreetly sound them all out before opening sensitive investigations. At the other end of the spectrum, a Security Council

20 *Sierra Leone war 'hero' on trial* (BBC News, June 10, 2004).

reference would only come after long informal consultations, since a veto would be in no-one's interest. And even if there is no political objection raised, a state can still discourage an investigation by pointing out privately how difficult the investigation will be, and how little evidence it suspects is available.

In turn, this is because the ICC is fundamentally dependent on states for its effectiveness. Money, personnel, witnesses, logistics, transport, investigation assistance, targeting, arrests, transfers, and many other elements are not really feasible without international help. A simple statement that "we have no information on that, sorry" may be enough to slow down or stop a promising investigation. Witnesses and documents may mysteriously disappear and arrests may never take place. (By contrast, leads, discreet briefings and hints about where to look will be very important in guiding the ICC's work, and these, of course, can be manipulated.)

6.4 The International Criminal Court and Africa

The result of the high-level politics of international criminal justice as described above is that it is likely that the only real action the ICC is likely to be able to undertake will be against small, poor, friendless states, especially in Africa. It is no coincidence that, as this piece was initially being written, Burma was being suggested as the first non-African target: a small, poor, isolated nation whose government has been at odds with the West for decades.

If we accept that Africa will be the main, if not the only area of activity for the ICC, what follows? First, western states are likely to have a large influence on what cases are addressed. The Darfur case may well be iconic here. The Save Darfur Campaign, without which the ICC cases would never have been brought, was a deliberate and well-funded attempt to use atrocity propaganda (once more partly based on reality) to mobilise western opinion to demand military interventions and trials. None of its substantial budget was ever spent in Africa: all went on lobbying and public relations in the US, including the funding of local groups, at universities and elsewhere.[21] The campaign was successful in purchasing the support of many American politicians, and led to the Hollywood star and public face of the Nespresso coffee-maker, George Clooney, being allowed to address the Security Council on the subject. More importantly, its simplistic Arab/African stereotype

21 See Mahmood Mamdani, Saviours and Survivors: Darfur, Politics and the War on Terror 48-71 (2009).

seems to have influenced the ICC as well.[22] This is likely to represent the pattern for the future.

Second, propaganda about crimes in Africa will serve to deflect attention from crises elsewhere. It cannot be a coincidence that the Save Darfur campaign was launched at a time when two wars begun by the United States, in Afghanistan and Iraq, were reaching a peak of destructiveness. The energy of human rights groups and others, which might have demanded withdrawal by the US from these wars, was deflected into other, and safer, channels.

Third, because the ICC is a permanent organization, it will need to take care always to look busy, to avoid having its budget cut. The means that even small-scale incidents in Africa (such as recently in Guinea) will be grist to the mill. It means in turn that for the foreseeable future the typical western narrative of Africa will continue to be of violence and conflict. Issues such as health and education, or the effects of world trade practices, will tend to be squeezed out for lack of time. But everybody knows that the main problems of Africa are not war crimes, or even war. The major causes of suffering and death in Africa lie elsewhere.

Fourth, as a consequence, the ICC will perpetuate the image of Africa under international tutelage, unable to address its own problems, and depending on western justice, as it depends on the IMF and the World Bank for money.

Fifth, because Africans have little control over where the ICC decides to investigate, their own attempts to manage political crises in the continent may well be derailed by the ICC's activities, or even rumours about them. Immunity from ICC investigations is likely to be a routine demand at the start of peace negotiations in the future, although of course no state can grant that. The tension between ICC investigations and the search for peaceful solutions is often presented as one of "justice vs. peace", or more controversially as sordid political calculation against the blinding light of truth. In practice, as we have seen, justice has little to do with it. Rather, we are faced with a conflict between the instinct for revenge and the instinct to pass on. And the instinct for revenge frequently comes from outside, rather than from Africa. However, if you are a western NGO or a Hollywood star, seeking revenge under the label of "justice", then you are, as Mamdani puts it, seeking "the right to punish but without being held accountable."[23] If a massive Sudan-style publicity campaign

22 A thorough (and overwhelming) critique of the ICC in Sudan is ALEX DE WAAL, A CRITIQUE OF THE PUBLIC APPLICATION BY THE CHIEF PROSECUTOR OF THE ICC FOR AN ARREST WARRANT AGAINST SUDANESE PRESIDENT OMAR AL BASHIR (2009).

23 *Id.* at 300.

in the future leads to a Security Council reference to the ICC, and a dormant war breaks out again, then, well, it is not our problem. Justice has been served.

Conversely, the very independence of the ICC may cause a wholly new series of problems for African conflicts as circumstances change on the ground. Thus, the reference of Libya to the ICC, by the Security Council (three of whose five Permanent Members are opposed to the Court) seemed initially a clever idea to destabilize Khadafy. Once it became clear that the Libyan leader would not go easily, however, doubts began to set in, and by the time of his killing in October 2011, mention of the indictment had effectively disappeared from the international discourse. It had become clear that the first rule of any normative system was in play here: be careful what you ask for, because you might get it.

Sixth, the ICC's western-influenced brand of retributive personal justice may be inappropriate to many – perhaps most – post-conflict situations. African states have begun to make use of traditional dispute resolution mechanisms which draw on deeply-embedded social structures and practices. This may be the pragmatic way forward in certain cases, but it will not be possible if the ICC is able to operate independently to bring criminal charges.

Finally, the way that the ICC investigates and brings charges will also inevitably shape understanding and discussion of African security problems. The use of the discourse of "ethnicity" and "genocide" in Rwanda, for example, is explained by the relentless ethnicization of African society by western thinkers over the last century. It seems to have begun as a simple mistake in the *Akaycsu* case, and was too embarrassing to correct later. This ethicized vision is helpful, because it reinforces western perceptions of Africa as a place of brutal ancient ethnic hatreds and endless tribal violence, rather than as an area where many of the growing pains of western civilization itself are being replicated. An accusation of genocide, even if the term is now meaningless, remains a powerful political weapon. It is for this reason, rather than any legal concerns, that the ICC Prosecutor is trying to have the President of Sudan prosecuted for genocide, when ironically, as one Sudanese expert noted, most Sudanese are "unclear about the concept of genocide, which so absent from the country's political culture".[24] But then nobody is going to ask Africans what they think.

Many Africans concede, if sometimes reluctantly, all or most of the above. Two arguments are made in reply, one serious and one silly. The silly argument is that "you want them to get away with it then!" This is not really an argument at all, but a kind of moral blackmail. Not only does it imply once more that the guilt of all accused (and many who have not

24 Nesrine Malik, The ICC's Blunder on Sudan, THE GUARDIAN, February 4, 2010.

yet been accused) can be assumed without a trial, it is also dangerous and misleading in the implicit alternative it proposes. People have been "getting away with it" for centuries, and will continue to do so. In domestic jurisdictions, crimes are not reported or not investigated, the wrong people are arrested or prosecuted, innocent people convicted and guilty people set free. And in every state through history, wealth, privilege and power have conferred at least a degree of impunity. Nothing is more dangerous and irresponsible than to suggest that anything different will result from vastly more complex and difficult investigations and trials by the ICC. Indeed, as we have seen, the result may well be to *increase* impunity by turning the ICC into a spectacle of Human Rights Theatre, whilst major powers continue to act as they wish.

A more sustainable argument consists of saying that Africans have supported the ICC, have signed and ratified the statute in large numbers and in some cases have asked the ICC to become involved. This is true as far as it goes but is not really the point. African states had effectively no influence on the preparations for the Rome Statute negotiations, or on those negotiations themselves. They also had little choice but to sign. Only large and powerful states (China, Russia), or states protected by them (Israel) could afford to stand aside. Not signing would have been unthinkable for African states, especially since major supporters of the ICC were also major donors. Moreover, few African states seem to have given much thought to the consequences of signature – discussions with government and military personnel some years later revealed widespread ignorance about what the Statute said, or even that it existed. And of course doing what foreign powers want, and manipulating it to your benefit, has been a necessary survival skill in Africa for a long time.

6.5 CONCLUSION

In the end, the question is whether Some Justice is better than No Justice. Often, the answer is yes. In some cases (as with ICTY) justice of a sort was done, without favour. In other cases (such as ICTR) artificial limits on the court's mandate severely undermined its credibility. Although the ICC is likely to represent Some Justice, it will do so in a very partial way. Imagine a country with a functioning judicial system, but where only petty criminals are ever prosecuted. Wealth and power provide almost total impunity, and finding a patron, or buying protection, is usually enough to ensure that you are never bothered by the police. Even if the prisons were full, few would regard such a system as effective or acceptable.

That is the risk with the ICC, and recognition of that fact may lie behind the hostility of African states to the indictment of President Bashir. Beyond the specific details of the case, there is a much more important issue of Africa's place in the international system of which the ICC is part, and its treatment in comparison with other regions. In effect, a shot has been fired across the bows of the West, and of its concept of the ICC as mainly Human Rights Theatre for Africans. If this resistance is not successful, then behind a façade of universal justice, the ICC may become simply a place to try Africans, as well as a way of keeping Africans in their place.

7 Is the International Criminal Court Targeting Africa?

*Reflections on the Enforcement of International Criminal Law in Africa**

Ntombizozuko Dyani

7.1 Introduction

Not only was Africa seen as a dark continent because of its history of colonialism, but also as a hopeless case even after independence from the colonial masters over 50 years ago because of the ongoing conflicts.[1] Indeed Africa is a complex continent; however recent history shows that Africa strives to be seen as progressive as other continents. Hence, it has been seen as a leader with most signatures and ratifications when it comes to the Rome Statute establishing the International Criminal Court (the ICC).[2] However, lately there has been a tension between African Union (AU) and the ICC, with the latter being accused of targeting Africans in its cases.[3] To date, three African states parties to the Rome

---

* The chapter forms part of the thesis submitted in partial fulfilment for the SJD degree at the University of Wisconsin-Madison, USA. This publication was made possible (in part) by a grant from the Carnegie Corporation of New York. The statements made and views expressed are, however, solely the responsibility of the author.

1 See Martin Meredith, The State Of Africa: A History Of Fifty Years Of Independence 681 (2005), where he observes that in reality fifty years after the beginning of the independence era, Africa's prospects are bleaker than ever before. Already the world's poorest region, it is falling behind all other regions of the world.

2 The Rome Statute was adopted by delegates from around the world gathered at the Food and Agriculture Organization building at a UN Conference of Plenipotentiaries on Establishment of an International Criminal Court, Rome, Italy, June 15–July 17, 1998. See Philippe Q. C. Kirsch & Darryl Robinson, *Reaching Agreement at the Rome Conference, in* The Rome Statute of the International Court: A Commentary 1 (Antonio Cassese, Paola Gaeta & John RWD Jones eds., 2002). As of 22 June 2011, 116 countries are States Parties to the Rome Statute of the ICC. Out of them 32 are African States, 15 are Asian States, 18 are from Eastern Europe, 26 are from Latin America and the Caribbean, and 25 are from Western Europe and other States. See <www.icc-cpi.int/Menus/ASP/states+parties> (Accessed August 20, 2011).

3 African Union (AU) Commissioner Jean Ping was reported to have told reporters that the ICC is 'discriminatory' and only go after the crimes committed in Africa, without seeing, those that were committed by the Western powers in places like Iraq, Afghanistan and Pakistan. See *African Union rejects Gaddafi Arrest Warrant*, BBC News Update, June 27, 2011. Available at: <www.bbcnewsupdate.com/african-union-rejects-gaddafi-arrest-warrant.html> (Accessed August 29, 2011). Also See the AU Assembly Decision on the Situation in Libya, Assembly/AU/Dec. 385 (XVII), where the Assembly notes "that the warrant of arrest ...

Statute – Uganda,[4] the Democratic Republic of Congo (the DRC)[5] and the Central African Republic[6] – have referred situations in their territories to the ICC; the United Nations (UN) Security Council has referred two situations involving non state parties to the Rome Statute – Sudan[7] and Libya;[8] and the Prosecutor has initiated an investigation into Kenya, a state party to the Rome Statute.[9] These are the only cases that are currently before the

---

seriously complicates the efforts aimed at finding a negotiated political solution to the crisis in Libya" and decides that member states "shall not cooperate in the execution of the arrest warrant". Also see the AU Assembly Decision on the Meeting of African States Parties to the Rome Statute of the ICC, Assembly/AU/ Dec. 245 (XIII) July 2009, where the AU Assembly decided not to cooperate with the ICC in the execution of the arrest warrant issued against President Al Bashir of Sudan. On the arrest warrant Mustafa Osman Ismail, an adviser to al-Bashir was quoted as saying "They do not want Sudan ... to become stable," "[t]he court is only one mechanism of neo-colonialist policy used by the West against free and independent countries." See Al Jazeera, *Mixed reaction to Bashir warrant*, March 5, 2009. Available at: <http://english.aljazeera.net/news/africa/2009/03/2009357272395326.html> (Accessed August 29, 2011). See also, Dire Tladi, *The African Union and the International Criminal Court: The battle for the Soul of International Law*, 34 SOUTH AFRICAN YEARBOOK OF INTERNATIONAL LAW 57 (2009), discussing the AU's decision not to cooperate with the ICC after the latter issued an arrest warrant against Al Bashir.

4 ICC Press Statements, President of Uganda refers situation concerning the Lord's Resistance Army (LRA) to the ICC, ICC-20040129-44, (January 29, 2004). Currently, the case of *The Prosecutor v. Joseph Kony, Vincent Otti, Okot Odhiambo and Dominic Ongwen* is being heard before the Pre-Trial Chamber II. In this case, five warrants of arrest have been issued against [the] five top-members of the Lord's Resistance Army (LRA). Following the confirmation of the death of Mr Lukwiya, the proceedings against him have been terminated. The four remaining suspects are still at large. Available at <www.icc-cpi.int/Menus/ICC/Situations+and+Cases> (Accessed September 22, 2011).

5 ICC Press Statements, Prosecutor receives referral of the situation in the Democratic Republic of Congo, ICC-OTP-20040419-50, (April 19, 2004). Currently, four cases are being heard before the relevant Chambers on the situation in the DRC: *The Prosecutor v. Thomas Lubanga Dyilo*; *The Prosecutor v. Bosco Ntaganda*; *The Prosecutor v. Germain Katanga and Mathieu Ngudjolo Chui*, and *The Prosecutor v. Callixte Mbarushimana*. Two cases are at the pre-trial stage. The proceedings against Thomas Lubanga Dyilo as well as Katanga and Ngudjolo Chui are at the trial stage. The accused, Thomas Lubanga Dyilo, Germain Katanga, Mathieu Ngudjolo Chui, and Callixte Mbarushimana are currently in the custody of the ICC. The suspect Bosco Ntaganda remains at large. See ICC website, *supra* note 4.

6 ICC Press Release, Prosecutor Receives Referral Concerning Central African Republic, ICC-OTP-20050107-86, (January 7, 2005). Currently, the case *The Prosecutor v. Jean-Pierre Bemba Gombo* is at the trial stage.

7 UN Security Council Resolution 1593, S/RES/1593 (2005), March 31, 2005. Currently, four cases are being heard before the Pre-Trial Chamber I: *The Prosecutor v. Ahmad Muhammad Harun ('Ahmad Harun') and Ali Muhammad Ali Abd-Al-Rahman ('Ali Kushayb')*; *The Prosecutor v. Omar Hassan Ahmad Al Bashir*; *The Prosecutor v. Bahar Idriss Abu Garda* and *The Prosecutor v. Abdallah Banda Abakaer Nourain and Saleh Mohammed Jerbo Jamus*. The suspect Bahr Idriss Abu Garda appeared voluntarily for the first time before Pre-Trial Chamber I on May 18, 2009. He is not in custody. The three other suspects remain at large.

8 UN Security Council Resolution 1970 (2011), February 26, 2011, S/RES/1970 (2011). On March 3, 2011 the ICC Prosecutor announced his decision to open an investigation in the situation in Libya, which is assigned by the Presidency to Pre-Trial Chamber I. Arrest warrants for President Gaddafi and two others were issued on June 27, 2011.

9 On November 6, 2009, the Presidency of the ICC issued a decision assigning the situation in the Republic of Kenya to Pre-Trial Chamber II. On March 31, 2010, the Pre-Trial Chamber II granted the Prosecutor authorization to open an investigation in the situation in Kenya. On March 8, 2011, Pre-Trial Chamber II, by majority, gave its decisions on the applications submitted by the Prosecutor to summon William Samoei Ruto, Henry Kiprono Kosgey, Joshua Arap Sang, as well as Francis Kirimi Muthaura, Uhuru Muigai Kenyatta and Mohammed Hussein Ali to appear before the Court on April 7, 2011. Available at: <www.icc-cpi.int/Menus/ICC/Situations+and+Cases> (Accessed September 22, 2011).

ICC and all of them come from Africa. One scholar has correctly observed that this tension arose after a warrant arrest was issued against an African head of state by the ICC.[10] Is the ICC targeting Africans? The answer is: it depends. Certain factors have to be taken into account before one can conclude whether or not Africa is being targeted by the ICC or if Africa is an easy target. For example, what is the significance of the fact that the crimes are under the jurisdiction of the ICC? And what obligations do (African) states have when it comes to these international crimes?

The ICC has jurisdiction over four categories of crimes, namely, genocide, crimes against humanity, war crimes and aggression.[11] Currently the ICC has jurisdiction over genocide, war crimes and crimes against humanity and not the crime of aggression.[12] The crimes under the jurisdiction of the ICC are crimes that shock human conscience and are most likely committed as some form of policy.[13] Therefore their prohibition is argued to have reached the status of customary international law (CIL) and the status

10 Richard Goldstone, *Does the ICC Target Africa*? 2 Equality of Arms Review 1, 3 (2009), where he notes that the African Union (the AU) "was notably silent as the ICC prosecuted erstwhile rebel leaders and political opponents of national governments, but now supports a deferral of proceedings against President Al Bashir". Also see Chris Black, *Some Reasons for Considering Why the ICC may not be considered as an Anti-African Institution*, African Yearbook of International Humanitarian Law 137 (2010), advancing several arguments against the proposition that the ICC is targeting Africans. For other scholars discussing the relationship between the ICC and Africa, see Chikeziri Sam Igwe, *The ICC's Favourite Customer: Africa and International Criminal Law*, 41 Comparative & International Law of South Africa 294 (2008), surveying the practice of international criminal law in Africa with reference to the ad hoc criminal tribunals in Africa and the implementation of the Rome Statute by several African States; Charles C. Jalloh, Dapo Akande & Max du Plessis, *Assessing the African Union's Concerns about Article 16 of the Rome Statute of the International Criminal Court*, 4 African Journal of Legal Studies 5 (2011), analyzing the merits of the AU's criticisms and its proposal for amendments of Art. 16 of the Rome Statute with reference to President Al Bashir's arrest warrant.

11 See Art. 5 of the Rome Statute, which states that "the jurisdiction of the Court shall be limited to the most serious crimes of concern to the international community as a whole".

12 The crime of aggression was not defined with other crimes at the adoption of the Rome Statute and it has since been defined and adopted in 2010 during the *Kampala Review Conference* and will come into force on January 17, 2017. It is included in Art. 8*bis* of the Rome Statute Amendment, see Resolution RC/Res.6 of June 11, 2010, adopted by consensus at the 13th Plenary Meeting on June 11, 2010. Depositary Notification CN 651.2010 Treaties. Available at <http://treaties.un.org> (Accessed November 29, 2010). Paragraph 3 of Art. 15*bis*, titled "Exercise of jurisdiction over the crime of aggression" states that the ICC "shall exercise jurisdiction over the crime of aggression in accordance with this article, subject to a decision to be taken after January 1, 2017 by the same majority of State Parties as is required for the adoption of an amendment to the Statute".

13 See para. 2 of the Preamble to the Rome Statute, which states that state parties are mindful that during this century millions of children, women and men have been victims of unimaginable atrocities that deeply shock the conscience of humanity. The definitions of these crimes are to be found in Arts. 6, 7, 8 and 8*bis* of the Rome Statute respectively. What is of importance is that the definitions include for example "acts committed with intent to destroy, in whole or in part, a national, ethnical, racial or religious Group" (Art. 6), "acts when committed as part of a widespread or systematic attack directed against a civilian population" (Art. 7), and "committed as part of a plan or policy or as part of a large-scale commission" (Art. 8).

of *jus cogens*.[14] Crimes that have acquired the status of *jus cogens* lead to consequences that include the duty to prosecute or extradite; to provide legal assistance; to eliminate statutes of limitations; to be considered as obligations *erga omnes*,[15] the consequence of which is that immunity cannot be granted.[16] It is also important to note that international crimes are committed by individuals[17] and therefore international law calls for

14 The doctrine of *jus cogens* in international law derives primarily from the Vienna Convention on the Law of Treaties, May 23, 1969, UN. Doc. A/CONF.39/27 (with annex) (hereinafter "Vienna Convention") which defines *jus cogens*, as '[a] peremptory norm of general international law accepted and recognized by international community of states as a whole from which no derogation is permitted and which can be modified only by a subsequent norm of a general international law having the same character'. *Id.* Art. 53. Also see: Cherif M. Bassiouni, *Universal Jurisdiction for International Crimes: Historical Perspectives and Contemporary Practice*, 42 VIRGINIA JOURNAL OF INTERNATIONAL LAW 81, 108 (2001), where he lists the *jus cogens* international crimes as piracy, slavery, war crimes, crimes against humanity, genocide, apartheid and torture; CHERIF M. BASSIOUNI & EDWARD M. WISE, AUT DEDERE AUT JUDICARE: THE DUTY TO EXTRADITE OR PROSECUTE UNDER INTERNATIONAL LAW 52 (1995), where they argue that a number of rules prohibiting international offences such as aggression, genocide, and serious breaches of international humanitarian law, are widely held to constitute rules of *jus cogens*; CHERIF M. BASSIOUNI, CRIMES AGAINST HUMANITY IN INTERNATIONAL CRIMINAL LAW 217 (1999), where he argues that since World War II, a number of international and regional instruments along with numerous United Nations resolutions reaffirm and provide support for the assertion that the protected interests whose violations are criminalized in crimes against humanity have become *jus cogens*; THEODORE MERON, WAR CRIMES LAW COMES OF AGE 233(1998), where he argues that the core prohibitions of crimes against humanity and the crime of genocide constitutes *jus cogens* norms; and Cherif M. Bassiouni, *Accountability for International Crime and Serious Violations of Fundamental Human Rights: Searching for Peace and Achieving Justice: The Need for Accountability*, 59 LAW & CONTEMPORARY LAW PROBLEMS 9, 17 (1996) (hereafter, , where he contends that crimes against humanity, genocide, war crimes and torture are international crimes that have risen to the level of *jus cogens*.

15 The doctrine of obligations *erga omnes* was introduced in the obiter dictum of the International Court of Justice (ICJ)in the *Barcelona Traction* case, where it was stated:

> An essential distinction should be drawn between the obligations of a State towards the international community as a whole, and those arising vis-à-vis another State in the field of diplomatic protection. By their very nature the former are the concern of all States. In view of the importance of the rights involved, all States can be held to have a legal interest in their protection; they are obligations *erga omnes*

Barcelona Traction Light and Power Co. Ltd (Belgium v. Spain), 1970 ICJ Rep. 3, 32 (Judgment of February 5).

16 Bassiouni, *Accountability for International Crime and Serious Violations of Fundamental Human Rights: Searching for Peace and Achieving Justice: The Need for Accountability supra* note 14, 17. Also see ANDRE DE HOOGH, OBLIGATIONS ERGA OMNES AND INTERNATIONAL CRIMES: A THEORETICAL INQUIRY INTO THE IMPLEMENTATION AND ENFORCEMENT OF THE INTERNATIONAL RESPONSIBILITY 45-46 (1996). THEODORE MERON, HUMAN RIGHTS AND HUMANITARIAN NORMS AS CUSTOMARY LAW 192 (1989), arguing that the opinion of the ICJ contains "an indication that the court did not intend to bestow *erga omnes* character upon all human rights, but only on rights which have matured into customary or general law of the nations"; and Kenneth C. Randall, *Universal Jurisdiction Under International Law*, 66 TEXAS LAW REVIEW 785, 830 (1988), where he argues that while authoritative list of obligations *erga omnes* and *jus cogens* norms do not exist, any such list likely would include the norms against hijacking, hostage taking, crimes against internationally protected persons, *apartheid*, and torture.

17 Diane F. Orentlicher, *Settling Accounts: The Duty to Prosecute Human Rights Violations of a Prior Regime*, 100 YALE LAW JOURNAL 2537, 2552 (1991), observing that although international law generally establishes rights and duties between and among states, international criminal law imposes obligations on individuals making them liable to criminal punishment.

individual criminal responsibility.[18] It follows therefore that states have a legal duty to prosecute individuals that are accused of having committed these crimes.

In this chapter I attempt to answer the question of whether or not the ICC is targeting Africans. I do not claim that I have all the answers, however, I attempt to answer the following questions: What are the legal obligations of states under international law, and in particular, the Rome Statute with regards to the international crimes and the ICC? Is there a limitation to the jurisdiction of the ICC? Can the ICC issue an arrest warrant for an incumbent head of state and senior officials? If so, what effect does such arrest warrant have on the obligations of states in international law? In this section I have briefly dealt with the significance of the international crimes and the second section will deal with the duty of states to prosecute perpetrators of international crimes. In that section I also deal with the obligation of the states parties to the Rome Statute to implement the Statute in their respective jurisdiction in order to be able to prosecute perpetrators of the crimes. After all the primacy of prosecution of international crimes lies with the states and it is only if they are unable or unwilling to prosecute that the ICC will step in through the principle of complementarity. The principle of complementarity is therefore discussed in section three of this research. Section four and five then deal with instances where the ICC even though it has jurisdiction might be barred from prosecution either because of amnesties (section 4) or immunities (section 5). In section four I also deal with the issue of the deferral of prosecutions by the ICC at the request of the Security Council in instances of threat to international peace and security and consider whether the ICC might be barred from prosecution in cases of amnesties because of a deferral. I also touch upon the request of the AU to the Security Council for a deferral in the cases of Sudan and Libya. In section 5 I deal with immunities in cases of incumbent heads of state and consider whether or not the African states have an obligation to comply with the request to cooperate with the

18 The principle of individual criminal responsibility was established by Art. 6 of the Nuremberg Charter which states that "[t]he Tribunal established by the Agreement referred to in Art. 1 hereof for the trial and punishment of the major war criminals of the European Axis countries shall have the power to try and punish persons who, acting in the interests of the European Axis countries, whether as individuals or as members of organizations, committed any of the following crimes." And subsequent to that the International Military Tribunal (IMT) held that "crimes against humanity are committed by men, not by abstract entities, and only by punishing individuals who commit such crimes can the provisions of international law be enforced". See (1947) I *Trial of the Major War Criminals before the International Military Tribunal* 171, 223 as quoted in Cherif M. Bassiouni, Crimes Against Humanity in International Criminal Law, *supra* note 14 at 370. Also see Art. 49 of the Geneva Convention I, Art. 50 of the Geneva Convention II, Art. 129 of the Geneva Convention III and Art. 149 of the Geneva Convention IV, which respectively provide that each contracting state must ensure that its legislation provides effective penal sanctions for persons 'alleged to have committed, or to have ordered to be committed, such grave breaches' defined in the Conventions; Art. 7 of the ICTY Statute; Art. 6 of the ICTR, Art. 6 of the SCSL and Art. 25 of the Rome Statute – which provides that a person who commits a crime within the jurisdiction of the Court "shall be individually responsible for punishment".

ICC in arresting and surrendering President Al Bashir and President Muammar Gaddafi to face prosecutions before the ICC. Finally I conclude by answering the question whether or not the ICC is targeting Africans.

7.2 The Duty to Prosecute or Extradite Perpetrators of International Crimes

International law imposes a duty on every state to prosecute or extradite the perpetrators of international crimes to other states that may be ready and willing to prosecute them, under the *aut dedere aut judicare* principle.[19] This duty flows from treaties and CIL. The establishment and operations since the beginning of the 90s of several international criminal tribunals such as the International Criminal Tribunals for the former Yugoslavia[20] and Rwanda[21] and the Special Court for Sierra Leone,[22] amongst others, is argued as evidence of an international resolve to ensure that those most responsible for core international crimes do not escape punishment.[23] A number of activities of the UN and other intergovernmental organizations reinforce the view that the prosecutions and punishment of international crimes are duties of states under customary law.[24] Furthermore, decisions of international and national courts support that the duty to prosecute and punish

19 Bassiouni & Wise, *supra* note 14, at 3, arguing that the expression *aut dedere aut judicare* is an obligation which requires a state that has hold of someone accused of committing a crime of international concern either to extradite the offender to another state which is prepared to try him or to take steps to have him prosecuted before its own courts.

20 The International Criminal Tribunal for the Former Yugoslavia (ICTY) was established to prosecute "Persons Responsible for Serious Violations of International Humanitarian Law Committed in the Territory of the Former Yugoslavia since 1991", S.C. Res. 827 (May 25, 1993). The Statute of the ICTY is contained in UN. Doc. S/25704, Annex (May 3, 1993).

21 The ICTR was established for the "Prosecution of Persons Responsible for Genocide and Other Serious Violations of International Humanitarian Law Committed in the Territory of Rwanda and Rwandan Citizens responsible for Genocide and other Violations in the Territory of Neighboring States, between January 1, 1994 and December 31, 1994", SC Res.955 (November 8, 1994). The Statute of the ICTR is attached to SC Res. 955 as an Annex.

22 The SCSL was set up jointly by the Government of Sierra Leone and the United Nations pursuant to Security Council Resolution 1315 (2000) of 14 August 2000. It is mandated to try those who bear the greatest responsibility for serious violations of international humanitarian law and Sierra Leonean law committed in the territory of Sierra Leone since 30 November 1996.

23 Ken Obura, *Duty to Prosecute International Crimes under International Law*, in PROSECUTING INTERNATIONAL CRIMES IN AFRICA 11, 24 (Chacha Murungu & Japhet Blegon eds., 2011).

24 For example, reports prepared by Special Rapporteurs, Special Representatives and Working Groups appointed by the Commission on Human Rights of the United Nations to report on human rights conditions in particular countries or on particular types of Human Rights violations have repeatedly condemned government's failure to punish torture, disappears and extra-legal executions. See Orentlicher, *supra* note 17 at 2583. Also see Meron, *supra* note 16 at 92, arguing that "the repetition of certain norms in many human rights instruments is [in] itself an important articulation of state practice".

international crimes is part of CIL.[25] Even for those states who might be persistent objectors to the crystallization of a norm to have reached the status of CIL,[26] there are several treaties that require the investigation, prosecution and subsequent punishment of perpetrators of international crimes.[27]

Furthermore, the Rome Statute states in its preamble that

> Recognizing that such grave crimes threaten the peace, security and well-being of the world, Affirming that the most serious crimes of concern to the international community as a whole must not go unpunished and that their effective prosecution must be ensured by taking measures at the national level and by enhancing international cooperation, Determined to put an end to impunity for the perpetrators of these crimes and thus contribute to the prevention of such crimes, Recalling that it is the duty of every State to exercise its criminal jurisdiction over those responsible for international crimes.[28]

From this, it follows that the state has two choices: to prosecute perpetrators of international crimes domestically or to hand them over to the ICC through the principle of complementarity. In order to be able to prosecute perpetrators of international crimes states need to have an effective legal system. This means that they need to have a law in place that allows

25 See for example *S v. Basson* 2005 (1) SA 171 (CC), para 37, stating that the international law obliges states to prosecute and punish crimes against humanity and war crimes. The international criminal tribunals for the former Yugoslavia and Rwanda have, respectively, also prosecuted and convicted individuals for crimes against humanity, war crimes and genocide.

26 On the persistent objector see Iain Brownlie, Principles of Public International Law 11-12 (7th ed., 2008) 11-12.

27 For example see the Geneva Conventions of August 12, 1949: Art. 50 of the Geneva Convention for the Amelioration of the Condition of the Wounded and Sick in Armed Forces in the Field (Geneva Convention I), Art. 51 of the Geneva Convention for the Amelioration of the Condition of the Wounded, Sick, and Shipwrecked Members of the Armed Forces at Sea (Geneva Convention II), Art. 130 of the Geneva Convention Relative to the Treatment of Prisoners of War (Geneva Convention III), and Art. 147 of the Geneva Convention Relative to the Protection of Civilian Persons in Time of War (Geneva Convention IV); the Protocols Additional to the Geneva Conventions of December 12, 1977: Art. 4 of Protocol I Relating to the Protection of Victims of International Armed Conflicts, and Arts. 11, 85, and 86 of Protocol II Relating to the Protection of Victims of Non-International Armed Conflicts; Art. IV of the Genocide Convention of 1948; Art. 4 of the Convention Against Torture and Other Cruel, Inhuman, or Degrading Treatment or Punishment (the Torture Convention); Art. 6 of the Slavery Convention of 1926; Arts. 1 and 2 of the International Convention on the Suppression and Punishment of the Crime of Apartheid of 1949; and Art. 4 (2) (b) and (e) of the Protocol on the Rights of Women in Africa. Treaties such as the Covenant on Civil and Political Rights of 1966 are silent about a duty to prosecute or to punish violations of the rights they ensure. But authoritative interpretations of these treaties make it clear that a state party fails in its duty to ensure the cluster of rights protecting physical integrity if it does not investigate violations and seek to punish those who are responsible. See Orentlicher, *supra* note 17, at 255.

28 Preamble to the Rome Statute, paras 3-6.

for them to prosecute. The first step for states party to the Rome Statute is to domesticate the Rome Statute. This in line with the principle of *pacta sunt servanda*,[29] which requires not only that states implement what has been provided for by the rule imposing an obligation, but also that they refrain from acts that could defeat the object and purpose of such a rule.[30] Simply put, a state that is a party to a treaty is bound to carry out the duties established by that treaty.[31] This legal obligation continues even if the government of the state changes or if it currently is not disposed to fulfilling the requirements of the treaty.[32] The Permanent Court of Justice articulated that 'a state which has contracted valid international obligations is bound to make in its legislation such modifications as may be necessary to ensure the fulfillment of the obligations undertaken'.[33] As the facts show, more than half of the African States have ratified the Rome Statute[34] and therefore it is expected of them to implement the Rome Statute by incorporating its provisions into their domestic laws.

7.3 The Complementarity Principle

In paragraph 6 of the preamble to the Rome Statute state parties recall that 'it is the duty of every State to exercise its criminal jurisdiction over those responsible for international crimes', and states also emphasize that the ICC 'shall be complementary to national criminal jurisdiction'.[35] Further to that Article 1 of the Rome Statute reinforces that primacy will be given to national courts to deal with international crimes under the jurisdiction of the ICC. Article 17 of the Rome Statute goes further and state that

1. Having regard to paragraph 10 of the Preamble and article 1, the Court shall determine that a case is inadmissible where:
   (a) The case has been investigated by a State which has jurisdiction over it and the State has decided not to prosecute the person concerned, unless the State is unwilling or unable genuinely to carry out the investigation or prosecution;

29 See Art. 26 of the Vienna Convention on the Law of Treaties of 1969, which states that states that 'every treaty in force is binding upon the parties to it and must be performed in good faith'.

30 See I. Lukashik, *New Thinking by Soviet Scholars: The Principle Pacta Sunt Servanda and the Nature of Obligation under International Law*, 83 American Journal of International Law 513, 515 (1989).

31 See Jonathan I. Charney, *Universal International Law*, 87 American Journal of International Law 529, 534 (1993).

32 Once a state voluntarily signs and ratifies a treaty, the state is bound by the provisions of such treaty. This rule is formulated in Art. 27 of the Vienna Convention, which states "a party may not invoke the provisions of its internal law as justification for its failure to perform a treaty".

33 *Exchange of Greek and Turkish Populations*, Advisory Opinion, 1925 P.C.I.J. (ser. B) No. 10 (Feb. 21) para. 52. Also see Charney, see note 50, at 534.

34 Currently 32 African States ratified the Rome Statute with Tunisia being the latest state to do so on June 21, 2011. See <www.icc-cpi.int/Menus/ASP/States+Parties/African%20States> (Accessed September 21, 2011).

35 Para. 10 of the Preamble to the Rome Statute.

(b) The case has been investigated by a State which has jurisdiction over it and the State has decided not to prosecute the person concerned, unless the decision resulted from the unwillingness or inability of the State genuinely to prosecute.
(c) The person concerned has already been tried for conduct which is the subject of the complaint, and a trial by the Court is not permitted under article 20, paragraph 3;
(d) The case is not of sufficient gravity to justify further action by the Court.

Looking at the relevant provisions of the Rome Statute, the principle of complementarity rests on two basic pillars: respect for the primary jurisdiction of states; and efficiency and effectiveness.[36] This exercise is entirely dependent on the ICC as Article 19(1) of the Rome Statute provides that the ICC 'shall satisfy itself that it has jurisdiction in any case brought before it' and 'may, on its own motion, determine the admissibility of a case in accordance with article 17'. Therefore, the acceptance of a situation will depend entirely on the ICC irrespective of who referred the situation. I discuss these terms below.

The Rome Statute states that 'unwillingness' is determined by looking at the following:
(a) The proceedings were or are being undertaken or the national decision was made for the purpose of shielding the person concerned from criminal responsibility for crimes within the jurisdiction of the Court referred to in article 5;
(b) There has been an unjustified delay in the proceedings which in the circumstances is inconsistent with an intent to bring the person concerned to justice;
(c) The proceedings were not or are not being conducted independently or impartially, and they were or are being conducted in a manner which, in the circumstances, is inconsistent with an intent to bring the person concerned to justice.[37]

---

36 Nidal Jurdi, *Some Lessons on Complementarity for the International Criminal Court Review Conference*, 34 South African Yearbook of International Law, 28, 29 (2009). On the issue of complementarity and the difficulties faced by the ICC, see generally, Mohammed M. El-Zeidy, *The Ugandan Government Triggers the First Test of the Complementarity Principle: An Assessment of the First State's Party Referral to the ICC*, 5 International Criminal Law Review 83 (2005); P. Gaeta, *Is the Practice of "Self-Referrals" a Sound Start for the ICC?* 2 Journal of International Criminal Justice 1949 (2004); Claus Kress, *"Self-Referral" and 'Waivers' of Complementarity*, 2 Journal of International Criminal Justice 944 (2004); Nidal Nabil Jurdi, *The Prosecutorial Interpretation of the Complementarity Principle: Does it Really Contribute to Ending Impunity on the National Level?* 10 International Criminal Law Review 73 (2010); William A. Schabas, *Prosecutorial Discretion v. Judicial Activism*, 6 Journal of International Criminal Justice 731 (2008); William A. Schabas, *Complementarity in Practice: Some Uncomplimentarity Thoughts*, 19 Criminal Law Forum 5, 12 (2009); Antonio Cassese, *Is the ICC Still Having Teething Problems?* 4 Journal of International Criminal Justice 434 (2006); and Mahnoushi Arsanjani & Michael W. Reisman, *The Law-in-Action of the International Criminal Court*, 99 American Journal of International Law 385 (2005).

37 See Art. 17(2)(a)-(c).

If one of the criteria is satisfied, then the ICC will assume jurisdiction. The Rome Statute does not define any of the criteria; therefore it depends on the ICC to decide. This paragraph is argued to set 'too high a threshold for the ICC in order to assume jurisdiction'.[38] As the ICC has not yet dealt with this criterion one of the very few writers who have written about it argues that 'shielding the person from criminal responsibility' could mean for example, bypassing the normal criminal procedures by appointing as special investigator who is politically aligned with persons close to the accused; and the transfer of a case to secret tribunals (which could be against the principles of due process).[39] On the other hand, the second criterion is argued to include 'national proceedings which exceed the usual national practice and which are not convincingly explained', whereas, the third criterion is said to 'relate to the independence and impartiality of the proceedings'.[40] In this regard the argument is that the ICC 'must be satisfied that not only that there are doubts concerning the impartiality and independence of any proceedings, but that these doubts led the ICC to believe that the proceedings are being conducted in a manner inconsistent with bringing the person to justice'.[41]

On the other hand, in order to determine 'inability' in a particular case, the Rome Statute requires the ICC to consider whether, due to a total or substantial collapse or unavailability of its national judicial system, the state is unable to obtain the accused or the necessary evidence and testimony or otherwise unable to carry out its proceedings.[42] The purpose of including inability in the Rome Statute was to address a situation where there has been a collapse of the institutions of the country, including its judicial system. The State may be willing to prosecute but the ability to do so does not exist.[43] Therefore, the Rome Statute addresses two types of collapse: the total collapse and substantial collapse. In considering what constitutes total or substantial collapse, it is argued that the Court must consider whether at least one of the following factors exists: (1) the state is unable to obtain the accused; (2) the state is unable to obtain the necessary evidence and testimony; or (3) the state is unable to otherwise carry out its proceedings.[44]

However, there is a debate on the issue of complementarity – whether it is a two-prong or three-prong test. Some legal scholars argue that when it comes to the issue of

---

38 John T. Holmes, *Complementarity: National Courts versus the ICC*, *in* THE ROME STATUTE OF THE INTERNATIONAL CRIMINAL COURT: A COMMENTARY 667, 675 (Antonio Cassese, Paola Gaeta & John RWD Jones eds., 2002).

39 *Id.* 675-676.

40 *Id.* 676.

41 *Id.*

42 See Art. 17(3).

43 Holmes, *supra* note 38, at 677.

44 *Id.* at 678.

complementarity, the ICC has jurisdiction when a state is either unwilling or unable to investigate or prosecute a person alleged to have committed an international crime under the Rome Statute.[45] These legal scholars rely on the expressed terms in the Rome Statute – 'unwilling' or 'unable' to investigate or to prosecute as provided in Article 17 of the Rome Statute. On the other hand, there are some scholars who argue that there is a third scenario –'inaction' or 'inactivity' – which also gives the ICC jurisdiction to prosecute.[46] Inaction is not expressly mentioned in the Rome Statute. The Office of the Prosecutor (the OTP), in its informal expert paper on the principle of complementarity,[47] observes that although it is common to emphasize the 'unwilling' or 'unable' test in Article 17, the article in fact deals with three logically distinct circumstances. The office of the Prosecutor explains that in that the inaction scenario, none of the alternatives of Article 17(1)(a)-(c) are satisfied and there is no impediment to admissibility. Thus, there is no need to examine the factors of unwillingness or inability; the case is simply admissible in terms of Article 17.[48] Therefore, inaction refers to the most straightforward scenario where no state has initiated any investigation. In such a scenario, none of the alternatives of Article 17 are satisfied and there is no impediment to admissibility. Thus, there is no need to examine the factors of unwillingness or inability – the case is simply admissible under the clear terms of Article 17.[49] This interpretation of Article 17 of the Rome Statute has been criticized.[50] It is argued that while 'inaction' is consistent with Article 17, it has led to outcomes that are inconsistent with the intention of the drafters in adopting the complementarity mechanism, *i.e.*, keeping the ICC as a court of last resort while encouraging national jurisdiction to exercise their primary duty to prosecute.[51]

In spite of these criticisms, the inaction scenario has been confirmed by the Appeals Chamber of the ICC in *Katanga*, where it said that inactivity is a basis for the intervention of the ICC.[52] The Appeals Chamber therefore held that in the case of inaction, the

45 For example, Schabas, *supra* note 36.

46 Darryl Robinson, *The Mysteriousness of Complementarity*, 21 Criminal Law Forum 67 (2010).

47 ICC Office of the Prosecutor *Informal Expert Paper: The Principle of Complementarity in Practice* (2003). Available at <www.icc-cpi.int/iccdocs/doc/doc654724.PDF> (Accessed July 2, 2011).

48 *Id.* at 7.

49 See *Informal Expert Paper* 7 at para. 18.

50 See for example, Schabas, *supra* note 36; Arsanjani & Reisman, *supra* note 36; Jurdi 'The Prosecutorial Interpretation of the Complementarity Principle: Schabas, *supra* note 36; and Ada Y. Sheng, *Analyzing the International Criminal Court Complementarity Principle Through a Federal Court Lens* (2006), Paper 1249, available at <http://law.bepress.com/expresso/eps/1249> (Accessed May 20, 2011). For a different view see Robinson, *supra* note 46.

51 Nidal Jurdi, *Some Lessons on complementarity for the International Criminal Court Review Conference*, 34 South African Yearbook of International Law 28, 30 (2009).

52 *The Prosecutor v. Germain Katanga and Mathieu Ngudjolo Chui* (ICC-01/04-01/07) *Reasons for the Oral decision on the Motion Challenging the Admissibility of the Case* (September 25, 2009). Also see *The Prosecutor v. Lubanga* (ICC-01-04-01/06-8) Decision on the Prosecutor's Application for a Warrant of Arrest, Pre-Trial Chamber I, February 10, 2006.

question of unwillingness or inability does not arise. The Appeals Chamber stressed that the complementarity principle as enshrined in the Rome Statute strikes a balance between safeguarding the primacy of domestic proceedings vis-à-vis the ICC on the one hand, and the goal of the Rome Statute to put an end to impunity on the other hand. Therefore, if states do not or cannot investigate and where necessary prosecute, the ICC must be able to step in.[53] I believe that there was no need for the Appeals Chamber to stretch Article 17 of the Rome Statute by coining the third scenario 'inaction' the ICC can assume jurisdiction on the basis of unwillingness of the state to prosecute if it was concerned with striking the balance between safeguarding the primacy of domestic proceedings vis-à-vis the ICC.[54]

The law as is stands, however, is that the ICC will assume jurisdiction for unwillingness, inability and inaction on the part of the states. It is therefore up to the states to ensure that when an issue of investigating and subsequently prosecuting international crimes arises, they have the primacy to do so. In order to be able to deal with the crimes in question states need to have effective legal systems in place. This starts with the implementation of the Rome Statute which can be done by domesticating the Statute. If not, the ICC will take over the prosecutions.

Now that I have discussed the basis of the ICC assuming jurisdiction of the international crimes through the principle of complementarity, what could bar the ICC from prosecuting?

7.4 Amnesties and the ICC

Black's Law Dictionary defines amnesty as 'an act of forgiveness that a sovereign state grants to individuals who committed offensive acts'.[55] Amnesties for international crimes come into being mainly when states are going through periods of transition, often from war to peace, and extreme political upheaval, for example, the handing over of power from military regimes to democratic civilian governments.[56] These amnesties usually take the form of legislative or constitutional acts of states, are contained in treaties or political agreements, or may be declared as an exercise of the executive power. Most states have the possibility of granting amnesties within the framework of their constitutions for crimes committed in their national legal orders. The granting of amnesty for international crimes

53 *The Prosecutor v. Germain Katanga and Mathieu Ngudjolo Chui* (ICC-01/04-01/07) Reasons for the Oral decision on the Motion Challenging the Admissibility of the Case (September 25, 2009) para. 78.

54 See also, Schabas, *supra* note 36, at 757, arguing that this is an 'activist' interpretation of Art. 17 of the Rome Statute.

55 Bryan A. Garner, Black's Law Dictionary 99 (9th ed. 2009).

56 Yasmin Naqvi, *Amnesty for War Crimes: Defining the limits of International Recognition*, 85 International Review of the Red Cross, 583, 586 (2003).

has a long and varied history.[57] Amnesties have long been employed by governments whether to end civil wars, to negotiate peace or for political transitions.[58]

What kind of amnesty are we considering here? Are we talking about blanket amnesty or conditional amnesty? Blanket amnesty is when alleged perpetrators of crimes are granted unconditional or blanket amnesty for crimes committed.[59] Conditional amnesty, on the other hand, is often coupled with a truth and reconciliation commission where an alleged perpetrator reveals all that happened before amnesty can be granted to him or her.[60] Legal scholars argue that reconciliation between the international demand for prosecution of international crimes and the national appeal for political compromise involving amnesty can best be achieved by drawing a distinction between permissible and impermissible amnesties, and by limiting international recognition to the former.[61] Richard Goldstone believes that the works of truth commissions or judicial inquiries share with criminal prosecutions the ability to bring significant satisfaction to victims.[62] He also acknowledges that the cost of the TRC is that many victims of worst human rights abuses will be denied full justice as they will have to bear the pain of seeing the perpetrators walk away free of punishment.[63] However, he also realizes that the decision to opt for a TRC is itself an important compromise. Using the example of South Africa, he argues that if the African National Congress

57 For the history of national amnesties granted for international crimes see Andreas O'shea, Amnesty For Crime in International Law Practice 5-33(2002); and Yasmin Q. Naqvi, Impediments to Exercising Jurisdiction over International Crimes 76-85 (2010).

58 For example in Zimbabwe (Amnesty Ordinance 3 of 1979 and the Amnesty (General Pardon) Ordinance 12 of 1980; Clemency Order No. 1 of 1988 and 2000), Lesotho (Amnesty Act No. 7 of 1980); Uganda (Amnesty Act of 2000); and South Africa (Promotion of National Unity and Reconciliation Act 34 of 1995). Also See Naqvi, *id.* at 78-79.

59 This was done in Chile where Augusto Pinochet was granted amnesty by Amnesty Law 2191, a 1978 military decree that granted full and unconditional amnesty for crimes committed between 1973 and 1978 and which was upheld by the Supreme Court in 1990. See Naqvi, *supra* note 57, at 79.

60 John Dugard, *Dealing with Crimes of a Past Regime. Is Amnesty Still an Option?* 12 Leiden Journal of International Law 1001(1999), where he states that from time immemorial amnesty has been employed as a means of promoting a political settlement and advancing reconciliation in societies that have emerged from repression. An example of an amnesty which is argued to be permissible is that of the South African Truth and Reconciliation Commission. The South African Truth Commission was established by the Promotion of National Unity and Reconciliation Act 34 of 1995 which was aimed at reconciling the South Africans after the apartheid regime. The Truth and Reconciliation Commission had a dual task of compiling a complete picture of the human rights violations of the past and the facilitation of amnesty. The Amnesty Committee was to consider applications for and to grant amnesty if it was satisfied that the applicant has committed an act constituting gross human rights violations; made a full disclosure of all relevant facts and that the act to which the applicant relates was an act associated with a political objective. A person granted amnesty would not be criminally or civilly liable in respect of the act in question. The Amnesty Committee granted 849 amnesties and refused 5392 out of 7112 applications it received, see TRC 'Amnesty Hearings and Decisions'. Available at <www.justice.gov.za/trc/amntrans/index.htm> (Accessed August 23, 2011).

61 Dugard, *id.* at 1009.

62 Richard Goldstone, *Justice as a Tool for Peace-Making: Truth Commissions and International Criminal Tribunals,* 28 New York Journal of International Law and Politics 485, 491 (1995).

63 *Id.* at 493.

had insisted on Nuremberg style trials for the leaders of the former apartheid government, there would have been no peaceful transition. Further, if the former government had insisted on a blanket amnesty, then similarly the negotiations would have broken down. He is therefore, of the view that the TRC is a bridge from the old to the new. Professor John Dugard is also of the view that while (conditional) amnesties do not in principle bar the ICC or a State Party from exercising criminal jurisdiction over an individual who has been granted amnesty, the political reality is that in some instances it might be expedient or a requirement of justice not to push ahead with the prosecution of such a person.[64]

On the other hand, Antonio Cassese argues that if a court of another state having in custody persons accused of international crimes decides to prosecute them although in their national state they would benefit from an amnesty law, such court would not thereby act contrary to general international law, in particular the principle of respect for the sovereignty of other states.[65] Professor Bassiouni goes even further and argues that there must be prosecution for at least the four *jus cogens* crimes of genocide, crimes against humanity, war crimes and torture as there can be no impunity for such crimes.[66] He insists that

> [T]he implications of *jus cogens* are those of a duty and not of optional rights; otherwise *jus cogens* would not constitute a peremptory norm of international law. Consequently, these obligations are non-derogable in times of war as well as peace. Thus, recognizing certain international crimes as *jus cogens* carries with it the duty to prosecute or extradite, the non-applicability of statutes of limitation for such crimes, and universality of jurisdiction over such crimes irrespective of where they were committed, by whom (including Heads of State), against what category of victims, and irrespective of the context of their occurrence (peace or war). Above all, the characterization of certain crimes as *jus cogens* places upon the states the *obligatio erga omnes* not to grant impunity to the violators of such crimes.[67]

64 Dugard, *supra* note 60, at 1001. Also see Jeremy Sarkin, *The Necessity and Challenges of Establishing a Truth and Reconciliation Commission in Rwanda*, 21 HUMAN RIGHTS QUARTERLY 767, 767 (1999). Arguing that in countries emerging from the periods of great turmoil, particularly turmoil associated with gross human rights violations of human rights, the question of how to deal with the past has been a crucial part of the transformation process.

65 ANTONIO CASSESE, INTERNATIONAL CRIMINAL LAW 315 (2003).

66 Bassiouni, *Accountability for International Crime and Serious Violations of Fundamental Human Rights*, *supra* note 14, at 20; also see N. Roht-Arriaza, *State Responsibility to Investigate and Prosecute Grave Human Rights Violations in International Law*, 78 CALIFORNIA LAW REVIEW 449, 475 (1990).

67 Cherif M. Bassiouni, *International Crimes: Jus Cogens and Obligatio Erga Omnes*, 59 LAW & CONTEMPORARY PROBLEMS 63, 65-6 (1996). Also see other scholars who agree that international crimes should be prosecuted and punished pursuant to international law: Orentlicher, *supra* note 17; Michael Scarf *Swapping Amnesty for Peace*, 31 TEXAS INTERNATIONAL LAW JOURNAL 1 (1996); Roman Boed, *The Effect of a Domestic Amnesty*, 33 CORNELL INTERNATIONAL LAW JOURNAL 297 (2000); and Carla Edelenbos, Human Rights Violations: A Duty to Prosecute? 7 LEIDEN JOURNAL OF INTERNATIONAL LAW 5 (1994).

Therefore there is a strong view from legal scholars that states do not have the right to provide blanket amnesty to transgressors of *jus cogens* international crimes,[68] particularly leaders and senior executors.[69] Instead they have an obligation to see to it that all the legal consequences pertaining to these crimes are carried out in good faith.

Does international law recognize national amnesties granted by states for international crimes committed by the past regimes? Neither the language of criminal law treaties nor the general human rights law treaties requiring prosecution prohibit by their terms an amnesty granted to those accused of gross human rights violations.[70] More broadly, save for the Additional Protocol II, such endorsement is also absent in international humanitarian law.[71] There is no agreement between legal scholars as to whether or not customary international law prohibits amnesties in cases of international crimes. However most legal scholars agree that there is no consistency in state practice.[72]

68 Crimes against humanity, genocide, war crimes and torture are international crimes that have risen to the level of *jus cogens*. See Bassiouni, *Accountability for International Crime and Serious Violations of Fundamental Human Rights*, *supra* note 14, at 17.

69 Bassiouni, *Introduction to International Criminal Law*, *supra* note 14, at 129; Roht-Arriaza, *supra* note 66, at 475.

70 See Naomi Roht-Arriaza, *Special Problems of a Duty to Prosecute: Derogation, Amnesties, Statutes of Limitation and Superior Orders*, *in* Impunity and Human Rights in International Law and Practice 57 (Naomi Roht-Arriaza ed., 1995).

71 Art. 6(5) of the Additional Protocol II provides that '[a]t the end of hostilities, the authorities in power shall endeavor to grant the broadest possible amnesty to persons who have participated in the armed conflict, or those deprived of their liberty for reasons related to the armed conflict, whether they are interned or detained.' The International Committee of the Red Cross clarifies that:

> Art. 6(5) of Protocol II is the only and very limited equivalent in the law of non-international armed conflict of what is known in the law of international armed conflict as 'combatant immunity', *i.e.*, the fact that a combatant may not be punished for acts of hostility, including killing enemy combatants, as long as he respected international humanitarian law, and that he has to be repatriated at the end of active hostilities. In non-international armed conflicts, no such principle exists, and those who fight may be punished under national legislation, for the mere fact of having fought, even if they respected international humanitarian law. The '*traux preparatoires*' of [art.] 6(5) indicate that this provision aims at encouraging amnesty, *i.e.*, the sort of release at the end of hostilities. It does not aim at an amnesty for those having violated international humanitarian law.

Letter from Dr. Toni Pfanner, Head of the Legal Division, ICRC Headquarters, Geneva, quoted in Douglas Cassel, *Accountability for International Crime and Serious Violations of Human Rights: Lessons from the Americas: Guidelines for International Response to Amnesties for Atrocities*, 59 Law & Contemporary Problems 197, 218 (1996). See Roht-Arriaza, *supra* note 70, at 59.

72 For example see Dugard, *supra* note 60, at 102, arguing that it is doubtful whether international law has reached this stage as state practice hardly supports such rules. Modern history is replete with examples of cases in which successor regimes have granted amnesty to officials of the previous regime guilty of torture and crimes against humanity, rather than prosecute them. In many cases, notably that of South Africa, the UN has welcomed such a solution. Also see Ronald C. Slye, *The Legitimacy of Amnesties under International Law and General Principles of Anglo-American Law: Is a Legitimate Amnesty Possible?* 43 Virginia Journal of International Law 173, 177 (2002), arguing that international law and the domestic legal practice

There is also an increasing trend in international human rights bodies explicitly condemning amnesties for certain particularly grave offenses, even those granted by successor regimes. The Human Rights Committee has concluded, with respect to the prohibition of torture that amnesties are generally incompatible with the duty of states to investigate such acts; to guarantee freedom from such acts within their jurisdiction; and to ensure that they do not occur in the future.[73] It also confirmed its views that amnesties are incompatible with States' obligations under the ICCPR in a number of its communications.[74] A 1985 report on amnesty laws by a UN *Special Rapporteur* suggested that international crimes or crimes against humanity should not be subject to possible amnesty to avoid a situation in which 'the infringement of the 'human condition' is such that the right of oblivion may become a right of impunity'.[75] The Special Court for Sierra Leone has held that 'a state cannot sweep such crimes into oblivion and forgetfulness which other states have jurisdiction to prosecute by reason of the fact that the obligation to protect human dignity is a peremptory norm and has assumed the nature of obligations *erga omnes*'.[76] It is interesting to note that the Statute of the Special Court for Sierra Leone expressly states that 'an amnesty granted to any person falling within the jurisdiction of the Special Court in respect of the crimes referred to in Articles 2-4 of the present Statute shall not be a bar to prosecution'.[77]

It therefore seems that the shift in trend is to deny amnesty for international crimes. However, state practice suggests otherwise, and therefore the rule has not yet crystallized into CIL. The Rome Statute is also silent on amnesty. However, arguments are made that certain provisions of the Rome Statute can be interpreted in such a way that amnesty can be permissible to serve both the interests of peace and justice.[78] The ICC has not dealt with

---

of states at times permit and even –in some cases – require, amnesties. In contrast, see Daniel D. Ntanda Nsereko, *The Role of International Criminal Tribunals in the Promotion of Peace and Justice: The Case of the International Criminal Court*, 19 CRIMINAL LAW FORUM 373, 377-80 (2008), arguing that: "[f]rom the stand-point of customary international law, there already exists a respectable body of legal opinion to the effect that a state's right to grant amnesty does not extend to persons who are suspected of having committed crimes against the law of nations or *delicta juris gentium*."

73 Human Rights Committee, General Comment 20, Art. 7 (Forty-fourth session, 1992), Compilation of General Comments and General Recommendations Adopted by Human Rights Treaty Bodies, U.N. Doc. HRI/GEN/1/Rev.1 at 30 (1994).

74 Bassiouni, *supra* note 69, at 735.

75 Study on Amnesty Laws and their Role in the Safeguard and Promotion of Human Rights, *Preliminary Report by Louis Joinet, Special Rapporteur, UN Commission on for Human Rights*, UN Doc.E/CN.4/Sub.2/1985/16(1985).

76 *Prosecutor v. Kallon et al.*, Decision on Challenge to Jurisdiction: Lome Accord Amnesty, Case No. SCSL-2004-15-AR72(E), March 13, 2004.

77 Art. 10 of the SCSL Statute. The Statutes of the ICTY and the ICTR do not have similar provisions.

78 For example see Michael P. Scharf, *The Amnesty Exception to the Jurisdiction of the International Criminal Court*, 32 CORNELL INTERNATIONAL LAW JOURNAL 507 (1999), where he analyses certain provisions of the Rome Statute as possible exceptions to the jurisdiction of the ICC.

this question yet. However, the issue of deferral in terms of Article 16 of the Rome Statute needs further discussion to ascertain whether or not the ICC can refuse to hear a case where national amnesty was granted.

7.5 Amnesties and the UN Security Council Deferral in Terms of Article 16 of the Rome Statute

Article 16 of the Rome Statute provides '[n]o investigation or prosecution may be commenced or proceeded with under this Statute for a period of 12 months after the Security Council, in a resolution adopted under Chapter VII of the Charter of the United Nations, has requested the Court to that effect; that request may be renewed by the Council under the same conditions'. The Security Council's power to defer had been one of the thorniest issues in the negotiations leading to the adoption of the Rome Statute.[79] The history of Article 16 of the Rome Statute comes from the 1994 International Law Commission (ILC) draft which read:

> No prosecution may be commenced under this Statute arising from a situation which is being dealt with by the Security Council as a threat to or breach of the peace or an act of aggression under Chapter VII of the Charter, unless the Security Council otherwise decides.[80]

This draft was criticized because it was seen as the ILC viewing the Security Council as the gatekeeper of the ICC.[81] Because of the list of items 'being dealt with … as a threat or breach of the peace or an act of aggression under Chapter VII' on the agenda of the Security Council is more or less identical to the list of serious violations of international humanitarian law likely to attract the attention of an international prosecutor, the ILC provision would have had the effect of giving a veto on all potential prosecution.[82] As a result, Singapore produced a compromise proposal that subsequently became, with a few minor changes, the final version of Article 16 of the Rome Statute. Article 16 'attempted

---

79 Kirsch & Robinson, *supra* note 2, at 645.

80 Art. 23(3) of the Draft Statute of the International Criminal Court prepared by the ILC, Report of the International Law Commission on the Work of its Forty-Sixth Session, May 2-July 22, 1994, UN Doc. A/49/10, Chapter II.

81 William A. Schabas, *United States Hostility to the International Criminal Court: It's All about the Security Council* (2004) 15 European Journal of International Law 701, 715. Also see Yassin A. M'Boge, *In the Interests of Peace and the Interests of Justice: Security Council Deferrals as a Constructive Tool for Conflict Resolution, in* International Law & Armed Conflict: Challenges Of The 21st Century 363, 364-368 (Noëlle Quénivet & Shilan Shah-Davis eds., 2010), discussing the origins of the deferral power of the Security Council under Art. 16 of the Rome Statute.

82 Schabas, *id.*

to reconcile those who believed there was a legitimate role for some political interference in judicial proceedings, for example where delicate peace negotiations were being pursued and those who saw this as unacceptable'.[83]

It is important to note that on the issue of the arrests warrants issued against Presidents Al Bashir and Muammar Gaddafi by the ICC, the AU has, on numerous occasions, requested the Security Council to request the ICC, as per Article 16 of the Rome Statute, to defer the proceedings for a period of one year.[84] The Security Council has chosen to ignore these requests.[85] Even though these requests by the AU do not relate to amnesties, they still are important in this discussion because the Security Council can request the ICC to defer the proceedings in any matter that might threaten international peace and security.

In terms of Article 16 the Security Council has to act in accordance with its powers under Chapter VII of the UN Charter. Article 39 of the UN Charter provides that '[t]he Security Council shall determine the existence of any threat to peace, breach of peace, or act of aggression and shall make recommendations, or decide what measures shall be taken in accordance with Articles 41 and 42, to maintain or restore international peace and security'.[86] The Security Council has the legal authority to require the ICC to respect an amnesty if two requirements are met: (1) where the Security Council has determined the existence of a threat to the peace, a breach of the peace or an act of aggression under Article 39 of the UN Charter, and (2) where a resolution requesting the ICC's deferral is consistent with the purposes and principles of the UN with regard to maintaining international peace and security, resolving threatening situations in conformity with the principles of justice and international law, and promoting respect for human rights and fundamental freedoms under Article 24 of the UN Charter.[87] With reference to Chapter VII of the UN Charter,

83 Schabas, *supra* note 81at 716.

84 See the AU Decision on the Situation in Libya, Assembly/AU/Dec.385(XVII) and AU Assembly Decision on the Implementation of the Assembly Decisions on the ICC Doc.EX.CL/670(XIX), Assembly/AU/Dec.366(XVII), Malabo, Equatorial Guinea, where the AU stated that it "deeply regrets that the request by the AU to the UN Security Council to defer the proceedings initiated against President Bashir of the Sudan has neither been heard nor acted upon", (para. 9) It also requested the Security Council to activate the provisions of Art. 16 with a view to deferring the ICC process on Libya in the interests of justice as well as peace in the country.

85 *Id.*

86 Under Art. 41, the Security Council is empowered to use economic and diplomatic sanctions and to sever transportation and communication links in efforts to maintain or restore international peace and security. If the Security is of the view that such measures have been or will be inadequate to maintain or restore international peace and security, Art. 42 authorizes the Security Council to take such military action, as it considers necessary to achieve these ends.

87 Scharf, *supra* note 78, at 523. Art. 24 of the UN Charter states that:

1. In order to ensure prompt and effective action by the United Nations, its Members confer on the Security Council primary responsibility for the maintenance of international peace and security, and agree that in carrying out its duties under this responsibility the Security Council acts on their behalf.

Article 16 requires that (i) an affirmative of nine Security Council members, and (ii) the absence of individual vetoes from the five permanent members of the Security Council.[88]

Does Article 16 of the Rome Statute mean that there can be amnesty which will bar the ICC from exercising its jurisdiction for international crimes because of the deferral? It seems that in the interests of peace and security, Article 16 grants the Security Council a collective veto power to block investigations and prosecutions. However, it is important to note that a referral is for a period of 12 months subject to a renewal depending on the circumstances of each situation. After the deferral period ends, the ICC may resume the proceedings. Therefore, a deferral in terms of Article 16 of the Rome Statute does not mean that a perpetrator of international crimes can never be prosecuted by the ICC. Furthermore, it must be recalled that the ICC has the power to determine its own jurisdiction in terms of the Rome Statute.[89] It is therefore possible that the ICC would not necessarily be compelled by a Security Council resolution to terminate an investigation or prosecution were it to find that an amnesty contravenes international law. Besides, if we argue that the international crimes under the jurisdiction of the ICC are so serious that they shock human conscience and that their prohibition have acquired the status of *jus cogens* it will be difficult for the ICC to refrain from prosecution once the case find its way there.

On the other hand, there are cases where the interests of international peace and security will require the Security Council to act. In this instance, an argument that can be advanced is that issues of amnesty and should be left in the hands of international organizations such as the Security Council not the ICC. The ICC was established to prosecute international crimes and nothing else.[90] In fact, the Office of the Prosecutor has explained

2. In discharging these duties the Security Council shall act in accordance with the Purposes and Principles of the United Nations. The specific powers granted to the Security Council for the discharge of these duties are laid down in Chapters VI, VII, VIII, and XII.
3. The Security Council shall submit annual and, when necessary, special reports to the General Assembly for its consideration.

88 See Art. 27 of the UN Charter which states
1. Each member of the Security Council shall have one vote.
2. Decisions of the Security Council on procedural matters shall be made by an affirmative vote of nine members.
3. Decisions of the Security Council on all other matters shall be made by an affirmative vote of nine members including the concurring votes of the permanent members; provided that, in decisions under Chapter VI, and under paragraph 3 of Art. 52, a party to a dispute shall abstain from voting.

89 See Art. 19 of the Rome Statute which states that "The Court shall satisfy itself that it has jurisdiction in any case brought before it. The Court may, on its own motion, determine the admissibility of a case..."

90 Both and Art. 1 and paras. 4-6 of the Preamble to the Rome Statute provides:
The State Parties to this Statute,
Mindful that during this century millions of children, women and men have been victims of unimaginable atrocities that deeply shock conscience of humanity, [r]ecognizing that such grave crimes threaten the peace, security and well-being of the world, [a]ffirming that the most serious crimes of concern to the

that while the alternative approaches to justice (such as amnesties) should not be summarily dismissed, the ICC is entrusted with the specific Statute mandate to help ensure that the most serious crimes do not go unpunished.[91] This statement by the Office of the Prosecutor shows the difficulties that can be faced by the ICC should a case involving amnesties come before it. The issue of amnesty *versus* the prosecution of international crimes by the ICC remains unsolved. Where do we draw the line? Would granting amnesty bring about peace in the state concerned? Would it deter individuals from committing similar crimes in future knowing that there is a possibility that amnesty can be granted? That remains to be seen.

7.6 Immunity and the ICC

Immunity is broadly defined as '[a]ny exemption from a duty, liability, or service of process, especially such exemption granted to a public official'.[92] International law accords state officials, including heads of states certain immunities from the jurisdiction of foreign states. The predominant justification for such immunities is that they ensure the smooth conduct of international relations and, as such, they are accorded to those states officials who represent the state at the national level. It is important that states are able to negotiate with each other freely and that those agents charged with the conduct of such activities should be able to perform their functions without harassment by other states.[93] International law distinguishes between sovereign immunity, heads of state and government and foreign ministers immunity, and diplomatic and consular immunity.

international community as a whole must not go unpunished and that their effective prosecution must be ensured by taking measures at the national and by enhancing international cooperation, [d]etermined to an end to impunity for the perpetrators of these crimes and thus to contribute to the prevention of such crimes … Have agreed [to establish the ICC which] shall have the power to exercise its jurisdiction over the persons for the most serious crimes of international concern …

91 ICC Office of the Prosecutor *Informal Expert Paper: The Principle of Complementarity in Practice*, 23 (2003). Available at <www.icc-cpi.int/iccdocs/doc/doc654724.PDF> (Accessed September 23, 2011).

92 Bryan A Garner, Black's Law Dictionary 817 (9th ed. 2009).

93 The Joint and Separate Opinions of Judges Higgins, Kooijmans and Buergenthal in Arrest Warrant of April 11, 2000 (*Democratic Republic of Congo v. Belgium*) (2002) ICJ Rep. 3, para. 75. Also see Michael A. Tunks, *Diplomats or Defendants? Defining the Future of Head-of-State Immunity*, 52 Duke Law Journal 651, 656 (2002), where he states "Head-of-State immunity allows a nation's leader to engage in his official duties, including travel to foreign countries, without fearing arrest, detention, or other treatment inconsistent with his role as head of a sovereign State. Without the guarantee that they will not be subjected to trial in foreign courts, heads of state may simply choose to stay at home rather than assume risks of engaging in international diplomacy".

Diplomats and certain officials on state missions enjoy considerable immunities which are detailed in treaty law.[94] However, immunity does not mean impunity.[95] Although diplomats and consular officials may be immune from criminal jurisdiction in the host country, that immunity can be waived so long as the waiver is expressed.[96] Further, there is no immunity from criminal jurisdiction in the home country and 'it is a duty of all persons enjoying such privileges and immunities to respect the laws and regulations of the receiving state'.[97] Furthermore, the UN Secretary-General has the right and duty to waive immunity of any official in any case where the immunity would impede the course of justice and can be waived without prejudice to the interests of the UN. In the case of a Secretary-General, the UN Security Council has to waive the immunity.[98]

Heads of state, heads of government and foreign ministers enjoy the broadest scope of immunity from criminal jurisdiction of foreign states in general. The rationale behind the exemption from the criminal jurisdiction it two-fold: first, head of state immunity is premised on the concept that a state and its rulers are one for the purposes of immunity; second the notion that all states are equal with consequence that no state may exercise judicial authority over another.[99] There are two types of immunities accorded to state officials: immunity *ratione personae* (personal immunity) and immunity *ratione materiae* (functional immunity). I now discuss these below.

7.7 Immunity of Heads of State and Senior State Officials and Prosecutions for International Crimes

Functional immunity is grounded on the notion that a state is not accountable to other states for acts that he accomplished in his official capacity and that therefore must be attributed to the state.[100] Functional immunity attaches to the official act rather than the

94 Vienna Convention on Diplomatic Relations, 1961; Vienna Convention on Consular Relations, 1963; and the Convention on the Privileges of the United Nations, 1946.

95 Arrest Warrant of 11 April 2000 (*Democratic Republic of Congo v. Belgium*) [2002] ICJ Rep 3, para. 60. For criticism of the ICJ see Antonio Cassese, *When May Senior State Officials be tried for International Crimes? Some Comments on the Congo v Belgium Case,* 13 European Journal of International Law 853, 862 (2002). Also see Marina Spinedi, *State Responsibility v Individual Responsibility for International Crimes: Tertium Non Datur?* 13 European Journal of International Law 895 (2002); Dapo Akande & Sangeeta Shah, *Immunities of State Officials, International Crimes, and Domestic Courts,* 21 European Journal of International Law 815(2011).

96 See Art. 32 of the Vienna Convention on Diplomatic Relations and Art. 45 Vienna Convention on Consular Relations.

97 See Art. 41(1) of the Vienna Convention on Diplomatic Relations and Art. 55(1) of the Vienna Convention on Consular Relations.

98 See Art. 5, section 20 of the Convention on the Privileges of the United Nations.

99 Antonio Cassese, International Law 120 (2008).

100 *Id.*

status of the official acts, it may be relied on by all who have acted on behalf of the state with regard to their official acts.[101] This conduct-based immunity may be relied on by former officials in respect of official acts performed while in office as well as by serving officials.[102] This type of immunity constitutes a substantive defense, in that it indicates that the individual official is not to be held responsible for acts which are in effect, those of the state. Such acts are imputable only to the state and functional immunity is a mechanism for diverting responsibility to the state.[103] In *Attorney-General of Israel v. Eichmann* the Israel Supreme Court stated that:

> The theory of 'Act of State' means that the act performed by a person as an organ of the State – whether he was Head of State or a responsible official acting on Government's order – must be regarded as an act of the State alone. It follows that only the latter bears responsibility therefor, and it also follows that another State has no right to punish the person who committed the act, save with the consent of the State whose mission he performed. Were it not so, the first State would be interfering in the internal affairs of the second, which is contrary to the conception of the equality of states based on their sovereignty.[104]

This was confirmed in *Prosecutor v. Blaškić*[105] where the Appeals Chamber of the International Criminal Tribunal for the Former Yugoslavia stated that

> [State] officials are mere instruments of a State and their official action can only be attributed to the State. They cannot be subject of sanctions or penalties for conduct that is not private but undertaken on behalf of the State. In other words, State officials cannot suffer the consequences of wrongful acts which are not attributable to the State on whose behalf they act: they enjoy the so-called 'functional immunity'. This is a well-established rule of customary international law going back to the eighteenth and nineteenth centuries, restated many times since.[106]

However, after World War II, international courts and tribunals have since held that the functional immunity of a state can be relaxed in order for senior state officials to be

101 Akande & Shah, *supra* note 95, at 825.
102 *Id.*
103 Cassese, *supra* note 95, at 863.
104 *Attorney-General of Israel v. Eichmann* 36 ILR (1962) 5, 308-309.
105 *Prosecutor v. Blaškić (Objection to the Issue of Subpoena duces Tecum)* IT-95-14-AR 108 (1997) 110 ILR (1997) 607, 707.
106 *Id.* para. 38.

prosecuted. In this regard, Article 7 of the London Charter removed immunity of heads of state from prosecution for crimes against humanity and war crimes,[107] and the Tokyo Charter followed suit (in Art. 6).[108] Subsequent developments include numerous restatements of the rule, at both the international and national levels. Mention can be made of Article IV of the 1948 Genocide Convention, Principle III of the Nuremberg Principles adopted in 1950 by the General Assembly, Article III of the 1973 Apartheid Convention, and more recently, Articles 7(2) and 6(2) of the ICTY and ICTR, which provide, respectively, that '[t]he official position of any accused person, whether as Head of State or Government or as a responsible government official, shall not relieve such person of criminal responsibility nor mitigate punishment.' In practice, these tribunals have prosecuted and convicted senior government officials involved in international crimes.[109] Furthermore, the Appeals Chamber of the Special Court for Sierra Leone held in the case against Charles Taylor,[110] that the official position of a person – whether a state official or not – does not bar prosecution before international courts. The Appeals Chamber emphasized that the official position of Charles Taylor 'as incumbent Head of State at the time when [...] criminal proceedings were initiated against him is not a bar to his prosecution by this Court. As such, Charles Taylor was and is subject to criminal proceedings before the Special Court for Sierra Leone.'[111] Nationally, it was echoed in Pinochet that a grant of functional immunity would have been inconsistent with those provisions of the Torture Convention providing universal jurisdiction for torture.[112]

Article 27 of the Rome Statute states that

1. This Statute shall apply equally to all persons without any distinction based on official capacity. In particular, official capacity as a Head of State or Government, a member

107 Annex to Agreement for the Prosecution and Punishment of Major War Criminals of the European Axis (London Agreement), London, Aug. 8, 1945, 82 U.N.T.S. 279, 59 Stat. 1544, E.A.S. No. 472, *reprinted in* 39 American Journal of International Law 257 (1945).

108 The Charter of the IMT for the Far East, Jan. 19, 1946, T.I.A.S. 1589.

109 The Nuremberg Tribunal prosecuted Admiral Eric Radar, whom Hitler named Germany's head of state directly before his suicide; it also prosecuted high-ranking state officials. On the other hand, the Tokyo Tribunal did not prosecute Emperor Hirohito, the Japanese head of state, but did prosecute, convict and sentence high-profile government officials. The ICTR has prosecuted and convicted senior government officials of Rwanda involved in the genocide, including former Prime Minister Jean Kambanda, who pleaded guilty. See *Prosecutor v. Jean Kambanda*, Case No. 97-23S, Judgment of 4 September 1998. For the ICTY, see *Prosecutor v. Slobodan Milosevic* (IT-02-54), who later died in custody before the completion of the proceedings.

110 *Prosecutor v. Charles Taylor*, Case SCSL-03-01-I-059 (Decision on Immunity from Jurisdiction, Appeals Chamber, May 31, 2004).

111 *Prosecutor v. Charles Taylor* Case, *id.* at para. 45-53.

112 *R v. Bow Street Stipendiary Magistrate and Others, Ex parte Pinochet (No. 3)* (1999) 2 All ER 97, 114, 169-170, 178-179, 190. See also Andrea Bianchi, *Immunity versus Human Rights: The Pinochet Case*, 10 European Journal of International Law 237 (1999).

of a Government or parliament, an elected representative or a government official shall in no case exempt a person from criminal responsibility under this Statute, nor shall it, in and of itself, constitute a ground for reduction of sentence.
2. Immunities or special procedural rules which may attach to the official capacity of a person, whether under national or international law, shall not bar the Court from exercising its jurisdiction over such a person.

These developments show that an individual's official position does not exempt him or her from individual responsibility, as it was affirmed by the Nuremberg Tribunal:

> The principle of international law which under certain circumstances protects the representatives of a State, cannot be applied to acts which are condemned as criminal by international law. The authors of these acts cannot shelter themselves behind their official position in order to be freed from punishment in appropriate proceedings.[113]

More complex is the issue of personal immunities – whether customary or treaty law on personal immunities can be relaxed in the case of international crimes. Can a head of state or senior official rely on personal immunities in order to avoid an arrest warrant and the exercise of criminal jurisdiction by a foreign court? I discuss this below.

7.8 Can an Incumbent Head of State or Senior State Official Be Prosecuted in a Foreign State?

Personal immunity is based on the notion that any activity of a head of state or government, diplomatic agent or foreign minister must be immune from foreign jurisdiction in order to avoid foreign states either infringing upon sovereign prerogatives of states or interfering with the official functions of a foreign state agent under the pretext of dealing with an exclusively private act.[114] Personal immunity is commonly regarded as prohibiting absolutely the exercise of criminal jurisdiction by states. However, questions are raised as to whether or not a foreign court may exercise jurisdiction on an incumbent head of state or senior official. In this instance, Dapo Akande argues that '[j]udicial opinion and state practice on this point are unanimous and no case can be found in which it was held

113 *In re Goering and others* (1946), 13 ILR 203 at 221. See also *Khadhafi*, France, *Cour de Cassation*, decision of March 13, 2001, No. 1414, stating that "at this stage of development of international customary law, the crime charged [*i.e.*, terrorism], no matter how serious, does not fall within the exceptions to the principle of immunity from jurisdiction of foreign Heads of State in office," as quoted in Naqvi, *supra* note 56, at 264.
114 Cassese, *supra* note 95, at 862.

that a state official possessing personal immunity is subject to the criminal jurisdiction of a foreign state where it is alleged that he or she has committed an international crime.'[115] Indeed, in *Pinochet*, the House of Lords opined that if *Pinochet* had currently been a head of state, he would have enjoyed personal immunities and therefore could have been exempted from arrest and criminal jurisdiction in Great Britain.[116]

The International Court of Justice (the ICJ), in *Arrest Warrant* case,[117] went a step further:

> [T]he functions of a Minister for Foreign Affairs are such that, throughout the duration of his or her office, he or she when abroad enjoys full immunity from criminal jurisdiction and inviolability. That immunity and inviolability protect the individual concerned against any act of authority of another State which would hinder him or her in the performance of his or her duties.
>
> In this respect, no distinction can be drawn between acts performed by a Minister for Foreign Affairs in an 'official' capacity, and those performed in a 'private capacity' or for that matter, between acts performed before the person concerned assumed office as Minister for Foreign Affairs and acts committed during the period of office. Thus, if a Minister for Foreign Affairs is arrested in another State on a criminal charge, he or she is clearly thereby prevented from exercising the functions of his or her office. The consequences of such impediment to the exercise of those official [sic] functions are equally serious, regardless of whether the Minister for Foreign Affairs was, at the time of arrest, present in the territory of the arresting State on an 'official' visit or a 'private' visit, regardless of whether the arrest relates to acts allegedly performed in an 'official' capacity or a 'private' capacity. Furthermore, even the mere risk that by travelling to or transiting another State a Minister for Foreign Affairs might be exposing himself or herself to legal proceedings could deter the Minister

115 Dapo Akande, *International Immunities and the International Criminal Court*, 98 American Journal of International Law 407, 407 (2004). However, the ILC has taken the view that 'the absence of any procedural immunity with respect to prosecution or punishment in appropriate judicial proceedings is an essential corollary of the absence of any substantive immunity or defence. Its rationale is that it would be paradoxical to prevent an individual from invoking his official position to avoid responsibility for a crime only to permit him to invoke this same consideration to avoid the consequences of his responsibility." See *Comment on Article 7 of the 1996 ILC Draft Code of Crimes against the Peace and Security of Mankind*, 2(2) Yearbook of International of Law Commission 27 (1996). Art. 7 of the ILC Draft Code provides that "[t]he official position of an individual who commits a crime against the peace and security of mankind, even if acted as head of State or Government, does not relieve him of criminal responsibility or mitigate punishment".

116 Opinion of Lord Phillips of Worth Matravers, Judgment of the House of Lords of March 24, 1999, at 653.

117 *Arrest Warrant* case, *supra* note 95.

> from travelling internationally when required to do so for the purposes of the performance of his or her official functions.[118]

The ICJ, after carefully examining state practice, also concluded that:

> It has been unable to deduce from this state practice that there exists under CIL any form of exception to the rule according immunity from criminal jurisdiction and inviolability to incumbent Ministers for Foreign Affairs, where they are suspected of having committed war crimes or crimes against humanity.[119]

The ICJ also concluded that no obligations arise from treaties for a duty to prosecute that can lift the CIL immunity of incumbent foreign affairs ministers. It also opined that this immunity extends even in cases involving allegations of international crimes, which must be taken to apply to the serving state officials and diplomats possessing personal immunity.[120] This principle has since been widely applied by national courts.[121] Recall that personal immunities cease to apply once the official leaves office. Hence, in its dictum, the ICJ stated that immunity might be lifted in four instances:

> Accordingly, immunities enjoyed under international law by an incumbent or former Minister for Foreign Affairs do not present a bar to criminal prosecution in certain circumstances.
>
> First, such persons enjoy no criminal immunity under international law in their own countries, and may thus be tried in their own countries, and may thus be tried by those countries' court in accordance with relevant rules of domestic law.
>
> Secondly, they will cease to enjoy immunity from foreign jurisdiction if the State they represent or have represented decides to waive that immunity.

118 *Id.* paras 54-55.

119 *Id.* para. 58.

120 *Id.*

121 See, for example, *The Schooner Exchange v. M'Faddon* 11 U.S. (7 Cranch) 116, 138 (1812) per C.J. Marshall, recognizing that, under customary international law, 'the immunity which all civilized nations allow to foreign ministers' is coextensive with the immunity of the sovereign; *Tachiona v. Mugabe*, 169 F. Supp. 2d 259 (S.D.N.Y. 2001), (where The Schooner Exchange, *id.*, was applied and the district accepted the Department of State's suggestion of immunity and dismissed the action against the incumbent President Robert Mugabe of Zimbabwe and Foreign Minister Stan Mudenge).

> Thirdly, after a person ceases to hold the office of Minister for Foreign Affairs, he or she will no longer enjoy all the immunities accorded by international law in other states. Provided that it has jurisdiction under international law, a court of one state may try a former Minister for Foreign Affairs of another State in respect of acts committed prior or subsequent to his or her period of office, as well as in respect of acts committed during that period of office in a private capacity.
>
> Fourthly, an incumbent or former Minister for Foreign Affairs may be subject to criminal proceedings before certain international criminal courts, where they have jurisdiction....[122]

This dictum has been severely criticized, especially the third ground, which is argued to imply that international crimes can never be committed in an official capacity.[123] I disagree with this view because if the ICJ meant that international crimes can never be committed in an official capacity, then it would have made a similar distinction in the fourth ground – where international courts can lift the immunity of a foreign minister, whether for personal or official capacity. The rationale for the ICJ's distinction for domestic courts is based on the assumption that a foreign court cannot adjudicate on the domestic affairs of another state for reasons of state sovereignty. In this regard, if a foreign court institutes proceedings against a former head of state for international crimes committed in an official capacity, then the foreign state will be encroaching on the sovereignty of such state.[124]

However, a problem with this distinction might arise when the ICC is faced with the question of whether a case is admissible or not (in terms of the complementarity principle), based on the fact that a domestic court did not lift a functional immunity of a state official

122 *Arrest Warrant* case, *supra* note 95, at para. 61.

123 Cassese, *supra* note 95 at 868, arguing that

> These crimes are *seldom* perpetrated in such capacity. Admittedly, a civilian or a serviceman acting in a private capacity may indeed commit war crimes (think for instance of the rape or torture of an enemy civilian). It is however hardly imaginable that a foreign minister may perpetrate or participate in the perpetration of an international crime "in a private capacity." Indeed, individuals commit such crimes by making use (or abuse) of their official status. It is primarily through the position and rank they occupy that they are in a position to order, instigate, or aid and abet or culpably tolerate or condone such crimes as genocide or crimes against humanity or grave breaches of the Geneva Conventions.

See also Steffen Wirth, *Immunity for Core Crimes? The ICJ's Judgment in the Congo v. Belgium Case,* 13 Europe Journal of International Law 877, 891 (2002).

124 See also Spinedi, *supra* note 95, at 899, arguing that "it must be concluded that according to the Court, a state is under the obligation not to subject to its jurisdiction the organs of another state having committed such crimes even after the officials in question leave office ... though the possibility remains to invoke state responsibility at the international level for the same conduct".

on the basis of the ICJ's dictum.[125] The ICJ makes it clear, in this dictum, that although foreign courts are generally prohibited from exercising jurisdiction to the incumbent heads of state, in some circumstances, they can do so. However, it is highly unlikely that a state can waive immunity on an incumbent head of state. Nonetheless, it is important to examine the relationship between the ICC and national jurisdictions for international crimes in cases of immunity for international crimes.

7.9 The Rome Statute on Immunities for Incumbent Heads of State and Senior State Officials

Article 27(1) does not depart from CIL with regard to functional immunities.[126] It restates the CIL rule, whereby for the purpose of establishing criminal responsibility, the plea of acting in an official capacity is of no avail.[127] On the other hand, Article 27(2), at face value, simply restates a well-known principle that under international law, individuals are only entitled to enjoy personal immunities vis-à-vis the authorities of the state where they are authorized to discharge official functions. Therefore, these immunities cannot be relied upon before the ICC; hence they cannot preclude the ICC from the exercise of the Court's jurisdiction.[128] However, Article 27(2) must be read in conjunction with Article 98(1) of the Rome Statute, which explicitly covers personal immunities in international law. Article 98(1) states that:

> The Court may not proceed with a request for surrender or assistance which would require the requested State to act inconsistently with its obligations under international law with respect to the State or diplomatic immunity of a person or property of a third State, unless the Court can first obtain the cooperation of that third State for the waiver of the immunity.

Article 98(1) is part and parcel of the set of rules governing the question of cooperation with the ICC. It actually bars the ICC from proceeding with requests for the surrender or assistance whenever the requested state, in order to execute such requests, would be required to breach – vis-à-vis a third state – its international legal undertaking in the area of immunities.[129]

We need to recall the *Arrest Warrant* case where the ICJ, in its dictum, stated that the personal immunity of an incumbent head of state can be lifted by an international criminal court such as the ICTY, the ICTR, or the ICC. While the ICTY and the ICTR are

125 See above discussions above on how the principle of complementarity works under the Rome Statute.
126 See section 5.1 above for the full citation of Art. 27(1).
127 Gaeta & Jones, *supra* note 2, at 990.
128 *Id.*
129 *Id.*

constructions of the Security Council,[130] the ICC was created by a multilateral treaty, and as a result, it can only bind state parties to the Rome Statute in accordance with international law rules.[131] There is therefore a clear tension between Article 27(2) and Article 98(1) of the Rome Statute when it comes to states parties' cooperation with the ICC in cases of arrests and surrenders. State parties are therefore faced with the dilemma of having to abide by the Rome Statute and to also honor their other obligations under international law as contemplated by Article 98(1) of the Rome Statute. How can these two provisions be reconciled? The ICC has not yet dealt with this issue, and very few legal scholars have discussed the tension between Articles 27(2) and 98(1) of the Rome Statute. One such scholar is Professor Paola Gaeta,[132] who argues that these two provisions can be reconciled by scrutinizing Article 98(1) closely. According to Professor Gaeta, two interpretations can be made.[133] According to the first interpretation, Article 98(1) uses the term 'Third State' (which only appears in this provision), to be distinguished from the term 'Requested State.'[134] Therefore, it can be construed to refer to a state other than the state that is requested by the ICC to co-operate. Consequently it could be argued that the drafters of Article 98(1) used the expression precisely to indicate third states, *i.e.*, states other than the requested state, regardless of whether or not such a third state is party to the Rome Statue. The ICC cannot conduct trials *in absentia*, neither can it execute arrest warrants by itself; it relies on states' cooperation.[135]

Therefore, if we agree to this interpretation, then Article 27(2) would prove to be meaningless were one to hold the view that a waiver of immunity by the competent states, including state parties to the Rome Statute, would always be a necessary condition to the obligation of the requested state to execute arrest warrants or requests for transfer. By virtue of Article 98(1), the ICC would be permitted to exercise its jurisdiction only after obtaining a waiver of immunity from the competent states.[136]

According to the second interpretation, Article 98(1) could mean that a waiver of immunity is a necessary condition to the execution of arrest warrants or transfers only in those cases where the requested state is internationally obligated, as far as immunities are concerned toward a state not party to the Rome Statute.[137] Therefore, the expression 'Third State' in Article 98(1) must be taken to mean 'third state with regards to the [Rome] Statute' – that is, equivalent to 'State not Party.' Under this interpretation, the ICC's request

130 On the establishment of these tribunals, see *supra* notes 20 and 21.
131 Art. 34 of the Vienna Convention.
132 Gaeta & Jones, *supra* note 2.
133 *Id.* at 992.
134 *Id.*
135 *Id.*
136 *Id.*
137 *Id.* at 994.

for arrest or transfer must be preceded by a waiver of immunity only in limited cases, *i.e.*, when the requested state is legally bound vis-à-vis a state not party to the Rome Statute.[138] I argue that this interpretation is valid and therefore should be followed.[139] Next, I investigate the issue of arrest warrants issued by the ICC against two incumbent heads of state.

7.9.1 Are States Required to Arrest and to Surrender President Al Bashir?

In March 2009 and February 2011, the ICC Pre-Trail Chambers decided to issue arrest warrants against Omar Al Bashir, an incumbent president of Sudan,[140] and Muammar Gaddafi, the incumbent president (until recently) of Libya,[141] respectively, for international crimes committed in their respective territories. The Pre-Trial chambers also requested cooperation from states seeking the arrest and surrender of the presidents. Both Sudan and Libya are not state parties to the Rome Statute, and both cases were referred to the ICC by the Security Council[142] acting in terms of Article 13 of the Rome Statute,[143] which serves as a trigger mechanism for the jurisdiction of the ICC.[144]

In light of the arrest warrants issued by the ICC, the AU asked the Security Council to request the ICC to defer the arrest warrants for a year, as permitted in Article 16 of the Rome Statute.[145] However, the Security Council is yet to respond to such requests. In light of the fact that the Security Council has ignored the AU's requests, the AU passed decisions whereby it demanded its member states not to cooperate with the ICC on the request to arrest and to surrender the persons in question.[146] The natural question then arises: what

---

138 *Id.*

139 See Art. 38 of the ICJ Statute, which provides that the writings of legal scholars can be used as an interpretative tool.

140 *Prosecutor v. Omar Ahmed Al Bashir*, ICC-02/05 -01/09, March 4, 2009. See also the July 12, 2010 decision, which adds genocide to the crimes Al Bashir is accused of having committed, as the first warrant of arrest does not include it, pursuant to the Appeals Chamber Decision of February 3, 2010, ICC-02-0501/09-73.

141 *Prosecutor v. Muammar Mohammed Abu Minyar Gaddafi*, ICC-01/11, June 27, 2011.

142 See UN Security Council Resolutions, *supra* notes 7 and 8.

143 The obligations created by treaties are enforced through the principle of *pacta sunt servanda*, which states that 'every treaty in force is binding upon the parties to it and must be performed in good faith'. See Art. 26 of the Vienna Convention. See also Art. 34, which states that a treaty does not create obligations or rights for a third state without its consent.

144 Paola Gaeta, *Does President Al Bashir Enjoy Immunity from Arrest?* 7 Journal of International Criminal Justice 315, 324 (2009).

145 See the AU Decision on the Situation in Libya, Assembly/AU/Dec.385(XVII), and the AU Assembly Decision on the Implementation of the Assembly Decisions on the ICC Doc.EX.CL/670(XIX), Assembly/AU/Dec.366 (XVII), Malabo, Equatorial Guinea, where the AU decided that member states shall not cooperate with the execution of the arrest warrant of Gaddafi and reaffirmed that by receiving President Al Bashir, Kenya and Djibouti were discharging their obligations under Art. 23 of the Constitutive Act and Art. 98 of the Rome Statute.

146 *Id.*

does this mean for AU member states that are also parties to the Rome Statute? The AU Constitutive Act does not expressly state that the decisions of the AU Assembly, which is the supreme organ of the AU,[147] are binding. However, an argument can be advanced that the AU Assembly decisions are valid and therefore bind the AU member states given that Article 25 of the AU Constitutive Act states that any member state that fails to comply with the decisions and policies of the Union may be subjected to sanctions.

There are three views to the question of whether or not states are required to arrest and surrender President Al Bashir.[148] One view is that a state can surrender a person to the ICC once the person is no longer entitled to immunity because he or she has relinquished his or her post, or because the requesting state has managed to obtain a waiver of immunities from the foreign state that the person represents.[149] This is unlikely to happen. The second view is that if a state decides to disregard the personal immunity of the foreign state official and surrender him or her to the ICC, that state commits an international wrongful act, though that will have no bearing on the jurisdiction of the ICC under Article 27(1) of the Rome Statute.[150] This view is taken from the (second) interpretation of Article 98(1) discussed above, holding that state parties to the Rome Statute owe obligations to a non-state party to the Rome Statute and therefore cannot arrest nor surrender President Al Bashir. Thus, the ICC's request to state parties to surrender President Al Bashir is contrary to Article 98 of the Rome Statute and is an act *ultra vires*. State parties are therefore not bound to comply with the request to cooperate in this regard.[151]

The third view contends that the removal of immunity by Article 27 of the ICC is also applicable at the national level, when national authorities act in support of the ICC.[152] By virtue of the referral being done in terms of Chapter VII of the UN Charter, Sudan is to be treated as bound by the Rome Statute, as if it were a party to the Statute. This resolves the tension between Articles 27(2) and 98(1) of the Rome Statute. The rationale for this view is found in Article 25 of the UN Charter, which states that 'Members of the United Nations

147 Art. 6(2) of the AU Constitutive Act.

148 Gaeta, *supra* note 144; and Dapo Akande, *The Legal Nature of Security Council Referrals to the ICC and Its Impact on Al Bashir's Immunities*, 7 Journal of International Criminal Justice 333 (2009). See in general, Nidal Nabil Jurdi, The International Criminal Court and National Courts: A Contentious Relationship 199 (2011), discussing the complementarity principle and the Security Council deferral in Darfur.

149 Gaeta, *supra* note 144, at 326.

150 *Id.*

151 *Id.* She also contends that the fact that an ICC is endowed with jurisdiction over a particular case, but is deprived of enforcement powers, does not imply that national judicial authorities are permitted to do whatever an international court asks them to do; and more so if that court has been established by virtue of a treaty, like the ICC, its authority derives from an instrument based upon consent.

152 Akande, *supra* note 148, at 333.

agree to accept and carry out the decisions of the Security Council….'[153] The argument is that the Rome Statute operates in this case not as a treaty, but by virtue of being a Security Council resolution; thus, the removal of immunity operates even with regard to non-state parties.[154] If we agree with the latter argument, then the ICC operates on two heads: as an independent court created by a multilateral treaty, and as an instrument of the Security Council. This could not be what was intended by the drafters of the Rome Statute. The history of this provision shows that it was designed to make available to the Security Council the jurisdictional mechanism created by the Rome Statute, but that it would not add to (nor restrict) the powers of the Security Council, as defined in the UN Charter.[155] Accordingly, the final version of Article 13(b) simply provides for the possibility of referral to the prosecutor by the Security Council 'acting under Chapter VII of the [UN] Charter.'[156] Therefore, the exercise of the power of referral by the Security Council is submitted to specific conditions, both arising from its competence under the UN Charter and from the inherent characteristics of a permanent international criminal court.[157] Furthermore, according to Article 13(b), the Security Council could only refer a 'situation in which one or more of such crimes [referring to Art. 5] appears to have been committed.' In this regard, the exercise by the Security Council of its powers under Chapter VII is submitted to the control of legality of the jurisdictional organs of the ICC.[158] So, even though the Rome Statute remains ambiguous as to the issues of admissibility in the case of referral by the Security Council, in defining the general principles of admissibility, Article 17 does not distinguish between the different trigger mechanisms.[159] The ICC is an independent court that operates according to the Rome Statute, and it is responsible for determining its own jurisdiction, as stated in Article 19 of the Rome Statute. The logical conclusion, therefore, is that if there were an explicit obligation from the resolution that referred the case to the ICC requiring all UN member states to cooperate and to arrest and surrender Al Bashir, then the state parties to the Rome Statute would be able to do so without having to commit a wrongful act.[160]

If one accepts that the arrest warrants against President Al Bashir and President Gaddafi were results of the referral by the Security Council and therefore binding on the states

153 *Id.*
154 *Id.* at 339.
155 Condorelli & Villalpondo, *supra* note 79, at 629.
156 *Id.*
157 *Id.*
158 *Id.* at 633.
159 Art. 17 of the Rome Statute discussed, *supra*.
160 Akande, *supra* note 148, at 343; and Gaeta, *supra* note 144, at 330. The Resolution (pertaining to the referral) indicates that Sudan and all other parties to the conflict shall cooperate fully, whereas other states not party to the conflict are urged to cooperate fully with the ICC. Therefore the language of the resolution is clear that only Sudan and the parties to the conflict are obliged to cooperate. The same language is used in the resolution pertaining to Libya. See Resolution 1593 and Resolution 1970; *supra* notes 7 and 8 (respectively).

(in terms of Art. 24 of the UN Charter), does every resolution that the Security Council passes bind UN member states? It depends on the wording, context and intent of such a resolution.[161] For example, those resolutions that merely 'recommend,' 'call upon' or 'urge' states to do or refrain from doing something are not binding on UN member states.[162] On the other hand, 'decisions' taken under Chapter VII of the UN Charter to maintain or to restore international peace and security are the most important category of binding resolutions.[163] Both resolutions of the Security Council on the referral of the situations in Sudan and in Libya do not use binding language on all UN member states; instead they employ the binding language only to Sudan and to Libya.[164] Therefore, it is reasonable to argue that UN member states and, in particular, African states are not bound by the resolution to arrest them, such states will be going against their obligations to Sudan under CIL. Therefore, while the arrest warrants issued are not unlawful, it would be unlawful to force the states to act against their obligations as envisaged in Article 98 of the Rome Statute.

Two arguments are advanced by this discussion on immunities and the Rome Statute with regard to the African states and the arrest warrants issued against the two presidents: (1) while Article 27 of the Rome Statute lifts the immunity of incumbent heads of states, state parties to the Rome Statute are not under any legal obligation to arrest and to surrender Al Bashir and Muammar Gaddafi by virtue of Article 98 of the Rome Statute, as analyzed above; and (2) AU member states are not under any legal obligation to surrender the persons in question, and instead they are under a legal obligation to abide by the decisions of the AU Assembly. However, this does not in any case absolve Al Bashir from facing the

161 Alan Boyle & Christine Chinkin, The Making Of International Law 229 (2007).

162 *Id.*

163 *Id.* See also Michael C. Wood, *Interpretation of Security Council Resolutions*, 2 Max Planck Yearbook of United Nations Law 73, 82 (1998), arguing that when the Security Council intends a provision to be binding, the resolution contains or refers to an Art. 39 determination, and includes the words "acting under Chapter VII" or reference to an appropriate article thereof, as well as the word 'decides". *Cf.* Ian Brownlie, Principles of Public International Law 692-693 (2008), arguing that to give legal significance to an omission of an organ to condemn is problematic, as this omission turns often on the political attitude of the majority in the organ concerned.

164 In Resolution 1593 pertaining to Darfur, Sudan, paras. 2 and 3, the Security Council *decided* that the *government of Sudan and all other parties to the conflict* in Darfur *shall* cooperate and provide any assistance to the ICC and the prosecutor, *urged* all states and regional and other organizations to cooperate fully, and also *invited* the ICC and the AU to discuss practical arrangements to facilitate the work of the prosecutor and of the ICC. In contrast, Resolution 1970 pertaining to the Libyan situation, paras 4 and 5 also used the same binding phrases '*decides*' and '*shall*' with regard to the Libyan authorities and *urged* all (other) states to cooperate fully. This is in comparison to para 17 of Resolution 1970, where the Security Council decided that "all Member States *shall* freeze without delay all funds, other financial assets and economic resources which are on their territories, which are owned or controlled, directly or indirectly by individuals or entities listed [...]" [emphasis added].

charges at a later stage, once they leave office.[165] Furthermore, while states are not legally obliged to arrest and to surrender these individuals, they are also not prohibited from doing so as long, as they are prepared to face the consequences of committing an internationally wrongful act. Consequently, arresting and surrendering them will not have any bearing on the lawfulness of the proceedings before the ICC.[166]

7.10 CONCLUSION

It may be easy to conclude that the ICC is not targeting Africans because African states have voluntarily ratified the Rome Statute and therefore the consequences that flow from such ratification are that the ICC will prosecute Africans if African states are unwilling or unable to do prosecute. Therefore, it all depends on the African states to domesticate the Rome Statute and ensure their own domestic prosecutions of their own people. It is also important to note that there might be those African states that will be unwilling to prosecute not because they do not have effective legal systems but because they are shielding the perpetrators. That will be clear cases falling under the jurisdiction of the ICC. Let us not forget the fact that AU only found a problem with the ICC after it indicted President Al Bashir – a colleague. Nothing was said by the AU when some of their leaders, in particular, President Museveni of Uganda, have expressly sought the intervention of the ICC. In this regard, in its letter of referral Uganda made reference to the 'situation concerning the "'Lord's Resistance Army' in northern and western Uganda."[167] It is argued that this implied that only the LRA and not the Ugandan government would be the subject of investigations.[168] The prosecutor has also been criticized for only investigating the LRA and not investigating the government forces as well. Hence, it is argued that

> [T]he OTP has branded the LRA leaders criminals from the moment it received the referral. When the Prosecutor had yet to conduct an official investigation the ICC press release announcing the referral already mentioned 'locating and arresting the LRA leadership' as key issue. The Prosecutor has continued to present the LRA as a criminal organization, even suggesting that for this reason the operations of those who combat the LRA cannot be questioned. When challenged in a public debate in London about the absence of investigations into the Ugandan government, the Prosecutor 'interrupted one

165 As per the ICJ judgment in *Arrest Warrant Case*, *supra* note 95.

166 Gaeta, *supra* note 144, at 332.

167 ICC, "President of Uganda Refers Situation Concerning the Lord's Resistance Army (LRA) to the ICC", ICC-20040129-44En, January 29, 2004. Also see Schabas, *supra* note 36, at 752; and Sarah M.H. Nouwen & Wouter G. Werner, *Doing Justice to the Political: The International Criminal Court in Uganda and Sudan*, 21 EUROPEAN JOURNAL OF INTERNATIONAL LAW 941, 951 (2011).

168 Nouwen & Werner, *id*. at 951.

> of his most insistent questioners and, pointing an accusatory finger, burst out: 'If you want to support the LRA, fine! But you should know they are a criminal organization.'[169]

In his defense, the Prosecutor has argued that the crimes committed by the LRA are far worse than the crimes committed by the Ugandan government forces.[170]

At the same time, is it also not legitimate to ask: is Africa the only continent that these atrocities are being committed? The OTP has confirmed that there are other situations that it has considered such as in Iraq and it found that those situations have not been that grave as compared to Africa.[171] One may criticize the attitude of the OTP and conclude that the ICC is targeting Africans because it is hard to believe that in Iraq, for example, the atrocities committed there do not shock the conscience of the OTP.[172] Therefore, there is some legitimacy to questioning the intention of the ICC in only prosecuting Africans and therefore on these bases one can conclude that the ICC is targeting Africans.

It may be so, but what does Africa do if it is being targeted? Does it not comply with its obligations under the Rome Statute? I do not think that should be the case. These are serious crimes that cannot be swept under the 'we are the target' rug. I have shown that international crimes are so serious that not even amnesties and immunities can be invoked

169 *Id.* at 952.

170 See ICC OTP "Statement by the Chief Prosecutor on the Uganda Arrest Warrants", The Hague, October 14, 2005, 2-3, where the Prosecutor said "[t]he criteria (*sic*) for selection of the first case was gravity. We analyzed the gravity of all crimes in Northern Uganda committed by the LRA and Ugandan forces. Crimes committed by the LRA were much more numerous and of much higher gravity than alleged crimes committed by the UPDF. We therefore started with an investigation of the LRA".

171 The OTP said the following with regards to Iraq:

> The Office considers various factors in assessing gravity. A key consideration is the number of victims of particularly serious crimes, such as willful killing or rape. The number of potential victims of crimes within the jurisdiction of the Court in this situation – 4 to 12 victims of willful killing and a limited number of victims of willful killing and a limited number of victims of inhuman treatment –was of a different order than the number of victims found in other situations under investigation or analysis by the office. It is worth bearing in mind that the OTP is currently investigating three situations involving long-running conflicts in Northern Uganda, the Democratic Republic of Congo and Darfur. Each of the three situations under investigation involves thousands of willful killing as well as intentional and large scale sexual violence and abductions. Collectively, they have resulted in the displacement of more than 5 million people. Other situations under analysis also feature hundreds or thousands of such crimes. Taking into account all the considerations, the situation did not appear to meet the required threshold of the Statute.

See ICC OTP, Communication Concerning the Situation in Iraq 8 (February 9, 2006). Also see ICC OTP "Criteria for Selection of Situations and Cases", unpublished draft document of the Office of the Prosecutor, June 2006, 9, where the OTP stated that "[a]t present, the gravest admissible situations within the jurisdiction of the [ICC] have been in one continent, Africa".

172 For such criticisms, see Schabas, *supra* note 36; and Kevin Jon Heller, *Situational Gravity under the Rome Statute*, *in* Future Directions in International Criminal Justice 1 (Carsten Stahn & Larissa van den Henk eds., 2009).

to bar prosecutions. What Africa needs to do is to strengthen their domestic laws and to also ensure that its legal system is effective – from having a system that is not full of unnecessary delays to having impartial prosecutors and judges that are fully aware of the international crimes and also know how to deal with them. It is only in this way that the African states cannot be targeted by the ICC because the ICC only operates through the principle of complementarity. If the African states do not prosecute as they are required in international law, then they risk being the easy targets of the ICC.

Part III
Africa and the Complementarity Principle of the Rome Statute of the International Criminal Court

Implications for Domestic Rule of Law and Justice

8 Taking Credible Ownership of Justice for Atrocity Crimes in Africa

The African Union and the Complimentarity Principle of the Rome Statute

Vincent O. Nmehielle

8.1 Introduction

Everyone would agree that the entry into force on July 1, 2002 of the Rome Statute of the International Criminal Court (Rome Statute)[1] was a very important milestone in the global quest to fight and possibly end impunity that was associated with the commission of egregious human rights violations in the various forms that they took. One vital importance of the International Criminal Court (ICC or the Court) is that it is a permanent international court vested with jurisdiction to deal with international crimes such as war crimes, genocide, crimes against humanity and the crime of aggression.[2] This is unlike the *ad hoc* arrangements of the Nuremberg and Tokyo trials in the aftermath of World War II, the United Nations International Criminal Tribunal for the former Yugoslavia, or the United Nations Criminal Tribunal for Rwanda that dealt specifically with such international crimes that were committed during specific situations that each of those *ad hoc* arrangements represented. The eventual establishment of the ICC in 2002 with the election of the judges of the court, the Prosecutor and members of his office, and the constituting of the Registry demonstrated that the ICC has come to stay as the world's permanent court with nearly universal international criminal jurisdiction.

It is equally true that Africa as a region was an active and enthusiastic participant in the negotiations leading to the adoption of the Rome Statute on July 17, 1998 in Rome. Indeed, African States were in the forefront in the discussions to establish the ICC, which they perceived as a possible deterrence to the vicious atrocities that were rampant in African conflicts as represented by the Rwanda genocide, among other such brutal conflicts in the continent. To show unflinching African support for the ICC, Senegal, an African state

---

1 Rome Statute of the International Criminal Court, July 17, 1998, 2187 U.N.T.S 90 and corrected by process-verbaux of November 10, 1998, July 12, 1999, November 30, 1999, May 8, 2000, January 17, 2001 and January 16, 2002.

2 For the jurisdiction of the ICC, see Art. 5 of the Rome Statute. Art. 6 defines the crime of genocide, Art. 7 defines crimes against humanity, and Art. 8 defines war crimes.

was the first state to ratify the Rome Statute on February 2, 1999. Presently, Africa has 33 member states to the Rome Statute, Cape Verde being the most recent African state to accede to the Rome Statute on 11 October 2011 after Tunisia, which joined the Rome Statute regime on June 22, 2011.[3]

Despite this elaborate African participation in the ICC, recent events appear to have dampened Africa's interest in and support for the ICC. These events relate to the indictment of President Omar Al-Bashir of The Sudan, arising from alleged atrocities committed in the Darfur region of The Sudan. The indictment of Al Bashir was based on a referral by the United Nations Security Council (UNSC) under Article 13(b) of the Rome Statute.[4] This was the first time the UNSC had referred a case to the Prosecutor of the ICC.[5] As a result of Africa's commitment to finding a political and peaceful solution to the Darfur conflict, the African Union (AU), as the African umbrella inter-governmental organization sought a deferral of the Al-Bashir indictment and prosecution under Article 16 of the Rome Statue and made a request to the UNSC in that regard, which request was not acted upon by the UNSC.[6] This prompted the AU Assembly to adopt a decision directing its members not to cooperate with the ICC relative to the arrest and surrender of President Al-Bashir.[7]

---

3 See African States Parties to the ICC Statute as enumerated on the ICC website <www.icc-cpi.int/Menus/ASP/states+parties/African+States/> (Accessed October 20, 2011) as follows: Burkina Faso, November 30, 1998 (16 April 2004); Senegal, February 2, 1999; Ghana, December 20, 1999; Mali, August 16, 2000; Lesotho, September 6, 2000; Botswana, September 8, 2000; Sierra Leone, September 15, 2000; Gabon, September 20, 2000; South Africa, November 27, 2000; Nigeria, September 27, 2001; Central African Republic, October 3, 2001; Benin, January 22, 2002; Mauritius, March 5, 2002; Democratic Republic of the Congo, April 11, 2002; Niger, April 11, 2002; Uganda, June 14, 2002; Namibia, June 20, 2002; Gambia, June 28, 2002; United Republic of Tanzania, August 20, 2002; Malawi, September 19, 2002; Djibouti, November 5, 2002; Zambia, November 13, 2002; Guinea, July 14, 2003; Congo, May 3, 2004; Burundi, September 21, 2004; Liberia, September 22, 2004; Kenya, March 15, 2005; Comoros, August 18, 2006; Chad, January 1, 2007; Madagascar, March 14 2008; Seychelles, August 10, 2010; Tunisia, June 22, 2011; Cape Verde October 11, 2011.

4 The UN Security Council referral was pursuant to its Resolution 1593 of March 31, 2005, S/RES/1593 (2005) under which the UNSC, "Acting under Chapter VII of the Charter of the United Nations . . . decides to refer the situation in Darfur since July 1, 2002 to the Prosecutor of the International Criminal Court."

5 See Charles Jalloh, Dakpo Akande and Max du Plessis (hereinafter Jalloh, et al), *Assessing the African Union Concerns about Article 16 of the Rome Statute of the International Criminal Court*, 4 AFRICAN JOURNAL OF LEGAL STUDIES 5, 6 (2011).

6 *Id.* at 8.

7 *Id.* According to its Assembly's Decision on the Meeting of the African States Parties to the Rome Statute of the International Criminal Court, Doc. Assembly/AU/13(XIII), adopted at its 13th Ordinary Session at Sirte, Libya July 1-3, 1999, the AU resolved "that in view of the fact that the request by the African Union has never been acted upon, the AU Member States shall not cooperate pursuant to the provisions of Art. 98 of the Rome Statute of the ICC relating to immunities, for the arrest and surrender of President Omar El Bashir of The Sudan. . ." The AU has reaffirmed this decision in its Assembly Decision on the Implementation of the Decisions on the International Criminal Court, Doc. EX.CL/639(XVIII), adopted at its 16th Ordinary Session January 30-31, 2011 at Addis Ababa, Ethiopia.

The AU has continued to express dissatisfaction with what it perceives as an uneven landscape of international criminal justice in view of the fact that virtually all the cases currently going on in the ICC are against African indictees. There is therefore a sense in the African Union that Africa is being targeted by the ICC as an instrument of powerful western states. This decision of the AU not to cooperate with the ICC places the 33 African member states of the Rome Statute in a difficult position relative to the treaty obligation that they voluntarily undertook when they ratified or acceded to the Rome Statute on the one hand, and their commitment and allegiance to the African Union should they choose to ignore the decision of the AU, on the other. This has further been complicated by the Kenya six[8] indictments and the recent referral by the UNSC of the Libya situation to the ICC and the ensuing indictment of the late Muammar Gaddaffi, his son and his security adviser.[9] To show that the African Union is serious about not cooperating with the ICC, its Assembly directed its organs to pursue a measure whereby a criminal chamber would be established within the African Court of Justice and Human Rights, which Chamber would be vested with jurisdiction for international crimes in Africa.[10]

8 The Kenya Six indictments comprise of two cases brought against the two factions (supporters of the Prime Minister Raila Odinga and those of President Mwai Kibaki) in the Kenyan election-induced conflict of 2008 that led to the killing of over 1,000 Kenyans: *The Prosecutor v. William Samoei Ruto, Henry Kiprono Kosgey and Joshua Arap Sang*, ICC-01/09-01/11 and *The Prosecutor v. Francis Kirimi Muthaura, Uhuru Muigai Kenyatta and Mohammed Hussein Ali*, ICC-01/09-02/11.

9 Pursuant to UN Security Council Resolution 1970 of February 26, 2011, S/RES/1970 (2011), the situation in Libya was referred to the ICC. On February 27, 2011, the Prosecutor of the ICC issued a warrant of arrest against Gadaffi, his son and his chief of military intelligence for crimes against humanity after a Pre-Trial Chamber found that "there are reasonable grounds to believe" that the crimes were committed. See <www.icc-cpi.int/Menus/ICC/Situations+and+Cases/Situations/ICC0111/Situation+Index.htm> (Accessed August 24, 2011) referring to ICC-01/11-01/11. *The Prosecutor v. Muammar Mohammed Abu Minyar Gaddafi, Saif Al-Islam Gaddafi and Abdullah Al-Senussi.*

10 See AU Assembly's Decision on the Meeting of the African States Parties to the Rome Statute of the International Criminal Court, Assembly/AU/13(XIII) (Decision on the Meeting of African States Parties to the Rome Statute), adopted at its 13th Ordinary Session at Sirte, Libya July 1-3, 2009, Para 5. Here the AU requested its Commission "to ensure the early implementation of Decision Assembly/Dec.213(XII), adopted in February 2009 mandating the Commission, in consultation with the African Commission on Human and Peoples' Rights and the African Court on Human and Peoples' Rights to examine the implications of the Court being empowered to try serious crimes of international concern such as genocide, crimes against humanity and war crimes, which would be complementary to national jurisdictions and processes for fighting impunity." Since the 13th Ordinary Session, this request has continually been reiterated in other AU Sessions. In this regard, the AU Commission has initiated the drafting of a Protocol pursuant to a workshop on the expansion of the jurisdiction of the African Court of Justice and Human Rights that was held in Midrand, South Africa from November 8-12, 2010. Following the workshop, a Draft Protocol on Amendments to the Statute of the African Court of Justice and Human Rights, Legal/ACJHRPAP/4 (II) has been tabled. This Draft Protocol seeks to establish a third Chamber for the African Court of Justice and Human Rights to deal with International Criminal Law, thus vesting the Court with jurisdiction for international crimes such as war crimes, genocide and crimes against humanity among other crimes such as piracy, corruption, terrorism, crimes against unconstitutional change of government, corruption, corporate criminal liability and the like.

The perception that the ICC is targeting Africa in its prosecutions of alleged perpetrators of atrocity crimes is indeed quite attractive in terms of passionately protesting what some in the AU and in Africa generally may perceive as international criminal justice experimentation with African leaders and citizens. This should not, however, mean that there should be no concerns on the part of Africans generally and the AU in particular regarding the rampant occurrence of atrocity crimes in the continent.

It therefore becomes very important to inquire into how Africa can be taken seriously in its commitment to end impunity in the continent. This is against the background that under the Constitutive Act of the African Union, the continent represented by the AU undertook to end impunity for atrocity crimes in the continent in the aftermath of the Rwandan genocidal massacre and the deafening silence of the international community in dealing with its prevention. Most importantly, the Rome Statute makes the ICC a court of last resort, giving primary jurisdiction to the domestic justice system. In the opinion of this author, this gives Africa the most important singular opportunity to take ownership of the justice process in dealing with atrocity crimes in the continent. This ownership must be credible in the spirit of a determination to end impunity within the injunctions of the Constitutive Act of the African Union and the obligations undertaken by African member States of the Rome Statute. The AU must be in the forefront in requiring its member states to ensure and to establish viable domestic systems that are truly able and willing to deal with impunity for atrocity crimes.

This chapter therefore focuses on the issue of how the complementarity principle enshrined in the Rome Statute can serve to enable credible domestic prosecution of atrocity crimes in Africa and the role of the AU in that regard. The chapter argues that the future of international criminal justice in Africa is in the hands of African States if only they take the domestic measures necessary to fully implement and benefit from the complementarity principle of the Rome Statute. The chapter makes the point that it is not just enough to cry foul at the skewed nature of international criminal prosecutions generally and in the ICC (despite this reality) in particular, but that Africa must find a way of effectively dealing with the seeming daily occurrence of atrocity crimes in its various territories. It is a reality, as demonstrated by recent conflicts and violent disturbances in countries such as Kenya, Ivory Coast, Nigeria, and Libya that impunity in the commission of atrocity crimes is rife in the continent. The continent collectively within the umbrella of the AU and as individual states must deal with this problem if she must be taken seriously, not just by its global counterparts, but also by its citizens, who are usually the victims of the crimes. Thus, she can meaningfully prevent what she perceives as international criminal justice witch-hunting by fully committing to and realizing the benefits of the complementarity principle of the ICC Statute.

Accordingly, having set background above in the first section, the second section of the chapter articulates why the AU is important and should influence the implementation of the complementarity principle in Africa by drawing on an assumption that the AU, as a regional authority, has already rejected impunity as evident in its constitutive instrument. The third section reviews the significance of the complementarity principle in the Rome Statute. The argument here is that the Rome Statute is quite clear that the ICC's jurisdiction is complementary to domestic jurisdiction and places domestic systems in a position to assume primary jurisdiction and to take credible ownership of justice for atrocity crimes. All that the domestic system needs to do is to clearly and credibly demonstrate that it meets the requirements inherent in the complementarity principle as articulated in the Rome Statute. The emphasis here is that the point must not be lost on anyone that the ICC is only a court of last resort and cannot assume a role that it is not designed to play.

The fourth section examines how the complementarity principle can be implemented in Africa, taking into account the AU's recognition of the importance of the principle in its decisions on the work of the ICC in Africa. The section argues that beyond reiterating the importance of the complementarity principle and urging African States Parties to the ICC to take steps in that regard, the AU must itself proactively engage its member states to credibly actualize complementarity. Such proactive steps could include establishing minimum standards aimed at achieving complementarity such as requiring domestication of the Rome Statute and comprehensive legal and judicial reform. The chapter in section 5 briefly discusses the AU's engagement with the ICC and how it can draw from the European Union model whereby there is proactive engagement with the ICC in the spirit of a genuine desire to encourage its member states to effectively deal with atrocity crimes. Such engagement does not mean succumbing to the whims of any institution but one that meaningfully articulates Africa's relevance to the work of the ICC and vice versa in a cooperative manner.

The chapter in section 6 very briefly examines the proposed AU international crimes chamber as an enlargement of the jurisdiction of the African Court of Justice and Human and Peoples' rights relative to the principle of complementarity under the Rome Statute that the AU endorses. The argument in the section is that considering the complementarity emphasis of the Rome Statute, which is also endorsed in the proposed AU mechanism, the establishment of the criminal chamber may not be expedient after all. The reasoning here is that the criminal chamber is likely to be in the same position as the ICC – endowed with limited jurisdiction as a court of last resort, which must defer to domestic systems. Therefore, the emphasis should be on making African domestic systems effective in truly dealing with atrocity crimes.

The chapter concludes that if Africa does not find credible domestic ways of taking ownership of justice for atrocity crimes in the continent, she will continue to be the field that produces the raw material needed for the ICC to experiment, make its mistakes and perfect its prosecutorial strategy in the enforcement of international criminal law. The African Union must therefore lead the way for African states (not because all members of the AU are parties to the Rome Statute but because of its normative stance against impunity) to take credible ownership of justice for atrocity crimes by engaging with its member states to credibly seize the opportunity presented by the complementarity principle of the Rome Statute.

8.2 THE AFRICAN UNION HAS REJECTED ATROCITY CRIMES AND IMPUNITY

The central assumption of this chapter, which may appear too optimistic and possibly laughable from the perspective of some, remains that the AU, at least in principle, has in fact, rejected and would not tolerate the commission of atrocity crimes and impunity for egregious violations of human rights. To accept otherwise would amount to total disregard of the foundational objectives and principles of the African Union as contained in its Constitutive Act. Prominent cardinal objectives of the AU in this regard are clearly provided for in Article 3(f), (g) and (h) of the Constitutive Act under which the AU agreed to:

(f) promote peace, security, and stability on the continent;
(g) promote democratic principles and institutions, popular participation and good governance;
(h) promote and protect human and peoples' rights in accordance with the African Charter on Human and Peoples' Rights and other relevant human rights instruments.

In the same vein, Article 4(h) of the Constitutive Act provides a very vital exception to the general principle in international relations of "non-interference by any Member State in the internal affairs of another" that is contained in Article 4(g). As a first in any regional intergovernmental organization's constitutive instrument the AU's Constitutive Act in the said Article 4(h) recognizes as a principle of the AU, "the right of the Union to intervene in a Member State pursuant to a decision of the Assembly in respect of grave circumstances, namely: war crimes, genocide and crimes against humanity." Similarly, it is also a principle of the AU for its member States to ensure "respect for democratic principles, human rights, the rule of law and good governance." While it may be said that the challenge for the AU Assembly is when (in terms of political will and timelines) it would make that important "decision" to intervene during the 'grave circumstances' envisaged in Article 4(h), the point remains that the commission of war crimes, genocide and crimes against humanity in any African state is a very serious matter and provides enough reason to warrant the violation of the sacred principle of non-intervention in another sovereign state's internal affairs. The lessons of Rwanda were evidently in the minds of many Member States of the AU when its Constitutive Act was adopted. Notwithstanding the political maneuvering that may affect a decision to characterize a grave circumstance as genocide, deciphering and agreeing that war crimes and crimes against humanity have been committed should ordinarily not be complicated.

Africa's rejection of atrocity crimes and impunity is further evidenced by the participation of a large number of African States in the negotiations leading to the adoption of the Rome Statute as alluded to in the introduction. One needs to keep in mind that the Rome Statute was adopted on July 17, 1998 almost two years before the AU Constitutive Act, which was adopted on July 11, 2000. Thus, in addition to the lessons of the Rwandan and possibly the Sierra Leonean civil wars, there can be no doubt that the AU Constitutive Act's recognition of genocide, war crimes and crimes against humanity as "grave circumstances" requiring the Union's intervention in a member state, may have been influenced by the Rome Statute, or the momentum around the need to curtail impunity within the period leading to the adoption of the Rome Statute. One would therefore be correct to say that the AU as a regional body must mean what it said and said what it meant when its Constitutive Act was adopted – the need for Africa to decisively deal with impunity and grave human rights violations on the continent. To do otherwise would be a failure of leadership at the regional supranational level.

8.3 Why Complementarity is of Vital Importance in the ICC Process[11]

The jurisdiction of the ICC is complementary to that of national courts as articulated in paragraph 10 of the Rome Statute's preamble and in the substantive Article 1 of the Statute. In the said preambular paragraph the States Parties emphasized "that the International Criminal Court established under this Statute shall be complementary to national criminal jurisdictions." In the same vein, Article 1 describes the Court as "a permanent institution" that "shall have the power to exercise its jurisdiction over persons for the most serious crimes of international concern, as referred to in this Statute, and shall be complementary

11 On complementarity, see generally, William Schabas, An Introduction to the International Criminal Court 174-191 (2007); Robert Cryer, Hakan Friman, Daryl Robinson & Elizabeth Wilmshurst, An Introduction to International Criminal Law and Procedure (hereinafter, Robert Cryer, et al.) 127-132 (2007), and Benson Olugbo, *Positive Complementarity and the Fight Against Impunity in Africa, in* Prosecuting International Crimes in Africa 249-274 (Chacha Murungu & Japhet Biegon eds., 2011).

to national criminal jurisdictions." Article 17 of the Rome Statute fully demonstrates the importance of this complementary relationship that should exist between the ICC and the domestic criminal accountability jurisdiction of member states. To emphasize this importance it is necessary to reproduce fully the provisions of Article 17, which has set out the parameters that govern this relationship:

1. Having regard to paragraph 10 of the Preamble and article 1, the Court shall determine that a case is inadmissible where:
   (a) The case is being investigated or prosecuted by a State which has jurisdiction over it, unless the State is unwilling or unable genuinely to carry out the investigation or prosecution;
   (b) The case has been investigated by a State which has jurisdiction over it and the State has decided not to prosecute the person concerned, unless the decision resulted from the unwillingness or inability of the State genuinely to prosecute;
   (c) The person concerned has already been tried for conduct which is the subject of the complaint, and a trial by the Court is not permitted under article 20, paragraph 3;
   (d) The case is not of sufficient gravity to justify further action by the Court.
2. In order to determine unwillingness in a particular case, the Court shall consider, having regard to the principles of due process recognized by international law, whether one or more of the following exist, as applicable:
   (a) The proceedings were or are being undertaken or the national decision was made for the purpose of shielding the person concerned from criminal responsibility for crimes within the jurisdiction of the Court referred to in article 5;
   (b) There has been an unjustified delay in the proceedings which in the circumstances is inconsistent with an intent to bring the person concerned to justice;
   (c) The proceedings were not or are not being conducted independently or impartially, and they were or are being conducted in a manner which, in the circumstances, is inconsistent with an intent to bring the person concerned to justice.
3. In order to determine inability in a particular case, the Court shall consider whether, due to a total or substantial collapse or unavailability of its national judicial system, the State is unable to obtain the accused or the necessary evidence and testimony or otherwise unable to carry out its proceedings.

From the above provisions of Article 17, it is quite clear that there must be an unambiguous demonstration that a state is "unwilling or incapable genuinely" to undertake the investigation and prosecution of a case that it has jurisdiction to prosecute within the Rome Statute. The indicators for unwillingness to prosecute are quite clear – "shielding" an accused person from "criminal responsibility"; a delay that is "unjustified" and that betrays intention to prosecute; lack of impartiality and independence in a trial. In the same vein, a state is "unable" to prosecute where there is a "substantial collapse or unavailability of its national judicial system. In addition, this will be the case where a state cannot find the accused person or is not in a position to procure necessary witnesses or evidence.

It is safe to say that agreement on Article 17 at the Rome Conference became the pivotal foundation of the Rome Statute. As suggested by Cryer, et al, it may not have been possible to adopt the Rome Statute without giving States the primary opportunity and responsibility to deal with international crimes in their jurisdictions.[12] This is important because states are not in the habit of surrendering their jurisdiction easily to an international institution, particularly a court or tribunal. Normally, a state would be more equipped to obtain the best evidence and to procure the necessary witnesses to effectively prosecute a case within its jurisdiction than would an international court[13] that is far removed from the territory of the crime. The logistics of investigating in a foreign country and procuring witnesses by the prosecutorial team of the ICC or any other international court vested with criminal jurisdiction can be an extremely daunting and expensive exercise. It follows therefore that ensuring effective domestic justice systems is primarily the best way of dealing with such cases that are implicated in international criminal justice processes.

Accordingly, unless a state genuinely (in the interest of fair trial considerations to avoid persecutive domestic prosecution of opponents, or where the crime is of enormous gravity) surrenders the case to the ICC, there is nothing that should prevent a state from assuming jurisdiction for crimes covered by the Rome Statute. To just assume that a state is "unwilling or unable" in the full ramifications of those concepts, to deal with cases that arise within its jurisdiction would be too condescending and patronizing. There appears to be this blanket assumption regarding African domestic courts. While there may be challenges in the domestic judiciaries and justice systems of many African states, it cannot be said that African states will automatically either be "unwilling" or "unable" to effectively deal with international crimes, unless we are talking of a failed state like Somalia. In some of the current African cases before the ICC, one is led to believe that the assessment of States' unwillingness or inability may have been hastily made by the ICC Prosecutor and by extension, the Court's Pre-Trial Chamber when one looks at the Court's first case of *Prosecutor v. Lubanga Dyilo*[14] where the Pre-Trial Chamber found that the case was admissible on the charge of recruiting child soldiers even though Lubanga had been in

12 Robert Cryer *et al.*, *supra* note 11, at 127.

13 *Id.*

14 *Prosecutor v. Lubanga Dyilo* ICC-01/04-01/06. Decision on the Prosecutor's Application for a Warrant of Arrest (February 10, 2006).

the custody of the government of the Democratic Republic of Congo (DRC) for a year for other serious crimes rather than specifically for the crime on which the ICC was trying him. Thus, 'inaction' on the part of the DRC relative to the conscription of child soldiers charge became the basis of the failure of an argument for domestic jurisdiction based on complementarity in that case.[15] While scholars appear worried by this somewhat controversial interpretation of admissibility, taking the circumstances of the case into account, the element of self-referral of the case by the DRC to the ICC weakened the well-placed criticism of the Pre-Trial Chamber's admissibility decision.[16] However, it may not be out of place for one to argue that the eagerness of the prosecutor to bring the *Lubanga* case before ICC and that of the Pre-Trial Chamber to find it admissible (the overriding self-referral by the DRC not withstanding) was as a result of the fact that the ICC was in a hurry to start actual prosecution of cases, since it appeared to have been idle for a very long time after the operationalization of the Court.

From where this author stands on the significance of the complementarity principle in relation to Africa, the thinking should rather be on how to make African states more willing and able to take on the prosecution of such cases covered by the Rome Statue, while at the same time being vigilant to transfer cases to the ICC based on clearly thought out criteria, which would depend on the circumstances of the particular cases even where a state may be willing and able to prosecute the case. It cannot be accepted that the agreement of states in Rome to vest primary criminal jurisdiction on domestic courts cannot be implemented in Africa. That is indeed the crux of the matter.

The Office of the Prosecutor (OTP) of the ICC in its 2003 policy paper clearly recognized the primacy of the domestic systems in dealing with the crimes created by the Rome Statute as the real import of the complementary principle, without which the ICC would be inundated with a huge caseload that it is not equipped to handle.[17] The policy paper also articulated the facilitative role of the OTP to encourage states:

> [T]o carry out their primary responsibility of investigating and prosecuting crimes. In any assessment of these efforts, the Office will take into consideration the need to respect the diversity of legal systems, traditions and cultures. The

15 *Id.* para. 37-39.

16 For an analysis of this decision and other similar decisions, see WILLIAM SCHABAS, *supra*, note 11 at 178-182. See also ROBERT CRYER *et al.*, *supra*, note 11, at 128.

17 ICC-OTP, Paper on some policy issues before the Office of the Prosecutor 3-5 (2003) (Paper on file with this author).

> Office will develop formal and informal networks of contacts to encourage States to undertake State action, using means appropriate in the particular circumstances of a given case. For instance, in certain situations, it might be possible and advisable to assist a State genuinely willing to investigate and prosecute by providing it with the information gathered by the Office from different public sources.[18]

This position of the Prosecutor speaks to the notion of positive complementarity – a concept that enables the OTP to implement "a proactive policy of cooperation aimed at promoting national prosecutions."[19] The OTP's definition of its role as promoting positive complementarity is quite clear. It is one where the OTP "will encourage genuine national proceedings where possible, including in situation countries, relying on its various networks of cooperation, but without involving the Office directly in capacity building or financial or technical assistance."[20] The engagement of the OTP with state parties to the Rome Statute on the basis of positive complementarity must be understood from the clear point of view of the OTP that it cannot provide capacity building, financial or technical assistance directly for the member states in encouraging them to implement domestic measures aimed at meeting their obligations under the ICC. To expect the OTP to provide these kinds of assistance to state parties must be naïve because the resources available to the ICC are limited and should only be used for direct ICC operations. Thus, positive complementarity must be understood in the context of proactive initiatives from the ICC in cooperation with state parties for the advancement of the Rome Statute's objectives.

The cooperation inherent in positive complementarity should not necessarily be between the ICC and member states of the Rome Statute only. It should exist between the ICC and regional organizations such as the African Union. In the context of Africa, this cooperation is vital for the success of ICC's work in the continent because of the continent's relevance in this regard, which is likely to remain the case for quite a while. In fact, this relationship should be pursued by both the ICC and the African Union on the one hand, and the ICC and African Member States of the Rome Statue on the other in the process. The seeming currently frosty relationship between the ICC and the African Union is a product of a lack of early meaningful engagement and cooperation between both institutions in

18 *Id.* at 5.

19 OTP-ICC, Prosecutorial Strategy 2009-2012 (1 February 2010), para. 16 (Strategy document on file with this author).

20 *Id.* para. 17.

the work of the ICC in Africa.[21] That said this author believes, however, that the African Union should have a direct and engaged interest in ensuring that its member states that are party to the ICC achieve complementarity.

8.4 Implementing the Complementarity Principle in Africa

The AU as a regional organ (though not a party to the Rome Statute) is well aware that complementarity is vital and this is important for the ICC and other stakeholders in their engagement with both the AU and its member states that are parties to the Rome Statute. In its 2009 'Decision on the Meeting of the African States Parties to the Rome Statute of the International Criminal Court,'[22] the AU Assembly recognized the importance of complementarity. In that Decision, the Assembly urged "Member States to initiate programs of cooperation and capacity building to enhance the capacity of legal personnel in their respective countries regarding the drafting and safety of model legislation dealing with serious crimes of international concern, training of members of the police and the judiciary, and the strengthening of cooperation amongst judicial and investigative agencies."[23] An important question that one must ask relative to the AU's awareness of the importance of complementarity in the processes required under the Rome Statute is, beyond the decisions that urge its member states to take steps to implement complementarity, what other proactive steps has the AU undertaken to ensure that these states actually take the issue of complementarity seriously? It is in the AU's interest that domestic systems are effective and can deal with the requirements of the Rome Statute. The reason the AU has to do this is two-fold: 1) the AU cannot be said to be in favor of egregious human rights violation and the perpetration of impunity. Thus, it must be bold to require its member states that are parties to the Rome Statute to practicalize the complementarity principle; 2) the AU cannot be seen to be taking decisions as a regional body on an issue concerning how it perceives the ICC to be functioning in Africa without being part of the solution to ensuring a proper functioning of the ICC regime on the continent. In this regard, there must

21 The recent ICC-AU joint seminar on technical aspects of the Rome Statute is an encouraging sign of a great need for some cooperation that will foster a good working relationship between the ICC and the AU. The importance of this event can be seen from some of the critical objectives of the conference that were outlined as follows – to "Foster understanding of the criteria of selection of situations and cases before the ICC; Explore the relationship between justice and peace and to describe the role of international and regional organizations in fulfilling these two objectives; Lay the ground for developing a system of exchange and communication between the ICC and the African Union as well as other relevant stakeholders." See Media Advisory on the ICC-AU Joint Seminar on Technical Aspects of the Rome Statute held on July 18-19, 2011 in Addis Ababa, Ethiopia, p. 2 (on file with this author).

22 See AU Assembly's Decision on the Meeting of the African States Parties to the Rome Statute of the International Criminal Court, Assembly/AU/13(XIII) (Decision on the Meeting of African States Parties to the Rome Statute), adopted at its 13th Ordinary Session at Sirte, Libya July 1-3, 2009.

23 *Id.* para. 9.

be ways that the AU can influence its members aligned to the Rome Statute regime to implement complementarity. The AU, as a regional body or institution that is normatively interested in confronting impunity should establish what could be considered minimum standards for practically implementing complementarity as outlined below, which this author would readily admit is not an exhaustive list.

8.4.1 *Domesticating the Rome Statute*

The first most important step is to encourage African States parties to the Rome Statute to domesticate the Statute. Making the Rome Statute part of domestic law must be made a priority. Of the 33 African States parties to the Rome Statute, between 2001 and 2011, South Africa, Burkina Faso, Senegal, Uganda and Kenya are the African states that this writer is aware have implemented domestic legislation that give effect to the Rome Statute in their jurisdictions. If the AU is unhappy with its citizens being tried by the ICC, it must encourage credible domestic ownership of justice for atrocity crimes. It is not enough that some of its member states have ratified the Rome Statute without doing more. The AU must engage African States parties to the Rome Statute to domesticate the Statute.

8.4.2 *Judicial Reform Geared Toward Domestic Implementation of the Rome Statute*

Alongside the domestication of the Rome Statute, the AU must be prepared to require concerted efforts to initiate elaborate judicial reform in the African States Parties to the Rome Statute. In some states, it will be necessary to require them to create an international crimes court or chamber within presently existing court structures that is vested with international criminal jurisdiction for crimes covered in the Rome Statute. A recent example in this regard (which this author is not aware of any influencing role of the AU) is Uganda, which has created an International Crimes Division of its High Court that was established in 2008.[24] The Ugandan Court opened its first trial of a leader of the Lord's Resistance Army in July 2011.[25] The ICC seems to have put its work in Uganda on

24 See the Judiciary of the Republic of Uganda, Establishment of International Crimes Division of the High Court at <www.judicature.go.ug/index.php?option=com_content&task=view&id=117&Itemid=154> (Accessed October 28, 2011).

25 The trial began on July 11, 2011, the first of such trial (*Uganda v. Thomas Kwoyelo*) in Africa relating to the giving of effect to domestic implementation of crimes covered in the ICC Statute. On the Ugandan International Crimes Division first case, see Judith Christabella Aceng, *Opening of first War Crimes Trials at the International Crimes Division of the High Court of Uganda* at <www.ucicc.org/index.php?view=article&catid=35%3Awhats-new-&id=123%3Aopening-of-first-war-crimes-trials-at-the-international-crimes-division-of-the-hugh-court-of-uganda&format=pdf&option=com_content> (Accessed October 28, 2011).

hold – rather choosing to shift activities to Kenya. In this regard, one is tempted to ask a question – could it be because of the seeming serious domestic justice mechanisms initiated by Uganda relative to its situations? While the ICC's seeming withdrawal from Uganda may well be because of other sundry considerations, this author is of the view that Uganda's step in initiating domestic mechanisms for the prosecution of atrocity crimes may be a factor. Uganda's step in this regard is commendable from the point of view of complementarity. Indeed, it may not be perfect, but it is a starting point and it is bound to benefit from further development and fine-tuning of the mechanism over time.

Any judicial or legal reform will involve the appointment and training of judges and other court officials that would function in the registry of the specialized crimes courts, chambers or divisions of existing courts. It will also involve comprehensive equipping of such courts with the necessary tools needed to enable them to achieve their mandate.

8.4.3 *Reform of Prosecutorial and Allied Services*

Just as the judiciary needs to be reformed to enable such African states that lack capacity in dealing with crimes covered in the Rome Statute to stem the capacity gap, so also is the need to reform the prosecutorial authorities and systems in place in those countries. This will involve the training of new prosecutors in international crimes prosecution and the provision of all necessary prosecutorial facilities to make the prosecution of such crimes as professional and credible as expected. An allied service to effective prosecution is effective investigative services. There must be a new crop of investigators to deal with this new area in many of the states that are party to the Rome Statute.

8.4.4 *Witness Management and Witness Protection*

A very important aspect of prosecuting and defending international crimes is the ability for effective witness management. The kind of crimes that the Rome Statute deals with usually attracts a large number of witnesses both for the prosecution and the defense. Effectively procuring these witnesses will require some special skills that may be lacking in a number of African states. More importantly instituting effective witness protection measures is vital for the safety and security of witnesses that may genuinely be in danger for testifying in such cases. Indeed, complementarity would mean having a robust witness management programme in place in member states of the Rome Statute.

8.4.5 *Effective Public Defender System*

In the interest of fair trial and equality of arms between the prosecution and the defense, every state must be in a position to have a credible and effective public defender system that caters to accused persons who may be indigent. It is definitely not going to be in all cases that accused persons are persons of means who would obtain the best legal defense available no matter the cost just to clear their names. Domestic prosecution of the crimes contained in the Rome Statute must meet the threshold of international standards of justice relative to ensuring adequate defense for accused persons. There is a danger of adverse public opinion against those accused of committing war crimes, genocide and crimes against humanity. They must therefore be afforded the opportunity for the best possible defense. The existence of effective and adequate defense only reinforces the credibility of the entire process of ensuring justice in the prosecution of these types of crimes whether domestically or internationally. Effective and adequate defense is therefore a very vital element of complementarity.

The AU must confront its perceived wrong moves of the ICC in Africa with credible solutions that convey a proactive stance in dealing with egregious violations of human rights that assume the dimension of international crimes as recognized in the Rome Statute. Without more from the AU as a regional authority, it will be very difficult to convince even well-meaning Africans that the organization is serious in this regard.

8.5 AFRICAN UNION'S ENGAGEMENT WITH THE ICC: USING THE EUROPEAN UNION'S MODEL

The relationship between the ICC and the European Union (EU) is quite a cordial one. It is widely known that the EU played a very pivotal role in the establishment of the ICC at a time that the United States abandoned its leading role in initiating the global movement for the creation of a permanent international criminal tribunal. When the United States eventually decided to undermine the ICC, the EU took it upon itself to make sure that the non-involvement of the United States did not result in the stillbirth of the ICC. This is mainly because of the EU's resolve at tackling impunity for gross human rights violations in the world. In this regard the EU is a pivotal financier of the ICC.[26] The EU recognizes

26 See ANTONIS ANTONIADIS & OLYMPIA BEKOU (hereinafter Antoniadis & Bekou), *The European Union and the International Criminal Court: An Awkward Symbiosis in Interesting Times* 3 (2007) (On file with this author).

that it is not a party to the Rome Statute as a supranational European entity, but rather that its constituent states are the parties. However, it has, as an organizing European entity taken steps that ensure a strong partnership with the ICC – a partnership that its component states have come to understand as vital and which partnership informs how each EU state regards its obligation under the Rome Statute. In this regard, the EU adopted a Common Position on the International Criminal Court.[27] The provisions of the Common Provisions Declaration form the foundation of the EU's commitment to the ICC, which commitment its constituent states are bound to take seriously. One principle that is of great importance in this regard is the universal accession to the Rome Statue.[28] Similarly, the EU has undertaken to make the acceptance, ratification or accession of the Rome Statue part of its foreign policy by raising them in negotiation with third states.[29]

Furthermore, the EU-ICC partnership is strengthened by the EU-ICC Agreement.[30] This Agreement creates areas of cooperation with the ICC that would enable the ICC to achieve its mandate. An area where the EU commitment has been shown beyond all others is in the domestic implementation of the Rome Statute. Among all parties to the Rome Statute, majority of the states that have domestically implemented the Statute is found in the EU. The EU in March 2011 adopted a new Decision on the international Criminal Court, which repeals the Common Position of 2003.[31] The new Decision, among other things, reiterates EU's support for the ICC; it contains commitment on ensuring global domestic implementation of the Rome Statute; it commits EU member states to take necessary measures to implement complementarity at national level; and its willingness to share experience with other states parties that may be interested in the implementation of the Rome Statute.[32]

Indeed, the EU-ICC engagement has good lessons that Africa, under the guidance of the AU can learn from. The overall AU-ICC engagement can commence on the same basis as that of the EU. While the various independent African states that are parties to the Rome Statute undertook individual treaty obligations, it is important to involve the AU in a buy-in against impunity in line with Article 4 of its Constitutive Act. A positive common position by the AU will definitely impact its member states' commitment to their obligation freely undertaken when they ratified or acceded to the Rome Statue. It therefore follows in

27 Council Common Position 2003/444/CFSP of June 16, 2003 on the International Criminal Court, O.J.L 150/67, 18.6.2003 referred to and cited in ANTONIADIS & BEKOU, *supra* note 26 at 5.

28 COUNCIL COMMON POSITION (doc.10400/03) CFSP, Pmbl 7 (on file with this author).

29 *Id.* Art. 2(1).

30 ANTONIADIS & BEKOU, *supra* note 26 at 5, citing Council Decision 2006/313/CFSP of 10 April 2006. O.J. L 115/49, 28.4.2006.

31 COUNCIL DECISION 2011/168/CFSP of March 21, 2011 (on file with this Author).

32 *Id.* Art.s 1, 2, 3 and 5.

terms of strategy for Africa and the ICC, that more energy and resources should be channeled to engaging the AU at the highest level. Vital aspects of this engagement is making investments in judicial and other reforms across Africa in line with the issues raised in the preceding section of this chapter. To this end, development partners should look to engaging prominent African states parties to the Rome Statute that are also prominent members of the African Union in terms of their positions as regional powers within the continent and whose contributions are substantial in the AU. These states should influence the AU as an entity to see the ICC in a positive light and engage with it from that perspective.

8.6 COMPLEMENTARITY AND THE PROPOSED AFRICAN UNION CRIMINAL CHAMBER

As indicated in the introductory part of this chapter, it is important to briefly interrogate the notion of an AU Criminal Chamber relative to complementarity. I deal with a more holistic examination of this issue elsewhere.[33] Therefore, I only raise a minute aspect of this new phenomenon and do not go into an intricate examination of the subject. The African Union's decision to explore the setting up of a criminal chamber as part of the African Court of Justice and Human Rights[34] can be said to be a reaction to the regional body's strong feeling that Africa was being targeted by the ICC. In the same vein, the African Union believes strongly that African views on enforcing the Rome Statute in Africa relative to the Union's initiatives for peaceful resolution of conflicts in the region are not being taken seriously by the international community in its various representations. It is quite clear that the refusal of the UNSC to attend to the AU's deferral request under Article 16 of the Rome Statute regarding the indictment of President Al Bashir of Sudan triggered this new attitude of the AU.

One very important point that must be taken away from the above scenario is that the AU does not appear to be saying that it does not want accountability in Africa for egregious violations of human rights. To be sure, as I have indicated earlier, the Constitutive Act of the African Union clearly calls for measures to deal with such violations in very strong terms.[35] The very fact that the AU is advocating for a criminal chamber within its regional human rights accountability mechanism is an indication that it is interested in dealing with impunity. The undertone that one can clearly glean from AU's objection is the need for Africa to take control of the prosecution and trial of African accused persons under its own

33 *See* generally Vincent O. Nmehielle, *Saddling the New African Regional Human Rights Court with International Criminal Jurisdiction: Innovative, Obstructive, Expedient* (Forthcoming and on file with this author; based on a paper presented at the International Conference on Africa and International Law: Taking Stock ad Moving Forward at Albany Law School, Albany, New York, April 12-14, 2012).

34 AU Assembly's Decision on the Meeting of the African States Parties to the Rome Statute of the International Criminal Court, *supra* note 10.

35 See Art. 4(h) of the AU Constitutive Act.

home-grown system. If this thinking is right, then, there may be a question as to whether there is any need to reinvent the wheel, since the complementarity principle of the Rome Statute already allows domestic systems to do so. Thus, there is need to seriously engage with the African Union to empower its Member States to embark on credible implementation of the complementarity principle by taking credible ownership of such trials in their various domestic systems that are designed for that purpose. It is clear from the recent Decision of the AU Assembly that the creation of a Criminal Chamber of the African Court is purely an avenue to seek "how best Africa's interest can be fully defended and protected in the international judicial system."[36] Any commentator or observer is likely to see this move as indeed reactionary due to a perceived "Africa backlash" on the ICC.

Another issue that must be interrogated is the impact of this decision on African member states to the Rome Statute. Of course, there is the issue of conflict of obligations for these states relative to their commitment under the Rome Statute regime on the one hand, and to their primary regional organization – the AU, on the other. It follows then that there is a need to engage the AU as a regional organization on the one hand, and these African States parties – as those with a treaty obligation on effective implementation of the Rome Statute in their domestic systems, on the other. There is no denying the fact that Africa needs the mechanism within the Rome Statute and the mechanism needs Africa. Unfortunately, Africa appears to be the region that currently makes the work of the ICC relevant. In this engagement, there must be some acceptance that it is not every case that emanates from Africa that needs to go to the ICC. Credible and sincere efforts must be brought to bear to encourage and enable African states to domestically deal with these cases.

From the point of view of complementarity, the Criminal Chamber will face the same challenges as the ICC in terms of a limited mandate that makes it a court of last resort because domestic courts have primary jurisdiction. There is also the problem of limited resources available to the Chamber in exercising its mandate. The argument for effective complementarity in individual African states' domestic systems as against an AU centralized criminal court or chamber can also be made from the angle of adequate or inadequate resourcing of African regional institutions. Currently, the African Commission on Human and Peoples' Rights as well as the African Court on Human and Peoples' Rights still need more resources and facilities for their full and effective functioning. The judges of the Human Rights Court, apart from the President are engaged on part-time basis. It cannot be envisaged that judges of the Criminal Chamber should serve part-time. An

36 Decision on the Implementation of the Assembly Decisions on the International Criminal Court, Assembly/AU/Dec.366(XVII), adopted at the 17th Ordinary Session of the AU Assembly, June 30 -July 1, 2011 in Malabo, Equatorial Guinea, para. 8.

African Criminal Chamber must operate on full-time basis and this has huge implications for costs. The creation of a Criminal Chamber will lead to the appointment of more judges and other personnel for the Chamber. A prosecutor, prosecutorial and investigative personnel must be appointed for his or her office to function effectively.

The AU appears to have the principle of complementarity at the back of its mind in exploring ways for the establishment of the Criminal Chamber. In this regard, draft Article 46H(1) of the Draft Statute of the African Court of Justice and Human and Peoples' Rights annexed to the Draft Protocol on Amendments to the Protocol on the Statute of the African Court of Justice and Human Rights[37] makes provision for concurrent jurisdiction between the proposed criminal chamber and "the Courts of African Regional Economic Communities as appropriate, and the national Courts of States Parties" over crimes covered in the Statute of the Court and the Protocol. Even though the term "concurrent jurisdiction" is used in the above draft article, the import of the provision is one of complementarity as clearly indicated in Article 46H(2) that provides:

The Court shall determine that a case is inadmissible where:

a) The case is being investigated or prosecuted by a State which has jurisdiction over it, unless the State is unwilling or unable to carry out the investigation or prosecution;
b) The case has been investigated by a State which has jurisdiction over it and the State has decided not to prosecute the person concerned, unless the decision resulted from the unwillingness or inability of the State to prosecute;
c) The person concerned has already been tried for conduct which is the subject of the complaint;
d) The case is not of sufficient gravity to justify further action by the Court.

This provision mirrors the admissibility requirements of Article 17 of the Rome Statute. In this regard one may begin to question how expedient it is to have this Chamber since the Rome Statute is quite clear that the jurisdiction of the ICC is complimentary to that of domestic courts. If in effect, the jurisdiction of the Chamber is complementary to that of national courts of member states, then we are back to the same position as under the Rome Statute. Without going into the full merit or otherwise of establishing the criminal chamber (which is reserved elsewhere), one is tempted to reiterate the point that the emphasis should have been on ensuring proper implementation of the principle of complementarity under the Rome Statute by the African states parties to the Statute.

37 Draft Protocol on Amendments to the Protocol on the Statute of the African Court of Justice and Human Rights, Legal/ACJHRPAP/4 (II) Rev. 2.

8.7 Conclusion

There is clear evidence of Africa's genuine support for the establishment of the ICC and the region's commitment to end impunity for gross and egregious human rights violations. The replacement of the Organization of African Unity with the AU signaled a clear intention of Africa to break from its challenging post-colonial past that has been filled with violent conflicts and mass atrocities. Thirty-three states out of 54 states of the African Union are parties to the Rome Statute. These states have not denounced their obligations under the Rome Statute and would not do so any time soon despite the seeming frosty relationship between the AU and the ICC. Indeed, there is no denying the fact that the highly toxic international politics at the level of the UNSC and the somewhat abrasive attitude of the first Prosecutor of the ICC is alienating the African Union on the one hand and some African member states to the Rome Statute on the other. Still, the point is made that the ICC is very relevant for the Africa as it is for the rest of the world. Africa must therefore be made to feel an integral part of the international system. Her voice represented by the AU should be heard in the various contributions that are made for effective international criminal justice. Just as the EU is engaged in ensuring the realization of the benefits of the complementarity principle in its member states that are party to the Rome Statute, the AU must be in the forefront in engaging its own member states. To this end, there should be increased engagement with African states on domestic prosecutions in the spirit of the Rome Statute. This will give Africa credible ownership of dealing with atrocity crimes on the continent. No African state can be said to be in favor of impunity. Thus, effectively implementing the complementarity principle is indeed the way forward in advancing international criminal justice accountability in Africa. All stakeholders in the quest to achieve global respect for international criminal justice, including the ICC need to truly engage the AU and the African States Parties to the Rome Statute on effective complementarity.

The AU on its part must be responsive by credibly making the issue of effective complementarity a departure point of its resolve to deal with impunity in the continent. The ICC can only be put out of work in Africa if effective domestic systems are in place to deal with atrocity crimes and if egregious violations of human rights on the continent with impunity are truly dealt with by the AU in the spirit of its Constitutive Act and other numerous normative instruments. The AU must move and be seen to move beyond fine ideals and aspirations tucked away in treaties but without meaningful implementation. Africa through the AU must gain the respect of its peers by protecting her citizens against tyranny and misrule.

9 The Complimentarity Principle Put to the Test

Uganda's Experience

Caroline Nalule and Rachel Odoi-Musoke

9.1 Introduction

When compared to other courts of an international nature, such as the International Court of Justice, the International Criminal Court (hereinafter referred to as 'ICC' or 'the Court') came into existence with a difference, namely that it almost has universal jurisdiction over individual perpetrators of the most atrocious crimes in international law. Important to note here are the aspects of universal jurisdiction as well as that of individual responsibility whereby individuals could no longer hide behind the blanket of state sovereignty for serious crimes that they may have committed. It has been argued that since the crimes within the jurisdiction of the ICC are so serious, they create an obligation on all States, whether party or not to the Rome Statute of the International Criminal Court[1] (hereinafter referred to as 'the Rome Statute'). More so, it adopted the position of Article 1 of Additional Protocol II to the 1949 Geneva Conventions, by extending its jurisdiction over non-traditional subjects of international law, to include non-State actors to an armed conflict, provided that their actions fall within the crimes that the Court can prosecute.

The establishment of the ICC was greatly supported and welcomed by many African States,[2] which could be attributed to the fact that there were several armed conflicts on the African continent most of which were characterized by serious violations of international human rights and humanitarian law. This could partly explain why all the cases or situations

1 Federica Gioia, *State Sovereignty, Jurisdiction, and 'Modern' International Law: The Principle of Complementarity in the International Criminal Court*, 19 Leiden Journal of International Law 1095, 1102-1105 (2006).

2 Judging from the signatories, the African States were 42 out of the 139 signatories to the Rome Statute making a 30% support from the African States. Refer to <http://treaties.un.org/Pages/ViewDetails.aspx?src=TREATY&mtdsg_no=XVIII-10&chapter=18&lang=en> (Accessed May 26, 2010). Presently 30 African countries have ratified the Statute making it the biggest regional bloc to have done so.

currently before the ICC concern African States.[3] One of such cases, which shall be the focus of the present discourse, is one referred by the Government of Uganda to the ICC in December 2003.[4] The situation that was referred for investigation and eventual prosecution, if need be, was against the Lord's Resistance Army (LRA), an insurgent group that has wreaked havoc and caused so much suffering in the northern part of Uganda for over twenty years.

This chapter examines the progress made in handling the post-conflict situation in Uganda and how it has generally put the complementarity principle to test in a rather unprecedented way. Before we look at how the complementarity principle has been applied in Uganda, it is necessary to give a background to the nature and status of the case before the ICC.

9.2 BACKGROUND TO THE CASE OF UGANDA BEFORE THE ICC

Uganda's political history since it gained independence in October 1962 has been marred by coups, dictatorship and tribal conflicts based on which tribe was deemed to be in power. In January 1986, the National Resistance Army/Movement (NRA/M) led by Yoweri Kaguta Museveni who hails from the Southern part of Uganda, overthrew the government of the day that was led by General Tito Okello Lutwa, from the Northern part of Uganda specifically from Acholiland. As a result of this coup, a number of insurgent groups rose up in the North and one would not be wrong to assert that there had not been much stability in the Northern part of Uganda for about twenty years since 1986. One of the many insurgent groups that came up was the LRA led by Joseph Kony who had originally been part of the Holy Spirit Movement led by Alice Lakwena, who was later defeated. The LRA has proven to be the most adversarial, persevering and elusive insurgent group that the Government of Uganda has had to deal with over the years. Although the LRA claimed that it was initially fighting for the Restoration of the Ten Commandments, hence, its name, it seems to have broken each and every one of those commandments to unimaginable extremes. The LRA has been accused of committing a number of atrocities ranging from murder, rape, abduction of children, sex slavery, mutilations, massacres, not to mention recruitment of child soldiers, on a mass scale. Most bizarre was that these atrocities were committed against Kony's

3 There are currently six situations or cases being handled by the ICC: The situation in Uganda – *The Prosecutor v. Joseph Kony, Vincent Otti, Okot Odhiambo and Dominic Ongwen*, the situation in the Democratic Republic of Congo – *The Prosecutor v. Thomas Lubanga*; *The Prosecutor v. Bosco Ntaganda*; *The Prosecutor v. Germain Katanga and Mathieu Ngudjolo*; the situation in Darfur, Sudan – *The Prosecutor v. Ahmad Harun and Ali Kushyab*; *The Prosecutor v. Omar Al Bashir*; *The Prosecutor v. Bahar Idriss*; the situation in the Central African Republic – *The Prosecutor v. Jean-Pierre Bemba*; the situation in the Republic of Kenya; and finally the situation in Libyan Arab Jamahiriya that was referred by the United Nations Security Council.

4 Press Conference, Office of the Prosecutor, The Investigation in Northern Uganda, (October 14, 2005), available at <www.icc-cpi.int/NR/rdonlyres/2919856F-03E0-403F-A1A8-D61D4F350A20/277306/Uganda_PPpresentation7.pdf> (last accessed May 26, 2010).

own kinsfolk, the Acholi people, moving away from the earlier thinking and perception that the LRA war was intended to overthrow the Southern-dominated government.

The Government of Uganda has employed various tactics over the years in an attempt to end the rebellion, but to no avail. The tactics have ranged from military offensives and operations both within and outside Uganda where the LRA had hideouts; peace talks initiated by various groups including religious groups; and amnesty offered by the government, but none of these seem to have proven successful.

On July 1, 2002, Uganda ratified the Rome Statute and this later turned out to be one of the ways by which Joseph Kony and his outfit would be pursued. As it were, in December 2003, President Yoweri Museveni, on behalf of the Government of Uganda, referred the situation of the LRA to the ICC Prosecutor to investigate in accordance with Article 14 of the Rome Statute. Following this, on July 29, 2004, the Chief Prosecutor of the ICC, announced that his office would begin preliminary investigations into crimes committed by the Lord's Resistance Army (LRA) during its 18-year war against the Government of Uganda.[5] The case was investigated and the Prosecutor, having been satisfied that the LRA leaders had a case to answer, had five arrest warrants issued, on July 8, 2005 against Joseph Kony, Vincent Otti, Raska Lukwiya,[6] Okot Odhiambo and Dominic Ongwen, the top commanders of the LRA.

The LRA seemed to have a change of heart and agreed to hold peace talks with the Government of Uganda. These talks were to be brokered by Riek Machar, the Deputy Vice President of the Government of Southern Sudan. The talks commenced in 2006, during which various agreements were signed[7] that would eventually culminate into the Final Peace Agreement. The Final Peace Agreement was supposed to be signed in November 2008, but Joseph Kony did not

5 Press Release, Prosecutor of the International Criminal Court opens an investigation into Northern Uganda (July 29, 2004), available at <www.icc-cpi.int/menus/icc/press%20and%20media/press%20releases/2004/Prosecutor%20of%20the%20international%20criminal%20court%20opens%20an%20investigation%20into%20nothern%20uganda> (last accessed May 8, 2010).

6 Proceedings against Raska Lukwiya were terminated on July 11, 2007 following news and confirmation of his death. *See* <www.icc-cpi.int/menus/icc/situations%20and%20cases/situations/situation%20icc%200204/related%20cases/icc%200204%200105/court%20records/chambers/pre%20trial%20chamber%20ii/decision%20to%20terminate%20the%20proceedings%20against%20raska%20lukwiya?lan=en-GB> (last accessed May 8, 2010). Although there has been news that Vincent Otti was also killed by Kony himself see Fortunate Ahimbisibwe & Gerald Tenywa, *Vincent Otti is Confirmed Dead*, The New Vision, November 21, 2007, this is yet to be confirmed by the Pre-trial chamber. As such his arrest warrant is still pending.

7 The following Agreements were signed between the Government of the Republic of Uganda and the Lord's Resistance Army/Movement: Agreement on Cessation of Hostilities (Agenda Item No. 1) signed on August 26, 2006; Agreement on Comprehensive Solutions (Agenda Item No. 2) signed on May 2, 2007; Agreement on Accountability and Reconciliation (Agenda Item No. 3) signed on June 29, 2007; Agreement on a Permanent Ceasefire (Agenda Item No. 4) signed on February 23, 2008; Agreement on Disarmament, demobilization and Reintegration (Agenda Item No. 5) signed on February 29, 2008; and Agreement on Implementation and Monitoring Mechanisms (Agenda Item No. 6) signed on February 29, 2008.

appear to sign and subsequent efforts to get the LRA to renegotiate and sign have proved futile. Currently, Joseph Kony and his rebels are said to be moving between the Democratic Republic of Congo and the Central African Republic leaving a trail of rampant atrocities.[8]

Of particular importance to us, however, is what was agreed upon as Agenda Item 3 during the peace talks. This comprised one of the agreements that was signed and which would have formed part of the Final Peace Agreement. Agenda Item 3 was on Accountability and Reconciliation and one of the terms of the agreement that was made was that "[t]he choice of forum for the adjudication of any particular case shall depend, amongst other considerations, on the nature and gravity of the offending conduct and the role of the alleged perpetrator in that conduct."[9] The Agreement goes ahead to provide in Clause 4.4. that "accountability mechanisms shall be implemented through the adapted legal mechanisms in Uganda." To further expound on this, Clause 5.1. provides that the parties:

> [A]ffirm that Uganda has institutions and mechanisms, customs and usages as provided for and recognized under national laws, capable of addressing the crimes and human rights violations committed during the conflict. The Parties also recognize that modifications may be required within the national legal system to ensure a more effective and integrated justice and accountability response.

The agreement also provides for alternative justice mechanisms with the major objective of reconciliation.[10] Such mechanisms would be utilized in tandem with the formal justice mechanisms.

Without explicitly making provision for where the LRA leaders would be tried, the Agreement, in Clause 6.1, provided "formal courts provided for under the Constitution shall exercise jurisdiction over individuals who are alleged to bear particular responsibility for the most serious crimes, especially crimes amounting to international crimes, during the course of the conflict." Joseph Kony and the other fugitives would fall squarely within this provision as they are generally considered to bear particular responsibility for the most serious crimes. The position seems to have been made more explicit in the Agreement on Implementation and Monitoring Mechanisms signed on February 29, 2008. There were

8 Press Release, United Nations Office for the Coordination of Humanitarian Affairs, D.R. Congo: UN Humanitarian Chief Condemns LRA Violence" (May 1, 2010) available at <www.reliefweb.int/rw/rwb.nsf/db900SID/MYAI-8532T9?OpenDocument> (last accessed May 8, 2010). *See also,* Human Rights Watch, *Trail of Death: LRA Atrocities in North Eastern Congo* (Human Rights Watch, 2010). Further information also available at <www.hrw.org/news/2011/05/23/uscentral-africa-protect-civilians-lra-abuses> (last accessed September 14, 2011).

9 Agreement on Accountability and Reconciliation of August 26, 2006 (hereinafter referred to as "Agenda Item No. 3"), at Clause 4.3.

10 *Id.* Clause 5.3.

specifically two clauses that are worth noting: Clause 36 provided that the Government would, soon after signing the Final Peace Agreement, give priority to commencing criminal investigations and establishing a Special Division of the High Court. Clause 37 is of particular importance; it provided "[o]n the basis of steps taken under clause 36 . . . the Government shall request the UN Security Council to adopt a resolution under Chapter VII of the Charter of the United Nations, requesting the International Criminal Court to defer all investigations and prosecutions against the leaders of the LRA."

This shift in position clearly created much confusion and uncertainty as to where Joseph Kony and the others would be prosecuted, if arrested. The situation was made worse by the failure of Kony to sign the Final Peace Agreement, thus raising questions as to the status or binding force of the numerous agreements that had been signed and could be said to be binding and enforceable. It is at this point in time that the issue of complementarity really came to the fore and it prompted the Court to invoke its *proprio motu* powers under Article 19 of the Statute to make a determination on the admissibility of the case.

In the following section, we deal with the applicability of the complementarity principle in Uganda's situation and how it has been put to the test, particularly when one considers that Uganda referred the case to the ICC; that it was investigated and almost at the point of prosecution, but with a possibility that the Government of Uganda could at some point seek to reclaim its jurisdiction over the case. The turn of events begged the question whether Uganda did actually not "put the cart before the horse" when it opted for the self-referral. The analysis of the circumstances is made here in light of the Court's decision on admissibility of the case and whether Uganda could make a case for exercising jurisdiction over the case. Now that it seems to have found a way to exercise jurisdiction, the Government of Uganda would still have to prove not so much its willingness as its ability to prosecute the case. The following discussion leads us into examining how far the Government of Uganda has gone to demonstrate its ability and the challenges that it stands to face in trying the wanted LRA leaders as opposed to the ICC in The Hague.

9.3 "Putting the Cart before the Horse"?

The complementarity principle as laid out in Article 17 of the Rome Statute, provides that a case will be inadmissible where: (a) it is being investigated or prosecuted by a State which has jurisdiction over it, unless the State is unwilling or unable genuinely to carry out the investigation or prosecution; or (b) the case has been investigated by the State which has jurisdiction over it and the State has decided not to prosecute the person concerned, unless the decision resulted from the unwillingness or inability genuinely of the State to prosecute. The principle has been explained as "reconciling the States' persisting duty to exercise jurisdiction over international crimes with the establishment of a permanent international criminal court having competence over the same crimes."[11]

Considering Uganda's referral of the case to the ICC to investigate and prosecute under Article 14, one would say that this self-referral ruled out the applicability of Article 17. More so when one considers that at the time of the referral, the Government of Uganda endorsed the Court's jurisdiction over the case by pointing out that the Ugandan judicial system had been unable to secure the arrest of the alleged perpetrators mainly because they operated from bases in Southern Sudan where Uganda had no jurisdiction. As such the Court was the "most appropriate forum for the investigation and prosecution of those bearing the greatest responsibility for the crimes within the referred situation."[12]

El Zeidy argues that Uganda's or any State's self-referral for that matter, could possibly imply a waiver of the complementarity principle. He says that "a State might prefer to defer the situation in question by referring it to the ICC without waiting for an admissibility ruling (*i.e.* without the Court technically determining that the State is unwilling or unable to proceed)."[13] He goes on to argue that this is so because an obvious interpretation of Article 17 would be that the ICC only takes over jurisdiction where a concerned State has shown neither willingness nor ability to prosecute.[14] By referring the case to the ICC, without first awaiting the examination by the Court, the country is waiving its jurisdiction over the investigation and prosecution of the case to the ICC.

At this point it needs to be mentioned that Uganda's decision to refer its situation to the ICC was not made purely out of the unwillingness or inability to prosecute. At the point in time that the referral was made, the conflict in northern Uganda had been raging on for close to twenty years and almost the entire population of northern Uganda had been forced into internally displaced persons camps and rendered virtually destitute and totally reliant on humanitarian assistance. The LRA were operating on both sides of the border, compelling the Ugandan forces to pursue them into a foreign territory, particularly in Southern Sudan. Despite a number of military operations carried out with the cooperation of the Government of Sudan, Kony and his top commanders still managed to get away. It could be suggested therefore that it was the inability to arrest, rather than the inability or unwillingness to prosecute that compelled the self-referral and therefore the State was not

11 *The Prosecutor v. Joseph Kony et al.*, ICC-02/04-01/05 -377, Decision on the Admissibility of the Case under Art. 19(1) of the Statute, para. 34 (March 10, 2009).

12 *Id.*, para. 37. These were confidential documents that were cited during the course of the proceedings as the reference to them was deemed by the Pre-Trial Chamber not to be prejudicial to their current status.

13 M. El Zeidy *The Ugandan Government Triggers the First Test of the Complementarity Principle: An Assessment of the First State's Party Referral to the ICC*, 5 INTERNATIONAL CRIMINAL LAW REVIEW 83, 100 (2005).

14 *Id.*

abdicating its jurisdiction to the ICC. Importantly also, one should note that nine years after the issuing of the arrest warrants, Joseph Kony and his commanders have not yet been apprehended.

The question therefore, could be that should Uganda succeed in securing the arrest of the LRA commanders, would it be justified in seeking a withdrawal of the arrest warrants? The issue to consider here is whether after investigating the case and issuing arrest warrants, the complementarity principle would then be brought into play at the point of prosecution. Would the ICC hand over the findings of its investigations to the Government of Uganda or would the latter initiate its own investigations as seems to be implied in Agenda Item No. 3? The use of the conjunction "or" as opposed to "and" in Article 17, with reference to investigation or prosecution by a State with jurisdiction would seem to imply that the complementarity principle can be applied at either the investigation or prosecution stage of a case, for purposes of the ICC determining the admissibility of the case. This was affirmed by Pre-Trial Chamber II in its decision on admissibility of the situation in Uganda in which, after a careful consideration of the provisions of Article 19, it was held that "the corpus of these provisions delineates a system whereby the determination of admissibility is meant to be an on-going process throughout the pre-trial phase, the outcome of which is subject to review depending on the evolution of the relevant factual scenario."[15]

During the admissibility proceedings, however, the Government of Uganda, despite having made ambiguous submissions prior to the hearing, relented that it had no objection to the Court's jurisdiction and that the case was admissible. In order to clear the ambiguity created, it submitted that the:

> framework and processes envisaged in the Agreement and the Annexure had been agreed upon in anticipation of a comprehensive peace agreement whose legal significance, importance and credibility was to be confirmed by its execution by Joseph Kony and the Government of Uganda; and that failure for the former to execute the Agreement resulted in the Agreement being of no legal force.[16]

Though this appears to be the official position of the Uganda Government as relayed to the Court, there seems to be another general and domestic view that the proceedings on admissibility were premature and that the Court should have waited for the Government

15 *The Prosecutor v. Kony et al.*, ICC-02/04-01/05 -377, para. 28.

16 *Id.* para. 8. It further submitted that the mechanisms envisaged under the Agreement were meant to apply to individuals other than those already indicted; and that the provisions of the Agreement were irrelevant to the four fugitives. *See* para. 12.

to pursue the domestic implementation of the Statute together with other mechanisms agreed upon in the various agreements.[17] The persons most affected by the LRA seem to be strongly advocating for peace and if the probability of peace talks was to arise yet again, the Government may have to seriously consider that option, which might then call for another admissibility ruling. Furthermore, although the Government of Uganda seems to have refuted the binding nature of the agreements in its submissions to the Pre-Trial Chamber, the matter would, in our view, still be subject to judicial scrutiny and determination.

The Court, nonetheless, settled the issue of who has the ultimate authority to determine the admissibility of the case saying that "it is for the Court, and not for Uganda to make such a determination."[18] This position as well as the Court's decision was later confirmed by the Appeals Chamber upon appeal by the Defense Counsel.[19] The decision of the Court was,

> [P]ending the adoption of all relevant legal texts and the implementation of all practical steps, the scenario against which the admissibility of the Case has to be determined remains therefore the same as at the time of issuance of the Warrants, that is one of total inaction on the part of the relevant national authorities; and accordingly, there is no reason for the Chamber to review that positive determination of the admissibility of the Case at that stage.[20]

Indeed, the circumstances since the decision was made have changed on the local scene and it is these changes that we seek to examine to decide whether Uganda is in position to investigate and prosecute the cases regarding the LRA indictees. We evaluate the extent to which the Government of Uganda has made progress to demonstrate its ability and willingness to prosecute. We shall start by the examination of the willingness criterion and then proceed to what has been put in place to demonstrate ability.

9.4 Examining Uganda's Willingness to Prosecute the LRA

Article 17(2) of the Rome Statute lays out what the Court would consider as unwillingness on the part of a State: a) where the proceedings seem to be undertaken for the purpose of shielding the person concerned from criminal responsibility; b) there has been

17 *Id.*, para. 9. The Office of Public Counsel for Victims (OPCV) submission was to the effect that the Proceedings should either be suspended or declared admissible pending the effective establishment of the legal and judicial machinery envisaged in the Agreement and the Annexure. See also the views expressed by some Ugandan leaders ICC failed the Kony talks, says Oulanyah, The New Vision, May 27, 2010.

18 *Id.*, para. 51.

19 *The Prosecutor v. Joseph Kony et al.*, ICC-02/04-01/05 OA3 Appeals Chamber, Judgment on the appeal of the Defence against the "Decision on the admissibility of the case under article 19(1) of the Statute" of 10 March 2009, (September 16 2009).

20 *The Prosecutor v. Kony et al.*, ICC-02/04-01/05 -377, para. 52.

an unjustified delay in the proceedings which in the circumstances is inconsistent with an intent to bring the person concerned to justice and; c) the proceedings are not being conducted independently or impartially and are being conducted in a manner which, in the circumstances, is inconsistent with bringing the person concerned to justice.

The issue to be considered here is whether the Government of Uganda satisfies any or all the above criteria in order for it to be said that it was unwilling to investigate or prosecute. This can only be gathered from its actions or omissions as the case may be. So far, there is no proof that the decision to handle the case domestically was made to shield any person responsible from criminal responsibility. On the contrary, it was the view of some observers that the ICC's investigation was biased in the sense that they did not look into the crimes committed by the Government forces, the Uganda Peoples' Defense Forces (UPDF). The Prosecutor, however, did later try to allay these suspicions by announcing that an analysis by the ICC had revealed that the crimes committed by the LRA were much more numerous and of much higher gravity than alleged crimes committed by the UPDF.[21] Nevertheless, there are those that still think the contrary.[22]

Furthermore, looking at the terms agreed upon under Agenda Item No. 3, they seem to be impartially drafted, that is to say, that any individual accused of committing serious crimes, be it LRA or UPDF could be made accountable. For example, clause 4.1. provides, "[F]ormal criminal and civil justice measures shall be applied to any individual who is alleged to have committed serious crimes or human rights violations committed during the conflict. Provided that State actors, shall be subjected to existing criminal justice processes and not special justice processes under this Agreement." The Agreement, therefore, covers both State and non-State actors and the proviso that applies to the State actors does seem to remove them from the purview of the Rome Statute, but that would not make their offences seem of less gravity. Assuming that the said State actors would probably be soldiers, they would be prosecuted under the laws governing the armed forces, which incorporate humanitarian law. The framework proposed under the Agreement would as such go beyond the narrow focus of the Statute and the Court in terms of the persons to be prosecuted.

As we shall see shortly, the Government has gone ahead to put in place mechanisms that would ensure that the perpetrators of the most serious crimes are brought to book. Any delay that has been occasioned in putting such mechanisms and institutions in place can

21 ICC, Statement by the Chief Prosecutor, Mr, Louis Moreno Ocampo, (October 14, 2005). Available at <www.icc-cpi.int/NR/rdonlyres/2919856F-03E0-403F-A1A8-D61D4F350A20/277305/Uganda_LMO_Speech_141020091.pdf> (last accessed May 8, 2010). [hereinafter Statement by the Chief Prosecutor].

22 *See ICC Accused of Favouring Government*, in THE DAILY MONITOR, May 7, 2010.

hardly be attributed to a general lack of unwillingness on the part of the State to make the perpetrators accountable.

Whether or not the proceedings shall be conducted independently or impartially remains to be seen, but so far the Ugandan Courts (particularly the higher Courts, that is, from the High Court to the Supreme Court) have been able to exhibit a high level of independence. This does not mean, however, that there is never any kind of interference. There have been numerous occasions when the judgments of the Courts have attracted criticisms from the highest political office. For instance, when the Constitutional Court ruled in June 2004 that the Referendum (Political Systems) Act, 2000 was unconstitutional, the President interpreted this as usurping the power of the people and the parliament and went on to state that "government will not allow any institution even the Court to usurp the power of the constitution in any way".[23] Perhaps, the ultimate test for the judiciary was in 2005 and 2007 when the High Court was hearing the bail application of some treason suspects allegedly linked to the opposition leader, Dr. Kiiza Besigye. On both occasions, the Court was surrounded by armed men belonging to the security forces and they re-arrested the suspects upon being granted bail. Even in these circumstances, the judiciary came out strongly to condemn these attacks which were, by all means, a flagrant flouting of judicial independence.[24] Concerns, however, still exist regarding the possibility of intimidation and interference, but the judiciary has been not deterred in asserting its independence. Indeed there has been a general improvement in the perception of judicial independence as evidenced by Uganda's improved ranking with regards to Judicial Independence in the Global Competitiveness Index, which now places Uganda 70th out of 139 countries and 15th in Africa.[25] There is no doubt, therefore that the Ugandan courts would not shy from their duty in international criminal trials.

9.5 Examining Uganda's Ability to Prosecute the Perpetrators of the Most Serious Crimes

The Court would determine a State's inability by considering whether, due to a total or substantial collapse or unavailability of its national judicial system, the State is unable to obtain the accused or the necessary evidence and testimony or otherwise unable to carry out its proceedings.[26] While the issue of the collapse of the judicial system would not arise,

23 *See* INTERNATIONAL BAR ASSOCIATION HUMAN RIGHTS INSTITUTE, JUDICIAL INDEPENDENCE UNDERMINED: A REPORT ON UGANDA 21 (2007).

24 *Id.* at 25-31.

25 WORLD ECONOMIC FORUM GLOBAL COMPETITIVENESS REPORT, 2010-2011 (2010).

26 Rome Statute of the International Criminal Court art 17(3), July 17, 1998, 2187 U.N.T.S 90. [hereinafter Rome Statute].

in the case of Uganda,[27] debate would ensue around the ability of the judicial system to obtain the accused or the necessary evidence or to carry out the proceedings. Gioia argues that "a national judicial system should be considered 'unavailable' when its substantive provisions do not allow the conducts corresponding to the crimes provided for in the Statute to be punished in terms which adequately reflect their gravity, thus triggering the stepping in of the Court."[28] Until recently (as recently as March 2010), Uganda, which is a dualist State, had not yet domesticated the Rome Statute. Technically it lacked the proper legal regime under which it could effectively prosecute the perpetrators of serious atrocious crimes.[29] Although it was being argued that the Geneva Conventions could be applied,[30] there is no precedent in Uganda, where the Geneva Conventions or other *jus cogens* norms have been applied to prosecute any individual.

Agenda Item No. 3 took all this into consideration and it is stipulated therein that modifications would be made in the existing legal system to ensure a more effective and integrated justice and accountability response. The Government of Uganda also undertook to establish necessary legislation, policies and procedures to establish the framework for addressing accountability. We shall now proceed to discuss how far it has gone in these undertakings which, in our view, would be used as a basis for judging its 'ability' or 'inability' as the case may be. As events unfold, the greater challenge seems to be the prevailing amnesty, which has taken on a new dimension as the formal trials commence. This will be considered at length later in the chapter.

9.5.1 Legislative Reform

The efforts to domesticate the Rome Statute commenced in mid-2004 with the first International Criminal Court Bill (No. 10 of 2004) being gazetted on May 28, 2004. The Bill was re-tabled in 2006 following its lapse with the expiry of the term of the Parliament in 2006. It was finally debated and passed into law in March 2010. The passage of this law served a threefold purpose: the Government of Uganda was able to fulfill one of its obligations under the Rome Statute, it also demonstrated a commitment by the Government to fulfill

27 The Constitution of the Republic of Uganda, 1995 clearly lays out the hierarchy of the Court system in Uganda with the High Court having unlimited original jurisdiction; appeals from the High Court lie to the Court of Appeal, which also doubles as the Constitutional Court; and the Supreme Court serves as the highest appellate Court. *See* UGANDA. CONST(1995) Arts. 129-139.

28 Gioia, *supra* note 1, at 1107.

29 The Penal Code Act, Cap. 120, (2000)(Uganda) only provides for the crimes of murder, kidnap with intent to murder, rape, defilement, assault occasioning actual bodily harm, as some of the possible crimes for which the perpetrators of the serious crimes could be charged.

30 The Geneva Conventions have been domesticated in Uganda under the Geneva Conventions Act, Cap. 363, (2000)(Uganda).

its obligations under the Agenda Item No. 3, and finally, as some sections of the public believe, it readied Uganda to host the ICC Review Conference scheduled for June 2010.[31] The purpose of the law as stated in Section 2 of the Act is as follows:

a) to give the force of law in Uganda to the Rome Statute;
b) to implement obligations assumed by Uganda under the Rome Statute;
c) to make further provision in Uganda's law for the punishment of the crimes of genocide, crimes against humanity and war crimes;
d) to enable Uganda to co-operate with the ICC in the performance of its functions, including the investigation and prosecution of persons accused of having committed the crimes referred to in the Rome Statute;
e) to provide for the arrest and surrender to the ICC of persons alleged to have committed crimes referred to under the Rome Statute;
f) to provide for various forms of requests for assistance to the ICC;
g) to enable the Ugandan courts to try, convict and sentence persons who have committed crimes referred to in the Rome Statute;
h) to enable the ICC to conduct proceedings in Uganda; and
i) to enforce any sentence imposed or order made by the ICC.

The Act is divided into ten parts: part 1 contains the preliminary matters such as the purpose, interpretation and application of the Rome Statute in Uganda; part 2 provides for international crimes and offences against the administration of justice; part 3 contains general provisions relating to requests for assistance; part 4 provides for arrest and surrender of persons to the ICC; part 5 contains provisions on domestic procedures for other types of co-operation including locating and identifying persons or things, taking evidence, facilitating appearance of witnesses, to mention but a few; part 6 provides for enforcement of penalties; part 7 contains provisions on protection of national security or third party information; part 8 provides for investigations or sittings of the ICC in Uganda; part 9 provides for requests for assistance to the ICC; and part 10 contains miscellaneous provisions. The Rome Statute is incorporated in the Act as Schedule 1, while Schedule 2 is the Agreement on the Privileges and Immunities of the ICC.

---

31 See *ICC Bill: Why Did MPs Trap Museveni and Save Kony*, THE INDEPENDENT MAGAZINE, March 31, 2010. Civil Society Organizations had also earlier expressed the warning that if Uganda failed to domesticate the Rome Statute, it would fall short of fulfilling the preconditions of hosting the 2010 ICC Review Conference that had been slated to take place in Kampala – The International Criminal Court Bill, 2006: Civil Society Organizations Perspectives, Speaking Notes made at a workshop organized by the Uganda Human Rights Commission on the ICC Bill, Hotel Africana, Kampala, (December 12, 2008).

The Act apparently focuses on setting out the terms of mutual co-operation between the ICC and the Government of Uganda in various aspects of the proceedings that would ensue following a request for co-operation from the ICC. In this respect it is a purely domesticating Act probably because the Act which retained for the most part its 2004 form pre-dated the Peace talks held in Juba, Southern Sudan and therefore the conclusions contained in Agenda Item 3. Section 18 of the Act which provides for jurisdiction is ambiguous in as far as it fails to explicitly state whether it is the Courts of Uganda that shall exercise the jurisdiction. When compared to similar Acts in South Africa and Kenya, these explicitly provide for the jurisdiction of the respective High Courts as the Courts with jurisdiction to conduct proceedings in matters regarding offences of genocide, war crimes and crimes against humanity.[32] Despite coming into place much later than the South African and Kenyan Acts from which it could have borrowed the language, the Ugandan Act, fails to explicitly provide for the jurisdiction of the High Court of Uganda, which seems to have been intentional so as to avoid the issue of parallel jurisdictions of the ICC and the Ugandan Courts, which has been a matter of debate since conclusion of the agreement on accountability and reconciliation between the Government of Uganda and the LRA.

The Act interestingly provides for various situations where there are competing requests for surrender of a person between the ICC and any other country. In the case where a competing request is from a State party to the Rome Statute, the request from the ICC would take priority, if the ICC has made a decision that the case is admissible.[33] A comprehensive reading of the ICC Act necessarily leaves one with the impression that should Kony be arrested, he would be handed over to the ICC in the Hague and the Government of Uganda would be compelled to abide by the co-operation provisions it has set out in the law as well as under the Rome Statute. That would, probably, leave the Ugandan courts to deal with other alleged perpetrators who do not have international arrest warrants pending against them.

9.5.2 *Justice Sector Reforms*

As part of the preparatory steps for the prosecution of persons indicted for serious crimes under international law, one of the biggest reforms undertaken within the justice sector was the creation of the Transitional Justice Working Group under the Justice Law and Order Sector and the War Crimes Division (which has since been renamed, the International Crimes Division) of the High Court. This division was duly constituted and

32 The Implementation of the Rome Statute Act of the International Criminal Court Act 27 (2002) (S.Afr) paras 4 & 5 provide for the jurisdiction of South African Courts and institution of proceedings in South African Courts; while para. 8 of the International Crimes Act, (2008) (Kenya) explicitly provides for the jurisdiction of the High Court in trying and punishing crimes under the Act.

33 The International Criminal Court Act No. 10 (2010) (Uganda) para. 41(2).

currently comprises of four judges and a registrar. Relatedly, International Crimes Units were also constituted in the Directorate of Public Prosecutions and the Uganda Police Force to handle the investigation and prosecution of international crimes. The officials of these units have been provided with specialized training, including benchmarking visits to The Hague, South Africa and Sierra Leone, in order to enhance their competence in investigating and adjudicating cases of this nature.

The International Crimes Division is currently handling its first trial of Thomas Kwoyelo who is being prosecuted under Uganda's Penal Code Act and the Geneva Conventions since the ICC Act was not in force at the time he was arrested, and charged with 12 counts and 53 alternative charges amounting to crimes against humanity under the Geneva Conventions Act and other penal legislations in Uganda. In the course of the trial, counsel for the defense raised an objection citing the unconstitutionality of the prosecution and the matter was referred to the Constitutional Court for determination. Indeed the proceedings so far have addressed some of the concerns that have been raised in this paper and indicate that the case could set the ground for a test of domestic prosecutions and the principle of complementarity.

9.6 Challenges Posed by Domestication of the Rome Statute

Despite the above mentioned changes that have had to be made in order for the Government of Uganda to prove its ability to prosecute the LRA rebels, the very fact of domestication of the Rome Statute has raised a number of controversial issues that present a rather challenging situation in the efforts to end the conflict in Northern Uganda and put in place some lasting solutions. Whatever approach that is adopted to address these challenges would have to be very carefully balanced in order to adequately satisfy the demands, aspirations and needs of all the parties involved, that is the international community, the people of Uganda especially those in the affected areas, but most importantly, the victims of the conflict without necessarily ignoring those that were involved in the commission of some of the most serious crimes. While some of these issues seem to have been solved by the ICC Act, there are some key issues that continue to be the subject of on-going consultations without necessarily getting any closer to finding the most appropriate solution to them.

9.6.1 Ratione Temporis *under the Rome Statute*

As noted earlier, the LRA began its activities in the late 1980s and has since been engaging in acts that would no doubt fall within the *ratione materiae* of the ICC had it been in existence then. The Court's jurisdiction is, however, limited to only those crimes that were committed after the Rome Statute came into force in Uganda, that is, in 2002.[34] Hence, some of the well-documented atrocities, such as the abduction of the Aboke girls and the Atiak massacre committed by the LRA at the height of the insurgency will not be the subject of the prosecution unless they can be proved to be 'continuing crimes'.[35] The ICC Act itself was enacted eight years after the Rome Statute was ratified and some 23 years after Kony started committing the acts for which he has been indicted. The Act, however, takes effect from the date of gazetting in July 2010 and cannot stretch back beyond this lest it violates the principle of non-retroactivity of laws. Agenda Item No. 3, in Clauses 2.2 and 2.3 provide, respectively, that "the accountability processes stipulated in the agreement shall relate to the period of the conflict"; and that "a comprehensive, independent and impartial analysis of the history and manifestations of the conflict, especially the human rights violations and crimes committed during the course of the conflict, is an essential ingredient for attaining reconciliation at all levels". What is envisaged in the Agreement clearly goes beyond what the international criminal justice system under the auspices of the ICC can provide. It is, therefore, most unlikely that the formal justice mechanisms shall meet the needs of the people of Uganda and those of the northern region in particular who would like to see the conflict resolution and peace-building process adopt a more holistic approach.

9.6.2 Whether or not to Lift the Presidential Immunity

Article 98(4) of the Constitution of the Republic of Uganda, 1995 confers immunity on a sitting president against any civil and criminal proceedings that may be brought against him or her in any court. The Rome Statute completely disregards the official capacity of an individual who is considered to bear criminal responsibility under the Statute[36] and offers no immunities that would usually be provided for under national laws. In this regard, Article 27(2) of the Statute further provides, "[I]mmunities or special procedural rules which may attach to the official capacity of a person, whether under national or international law, shall not bar the Court from exercising its jurisdiction over such a person." The ICC Act reiterates the position of the Rome Statute in Section 25 where it provides that

34 Art. 11(2) of the Rome Statute clearly stipulates that the Court may only exercise jurisdiction in respect of those crimes committed after the entry into force of the Statute in that specific State.

35 This is whereby an act or events that would constitute elements of a crime were committed prior to the coming into force of the law, but they have continued even after the law has come into force and as such the Court may take them into account especially if they are relevant to the fact in issue. *See Prosecutor v. Anatole Nsengiyumva*, ICTR-96-12-I, Decision on the Defence Motions objecting to the Jurisdiction of the Trial Chamber on the Amended Indictment, paras. 7-8 (April 13, 2000).

36 Art. 27(1) is specific that "... official capacity as a Head of State or Government ... shall in no case exempt a person from criminal responsibility under this Statute ... ".

the existence of any immunity or special procedural rule attaching to the official capacity of any person is not a ground for refusing to arrest or surrender that person to the ICC or rendering any related assistance.

This naturally raised concern in several spheres and begged a deeper consideration of the provisions of the bill in relation to the Constitution. The way that Kenya dealt with a similar problem was to provide for the immunity of the head-of-state while including an exception for cases of cooperation with the ICC.[37] Unfortunately, the new Kenyan Constitution came into place after Uganda had passed its International Criminal Court Act, and the policy makers could not make use of this precedent. As such, in the final discussions by the Leadership structures of the Justice Law and Order Sector[38] and in the considerations by Parliament, it was conceded that the question of Official Immunity would have no place in the international sphere but that the High Court and therefore the International Crimes Division would remain subject to the provisions of the Constitution. The Constitution provides for the official immunity from all forms of prosecution for some leaders, particularly the Head of State. It was recognized, however, that this immunity is only with regard to domestic prosecution and by virtue of the international treaties, cannot extend to international tribunals such as the ICC. In this regard therefore, regardless of the provisions of the Rome Statute and the ICC Act, the official immunity of the President could be upheld in the Ugandan courts in which case the courts would be unable to prosecute such a person. In light of, Article 27 of the Vienna Convention on the Law of Treaties, Uganda may not invoke the provisions of its internal law as justification for its failure to perform a treaty; and so the position of the Ugandan government as regards presidential immunity under the ICC Act may not hold under international law.

9.6.3 *The Death Penalty versus Life Imprisonment*

The Constitution of the Republic of Uganda provides for the deprivation of one's right to life where this is done in accordance with a sentence passed by a competent court of law and confirmed by the highest appellate court in Uganda. The Supreme Court of Uganda[39] recently affirmed the constitutionality of the death penalty in Uganda for what

37 KENYA. CONST, (2010) Art 143(1) and (4).

38 The Justice Law and Order Sector is a Sector Wide Approach to planning, budgeting and reforms that is being implemented in Uganda and brings together 15 Ugandan institutions with mandates that centre around the rule of law and administration of Justice. The Leadership structures comprise of the Steering Committee, made up of Permanent Secretaries and the Leadership Committees which are comprised of the Ministers, Heads of Institutions and the Chief Justice, being the policy and political leadership of the Sector.

39 *Susan Kigula v. Uganda*, Supreme Court Constitutional Appeal No. 3 of 2006, judgment delivered on January 21, 2009.

are considered serious crimes under the Penal Code Act.[40] The Rome Statute, on the other hand, provides for life imprisonment as the maximum penalty that can be handed down under the Statute.[41] It also provides in Article 23 that a person convicted by the Court shall be punished only in accordance with this Statute. Initially, the ICC Bill had prescribed the death penalty for persons found guilty of the most serious international crimes[42] and the argument for setting such a higher penalty was that Article 80 of the Rome Statute allows for the application by State parties of penalties that are prescribed in their national laws. The position seems to have changed at the time of passing the Act as it retains life imprisonment as the maximum penalty in accordance with the Rome Statute. The controversy here is the absurd state of affairs that shall ensue when a person found guilty of a single case of murder under the Penal Code Act may be sentenced to death, while a person convicted of crimes under the ICC Act, shall be sentenced to life imprisonment! It is very likely that the majority of Ugandans who supported the retention of the death penalty in the Constitution during the Constitutional review process would view this as a gross injustice.

9.6.4 *The Victim-Perpetrator Dichotomy*

One of the complexities in the LRA situation is drawing a dichotomy between a victim and a perpetrator during a conflict that has spanned over two decades. It is a well-known fact that one of the tactics employed by the LRA was the abduction of children whom they would then profoundly terrorize and force to commit heinous crimes, often against their own kinsfolk as a first step towards indoctrinating them and eventually conscripting them into the rebel ranks.[43] Over the years, these children have become adults and have risen through the rebel hierarchy and in turn committed some of the crimes that would fall under the Rome Statute. The Statute provides in Article 26 that "the Court shall have no jurisdiction over any person who was under the age of 18 at the time of the alleged commission of the crime". This aspect of the Rome Statute has been incorporated in the ICC Act.[44] The dilemma here is that some of the most atrocious crimes have been committed by children! There is also a scenario where there is evidence that a person committed some of the most serious crimes while he or she was below 18 years, but there seems to be no

40 The Penal Code Act prescribes the death penalty for serious offences such as murder, treason, aggravated robbery, kidnap with intent to murder etc.

41 Rome Statute, *supra* note 26 at Art. 77(2).

42 For instance, Clause 7(3) (a) was to the effect that the penalty for genocide, or conspiring with, or agreeing with any person to commit genocide is, if the offence involves the wilful killing of a person, the same as the penalty for murder prescribed by the Penal Code Act.

43 Refugee Law Project (RLP), *Behind the Violence: Causes, Consequences and the Search for Solutions to the War in Northern Uganda*, 20-23 (Refugee Law Project Working Paper No. 11 RLP: Kampala, 2004) [hereinafter *Behind the Violence*]. See also, Statement by the Chief Prosecutor, *supra* note 21.

44 Section 5(b) of the Act incorporates the entire Part 3 of the Rome Statute under which Art. 26 falls.

evidence of crimes committed after the person became an adult, although that person has continued to be part of the LRA until the time of arrest. To further compound the problem, the age of criminal responsibility in Uganda is 12 years and therefore the domestic legal system provides no bar to the prosecution of child soldiers.

The communities too have their concerns about the prosecution of these children. A prevailing point of view in Northern Uganda is that the rebels are their children and that subjecting them to formal justice procedures would not only defeat their aspirations for peace and reconciliation, but would also be deemed as a social injustice. The argument here is that the State failed in its obligations to protect the people, especially the children, from the rebels by not providing adequate security. They were abducted[45] and subjected to gross human rights violations by the rebels, the State still failed to rescue them while the rebels exploited them and turned them into criminals; and now the same State is turning round and prosecuting them for crimes that were committed under circumstances forced upon them. The argument made by the people of Northern Uganda and whose views seem to be adequately taken into account under Agenda Item No. 3 that the transitional justice process should promote peace and reconciliation more than retribution becomes more plausible though in itself it creates another implementation challenge.

9.6.5 *The ICC Process and Amnesty*

Uganda enacted an Amnesty law in 2000 as one of the ways to end the many armed conflicts that were taking place at the time. According to Section 2 of the Act, the 'amnesty is declared in respect of any Ugandan who has at any time since the 26th day of January 1986, engaged in or is engaging in war or armed rebellion against the Government of the Republic of Uganda . . .'[46] This does necessarily apply to members of the LRA. A number of former rebels, totaling about 26,000 to date have been granted amnesty under the Amnesty Act.[47] The Amnesty Act, under Section 2A, provides for exclusion via a statutory instrument, of persons the Government deems ineligible for amnesty. However, no

45 It has actually been alleged that the army deployment was plainly inadequate in some places and that the army was in a number of instances poorly equipped to ward off any rebel attacks. See *Behind the Violence*, *supra* note 43, at 29-32.

46 The Act was initially meant to be in place for a period not exceeding six months (Section 16 of the Amnesty Act), but has since been extended with the latest extension being for a period of 24 months from May 25, 2010. See Amnesty Act (Extension of Expiry Period) Instrument, (2010) (Uganda).

47 By August 2008, 22,930 rebels had been granted amnesty of which 10,813 were former LRA rebels. See Information Counseling and Referral Services, Preliminary Analysis: Reporter Profiling from the Amnesty Commission of Uganda (November 2008) available at <http://reliefweb.int/node/333758>. Some of the LRA former rebels that were granted amnesty included former LRA commanders like Sam Kolo and Kenneth Banya.

such instrument has been issued to date. According to the Amnesty Commission, if either Joseph Kony or any of his top commanders were to appear before them, there is nothing in the law that would bar them from being granted amnesty.[48]

This question arose in the case of Thomas Kwoyelo who was captured in battle in the Democratic Republic of Congo and indicted in the High Court.[49] In the period preceding his trial, he made a declaration renouncing rebellion and applied for a grant of Amnesty under the Act. At his hearing before the High Court, Kwoyelo objected to the proceedings on the ground that he had applied for amnesty and his application had been submitted to the Director of Public Prosecutions (DPP) as required under Section 3(3) of the Act,[50] but by the time of the hearing the DPP had not responded to the application for amnesty. This matter was referred to the Constitutional Court[51] for interpretation and both parties raised Constitutional objections around amnesty which were considered by the Court. The Applicant, Kwoyelo argued that he had been discriminated against as he had applied for amnesty and had not been granted the same whereas several other persons in similar situations to his had been granted amnesty. The State on its part argued that the Amnesty Act was unconstitutional as it contravened the powers of the DPP to initiate or stop prosecutions without interference from any quarters. The Constitutional Court ruled that since 2000 when the Amnesty Act was enacted, the DPP had sanctioned the grant of amnesty to 24,066 persons and that there was no objective or reasonable explanation for the DPP not to act on the application by Kwoyelo. The court reasoned that the applicant had acquired a legal right to be granted amnesty or pardon under the Act like all other persons who had renounced rebellion and was "deemed to have been granted amnesty . . ." once he made the declaration to the Prison Officer. The court further opined that the Act allowed the Minister to exempt certain individuals from amnesty but this had never been done, and that the DPP was at liberty to prosecute government officers and rebels who had not applied for amnesty. The Court came to the conclusion that the applicant had shown a case that the Amnesty Commission and the Director of Public Prosecutions had not accorded him equal treatment under the Amnesty Act, hence violating his constitutional right to equality before the law. The Court made an order that the lower court (the High Court, International Crimes Division)

48 Remarks presented by the Amnesty Commission Principal Legal Officer at a workshop organized by the Uganda Human Rights Commission on the ICC Bill, Hotel Africana, Kampala, (December 12, 2008).

49 High Court -00-ICD-Case No. 02/10.

50 "The section provides that a reporter to whom sub section (2) applies shall not be released from custody until the Director of Public Prosecutions has certified that he or she is satisfied that – (a) the person falls within the provisions of section 2; and (b) he or she is not charged or detained to be prosecuted for any offence not falling under section 2." Section 3 ((1) and (2) gives the mode by which a person can seek amnesty and include a person in detention making a declaration to a Prison Officer or judge or magistrate. In the case of Kwoyelo, the declaration was made to a Prison Officer.

51 Constitutional Petition No. 036/11 (Reference). Ruling made on September 22, 2011.

cease the trial. The ruling of the Constitutional Court raises grave concerns for the prosecution of war crimes and crimes against humanity in the Ugandan context. For as long as the Amnesty Act exists in its current form, it would loom precariously over the possibility of any trial of an LRA or other rebel combatants in the domestic courts and possibly provide the ICC with a clear instance of "... willing but unable to prosecute".

Considering that Kony and the other indicted persons are wanted by the ICC, which Kwoyelo was not, one could argue that the Constitutional Court would view the matter differently and arrive at a different decision, should the matter arise before it. This speculation notwithstanding, should such a ruling be applied to the indicted persons? Our view is that applying the ruling to the indicted persons would obviously amount to a blatant breach of Uganda's obligations under the Rome Statute, which requires that at least the indictees undergo trial or prosecution;[52] and considering international jurisprudence which generally regards amnesties for perpetrators of human rights violations as a deprivation of the right to an effective remedy;[53] in the circumstances, an amnesty to the fugitive LRA top commanders would not be recognized and would be considered as a manifestation of Uganda's inability to bring the perpetrators to justice.

9.6.6 *The ICC Process and Traditional Justice Mechanisms*

Agenda Item No. 3 clearly stipulates that national legal arrangements, consisting of formal and non-formal institutions and measures, for ensuring justice and reconciliation with respect to the conflict shall be promoted.[54] According to Hon. Justice James Ogoola, then Principal Judge of the High Court of Uganda and Chairperson of the Transitional Justice Working Group, formal mechanisms can only take care of one tenth of the perpetrators, while 90% will be taken care of by traditional mechanisms.[55] The traditional justice mechanisms mentioned here come in many forms depending on the various communities in the affected areas. Some of the proposed mechanisms are *Culo Kwor, Mato Oput, Kayo Ocuk, Ailiuc* and *Tonu ci Koka*. All these mechanisms involve the perpetrator confessing and telling the truth, renouncing their deeds and offering reparations. Such reparations may include undergoing some rituals and may be making material restitution to the offended individuals and also taking on some life-long obligations towards the victims such as

52 The preamble to the Rome Statute emphasizes that 'the most serious crimes of concern to the international community must not go unpunished and that their effective prosecution must be ensured ....'

53 See decision of the Human Rights Committee in *Hugo Rodriguez v. Uruguay*, Communication No. 322/1988, U.N. Doc. CCPR/C/51/D/322/1988 (1994).

54 Agenda Item No. 3, *supra* note 7 Clause 2.1.

55 Justice Ogoola, J., *Opening Remarks*, *in* Beyond Juba, Report on the Proceedings of the Jlos Transitional Justice Working Group Round Table Discussion, 4 (2009).

providing for some or all of their basic needs. The case for this option, which aims more at rehabilitation and restoration than punishment, is made stronger when considered in light of the fact that most of the rebels were abducted in childhood and have been brainwashed and turned into perpetrators of serious crimes. For the very reasons given as to why the amnesty would amount to a breach of Uganda's obligations under the Rome Statute, so would the traditional justice mechanisms if applied to the LRA top commanders.

The challenge that Uganda now faces, is to decide which procedure takes precedence over the other and in what circumstances? The situation becomes more complex with regard to the lower ranking rebels who are arrested or who surrender. The question remains as to which mechanism should handle the various cases and what filter mechanism will be used to determine the correct forum for each individual. The Transitional Justice Working Group under the Justice, Law and Order Sector has formed sub-committees on formal mechanisms, traditional justice mechanisms and truth telling and national reconciliation to consider these issues. An additional sub-committee on integrated systems has been established to design the linkage between the various different systems and define the method of referral and interaction between the various systems. The sub-committees have been carrying out consultations both within and outside Uganda and have recently completed countrywide grassroots consultations on the establishment of a Truth Telling and National Reconciliation mechanism and the use of traditional justice mechanisms as complementary or alternative modes of accountability and reconciliation. The final report and policy options will be presented to the Justice Law and Order Sector and thereafter to the Executive in the course of time and proposals made on alternative measures to the formal prosecutions. It is anticipated that their findings and recommendations will also provide guidance on how all these mechanisms can operate effectively in tandem with each other.

9.6.7 *Victim and Witness Protection*

The ICC has an elaborate victim and witness protection regime clearly laid out under the Statute as well as the Rules and regulations.[56] At the domestic level, the Government is still in the process of drafting a witness protection law, which should provide the appropriate framework to ensure the protection and support of witnesses and victims. The real challenge, however, would lie in having an effective witness protection system that works in practice. Drawing from the Kenyan experience, with a Witness Protection Act since 2008,

56 The Rome Statute, *supra* note 26 art 68; also Rules of Procedure and Evidence, ICC-ASP/1/3 available at <www.icc-cpi.int/NR/rdonlyres/F1E0AC1C-A3F3-4A3C-B9A7-B3E8B115E886/140164/Rules_of_procedure_and_Evidence_English.pdf Rules 85-88> and also Regulations of the Court, available at <www.icc-cpi.int/NR/rdonlyres/B920AD62-DF49-4010-8907-E0D8CC61EBA4/277527/Regulations_of_the_Court_170604EN.pdf Regulations>, 41-42.

they are still facing serious challenges in implementation: funding is inadequate, there is lack of trust in state institutions, and witnesses still face threats of all kinds.[57] Even if a witness protection law was passed in Uganda, it would take a long time before it is implemented as envisaged under the Rome Statute. This is so because there is no recognizable or functional existing witness protection regime in Uganda. Furthermore, while the Sierra Leonean model, cited as a new international criminal justice model for protecting African witnesses,[58] would be one that Uganda could copy, the funding for the same may not be readily available. It must be noted that Sierra Leone as a country does not fund the witness protection programme of the Special Court for Sierra Leone, but rather the court itself, which is an international organization in its own right.

9.6.8 *Compensation and the Trust Fund*

Article 79 of the Rome Statute provides for the establishment of the Trust Fund for the benefit of victims of crimes. This provision has been incorporated into the Ugandan law by virtue of Section 5(f) of the ICC Act. Currently, there is no victim compensation fund in Uganda, despite numerous recommendations by the Uganda Human Rights Commission (UHRC) to the Government of Uganda to establish the same for victims of human rights violations. In cases where UHRC has made compensation orders against government, payment of victims has been delayed with the concerned ministry citing budgetary constraints. Furthermore, although under the ICC arrangement, it is the convicted person who bears the reparations to victims,[59] the persons envisaged to be prosecuted within Uganda (individuals other than the four indicted men)[60] might not be in position to pay the amount of the reparations that the court may make against them. The question of compensation and reparations is therefore a fundamental issue that is being considered by the justice sector and it is anticipated that the recommendations that it makes will inform the development of a comprehensive policy on reparations and compensation of victims.

9.7 Conclusion

The situation in Uganda seems to be unfolding in a manner that was never envisaged by the drafters of the Rome Statute. Various factors, including the failure to execute the arrest warrants, the suspicions with which some sections of the public view the ICC,

57 C. Mahony, The Justice Sector Afterthought: Witness Protection in Africa 111 (2010).
58 *Id.* at 7.
59 Rules of Procedure and Evidence *supra* note 56, Rule 98 (1).
60 That is if we are go by the submissions of the Government of Uganda during the admissibility proceedings, *The Prosecutor v. Kony et al.*, ICC-02/04-01/05-377.

the continuing activities of the LRA, and the vacillating position of the Government of Uganda – all add to the complexity of the matter.

Given the view that still persists in some circles domestically that Uganda should be left to conduct the prosecutions of Joseph Kony and the others, and that peaceful solutions to the conflict should still be vigorously pursued by the Government and all concerned, the question of admissibility may still arise before the ICC. It has been pointed out by a number of writers that one of the greatest weaknesses of the Rome Statute is that it still continues to pay a considerable amount of allegiance to the principle of State sovereignty.[61] This is clearly discerned from the Preamble paragraphs 4 and 6, which emphasize that prosecution for the most serious crimes of concern to the international community, must be ensured by taking measures at the national level and by enhancing international cooperation; and that it is the duty of every State to exercise its criminal jurisdiction over those responsible for international crimes. This probably explains why under Article 17, the ICC can only act where the State has demonstrated its unwillingness or inability to genuinely to investigate or prosecute. This being the case, the ICC must endeavor not to compromise a State's jurisdiction to handle its internal matters. Hence, the Government of Uganda has now tried, in the exercise of its sovereignty to reclaim its jurisdiction over the case against the LRA. However, Uganda's vacillating position regarding its relationship with the ICC – as evidenced by the timing of its referral of the LRA situation to the ICC; its subsequent undertakings in the agreement with the LRA, its submissions before the Pre-trial Chamber; the subsequent passage of an ICC Act which adopted the Rome Statute lock, stock, and barrel and clearly failed to contextualize it – do not reflect quite well on its ability to prosecute the four fugitive LRA commanders. The Constitutional Court ruling in the Kwoyelo case clearly indicates that there are still gaps in Uganda's Rome Statute domestication process, which situation does not augur well with its efforts to prove that it fulfills the requirements of complementarity under the Rome Statute.

In our humble view, should Joseph Kony and the three others be arrested, their trial would probably take place in The Hague while the Ugandan system deals with any lower ranking or future perpetrators who might be arrested.

61 Gioia, *supra* note 1, at 1096. See also, H. Van der Wilt & S. Lyngdorf, *Procedural Obligations under the European Convention on Human Rights: Useful Guidelines for the Assessment of 'Unwillingness' and 'Inability' in the Context of the Complementarity Principle*, 9 International Criminal Law Review 29, 44 (2009). See M.C. Bassiouni, *ICC – Quo Vadis*, 3 Journal of International Criminal Justice, 423 (2006), cited in Nidal Nabi Jurdi, *The Prosecutorial Interpretation of the Complementarity Principle: Does it Really Contribute to Ending Impunity on the National Level?* 10 International Criminal Law Review 73, 74 (2010).

Part IV
The Limits of the International Criminal Court in Achieving Peace and Justice in Africa

10 Peace, Justice and the International Criminal Court

Limitations and Possibilities

*Janine Natalya Clark**

10.1 Introduction

A core debate within the transitional justice literature concerns the relationship between peace and justice. The International Criminal Court (ICC) not only features prominently in such debates but is often invoked in support of the contention that justice poses a threat to peace. In the words of one scholar, "The ICC might be seen . . . not just as a challenge to impunity, but also as a potential challenge or impediment to peace negotiations and agreements . . . ".[1] This chapter directly engages with such arguments but seeks to portray the ICC neither as an obstacle to peace nor as an instrument of peace. Rather, it aims to offer a more nuanced, exploratory analysis focused on both the Court's limitations and possibilities as a tool of justice and peace. Stressing that 'justice' is far broader than criminal trials alone, it maintains that we should not over-rely upon the ICC to deliver either peace or justice. The latter's work must form part of a broader, more holistic transitional justice strategy that combines retributive and restorative justice elements. The fact, however, that the Court itself, to some extent, embodies both types of justice not only represents a significant development in international criminal law[2] but also serves to underline that the Court has potential in respect of both justice and peace.

---

* This contribution previously appeared in Janine Natalya Clark, *Peace and Justice and the International Criminal Court: Limitations and Possibilities*, 9(3) Journal of International Criminal Justice 521 (2011) and is reprinted with kind permission of the publisher.

1 Chanda Lekha Sriram, *Conflict Mediation and the ICC: Challenges and Options for Pursuing Peace with Justice at the Regional Level*, *in* Building a Future on Peace and Justice: Studies on Transitional Justice, Peace and Development – the Nuremberg Declaration on Peace and Justice 303, 305 (Kai Ambos, Judith Large & Marieke Wierda eds., 2009).

2 As one commentator observes, 'The notion that international justice should not only address traditional retributive justice, namely the punishment of the offender, but also restorative justice, namely having victims participate in the proceedings as well as providing them with reparation for their injuries, has gained increasing recognition with the establishment of the ICC. The ICC departed here from the overall retributive justice approach as applied by the International Criminal Tribunal for the former Yugoslavia (ICTY) and the International Criminal Tribunal for Rwanda (ICTR)'. Ann Marie de Brouwer, *Reparation to Victims of Sexual Violence: Possibilities at the International Criminal Court and the Trust Fund for Victims and their Families*, 20 Leiden Journal of International Law 207, 208 (2007).

Divided into three substantive sections, the first part of the chapter examines some of the difficulties that the ICC faces in dispensing justice, including its dependence on state co-operation and the contested nature of 'justice'. The second part of the chapter looks at how, despite these challenges, the ICC can nevertheless deliver some level of justice, notably by introducing greater clarity in respect of the restorative justice elements of its mandate, by increasing the visibility of its work and by working with local courts to facilitate the holding of national trials. Bringing to the fore the complex and much-debated relationship between justice and peace, and focusing on the case of northern Uganda (Acholiland) as being particularly illustrative in this regard, the final part explores whether the ICC can deliver peace. While underscoring that the relationship between criminal trials and peace remains empirically under-researched, it argues that the ICC can potentially contribute to peace but only as part of a comprehensive approach to justice that is deeper and thicker than criminal trials alone. In short, 'A tribunal can be but one step in a process seeking to ensure peace [. . .]'.[3]

10.2 The ICC's Limitations as an Instrument of Justice

According to supporters of international criminal trials, the dispensing of justice helps to, inter alia, individualize guilt, curb victims' desire for revenge and foster peace-building and reconciliation.[4] Notwithstanding the popularity of such arguments, it is striking that their advocates often fail to critically engage with the concept of justice, as if its meaning were somehow self-explanatory. Arendt's insistence that the sole purpose of a criminal trial is to render justice can be read as epitomizing this trend.[5] Yet while justice most obviously entails the prosecution, fair trial and punishment of those who violate the law, such a formalized, procedural understanding fails to capture the richness of justice. Embedded within the macro concept of justice, for example, is the notion of restorative justice, a non-punitive approach focused on addressing the multiple needs (of victims, perpetrators and affected communities alike) that crime creates. Adding to the complexities inherent in defining 'justice', it is in many ways a deeply subjective notion; 'delivering justice usually means different

3 Martha Minow, Between Vengeance and Forgiveness: Facing History After Genocide and Mass Violence 50 (1998).

4 Neil J. Kritz, *Coming to Terms with Atrocities: A Review of Accountability Mechanisms for Mass Violations of Human Rights*, 59 Law and Contemporary Problems 127-152 (1996); Payam Akhavan, *Justice in The Hague, Peace in the Former Yugoslavia? A Commentary on the United Nations War Crimes Tribunal*, 20 Human Rights Quarterly 737 (1998); Antonio Cassese, *On the Current Trends Towards Criminal Prosecution and Punishment of Breaches of International Humanitarian Law*, 9 European Journal Of International Law 2 (1998); Kingsley Chiedu Moghalu, *Reconciling Fractured Societies: An African Perspective on the Role of Judicial Prosecutions, in* From Sovereignty Impunity to International Accountability: the Search for Justice in a World of States 197 (Ramesh Thakur & Peter Malcontent eds., 2004).

5 Hannah Arendt, Eichmann in Jerusalem: a Report on the Banality of Evil 5 (revised edition, 1977).

things to different people'.[6] This in turn means that justice can be a highly divisive and polarizing notion, as highlighted by the contrasting ways in which Bosnian Serbs and Bosnian Muslims reacted to the news of the arrest, in July 2008, of the indicted war criminal Radovan Karadzić. While members of one group protested, members of the other celebrated.[7] If, therefore, justice is quintessentially a 'disputed matter',[8] an inevitable challenge will always be one of trying to establish a broad consensus that 'justice' has been done.

If, on a conceptual level, justice is a far less straightforward concept than the transitional justice literature often seems to imply, the pursuit of justice also poses fundamental practical challenges. This first section of the chapter will therefore explore a combination of conceptual and practical issues that arguably limit the extent to which the ICC can deliver justice (whether understood in a narrow, retributive sense or in a broader, restorative sense), and more particularly justice that is perceived as such on the ground. It will focus specifically on allegations of political bias (the notion that prosecutorial decisions are based on political considerations) and selective justice (the idea that there are incomprehensible gaps in respect of ICC trials), as well as the Court's dependence on state co-operation.

10.2.1 Allegations of Political Bias and Selective Justice

If beauty is in the eye of the beholder, the same is similarly true of justice.[9] Hence, it must not only be done but must also be *seen* to be done. To date, however, the ICC has encountered significant difficulties in this latter regard. Questions have been raised, for example, concerning the quality and impartiality of any 'justice' dispensed by a court that to date is only focusing on crimes committed in Africa. This perceived geopolitical bias in turn encourages the idea that the ICC is an institution which reflects and consolidates existing international power structures. In 2009, for example, according to the ICC's Outreach Unit, people in Uganda frequently posed questions such as: 'Why is it that powerful countries like the United States, Russia and China are not parties to the Rome Statute?' and

6 H. van der Merwe, *Delivering Justice During Transition: Research Challenges, in* ASSESSING THE IMPACT OF TRANSITIONAL JUSTICE: CHALLENGES FOR EMPIRICAL RESEARCH 115, 138 (Hugo van der Merwe, Victoria Baxter & Audrey R. Chapman eds., 2009).

7 Janine Natalya Clark, *The State Court of Bosnia and Hercegovina: A Path to Reconciliation?* 13 CONTEMPORARY JUSTICE REVIEW 371, 375 (2010).

8 Daniel Philpott, *Beyond Politics As Usual: Is Reconciliation Compatible With Liberalism? in* THE POLITICS OF PAST EVILS: RELIGION, RECONCILIATION, AND THE DILEMMA OF TRANSITIONAL JUSTICE 11, 15 (Daniel Philpott ed., 2006).

9 Eric Stover & Harvey M. Weinstein, *Introduction: Conflict, Justice and Reclamation, in* MY NEIGHBOUR, MY ENEMY: JUSTICE AND COMMUNITY IN THE AFTERMATH OF MASS ATROCITY 1, 4 (Eric Stover & Harvey M. Weinstein eds., 2004).

'Why are all the cases before the ICC coming from Africa? Is the Court a new tool for Western imperialism in Africa?'[10]

Particular decisions and actions taken by the ICC's Prosecutor, Luis Moreno-Ocampo, have further fuelled allegations of political bias. For example, in northern Uganda both the rebel Lord's Resistance Army (LRA) and the Ugandan army, the United People's Defence Force (UPDF), have committed serious war crimes and human rights violations,[11] yet to date Moreno-Ocampo has only issued indictments against five LRA commanders – Joseph Kony, Vincent Otti, Okot Odhiambo, Dominic Ongwen and Raska Lukwiya (since deceased). The Prosecutor has justified this decision on the grounds of gravity;

> Some people say that the only way to retain our impartiality is to prosecute both the LRA and the UPDF. However, I think that impartiality means that we apply the same criteria equally to all sides. A major criterion is gravity. There is no comparison of gravity between the crimes committed by the Ugandan army and by the LRA – the crimes committed by the LRA are much graver than those committed by the Ugandan army.[12]

Such distinctions, however, are unlikely to resonate with victims of UPDF crimes, thus exposing a critical disconnect between judicial-based and grassroots understandings of impartiality. When Moreno-Ocampo and Uganda's President Museveni held a joint press conference in January 2004, for example, to announce that the ICC would begin preliminary investigations in northern Uganda, little consideration appears to have been given to how this event would be perceived on the ground.[13] One commentator thus maintains

---

10 International Criminal Court, 'Outreach Report 2009' (2009), available at: <www.icc-cpi.int/NR/rdonlyres/8A3D8107-5421-4238-AA64-D5AB32D33247/281271/OR_2009_ENG_web.pdf> (Accessed April 3, 2010). Goldstone and Smith thus maintain that '. . .without expanding to other corners of the world, the ICC does indeed risk being branded, at best, as a selective prosecutor, and at worst, as a purveyor of racially conscious justice'. Richard J. Goldstone & Adam M. Smith, International Judicial Institutions: The Architecture of International Justice at Home and Abroad 113 (2009).

11 According to Branch, '. . .there is a clear record of international violence perpetrated by both the rebels and the government forces in northern Uganda, many within the ICC's temporal mandate. In dominant international portrayals of the conflict, however, government violence has been downplayed, if not entirely ignored'. Adam Branch, *Uganda's Civil War and the Politics of ICC Intervention,* 2 Ethics and International Affairs 179, 182 (2007).

12 Luis Moreno-Ocampo, *Keynote Address: Integrating the Work of the ICC into Local Justice Initiatives,* 21 American University International Law Review 497, 501 (2006).

13 Of course, the Office of the Prosecutor (OTP), which Ocampo represents, is not synonymous with the entire ICC. Local communities, however, particularly if they have little knowledge of the Court's structure, may conflate the two. During the author's fieldwork in Bosnia-Hercegovina (2008-2009), for example, which focused on exploring the ICTY's impact on inter-ethnic relations in the country, Serb interviewees were particularly critical of Carla Del Ponte, a former Chief Prosecutor. Accusing her of anti-Serb bias, they made no distinction between Del Ponte, as the head of the OTP, and the ICTY as a whole.

that, 'Until the ICC makes its impartiality evident in practice, and until it establishes its independence from the Ugandan government in more than just its rhetoric . . . its capacity to establish justice or conform to the rule of law in Uganda will be seriously impaired'.[14] Given that the ICC is entirely dependent on state co-operation, however (see below), and in this case on the co-operation of the Ugandan government,[15] matters are not quite as straightforward as Branch suggests. The practical realities confronting the Court and the very difficult and sensitive contexts in which it operates will arguably constrain, to some degree, its ability to deliver impartial justice.[16]

Polemics surrounding the neutrality of ICC justice are linked to the problem of selective justice which, once again, has less to do with the Court itself than with the circumstances in which it is functioning. When mass atrocities have occurred over a period of time, difficult decisions must necessarily be made about which crimes to prosecute and during which timeframe. The ICC is dealing only with war crimes, crimes against humanity, genocide and the crime of aggression committed since July 1, 2002, the date upon which the Rome Statute entered into force. This is not to call into question the cardinal legal principle of non-retroactivity. The issue, however, is that significant disconnects may arise between legal principles and their grassroots interpretation. In short, '. . . while a timeline starting on July 1, 2002 makes perfect sense from the perspective of the negotiating history of the Statute, from the point of view of the situations under investigation it seems very artificial'.[17] According to the Victims' Rights Working Group (VRWG), for example, there is still a widespread belief among victims that the rationale for the Court's temporal jurisdiction is to protect certain groups and individuals from the risk of prosecution.[18] This critical gap between legal/policy decisions and the everyday lives of those directly affected thus raises fundamental questions regarding the extent to which a court like the ICC can deliver justice that is perceived as such on the ground.

14 Branch, *supra* note 11, at 189.

15 One example of this is 'investigators' use of Ugandan government vehicles and officials to facilitate their enquiries on the ground . . .'. TIM ALLEN, TRIAL JUSTICE: THE INTERNATIONAL CRIMINAL COURT AND THE LORD'S RESISTANCE ARMY 97 (2006).

16 VICTOR PESKIN, INTERNATIONAL JUSTICE IN RWANDA AND THE BALKANS: VIRTUAL TRIALS AND THE STRUGGLE FOR STATE COOPERATION 255 (2008).

17 Marlies Glasius, *What is Global Justice and Who Decides? Civil Society and Victim Responses to the International Criminal Court's First Investigations*, 31 HUMAN RIGHTS QUARTERLY 496, 501 (2009). On this point, see also Sverker Finnström, *Reconciliation Grown Bitter? War, Retribution and Ritual Action in Northern Uganda*, *in* LOCALISING TRANSITIONAL JUSTICE: INTERVENTIONS AND PRIORITIES AFTER MASS VIOLENCE 135, 139 (Rosalind Shaw, Lars Waldorf & Pierre Hazan eds., 2010).

18 Victims' Rights Working Group (VRWG), The Impact of the ICC on Victims and Affected Communities: A Report of the Victim Rights Working Group (2010), available at: <www.redress.org/Stocktakingreport2010.pdf> (Accessed November 20, 2010).

That the ICC can only deal with a small number of cases – an estimated two or three per year – further encourages allegations of selective justice. According to the ICC's 2009 Outreach Report, for example, a commonly-asked question among Darfuri refugees in Eastern Chad and among the Darfuri diaspora was: 'Why is the international community only focusing on crimes committed in Darfur, when there are also crimes committed in other regions in Sudan?'[19] Similarly in the Democratic Republic of Congo (DRC), the VRWG reports that victims do not understand the Prosecutor's selection policy or the reasons why so few arrest warrants have been issued.[20] The Court's case against Jean-Pierre Bemba Gombo, the leader of the rebel *Mouvement de Libération du Congo* (MLC), has created additional confusion, owing to the fact that he is only being prosecuted for alleged war crimes and crimes against humanity committed in the Central African Republic (CAR) but not in the DRC itself.[21] This, according to Human Rights Watch, 'is a significant missed opportunity to bring justice for Congolese victims of crimes committed by MLC troops'.[22] Given that Bemba, a candidate in the DRC's 2006 presidential elections, is a former political and military rival of President Joseph Kabila, to whom he lost the aforementioned elections, his prosecution in The Hague has also generated controversy, by reinforcing the perception that 'the current strategy is one-sided and beneficial to Kabila'.[23]

Blumenson maintains that ICC prosecutions will be 'extremely selective' not least for practical reasons, including the Court's limited resources and weak enforcement powers.[24] The practical realities of dispensing justice in the aftermath of mass crimes, however, conflict with the very high expectations that the ICC has generated, not only among the relevant local populations but also within the international community itself.[25] The extent to

19 ICC, *supra* note 10.

20 VRWG, *supra* note 18.

21 According to the ICC Prosecutor, 'Jean-Pierre Gombo used an entire army as a weapon to rape, pillage and kill civilians in the Central African Republic. Today he is brought to account for deliberately failing to prevent, repress or punish mass atrocities committed by his men in the CAR'. ICC Press Release, 'Journalists in Bangui, Kinshasa and The Hague Put Questions to Parties and Participants in the Trial of Jean-Pierre Bemba Gombo' (2010), available at: <www.icc-cpi.int/NR/exeres/7BA1991C-707F-414F-AC34-9F15830ACA96.htm> (Accessed November 22, 2010).

22 Human Rights Watch, 'ICC: Q & A on the Trial of Jean-Pierre Bemba' (2010), available at: <www.hrw.org/en/news/2010/11/18/bemba-qa> (Accessed November 26, 2010). Prunier claims that during the Congo war, Bemba's troops practiced cannibalism in Ituri. Gerard Prunier, From Genocide to Continental War: the "Congolese" Conflict and the Crisis of the Contemporary Africa 310 (2009).

23 Mima Adjami & Guy Mushiata, 'Democratic Republic of Congo: Impact of the Rome Statute and the International Criminal Court' (2010), available at: <www.ictj.org/static/Publications/ICTJ_DRC_RSRC-ImpactofICC_bp2010.pdf> (Accessed November 22, 2010).

24 Eric Blumenson, *The Challenge of a Global Standard of Justice: Peace, Pluralism and Punishment at the International Criminal Court*, 44 Columbia Journal of Transnational Law 801, 818 (2006).

25 Antonio Cassese, *Is the ICC Still Having Teething Problems?* 4 Journal of International Criminal Justice 434, at 441 (2006); William W. Burke-White, *Proactive Complementarity: The International Criminal Court and National Courts in the Rome System of International Justice*, 49 Harvard International Law Journal 53, 54 (2008).

which the Court can actually deliver justice, therefore, will depend in part upon people's expectations. If these are too high, disappointment will inevitably follow.[26] It is imperative, therefore, that the Court itself is clear and open about what it can and cannot achieve, as opposed to being 'caught between an idealistic vision of a global court designed to prosecute the cases that domestic jurisdictions cannot or will not prosecute, and the pragmatic concerns of a new institution seeking judicial results to secure its legitimacy'.[27]

10.2.2 Dependence on State Co-Operation

Bodies set up to prosecute war criminals share a common characteristic – their dependence on states. These institutions have no powers of arrest and therefore require the co-operation of states in order to be able to fulfil their mandates. The late Antonio Cassese, the first president of the International Criminal Tribunal for the former Yugoslavia (ICTY), powerfully underlined this point. Using the Tribunal as an example, he argued that the ICTY 'remains very much like a giant without arms and legs – it needs artificial limbs to walk and work. And these artificial limbs are state authorities. If the cooperation of states is not forthcoming, the ICTY cannot fulfil its functions. It has no means at its disposal to force states to cooperate with it'.[28] This description of the ICTY is no less applicable to the ICC. Yet while the Court needs the co-operation of states, it is powerless to enforce this. Article 87(7) of the Rome Statute simply states that,

> Where a State Party fails to comply with a request to cooperate by the Court contrary to the provisions of this Statute, thereby preventing the Court from exercising its functions and powers under this Statute, the Court may make a finding to that effect and refer the matter to the Assembly of States Parties or, where the Security Council referred the matter to the Court, to the Security Council.[29]

---

26 The example of the International Criminal Tribunal for the former Yugoslavia (ICTY) illustrates this point. Orentlicher notes that '. . .there is a large distance between Bosnians' original expectations and their perceptions of what the ICTY has achieved seventeen years on. . . Some of these expectations [for example, the expectation that the Tribunal would prosecute virtually all war criminals] were unrealistic and laid the ground for disappointment'. D.F. Orentlicher, *That Someone Guilty Be Punished: The Impact of the ICTY in Bosnia* New York: Open Society Institute, 2010 14, available at <www.ictj.org/static/Publications/Orentlicher_BiH_OSJI-ICTJ_ThatSomeoneGuilty_pb2010.pdf> (Accessed December 15, 2010). See also Janine Natalya Clark, *The Limits of Retributive Justice: Findings of an Empirical Study in Bosnia and Hercegovina*, 7 Journal of International Criminal Justice 463, 467 (2009); *id. The Impact Question: The ICTY and the Restoration and Maintenance of Peace*, *in* The Legacy of the International Criminal Tribunal for the Former Yugoslavia (Bert Swart, Alexander Zahar & Goran Sluiter eds., 2011).

27 Phil Clark, *Law, Politics and Pragmatism: The ICC and Case Selection in Uganda and the Democratic Republic of Congo, in* Courting Conflict? Justice, Peace and the Icc in Africa 37, 39 (Nicholas Waddell & Phil Clark eds., 2008).

28 Cassese, *supra* note 4, at 13.

29 Rome Statute of the International Criminal Court (1998), available at: <http://untreaty.un.org/cod/icc/statute/99_corr/cstatute.htm> (Accessed April 30, 2010).

Critical, therefore, to the issue of whether the ICC can deliver justice is its relationship with states – and in particular those states that currently have cases before the Court[30] – and more specifically their readiness to work with the Court.[31] Hence, in keeping with the tenets of Realist theory in International Relations – and the basic idea that power is the defining feature of a state-centric international system – it can be argued that, 'The principal obstacles to the effectiveness of the ICC will always be *Realpolitik* and states' interests'.[32] The following example highlights this. On 22 August 2006, the ICC issued a warrant of arrest against Bosco 'the Terminator' Ntaganda, the military chief of staff of the National Congress for the Defence of the People (CNDP) in the DRC.[33] However, not only does Ntaganda remain at liberty but he and his militia group have been integrated into the Congolese army, the Armed Forces of the Democratic Republic of Congo (FARDC). Supported by the United Nations Organization Mission in the DRC (MONUC) – the UN peacekeeping force that was recently renamed the United Nations Organization Stabilization Mission in the DRC (MONUSCO) – the FARDC has absorbed the CNDP as part of its fight against the Democratic Liberation Forces of Rwanda (FDLR), an exile militia group of Rwandan Hutus. Human Rights Watch has strongly condemned such developments, insisting that, '[President Joseph] Kabila's government has a legal obligation to arrest Ntaganda, not to promote him'.[34] Similarly, Moreno-Ocampo has declared that, 'For such criminals, there must be no escape. Then peace will have a chance. Then victims will have hope'.[35] President Kabila himself, however, maintains that there are legitimate reasons for the Congolese authorities to work with Ntaganda. Highlighting the complex and heavily contested relationship between peace and justice, to be discussed in the final section, Kabila asks, 'Why do we choose to work with Mr Bosco, a person sought by the ICC? Because we want peace now. In Congo, peace must come before justice'.[36]

---

30 At the time of writing, these states are Uganda, the DRC, the CAR, the Sudan, Kenya and, most recently, the Ivory Coast and Libya.

31 Apropos of Darfur, for example, de Waal maintains that, 'While the current polarisation and estrangement between Sudan and the international community remains, it is unlikely that the ICC will be able to achieve the successful prosecution of even two individuals'. Alex de Waal, *Darfur, the Court and Khartoum: The Politics of State Non-Cooperation, in* Courting Conflict? Justice, Peace And The Icc In Africa 29, 35 (Nicholas Waddell & Phil Clark, eds., 2008). It should be noted in relation to the Sudan, however, that while four of the seven individuals indicted by the ICC remain at large, including President Omar al-Bashir, the remaining three – Bahr Idriss Abu Garda, Abdallah Banda Abakaer Nourain and Saleh Mohammed Jerbo Jamus – have all appeared before the Court.

32 Cherif M. Bassiouni, *The ICC – Quo Vadis?* 4 Journal of International Criminal Justice 421, 426 (2006).

33 This arrest warrant was subsequently unsealed on 28 April 2008.

34 Human Rights Watch, DR Congo: Arrest Bosco Ntaganda (2009), available at: <www.hrw.org/en/news/2009/02/02/dr-congo-arrest-bosco-ntaganda> (Accessed April 15, 2010).

35 Cited in Thijs Bouwknegt, 'ICC Arrest Warrant Against "Terminator" Bosco Ntaganda' (2008), available at: <http://static.rnw.nl/migratie/www.rnw.nl/internationaljustice/icc/DRC/080429-ICC-Ntaganda-redirected> (Accessed April 15, 2010).

36 Cited in David Smith, 'The Terminator' Lives in Luxury While Peacekeepers Look On (2010), available at: <www.guardian.co.uk/world/2010/feb/05/congo-child-soldiers-ntaganda-monuc> (Accessed April 15, 2010).

That the ICC is strongly dependent on state co-operation is likely to affect which cases it decides to prosecute. Is it, for example, a coincidence that the ICC's first cases in the DRC – Thomas Lubanga Dyilo, Germaine Katanga and Mathieu Ngudjolo Chui – all centre on crimes committed in Ituri? One scholar notes that, 'Of the various conflicts in the DRC, that in Ituri is the most isolated from the political arena in Kinshasa', as a result of which '. . . investigations and prosecutions in Ituri display the least capacity to destabilise the current government'.[37] The Court, in other words, needs to tread carefully. In order to conduct its investigations in the DRC, and in order to ensure the safety and security of its staff, it is essential that the ICC has the support and co-operation of the government in Kinshasa. Hence, while the Prosecutor maintains that gravity is a key criterion for selecting which cases to prosecute,[38] there are political and pragmatic considerations that may also enter into the equation.[39] The difficulty is that the exigencies of *Realpolitik* are unlikely to be readily understandable to victims on the ground, thus further underscoring the immense challenges that the ICC faces in delivering justice.

It must be emphasized that 'No mechanism will ever deliver perfect justice'[40] and the ICC is no exception. Furthermore, in the aftermath of such grave offences as mass rape, torture and crimes against humanity, we cannot rely solely upon a judicial institution to deliver justice; there is more to justice than the prosecution and trial of war criminals. Nevertheless, as the first permanent international criminal court, the ICC is a critical part of the justice equation – although only one part.[41] Hence, it is important to explore how it might realize its potential as an instrument of justice. It is argued that it can so do in three main ways – by clarifying and facilitating the exercise of victims' rights, by increasing the visibility of its work and by working with local courts in accordance with the cardinal principle of complementarity.

37 Clark, *supra* note 27, at 40. On October 11, 2010, however, in accordance with a sealed arrest warrant issued by the ICC on September 28, 2010, French authorities arraigned Callixte Mbarushimana, one of the FDLR leaders. Mbarushimana stands accused of committing war crimes and crimes against humanity in North and South Kivu. He is the first senior figure arrested on behalf of the ICC for crimes perpetrated in the Kivus.

38 Moreno-Ocampo, *supra* note 12 at 498.

39 This is true not only in the particular case of the ICC. For example, one of the reasons why the International Criminal Tribunal for Rwanda (ICTR) has so far chosen not to issue any indictments for crimes committed by the Rwandan Patriotic Front (RPF) is to avoid antagonizing or alienating the Rwandan government, largely composed of former members of the RPF. That the Tribunal is only trying Hutus, however, has inevitably given rise to allegations of bias; '. . .the void in prosecutions created by the absence of any RPF individuals accused of crimes has . . . been the source of much criticism regarding the achievement of justice on the part of the ICTR'. Nicholas A. Jones, THE COURTS OF GENOCIDE: POLITICS AND THE RULE OF LAW IN RWANDA AND ARUSHA (2010).

40 Blumenson, *supra* note 24, at 867.

41 Goldstone & Smith, *supra* note 10, at 142.

10.3 THE ICC'S POTENTIAL AS AN INSTRUMENT OF JUSTICE

While victims are a key constituency in deciding whether and to what extent justice has been done, historically they have played only a marginal role in trial proceedings. This, however, is now starting to change, and the Rome Statute epitomizes this development. It has thus been argued that 'From the victims' perspective, it is not far-fetched to say, the Rome Statute is a momentous advance compared to the ad hoc tribunals for not only the former Yugoslavia and Rwanda, but also Nuremberg and Tokyo'.[42] The Statute contains important restorative justice elements – namely Article 68 on the participation of victims in the trial process, Article 75 on the possibilities of reparative justice and Article 79 on the establishment of a Trust Fund for victims. While such provisions are to be welcomed, they are not enough in and of themselves. In order to potentially deliver a more victim-centred justice, it is argued that the Court needs to introduce greater clarity and understanding in relation to the restorative aspects of its mandate.

10.3.1 *Justice through Increased Clarity and Communication*

It is critical that victims fully understand and have the opportunity to exercise their rights under the Rome Statute. In other words, these rights must be clear and accessible. The current application process for victims to participate in ICC proceedings, however, has been criticized as overly complicated. According to the VRWG, 'The application forms are lengthy and abstract, there is little feedback about the processing of applications and the procedures are slow and remote'.[43] Victims, moreover, have described the process as 'bureaucratic', 'heavy and long', 'heavy and slow' or 'heavy and strict'.[44] At the same time, the process needs to be transparent. As of April 2010, for example, the ICC had received 2,035 applications for participation but had only granted 760 of these.[45] Victims need to understand this process, to help ensure that the rejection of their applications is not interpreted as a dismissal or negation of their suffering and trauma. It is therefore important for the Court to work closely with local victims' organizations, in order to better understand what victims want and need, to gain valuable grassroots insight into how its work is perceived on the ground and to give victims a voice not only within the courtroom but

42 M. Henzelin, V. Heiskanen & G. Mettraux, *Reparations to Victims before the International Criminal Court: Lessons from International Mass Claims Processes*, 17 CRIMINAL LAW FORUM 317, 317-318 (2006).

43 VRWG, *supra* note 18.

44 *Id.*

45 ICC, Registry and Trust Fund for Victims: Fact Sheet, Review Conference of the Rome Statute, RC/ST/V/INF.3 (2010), available at: <www.icc-cpi.int/iccdocs/asp_docs/RC2010/Stocktaking/RC-ST-V-INF.3-ENG.pdf> (Accessed November 21, 2010).

also in identifying how the Court's complex procedures can be improved and made more accessible.

Victims must be able not only to avail themselves of their rights. They must also have realistic expectations of what the Court can deliver, not least with respect to reparations. This is an area in which the potential for deep disappointment among victims is considerable.[46] Since the ICC has only recently completed its first trial, no reparations payments have been made to date under Article 75 of the Rome Statute. Victims are, however, already benefitting from the Court's Trust Fund,[47] which was officially established on September 9, 2002. According to a recent report by the Bureau on Stocktaking, the Trust Fund has so far received a total of €4.9 million from 24 states, of which '[a]pproximately €2.7 million has been available to projects in northern Uganda and the Democratic Republic of Congo'.[48] These projects include physical rehabilitation for victims of war, empowerment of victims through agricultural development, assistance for victims of sexual and/or gender-based violence and aid and support for victims of torture and/or mutilation.[49]

Notwithstanding the very valuable work that the Trust Fund is facilitating, it goes without saying that it cannot help everyone. Inevitably, this can have a significant impact on those who miss out, contributing to the belief that their suffering is being overlooked; '. . . many who have not had a chance to benefit from the Trust Fund's projects have been dispirited, fearing that their chance might have been lost'.[50] This situation, moreover, may exacerbate

46 The example of South Africa is particularly illustrative in this regard. South Africa does not have any cases before the ICC. It favoured a restorative justice-based approach – in the form of a truth reconciliation commission (TRC) – to dealing with its apartheid past. The important point is that while reparative justice was a core element of the TRC process, it resulted in high levels of dissatisfaction among victims. According to Jobson, for example, 'The awarding of final reparations by government was inordinately delayed. The payments themselves were limited [a one-off payment of 30,000 Rand] and much reduced from the original recommendations of the TRC [a payment of between 22,000 Rand and 25,000 Rand for six successive years [. . .]' Marjorie Jobson, *The TRC's Unfinished Business: Reparations*, *in* TRUTH AND RECONCILIATION IN SOUTH AFRICA: TEN YEARS ON 45, 47 (Charles Villa-Vicencio & Fanie du Toit eds., 2006).

47 Art. 79 (1) of the Rome Statute stipulates that 'A Trust Fund shall be established by decision of the Assembly of States Parties for the benefit of victims of crimes within the jurisdiction of the Court, and of the families of such victims'. Rome Statute, *supra* note 29.

48 Report of the Bureau on Stocktaking, "The Impact of the Rome Statute System on Victims and Affected Communities", ICC-ASP/8/49 (2010), available at: <www.icc-cpi.int/iccdocs/asp_docs/ASP8R/ICC-ASP-8-49-ENG.pdf> (Accessed November 21, 2010).

49 The Trust Fund for Victims, "Programme Progress Report: November 2009" (2009), available at: <www.trustfundforvictims.org/sites/default/files/imce/TFV%20Programme%20Report%20November%202009.pdf> (Accessed November 21, 2010); 'Recognizing Victims and Building Capacity in Transitional Societies – Spring 2010 Programme Progress Report' (2010), available at: <www.trustfundforvictims.org/sites/default/files/imce/TFV%20Programme%20Report%20Spring%202010.pdf> (Accessed November 21, 2010).

50 Gaëlle Carayon, *The ICC's Impact on Victims and Affected Communities*, 16 VRWG Bulletin (2010), available at: <www.vrwg.org/English%2016Final.pdf> (Accessed November 20, 2010).

the aforementioned problem of selective justice. According to the VRWG, for example, many victims and affected communities in Uganda and the DRC have raised questions regarding the criteria used to determine which projects receive funding.[51]

The risk of unmet expectations is only likely to increase once the ICC makes its first reparations award under Article 75. While this risk cannot be entirely eliminated, it can be managed. Firstly, one difficulty at present is a lack of clear guidelines in respect of reparations. In short, 'The Statute and the Court's Rules of Procedure and Evidence [. . .] provide little insight as to how the Court is expected to process the waves of reparation claims that are expected to reach its shores'.[52] Article 75, for example, is very general and lacks detail. Over time, however, as the Court begins to deal with reparations claims, its jurisprudence can be expected to bring greater clarity to the issue, in the same way that it has vis-à-vis the participation of victims.[53] Secondly, the Court needs to invest more time and resources in outreach work. Communication and engagement with local communities, both directly and through victims' organizations, are critical tools for helping to ensure that people understand the Court, that victims are informed of their rights and how to exercise them and that they appreciate that limitations inevitably exist in respect of what can and cannot be achieved.[54]

Outreach therefore has a critical role to play in relation to justice. Not only can it help to create greater understanding and to manage victims' expectations in relation to the restorative justice components of the Court's mandate. It is also important for increasing the visibility of the Court's work, thereby helping to ensure that justice is not only done but also seen to be done.

10.3.2 Justice through Increased Visibility

Like the ICTY and the International Criminal Tribunal for Rwanda (ICTR), based in The Hague and Arusha (Tanzania) respectively, what the ICC is essentially delivering is 'remote justice',[55] and this is more difficult to see from the perspective of affected local

51 VRWG, *supra* note 18.

52 Henzelin *et al.*, *supra* note 42, at 320.

53 Dadimos Haile, The Modalities of Victims' Participation Evolve in the Katanga/Ngudjolo Trial, 16 VRWG Bulletin (2010), available at: <www.vrwg.org/English%2016Final.pdf> (Accessed November 20, 2010).

54 De Brouwer, *supra* note 2, at 222.

55 This term is borrowed from Gabrielle Kirk MacDonald, a former judge at the ICTY. Judge Kirk McDonald described as "remote" the justice being dispensed by a tribunal that is geographically, linguistically and procedurally removed from the people of the former Yugoslavia. Kirk G. McDonald, *Problems, Obstacles and Achievements of the ICTY*, 2 Journal of International Criminal Justice 558, 569 (2004).

communities. Nevertheless, the Court can improve and enhance the visibility of its work by making every effort to ensure that local populations are familiar with and understand what it is doing and why. This is crucial; 'Recent experience has brought home the need for concerted efforts to ensure that, when prosecutions or truth commissions are instituted, their work is known and understood by the societies on whose behalf they operate'.[56] While the ICTY, created in 1993, was the first tribunal to establish an Outreach Unit, it did not recognize the necessity of reaching out to and communicating with local communities until 1999 – six years too late.[57] Of course it would have been extremely difficult for the ICTY to begin outreach work in 1993, owing to the fact that the war in Bosnia-Hercegovina was still raging. Yet this war ended in 1995. That the Tribunal waited another four years to commence any outreach activities meant that valuable opportunities to counter anti-ICTY media and political propaganda (particularly in Serbia) were missed.

Learning from the ICTY's mistakes, subsequent tribunals have heeded the importance of early outreach work, including the ICC. According to its outreach strategy, 'Justice must be both done and seen to be done. Hence, in order for the Court to fulfil its mandate, it is imperative that its role and judicial activities are understood, particularly in those communities affected by the commission of crimes under the Court's jurisdiction'.[58] The ICC began outreach work in the DRC and Uganda in 2004, extending this to the CAR and Darfur in 2007. Defining outreach as 'a process of establishing sustainable, two-way communication between the Court and communities affected by situations that are the subject of investigations or proceedings',[59] the Court's outreach activities are broad and diverse and informed by a bottom-up ethos.[60] They include the production of radio and television programmes such as 'ICC at a Glance' and 'News from the Court'; trainings for journalists; town-hall style/village meetings; the use of an internet-based Short Message Services system; the holding of workshops and seminars; focus group discussions; the dissemination of outreach materials and legal texts; and mass outreach meetings. Furthermore, there is a

56 Diane F. Orentlicher, *Settling Accounts Revisited: Reconciling Global Norms with Local Agency*, 1 International Journal of Transitional Justice 10, 16 (2007).

57 Janine Natalya Clark, *International War Crimes Tribunals and the Challenge of Outreach*, 9 International Criminal Law Review 99 (2009).

58 ICC, Strategic Plan for Outreach of the International Criminal Court, *ICC-ASP/5/12* (2006), available at: <www.icc-cpi.int/NR/rdonlyres/FB4C75CF-FD15-4B06-B1E3-E22618FB404C/185051/ICCASP512_English1.pdf> (Accessed April 3, 2010).

59 International Criminal Court, 'Integrated Strategy for External Relations, Public Information and Outreach' (2007), available at: <www.icc-cpi.int/NR/rdonlyres/425E80BA-1EBC-4423-85C6-D4F2B93C7506/185049/ICCPIDSWBOR0307070402_IS_En.pdf> (Accessed April 3, 2010).

60 According to the ICC's 2009 Outreach Report, 'The Outreach Unit communicates its messages using a bottom-up approach, taking into account the specific information needs of each of the target audiences. By working in this way, the Outreach Unit aims to give these communities ownership, rendering it an institution that works for them and in their name'. ICC, *supra* note 10.

strong emphasis placed on working and developing relationships with local partners and intermediaries, 'particularly where ICC staff are unable to contact the general public due to lack of resources, logistical or other constraints or security concerns'.[61]

Outreach work, however, poses enormous challenges for the ICC, particularly since all of the cases that it is currently dealing with are Africa-based. To highlight some of the key challenges, the Court is geographically, linguistically[62] and procedurally removed from the African Continent; there are significant security issues in the countries concerned; poor infrastructure makes travel extremely difficult, particularly to remote rural areas; and the ICC faces hostile propaganda from media and politicians in countries like the Sudan. The extent to which people understand the Court, however, has been shown to affect how they perceive it,[63] and the way in which local communities view the ICC is critical to the issue of whether and to what extent it can deliver justice. It is thus essential that the Court continues to develop and to expand its outreach programme.[64] International criminal justice 'does not necessarily imply geographic remoteness or antiseptic procedures divorced from local realities'[65] and it is hoped that the ICC can demonstrate this.

If outreach is one potential solution to the problem of 'remote justice', there are also implicit suggestions contained within the Rome Statute itself as to how the issue might be addressed. For example, while Article 3(1) states that, 'The seat of the Court shall be established at The Hague in the Netherlands', Article 3(3) adds that, 'The Court may sit elsewhere, whenever it considers it desirable, as provided in this Statute'. Article 4(2) further stipulates that, 'The Court may exercise its functions and powers. . .on the territory of any State Party and, by special agreement, on the territory of any other State'.[66] Rule 100(1) of the Court's Rules of Procedure and Evidence reiterates this, stating that 'In a particular

---

61 ICC, *supra* note 58.

62 The ICC's working languages are English and French. More broadly, its official languages are English, French, Spanish, Russian, Arabic and Chinese.

63 *Id.*

64 Apropos of northern Uganda, for example, where it is widely believed that the ICC itself has the powers to arrest LRA leaders, Pham and Vinck maintain that "The ICC should develop a strategy to manage expectations and explain the process of arresting the LRA until they are apprehended". Phuong Pham & Patrick Vinck, *Transitioning to Peace: A Population-Based Survey on Attitudes about Social Reconstruction and Justice in Northern Uganda* (2010), available at <www.law.berkeley.edu/HRCweb/pdfs/HRC_Uga2010final_web.pdf> (Accessed January 21, 2011). The Court itself acknowledges that ". . .a lot more needs to be done to increase the Court's visibility within the affected communities". ICC, *supra* note 58.

65 Payam Akhavan, *The Lord's Resistance Army Case: Uganda's Submission of the First State Referral to the International Criminal Court*, 99 The American Journal of International Law 403, 421 (2005).

66 Rome Statute, *supra* note 29.

case, where the Court considers that it would be in the interests of justice, it may decide to sit in a State other than the host State'.[67]

Were the Court to conduct some of its trials not in The Hague but in those countries where the crimes that it is prosecuting took place, this would give its work a greater immediacy – in terms of geographical proximity, visibility and increased ease of access – akin to that of a hybrid court like the Special Court of Sierra Leone. This in turn could help to foster a sense of local ownership, by allowing communities to actually witness the justice process and be a part of it – rather than simply distant onlookers. Without this local engagement and interest, the ICC risks being perceived as a distant and incomprehensible 'foreign' institution with little relevance to people's everyday lives, a commonly-held view of the ICTY in BiH.[68]

In-situ trials would of course pose significant practical, logistical and in some cases security challenges. Certainly, it would not be feasible to hold in-country trials in states where conflict is ongoing (for example, the DRC) or where the government is opposed to the ICC (as in the case of the Sudan). To overcome such obstacles, one possibility would be to establish a regional chamber of the Court. This might encourage witnesses to come forward;[69] it would require a lesser degree of co-operation with the state in which the crimes being prosecuted took place, thus helping to avoid fuelling perceptions of bias and impartiality; and it would still allow the Court to deliver a more visible and accessible justice than it is currently doing. A second possibility would be for the Court to hold a limited number of in-country hearings, where circumstances permit. Extensive consultation with victims' organizations would, however, be a critical prerequisite, in order for the Court to identify those cases of particular importance to victims and local communities.

In addition to conducting regional or in-situ proceedings, a third and final way for the ICC to deliver justice is to work closely with local courts, as well as the broader international

67 ICC Rules of Procedure and Evidence, ICC-ASP/1/3, available at: <www.icc-cpi.int> (Accessed April 30, 2010).
68 Clark, *supra* note 26, at 484.
69 Ford observes that "One of the most interesting results of the ICC's exploration of moving part of the Lubanga trial to the DRC was that even though the parties and the Trial Chamber seemed to agree that having local hearings was desirable, the witnesses were overwhelmingly opposed to testifying in the DRC". Stuart Ford, *The Promise of Local or Regional ICC Trial Chambers: Incorporating the Benefits of the Hybrid Tribunals into the ICC* (2010), available at: <http://ssrn.com/abstract=1605294> (Accessed November 24, 2010).

community, in order to facilitate the holding of domestic trials.[70] This in turn would help to address the 'impunity gap' created by the very limited number of ICC prosecutions.

10.3.3 Justice through Increased Co-Operation

Complementarity is one of the core principles of the Rome Statute. Article 1 provides that the Court's jurisdiction 'shall be complementary to national criminal jurisdictions'; and Article 17 underlines that primacy of jurisdiction rests with states themselves, not with the ICC.[71] The ICC thus has a valuable role to play in working with and assisting these national courts, thereby contributing to the delivery of a more local justice. In other words, just as States Parties should co-operate with the Court, there is also significant potential for 'reverse co-operation'.[72] The type and extent of support that the Court should provide, however, is much debated and a number of different concerns have been expressed. One such concern is that aiding countries to conduct their own national trials should neither detract from the Court's primary function of prosecuting those who commit heinous crimes nor over-burden it. Baylis, for example, is sceptical of the idea that the ICC 'might devote any substantial resources to assisting with national trials', based in part on the Court's resource constraints.[73] Burke-White notes that the provision of direct technical assistance to States would be particularly demanding on the Court's limited resources, and hence 'must be pursued with the utmost caution'.[74]

A second concern is that by providing assistance and training to national courts, the Court may risk antagonizing communities on the ground, even though the aim would be to help those communities. If, for example, local people have very negative perceptions of the ICC,

70 Recent research by Pham and Vinck in northern Uganda revealed that among the 2,498 respondents, there was more support for trials in Uganda by Ugandan courts (35%) than for trials at the ICC, whether in The Hague (28%) or in Uganda (22%). Pham & Vinck, *supra* note 64. According to similar research in the DRC in 2007, 85% of the 2,620 respondents in Ituri, North and South Kivu expressed a preference for trials held in the DRC. Of this 85%, moreover, 82% expressed the view that the international community should aid domestic courts. Patrick Vinck, Phuong Pham, Sulima Baldo & Rachel Shigekane, *Living with Fear: A Population-Based Survey on Attitudes about Peace, Justice and Social Reconstruction in Eastern Democratic Republic of Congo* (2008), available at: <http://escholarship.org/uc/item/9738b4pm#page-2> (Accessed January 21, 2011).

71 Rome Statute, *supra* note 29.

72 Art. 93(10)(a) of the Rome Statute stipulates that 'The Court may, upon request, cooperate with and provide assistance to a State Party conducting an investigation into or trial in respect of conduct which constitutes a crime within the jurisdiction of the Court or which constitutes a serious crime under the national law of the requesting State'. *Id.*

73 Elena A. Baylis, *Reassessing the Role of International Criminal Law: Rebuilding National Courts through Transnational Networks*, 50 Boston College Law Review 1, 22 (2009).

74 Burke-White, *supra* note 25, at 94.

they may resent its 'interference' in their country's internal affairs, particularly if this is seen as undermining local ownership of the judicial process. If, moreover, the ICC Prosecutor is seen to be co-operating with local prosecutors, this could further encourage allegations of political bias. In short, '. . .dialogue and partnership with states may compromise the independence and appearance of impartiality of the Prosecutor'.[75] The Office of the Prosecutor (OTP) itself has similarly recognized this. In its 2009-2010 Prosecutorial Strategy, for example, it underlines apropos of the preliminary examination phase that 'The Office cannot be the adviser to national jurisdictions as it would risk tainting future proceedings'.[76]

A third important concern is that the Court's efforts to foster meaningful complementarity could engender 'legal mimicry' at the expense of a more nuanced and culturally sensitive legal process. Drumbl, for example, opines that complementarity 'may encourage heterogeneity in terms of the number of institutions adjudicating international crimes, but homogeneity in terms of the process they follow and the punishment they mete out'.[77] Such homogeneity, in turn, means that 'the content of local practices may be excluded regardless of the legitimacy with which these practices are received'[78], thereby further obstructing a sense of local ownership of the process.

In view of the complex questions and challenges that complementarity thus raises, it is perhaps unsurprising that the Court has adopted a somewhat cautious approach to the issue. In its 2009-2012 Prosecutorial Strategy, for example, the OTP articulates its policy of 'positive complementarity'. According to this '. . .the Office will encourage genuine national proceedings where possible' by, inter alia, providing information to national judiciaries, sharing databases of non-confidential materials and inviting local officials and lawyers from those countries in which the Court is conducting its investigations to participate in the OTP's investigative and prosecutorial activities. The Strategy also, however, sets limits upon what this positive approach to complementarity entails. It thereby endorses the definition of positive complementarity put forward in the Report of the Bureau of Stocktaking, wherein the term is used to refer to:

> all activities/actions whereby national jurisdictions are strengthened and enabled to conduct genuine national investigations and trials of crimes included in the Rome Statute, without involving the Court in capacity building,

75 Carsten Stahn, *Complementarity: A Tale of Two Notions*, 19 CRIMINAL LAW FORUM 87, 108 (2008).

76 Office of the Prosecutor (OTP), Prosecutorial Strategy 2009-2012 (2010), available at: <www.icc-cpi.int/NR/rdonlyres/66A8DCDC-3650-4514-AA62-D229D1128F65/281506/OTPProsecutorialStrategy20092013.pdf> (Accessed September 30, 2010).

77 MARK A. DRUMBL, ATROCITY, PUNISHMENT AND INTERNATIONAL LAW 143 (2007).

78 *Id.*

> financial support and technical assistance, but instead leaving these actions and activities for States, to assist each other on a voluntary basis.[79]

While it remains to be seen exactly how this policy of positive complementarity will translate into practice, three important points should be made. The first is that while both the ICTY and the ICTR, in contrast to the ICC, have primacy of jurisdiction over national courts, one of the criticisms of these ad hoc tribunals has been that they have not done enough to aid and to reach out to local judiciaries. A former ICTY Deputy Prosecutor, for example, has argued that both tribunals 'have had little impact on the legal infrastructure in these countries [in the former Yugoslavia and Rwanda]'.[80] Since adopting its Completion Strategy in 2003, the ICTY in particular has now started to invest considerable time and resources in local judiciaries in the former Yugoslavia, including via training programmes and the transfer of materials and expertise. However, while such capacity-building work is likely to constitute one of the ICTY's most important and valuable legacies, it arguably should have started much earlier, particularly given that local courts in the former Yugoslavia will have the main responsibility for prosecuting war crimes cases once the Tribunal closes its doors. The fact, therefore, that the ICC, at a relatively early stage of its existence, has sought to clarify and to concretize the notion of complementarity is to be welcomed.

The second point is that while the ICC has a central role to play in facilitating domestic prosecutions, the onus in this regard does not lie solely with the Court. The Preamble of the Rome Statute, for example, emphasizes that '. . .the most serious crimes of concern to the international community as a whole must not go unpunished and that their effective prosecution must be ensured by taking measures at the national level and by enhancing international cooperation'.[81] Hence, the broader international community should be involved in assisting national courts to conduct their own trials. Indeed, the Report of the Bureau on Stocktaking insists that 'Activities aimed at strengthening national jurisdictions. . .should be carried out by States themselves, together with international and regional organizations and civil society, exploring interfaces and synergies with the Rome Statute system'.[82] If, therefore, one way in which the ICC can deliver justice is through increased co-operation, this includes greater co-operation between the Court and States

79 Report of the Bureau on Stocktaking, *Taking Stock of the Principle of Complementarity: Bridging the Impunity Gap*, ICC-ASP/8/51 (2010), available at: <www.icc-cpi.int/iccdocs/asp_docs/ASP8R/ICC-ASP-8-51-ENG.pdf> (Accessed November 20, 2010).

80 Tolbert David & Andrew Solomon, *United Nations Reform and Supporting the Rule of Law in Post-Conflict Societies*, 29 Harvard Human Rights Journal 29, 37 (2006). It is important to reiterate, however, that the Rwandan government has consistently obstructed the ICTR's work, notably the latter's efforts to prosecute members of the rebel Rwandan Patriotic Front (RPF). The RPF's former leader, Paul Kagame, is today the President of Rwanda. See, for example, Peskin, *supra* note 16.

81 Rome Statute, *supra* note 29.

82 Report of the Bureau on Stocktaking, *supra* note 79.

Parties in general. That is to say that, 'As in the case of all international and hybrid courts, the ICC has to work as part of a broader rule-of-law network'.[83]

The third and final point is that through the operationalization of complementarity, the Court can potentially have a significant catalytic effect.[84] This is illustrated by the establishment in 2008 of a War Crimes Division of Uganda's High Court and, more recently, by the country's adoption of the International Criminal Court Act 2010, thereby incorporating the Rome Statute into Ugandan law. As one commentator underlines, 'Even when the Court is already investigating crimes under its jurisdiction, its intervention is still capable of acting as a catalyst for both legislative change and the building of capacity on the domestic level'.[85] If further concrete examples of the Court's catalytic effects emerge, a detailed analysis of these effects would be an important area for research. This would help us to gauge whether and to what extent the Court is indirectly delivering some level of justice. Perhaps more significantly, these effects would provide a useful criterion for measuring the Court's impact, thereby helping to address a significant 'impact gap' within the transitional justice literature. This gap is particularly pronounced vis-à-vis the impact of criminal trials on peace and reconciliation.[86] It is to this relationship between justice and peace that the final part of the chapter now turns.

10.4 THE PEACE AND JUSTICE DEBATE

Thus far, this chapter has focused on the ICC as an instrument of justice, evaluating both its limitations and possibilities. Can it also, however, be an instrument of peace? This is a question that goes to the heart of scholarly debates regarding the relationship between peace and justice, the extent to which the two concepts are compatible and which of the two needs to come first. Uganda features prominently in such discussions and will therefore form the main focus of this final section, which begins by briefly examining two main viewpoints within the transitional justice literature on the nexus between justice and peace.

---

83 International Centre for Transitional Justice (ICTJ), *Victims and the ICC Review Conference: Interview with David Tolbert, President of the ICTJ* (2010), available at: <www.ictj.org/static/Newsletter/Transitions_June_2010.pdf> (Accessed November 20, 2010).

84 According to the OTP's Prosecutorial Strategy, for example, "The preliminary examination offers a first opportunity for the Office to act as a catalyst for national proceedings", OTP, *supra* note 76.

85 Marieke Wierda, Stocktaking: Complementarity, ICTJ Briefing, (2010), available at: <www.ictj.org/static/Publications/ICTJ_RSRC-Complementarity_bp2010.pdf> (Accessed November 20, 2010).

86 Delpla, for example, remarks of the ICTY that "its impact in terms of its purported contribution to peace and reconciliation has been extrapolated rather than observed. It has been mainly derived from other historical experiments, such as the Nuremberg trials, for its alleged pedagogical value, or the South Africa Truth and Reconciliation Commission, for its supposed reconciliatory effect". Isabelle Delpla, *In the Midst of Injustice: The ICTY from the Perspective of some Victims Associations, in* THE NEW BOSNIAN MOSAIC: IDENTITIES, MEMORIES AND MORAL CLAIMS IN A POST-WAR SOCIETY 211, 216 (Xavier Bougarel, Elissa Helms & Ger Duijzings eds., 2007).

10.4.1 Peace versus Justice/Peace via Justice

The first viewpoint regards peace and justice as being in tension, such that we need to choose one or the other. Historically, it is this notion of 'peace versus justice' that has tended to prevail. Following the return to civilian rule in Argentina in 1983, for example, the military junta accorded itself immunity from criminal prosecutions. Although the new government subsequently repealed this amnesty, threats from the military ultimately led to the passing of new quasi-amnesty laws,[87] which the government considered more conducive to long-term peace and stability than criminal trials. Similarly, South Africa dealt with the legacy of the apartheid years by establishing a truth and reconciliation commission (TRC) and amnestying those who fully confessed to their crimes, in the conviction that what the country most needed to heal and move forward was truth. The new African National Congress (ANC) government, led by Nelson Mandela, judged that criminal trials risked doing more harm than good.[88]

More recently, there has been a shift away from the notion that we have to choose between peace and justice to a very different viewpoint – the idea that we need to have justice *in order* to have peace. This 'peace via justice' position can be particularly associated with the ICTY and ICTR, both of which are based on the premise that there can be no peace without justice. To cite Graham Blewitt, a former Deputy Prosecutor at the ICTY, '. . .the ICTY is essentially an instrument of peace: the criminal prosecution of persons responsible for serious violations of international humanitarian law is regarded as being central to the peace process in the former Yugoslavia'.[89] Notwithstanding such confident assertions, the actual effects of criminal trials and the extent to which they do in fact aid social peace and stability remain empirically under-explored.[90] Arguably one reason for this is that the task of actually measuring impact presents significant challenges. Peace, for example – not

87 Priscilla B. Hayner, UNSPEAKABLE TRUTHS: TRANSITIONAL JUSTICE AND THE CHALLEMGE OF THE TRUTH COMMISSIONS 46 (2nd ed. 2011).

88 Desmond Tutu, NO FUTURE WITHOUT FORGIVENESS 27 (1999).

89 G.T. Blewitt, *The International Criminal Tribunal for the Former Yugoslavia and Rwanda, in* JUSTICE FOR CRIMES AGAINST HUMANITY 145, 146 (Mark Lattimer & Philippe Sands eds., 2006).

90 Moghalu, for example, remarks that "There is no empirical proof of any situation. . .where trials have in and of themselves created reconciliation". Kingsley Chiedu Moghalu, *Prosecute or Pardon? Between Truth Commissions and War Crimes Trials, in* PEACE VERSUS JUSTICE? THE DILEMMA OF TRANSITIONAL JUSTICE IN AFRICA 69, 90 (Cha.L. Sriram & S. Pillay eds., 2009). It has been suggested, therefore, that "The expectations of the international community for trials should be limited to an agreement that retributive punishment is appropriate and sufficient in and of itself; that reconciliation processes may be of another order entirely, and that the relationship between justice and reconciliation remains unclear". Harvey M. Weinstein, Laurel E. Fletcher, Patrick Vinck & Phuong N. Pham, *Stay the Hand of Justice: Whose Priorities Take Priority? in* LOCALIZING TRANSITIONAL JUSTICE: INTERVENTIONS AND PRIORITIES AFTER MASS VIOLENCE 27, 31 (Rosalind Shaw & Lars Waldorf eds., 2010).

in the negative sense of an absence of conflict but in the thicker, more positive sense of reconciliation – is an intangible concept that cannot be easily measured or quantified. Gauging impact, moreover, necessarily raises difficult issues pertaining to causation, particularly when the court in question is not based in-country. Fundamentally, the impact of transitional justice processes 'can be difficult to ascertain or quantify because it may be highly collinear with other factors, contingent on precise constellations of circumstances, modified by numerous variables and subject to complex interaction effects'.[91]

While various commentators have addressed the relationship between justice and peace (reconciliation), they have focused more on whether justice *can* foster reconciliation as opposed to whether it has *actually* done so in practice.[92] Until this 'impact gap' is sufficiently addressed,[93] the relationship between criminal trials and peace will continue to be highly ambiguous and open to speculation. The ICC's investigations, and in particular

91 David Backer, *Cross-National Comparative Analysis, in* ASSESSING THE IMPACT OF TRANSITIONAL JUSTICE: CHALLENGES FOR EMPIRICAL RESEARCH 23, 159 (Hugo van der Merwe, Victoria Baxter & Audrey R. Chapman eds., 2009).

92 See, for example, Aleksandar Fatic, RECONCILIATION VIA THE WAR CRIMES TRIBUNAL? (2000); Michael Humphrey, *International Intervention, Justice, and National Reconciliation: The Role of the ICTY and ICTR in Bosnia and Rwanda*, 2 JOURNAL OF HUMAN RIGHTS 495 (2003); Lilian A. Barria & Steven D. Roper, *How Effective are International Criminal Tribunals? An Analysis of the ICTY and ICTR*; 9 THE INTERNATIONAL JOURNAL OF HUMAN RIGHTS 349 (2005); Rachel Kerr, *Peace through Justice? The International Criminal Tribunal for the Former Yugoslavia*, 7 SOUTHEAST EUROPEAN AND BLACK SEA STUDIES 373 (2007).

93 Increasingly, however, scholars are recognizing the importance of examining and devising ways to empirically test the impact of criminal tribunals. Orentlicher, for example, has undertaken very comprehensive research on the ICTY's impact both in BiH and in Serbia. Orentlicher, *supra* note 26; *id.*, *Shrinking the Space for Denial: The Impact of the ICTY in Serbia* (2008). Available at: <www.soros.org/initiatives/justice/focus/international_justice/articles_publications/publications/serbia_20080520/serbia_20080501.pdf> (Accessed December 1, 2009). While not focused exclusively on the issue of impact, extremely important work – in the form of population-based surveys – is also being done by staff at the Human Rights Centre at the University of California, Berkeley. See, for example, Phuong Pham *et al.*, WHEN THE WAR ENDS: A POPULATION-BASED SURVEY ON ATTITUDES ABOUT PEACE, JUSTICE AND SOCIAL RECONSTRUCTION IN NORTHERN UGANDA (2007); Phuong Pham et al., SO WE WILL NEVER FORGET: A POPULATION-BASED SURVEY ON ATTITUDES ABOUT SOCIAL RECONSTRUCTION AND THE EXTRAORDINARY CHAMBERS IN THE COURTS OF CAMBODIA (2009); Phuong Pham & Patrick Vinck, BUILDING PEACE, SEEKING JUSTICE: A POPULATION-BASED SURVEY ON ATTITUDES ABOUT ACCOUNTABILITY AND SOCIAL RECONSTRUCTION IN THE CENTRAL AFRICAN REPUBLIC (2010); Pham & Vinck, *supra* note 64 and 70. This author's own research has sought to empirically explore whether and to what extent the ICTY has contributed to peace (in the specific sense of reconciliation) in post-conflict BiH. It has found that overall the Tribunal has had little positive impact on reconciliation in BiH. Indeed, it has questioned whether it is in fact realistic for a complex judicial body, located in another country, to aid such a personal and individual process as reconciliation. See the following publications by Clark, *supra* note 26; *From Negative to Positive Peace: The Case of Bosnia and Hercegovina*, 8 JOURNAL OF HUMAN RIGHTS 360 (2009); *Judging the ICTY: Has It Achieved Its Objectives?* 9 JOURNAL OF SOUTHEAST EUROPEAN AND BLACK SEA STUDIES 123 (2009); *Transitional Justice in BiH: The International Criminal Tribunal for the Former Yugoslavia, in* THE DEVELOPMENT OF INSTITUTIONS ON HUMAN RIGHTS: A COMPARATIVE STUDY 83 (Lillian Barria & Steven Roper eds., 2010).

its intervention in northern Uganda, highlight this. They have helped to re-ignite debates concerning the nexus between peace and justice, and how we perceive this relationship will in turn critically influence our views on whether or not the Court can facilitate peace. If we lean towards the notion of peace versus justice, the ICC's ability – as a putative instrument of justice – to foster peace will be negligible. If, however, we adopt the alternative peace via justice position, clearly there is far more scope for the ICC to make a positive contribution to peace.

10.5 The ICC as an Obstacle to Peace

It has been argued that '. . .no one should underestimate the prospect of genuine "peace versus punishment" dilemmas',[94] and such dilemmas have particularly arisen in the context of the ICC's intervention in northern Uganda. When Moreno-Ocampo issued arrest warrants against five LRA commanders in 2005, this drew immediate criticism from both within and outside of Uganda. A major objection was that the arrest warrants contravened Uganda's Amnesty Act, passed in 2000 to allow those who renounced violence to return to their communities without fear of possible prosecution. Not only did the Act reflect the will of the people[95] but progress had been made since its adoption.[96] Linked to this is the more fundamental objection that the ICC's involvement in northern Uganda represents a threat to peace. According to this view, the ICC's work in Uganda is inimical to peace as it will discourage the very people upon whom peace depends – most notably the LRA leader Joseph Kony – from coming forward and signing a peace agreement. Scharf, for example, insists that it is unrealistic to expect leaders involved in conflict to agree to a peace deal if thereafter they face the risk of arrest and imprisonment.[97]

While such arguments cannot be simply dismissed, they must be seriously questioned. Most obviously, is it not misjudged to contend that the ICC's arrest warrants represent a

94 Blumenson, *supra* note 24, at 832.

95 Apuuli, for example, notes that, "According to recent studies, 70% of the people in the North [of Uganda] want conditional amnesty for Kony". Kasaija Phillip Apuul, *The ICC Arrest Warrants for the Lord's Resistance Army Leaders and Peace Prospects for Northern Uganda*, 4 Journal of International Criminal Justice 179, 184 (2006).

96 Allen, for example, notes that "By mid-2004, over five thousand adult former LRA fighters had surrendered and applied for it [amnesty]'. Allen, *supra* note 15, at 75.

97 Michael P. Scharf, *The Amnesty Exception to the Jurisdiction of the International Criminal Court*, 32 Cornell International Law Journal 507, 508 (1999). Similar arguments have been expressed within Uganda itself, in particular, by members of the Acholi Religious Leaders Peace Initiative (ARLPI), established in 1998. See, for example, Allen, *supra* note 15, at 85. Following the Juba peace talks in 2006, the LRA and representatives of the Ugandan government signed a Cessation of Hostilities Agreement. However, the peace talks ultimately collapsed and hence a final peace agreement was not signed.

threat to peace, given that there has been no real peace in northern Uganda since 1986?[98] Furthermore, to argue that the ICC will deter men such as Kony from signing a peace accord appears to assume that a peace agreement is a guarantee of peace. The reality, however, is far more complex; '. . .violence is not switched off like a tap by the mere agreement of a peace accord. Much violence is structural in nature and often immune to the provisions of a peace accord. . ..'[99] This highlights the important distinction between positive and negative peace,[100] which the Court's critics often gloss over.

The contention that the ICC's arrest warrants pose a threat to peace in northern Uganda not only conceptualizes peace in a very narrow, negative sense – as the absence of physical violence. It also privileges a very short-term view of peace. Understanding peace in a broader, positive sense and adopting a more long-term perspective, however, can bring an important new dimension to debates about the relationship between peace and justice. In the words of Mendéz, 'This removal [of people like Kony] by the fact that they are now under indictment may initially be seen as an obstacle to peace, but further down the road it may be exactly what is needed to get a stable peace in Northern Uganda.'[101] Finally, while critics of the ICC's work in Uganda submit that peace should come before justice,[102] the complexities and particularities of individual post-conflict societies demand contextually-sensitive and tailored responses rather than general formulae. Peace and justice, in other words, 'do not necessarily follow a linear peace-then-justice trajectory.'[103]

98 Today it might be argued that there is some level of negative peace in Uganda, largely due to the fact that the LRA has now shifted its campaign of terror and violence to the DRC and the CAR. According to the United Nations, for example, the LRA killed more than 1,200 civilians in the DRC in 2009. Xan Rice, Lord's Resistance Army Terrorises Congo after Ugandan Crackdown (2009), available at: <www.guardian.co.uk/world/2009/sep/14/lords-resistance-army-terrorises-congo> (Accessed April 18, 2010). In March 2010, LRA fighters kidnapped more than 50 people and killed ten people in the eastern prefecture of Haut-Mbomou in the CAR. Xan Rice, Lord's Resistance Army Rebels Kill 10 in the Central African Republic (2010), available at: <www.guardian.co.uk/world/2010/mar/23/lords-resistance-army-rebels-attack> (Accessed April 18 2010).

99 Roger Mac Ginty, NO WAR, NO PEACE: THE REJUVENATION OF STALLED PEACE PROCESSES AND PEACE ACCORDS 112 (2008).

100 According to Simpson, "At its most basic, this is a distinction between peace processes that prioritize ending violence in the shorter term, as opposed to building more durable peace through addressing the underlying causes of violence". Graeme Simpson, *One Among Many: The ICC as a Tool of Justice During Transition, in* COURTING CONFLICT? JUSTICE, PEACE AND THE ICC IN AFRICA 73, 74 (Nicholas Waddell & Phil Clark eds., 2008).

101 Jaer E. Méndez, cited in IRIN, *Justice for a Lawless World? Rights and Reconciliation in a New Era of International Law – Part II* (2006), available at: <www.irinnews.org/pdf/in-depth/RightsAndReconciliationPart2.pdf> (Accessed April 5, 2010).

102 Refugee Law Project, *Peace First, Justice Later: Traditional Justice in Northern Uganda* (2005), available at: <www.refugeelawproject.org/working_papers/RLP.WP17.pdf> (Accessed April 5, 2010).

103 Moreno-Ocampo, *supra* note 12, at 498.

If we adopt the position that peace and justice are fundamentally incompatible and in conflict, the ICC will inevitably represent a potential impediment to peace. Such dichotomous thinking, however, is ultimately unhelpful.[104] Undoubtedly, tensions between peace and justice can and do exist, yet this does not mean that we must make a choice between the two. Such Manichaeism will only entrench the very binaries that we need to overcome. Crucial to exploring and understanding the relationship between peace and justice is to conceptualize justice in a much fuller and deeper sense than merely criminal trials. In essence, 'Working for both peace and justice requires a broader and more holistic view of how both of these aims are achieved and the important connection between them'.[105]

10.5.1 The ICC as a Potential Facilitator of Peace

'Justice' is a multi-dimensional concept that encompasses judicial and non-judicial forms, retributive and restorative elements. To understand it solely or primarily as criminal trials, therefore, is not only erroneous[106] but also places a huge burden on judicial bodies like the ICC. To return to the case of northern Uganda, the Acholi people have their own indigenous forms of justice. The rite of *mato oput*, for example, is traditionally used when a member of one clan kills a member of another. Informed by restorative justice principles,[107] *mato oput* entails a process of mediation, confession, payment of compensation, a reconciliation ceremony during which two sheep are slaughtered and exchanged and finally the drinking of the *oput* root, to symbolize the washing away of bitterness between the two clans. Contrary to claims that the ICC's intervention in Uganda rides roughshod over such indigenous justice practices,[108] international criminal justice and traditional justice are not alternatives but rather complementary forms of justice that should be concurrently pursued (a point which has yet to be fully heeded in Uganda). As one legal authority underscores, '...it would be loading too much on the ICC to see it as the sole mechanism for delivering justice (in the fullest sense of the word)'.[109]

104 Janine Natalya Clark, *The ICC, Uganda and the LRA: Re-Framing the Debate,* 69 African Studies 14 (2010).

105 Priscilla Hayner, *Negotiating Justice: The Challenge of Addressing Past Human Rights Violations, in* Contemporary Peacemaking: Conflict, Peace Processes and Post-War Reconstruction 328, 336 (John Darby & Roger Mac Ginty eds., 2d ed. 2008).

106 Menkel-Meadow underscores that, "Just as military solutions to 'war' may not bring us peace, an exclusive focus on 'legal' needs and interests may not bring us justice. This is true, whether we like it or not". Carrie Menkel-Meadow, *Practicing 'In the Interests of Justice' in the Twenty-First Century: Pursuing Peace as Justice,* 70 Fordham Law Review 1761, 1774 (2002).

107 Zehr identifies 10 "signposts" of restorative justice. These include a focus on the harm caused, rather than on the laws broken; the restoration and empowering of victims; and the provision of opportunities for dialogue between victim and offender. Howard Zehr, The Little Book of Restorative Justice 40 (2002).

108 See, for example, Katherine Southwick, *Investigating War in Northern Uganda: Dilemmas for the International Criminal Court,* 1 Yale Journal of International Affairs 105 (2005).

109 Justice Albie Sachs, *Foreword, in* Courting Conflict? Justice, Peace and the ICC in Africa 6 (Nicholas Waddell & Phil Clark eds., 2008).

As part of a comprehensive justice strategy that includes but does not over-rely upon criminal trials, however, the Court can potentially contribute to peace in northern Uganda and elsewhere, in particular through the dispensing of justice that is accessible and comprehensible to local communities.[110] Of course, the emphasis must be on the word 'potentially'; to reiterate, the relationship between criminal trials and peace remains empirically under-explored and thus constitutes a critical area for future research. Yet simply by understanding justice as a more textured and multi-dimensional term than just criminal trials, our conceptual starting point can progress beyond narrow peace versus justice debates towards a more sophisticated '*peace and justice continuum* in which diverse accountability mechanisms can contribute to peace-building efforts, rather than compromise them'.[111]

That the ICC is still a young institution dealing with only a small number of cases means that its ability to actually contribute to peace remains to be seen. The fact that it may aid peace in one context, moreover, does not necessarily mean that it will do so in another. As Bassiouni underlines,

> Every post-conflict situation is *sui generis*, and the prospects for the Court's investigations and prosecutions will vary in each case depending upon a number of factors including the context and circumstances in which the crimes occurred, accessibility to evidence, logistical considerations and, above all, the political willingness of the interested states in providing support to the Court.[112]

The critical point, therefore, is that rather than viewing the ICC as either an obstacle to peace or as an instrument of peace, a more nuanced perspective is ultimately required. We need, in other words, to acknowledge and to examine both the Court's limitations and its potential, and thus to recognize that as regards the relationship between criminal justice

110 Mendéz, for example, argues that in a number of cases – including the Ivory Coast, Georgia and Guinea – the ICC has prevented violence. In 2004, for example, when he was a special advisor to the United Nations Secretary-General, Mendéz gave a press statement in the Ivory Coast, emphasizing that since the country had made the decision in 2002 to accept the ICC's jurisdiction, those individuals responsible for inciting hatred and violence faced the risk of criminal prosecution in The Hague. Recalling how it was later established that 'the prospect of ICC prosecution was carefully analyzed by persons in authority and their legal advisers', he notes that 48 hours after his press release was widely broadcast, calm returned to the country. For him, therefore, "...the incident is evidence that the threat of prosecution can stay the hand of perpetrators". Juan E. Mendez, "The Importance of Justice in Securing Peace", ICC Review Conference of the Rome Statute (2010), available at: <www.icc-cpi.int/iccdocs/asp_docs/RC2010/Stocktaking/RC-ST-PJ-INF.3-ENG.pdf> (Accessed November 24, 2010).

111 Simpson, *supra* note 101, at 75.

112 Bassiouni, *supra* note 32, at 423.

and peace, there are no clear-cut answers. Rather, 'efforts to prosecute war crimes suspects may both enhance and complicate efforts to achieve and maintain peace'.[113]

10.6 Conclusion

For one prominent legal scholar, 'Most intriguing about the response of trials to mass atrocities is the close proximity of idealism and cynicism surrounding the entire project'.[114] Seeking to carve a middle ground between these two extremes, this chapter has explored both the ICC's limitations and possibilities in delivering justice and peace. While identifying three particular ways in which the ICC can potentially realize its capacity as a vehicle of justice – namely increased clarity, increased visibility and increased co-operation – it has also emphasized that there is far more to justice than criminal trials. Hence, notwithstanding the important concessions to restorative justice within the Rome Statute, we cannot over-rely upon the ICC to deliver justice after mass atrocities. To cite Goldstone and Smith, '. . .the menu of how best to deal with such crimes has become enriched and multifaceted'.[115]

Turning to the Court's potential as an instrument of peace, this research has argued that while tensions can and do arise between peace and justice, this does not necessarily mean that the ICC represents a threat to peace. Rather than engaging in narrow peace versus justice debates, a 'dichotomous dilemma [that] is often overstated',[116] the way forward is to explore whether and how the ICC can contribute to peace as part of a comprehensive and holistic justice strategy. As Moreno-Ocampo himself underscores, '. . .we must think about an integrated approach and how to combine justice with other areas, such as rehabilitation and development, in order to produce better communities'.[117] That the Court has recognized the importance of restorative justice – notably by making provision for the participation of victims and for reparative justice – thus represents a significant starting point.

While no definitive conclusions can be drawn at this stage, the work of the Court has undoubtedly injected important new substance into discussions about the relationship between criminal trials, justice and peace. To the extent that such debates to date have tended to adopt a more theoretical focus, it is hoped that the polemics surrounding the

113 Peskin, *supra* note 16, at 257.
114 Minow, *supra* note 3, at 28.
115 Goldstone & Smith, *supra* note 10, at 142.
116 Chand Lekha Sriram, *Introduction: Transitional Justice and Peacebuilding*, in Peace Versus Justice? The Dilemma Of Transitional Justice In Africa 1 (Chand Lekha Sriram & Suren Pillay eds., 2009).
117 Moreno-Ocampo, *supra* note 12, at 503.

ICC will provide the catalyst for more empirical research in this area. Such research is essential for generating realistic expectations – 'One must not expect too much from justice, for justice is merely one aspect of a many faceted approach needed to secure enduring peace in a transitional society'[118] – and for providing critical insight into the strengths and weaknesses of criminal trials in post-conflict societies in Africa and elsewhere.

118 Richard J. Goldstone, *Justice as a Tool for Peacemaking: Truth Commissions and International Criminal Tribunals*, 28 NEW YORK UNIVERSITY JOURNAL OF INTERNATIONAL LAW AND POLICY 485, 485-486 (1996).

11 Multinational Corporate Complicity

A Challenge for International Criminal Justice in Africa

Eric Colvin and Jessie Chella

11.1 Introduction

There have been debates about the legitimacy of the focus by the International Criminal Court on crimes committed in Africa in comparison with other troubled regions of the globe. There have also been debates about whether there may be alternative, perhaps more appropriate, mechanisms for advancing peace, order and good governance in Africa. There is, however, another issue relating to the relationship between the Court and Africa which has attracted less attention: the Court's exclusive focus on local, African perpetrators of international crimes to the neglect of external parties who may arguably share responsibility for these crimes: in particular, multinational corporations. The Rome Statute of the International Criminal Court (ICC) does not at present permit the prosecution of corporations. Arguments are presented in this paper for amendments to the Statute in order to introduce corporate liability and to bring the characteristic modes of corporate involvement in international crimes within the scheme for accomplice liability.

The first references to the ICC concerned allegations of crimes committed in Africa by African perpetrators. All the resulting arrest warrants issued by the Court have been directed at these alleged local, African perpetrators.[1] Yet, attention to international crimes committed on African soil does not require a preoccupation with crimes committed only by Africans. Even if the perpetrators of crimes are Africans, external parties may be linked as accomplices. Such links are most likely to occur in cases where international crimes are

1 See Uganda: *The Prosecutor v. Joseph Kony, Vincent Otti, Okot Odhiambo and Dominic Ongwen*, Case No. ICC-02/04-01/05; Congo: *The Prosecutor v. Thomas Lubanga Dyilo*, Case No. ICC-01/04-01/06; *The Prosecutor v. Bosco Ntaganda*, Case No. ICC-01/04-02/06; *The Prosecutor v. Germain Katanga and Mathieu Ngudjolo Chui*, Case No. ICC-01/04-01/07; Sudan: *The Prosecutor v. Ahmad Muhammad Harun ("Ahmad Harun") and Ali Muhammad Ali Abd-Al-Rahman ("Ali Kushayb")*, Case No. ICC-02/05-01/07; *The Prosecutor v. Omar Hassan Ahmad Al Bashir*, Case No. ICC-02/05-01/09; *The Prosecutor v. Bahr Idriss Abu Garda*, Case No. ICC-02/05-02/09; Central African Republic: *The Prosecutor v. Jean-Pierre Bemba Gombo*, Case No. ICC-01/05-01/08.

connected with business operations. In pursuit of profit, businesses can become involved in international crimes in such ways as by providing access to infrastructure used for the commission of the crimes, or by supplying instruments or materials used in their commission, or by providing financial support for the perpetrators.

Moreover, as businesses increasingly operate on an international scale, the result may be increased instances of complicity of multinational businesses operating from one country in crimes committed in another country.[2] For example, it has been widely alleged that some multinational businesses seeking to obtain minerals from eastern parts of the Democratic Republic of the Congo have been complicit in crimes against humanity and war crimes committed by armed forces in the region.[3]

Allegations of the complicity of multinational businesses in international crimes have increased significantly in the last sixty years.[4] Africa has figured prominently in such allegations. Much of the African continent boasts of vast deposits of natural resources, which include: oil, diamonds, iron ores, coffee, timber and gold.[5] The presence of these natural resources has led to a significant number of African countries becoming the "new frontier for the extractives sector".[6] Extractive corporations operate in conflict zones characterized by unstable local environments where the rule of law is weak or non-existent or the governments face difficulty enforcing internationally recognized human rights.[7] The struggle to control natural resources has been one of the factors fuelling the conflicts in destabilized African countries. Granted, natural resources are not the only source of conflict in the African continent; however, the exploitation of these resources has contributed significantly to the on-going conflicts in the region.[8]

There is a major legal barrier to the prosecution of multinational businesses for involvement in international crimes. Business operations are now mainly conducted through the vehicle of corporations. Corporate criminal liability is established in many domestic jurisdictions. Moreover, recognition of the central role of corporations in modern commerce,

---

2 It has been claimed: "Most cases in which allegations and charges of corporate complicity have arisen concern multinational corporations." See Wim Huisman & Elies van Sliedregt, *Rogue Traders: Dutch Businessmen, International Crimes and Corporate Complicity,* 8 JOURNAL OF INTERNATIONAL CRIMINAL JUSTICE 803, 815 (2010).

3 See Final Report of the Panel of Experts on the Illegal Exploitation of Natural Resources and Other Forms of Wealth of the Democratic Republic of the Congo, U.N. Doc. S/2002/1146 (October 16, 2002).

4 International Commission of Jurists, *Corporate Complicity in International Crimes* (2008) Volume 1, 1.

5 See generally, Jonathan M. Winer & Trifin J. Roule, *Follow the Money: The Finance of Illicit Resource Extraction, in* NATURAL RESOURCES AND VIOLENT CONFLICT: OPTIONS AND ACTIONS (WORLD BANK, IAN BANNON & PAUL COLLIER eds., 2003)

6 Alyson Warhurst, *Insight: Human Rights are a Business Issue*, BUSINESSWEEK, December 14, 2007.

7 See Maplecroft, Media Release, *Human Rights Risk Extreme Throughout Much of Asia and Africa*, 3 <www.maplecroft.net/HR09_Report_Press_release.pdf> (last accessed October 24, 2009).

8 WORLD BANK, (BANNON & COLLIER eds., 2003) *supra* note 5.

and of the potential for criminal conduct to occur in the course of corporate operations, has led in recent years to some radical changes to the nature and scope of corporate criminal liability. Yet, international criminal law does not currently recognize corporate criminal liability in any form. Thus, Article 25(1) of the Rome Statute of the ICC provides: "The Court shall have jurisdiction over natural persons pursuant to this Statute." Corporate personnel can be prosecuted before the Court in their personal capacity. However, corporations themselves are immune from liability.

This chapter will examine: (1) the need to introduce corporate liability under the Rome Statute of the ICC for the purposes of international criminal law generally and to address issues arising in the specific context of international crimes committed in Africa; (2) the forms of corporate liability which may be appropriate, particularly with respect to the operations of multinational corporations; and (3) the amendments which may be made to the law of complicity for international crimes in order to accommodate the characteristic forms of corporate involvement. Of course, complicity must be of sufficient gravity to justify action by the Court.[9] The chapter will not, however, examine the issues of prosecutorial policy which would arise in relation to the use of the legal framework which we propose.

11.2 THE CASE FOR CORPORATE COMPLICITY LIABILITY

11.2.1 The Businesses and the Crimes

It is conceivable that multinational businesses might perpetrate international crimes as principals. Complicit perpetration is, however, more likely than actual perpetration. There are several ways in which this might occur.[10] The simplest cases would involve the provision of infrastructure, instruments or materials used in the commission of crimes. A business might even provide the instruments or materials used to actually perpetrate the crimes. For example, a Dutch businessman who sold poison gases to Saddam Hussein's Regime in Iraq was convicted by a Dutch court of complicity in war crimes arising from the subsequent use of the gases.[11] Alternatively, a multinational business might supply

9 See Art. 17(1)(d) of the ICC Rome Statute.

10 See generally, Wolfgang Kaleck & Miriam Saage-Maaß, *Corporate Accountability for Human Rights Violations Amounting to International Crimes*, 8 JOURNAL OF INTERNATIONAL CRIMINAL JUSTICE 699, 700-709 (2010); Hans Vest, *Business Leaders and Modes of Individual Criminal Responsibility under International Law*, 8 JOURNAL OF INTERNATIONAL CRIMINAL JUSTICE 851, 852-855 (2010).

11 See generally, Harmen G. van der Wilt, *Genocide, Complicity in Genocide and International v. Domestic Jurisdiction: Reflections on the van Anraat Case*, 4 JOURNAL OF INTERNATIONAL CRIMINAL JUSTICE 239 (2006); Harmen G. van der Wilt, *Genocide v. War Crimes in the Van Anraat Appeal*, 6 JOURNAL OF INTERNATIONAL CRIMINAL JUSTICE 557 (2008); Huisman & van Sliedregt, *supra* note 2, at 807-810.

logistic support for the commission of crimes, such as transport for the perpetrators. This was the kind of complaint made against an Australian mining company operating in the DRC, which allegedly allowed its vehicles to be borrowed for transporting troops to the place where they committed crimes.[12]

The acts alleged to make a business complicit might even appear neutral in effect, having legitimate as well as criminal consequences.[13] For example, complaints have been made about the conduct of a Canadian corporation engaged in natural resources extraction in the Sudan on the ground that its development of infrastructure such as roads and airports facilitated the commission of crimes against the local population by the Government of the Sudan.[14]

Where an appropriate *mens rea* such as intent or knowledge can be established, the provision of infrastructure, instruments or materials which facilitate the commission of crimes falls within conventional notions of complicity by aiding. More complex issues arise if multinational businesses engaged in manufacturing happen to purchase materials when international crimes have been committed in their extraction, as has been alleged with respect to certain mining operations in the DRC.[15] Such cases might be viewed simply as instances of beneficial complicity, in which advantage is taken of crimes but there has been no active involvement in their commission. On this view, traditional principles of criminal responsibility would exclude any liability for the crimes.[16] However, it might be argued that purchasers sustain on-going operations and thereby contribute to the commission of future crimes.[17] On this view, there could be complicity by aiding when the future crimes are committed, assuming at least some measure of foresight and therefore culpability with respect to what will happen.

---

12 See Global Witness Report, *Rights and Accountability in Development, Action against Impunity for Human Rights, and African Association for the Defence of Human Rights, "Kilwa Trial: A Denial of Justice" A Chronology, October 2004-July 2007* (July 17, 2007).

13 See the discussion in Christoph Burchard, *Ancillary and Neutral Business Contributions to "Corporate-Political Core Crime" Initial Enquiries Concerning the Rome Statute*, 8 JOURNAL INTERNATIONAL CRIMINAL JUSTICE 919 (2010).

14 See the action brought under the U.S. Alien Tort Claims Act: *Presbyterian Church of Sudan v. Talisman Energy, Inc.*, (Docket No. 07-0016-cv) U.S.C.A. 2nd Circuit, 2 October 2009. The Court rejected the claim on the ground that the appropriate mens rea could not be established. See also the discussion in Norman Farrell, *Attributing Criminal Liability to Corporate Actors; Some Lessons from the International Tribunals*, 8 JOURNAL INTERNATIONAL CRIMINAL JUSTICE 873, 884-885 (2010).

15 See Final Report of the Panel of Experts on the Illegal Exploitation of Natural Resources, *supra* note 3.

16 See discussion on limits of holding corporations liable in John Ruggie, *UN Special Representative of the Secretary-General on the Issue of Human Rights in Transnational Corporations and other Business Enterprises, Promotion and Protection of all Human Rights, Civil, Political, Economic, Social and Cultural Rights, including the Right to Development 'Clarifying the Concepts of "Sphere of Influence" and "Complicity"*, U.N. DoC., A/HRC/8/16 (May 15, 2008) (41).

17 See Burchard, *supra* note 11 at 932.

11.2.2 The Corporate Form

Modern businesses usually work through the corporate form. An alternative to prosecuting corporate personnel could be to prosecute the corporate entity. At the level of domestic criminal law, there has been increasing recognition of the worth of exposing corporate entities to criminal liability. Corporate criminal liability is well-established in the common-law jurisdictions. Moreover, although it was resisted by Western European legal systems for most of the twentieth century, it has become widely accepted in these systems in recent years.[18]

There are several rationales for corporate criminal liability.[19] Most obviously, it can allow sanctions against corporate assets that might otherwise be protected. This can deprive shareholders of profit and provide an incentive to improve future behavior. It can also generate funds for compensation for the victims of crime. There are other, less tangible, benefits which apply particularly to large corporate entities such as many of those involved in multinational business. In large corporate entities, individuals come and go and are easily replaced. The genesis of complicity in crime may lie more in the policies and culture of the corporation than in the individual characteristics of the personnel involved.[20] Imposing liability on individuals may therefore not appropriately express the condemnatory message that is desired. Moreover, it may even be impossible to identify and pursue the particular individuals who are responsible. This is a particular problem with multinational corporations, where the effective decision-makers may be far from the scene of the crimes, shielded by distance and by barriers of organizational complexity and cultural impenetrability.

Depending on the domestic law, a corporation might be prosecuted for complicity in an international crime in the jurisdiction where the crime occurred, the jurisdiction where it is incorporated or anywhere else asserting universal jurisdiction. There are several

18 Countries with legislative regimes for corporate criminal liability now include the Netherlands, Belgium, France, Portugal, Denmark, Norway, Finland, and Switzerland. Countries still lacking such regimes include Germany, Italy and Spain. *See* Sara Sun Beale & Adam G. Safwat *What Developments in Western Europe Tell Us About American Critiques of Corporate Criminal Liability*, 8 Buffalo Criminal Law Review 89, 105-106 (2004). Also, membership to the Organization for Economic Co-operation and Development (OECD) encourages member States to implement the necessary measures to criminalize corporate complicity in crimes.

19 On the various rationales for corporate liability in international criminal law, *see* Mordechai Kremnitzer *A Possible Case for Imposing Criminal Liability on Corporations in International Criminal Law*, 8 Journal of International Criminal Justice 909 (2010).

20 It has been argued that the dominant motive for corporate complicity in international crimes is loss minimization, with corporations operating in conflict-ridden regions seeking to recover their capital investment: Huisman & van Sliedregt, *supra* note 2 at 818.

countries which recognize corporate liability and also assert universal jurisdiction over international crimes.[21] In addition, a number of civil actions against corporations have been brought in the United States on the basis of universal jurisdiction under the Alien Tort Statute.[22]

A corporation cannot, however, be prosecuted for complicity in an international crime before an international tribunal. The ICC Rome Statute currently does not allow for corporate liability. Neither does the general body of international criminal law recognize any form of corporate criminal liability. The ICC as well as the existing *ad hoc* international institutions dealing with international crimes only exercise jurisdiction over natural persons.[23]

There is some adverse history to the idea of corporate liability in the international sphere. Article 23(5) and (6) of the Draft Statute for the Establishment of an International Criminal Court contained provisions dealing with the liability of legal persons.[24] However, these draft provisions were rejected by delegates at the Rome Conference deliberations.[25] Although the French Delegation presented a revized version of the controversial provision,[26] the amended proposals were also rejected. Some delegates strongly opposed the notion of corporate liability arguing that the doctrine was not even recognized in most of the existing legal systems at the time.[27]

---

21 Australia is an example. See Criminal Code (Cth) ss 12.1, 15.4, 268.117.

22 See Doug Cassel, *Corporate Aiding and Abetting of Human Rights Violations: Confusion in the Courts*, 6 Northwest University Journal of International Human Rights 304, 305-306 (2008); Jonathan Drimmer *Human Rights and the Extractive Industries: Litigation and Compliance Trends*, 3(2) Journal of World Energy Law and Business 121 (2010).

23 Art. 25(1) of the ICC Rome Statute provides only for jurisdiction over natural persons. See also, Art. 7 of the Statute of the International Criminal Tribunal for the Former Yugoslavia (as amended May 17, 2002), May 25, 1993; Art. 6 of the Statute of the International Criminal Tribunal for Rwanda; Art. 29new of the Law on the Establishment of the Extraordinary Chambers in the Courts of Cambodia for the Prosecution of Crimes Committed During the Period of Democratic Kampuchea; Art. 29 of the UN/Cambodia Agreement Law on the Establishment of the Extraordinary Chambers in the Courts of Cambodia for the Prosecution of Crimes Committed During the Period of Democratic Kampuchea; Art. 6 of the Sierra Leone Special Court Statute; Art. 15 of the Iraqi High Tribunal Statute.

24 See UN Plenipotentiaries on the Establishment of the International Criminal Court, Report of the Preparatory Committee on the Establishment of an International Criminal Court, "Draft Statute for the International Criminal Court", Rome, Italy, June 15-July 17, 1998 U.N. Doc. A/Conf.183/2/Add.1. (April 14, 1998).

25 Kai Ambos *Article 25: Individual Criminal Responsibility, in* Commentary on the Rome Statute of the International Criminal Court – Observers' Notes, Article By Article 746 (Otto Triffterer ed., 2d ed. 2008).

26 United Nations Working Group on General Principles of Criminal Law, Diplomatic Conference of Plenipotentiaries on the Establishment of an International Criminal Court, *Working Paper on Article 23, Paragraphs 5 And 6: Draft Statute of an International Criminal Court* (July 3, 1998), UN Doc. A/Conf./183/WGGP/L.5/Rev.2. (Hereafter "Draft Statute of an ICC").

27 Kai Ambos, *supra* note 25 at 743, 746 (Otto Triffterer ed., 2d ed. 2008). To date, there are a number of domestic jurisdictions that do not recognize criminal liability for corporate entities. These include: Brazil, Bulgaria, Luxembourg and the Slovak Republic.

Nevertheless, the trend among domestic jurisdictions towards recognizing corporate criminal liability is well established and has accentuated in the years since the text of the ICC Rome Statute was negotiated.[28] Corporate liability would be a welcome addition to the sphere of international criminal law, particularly with respect to multinational corporations which have the means to contribute to compensation for victims and the personnel of which it would be difficult and inadequate to pursue. Leaving corporate liability to domestic jurisdictions risks letting it fall through the net of liability, given the variability of domestic law and the vagaries of domestic law enforcement.

The introduction of corporate criminal liability in the international sphere would require the amendment of the ICC Rome Statute.[29] In designing any amendments, the questions to be addressed are: on what basis should corporations be held liable in international criminal law and, in particular, on what basis should they be held liable for complicity?

11.3 MODELS OF CORPORATE LIABILITY

There are two competing models of corporate liability found within domestic jurisdictions: derivative liability and non-derivative liability.[30] Under the derivative model, corporate liability must always be located through the liability of a human actor who is part of or an agent of the corporation. An individual first commits the offence; the culpability of the individual is then imputed to the corporation. In contrast, under the non-derivative model, the liability of the corporation is primary and not dependent on the liability of any individual. It is diagnosed through questions about the culpability of the corporation itself rather than imputed from another source. This paper proposes corporate criminal liability

28 See, Beale & Safwat *supra* note 18 at 105-106; Sara Sun Beale, *A Response to Critics of Corporate Criminal Liability*, 46 AMERICAN CRIMINAL LAW REVIEW 1481, 1493-1494 (2009).

29 Art. 123 of the ICC Rome Statute contains enabling provisions that provide a review to consider any amendments to the Rome Statute. The first of such reviews took place May 31–June 11, 2010. Art. 121 of the Rome Statute details the procedure to be followed by State Parties wishing to amend the Rome Statute at any time in the future after the first review conference has been held.

30 See generally, Eric Colvin, *Corporate Personality and Criminal Liability*, 6:1 CRIMINAL LAW FORUM 1(1995); Celia Wells, *Corporate Criminal Responsibility*, *in* RESEARCH HANDBOOK ON CORPORATE LEGAL RESPONSIBILITY 147-152 (Stephen Tully ed., 2005) and James Gobert & Maurice Punch, RETHINKING CORPORATE CRIME 146-153 (2003). For example, derivative liability is adopted in domestic jurisdictions such as the USA, South Africa and the United Kingdom. Non-derivative liability is found in Australia and Switzerland. These models are not mutually exclusive. Multiple bases for corporate liability have been implemented in several domestic jurisdictions. For example, Part 2.5, Division 12 of the Australian Criminal Code (Cth) contains provisions dealing with corporate liability which incorporate both derivative liability and non-derivative liability. Note that the term 'non-derivative liability' is used here to avoid confusion with the term "organisational liability". Non-derivative liability is generally described by academics as "organisational liability". This paper uses the term 'non-derivative liability' to distinguish it from derivative liability.

on the basis of non-derivative liability as the better model to transplant internationally and adopt within the ICC Rome Statute.

Derivative liability is the traditional model in most domestic jurisdictions. Legal theorists who support the derivative liability model tend to favor the nominalist view of legal personality. According to the nominalist view of legal personality, corporations are fictitious, artificial persons and essentially nothing more than collections of individuals.[31] There are two main varieties of derivative liability: vicarious liability and identification liability.[32] They differ in the range of persons whose individual liability can be imputed to the corporation.

When vicarious liability is adopted, the corporation can become liable for the conduct of any individuals if their actions fall within the ambit of their corporate employment or authority. Vicarious liability for corporations has been developed as a matter of common law by federal courts in the United States.[33] It has also been adopted by statute in South Africa.[34]

Under identification liability, a narrower range of actors can make the corporation liable. There are different versions of identification liability, encompassing narrower or broader ranges of persons with whom the corporation is identified. However, corporate liability is usually established only through the liability of specific individuals that act as the "directing minds" of the corporation.[35] Hence, the responsibility for corporate conduct and fault lies with the board of directors, the managing director, or other person to whom supreme power has been delegated. These persons are said to be acting *as* the company.[36] Literally, "what the senior executive does and thinks in the performance of his (or her) duties is identified with, and becomes the acts and thoughts of, the company itself."[37] Identification liability has been the traditional model for corporate liability in Australia, Canada and England, although there have been some changes in recent years.[38] It was also adopted in the American Model Penal Code.[39]

31 See Colvin, *supra* note 30 at 1-4; Jonathan Clough & Carmel Mulhern, THE PROSECUTION OF CORPORATIONS 4-5 (2002).

32 For discussions of derivative liability models, see Colvin *supra* note 30; Wells, *supra* note 30 at 147-152; Clough & Mulhern, *supra* note 31 at 146-153.

33 See for example, *United States v. Hilton Hotels Corp.*, 467 F.2d 1000 (9th Cir. 1972); *United States v. Bank of New England*, 821 F.2d 844 (1st Cir. 1987).

34 Criminal Procedure Act, No. 51 of 1977, Art. 332 (S. Afr.).

35 *Tesco Supermarkets Ltd v. Nattrass* [1972] AC 153 at 171 (HL).

36 Matthew Goode, *Corporate Criminal Liability*, 3, <www.aic.gov.au/publications/proceedings/26/goode.pdf> (last accessed December 7, 2008), discussing *Tesco Supermarkets Ltd v. Nattrass* [1972] AC 153, HL.

37 RUSSELL HEATON, CRIMINAL LAW 466 (2d ed., 2006). Gender neutral terms added.

38 See for example, *Tesco Supermarkets Ltd v. Nattrass* [1972] AC 153 (HL); *Canadian Dredge & Dock Co. v. The Queen* [1985] 1 S.C.R. 662 (Can.).

39 American Law Institute, *Model Penal Code*, Art. 2.07.

Several domestic jurisdictions have now moved towards the model of non-derivative liability for at least offences of negligence.[40] Non-derivative liability makes the corporate entity itself directly liable.[41] Legal theorists who support this model tend to favor the realist view of legal personality. According to the realist view of legal personality, corporate entities have an existence that is, to some extent, independent of the existences of their individual members. Corporations are more than the sum of their individual parts. They comprise institutionalized relationships embodying distinctive cultures which shape the outlook and channel the conduct of their members. They can therefore possess a separate legal personality which makes them appropriate subjects for criminal liability in their own right.[42] Hence, the culpability of the corporation itself rather than the culpability of its individuals is of primary concern.[43] The questions to be asked are what the corporation did or did not do, as an organization; what it knew or ought to have known about its conduct; and what it did or ought to have done to prevent crimes occurring. Non-derivative liability is established on the basis of "corporate policies, procedures, practices and attitudes; deficient chains of command and oversight; and corporate 'cultures' that tolerate or encourage criminal offences."[44]

When the question of corporate liability was before the Rome Conference on the establishment of an International Criminal Court, it was derivative liability that was contemplated. The amended proposals which were finally rejected were based on the identification version of derivative liability, with liability imputed from the liability of an individual "in a position of control":

5. Without prejudice to any individual criminal responsibility of natural persons under this Statute, the Court may also have jurisdiction over a juridical person for a crime under this Statute.

   Charges may be filed by the Prosecutor against a juridical person, and the Court may render a judgment over a juridical person for the crime charged, if:

   (a) The charges filed by the Prosecutor against the natural person and the juridical person allege the matters referred to in subparagraphs (b) and (c); and

40 See Beale & Safwat, *supra* note 18 at 136, 138; Beale, *supra* note 28 at 1496.

41 GOBERT & MAURICE, *supra* note 30 at 97.

42 CLOUGH & MULHERN, *supra* note 31 at 64-65.

43 The Australian Criminal Code (Cth) is an example of a domestic jurisdiction that adopts a non-derivative liability approach when dealing with corporate criminal liability.

44 Allens Arthur Robinson, *Corporate Culture as a Basis for the Criminal Liability of Corporations,* paper prepared for the UN Special Rapporteur to the Secretary General (February 2008) 6 <http://198.170.85.29/Allens-Arthur-Robinson-Corporate-Culture-paper-for-Ruggie-Feb-2008.pdf> (last accessed July 29, 2008); see also, Colvin, *supra* note 30; Celia Wells *International Trade in Models of Corporate Liability* (2002), The Centre for Business Relationships, Accountability, Sustainability and Society <www.brass.cf.ac.uk/uploads/cacorptoolkitcw0203.pdf> (last accessed December 7, 2008). Note that Celia Wells refers to this model as the "Holistic" Theory Model.

(b) The natural person charged was in a position of control within the juridical person under the national law of the State where the juridical person was registered at the time the crime was committed; and

(c) The crime was committed by the natural person acting on behalf of and with the explicit consent of that juridical person and in the course of its activities; and

(d) The natural person has been convicted of the crime charged . . .[45]

This proposal would provide the narrowest conceivable version of corporate liability and would also be practically very difficult to enforce. Its adoption could present near insuperable problems for enforcement against multinational corporations with wide physical separation of the head office from diffuse global operations. These difficulties might be alleviated by adopting a broader version of identification liability or by switching to the vicarious liability version of derivative liability. A wider range of individuals could then make the corporation liable. There would, however, still be the potentially difficult task of isolating the activities and culpability of specific individuals within what can be large and complex organizations. The difficulty can be particularly great when the organization is multinational in character. Moreover, any form of derivative liability faces the objections that it is artificial and arbitrary. There is no necessary relationship to culpability. A corporation's liability turns simply on the conduct of corporate personnel rather than on the presence of some form of corporate fault for this conduct.

Non-derivative liability offers a more attractive alternative for corporate liability generally and, in particular, for responding to the problem of multinational corporate complicity in international crimes. The Australian Commonwealth Criminal Code provides an example of what non-derivative liability can comprise which is particularly interesting because, unlike most schemes for non-derivative liability, it covers not only offences of negligence but also offences requiring subjective fault.[46]

For offences of negligence, a corporation can be held liable under the Australian Commonwealth Code even when no individual has the required fault element. The negligence of the corporation can be established by viewing its conduct "as a whole" – "that is, by aggregating the conduct of any number of its employees, agents or officers".[47] This

45 See Draft Statute of an ICC, *supra* note 26, Art. 23, paras. 5-6.

46 See Criminal Code (Cth). In Australia, criminal law is primarily a matter of jurisdiction for the states and territories rather than the Commonwealth. However, despite the lack of an express power to enact criminal law, the Commonwealth does possess a supplementary or incidental power to create criminal offences in areas over which it has specific constitutional jurisdiction, such as external affairs, international trade and commerce, and taxation. It can use penal sanctions in order to enforce its regulatory schemes in these areas.

47 Criminal Code (Cth) s. 12.4(2).

is particularly relevant where criminal negligence is in issue but, although organizational sloppiness has been pervasive, simple negligence is all that can be established against any single individual. For offences where intention, knowledge or recklessness is required, this fault element is attributed to a corporation that "expressly, tacitly or impliedly authorized or permitted the commission of the offence".[48] Authorization or permission can be attributed to a body corporate under various conditions. These include express, tacit or implied authorization or permission by the board of directors or a "high managerial agent", unless the corporation proves that it exercised due diligence to prevent the conduct, or the authorization or permission.[49] More radically, the conditions for authorization or permission also include the existence of a corporate culture that directed, encouraged, tolerated or led to non-compliance with the relevant provision. Authorization or permission is even established by the failure of the body corporate to create a corporate culture of compliance.[50]

The Rome Statute of the ICC would benefit from the introduction of some kind of non-derivative scheme of corporate liability. The provisions on subjective fault would be the critical elements in an ICC scheme, since liability for negligence is generally excluded for international crimes.[51] The advantage of the Australian scheme is that it allows subjective fault for corporations to be proved not only through identification with key personnel but also through criminogenic corporate cultures. For this purpose, "corporate culture" is defined in broad terms that encompass informal conduct and practices as well as stated policies and formal rules: "Corporate culture" is an attitude, policy, rule, course of conduct or practice existing within the body corporate generally or within the area of the body corporate in which the relevant activities take place."[52]

The focus on corporate culture is the key to non-derivative liability. However, the Australian scheme may cast the net of liability too widely for offences requiring forms of subjective fault. Under the Australian scheme, there are two ways in which a corporate culture can be linked to commission of an offence: either through a culture of noncompliance with the law or through the failure of a body corporate to develop a culture of compliance. The Australian scheme does not identify collective meanings for each type of subjective fault. Instead, it abandons the distinctions between types of subjective fault in favor of the uniform standard of a culture of noncompliance or a failure to develop a culture of compliance. Admittedly, a culture of noncompliance must positively favor

---

48 S. 12.3(1).

49 Ss. 12.3(2)(b), 12.3(3).

50 S 12.3(2)(d).

51 Art. 30(1) of the ICC Rome Statute states: "Unless otherwise provided, a person shall be criminally responsible and liable for punishment for a crime within the jurisdiction of the Court only if the material elements are committed with intent and knowledge."

52 Australian Criminal Code (Cth) s. 12.3(6).

the commission of the offence. This might be viewed as a collective form of subjective recklessness. The difficulty, however, is that the same scheme of liability applies for all offences requiring some form of subjective fault, including those offences which require intention or knowledge rather than just recklessness for their commission by individuals. Moreover, the alternative basis for liability, failure to develop a culture of compliance, involves a form of negligence rather than subjective fault. It is a questionable ground on which to hold a corporation liable for an offence involving any form of subjective fault.

An appropriate scheme of non-derivative corporate liability for offences of subjective fault in the ICC Rome Statute should incorporate collective meanings for terms, like "intention" and "knowledge", which are used in the Statute to specify distinctive mental states.[53] First, in order for a corporation to commit an offence "intentionally" in the sense of *purposefully*, it should be necessary that it was corporate *policy* to commit the offence rather than just that the corporate culture favored its commission. There could be a specific corporate directive for the offence to be committed. However, a policy might also be attributed to a corporation when it provides the most reasonable explanation for the corporation's conduct and would therefore be seen as an implied authorization by individual members or agents. Secondly, in order for a corporation to commit an offence "knowingly", it should be necessary not only that the corporate culture favored the commission of the offence but that knowledge of its commission was held somewhere within the corporation. The idea of collective knowledge might be invoked even where the relevant information is divided between corporate personnel.[54] For example, suppose that a multinational corporation purchases minerals the extraction of which involves crimes against humanity by the local suppliers and that the suppliers use the money to acquire guns and other instruments of crime. The corporation should not be held liable for knowingly aiding the crimes simply because its culture encouraged the morally blind pursuit of profit. The corporation should, however, be held liable if it had been warned how the money would be used, even if the warning had not reached the personnel making or authorizing the purchases.

---

53 See Colvin, *supra* note 30 at 38-41.

54 The foregoing suggestions could be expressed in statutory form in this way:

1. (a) Corporate intention to commit an offence may be established by proof that it was the policy of the corporation to commit the offence.
   (b) A policy may be attributed to a corporation where it provides the most reasonable explanation of the conduct of that corporation.
2. (a) Corporate knowledge of the commission of an offence may be established by proof that the relevant knowledge was possessed within the corporation and that the culture of the corporation caused or encouraged the commission of the offence.
   (b) Knowledge may be possessed within a corporation even though the relevant information is divided between corporate personnel.

Other schemes of non-derivative liability for offences of subjective fault might be devised. The crucial point, however, is that distinctions between forms of subjective fault should be respected in any scheme of corporate liability, even if the forms of subjective fault are conceived somewhat differently for corporations than for individuals.

11.4 Models of Complicity

As was discussed earlier, the involvement of corporations in international crimes is characteristically by way of complicity in the actions of others rather than through perpetration. Corporations and their personnel do not actually commit the crimes themselves. Instead, they are involved in such ways as supplying the instruments or materials for the commission of the crimes or providing logistic or financial support to the perpetrators. Modes of participation which are recognized in international criminal law include, *inter alia*: ordering, instigating, inducing, soliciting, inciting, planning, and aiding and abetting.[55] Complicity by aiding and abetting is the form of participation most often alleged against multinational corporations.[56]

Aiding and abetting is defined in the Rome Statute of the ICC. Article 25(3)(c) makes a person criminally responsible for a crime within the jurisdiction of the Court if the person: "For the purpose of facilitating the commission of such a crime, aids, abets or otherwise assists in its commission or its attempted commission, including providing the means for its commission."

This definition is relatively loose with respect to the conduct elements of aiding and abetting. Customary international law emerging from the *ad hoc* tribunals and special courts indicates that aiding and abetting can involve encouraging or providing moral support for the commission of a crime as well as providing practical assistance.[57] In addition, the provision of assistance, encouragement or moral support can be given before, during or after

55 See, Art. 6 of the International Military Tribunal Charter, Art. 2 of the Control Council Law No. 10, Art. 5 of the International Military Tribunal for the Far East Charter, Art. 7 of the ICTY Statute, Art. 6 of the ICTR Statute, Art. 25 of the ICC Rome Statute, Section 14 of Regulation No. 2000/15 for the Panels of Judges with Exclusive Jurisdiction over Serious Criminal Offences Established within the District Courts in East Timor, Art. 29new of the Extraordinary Chambers in the Courts of Cambodia Law on the Establishment of the Extraordinary Chambers in the Courts of Cambodia for the Prosecution of Crimes Committed During the Period of Democratic Kampuchea, Art. 29 of the UN/Cambodia Agreement on the Law on the Establishment of the Extraordinary Chambers in the Courts of Cambodia for the Prosecution of Crimes Committed During the Period of Democratic Kampuchea, Art. 6 of the SCSL Statute and Art.15 of the IHT Statute.

56 International Commission of Jurists, *supra* note 4 at 27.

57 *Prosecutor v. Furundzija* (Judgement) (International Criminal Tribunal for the former Yugoslavia, Trial Chamber, Case No. IT-95-17/1-T, 10 December 1998) [249].

the commission of the crime.[58] Furthermore, the aider and abettor can incur liability for assisting in the planning, preparation or execution stage of the crime.[59] The tribunals have differed from the ICC Statute in requiring that aiding make a "substantial contribution" to the commission of the crime.

The ICC definition of aiding and abetting is more specific with respect to its mental element. To constitute aiding and abetting, Article 25(3)(c) of the Statute requires that the action have been taken "for the *purpose* of facilitating the commission of such a crime". This differs from the *mens rea* adopted for aiding and abetting by the international tribunals, which is *knowledge* that the acts performed would assist the commission of the crime.[60]

The "purpose" approach contained in Article 25(3)(c) of the ICC Rome Statute was chosen by delegates at the Rome Conference deliberations on the Draft Statute for the Establishment of an International Criminal Court.[61] Under Article 23(7)(d) of the Draft Statute, a person would be criminally responsible if the person: [with [intent] [knowledge] to facilitate the commission of such a crime,] aids, abets or otherwise assists in the commission [or attempted commission] of that crime, including providing the means for its commission.

The Preparatory Committee were unable to agree upon Article 23(7)(d) of the Draft Statute provisions, as evidenced by the words which appear in brackets.[62] The matter was then resolved at the Rome Conference by introducing the "purpose test".[63] This was adopted from the provision on aiding in the Model Penal Code of the American Law Institute.[64] A similar "purpose" test was also used in the definition of aiding in a draft code prepared for England in the late 1870s, known as the 'Stephen Code' after its principal drafter, Sir James Stephen. The Stephen Code was never enacted in England but became the basis for the Canadian Criminal Code 1892 and the New Zealand Crimes Act 1893. "Purpose" is still a required element of aiding in these jurisdictions.[65]

---

58 *Prosecutor v. Milutinović* (Judgment) International Criminal Tribunal for the former Yugoslavia, Trial Chamber, ICTY Case No. IT-05-87-T, volume 1 of 4, 26 February 2009 91.

59 *Prosecutor v. Blaškić*, (Judgment) International Criminal Tribunal for the former Yugoslavia, Appeal Chamber, ICTY Case No. IT-95-14-A, 29 July 2004 48.

60 *Prosecutor v. Tadić* (Judgment) International Criminal Tribunal for the former Yugoslavia, Appeal Chamber, ICTY Case No. IT-94-1-A, July 15, 1999 229; *Prosecutor v. Orić* (Judgment) International Criminal Tribunal for the former Yugoslavia, Appeal Chamber, ICTY Case No. IT-03-68-A, July 3, 2008 43.

61 Draft Statute of ICC, *supra* note 26.

62 Cassel, *supra* note 22 at 310.

63 *Id.* at 310-311. The decision to adopt the purpose test was reached by the Working Group on General Principles of Criminal Law.

64 American Law Institute, *Model Penal Code*, Art. 2.06(3)(a). See, Ambos *supra* note 25 at 757. Ambos was an Observer at the Rome Conference deliberations.

65 See now, Canadian Criminal Code R.S.C. 1985 c. C-46, s 21(1)(1)(b); New Zealand Crimes Act (1961) (NZ), s. 66(1)(b).

The differences between the "knowledge" and "purpose" formulations of the *mens rea* for aiding and abetting are important. The former focuses on what is foreseen as to the consequences of the action while the latter focuses on the reasons why the action is taken. Under a "knowledge" test, an aider or abettor must act knowing what the consequences will be. Action taken in the hope but not the assurance of aiding or encouraging an offence may therefore not qualify More importantly for present purposes, however, a "purpose" test may exclude persons who happen to aid when acting for commercial reasons. The difficulty with what might be called "commercial aiders" is that, even though they may know full well that their actions will assist the commission of crimes, they may do so not for the purpose of facilitating their commission but rather for the purpose of making profit. Multinational corporations will characteristically fall into this category. The same problem would arise with an "intent" test if intent is given a narrow meaning which makes it equivalent with purpose, as it often is in international criminal law.

The issue is how a requirement for "purpose" is to be interpreted in the law of aiding and abetting. The Model Penal Code states that a person acts "purposefully" with respect to the nature or consequences of conduct when "it is his *conscious object* to engage in conduct of that nature or to cause such a result".[66] This fits with ordinary language, where the concept of purpose usually refers to an actor's *reasons* for doing what was done:

> My purpose in doing something is my reason for it, in the sense of what I am trying to do or what I want to accomplish by doing it. Hence, to specify a purpose is to give an explanation, whereas to specify an intention is not necessarily to do so. We do things *with* an intention, but *for* a purpose, since the intention may only accompany the action, whereas the purpose must be a reason for it. We do not naturally speak of "the reason or intention" and "the point or intention" in the way that we do speak of "the reason or purpose" and "the point or purpose" of an action.[67]

On this interpretation, an actor's purpose was to accomplish something if the prospect of its occurrence played a causal role in the decision to act.[68] The connection may have been of a "but for" kind, in which event the prospect would have been the sole purpose. Alternatively, there may have been several purposes, one of which can be isolated and used to ground criminal liability.

66 AMERICAN LAW INSTITUTE, MODEL PENAL CODE, Art. 2.02(2)(a)(i).
67 Alan R. White, *Intention, Purpose, Foresight and Desire*, 92 LAW QUARTERLY REVIEW 569, 574 (1976).
68 See ERIC COLVIN & SANJEEV S. ANAND PRINCIPLES OF CRIMINAL LAW 181 (3d ed., 2007).

Treating "purpose" as equivalent to "object" or "reason" is how Article 25(3)(c) of the ICC Statute has been interpreted by some commentators.[69] It has been argued that most commercial aiders or abettors are excluded. Thus, if a corporation or its personnel were to successfully raise the possibility that the reason they provided practical assistance for the commission of a crime was simply in order to make a profit, they would not be liable.[70]

This restrictive interpretation is not, however, accepted by everyone. There are two main ways in which it has been attacked.[71] One way challenges the application of the purpose test in cases of complex motivation. The other way challenges the proposition that the term "purpose" has a distinctive meaning which excludes mere knowledge of an outcome. Both challenges stem from a policy-based rejection of the idea that the commercial aider should be exempt from liability for the known consequences of aiding. In our view, both challenges are unsuccessful. We believe that exposing most commercial aiders to liability under the ICC Rome Statute would require the removal of the "purpose' provision in Article s 25(3)(c).

Some writers have sought to argue that at least some commercial aiders can fall within the ambit of ICC liability even if the "purpose" requirement is interpreted to mean that the person must act in order to aid.[72] The argument concerns the application of the "purpose" test in cases of complex motivation. Consider the example of a businessman who sold Zyklon B gas which was used in the gas chambers for the mass killings of Jews by the Nazis. Doug Cassel suggests that one of the purposes would have been to encourage continued mass killings of Jews: "Only so could they continue selling large quantities of gas to the Nazis for profit".[73] In Cassel's view, the killings constituted a secondary purpose of the sales. In other words, the gas was supplied for the secondary purpose of killing because the primary purpose of making continued profits was dependent on the killings occurring.

It is true that, if it is to be concluded that an actor's purpose in doing something did not include an outcome which was foreseen, then the actor must have been genuinely opposed or indifferent to it. Purpose is not negatived where an actor chose to bring about an outcome as a means of attaining some further objective. However, there are two major limitations to the application of this approach to commercial transactions.

69 See for example, Farrell, *supra* note 14 at 882-885; Burchard, *supra* note 13 at 939-941.

70 ROBERT CRYER ET AL, AN INTRODUCTION TO INTERNATIONAL CRIMINAL LAW AND PROCEDURE 377 (2d ed., 2010).

71 A third way has been proposed in Vest *supra* note 10 at 862. Vest has suggested that the general requirement for "intent and knowledge" under Art. 30(1) of the ICC Statute be used to give an expansive interpretation to the "purpose" requirement in Art. 25(3)(c). Vest rightly concedes, however, that the opening words of Art. 30(1), "Unless otherwise provided . . . 0", present a formidable obstacle to this interpretation.

72 Cassel, *supra note* 22 at 312-313; Vest, *supra* note 10 at 862.

73 *Id.* at 312.

The first is that it can only ground liability for aiding and abetting in on-going relationships in which a commercial supplier has not only the purpose of making profit from a specific transaction but also the purpose of making continued profits from involvement in a series of transactions. There is no liability in profit-driven single transactions because making a profit is not dependent on how the items supplied are used. The profit is made if even the items are thrown away or destroyed. The second limitation is that the relationship must be one in which crimes will necessarily be committed. This may fit the supply of items which could be used only for the purpose of committing crimes, such as the Zyklon B gas supplied to the Nazis. However, it does not fit the supply of items for multiple uses, such as vehicles. Moreover, it does not fit manufacturers who purchase materials knowing that crimes have been and will be committed in the course of their extraction. Such manufacturers can sustain on-going extraction operations and thereby contribute to the commission of future crimes. In most instances, however, the manufacturers will be indifferent or even opposed to the commission of the crimes. Their only purpose in making the purchases is to achieve a profit through their own subsequent dealings with the materials.

The Supreme Court of Canada has taken a more radical approach to the interpretation of "purpose" as the *mens rea* requirement for aiding under the Canadian Criminal Code.[74] In *Hibbert*,[75] the Court considered at length the meaning of the term "purpose" and arrived at the conclusion that purpose is synonymous with "intention" in the broad sense of this term which includes knowledge that an outcome will occur as well as purpose to make it occur.[76] This interpretation would bring the commercial aider within the ambit of liability regardless of why the aid was given, as long as its consequences were known.

The Supreme Court of Canada diagnosed two distinct meanings for the term "purpose". Speaking for the Court, Lamer C.J. said:

> It is impossible to ascribe a single fixed meaning to the term "purpose". In ordinary usage, the word is employed in two distinct senses. One can speak of an actor doing something "on purpose" (as opposed to by accident) thereby equating purpose with "immediate intention". The term is also used, however, to indicate the ultimate ends an actor seeks to achieve, which imports the idea of "desire" into the definition.[77]

74 R.S.C. 1985, c. C-46, s. 21(1)(b).
75 *R v. Hibbert* [1995] 2 S.C.R. 973, 40 C.R. (4th) 141.
76 See, for example, *R v. Chartrand* (1994) 31 C.R. (4th) 1, 21 (SCC); *R v. Woollin* [1999] A.C. 82 (HL); *Peters v. The Queen* (1998) 192 CLR 493, [68].
77 *R v. Hibbert* [1995] 2 S.C.R. 973, 40 C.R. (4th) 141, [27].

In the former meaning, "purpose" is synonymous with "intention", in the broad sense of this term which includes knowledge that an outcome will occur.[78] In the latter meaning, reference is made to "desire" but the basic idea appears to be the equation of purpose with reasons for acting. In most instances, a purpose to achieve some outcome will be accompanied by a desire for it. Nevertheless, it may be possible to act for some purpose which is distasteful: for example, if the lesser of two evils is chosen. It is therefore preferable to speak of objects or reasons rather than desire.

The Supreme Court took the view that "purpose" could carry either of these meanings in statutory provisions. The specific concern in *Hibbert* itself was the meaning of "purpose" in s. 21(1)(b) of the Canadian Criminal Code, which makes everyone a party to an offence who "does or omits to do anything for the purpose of aiding any person to commit it". An argument had been made that the appellant had acted out of fear and therefore did not have the *mens rea* for aiding an offence of aggravated assault. The Court rejected this argument on the ground that, in the context of s. 21(1)(b), purpose could be equated with intention. Therefore, *mens rea* could not be negated by evidence of having acted out of fear.[79] It was stressed in *Hibbert* that the decision was restricted to the interpretation of s. 21(1)(b) and that a different interpretation of "purpose" might be appropriate for some other statutory provision.[80]

The decision in *Hibbert* was expressly made in light of policy considerations. The Supreme Court of Canada was concerned that someone who aids an offence for solely commercial reasons should not escape liability. Indeed, the Court commented that it would be absurd if such a person could escape liability.[81]

Similar reasoning on the meaning of "purpose" is apparent in the Report of the International Commission of Jurists Expert Legal Panel on *Corporate Complicity in International Crimes*. It was argued that it makes little practical difference whether the *mens rea* standard for aiding and abetting is expressed as knowledge or purpose:

> [P]ractically speaking, if it is established that a corporate official had knowledge that an act would facilitate the commission of a crime, and yet proceeded to act, then the purpose to facilitate could be found to exist. The fact that the

78 The following analysis of the *Hibbert* decision is taken from Colvin & Anand, *supra* note 68 at 188-189.

79 It was said that, if fear was to be relevant, it could only be in the context of a special excusing defence of duress.

80 *R v. Hibbert* [1995] 2 S.C.R. 973, 40 C.R. (4th) 141, [30].

81 *R v. Hibbert* [1995] 2 S.C.R. 973, 40 C.R. (4th) 141, [32]; endorsing Allan W. Mewett & Morris Manning, Criminal Law 112 (2d ed., 1985).

> official knowingly aided a crime in order make a profit does not diminish his assistance; indeed it could be interpreted as providing a further incentive to facilitate the crime "on purpose".[82]

Such broad interpretations of "purpose" requirements are curious. The two meanings of purpose which have been diagnosed appear to refer to different phrases in which the term is used rather than different meanings for the term itself. When we speak loosely of something having being done "on purpose", we ordinarily mean that the action was accompanied by some purpose; it was deliberate, goal-oriented conduct rather than conduct which occurred by accident. A statement of this kind makes no claim about what the purpose actually was. In contrast, when it is said that action was taken "for the purpose of" something specific such as facilitating the commission of a crime, a claim is made about the nature of the purpose. This is the way that Article 25(3)(c) of the ICC Rome Statute is framed. It does not say that a person who, *acting on purpose*, aids, abets or otherwise assists a crime is criminally responsible. Instead, it makes a person criminally responsible who, "*for the purpose of facilitating the commission of such a crime*, aids, abets or otherwise assists in its commission . . . ." Article 25(3)(c), in its present form, should therefore mean that the specific purpose of, and therefore reasons for, an action must be identified if it is to make the actor liable.

Some writers have suggested that Article 25(3)(d)(ii) of the ICC Rome Statute might present a way of avoiding these difficulties with Article 25(3)(c). Article 25(3)(d) is a complicated provision. It provides for criminal responsibility on the part of a person who:

> (d) In any other way contributes to the commission or attempted commission of such a crime by a group of persons acting with a common purpose. Such contribution shall be intentional and shall either:
>
> (i) Be made with the aim of furthering the criminal activity or criminal purpose of the group, where such activity or purpose involves the commission of a crime within the jurisdiction of the Court; or
>
> (ii) Be made in the knowledge of the intention of the group to commit the crime

Under the first alternative, there is a purposive requirement for the contribution: the *aim* must be to further the criminal activity or purpose of the group. However, the suggestion has been that the second alternative, where "knowledge" of the intention of the group suffices for *mens rea*, would make the commercial aider liable.[83] Hans Vest has therefore

82 International Commission of Jurists, *supra* note 4.

83 Vest, *supra* note 14, at 864-865 (2010); Farrell, *supra* note 14 at 880-881.

described the second alternative as "a rescue clause" in relation to the restricted scope of aiding and abetting.[84]

Yet, it seems doubtful that such a broad interpretation of Article 25(3)(d)(ii) is justified, even if it is assumed that most international crimes are committed by groups acting with a common purpose. First, the opening words of Article 25(3)(d) refer to contributing in "any other way", so that the provision appears to establish a supplementary form of liability rather than a form which could supplant the others specified in Article 25(3). Its concern appears to be with contributions, such as assisting in the organisation of group meetings, which might be considered too remote from the commission of a crime to constitute aiding its commission. Secondly, Article 25(3)(d) specifies two forms of *mens rea* for the contribution. Under (i), there need only be the aim of furthering the criminal activity or criminal purpose of the group: there is no requirement for any state of mind respecting the specific crime committed. Under (ii), however, the requirement is for knowledge of "the intention of the group to commit *the* crime", presumably meaning the specific crime for which the contributor is to be held liable.[85] A commercial aider will rarely have this kind of specific knowledge. A commercial aider who knows that crimes will be committed is unlikely to know when, where and against whom they will be committed.

In the result, it must be concluded that exposing most commercial aiders to liability would require an amendment to the ICC Rome Statute. The objective would be to ensure that there is liability when a person knowingly as well as purposefully aids the commission of a crime. This would bring the *mens rea* for aiding under the ICC Rome Statute in line with that adopted by the *ad hoc* institutions such as the ICTY, ICTR, SCSL and ECCC.[86]

There are two ways in which the objective can be accomplished. One is through broadening the express mental element in Article 25(3)(c) itself. For example, the provision could be amended to read so that it makes a person criminally responsible for a crime within the jurisdiction of the ICC if the person:

> (c) *Knowingly, or* for the purpose of facilitating the commission of such a crime, aids, abets or otherwise assists in its commission or its attempted commission, including providing the means for its commission;

84 Vest, *supra* note 10 at 865.

85 See Burchard, *supra* note 13 at 944.

86 E. van Sliedregt, The Criminal Responsibility of Individuals for Violations of International Humanitarian Law 93 (2003).

The other way in which the objective could be accomplished is through the deletion of any express mental element, so that the provision would simply read: "(c) Aids, abets or otherwise assists in its commission or its attempted commission, including providing the means for its commission;" The mental element would then be read into the provision in the same way as it is read into many other provisions in the ICC Rome Statute, by reference to the general provision on mental elements in Article 30(1): "Unless otherwise provided, a person shall be criminally responsible and liable for punishment for a crime within the jurisdiction of the Court only if the material elements are committed with intent and knowledge."

The expression "intent and knowledge" is generally understood to mean "intent *or* knowledge".[87] Article 25(3)(c) of the ICC Rome Statute presently operates as one of the exceptions contemplated by the opening words of Article 30(1). Bringing Article 25(3)(c) under the umbrella of Article 30(1) would mean the commercial aider would be liable for an international crime if it was known that the action would aid, even if the purpose was simply to make a profit. This would be simpler than amending the express reference to a mental element in Article 25(3)(c) itself.

Concerns are sometimes expressed that, if no more is required for *mens rea* than knowledge that a crime would be aided, the net of liability could capture persons engaged in ordinary business activities who make minor contributions to the commission of offences. In response, it might be contended that any legitimate concerns in this respect can be handled through the exercise of prosecutorial discretion, as they usually are in domestic jurisdictions which adopt the "knowledge" test. Alternatively, the ICC Statute could attempt to address the problem, for example by adopting the "substantial contribution" test formulated by the international tribunals for the *actus reus* of aiding and abetting.[88]

11.5 Conclusions

Corporate criminal liability has expanded in many domestic jurisdictions in response to the greater role of corporations in modern commerce and the expanding potential for criminal conduct to occur in the course of corporate operations. The challenge for international criminal justice is to respond to these developments. Corporate criminal liability needs to be introduced into the Rome Statute of the ICC. Moreover, the scheme of liability

87 See Antonio Cassese, International Criminal Law 176-177 (2003).

88 *Prosecutor v. Tadić* (Judgment) International Criminal Tribunal for the former Yugoslavia, Appeal Chamber, ICTY Case No. IT-94-1-A, 15 July 1999 229; *Prosecutor v. Orić* (Judgment) International Criminal Tribunal for the former Yugoslavia, Appeal Chamber, ICTY Case No. IT-03-68-A, July 3, 2008 43. *See* generally, Vest, *supra* note 10 at 860-861.

for aiding and abetting crimes under the Statute needs to be amended to take better account of the characteristic forms of corporate complicity.

Our particular concern has been with the potential complicity of multinational corporations which purchase and use materials tainted by the commission of international crimes in the course of their extraction. The personnel of such corporations could perhaps be made liable at present for their activities. However, in large corporate entities, individuals come and go and are easily replaced. It may be impossible to identify and pursue the particular individuals who are responsible. Even if it can be done, prosecution of the individuals may not appropriately express the condemnatory message that is desired about the activities of the corporation. We have therefore argued for the introduction of corporate criminal liability in the ICC Rome Statute. Moreover, we have argued for non-derivative liability, based on the role played by corporate cultures and policies in the genesis of criminal conduct. This avoids the need to establish the liability of some specific individual before the corporation can be made liable. It also avoids the artificiality and arbitrariness of simply attributing the liability of an individual to a corporation.

The introduction of corporate liability would by itself be insufficient to address multinational corporate involvement in its perhaps most characteristic form: the purchase of materials extracted in ways involving the commission of international crimes, with the result that on-going operations are sustained and a contribution is thereby made to the commission of future crimes. Even where the purchaser knows how the materials have been and will be produced, a barrier to liability may be presented by the requirement under the ICC Rome Statute that aid be given "for the purpose of facilitating the commission of such a crime". The barrier should be removed, so that the general *mens rea* requirement under the Statute, intent or knowledge, applies.

The challenge of developing corporate criminal liability in the international sphere has particular significance for the legitimacy of international criminal justice in Africa. Africa has been the scene of some horrendous crimes against humanity and war crimes since the ICC Rome Statute came into force. Such crimes are properly within the purview of the ICC. Nevertheless, questions about the legitimacy of the Court's involvement can be expected if action can only be taken against African perpetrators of crimes and complicit multinational corporations are immune from any liability. We have not proposed principles to guide the determination of whether complicity is of sufficient gravity to justify action by the Court. Issues of prosecutorial policy fall outside the scope of this paper. Our aim has simply been to argue for the removal of certain legal impediments to the prosecution of culpable actors.

Part V
Impunity and Justice

Any African International Criminal Justice Alternatives?

12 At the Crossroads

Deconstructing the Challenges of International Justice and the Fight against Impunity in Africa

Godwin Odo

12.1 Introduction

The signing of the Rome Statute on July 17, 1998,[1] establishing the International Criminal Court (ICC) represents a significant achievement in the quest to hold perpetrators of the gravest types of crimes accountable. For the first time, a permanent, independent court was created to try heinous crimes such as genocide, war crimes and crimes against humanity. The establishment of the ICC was spurred on by the perceived successes of the two ad-hoc tribunals: the International Criminal Tribunal for Yugoslavia (ICTY)[2] and the International Criminal Tribunal for Rwanda (ICTR).[3] The historic feat was hailed across the world in recognition of the diplomatic skills employed by negotiators of the treaty to arrive at a consensus on the draft and the Court's potential as a forum for international justice. According to Amnesty International,

> [t]he true significance of the adoption of the Statute may well lie, not in the actual institution itself in the early years, which will face enormous obstacles, but in the revolution in legal and moral attitudes towards worst crimes in the world. No longer will these crimes be simply political events to be addressed by diplomacy at the international level, but crimes which all states have a duty to punish themselves, or if they fail to fulfill this duty, by the international community in accordance with the rule of law.[4]

Before the coming into force of the Rome Statute, Africa had experienced a fair share of wars and conflicts. Conflicts in Liberia, Uganda, Sierra Leone, Burundi, Rwanda, Congo DRC, and Sudan have resulted in grave violations of human rights. Indeed, Africa is a

---

1 Rome Statute of the International Criminal Court, U.N Doc.A/CONF.183/9.
2 Established pursuant to Security Council Resolution 827 of May 25, 1993.
3 Established pursuant to Security Council Resolution 955 of November 8, 1994.
4 Amnesty International Report on the Rome Statute, August 1998, cited in Compilation of Core Documents of the International Criminal Court, V (2003).

victim and perpetrator of injustices. It is also a theatre of home-grown and externally generated and sustained conflicts.[5] Apart from the (ICTR) International Criminal Tribunal for Rwanda, which has been trying perpetrators of the Rwandan genocide and the Special Court for Sierra Leone (SCSL),[6] trying perpetrators of the atrocities committed during the war in that country, perpetrators of these acts have not been made to account for their deeds. It is not surprising therefore that Africa has remained a centre-piece of international justice mechanisms. In other words, Africa continues to be the object of enforcement of international criminal justice, through *ad hoc* tribunals (as we have seen), in foreign national jurisdictions using the principle of universal jurisdiction, and now the ICC.[7] Recent events in many African countries point to the fact that Africa will continue to remain a focus of international criminal justice.[8] However, it is this focus on Africa that has precipitated the greatest challenge to international justice on the continent. This controversy is reflected in the resolutions passed by the African Union at its summit of January 2009 which seemingly amounts to a direct challenge to international justice on the continent.

The objective of this chapter is to undertake a critical examination of the challenges facing the successful application of international justice and accountability mechanisms aimed at combating impunity in Africa. Specifically, the chapter seeks to deconstruct the resolutions passed by the Assembly of Heads of State and Government of the African Union at its 12th Ordinary Summit held in Addis Ababa, Ethiopia in January 2009. Thereafter, an attempt will be made to put forward suggestions aimed at addressing the concerns of critics of the application of international justice mechanisms in Africa and at the same time ensuring that perpetrators of grave crimes do not go unpunished.

Three decisions of the African Union in this regard merit an in-depth consideration. The first is the decision on the abuse of the principle of universal jurisdiction, including the request to the African Union Commission to, in collaboration with the African Commission on Human and Peoples' Rights and the African Court on Human and Peoples' Rights consider the possibility of conferring criminal jurisdiction on the Court; while the

5 Shadrack Gutto, *Africa's Contradictory Roles and Participation in the International Criminal Justice System, in* African Perspectives on International Criminal Justice 17, 19 (Evelyn A. Ankumah & Edward K. Kwakwa eds., 2005)

6 Established pursuant to Security Council Resolution 1315 of August 14, 2000 establishing the Special Court for Sierra Leone.

7 Gutto, *supra* note 5, at 20.

8 The International Criminal Court on June 27, 2011, issued a warrant of arrest for Libyan leader Colonel Muammar Qhaddafi, his son, Seif al-Islam and Chief of Intelligence Abdullah Senussi on charges of crimes against humanity, including murder and persecution, stemming from the first two weeks of the uprising in the North African country.

second relates to the application by the International Criminal Court Prosecutor for the indictment of the President of the Republic of Sudan Omar Hassan El Bashir,. Finally, the resolution on the trial of Hissene Habre of Chad by Senegal will also be examined.

12.2 African Union Resolution on the Abuse of the Principle of Universal Jurisdiction

Judicial powers of a court are primarily exercisable over persons or entities within its territory or sphere of operations or over acts that arise within its territory. This assertion also holds true of international crimes. The problem, however, is that the territorial and the national states do not always exercise their jurisdiction. They may be unable to do so because of lack of resources and capacity, or mere refusal to initiate proceedings because the accused are State officials or prefer 'softer' methods for achieving justice such as truth and reconciliation commissions.[9] However, the evolution of legal thought has extended jurisdictional competence of courts to situations where a court may exercise powers over persons who committed acts outside its territory but who consequently come within its territory.

Over the years, the basis of this practice which is referred to as universal jurisdiction has pitched States whose citizens have been subjected to this practice against those who exercise the powers outlined above. Specifically, countries in Europe have come against African and South American governments in this contestation as to the propriety of trying persons who commit offences anywhere in the universe in national courts other than where the acts were committed. The continued exercise of the power of universal jurisdiction by European courts led to the adoption of a resolution on the abuse of the principle of universal jurisdiction by the African Union at its Summit in Sharm El Sheik in July 2008.

At its Summit in Addis Ababa, the African Union noted the Progress Report of the Commission on the implementation of its earlier decision adopted in Sharm El Sheikh, Egypt in July 2008 on the abuse of the principle of universal jurisdiction and the work of the African Union-European Union (AU-EU) Technical Ad-Hoc Expert Group set up with the mandate to clarify the respective understanding of the principle on the African and European sides. The body reiterated its commitment to fighting impunity in conformity with the provisions of its Constitutive Act,[10] but expressed regret that in spite of its previous Summit decision calling for a moratorium, and whilst the African Union and the

9 Anne Pieter van der Mei, *African Perspectives on International Criminal Law Justice, in* AFRICAN PERSPECTIVES ON INTERNATIONAL CRIMINAL JUSTICE 29 (Evelyn A. Ankumah & Edward K. Kwakwa eds., 2005).

10 Art. 4(h) of the Constitutive Act of the African Union adopted at Lomé, Togo, July 11, 2000.

European Union were already in discussion to find a durable solution to this issue, a warrant of arrest was executed against Mrs. Rose Kabuye, Chief of Protocol to the President of the Republic of Rwanda, thereby creating tension between the AU and the EU. It appealed to all UN Member States, in particular the EU States to suspend the execution of warrants issued by individual European States until all legal and political issues have been exhaustively discussed at the level of the UN Security Council and the UN General Assembly.

The most interesting aspect of this decision was the request that the AU Commission should, in consultation with the African Commission on Human and Peoples' Rights and the African Court on Human and Peoples' Rights examine the implications of the Court being empowered to try international crimes such as genocide, crimes against humanity and war crimes and report to the Assembly in 2010. This aspect of the AU decision will be discussed later in the paper.

12.3 The Principle of Universal Jurisdiction

Universal jurisdiction is premised on the concept that certain crimes are so serious that all of humanity has reason to bring the perpetrators to justice, regardless of the place of the offence or of the nationality of the offenders or the victims.[11] The principle of universal jurisdiction stems from the postulate that some crimes are so serious that they harm the international community as a whole and that, as a consequence, States are entitled, if not required, to bring proceedings against the perpetrators regardless of the location of the crime and the nationality of the perpetrator, or of the victims.[12] Among those serious crimes are genocide, crimes against humanity, torture, some war crimes, apartheid and slavery.[13] This principle derogates from the usual rules of jurisdiction as recognized by international law and according to which there are four main criterions to establish jurisdiction. They are territorial jurisdiction: the state has legal jurisdiction to judge crimes committed in its territory; Active personality jurisdiction: the state has legal jurisdiction to judge crimes committed by its nationals; Passive personality jurisdictions: the state has jurisdiction to judge crimes committed against its nationals; and Protective principle: the state has legal jurisdiction to judge crimes deemed to constitute a threat to some fundamental national interests.[14]

11 Navi Pillay, *The Contribution of National Courts to International Criminal Justice: Some Comments on the Emerging Notion of Universal Jurisdiction, in* African Perspectives on International Criminal Justice 7, 8 (Evelyn A. Ankumah & Edward K. Kwakwa eds., 2005).

12 Track Impunity Always (TRIAL): Universal Jurisdiction, available at: <www.trial-ch.org/en/int-law/universal-jurisdiction.html> (Accessed March 17, 2011).

13 *Id.*

14 *Id.*

International law, both customary and conventional, regulates states' assertion of universal criminal jurisdiction. States by and large accept that customary international law permits the exercise of universal jurisdiction over the international crimes of genocide, crimes against humanity, war crimes and torture, as well as over piracy. Customary international law proscribes the crime of piracy and the exercise of universal jurisdiction over pirates is accepted in customary international law.[15] Article 19 of the 1958 Geneva Convention on the High Seas and Article 105 of the 1982 United Nations Convention on the Law of the Sea codify this customary rule that, "[o]n the high seas, or in any place outside the jurisdiction of any State, every State may seize a pirate ship or aircraft, or a ship or aircraft taken by piracy and under the control of pirates, and arrest the persons and seize the property on board."[16] In addition, numerous treaties oblige states parties to empower their criminal justice systems to exercise universal jurisdiction over the crimes defined in those treaties, although this obligation extends only to the exercise of such jurisdiction when a suspect is subsequently present in the territory of the forum state.[17]

Historically, universal jurisdiction can be traced back to the writings of early scholars of note, such as Grotius, and to the prosecution and punishment of the crime of piracy.[18] It was not until the end of the Second World War that the idea gained prominence and recognition with the adoption of the Four Geneva Conventions of 1949 in which State parties undertake to enact any legislation necessary to provide effective penal sanctions for persons committing or ordering to be committed any of the grave breaches of the Convention ... and to search for persons alleged to have committed, or to have ordered to be committed, such grave breaches and shall bring such persons regardless of their nationality before its own courts.[19]

Perhaps the most celebrated case involving the exercise of the principle of universal jurisdiction was the arrest of the former Chilean dictator, Augusto Pinochet in United Kingdom pursuant to a warrant issued against him by a Spanish magistrate *Judge Baltasar*

15 Report of the Commission on the Use of the Principle of Universal Jurisdiction by some Non-African States as Recommended by the Conference of Ministers of Justice/Attorneys General adopted at Thirteenth Ordinary Session of the Executive Council of the African Union, June 24-28, 2008, at Sharm El-Sheik, Egypt; EX.CL/411(XIII) para. 4, available at: <http://internationaljusticeafrica.org/documents/EX.CL%20 411(XIII)%20Study%20on%20universal%20jurisdiction.doc> (Accessed April 13, 2011).

16 1958 Geneva Convention on the High Seas, 450 U.N.T.S. 82; 1982 Convention on the Law of the Sea, 21 ILM 1261 (1982).

17 Report of the AU-EU Technical Ad Hoc Expert Group on the Principle of Universal Jurisdiction, Brussels, April 16, 2009, at 7.

18 Xavier Philippe, *The Principles of Universal Jurisdiction and Complementarity*, 88 INTERNATIONAL REVIEW OF THE RED CROSS 378 (2006).

19 Common Arts. 49, 50, 129, 146 & 85 of Additional Protocol 1 to the Four Geneva Conventions of 1949.

Garzon in 1998 for crimes of genocide and terrorism.[20] Thus, the legal rationale and authority for the actions of the Spanish judge may have been equivalent to the Roman concept of *actio popularis, or universal interest.*[21] A striking feature of the Pinochet case was that a Spanish judge had the authority to order Pinochet's arrest for crimes committed primarily in Chile and primarily against Chileans. There was no traditional jurisdictional nexus linking the alleged perpetrator and the prosecuting state. The alleged crimes had not been committed in Spain; Pinochet was not a Spanish national; and he was not in Spain at the time of his arrest. Furthermore, the alleged victims were not Spanish citizens, and, ostensibly, there were no protected Spanish economic interests at stake.[22] His detention became a leading symbol of the globalization of justice, and elevated and transformed the principle of universal jurisdiction – the ability of international community to pursue the prosecution of dictators, torturers and mass murderers beyond the borders of their home nations – into a precedent for future legal efforts against perpetrators of human rights crimes.[23]

Despite the cogency of the rationale behind the universal jurisdiction principle – to ensure that perpetrators of grave crimes do not go unpunished, it is attended by several challenges and pitfalls which form the basis of opposition by some critics who oppose its application. These include the absence of implementing national legislations, political will, the possibility of abuse of the principle, immunity for state officials and the practical obstacles to a fair trial where the principle is invoked. One of the vocal critics of this principle is Henry Kissinger, former United States Secretary of State who declares the exercise of the principle in the Pinochet case as a dangerous precedent. According to him:

> [t]he unprecedented and sweeping interpretation of international law in Ex parte Pinochet would arm any magistrate anywhere in the world with the power to demand extradition, substituting the magistrate's own judgment for the reconciliation procedures of even incontestably democratic societies where alleged violations of human rights may have occurred. It would also subject the accused to the criminal procedures of the magistrate's country, with a legal system that may be unfamiliar to the defendant and that would force the defendant to bring evidence and witnesses from long distances. Such a system goes far beyond the explicit and limited mandates established by

---

20 Human Rights Watch, *The Pinochet Prosecution*, available at: <www.hrw.org/campaigns/chile/index.html> (Accessed September 25, 2010).

21 Pillay, *supra* note 11, at 8.

22 *Id.*

23 Peter Kornbluh, Genocide and Crimes Against Humanity – Augusto Pinochet, available at <www.enotes.com/genocide-encyclopedia/pinochet-augusto> (Accessed September 22, 2010).

> the UN Security Council for the tribunals covering war crimes in the former Yugoslavia and Rwanda as well as the one being negotiated for Cambodia.[24]

Kissinger argues that the most important issue is the relationship of universal jurisdiction to national reconciliation procedures set up by new democratic governments to deal with their countries' questionable pasts. One would have thought, he states, that a Spanish magistrate would have been sensitive of the incongruity of a request by Spain, itself haunted by transgressions committed during the Spanish Civil War and the regime of General Francisco Franco, to try in Spanish Courts alleged crimes against humanity committed elsewhere. He concludes that "it is an important principle that those who commit war crimes or systematically violate human rights should be held accountable. But the consolidation of law, domestic peace and representative government in a nation struggling to come to terms with a brutal past has a claim as well. The instinct to punish must be related, as in every constitutional democratic political structure, to a system of checks and balances that includes other elements critical to the survival and expansion of democracy."[25]

In furtherance of the AU resolution, the 10th and 11th meeting of the AU-EU Ministerial Troika[26] considered the issue of universal jurisdiction and its impact on the relationship between the two bodies and constituted a Technical Ad Hoc Expert Group.[27] The terms of reference of the expert group include: To provide a description of the legal notion of the principle of universal jurisdiction, setting out the distinctions between the jurisdiction of international criminal tribunals and the exercise of universal jurisdiction and related concepts by individual states on the basis of their national laws; Outline the respective understandings on the African and EU sides regarding the principle of universal jurisdiction and its application; and make, as appropriate, recommendations for fostering a better mutual understanding between the AU and the EU of the purpose and the practice of universal jurisdiction.[28]

The Expert Group has concluded its work and submitted its report to the AU-EU Ministerial Troika for consideration. The group after a careful and detailed analysis of the issues came up with a total of seventeen recommendations aimed at promoting a better

24 Henry Kissinger, The Pitfalls of Universal Jurisdiction (2001), available at: <www.globalpolicy.org/component/content/article/163/28174/html> (Accessed March 17, 2011).

25 *Id.*

26 The meetings were held on September 16, 2008 (Brussels) & November 20-21, 2008 (Addis Ababa).

27 Members of the Expert Group include: Professor Antonio Cassese (Italy), Dr Mohammed Bedjaoui (Algeria), Professor Pierre Klein (Belgium), Dr Chaloka Beyani (Zambia), Dr Roger O'Keefe (Australia) Professor Chris Maina Peter (Tanzania).

28 Report of the AU-EU Technical Ad Hoc Expert Group on the Principle of Universal Jurisdiction, Brussels, April 16, 2009, at 2.

understanding of the principle of universal jurisdiction, maintaining a cordial relationship between the AU and EU, and strengthening national and regional mechanisms to ensure accountability for international crimes. Some of the highlights of the recommendations are: That all States should strive to put an end to impunity for genocide, crimes against humanity, war crimes and torture, and prosecute those responsible for such crimes. States are also legally bound to prosecute treaty crimes, whenever they are parties to such treaties;[29] when exercising universal jurisdiction over serious crimes of international concern such as genocide, crimes against humanity, war crimes and torture, states should bear in mind the need to avoid impairing friendly international relations.[30] Where national criminal justice authorities have initiated investigations and collected compelling evidence of serious crimes of international concern allegedly committed abroad against non-nationals by non-nationals, and where the suspect is a foreign state official exercising a representative function on behalf of his or her state, these authorities should consider refraining from taking steps that might publicly and unduly expose the suspects, thereby discrediting and stigmatizing them, curtailing their right to be presumed innocent until found guilty by a court of law and hampering the discharge of their official functions.[31]

In addition, the Group recommended that those national criminal justice authorities considering exercising universal jurisdiction over persons suspected of serious crimes of international concern are legally bound to take into account all the immunities to which foreign state officials may be entitled under international law and are consequently obliged to refrain from prosecuting those officials entitled to such immunities.[32] In prosecuting serious crimes of international concern, States should, as a matter of policy, accord priority to territoriality as a basis of jurisdiction, since such crimes, while offending against the international community as a whole by infringing universal values, primarily injure the community where they have been perpetrated and violate not only the rights of the victims but also the general demand for order and security in that community. In addition, it is within the territory of the state of alleged commission that the bulk of the evidence will usually be found.[33]

The extent to which the adoption and implementation of the report of the expert group will go in reducing the tension generated between the AU and the EU as a result of the application of the principle of universal jurisdiction remains to be seen. African States

29 Recommendation 1, Report of the AU-EU Technical Ad Hoc Expert Group on the Principle of Universal Jurisdiction, at 24.

30 *Id.* at 6.

31 *Id.* at 7.

32 *Id.* Recommendation 8.

33 *Id.* Recommendation 9.

have referred the delineation of the scope and application of the principle of Universal Jurisdiction to the General Assembly and the issue is presently under consideration by the Sixth Committee. At its 28th meeting on November 11, 2010, the Committee adopted draft resolution A/C.6/65/L.18 without a vote. Under the draft resolution, the General Assembly would request the Secretary-General to invite member States and relevant observers, as appropriate, to submit information and observations before April 30, 2011 on the scope and application of universal jurisdiction, including, where appropriate, information on the relevant applicable international treaties, their domestic legal rules and judicial practice, and to prepare and submit to the General Assembly, at its 66th session, a report based on such information and observations.[34]

12.4 African Union Resolution on the ICC Indictment of the President of Sudan

Another significant decision at the January 2009 Summit of the African Union relates to the application by the Prosecutor of the International Criminal Court for the indictment of His Excellency Omar Hassan Ahmed El Bashir, President of the Republic of Sudan. The AU expressed deep concern at the indictment of President Bashir; cautioned that the approval of this application would seriously undermine the delicate peace process underway in The Sudan; and urged the United Nations Security Council, in accordance with Article 16 of the Rome Statute of the International Criminal Court and as earlier requested by the Peace and Security Council of the AU to defer the process initiated by the ICC.

The Assembly of the Heads of States and Government reiterated once again its unflinching commitment to combating impunity and promoting democracy, the rule of law and good governance throughout the entire continent and condemned the gross violations of human rights in Darfur while urging that the perpetrators be apprehended and brought to justice. The AU Commission was requested to send a high-level delegation from the AU to the UN Security Council and to convene as early as possible, a meeting of the African Countries that are party to the Rome Statute of the ICC to exchange views on the work of the ICC in relation to Africa, in particular, in the light of the process initiated against African personalities, and to submit recommendations taking into account all relevant elements. Finally, the Assembly supported the decision by the Peace and Security Council of the African Union (PSC) to establish a High-Level Panel of Eminent Personalities under the chairmanship of the former President of the Republic of South Africa, H.E. Mr. Thabo

34 General Assembly of the United Nations, Legal –Sixth Committee Resolution 64/117, The Scope and Application of the Principle of Universal Jurisdiction: (Agenda item 86), available at: <www.un.org/en/ga/sixth/65/ScopeAppUniJuri.shtml> (Accessed April 13, 2011).

Mbeki, to examine the situation in depth, and to submit recommendations on how best the issues of accountability and combating impunity on the one hand, and reconciliation and healing, on the other hand could be effectively and comprehensively addressed.[35] It is instructive to note however, that both in the case of the indictment of President Bashir, and the leaders of the LRA in Northern Uganda, the peace negotiations were initiated after the indictments were issued by the ICC.[36]

Subsequent to the adoption of these resolutions by the AU, a panel of three ICC judges on March 4, 2009 issued an arrest warrant for President Bashir at the prosecutor's request. This represents the first time in history that a warrant will be issued against a serving Head of State by the ICC. On 12 July 2010, Pre-Trial Chamber 1 of the ICC, following an application by the ICC Prosecutor, issued a second warrant of arrest against the Sudanese President on charges of genocide.[37] This action has polarized Africa and indeed, the rest of the world and has led to the contestation as to whether or not the ICC is unduly focused on Africa, since its present situation countries are all on the continent.

On the one side, you have those who believe that the adoption of the indictment and issuance of a warrant of arrest sends a signal to high government officials who are engaged in, or may be involved in the commission of such crimes in future that the arm of the law will surely catch up with them, irrespective of their status and position. On the other side, there are those who believe that the action was most irresponsible on the part of the prosecutor and the Court in view of the delicate peace process in Sudan and the immunity a serving Head of State enjoys. Two prominent Africans, Nobel Laureate Bishop Desmond Tutu and Kofi Annan, former United Nations Secretary General have voiced support for the ICC action. Desmond Tutu stated as follows:

> I regret that the charges against President Bashir are being used to stir up the sentiment that the justice system — and in particular, the international court — is biased against Africa. Justice is in the interest of victims and the victims of these crimes are African. To imply that the prosecution is a plot by the West is demeaning to Africans and understates the commitment to justice we have seen across the continent. It's worth remembering that more than 20 African

---

35 AU General Assembly Decision on the Application by the Prosecutor of the International Criminal Court (ICC) for the Indictment of the President of the Republic of Sudan, Assembly/AU/Dec.221(XII) at 2.

36 Johan van der Vyver, *African Union's Responses to the Indictment of President Bashir by the International Criminal Court*, Research discussion at the Institute for International and Comparative Law, University of Pretoria, South Africa, March 15, 2011.

37 Report of the Chairperson of the Commission on the Situation in Darfur, PSC/PR/2(CCXXXVII), presented to the Peace and Security Council 237th Meeting at Ambassadorial Level, at 7-8; July 21, 2010, Kampala, Uganda.

> countries were among the founders of the International Criminal Court, and of the 108 nations that joined the court, 30 are in Africa. That the court's four active investigations are all in Africa is not because of prosecutorial prejudice — it is because three of the countries involved (Central African Republic, Congo and Uganda) themselves requested that the prosecutor intervene. Only the Darfur case was referred to the prosecutor by the Security Council. The prosecutor on his own initiative is considering investigations in Afghanistan, Colombia and Georgia.[38]

This position is reinforced by Kofi Annan when he observed as follows:

> In recent months, some African leaders have expressed the view that international justice as represented by the ICC is an imposition, if not a plot, by the industrialized West. In my view, this outcry against justice demeans the yearning of human dignity that resides in every African heart. It also represents a step backward in the battle against impunity.[39]

Concerns about the perceived targeting of Africa by international justice mechanisms was expressed by the Registrar of the International Criminal Tribunal for Rwanda, Adama Dieng at a press statement following the arrest of Rose Kabuye in Germany. According to him, "[l]aw is law but we must understand that we live in a complex world. I am not saying that we shouldn't defend the principles of justice but we should not build a perspective that international justice is towards an African. The International Criminal Court is only trying cases from Africa."[40] He said the ICTR's conviction of Jean Kambanda (former chief of Rwandan Government) for genocide and other serious violations of international humanitarian law send a strong signal to all leaders in Africa and elsewhere who could be tempted to use their power and influence to perpetrate gross violations of human rights.[41]

While there are merits in the arguments of those in support of the ICC's work and its present focus on Africa, the arguments of its opponents cannot be waved aside or wished away as being put forward in a bid to allow perpetrators of heinous crimes to walk free. Indeed some of them, like the ICTR Registrar are people known to have played an important role in the development of the African regional human rights system and international criminal justice on the continent.

---

38 Desmond Tutu, *Op-Ed,* New York Times, May 3, 2009.

39 Kofi Annan, *Op-Ed,* New York Times, June 30, 2009.

40 Berna Namata, Rwanda: ICTR Registrar Condemns Rose Kabuye's Arrest, available at: <http://allafrica.com/stories/200811130039.html> (Accessed March 17, 2011).

41 *Id.*

For a better appreciation of the scenario, let us take a critical look at the process by which the situations were taken up by the ICC and the composition of the ICC. It must be noted, that the jurisdiction of the ICC is based on the principle of complementarity, which allows the Court to assume jurisdiction only when the State is unable or unwilling to prosecute.[42] As earlier stated, of the four ICC situation countries in Africa, three (Uganda, Congo DRC and the Central African Republic) themselves referred the cases to the ICC pursuant to Article 14 of the Rome Statute, in contrast with the Sudanese referral which took place pursuant to a Security Council Resolution.[43] While it could be argued that the African Article 14 referrals were made despite the fact that the states in question may have been willing and able to prosecute, by inviting the permanent Court to investigate international crimes within their territories, those three nations put aside the sovereign pride that traditionally impeded state action towards punishment of gross humanitarian law violations.[44] In doing so, Uganda, the CAR and the DRC waived complementarity and put themselves on the line to offer the first test cases to an untested Court.[45] What this shows is that the ICC did not focus its searchlight on Africa with a view to taking up investigations and prosecutions. Rather, it was the governments of the concerned African States that requested the ICC to take up investigations. The present situation in Darfur represents a serious humanitarian catastrophe. While the peace process is underway, innocent civilians continue to lose their lives and property and also face forceful displacements that turn them into refugees.

Genuine as this argument may sound; an inverse analysis will expose its pitfalls. All three states that have made referrals to the ICC are experiencing ongoing conflicts and there are two sides to every conflict. But putting one side – the government – in a position to seize the ICC, the reality that is created is that incumbent governments now see the ICC as a potent weapon against recalcitrant rebels who lack the diplomatic facility of recognition. Some have criticized the ICC prosecutions in Uganda, the DRC and CAR for focusing on alleged abuses committed by rebel fighters to the exclusion of those reportedly committed by government troops.[46] Unwittingly, the ICC is now placed in an

42 In accordance with the complementarity principle provided for in Art. 17 of the Rome Statute of the International Criminal Court.

43 Security Council Resolution 1593 of March 31, 2005 referring the situation in Darfur to the International Criminal Court.

44 Charles C. Jalloh, *Regionalizing International Criminal Justice?*, 9 International Criminal Law Review. 455, 448 (2009).

45 Claus Kress, *'Self Referrals' and 'Waiver of Complementarit'*, 2 Journal of International Criminal Justice. 944 (2004).

46 Arieff, Margesson & Browne, International Criminal Court Cases in Africa: Status and Policy Issues (Congressional Research Service) April 2, 2010, at 26; available at: <http://fpc.state.gov/documents/organisations/141591.pdf> (Accessed March 16, 2011).

awkward position where it is perceived as being used to fight insurgency. The *volte face* by the Uganda government that later wanted to be allowed to negotiate with the Lord's Resistance Army Rebels because of its inability to arrest the indicted LRA commanders lays credence to this assertion and heightens the controversy of striking a balance between pursuing the demands for justice and fostering enduring peace in the affected communities.

One question that needs to be answered in trying to unravel the rationale behind the perceived one-sided focus on Africa is whether Africa is underrepresented at the ICC to warrant a biased focus on the continent. A sedate perusal of the list of judges of the ICC will reveal that there are five judges from Africa. Ghana, Uganda, Kenya, Botswana are all represented on the ICC bench, while the judge from Mali is the *Vice* President of the Court.[47] The *Deputy* Prosecutor also is from Gambia. Given the number and position of Africans serving on the ICC bench and the prosecutor's office, it is doubtful that the ICC's current focus on Africa is borne out of any racial or other prejudicial interests, albeit the fact that they hold deputizing positions and not principal ones.

Another insight into the possible basis for the perceived afro centric focus of the ICC is provided by Kevin Jon Heller. According to him, that is not to say that the OTP's single-minded emphasis on Africa is justified. It isn't. But it is important to understand why the emphasis is unjustified. The problem stems from the criterion the OTP uses to decide which situations it will investigate: the number of victims. That criterion explains the OTP's Africa obsession: In its view, the African situations are simply more serious than the other non-African situations because they involve far greater number of victims.[48]

Against the backdrop of these two contending views, a third has emerged. This group expresses reservations about the ICC indictment of Sudanese President, Omar Bashir, not on the basis of perceived bias or racial-based prejudices, but instead on the practical implications of the ICC indictment on the civilian populations in the Sudan in particular, and the Great Lakes region in general. Chidi Anselm Odinkalu, scholar and human rights activist, is a prominent protagonist of this view. He maintains that the greatest fears about the role that international justice is playing in Africa arise not from crimes behind us but in connection with a mass atrocity that some informed people foresee and all must

47 Judges of the International Criminal Court – Wikipedia, The Free Encyclopedia, available at: <http://en.wikipedia.org/wiki/Judges_of_the_International_Criminal_Court> (Accessed April 15, 2011).

48 Kevin Jon Heller, *Why is the Prosecutor So Focused on Africa? in* The Reckoning: The Battle for the International Criminal Court, Perspectives on International Justice and Human Rights, available at: <www.pbs.org/pov/reckoning/perspectives_heller.php> (Accessed March 16, 2011).

work to prevent – a disintegration of Sudan into a regional killing field.[49] Specifically in relation to the ICC indictment he subtly, but with conviction outlines his arguments as follows:

> [i]n authorizing the arrest of Sudan's President Al Bashir, ICC judges agreed that he has a case to answer for his alleged role in war crimes and crimes against humanity committed in Darfur. But the execution of the warrant without an adequately managed transition could create a power vacuum in Khartoum unleashing destabilizing tremors beyond Sudan's borders. Consequently, all nine countries that share a border with Sudan are on a war footing. Without a government for two decades, nearby Somalia is already a major destabilizing factor in the region. Uganda's murderous Lord's Resistance Army, long supported by Khartoum and whose leaders are also wanted by the ICC, is regrouping in vast ungoverned border territory between Sudan, Uganda and DRC. The 2005 'comprehensive' peace agreement (CPA) that ended Sudan's half century-long north-south war risks breakdown, while the Darfur crisis in western Sudan remains active. These uncertainties drive an undisguised arms race in the region. If the CPA collapses, many fear a transnational atrocity site like none this region has known.[50]

In effect, those who propound the view do not necessarily disagree with rationale behind the indictment of President Bashir, rather, their grouse is that the indictment and warrant should not have taken place without an enabling environment that guarantees the security and safety of civilians who as victims, have borne the brunt of these atrocities.

The crux of this argument lies in the often-forgotten interest of the victims who are at risk of suffering double victimization if war criminals, who are fugitives of the international justice system decide to unleash more terror on the populace with the reasoning that since they stand indicted, they may well continue with the crimes knowing that they will face justice whenever they are apprehended. This argument is not without merit. The action of the leaders of the Lord's Resistance Army in Northern Uganda in heightening their attacks on the civilian population following their indictment by the ICC sparked the great, yet unresolved debate of which among two concepts of peace and justice is more important than the other and should therefore be given primacy. While the quest by the ICC to hold

49 Chidi Odinkalu, *Saving International Justice in Africa, in* Debating International Justice in Africa, Oxford Transitional Justice Research Collected Essays 15 (2008-2010), available at: <www.fljs.org/uploads/documents/Justice_in_Africa.pdf> (Accessed March 17, 2011)

50 *Id.*

international criminals are commendable, it should in doing this refrain from acts that do not take into consideration the weak victims on whose behalf justice is pursued.

In his conclusion, Odinkalu asserts that "most victims need reassurance that when the neighborhood mass murderer arrives, their only defense is not in the promise of a warrant from a distance tribunal on thin resources. They are right in asking that the promise of justice should be accompanied by credible protection from reprisals".[51]

Since the indictment and issuance of the warrant of arrest against the Sudanese President, there has been an increased clampdown on human rights activists in Sudan. Many of them, including those who were involved in the process of gathering information which formed the basis of the ICC indictment, and who are potential witnesses if and when the trial goes underway, have been forced into exile. Several aid groups providing the much needed humanitarian services in the region have been expelled by the Khartoum based government who now invests time and resources in a campaign to discredit the ICC. This has resulted in the worsening of the already pathetic humanitarian crisis in Darfur – an unintended consequence of the ICC indictment and warrant of arrest against Bashir. These are practical issues which the ICC needs to address if it is to shore up its credibility which has been battered by critics of its perceived biased role in Africa.

12.4.1 Meeting of the African State Parties to the ICC

The ministerial meeting of African State Parties to the ICC was held from June 8-9 in Addis Ababa, Ethiopia. The meeting was organized in compliance with the AU decision,[52] which mandated the AU Commission to convene a meeting of African State Parties to the Rome Statute to exchange views on the work of the ICC in relation to Africa, particularly in the light of the proceedings instituted against certain African personalities. The meeting was well attended by African Union Member State Parties to the ICC.[53] The meeting after an extensive deliberation of the concept note developed by the AU Commission and presented on its behalf by Ben Kioko, Legal Counsel to the AU, arrived at certain recommendations.

---

51 *Id.*

52 AU General Assembly Decision on the Application by the Prosecutor of the International Criminal Court (ICC) for the Indictment of the President of the Republic of Sudan, Assembly/AU/Dec.221(XII).

53 Representatives of the following countries attended the meeting: Benin, Botswana, Burkina Faso, Burundi, Chad, Congo, Djibouti, Democratic Republic of Congo, Gambia, Ghana, Kenya, Lesotho, Liberia, Malawi, Mali, Mauritius, Namibia, Niger, Nigeria, Senegal, Sierra Leone, South Africa, Tanzania, Uganda and Zambia.

Contrary to fears that the meeting might lead to a mass withdrawal of African State parties to the ICC, the meeting reiterated the unflinching commitment of AU Member States to combating impunity and promoting democracy, the rule of law and good governance on the continent and urged the AU Commission to ensure early implementation of the Assembly decision mandating the AU Commission, in consultation with the African Commission on Human and Peoples' Rights and the African Court on Human and Peoples' Rights, to examine the implications of the Court being empowered to try international crimes such as genocide, crimes against humanity and war crimes, which would be complementary to national jurisdiction and processes. The State Parties called for the initiation and implementation of a programme of cooperation and capacity building to enhance the capacity of legal personnel in Member States regarding the drafting and scrutiny of model legislation dealing with international crimes, training of members of the police and judiciary, and the strengthening of cooperation among judicial and investigative bodies. It also urged any affected party to have recourse to legal processes regarding the appeal process and the issue of immunity as provided for in the Rome Statute. In this regard, the meeting reiterated the commitment of African State Parties to the ICC.[54]

It went further to suggest issues that can be addressed within the framework of the review conference as follows: Article 13 of the Rome Statute granting power to the UN Security Council to refer cases to the ICC; Article 16 of the Rome Statute granting power to the UN Security Council to defer cases for one year; Procedures of the ICC; Clarification on the immunity of officials whose states are not parties to the ICC and a comparative analysis of the implications of the practical application of Articles 27 and 98 of the Rome Statute. Finally, the meeting also put forward for consideration, the possibility of obtaining regional inputs in the process of assessing the evidence collected and in determining whether or not to proceed with prosecution, particularly against senior state officials and any other issues that might be of concern to member states. The Assembly of States and Government of the AU was called upon to present another resolution to the United Nations Security Council to invoke Article 16 of the Rome Statute by deferring proceedings against President Bashir as well as express grave concern that a request made by fifty three member states of the United Nations has been ignored.[55]

The outcome of the meeting represents a principled and considered approach to the challenges facing the work of the ICC in Africa. Although the AU is an umbrella body of African states, it must not be forgotten that each of these State Parties signed the Rome Statute in its individual capacity and not collectively. The international law principle of *pacta sunt*

54 Report of the Meeting of African State Parties to the Rome Statute of the International Criminal Court (ICC) at 6; June 6-8, 2009, Addis Ababa, Ethiopia.

55 *Id.*

servanda imposes an obligation on state parties to a treaty entered into voluntarily and in good faith to respect and implement obligations arising there from.

During the 13th AU Summit in Libya, the Assembly reviewed the recommendations of the Executive Council on the meeting of the African State Parties to the Rome Statute of the ICC and noted with grave concern the unfortunate consequences that the indictment has had on the delicate peace process underway in The Sudan and the fact that it continues to undermine the ongoing efforts aimed at facilitating the early resolution of the conflict in Darfur. The Summit decided that in view of the fact that the request by the African Union has never been acted upon, the AU member States shall not cooperate with the ICC pursuant to the provisions of Article 98 of the Rome Statute of the ICC relating to immunities, for the arrest and surrender of President Omar El Bashir of Sudan.[56] As a matter of international law, the Sirte decision was hollow. But as a political decision, it was clear: International justice on the continent is now at a major crossroads.[57] This decision has elicited mixed reactions from keen observers of African affairs. The variety of views was aptly captured by a Nigerian daily in its editorial as follows:

> Cynics have seen the decision as a self-protection measure by leaders who have crimes they fear to line up to answer for if the trial of Bashir is endorsed. Other critics have blamed the decision on the habits of governance which value impunity, mass cruelty and the denial of the dignity of citizenship when it serves the machinations of African rulers. Another school of thought sees it as evidence of disgraceful actions which ignore the moral values of the majority of peoples that African rulers claim to act on behalf of. Still others see it as another evidence of Western imperialism and interference in the affairs of less powerful and developing countries.[58]

The paper concludes that there is much validity to these views; and the indignation that fuels them deserves our attention and commendation.[59] Indeed, one week after this decision President Bashir cancelled his planned trip to Uganda after the country's State Minister for International Affairs told the press that Bashir faced arrest in Uganda. But Ugandan officials later issued a disclaimer saying the minister was not mandated to speak on behalf of the government on the issue and that Uganda was committed to the ICC, but wanted

56 Decision on the Meeting of African State Parties to the Rome Statute of the International Criminal Court (ICC) Doc. Assembly/AU/13(XIII).

57 Comfort Ero, *Understanding Africa's Position on the International Criminal Court, in* Debating International Justice in Africa, Oxford Transitional Justice Research Collected Essays 11 (2008-2010).

58 *Editorial,* Daily Trust, July 17, 2009.

59 *Id.*

to avoid an incident.[60] The trip was eventually called off. Another proposed visit to Nigeria by Bashir was also thwarted following intensive advocacy by NGOs who insisted that Nigeria has obligations to arrest him and hand him over to the ICC if he sets foot in the country.[61] President Bashir has however visited Kenya and Chad, two African State Parties to the ICC. Both countries refused to comply with warrant issued by the ICC which requires them to arrest and surrender Bashir to the Court. Following the visits, the Pre-Trial Chamber of the ICC issued a decision regarding the Kenya visit, in which it informed the United Nations Security Council and the Assembly of State Parties to the Rome Statute "in order for them to take any measure they may deem appropriate". The decision also stated as follows:

> [t]he Republic of Kenya has a clear obligation to cooperate with the Court in relation to the enforcement of such warrants of arrest, which stems both from the United Nations Security Council Resolution 1593 (2005) whereby the United Nations Security Council "urge[d] all states and concerned regional and other international organizations to cooperate fully with the Court, and from Article 87 of the Statute of the Court, to which the Republic of Kenya is a State Party.[62]

Dapo Akande argues that the ICC judges have to take a large share of the blame for this situation. Despite the assertion that Kenya has a clear obligation to arrest President Bashir, the matter is by no means clear. As is well known, a decent argument can be made that Bashir, being a serving head of State is immune from arrest in other States.[63] Despite very reasonable doubts and despite the importance of the issue, ICC judges in the Appeals and Pre-Trial Chamber have refused to address the immunity question and to clarify matters.[64]

In response to the decision of the Pre-Trial Chamber of the ICC, the African Union asserts that it regrets the decision of the Pre-Trial Chamber relating to the visit of President Omar El-Bashir of the Sudan to the Republic of Chad and the Republic of Kenya on July 21 and

60 Wanted Bashir, Drops Ugandan Trip, July 17, 2009, available at: <http://newsbbc.co.uk/2/hi/africa/8154730.stm> (Accessed July 28, 2009).

61 This advocacy was carried out under the auspices of the Nigerian Coalition on the International Criminal Court.

62 Decision Informing the United Nations Security Council and the Assembly of the State Parties to the Rome Statute about Omar Al-Bashir's presence in the territory of the Republic of Kenya (Pre-Trial Chamber 1) No. ICC-02-05-01/09 of August 27, 2010, at 3.

63 Dapo Akande, *ICC Reports Kenya and Chad to the UN Security Council over Bashir's Visits*, European Journal of International Law Analysis, available at: <www.ejiltalk.org/icc-reports-Kenya-and-chad-to-the-un-security-council-over-bashir's-visits >(Accessed April 15, 2011).

64 *Id.*

August 27 respectively[65] and decides, that by receiving President Bashir, the Republic of Chad and the Republic of Kenya were implementing various AU Assembly decisions on the warrant of arrest issued by the ICC against President Bashir as well as acting in pursuit of peace and stability in their respective regions.[66]

12.5 African Court on Human and Peoples' Rights and the Exercise of Criminal Jurisdiction

One of the reactions of the African Union to the perceived bias against Africa by the ICC and the abuse of the principle of universal jurisdiction is the mandate to the AU Commission in collaboration with the African Commission on Human and Peoples' Rights and the African Court on Human and Peoples' Rights to consider the possibility of conferring jurisdiction over international crimes on the Court.

The establishment of an African Court on Human and Peoples' Rights in January 2004, with powers to render decisions capable of being enforced against member States of the African Union and the subsequent election of judges to the Court in January 2006, represented an important advancement in the African human rights system. Hitherto, complaints against State Parties based on the African Charter on Human and Peoples' Rights were handled by the African Commission which could only make recommendations to the State Party concerned.[67]

Eight years after the coming into force of the protocol establishing the court, only three cases have come before the court. The first, filed by Mikelot Yogogombaye against Senegal challenging the proposed trial of Hissein Habre by Senegal has come before the court and was declared inadmissible by the Court, on the basis that Senegal has not made the declaration allowing individuals and NGOs to bring cases against it to the Court.[68]

The second case was brought before the Court by the African Commission on Human and Peoples' Rights against the Great Socialist People's Libyan Arab Jamahiriya alleging gross violation of human rights. The Court unanimously ordered provisional measures stating

65 Decision on the Implementation of the Decisions of the International Criminal Court Doc.EX.CL/639(XVIII) Assembly/AU/Dec.334(XVI) Assembly of the Union, Sixteenth Ordinary Session, January 30-31, 2011, Addis Ababa, Ethiopia.

66 *Id.*

67 Art. 45 of the African Charter on Human and Peoples' Rights adopted by the eighteenth Assembly of Heads of State and Government in June 1981, Nairobi, Kenya.

68 Judgment in the matter of *Michelot Yogogombaye v. The Republic of Senegal*, application No. 001/2008, available at <www.african-court.org/en/cases/latest-judgments/> (Accessed March 17, 2011).

that the Great Socialist People's Arab Jamahiriya must immediately refrain from any action that would result in loss of life or violation of physical integrity of persons, which could be a breach of the provisions of the Charter or of other international human rights instruments to which it is a party.[69]

In the third and most recent case,[70] the applicant, Mr. Femi Falana, a Nigerian-based lawyer, filed an application against the African Union, as a representative of its then 53 Member States (now 54), asking the Court to find Article 34(6) of the Protocol Establishing the Court as inconsistent with 1, 2, 7, 13, 26 and 66 of the African Charter on Human and People's Rights (African Charter) as, according to him, the requirement for a State to make a declaration to allow access to the Court by individuals and non-governmental organization is a violation of rights to freedom from discrimination, fair hearing and equal treatment, as well as his right to be heard. The respondent, the African Union, disputes the allegation of the applicant, and maintains that they are ill-founded, as the African Union is neither a part to the African Charter on Human and Peoples' Rights, nor to the Protocol establishing the Court, and is not the legal representative of its member states, which are Sovereign States. After hearing argument from both parties on the 22 and 23 March 2012, the Court reserved its ruling which will be delivered within ninety days.

The paucity of cases before the African human rights court has been a source of concern to many who have been waiting for the court to commence actual deliberation on substantive cases. The seat of the court is located in Arusha, Tanzania, which is now emerging as Africa's judicial capital.[71] The Court has adopted its 'Interim Rules of Procedure' which would guide the conduct of filing and prosecution of cases before the court.[72] A new protocol has been adopted by the AU merging the African Court on Human and Peoples' Rights with the AU Court of Justice, with each maintaining a separate chamber.[73]

While awaiting the outcome of the mandate to the AU Commission on the propriety of conferring the African Human Rights Court with criminal jurisdiction for international crimes, some perfunctory remarks are apposite. It is a trite principle of international law that a treaty is binding upon the parties to it and must be performed by them in good

69 *In the Matter of the African Commission on Human and Peoples' Rights v. Great Socialist People's Libyan Arab Jamahiriya*; Application No. 004/2011, Order for Provisional Measures, March 25, 2011 available at: <http://african-court.org/fileadmin/documents/Court/Cases/Order_for_Provisional_Measures_against_Libya.PDF> (Accessed March 21, 2011).

70 *Femi Falana v. The African Union* (Application 001/2011).

71 Arusha also hosts the International Criminal Tribunal for Rwanda (ICTR) and the East African Court of Justice (EACJ).

72 The Interim Rules of the Court was adopted on June 20, 2008.

73 Protocol on the Statute of the African Court of Justice and Human Rights adopted at the 11th African Union Summit at Sharm el Sheikh, Egypt, 2008.

faith.[74] Conversely, a State cannot be bound by treaties to which it is not a party. As at today, thirty one African States have signed the Rome Statute of the ICC,[75] whereas only twenty five African States have ratified the Protocol on the Establishment of the African Court on Human and Peoples' Rights.[76] Out of the twenty five states, only Burkina Faso, Mali, Malawi and Tanzania have made the declaration allowing individuals and non-governmental organizations with observer status at the African Commission on Human and Peoples' Rights to bring cases against them before the Court, in accordance with Article 34(6) of the Protocol.[77]

The implication of this is that more African States have ratified the Rome Statute of the ICC than have the Protocol establishing the African Court on Human and Peoples' Rights, which is the AU's own treaty. If the poor status of ratification of the protocol is not addressed, the implication is that, if the African Court acquires criminal jurisdiction for international crimes, AU State Parties who have not ratified the protocol may refuse to do so with a view to avoiding the jurisdiction of the Court over persons within its territories. Conferring this additional jurisdiction on the court would require an amendment to the existing protocol, or an entirely new protocol, and the usual slow pace of ratification of treaties by African States may have the effect of delaying the coming into force of such a protocol.

12.6 AU RESOLUTION ON THE TRIAL OF HISSEIN HABRE BY SENEGAL

The AU at its summit in July 2006 in the Gambia, mandated Senegal to prosecute and ensure that Hissene Habre is tried, on behalf of Africa for crimes committed when he was Head of State in Chad, by a competent Senegalese court with guarantees for fair trial.[78] Habre is under nominal arrest in Senegal where he has spent the last 20 years in exile.[79] Prior to the AU Resolution, domestic criminal proceedings accusing him of complicity in torture and crimes against humanity started in Senegal in early February 2000, but were eventually dismissed by the Dakar Appeals Court – a decision then confirmed by the Senegalese Court of Cassation – on the basis that Senegal had not adopted the incorporating legislation necessary to implement the relevant international rules criminalizing crimes

74 Art. 26, Vienna Convention on the Law of Treaties, 1969.

75 African State Parties to the International Criminal Court, available at: <www.icc-cpi.int/Menus/ASP/states=parties/African=States> (Accessed April 15, 2011).

76 List of countries which have signed, ratified/acceded to the Protocol to the African Charter on Human and Peoples' Rights, available at: <www.africa-union.org> (Accessed September 22, 2010).

77 Coalition for an Effective African Court on Human and Peoples' Rights, Background to the African Court, available at: <www.africancourtcoalition.org> (Accessed April 17, 2011).

78 Assembly/AU.Dec.03(VI) August 2, 2006.

79 Valentina Spiga, *Non-retroactivity of Criminal Law: A New Chapter in the Hissene Habre Saga*, JOURNAL OF INTERNATIONAL CRIMINAL JUSTICE 1 (2011).

against humanity, and that the Code of Criminal Procedure did not include torture among the offences committed by foreigners outside Senegal over which national courts could assert jurisdiction.[80]

Senegal has subsequently put in place a legal framework that permits the trial of Habre by amending its constitution and laws to permit the prosecution of genocide, crimes against humanity, war crimes and torture no matter when and where the acts occurred.[81] However, Senegal has been putting off Habre's trial for years, saying it would not proceed until it received international funding for anticipated trial costs.[82] The AU therefore called on member states, the EU and other partner countries to make their contributions directly to the African Union Commission which should report back at the next summit.

This AU decision was reviewed at its 12th Ordinary Summit in Addis Ababa, Ethiopia and yet again came up for consideration at its Summit in Libya in July 2009. The Assembly expressed regret that in spite of its previous Assembly decision calling on all Member States of the AU to make voluntary contributions to the budget estimated for the trial of Hissene Habre, there has been no positive reaction from member states. The AU reiterated its appeal to Member States to contribute to the budget of the trial and requested the government of Senegal and the AU Commission in collaboration with the partners, particularly the European Union to consider the possibility of organizing a donor's conference as soon as possible.[83] On November 24, 2010, international donors met in Dakar and fully funded the $11.7 million budget for the trial.[84]

Interestingly, Habre had filed a case against Senegal at the ECOWAS Community Court of Justice challenging his proposed trial by Senegal on the grounds that the law on which Senegal intended to try him was not in place when the alleged offences he is accused of were committed, contrary to accepted principles of non-retroactivity in criminal law under both domestic and international law. Senegal contended that the legislative changes were undertaken in order to conform national legislation to the international engagements of the state. Accordingly, the retroactive jurisdiction of its domestic courts would not introduce new crimes with retroactive effects, since genocide, crimes against humanity and war crimes were already criminalized by international law.[85]

80 *Id.* at 2.

81 Alex Thurston, UN Pressures Senegal to Act on Hissene Habre, Sahel Blog, available at: <http://sahelblog.wordpress.com/2011/01/19/un-pressures-senegal-to-act-on-hissene-habre> (Accessed March 14, 2011).

82 Human Rights watch, Senegal Must Prosecute or Extradite Hissene Habre, available at: <www.hrw.org/en/news/2011/01/18/united-nations-senegal-must-prosecute-or-extradite-hiss-ne-habr>, (Accessed March 14, 2011).

83 Decision on the Hissene Habre Case. Doc.Assembly/AU/Dec.246(XIII).

84 Human Rights Watch, *supra* note 81.

85 Spiga, *supra* note 78, at 5.

In its judgment, the ECOWAS Court held that Habre's trial should be carried out by "a special ad hoc procedure of an international character"[86] and that the mandate assigned by the African Union to Senegal should be carried out in accordance with the 'international custom' relating to the establishment of ad hoc jurisdictions.[87] The Court appears to assert that any proposed trial of Habre by a Senegalese court would amount to the violation of the non-retroactivity principle.

This decision of the ECOWAS Court has been described as flawed for a number of reasons.[88] First of all, the Court after correctly interpreting the provisions of Article 15(1) of the ICCPR, failed to rely on it albeit the fact that the relevant offences were criminalized under international rules at the moment of their alleged commission. It instead, placed reliance on Article 15(2) as the basis for the establishment of the ad hoc tribunal when in fact there was no general principle of law common to all nations prohibiting crimes against humanity and war crimes at the moment of the facts allegedly committed by Habre. Another flaw in the Court's reasoning is that in holding that a Senegalese incorporating law would violate the principle of non-retroactivity, the Court fails to notice that any ad-hoc tribunal statute would fail for the same reason. Rather than looking at the time of adoption of the law, the Court should have looked to the existence of a rule of international law applicable at the moment of the commission of the facts.

There is much validity in the rationale behind the criticism of the judgment of the ECOWAS Court, but it must however be noted that the Court did not declare Senegal's incorporating law as not applicable for the purposes of trying Habre and wash its hands off the case, it went further to propose the establishment of an ad hoc tribunal as a basis on which Habre can be tried.

Following the ECOWAS decision, the African Union has proposed that an Extraordinary African Chambers will be created within the Senegalese Judicial system with the Presidents of the trial court and the appeals court appointed by the African Union to prosecute the person or persons "who bear the greatest responsibility" for genocide, crimes against humanity, war crimes and torture committed in Chad from June 1982 to December 1990.[89]

Recent events in Senegal appear to put to question, the commitment of the Senegalese government to bring Habre to trial. President Wade of Senegal had declared that he has had enough of the Hissene Habre case and that he was returning it to the African Union.[90]

86 Human Rights Watch, *supra* note 81.
87 Spiga, *supra* note 78.
88 *Id.*
89 Human Rights Watch, *supra* note 81.
90 *Id.*

The United Nations Committee on Torture has recently written to Senegal through its Rapporteur stating that "financing is today at [Senegal's] disposition, thanks to the raising of funds from many sources," and that, "the Committee wishes therefore to remind [Senegal] of its obligation under the Convention Against Torture, to submit the case to its competent authorities for the purpose of prosecution or failing that, since Belgium has made an extradition request, to comply with that request" or another extradition request made pursuant to the Convention.[91]

The Belgian extradition request is now a subject of a case at the International Court of Justice whereby Belgium is seeking a determination of Senegal's obligation to extradite Hissene Habre to Belgium to face trial.[92] This has complicated matters for both the AU and Senegal since Senegal has not taken any concrete action to bring Habre to trial. This delay appears to have led to a rethink on a new venue for an African trial for Habre. Rwanda recently offered to host the trial and the AU Assembly by its recent decision is considering that offer and has requested consultation between the AU Commission, Senegal and Rwanda in that regard.[93]

12.7 Conclusion

In the foregoing part of this chapter, I have reviewed the status on international justice mechanisms in Africa and the substance and implications of the resolutions reached at the 12th Summit of the African Union as well as the variegated arguments in support and against them. My task in the concluding part of this piece is to attempt to distill the cardinal principles and processes that seek to advance the cause of international justice while at the same time responding to the challenges encountered in the operation of the system in Africa.

12.7.1 Between Leaders' and Citizens' Perceptions

Recent opinion polls appear to reinforce the argument that the views of leaders of some African countries on appropriate mechanisms for dealing with international crimes differ with those of their citizens. A WorldPublicOpinion.org poll of seven largely Muslim and African nations indicates that contrary to the position of their governments, the public in four nations approve of the indictment of the Sudanese President by the ICC for war

91 Letter to Senegal dated January 12, 2011 from the United Nations Committee against Torture urging Senegal to prosecute or extradite Hissene Habre.

92 See *The case concerning Questions relating to the Obligation to Prosecute or Extradite (Belgium v. Senegal)* filed by Belgium in ICJ on 19 February 2009.

93 See Decision on the *Hissene Habre Case*, Assembly/AU/Dec.401(XVIII) at the 18th Ordinary Session in Addis Ababa in January 2012, Paras. 2 and 5.

crimes and crimes against humanity in Darfur.[94] Of the three African countries in which the poll was conducted, Kenya recorded a 77% support for the indictment while Nigeria recorded 71%. In Egypt, 52% disapproved as against 47% in support.

In a related development, a 2009 public opinion poll has revealed that 62% of Kenyans want perpetrators of the post-election violence in Kenya to be tried by the ICC.[95] President Mwai Kibaki and Prime Minister Raila Odinga favor the local option. Former UN Secretary General, Kofi Annan, had handed over a sealed envelope containing the names of ten top suspects of the Kenyan violence to the ICC Prosecutor, Luis Moreno-Ocampo.[96] In December 2010, Ocampo named six high-profile figures accused of crimes against humanity.[97] Kenya has however, submitted a request to the UN Security Council to consider positively the (African Union) Resolution endorsing Kenya's request for a 12-month deferral to allow the country complete reforms and embark on local trials.[98]

12.7.2 Building Domestic Capacity for the Prosecution of International Crimes

The variance between the views of leaders and followers may be traced to the lack of confidence on the ability of national judicial mechanisms to dispense justice without fear or favor and devoid of political interference. To address this, member States of the AU should entrench the principles of democracy, rule of law and independence of the judiciary. The AU should intensify the campaign for the ratification of the African Charter on Democracy, Elections and Good Governance and abide by its principles. This will promote enduring democracy across the continent. In line with one of the recommendations of the AU-EU Technical Ad Hoc Expert Group, the AU should encourage member states that are yet to do so to develop national legislations for the prosecution and punishment of

94 World Public Opinion, Many Approve of ICC Indictment of Bashir: Poll of 7 Muslim and African Nations (2009), available at: <www.worldpublicopinion.org/pipa/articles/btjusticehuman_rightsra/624.php?lb=bthr&pnt=624&nid=&id> (Accessed March 15, 2011).

95 See International Criminal Court OTP Weekly Briefing Issue #20 (2010), available at: <www.icc-cpi.int/NR/nrdonlyres/BEDF7DF7-76FD-4116-8D08-A92E2454CC9A/281459/OTPWBJanuary_Issue20.pdf> (Accessed March 15, 2011). See also Felicity Conrad, The ICC's Investigation in Kenya into Crimes Against Humanity: Potential and Challenges, The American Non-Governmental Organizations Coalition for the International Criminal Court (2010), available at: <www.amicc.org/docs/kenya_investigations.pdf> (Accessed March 15, 2011).

96 Francis Obinor, *Most Kenyans want violence suspects tried by ICC*, Guardian Newspaper, July 20, 2009.

98 The six include suspended Education Minister William Ruto, Finance Minister Uhuru Kenyatta and Industrialization Minister Henry Kosgey, Secretary to the Cabinet Francis Kirimi Muthaura, former Police Chief Mohammed Hussein Ali and radio executive Joshua Arap Sang.

98 Margaret Kalekye, UNSC Confirms Receiving Kenyan Request for Deferment of ICC Trials, Bernama; March 9, 2010.

international crimes. A programme of legal training, capacity building and judicial cooperation among member states in relation to international crimes and law should be initiated by the AU as recommended by the Meeting of African State Parties to the ICC and the Expert Group on universal jurisdiction.

It must be restated that under the complimentarity principle as provided for in the Rome Statute of the ICC, it is only when states are unwilling or unable to prosecute perpetrators of international crimes that the ICC steps in. African States should learn from the example of Senegal's attempt to try Habre in its domestic court and the legal hurdle of non-retroactivity which formed the basis of the dismissal of the case. Countries must not wait until there is an alleged perpetrator within their jurisdiction before taking steps to enact relevant incorporating legislation. The more the states in Africa with operative incorporating legislation that allows for the trial of perpetrators of international crimes, the smaller the potential place of refuge of such perpetrators. This will serve as a deterrent to future perpetrators. African states are parties to treaties permitting and, in some cases, requiring, the exercise of criminal jurisdiction but provision to operationalize the principle at national level is weak.[99] In addition to the enactment of implementing legislation, African states should promote the expansion and utilization of the principle of universal jurisdiction based on the Cairo-Arusha Principles.

12.7.3 Promoting Better Collaboration between the AU and the ICC

Another important step to promote better relations between the ICC and the AU is to intensify the ongoing dialogue between both institutions and hasten the approval and implementation of the proposal for the ICC to open a liaison office with the AU in Addis Ababa. The African Union's decision to reject for now, the proposal for the establishment of the liaison office[100] should be reconsidered. The current relations between the AU and the ICC do not augur well for the credibility of the Court in Africa.

Unfortunately, rather than improving, it appears to be deteriorating. In its recent summits in Kampala[101] and Addis Ababa,[102] the AU reiterated its earlier resolutions relating to the ICC, the trial of Hissene Habre and the exercise of universal jurisdiction. Indeed, the

99 International Refugee Rights Initiative, *In the Interests of Justice? Prospects and Challenges for International Justice in Africa* 62 (2008).

100 Decision on the Progress Report of the Commission on the Implementation of Decision Assembly/AU/DEC 270(XIV) on the Second Ministerial Meeting on the Rome Statute of the International Criminal Court (ICC) Doc. Assembly/AU/10/XV Adopted by the Fifteenth Ordinary Session of the Assembly of the Union, July 27, 2010, Kampala, Uganda.

101 Fifteenth Ordinary Session of the Assembly of the African Union, July 25-27, 2010.

102 Sixteenth Ordinary Session of the Assembly of the African Union, January 30-31, 2011.

Assembly expressed concern over the conduct of the ICC Prosecutor, Mr. Moreno Ocampo who has been making egregiously unacceptable and condescending statements on the case of President Hassan Omar El-Bashir of The Sudan and other situations in Africa.[103] The African Union also expressed deep regrets over the decision of the Pre-trial chamber 1 of the ICC informing the UN Security Council and the Assembly of the State Parties to the Rome Statute about the visit of President Omar El-Bashir of the Sudan to the Republic of Chad and the Republic of Kenya on July 21 and August 27 respectively.[104] The AU endorsed Kenya's request for a deferral of the ICC investigations and prosecutions in relation to the 2008 post election violence under Article 16 of the Rome Statute to allow for a National Mechanism to investigate and prosecute the cases under a reformed judiciary provided for in the new constitutional dispensation, in line with the principle of complementarity.[105]

It has to be noted that the reliance placed on Article 16 by the African Union in requesting for a deferral of investigation or prosecution by the ICC in the Kenyan situations is misconceived. Article 16 empowers the UN Security Council to defer investigations for twelve months to "maintain or restore in international peace and security" but not as a measure to allow states to put in place national mechanisms with a view to fulfilling their obligation to prosecute under the complementarity principle of the Rome Statute. While national trials are not a basis for an Article 16 deferral, they could form the basis of an admissibility challenge under article 19 of the Rome Statute.[106] Article 19 provides the Kenyan government with the right to challenge the admissibility of a case on the basis that it is already being investigated and/or prosecuted in Kenya. This is distinct from deferral under Article 16, and is made to the Court, not the Security Council.[107]

The ICC on the other hand needs to ensure that the quest for justice should as much as possible take into consideration the interests of enthroning lasting peace in societies that have experienced some form of conflict. As a learned commentator has stated, criminal prosecutions has become such an overwhelming objective that the tribunals appear to have abandoned the broader and more grandiose ambition of "contributing to national reconciliation and the restoration and maintenance of peace."[108] He argues that the objectives of using criminal prosecution to reestablish social equilibrium and promote reconciliation,

103 Assembly/AU/Dec.296(XV), at 2.

104 Chad and Kenya are the only State Parties to the Rome Statute that President Bashir has visited since his indictment by the International Criminal Court.

105 Coalition for an Effective African Court on Human and Peoples' Rights, Background to the African Court, *supra* note 76.

106 Human Rights Watch, Africa: Countries Should Reconsider Support for the Deferral of Kenya's ICC Investigations (2011), available at: <http://allafrica.com/stories/201103030164html> (Accessed March 15, 2011).

107 *Id.*

108 Okechukwu Oko, *The Challenges of International Criminal Prosecutions in Africa*, 31 Fordham International Law Journal. 349 (2008).

though laudable and rhetorically inspiring, are simply unattainable.[109] The hope that international criminal prosecutions will reconcile mutually distrusting ethnic groups with a long history of reciprocal antagonism is quaint, perhaps even naïve. He concludes by further stating that, "international criminal prosecutions launched in Africa, amid much publicity and high expectations are on the verge of irrelevance. After more than ten years of international criminal prosecutions in Africa, it is becoming increasingly obvious that criminal prosecution is a weak reed on which to hoist the strategy of reestablishing social equilibrium and reconciling intergroup hostilities in post conflict African societies".[110]

To assert or assume, that the pursuit of justice equals peace is to adopt a simplistic approach to a complex problem. The Court should seek to build understanding and ownership of its activities and focus on building local capacity to advance positive complementarity, since overall; it can only handle the very high profile cases, leaving the national systems to deal with those that bear lesser responsibility for international crimes. The ICC must also evolve a mechanism for the receipt and consideration of local input[111] prior to the issuance of indictments and commencement of prosecutions and must develop a plan of how to promote enduring peace and reconciliation, beyond prosecutions.

12.7.4 Prospects of an African Alternative to the ICC

The mandate given to the AU Commission to work in collaboration with the African Commission on Human and Peoples' Rights and the African Court on Human and Peoples' Rights and consider the possibility of conferring jurisdiction for international crimes on the Court is still outstanding. Besides the legal and practical problems facing such a proposition, it is worthy to note that international criminal trials are special trials that require seasoned and well trained prosecutors and judges. Without any intention of being disrespectful, it is doubtful if the Court as presently constituted will be in a position to undertake the nature of criminal trials envisaged. The AU must however show that the intended aim of conferring criminal jurisdiction on the court is not to allow perpetrators of such crimes to avoid being called to account. Assuming that the proposal is pursued, a condition precedent shall be the universal ratification of the new or amended protocol by all member states of the African Union, so that no State or individual will seek to avoid the hands of justice on the ground that they are not party to the treaty that established the court nor confers it with criminal jurisdiction.

109 Okechukwu Oko, *The Limits of Prosecution, in* Debating International Justice in Africa, Oxford Transitional Justice Research Collected Essays, 21-23 (2008/2010).

110 *Id.*

111 This includes the societal norms, principles and mechanisms for dealing with deviant behavior of the worst nature and must not necessarily be sourced through the government since, as we have seen from the Sudan and Kenyan indictments, perpetrators are people holding high positions in government.

However, I do not see conferring criminal jurisdiction on the existing African Court as the only viable and principled response to the problems facing international justice and the fight against impunity in Africa. As a legal proposition, such a regional Court confronts an insurmountable risk of being incompatible with the norms and standards of the Constitutive Act of the African Union and of the UN Charter.[112]An extension of the jurisdiction of the Court would create a regional African exceptionalism to international criminal law and international justice, ultimately damaging the credibility and effectiveness of Africa's regional human rights system. In the space between an African exceptionalism and an ineffectual regional system, an African impunity gap could become institutionalized, rendering international criminal law irrelevant to Africa. This outcome is both undesirable and avoidable.[113] There is a serious risk that the creation of a regional criminal court by and for African countries will undermine effective accountability for international crimes in Africa, erode existing norms, institute a corrosive system of forum shopping for international crimes, prevent Africa's regional human rights system from fulfilling its potential, and derail the protection of human rights in Africa. Far from contributing to effective accountability for international crimes, such a regional criminal court would preclude accountability in any form.[114] The timing of the new quest to confer criminal jurisdiction on the African Court following the indictment of Bashir by the ICC, and the fact that the proposal had earlier been made to the African Union but was rejected[115] raises serious questions as to the underlying motives for the action.

12.7.5 *Building on the Legacies of the ICTR*

As the International Criminal Tribunal for Rwanda prepares to wind up operations, the AU should be proactive in preserving the legacies of the tribunal and negotiate with the United Nations with a view to utilizing the human and infrastructural resources that

112 Implications of the African Court on Human and Peoples' Rights Being Empowered to try International Crimes such as Genocide, Crimes Against Humanity, and War Crimes, An opinion submitted in response to the decision of the Assembly of Heads of State and Government of the African Union requiring the African Union Commission in collaboration with the African Commission on Human and Peoples' Rights and the African Court on Human and Peoples' Rights to consider the possibility of conferring criminal jurisdiction over international crimes on the Court. The following organizations authored this submission: Coalition for an Effective African Court on Human and Peoples' Rights (CAEC); Darfur Consortium; East African Law Society (EALS); International Criminal Law Centre of the Open University of Tanzania (ICLC); Open Society Justice Initiative; Pan-African Lawyers Union (PALU); Southern Africa Litigation Centre (SALC) and West African Bar Association (WABA) at 5.

113 *Id.* at 21.

114 *Id.* at 22.

115 The proposal to confer criminal jurisdiction on the merged courts was made by the Working Group on the Draft Single Instrument Relating to the Merger of the African Court on Human and Peoples' Rights and the Court of Justice of the African Union.

has served the ICTR for the benefit of its member states. Indeed with proper engagement with the ICC and the United Nations, the facilities of the ICTR may be transformed into a chamber of the ICC to undertake trials of cases arising from Africa and reduce costs associated with moving victims, suspects and witnesses to The Hague. It could become a vehicle for the advancement of positive complementarity by the ICC.

12.7.6 Prompt Trial of Hissein Habre

The African Union should strive to ensure that the trial of Hissene Habre by an ad hoc international tribunal as recommended by the ECOWAS Court is carried out timely, with all the guarantees of a free and fair trial. Lack of funds had been the reason for the undue delay in commencing the trial of Habre. Now that the funds have been secured, any further delay will question the sincerity and genuine desire of the African Union to bring Habre to trial. This test case will show the world that when the occasion arises, Africa is not only committed to fighting impunity, but can also try any citizen of member states that are accused of any of the international crimes.

The AU Assembly Resolution requesting the Commission to undertake consultations with the government of Senegal in order to finalize the modalities for the expeditious trial of Hissene Habre through a special tribunal with an international character consistent with the Economic Community of West African States (ECOWAS) Court of Justice Decision[116] must be followed up with concrete action. However, uncertainty in this regard remains with the likelihood of Rwanda serving as the new host of the Habre trial. Whatever the case, the important thing is that Habre needs to be brought to trial for the credibility of the AU's supposed stand against impunity.

12.7.7 The Responsibility to Protect

Genocide, war crimes and crimes against humanity are grave international crimes. When they are about to be committed, or are actually being committed anywhere in Africa, the African Union as an institution should intervene and live up to its commitment to fight impunity. This would be in line with the provisions of Article 4(h) of its Constitutive Act. One way to realize this commitment is to rely on an emerging concept in international norms called 'The Responsibility to Protect' – the idea that sovereign states have a responsibility to protect their own citizens from avoidable catastrophe – from mass murder and rape, from starvation – but that when they are unwilling to do so, that responsibility

116 Decision on the *Hissene Habre Case*, Doc.Assembly/AU/9(XVI).

must be borne by the broader community of states.[117] This norm sets out the principles relating to humanitarian intervention. The development of this norm can be traced to the ethnic cleansing committed by the Serb Army against the Muslim Albanian population in Kosovo. According to Richard Goldstone,

> [t]he NATO powers felt obliged to intervene. A threatened veto by the Russian Federation resulted in the NATO powers using military force without the authority of a resolution of the Security Council. It was thus in violation of the United Nations Charter and illegal. The intervention was for one purpose only – a humanitarian effort to save the lives and property of victims. There was no ulterior motive. The global community generally approved of that intervention. When after the military campaign was over, Russia proposed a Security Council resolution to condemn the intervention, it was overwhelmingly defeated in a vote of 13 to 2. The problem that remained was a gap between international law that made the intervention illegal and the morality of protecting innocent people from war crimes perpetrated by a foreign government.[118]

There are five guidelines or criteria that must be met before an intervention can be regarded as legitimate. They are: Is the harm sufficiently serious to justify the use of military force? In the case of internal threats, does it involve genocide and other large-scale killing, ethnic cleansing, or serious violations of international humanitarian law, actual or imminently apprehended? Is it clear that the primary purpose of the proposed military action is to stop or avert the threat? Has every non-military option for meeting the threat been explored, with reasonable grounds for believing that other measures will not succeed? Are the scale, duration and intensity of the proposed military action the minimum necessary to meet the threat? Finally, is there a reasonable chance of the military action being successful in meeting the threat with the consequences of action not likely to be worse than the consequences of inaction?[119]

Despite the "total rejection of impunity" which has been embraced at the political level by the AU Assembly, the lack of condemnation of serious violations of human rights on the continent and the continued escalation of conflicts and instability call into question the real commitment of African leaders.[120] Several African States have been at the forefront

117 The Responsibility to Protect: Report of the International Commission on Intervention and State Sovereignty, VII.

118 Richard J. Goldstone, *Preventing and Prosecuting Crimes Against Humanity in the 21st Century*, at 6-7; Distinguished Lecture on Human Rights and International Justice, Organized by The John D. & Catherine T. MacArthur Foundation; February 14, 2005, Abuja, Nigeria.

119 *Id.* at 8.

120 International Refugee Rights Initiative, *supra* note 96.

in dealing with impunity. But while we can cite many good examples, we cannot continue to defend states who fail to protect citizens. Instead the AU must work more effectively to enforce accountability; it should translate its declarations on the fight against impunity into concrete actions that result in the protection of Africa's citizens.[121]

The adoption and implementation of this norm by the AU will ensure that citizens of African States are protected from these crimes when they are being committed by the government and highly placed state officials, as has happened in the past; or when the government fails to protect its citizens. The mobilization of the proposed African Union Standby Force will be important in the application of this norm when the need arises.

In summary, besides the adoption and implementation of the responsibility to protect norm, the African Union needs to strengthen existing mechanisms for the promotion and protection of human rights in Africa, including cases of gross human rights violations – a prelude to international crimes. This it can achieve through adequate budgetary provisions for the institutions charged with such mandate, establishing and effectuating mechanisms for state compliance with the provisions of human rights instruments and positively reaffirming its commitment to fight impunity in accordance with its Constitutive Act. Another important step would be for the African Union to improve the level of compliance by member states with the decisions of these regional and sub regional human rights mechanisms. The development and implementation of a capacity building programme aimed at strengthening the legal and law enforcement capacity of national jurisdictions to deal with international crimes will go a long way in addressing the concerns facing international justice in Africa.

It is possible to envisage a future without mass atrocities in Africa, and, indeed, a future in which there is no need for a regional or international court to try international crimes in Africa, because effective national and regional mechanisms of justice exist on the continent.[122]

It is hoped that we can truly say 'never again' will mass atrocities like the ones in Rwanda, Burundi, Sierra Leone, Congo, Liberia, Uganda and Darfur, be allowed to occur in Africa, and, if, and when they occur, the perpetrators will surely be accountable for their deeds under capable national jurisdictions or through international justice mechanisms, if the national jurisdictions are unable or unwilling to deliver justice to victims and perpetrators of international crimes alike as well as the communities whose societal norms have been desecrated by the gravity of the crimes committed.

121 Comfort Ero, *supra* note 57, at 14.
122 *Supra* note 108, at 23.

13 The African Union High-Level Panel on Darfur

*A Precedent for Regional Solutions to the Challenges Facing International Criminal Justice?**

Lutz Oette

13.1 Introduction

Responses to the arrest warrant issued by the International Criminal Court (ICC) against Sudan's President Omar al-Bashir in early 2009, coming amidst growing resentment over the exercise of universal jurisdiction against African leaders, have brought in sharp relief the mounting unease with, if not outright opposition to the use of international criminal justice mechanisms in Africa. This is emblematic of a wider soul-searching concerning the utility, fairness and future course of international criminal justice, which has dampened the enthusiasm that marked the heydays of the Rome Conference (1998) and the coming into force of the Rome Statute (2002). The mismatch between great expectations and limited success coupled with institutional weaknesses is not entirely surprising for a relatively young institution such as the ICC. However, developments over the last decade have given rise to more fundamental challenges that call into question both the theoretical underpinnings of international criminal law and the still rather fragile architecture of its institutions. The conceptual challenge concerns the adequacy of giving primacy to a criminal law approach in response to mass crimes. This is particularly pronounced in the course of armed conflicts in the African context, as exemplified in the debates about peace, justice and reconciliation in respect of Northern Uganda, Darfur and beyond.[1] The institutional challenge concerns the nature, role and politics of bodies tasked with applying international criminal law and advancing international criminal justice. The ability of the ICC effectively to prosecute serious international crimes without political interference or bias is of critical importance in this regard as many states, particularly in Africa, preferred the ICC to other mechanisms such as ad-hoc tribunals and to the exercise of universal jurisdiction, which were seen as limited or susceptible to unfair targeting of weaker states.

* The opinions expressed in this article are those of the author alone.

1 See in particular Payam Akhavan, *Are International Criminal Tribunals A Disincentive To Peace?: Reconciling Judicial Romanticism With Political Realism*, 31 Human Rights Quarterly 624 (2009).

The African Union (AU) High-Level Panel on Darfur (AUPD), which was set up as part of the AU's call to defer the al-Bashir case pursuant to Article 16 of the Rome Statute and tasked with recommending what should be done in the Darfur situation,[2] constitutes a critical test case for the AU to demonstrate its ability to fashion viable regional responses to international crimes. This chapter examines how the AUPD has addressed the conceptual and institutional challenges identified above and to what degree it has contributed to developing an 'African' approach to international criminal justice. To this end, it considers the AUPD's report and recommendations, with a particular focus on the objectives of justice and reconciliation. This is accompanied by an examination of the AU's role in the process of defining the AUPD's mandate, supporting its work and overseeing implementation of its recommendations, which is also with a view to determining whether an AUPD-type approach can serve as a model in other situations characterized by the commission of international crimes.

13.2 Conceptual and Institutional Challenges Concerning International Criminal Justice in Africa

Re-reading the statements made by the African delegates on the occasion of the adoption of the Rome Statute in 1998 is a rather strange experience. It is at once exhilarating and deflating, recalling the collective pride and enthusiasm of having contributed to the establishment of a historic institution and highlighting a sense of disillusionment with international criminal justice thirteen years on. African delegates at the Rome Conference stressed the need for a strong and independent institution capable of combating impunity effectively with a view to preventing mass atrocities such as those committed in Rwanda or Sierra Leone in the 1990s.[3] These delegates also emphasized the principles of the ICC's universality and complementarity as prerequisites for its effective functioning.[4] This included the Organisation of African Unity (OAU), the AU's predecessor, which lent its support to the ICC.[5] Notably, one searches in vain for any reference to, let alone preference for regional mechanisms. Many

2 African Union, Peace and Security Council, Decision PSC/MN/Comm(CXLII), *Communiqué of the 142nd Meeting* (July 21, 2008).

3 See in particular statements at the Rome Conference by Dr. A.M. Omar, Minister of Justice, Republic of South Africa on behalf of the Southern African Development Community (SADC) (June 15, 1998); S.E. Jacques Baudin, Minister of Justice, Republic of Senegal (June 16, 1998); Hon. S. Amos Wako, Attorney-General of the Republic of Kenya (June 16, 1998); Mr. Mothusi Nkgowe, Minister/Deputy Permanent Representative of Botswana (June 18, 1998); and H.E. Mr. Vincent Kirabokyamaria, Uganda Republic Ambassador to Italy (June 18, 1998). See also statement by Tiyanjana Maluwa, OAU Legal Counsel (June 17, 1998). See <www.un.org/icc/index.htm> (Accessed on November 22, 2011).

4 Id. See also the statements by H.E. Aanaa Naamua Enin, Ambassador to Italy of the Republic of Ghana (June 16, 1998) and Maitre Ruberwa Manywa, Cabinet Director of the Ministry of Foreign Affairs, Democratic Republic of Congo (June 18, 1998).

5 See statement by Tiyanjana Maluwa, OAU Legal Counsel (June 17, 1998) *id.*

African states subsequently became parties to the Rome Statute and African nationals are well-represented in the court's structure.[6] This account, which demonstrates the significant contribution made by African states to the ICC, raises the question of what happened since, or, from the standpoint of an ICC advocate, of what went wrong.

The parallel but interrelated challenges to the conceptual foundations and institutional workings of international criminal justice may provide an explanation. First, the rationale of international criminal law has been called into question, namely that the prosecution of individuals for serious large-scale crimes by international institutions representing the 'international community' will act as deterrent, provide justice to victims and contribute to peace.[7] The fact that international prosecutions target few individuals for mass crimes, instead of focusing on the collective nature of events, is seen to account for the perceived inadequacy of the current model and its limited apparent deterrent effect.[8] This is arguably particularly pronounced in the African context and doubts have been expressed as to whether the paradigm of prosecuting a selected number of individuals for international crimes bearing the greatest responsibility is best suited in such circumstances.

The nature of conflicts and African modes of justice and reconciliation have been invoked to argue that 'international criminal tribunals based on Western notions of justice' are inadequate[9] if not altogether counterproductive because they 'can do very little to re-establish social equilibrium and arrest the advancing decrepitude threatening to engulf Africa'.[10] This reasoning implies that retributive justice is out of place in the African context.[11]

---

6 33 out of 119 ICC states parties were from Africa and five out of the eighteen ICC judges were Africans as of November 2011. See <www.icc-cpi.int/Menus/ASP/states+parties/> and <www.icc-cpi.int/Menus/ICC/Structure+of+the+Court/> (Accessed on 22 November 2011). See for an account of Africa's contribution to the ICC, Max Du Plessis, *The International Criminal Court and its work in Africa: Confronting the Myths*, Institute of Strategic Studies Paper 173, (November 2008) 3-5.

7 See Mark A. Drumbl, *A Hard Look at the Soft Theory of International Criminal Law*, *in* L.N. Sadat & M.P. Scharf (eds.), THE THEORY AND PRACTICE OF INTERNATIONAL CRIMINAL LAW, ESSAYS IN HONOR OF M. CHERIF BASSIOUNI 1-18 (2008), and Kenneth A. Rodman, *Darfur And the Limits of Legal Deterrence*, 30 HUMAN RIGHTS QUARTERLY 529-560 (2008).

8 Drumbl, *supra* note 7 at, 14-15.

9 Tim Kelsall, *International Criminal Justice and Non-Western Cultures*, Oxford Transitional Justice Research Working Paper Series: *International Criminal Justice in Africa* (April 12, 2010), available at <www.csls.ox.ac.uk/documents/Kelsall_InternationalCriminalJustice_Final.pdf> (Accessed November 22, 2011), argues that the basic doctrines, jurisprudence and procedure of international criminal justice are of Western origin. As a consequence, 'this can cause problems when the jurisprudence has a poor sociological fit', *e.g.* in relation to the principle of command responsibility, and is seen as alien in the African context, in particular adversarial proceedings.

10 Okechukwu Oko, *The Challenges of International Criminal Prosecutions in Africa*, 31 FORDHAM INTERNATIONAL LAW JOURNAL 343, 354 (2007-2008).

11 For a critique of this view, see Godfrey M. Musila, *In the Face of Impunity, We Play Politics with International Criminal Tribunals*, INSTITUTE FOR SECURITY STUDIES (8 August 2008): "...it is not true that retributive justice – punishment of offenders – is alien to African notions of justice".

Rwandan and Ugandan responses to mass crimes, including recourse to 'traditional' methods of justice, namely Gacaca and Mato Oput respectively, have triggered debates about the need for indigenous approaches to mass crimes that address violations within the local environment.[12] While some herald the preference for local mechanisms with an emphasis on reconciliation as evidence of genuine or 'African' solutions, others have pointed to the risk of political manipulation and lack of adequate accountability.[13]

Second, there are growing concerns over the legitimacy and efficacy of international institutions tasked with prosecuting international crimes, in particular the ICC. The ICC was based on a collective understanding, which relies on a division of labour between national systems and the international body known as complementarity that gives primacy to national investigations and prosecutions.[14] This system is characterized by its simultaneous affirmation of the universality of international criminal law and the upholding of state sovereignty.

The interplay between national and international prosecutions in the Rome Statute differs from the exercise of universal jurisdiction, *i.e.* the principle that some crimes are of such an egregious nature that all states have an interest in prosecuting, if not a duty to prosecute suspects before their national courts irrespective of where and by or against whom the crime was committed.[15] The application of this principle in a series of cases against African officials over the last decade has fuelled perceptions that international criminal law serves as a tool used by strong states against weaker states or entities, which has been portrayed as having neo-colonial overtones.[16] The AU has taken up the issue at an institutional level by rejecting the 'abuse' of universal jurisdiction,[17] while stressing its

12 See Luc Huyse & Mark Salter (eds. 2007), TRADITIONAL JUSTICE AND RECONCILIATION AFTER CONFLICT: LEARNING FROM AFRICAN EXAMPLES. See for a critical account, T. Allen, *Ritual (Ab)use? Problems with Traditional Justice in Northern Uganda, in* COURTING CONFLICT? JUSTICE, PEACE AND THE ICC IN AFRICA 47-54 (Nicholas Waddell & Phil Clark eds., 2008)

13 Compare, for example, MAHMOOD MAMDANI, SAVIORS AND SURVIVORS: DARFUR, POLITICS AND THE WAR ON TERROR 282-288 (2009); and Comfort Ero, *Understanding Africa's Position on the International Criminal Court*, Oxford Transitional Justice Research Working Paper Series: International Criminal Justice in Africa, (April 10, 2010), available at <www.csls.ox.ac.uk/documents/Ero_Africas_PositionFinalOTJR.pdf> (Accessed November 22, 2011) as well as Musila, *supra* note 11.

14 See Markus Benzing, *The Complementarity Regime of the International Criminal Court: International Criminal Justice between State Sovereignty and the Fight against Impunity, in* 7 MAX PLANCK UNITED NATIONS YEARBOOK, 591-632 (A. von Bogdandy & R. Wolfrum eds., 2003).

15 See Luis Angel Benavides, *The Universal Jurisdiction Principle: Nature and Scope*, 1 ANNUARIO MEXICANO DE DERECHO INTERNACIONAL 19-96 (2001).

16 COUNCIL OF EUROPE, THE AU-EU EXPERT REPORT ON THE PRINCIPLE OF UNIVERSAL JURISDICTION (April 16, 2009) Doc. 8672/09, para.37.

17 Assembly of the African Union, 'Decision on the Report of the Commission on the Abuse of the Principle of Universal Jurisdiction', Doc EX.CL/411 (XIII) (June 30 and July 1, 2008) and 'Decision on the Abuse of the Principle of Universal Jurisdiction', Assembly/AU/Dec. 240 (XII) (February 4, 2009).

commitment to accountability and justice for international crimes with reference to the AU Constitutive Act.[18] Implicit in this opposition to universal jurisdiction is the perceived bias of international criminal justice, particularly if exercised unilaterally.

This perception was initially primarily confined to universal jurisdiction and ad-hoc tribunals but now appears to have also engulfed the ICC. Several factors have contributed to this development. All seven ICC situations to date concern African countries while the ICC has not yet investigated situations elsewhere that have been characterized by allegations of international crimes, which includes measures taken in the post 9/11 context. The first instance in which the UN Security Council referred a situation to the ICC Office of the Prosecutor (OTP) concerned an African country, namely Darfur/Sudan (which was later followed by Libya).[19] This has reinforced views that international criminal law and its institutions are predominantly employed against states that are weak and have limited support.[20] These perceptions matter as they undermine the ICC's claim to universality as it is, rightly or wrongly, increasingly associated with Western power interests, turning it into a political instrument rather than an impartial international body.[21] The supposed bias also undermines a central tenet of international criminal law, or indeed any criminal law and the rule of law, namely that like cases are treated alike and that no one should be above the law regardless of his or her position. There is thus a close link between accusations of western notions of justice, institutional bias and the call for alternative African and regional approaches to justice for international crimes.

The debate surrounding the al-Bashir case invites two contrasting readings of the nature of the challenges that international criminal justice poses in the current situation. One position would postulate that universal notions and international mechanisms are Western dominated and detached, and have failed to address key issues in the African context, rendering them inadequate if not ineffective. Such reading may appear surprising in relation to the ICC given that African states had been supportive of the Court and that three

18 *Id.* Art. 4(h) of the AU Constitutive Act provides 'the right of the Union to intervene in a Member State pursuant to a decision of the Assembly in respect of grave circumstances, namely: war crimes, genocide and crimes against humanity'.

19 S/RES/1593 (2005) on Darfur, Sudan, and S/RES/1970 (2011) on Libya.

20 See statement of the Algerian delegate in debates on the referral of the Darfur situation, UN Security Council Verbatim Record, UN Doc. S/PV.5158 (31 March 2005) and O. Oko, *The Limits of Prosecutions*, Oxford Transitional Justice Research Working Paper Series: *International Criminal Justice in Africa*, 10 March 2010, 2, available at <www.csls.ox.ac.uk/documents/Oko_Limits_Final_OTJR.pdf> (Accessed 22 November 2011).

21 See for a brief account of key arguments, A. Branch, *What the ICC Review Conference Can't Fix*, Oxford Transitional Justice Research Working Paper Series: *International Criminal Justice in Africa* (15 March 2010), available at <www.csls.ox.ac.uk/documents/AdamBranchICC_Final.pdf> (Accessed 22 November 2011) and Mamdani, *supra* note 13 at 283, 284.

states have referred situations to the ICC, albeit in some instances apparently following some prodding by the OTP.[22] It would suggest a change in attitude born out of a realisation of the ICC's limits as well as of its politics and conduct in relation to specific situations, especially in the course of ongoing conflict as in Sudan.[23] This change in understanding of international criminal justice in general and the ICC in particular does not necessarily suggest a fundamental challenge to the principles of accountability and justice but questions its impartial use and lack of sensitivity to regional particularities, thus making it potentially more context-specific. The charges against 'Western' bias and imperialism echo the cultural relativism debate in the human rights discourse of the 1990s.[24]

Alternatively, the growing opposition may be read as evidence that international criminal justice and the ICC are becoming, or are threatening to become, more effective. Political leaders have an incentive to forestall any possibility that they would be prosecuted and efforts at the AU level could be interpreted as pre-emptive moves to this end. As in previous debates about the enforcement of international human rights standards, it is not always entirely clear to what degree the current debate reflects genuine concerns and a need for adjustments or a desire to preserve a culture of impunity, at least for political leaders.[25] What is clear is that latest developments have opened up a debate that squarely poses the question of the future course of international criminal justice in Africa, and what forms it should take. The al-Bashir case has presented an opportunity for the AU to take a lead in reflecting on, and implementing suitable regional approaches in response to international crimes falling within the jurisdiction of the ICC. This follows earlier, rather inconclusive efforts to find African ways of holding Hissène Habré accountable that were taken in response to the exercise of universal jurisdiction by European states.[26] The opportunity inherent in these developments is a challenge for the AU both to define the nature of any regional approaches and to demonstrate its capacity to effectively implement measures taken towards this end.

---

22 See in this context Phil Clark, *Law, Politics and Pragmatism: The ICC and Case Selection in the Democratic Republic of Congo and Uganda*, in Waddell & Clark, *supra* note 12 at 37-45.

23 Although, as Ero, *supra* note 13, emphasizes '[t]he continent is composed of fifty-three states whose views on the ICC's role are more varied and complex than is often imagined'.

24 For an account of the Asian values debate, William Twining, General Jurisprudence: Understanding Law From A Global Perspective 198, 199 (2009); and for a critical view at the time, see Ghai Yash, *Asian Perspectives on Human Rights,* 23 Hong Kong Law Journal 342-357 (1993). For a prominent African critique of the human rights discourse, *see* Makau Mutua, *Savages, Victims and Saviors: the Metaphor of Human Rights*, 42 (1) Harvard International Law Journal 201-245 (2001).

25 See for parallels in the Asian values debate, Ghai, Ghai Yash, *Asian Perspectives on Human Rights,* 23 Hong Kong Law Journal 342-357 (1993).

26 See Report of the Committee of Eminent African Jurists on the Case of Hissène Habré, African Union, May 2006.

13.3 THE ROLE OF THE AUPD IN THE DEVELOPMENT OF REGIONAL RESPONSES TO INTERNATIONAL CRIMES

13.3.1 Background

Following the recommendations of the UN Commission of Inquiry on Darfur that had found evidence of war crimes and crimes against humanity, the UN Security Council referred the Darfur situation to the ICC OTP in March 2005.[27] Two years later, the ICC issued arrest warrants against Ahmad Haroun and Ali Kushayb.[28] The Government of Sudan (GoS) refused to cooperate with the ICC on the enforcement of the arrest warrants.[29] Following the OTP's application in June 2008, the ICC's Pre-Trial Chamber I issued an arrest warrant against Sudan's president al-Bashir in March 2009 on counts of crimes against humanity and war crimes. This was complemented by a further arrest warrant on counts of genocide issued in July 2010 following an appeal by the OTP.[30]

The OTP's application triggered an extensive debate that pitted proponents of a criminal justice approach against those arguing that an arrest warrant would be detrimental to the peace process and a political solution to Sudan's problems.[31] Several UN Security Council member states supported a deferral of the al-Bashir case and endorsed the AU's position,[32] which had called for a deferral pursuant to Article 16 of the Rome Statute.[33] The AU proposed a regional solution based on the principle of accountability and reconciliation. In February 2009, the AU Peace and Security Council established the AUPD, which has also been referred to as the Mbeki Panel after its chairman, the former South African President Thabo Mbeki. The AUPD was given a broad mandate to 'examine the situation in depth

27 Report of the International Commission of Inquiry on Darfur to the United Nations Secretary-General pursuant to Security Council resolution 1564 of 18 September 2004 (25 January 2005), para. 573; UNSC Resolution 1593 (March 31, 2005).

28 See *The Prosecutor v. Ahmad Muhammad Harun ("Ahmad Harun") and Ali Muhammad Ali Abd-Al-Rahman ("Ali Kushayb")*, Warrant of Arrest for Ahmad Harun, ICC-02/05-01/07-2 (27 April 2007), and Warrant of Arrest for Ali Kushayb, ICC-02/05-01/07-3 (April 27, 2007).

29 See *The Prosecutor v. Ahmad Muhammad Harun ("Ahmad Harun") and Ali Muhammad Ali Abd-Al-Rahman ("Ali Kushayb")*, Decision informing the United Nations Security Council about the lack of cooperation by the Republic of the Sudan, ICC-02/05-01/07 (23 May 2010).

30 Second Warrant of Arrest against Omar Hassan Ahmad Al Bashir, *Case of the Prosecutor v. Omar Hassan Ahmad Al Bashir* (ICC-02/05-01/09), Pre-Trial Chamber (July 12, 2010).

31 See Lutz Oette, *Peace and justice, or neither? The repercussions of the al-Bashir case for international criminal justice in Africa and beyond*, 8(2) JOURNAL OF INTERNATIONAL CRIMINAL JUSTICE 345-364 (2010).

32 *Id.*

33 Art. 16 of the Rome Statute reads: 'No investigation or prosecution may be commenced or proceeded with under this Statute for a period of 12 months after the Security Council, in a resolution adopted under Chapter VII of the Charter of the United Nations, has requested the Court to that effect; that request may be renewed by the Council under the same conditions'.

and submit recommendations to Council on how best the issues of accountability and combating impunity, on the one hand, and reconciliation and healing, on the other, could be effectively addressed'.[34] The mandate was to be carried out '...with the active involvement of the AU and its relevant institutions and, as necessary, the support of the larger international community'.[35]

13.3.2 *Approach*

The AUPD was the first body of its kind tasked with developing AU-led responses to international crimes under investigation by the ICC. It took a broad view of the nature of the conflict, which it located in the national context and called the 'Sudanese crisis in Darfur'.[36] It attributed the conflict to a pattern of 'a weak and divided periphery subordinated to a powerful centre', with Darfur, which had been an independent Sultanate until 1916,[37] becoming economically and politically marginalized following its incorporation into Sudan.[38] This is part of a broader structure that reflects a failure of 'successive governments in the independence era... to ...transform Sudan into a nation in which all its citizens equally feel a shared sense of pride and belonging'.[39] Land conflicts, environmental factors, the breakdown of law and order and the proliferation of small arms have resulted in tens of thousands of violent deaths at the height of the crisis, large-scale rape, war crimes and other international crimes, a humanitarian crisis characterized by mass displacement and impoverishment, and the collapse of the social fabric in Darfur.[40]

The Panel undertook its work from March to September 2009 and organized, *inter alia*, several public meetings in Darfur and Khartoum that were attended by a large number of persons to discuss the issues falling within its mandate.[41] Its consultative and participatory approach was widely commended for providing the opportunity for a large number of Sudanese and other stakeholders to share their views on peace, justice and reconciliation.[42] Considering that the AUPD carried out its mandate in a challenging and highly

---

34 African Union, Peace and Security Council, Decision PSC/MN/Comm(CXLII), *Communiqué of the 142nd Meeting* (July 21, 2008). See on the AUPD's mandate *Darfur: The Quest for Peace, Justice and Reconciliation*, Report of the African Union High-Level Panel on Darfur (AUPD), PSC/AHG/2 (CCVII) (October 29, 2009) 1, 2.
35 Report of AUPD *supra* note 34 at 1-2, para. 3.
36 *Id.* at para. 9.
37 See R.S. O'FAHEY, THE DARFUR SULTANATE: A HISTORY (2008).
38 AUPD Report *supra* note 34 at 13, para. 55.
39 *Id.* at para. 48.
40 *Id.* at 14-28.
41 *Id.* at 5-6 paras 19, 20.
42 *Id.* 5-8, paras 19-35.

politicized situation, its successful approach was itself a notable achievement that may serve as model for AU responses in similar situations.

13.3.3 *Vision of Panel*

The AUPD stressed the interrelationship between accountability and reconciliation as well as their instrumental link to peace.[43] It took a nuanced approach to the question of accountability by stressing its importance as a means to provide justice and establish the rule of law while situating any measures taken towards these ends in the broader context of the peace process.[44] In so doing, it complemented a pure criminal law paradigm with reconciliation and measures to address the socio-economic causes of conflict and violations. It also emphasized 'democratic governance' as a 'crucial fourth component to the Panel's vision',[45] implying that the three other objectives cannot be achieved without a parallel political transformation. The proposed solution is informed by a holistic understanding that reflects current approaches to post-conflict justice.[46] As such, it constitutes a familiar combination of measures adjusted to the particulars of the situation. The actors involved, the approach taken and the recommended action have given the process a regional imprimatur that highlights the importance of adopting a contextual response to the Darfur crisis in Sudan.

13.3.4 *Notion of Justice and Reconciliation*

The AUPD used the terms justice and reconciliation throughout its report without setting out its own definitions thereof. Instead, in line with its overall approach of promoting ownership, it was guided by the Sudanese stakeholders' understanding of these concepts.[47] The Panel noted that 'although they frequently prefaced their positions with support for international justice, the people of Darfur demonstrated a varied and rich understanding of justice and reconciliation. Their most immediate demand was for protection and security guarantees, followed by a political settlement that can lead to an equitable distribution of wealth, development, the rule of law and a political system that gives them a significant say over their own affairs within Darfur'.[48] Its findings were that no 'single conception of

43 *Id.* at 3, para. 10.
44 *Id.* xv-xvii, paras 12, 16-20, 88 and 317-319.
45 *Id.* 3, para. 11.
46 See for example Naomi Roht-Arriaza & Javier Mariezcurrena, Transitional Justice in the Twenty-First Century: Beyond Truth Versus Justice (eds. 2006).
47 AUPD Report, note 34 above, 51, para. 202.
48 *Id.* 51, 52, para. 203.

justice' can meet the needs expressed.[49] Significantly, the AUPD found that Darfurians 'like other Sudanese the Panel spoke with, demonstrated their comfort with the pluralism of their legal heritage, drawing on their traditional culture, religious jurisprudence, while calling for sound, reliable and independent formal institutions of justice'.[50]

The AUPD was similarly cautious to avoid a particular definition of reconciliation. Instead, it argued that 'reconciliation, the term used to describe the process of helping communities overcome grief, anger, animosity and mistrust, and achieve healing, is seen as the key to renewing and strengthening social relations and the foundation for durable peace. But its meaning is elastic...Security, truth, justice, reparations, the absence of discriminatory practices, acknowledgment, remorse and forgiveness are commonly regarded as essential prerequisites...'[51]

As a result of its consultations, the AUPD drew the conclusion that 'an outcome which would promote national justice and reconciliation proceedings is therefore required. Its principal goal would be to give the people of Darfur access to a credible, comprehensive and coherent system of justice within their own country, implemented in close consultations with Darfurians and Sudanese more generally, and Sudan's partners, including the [AU]. Criminal justice will play an important role, but not an exclusive one, and must be underpinned by procedures that allow meaningful participation of victims, as well as reparations and other acts of conciliation'.[52] The way in which the AUPD formulated this goal reflects its process-oriented approach, which it favoured over ascribing fixed meanings to the notions of justice and reconciliation.

13.3.5 *Justice and Accountability*

The AUPD navigated a delicate course when considering appropriate mechanisms to hold accountable those suspected of having committed international crimes in Darfur. It recognized the role of the ICC but downplayed its significance,[53] stressing the importance of complementarity and national criminal justice mechanisms.[54] In its

49 Such justice includes 'provision of security and the rule of law, through measures such as disarming the militia, an end to predatory policing, and the need for security agencies that act in their collective interests'. *Ibid.*

50 *Id.*

51 *Id.* 72, para. 260.

52 *Id.* 52, para. 205.

53 *Id.* 65, 66, paras 244, 245 and 93, para. 339.

54 *Id.* xix, paras 25; 69, paras 255; 91, 92, and 336.

recommendations, the AUPD emphasized that justice and reconciliation should be pursued in an integrated and coordinated manner.[55] According to the AUPD, the people of Darfur 'understand "justice" broadly to encompass processes of achieving equality, obtaining compensation and restitution, establishing the rule of law, as well as criminal justice. They will therefore expect a package of interventions which deal with all these aspects of justice, and which do not prefer any one measure above the other'.[56] As a result, the AUPD proposed a series of measures consisting of legislative reforms, capacity building, and the setting up and strengthening of adequate mechanisms.[57] These mechanisms consist of traditional justice mechanisms, the Special Courts and a proposed Hybrid Court, all of which are considered to play an important and interrelated role in dealing with crimes of differing levels of gravity. The AUPD suggested 'the establishment of a Hybrid Court to deal particularly with the most serious crimes, to be constituted by Sudanese and non-Sudanese judges and senior legal support staff, the latter two groups to be nominated by the African Union'.[58] The rationale for the recommended Hybrid Court, namely that 'faith in [Sudan's] criminal justice system has been severely eroded',[59] is seemingly at odds with the proposal to locate it within the Sudanese legal system instead of establishing such court as an independent entity operating outside the national system, such as the Special Court for Sierra Leone. This proposal appears to reflect a compromise in the approach taken based on the belief in both the transformative impact that the involvement of external actors would entail and the introduction of substantial changes to the Sudanese legal framework needed to make the Hybrid Court effective. The recommendation to strengthen the system of Special Courts raises similar question in light of their poor record to date. In terms of their respective roles, it appears that the Special Courts should be 'the principal forum for delivering criminal justice for crimes relating to the conflict in Darfur'[60] whereas the Hybrid Court 'shall exercise ... jurisdiction over individuals who appear to bear greatest responsibility for the gravest crimes',[61] thus suggesting a degree of complementarity between the two mechanisms. It is noteworthy that the AUPD undertook a detailed study of relevant Sudanese legislation and the state of the judiciary,[62] and proposed specific reforms, such as the removal

55 *Id.* at xix, para. 25, and 88, 89, 317-320.

56 *Id.* at 88, para. 317.

57 *Id.* at xix, para. 25, and 88, 89, para. 320.

58 *Id.* at xix, para. 25(b). See on the hybrid court also 66-69, paras 246-254, and 89-91, paras 322-333.

59 *Id.* at xvi, para. 16. See also 66, para. 246, and 68, para. 252.

60 *Id.* at 88, para. 320 (a).

61 *Id.* at para. 320 (b). See also 68, para. 254.

62 For an analysis of the AUPD's assessment of Sudan's law in respect of two important prerequisites for effective prosecutions for international crimes, namely retroactivity and command responsibility, *see* M.A. Babiker, '*The International Criminal Court and the Darfur crimes: The dilemma of peace and supranational justice*', 5 International Journal of African Renaissance Studies 1, 82, 93-96 (2010).

of immunities for officials.[63] This signifies both the importance accorded to national approaches and the great care taken in showing that Sudan is not viewed as having been capable of prosecuting international crimes committed in Darfur, GoS assertions to the contrary notwithstanding.[64]

13.3.6 *Reconciliation and Reparations*

The AUPD recommended a series of measures to promote reconciliation while emphasising the latter's nexus with justice, in particular in form of acknowledgment of responsibility and reparations.[65] Its functional approach to reparations as part of a broader reconciliation strategy is captured in the AUPD's view according to which 'reparations, including collective and individual compensation for the losses and damages which all affected Darfurians have endured, reconstruction of homes and villages and provision of basic services, are an important part of attending to their economic and psychological needs and their social rehabilitation. They must, therefore, in the view of the Panel, form a key element of strategies for reconciliation'.[66] The AUPD also stressed the need to build on the commitment to provide compensation contained in the Darfur Peace Agreement.[67] However, it failed to equally stress that reparation is a right of victims, the purpose of which is to make good, or undo as much as possible, the harm suffered as a result of a violation.[68] The question of reparations could or even should have equally been addressed under the separate rubric of justice as victims' right to reparation under international law is conceptually different from any reconciliation although it would ideally foster the latter.[69]

The AUPD also stressed the need for socio-economic development to address the causes of conflict.[70] Post-conflict development is important but conflating reparation measures with development measures risks depriving reparations of their specific function of public

63 AUPD Report, *supra* note 34 at xix, para. 25 (c) and (d); 56-63, paras 215-238; and 91, 92, para. 336. In this context see also Mohammed Abdelsalam Babiker, *The Prosecution of International Crimes under Sudan's Criminal and Military Laws: Developments, Gaps and Limitations*, *in* L. Oette (ed.), Criminal Law Reform and Transitional Justice: Human Rights Perspectives for Sudan (2011) 161-181.

64 AUPD Report, *supra* note 34 at 51-71, paras 203-259 and 89, para. 321.

65 *Id.* at 94, para. 341.

66 *Id.* at 75, para. 265.

67 *Id.* at para. 266. On the question of reparations see also International Centre for Transitional Justice, *Reparation and the Darfur Peace Process: Ensuring Victims' Rights* (November 2007).

68 See *id.* See also *Case Concerning the Factory at Chorzów, Claim for Indemnity (Jurisdiction)*, 1927, P.C.I.J., Series A, No. 9, 29.

69 See on the right to reparation in particular 'Basic principles and guidelines on the right to a remedy and reparation for victims of gross violations of international human rights law and serious violations of international humanitarian law', UN General Assembly Resolution 60/147 (UN Doc. No. A/RES/60/147 (2006).

70 AUPD Report, *supra* note 34 at xx, para. 28, and 75, para. 267.

acknowledgment of wrongdoing and vindication for victims.[71] Rightly, the AUPD kept these two elements conceptually distinct while acknowledging their interrelationship.[72]

As the main institutional vehicle for the reconciliation process, the AUPD recommended the 'establishment of a Truth, Justice and Reconciliation Commission (TJRC) to promote truth telling and appropriate acts of reconciliation and to grant pardons as considered suitable'.[73] The TJRC should be 'independent and composed of persons of high moral standing', and should include Darfurians, women and jurists,[74] the latter two presumably to ensure gender representation and legal expertise. Somewhat surprisingly, it did not list other professions or backgrounds that may be of equal value. The TJRC's proposed mandate is broad, including truth-telling and making recommendations on reparations, prevention and reconciliation, and is similar to that of other TJRC's set up recently.[75] The AUPD recommended that the TJRC should have the 'the power to grant pardons to individuals'[76] without specifying the conditions thereof.[77] It thus left one of the defining challenges for such commissions unresolved, namely how to entice perpetrators of serious crimes to come forward without offering them freedom from punishment that may be in contravention of international standards.

13.3.7 *Assessment*

In essence, the AUPD's approach seeks to support contextual and positive complementarity by strengthening the national legal system and processes in Sudan, complemented by AU supported hybrid mechanisms, with an emphasis on both justice and reconciliation. The AUPD's recommendations combine international criminal justice and transitional

71 See Naomi Roht-Arriaza & Katherine Orlovsky, *A Complementary Relationship: Reparations and Development*, *in* PABLO DE GREIFF & ROGER DUTHIE (Eds., 2009) TRANSITIONAL JUSTICE AND DEVELOPMENT: MAKING CONNECTIONS 170-213 (2009). On the functions of reparations in post-conflict societies, see Pablo de Greiff, *Justice and Reparations*, *in* THE HANDBOOK OF REPARATIONS 451-478 (PABLO DE GREIFF ed., 2006).

72 See AUPD Report, *supra* note 34 at xix, xx, paras. 27, 28; 74, 75, 264-267; 95-97, 345(f) and (g); 346, 350 and 351. However, the AUPD's use of 'delivering social and economic justice' for restitution and relocation of Internally Displaced Persons (IDPs) (for example in paras. 95, 96, 346-348) is misleading as these measures are commonly understood to form part of reparations. See in particular 'Basic Principles', note 69 above.

73 *See* AUPD Report, at xix, para. 25(e).

74 *Id.* at 95, para. 345(a).

75 *Id.* at 95, para. 345. Compare, for example, The Truth and Reconciliation Commissions of Liberia, which also includes an explicit gender dimension. See <https://www.trcofliberia.org/> (Accessed November 22, 2011).

76 *See* AUPD Report, *supra* note 34 above, 95, para. 345(e).

77 *Id.* at 76, para. 269: 'To persuade perpetrators to make full and truthful confessions, or to accept responsibility for their crimes, there must be incentives for them to appear before the TRJC and disclose their actions, in order to disown the past and move forward'.

justice approaches in a comprehensive fashion. They provide a remarkable blueprint for a process that seeks to address root causes of conflict and injustices in Sudan. The AUPD's primary achievement to date is to have opened perspectives and opportunities for Sudanese engagement with AU support. However, this very fact means that it carries the risk of promising more than what can be delivered.

13.3.8 Implementation

The AUPD appears to put a lot of faith in a process-oriented approach of implementation to effectuate the transformation needed to ensure lasting peace based on justice and reconciliation. It emphasizes the agency of the 'Sudanese people' in the process, which itself is subject to further negotiations.[78] Such an approach is perhaps inevitable in seeking to find a solution that commands broad national support in Sudan but carries the risk of watering down if not undermining altogether key elements of the AUPD's recommendations. It is already becoming clear that the ultimate success of the process will depend heavily on the political will and commitment of the actors concerned, in particular the GoS. However, recent experiences in Sudan cast doubt on the AUPD's apparent assumption that a comprehensive transformation is not only needed but also possible. This concerns in particular the failure to bring about the 'democratic transformation' envisaged in the Comprehensive Peace Agreement (CPA) between the GoS and the Sudan Peoples' Liberation Movement/Army (SPLM/A)[79] that had ended the armed conflict in the South of Sudan in 2005.[80]

The AUPD contemplated a proactive role for the AU throughout the process, from the initial work of the AUPD to the implementation of its recommendations by the AU High Level Implementation Panel (hereinafter AUHLIP) that has been established for that purpose.[81] This constitutes a major test that will have repercussions for future interventions, namely to demonstrate the AU's capacity to effectively engage with a recalcitrant state as part of a broader political process. The difficulties of this process have already become apparent. The

78 In form of the Global Political Agreement mentioned throughout the AUPD Report and being negotiated at the time of writing.

79 See the Chapeau of the Comprehensive Peace Agreement: 'The Parties further acknowledge that the successful implementation of the CPA shall provide a model for good governance in the Sudan that will help create a solid basis to preserve peace and make unity attractive and therefore undertake to fully adhere to the letter and spirit of the CPA so as to guarantee lasting peace, security for all, justice and equality in the Sudan'.

80 See on the CPA, S. Basha, '*The Comprehensive Peace Agreement – A Synopsis*', *in* B. Raftopoulos And K. Alexander (Eds.), Peace In The Balance: The Crisis In Sudan, Institute For Justice And Reconciliation (2006) 23-38, and, for a recent assessment, E. Thomas, *Against the Gathering Storm: Securing Sudan's Comprehensive Peace Agreement*, A Chatham House Report (2009), available at <www.chathamhouse.org/sites/default/files/public/Research/Africa/0109sudan_r.pdf> (Accessed November 22, 2011).

81 African Union Peace and Security Council, Communiqué of the 207th Meeting, PSC/AHG/COMM.1(CCVII) (October 29, 2009).

GoS responded equivocally to the proposals to establish a Hybrid Court.[82] In early 2010, it enacted legislation that maintained immunities for members of the security forces,[83] contrary to the recommendations made by the AUPD just a few months earlier.[84] The AUHLIP has mainly focussed on the Darfur peace process, the April 2010 elections and the 2011 referendum about Southern Sudan's independence.[85] The AUPD/AUHLIP can be credited with having contributed to a greater awareness of the importance of justice and reconciliation amongst the actors engaged in the Darfur peace talks that resulted in the Doha Document for Peace in Darfur, an agreement that includes provisions on human rights, reparation, as well as justice and reconciliation.[86] However, there is an evident risk that a political approach may be prioritized over one of bringing about structural reforms and building institutions. This raises the question of the AUHLIP's capacity and a potential overreach, *i.e.* engaging in multiple parallel tasks might limit the effectiveness of its work. Lacking, delayed or selective implementation risks undermining the credibility of the process and the legitimacy of the AUPD's work. Effective implementation is therefore a crucial yardstick for the success of the process-oriented approach taken by the AUPD.

These developments also pose the broader institutional question for the AU as to whether the Darfur situation has actually been the most suitable for an AUPD-style mode of intervention. It is reasonable to assume that the GoS committed itself to this process primarily for reasons of political survival, namely to deflect attention from the Bashir arrest warrant and in

82 'Sudan reiterates rejection of Darfur Hybrid Courts', Sudan Tribune (November 1, 2009), available at <www.sudantribune.com/spip.php?article32973> (Accessed November 22, 2011). See also the draft of a GoS document, Office of the Presidential Advisory, 'Towards a New Strategy for Achieving Comprehensive Peace, Security and Development in Darfur', August 2010, in which it welcomed the AUPD's role and declared its readiness to engage with the panel while confining its commitment to national justice mechanisms, namely supporting the work of the special prosecutor for Darfur and related national tribunals. The draft is notable for its omission of any mention of the Hybrid Courts, which can be understood as an implicit rejection. Several English versions of the draft strategy were available online in September 2010, see <http://blogs.ssrc.org/sudan/wp-content/uploads/2010/09/Office-of-the-Presidential-Advisor-Darfur-strategy.doc> (Accessed September 10, 2010) and <www.smallarmssurveysudan.org/pdfs/facts-figures/darfur-peace-process/HSBA-Darfur-Peace-Process-New-Strategy.pdf> (Accessed September 10, 2010).

83 See Art. 52(3) of Sudan's National Security Act, 2010.

84 Note 63 above.

85 See Presentation by the Chairperson of the AU High Level Implementation Panel for Sudan to the UN Security Council: UNHQ, New York (June 14, 2010), available at <www.unisa.ac.za/contents/colleges/docs/TMLI-UNSC.pdf> (Accessed November 22, 2011) as well as further briefings to the UN Security Council, such as on February 9, 2011, available at <www.unisa.ac.za/contents/colleges/docs/Remarks%20of%20the%20Chairperson%20of%20AU%20High%20%209%20Feb%202011.pdf> (Accessed November 22, 2011) and on June 20, 2011, available at <www.un.org/News/Press/docs/2011/sc10286.doc.htm> (Accessed November 22, 2011). See also Communique of the 271st meeting of the AU Peace and Security Council, 8 April 2011, para.12, available at <www.securitycouncilreport.org/atf/cf/%7B65BFCF9B-6D27-4E9C-8CD3-CF6E4FF96FF9%7D/RO%20PSC%20PR%20Comm_CCLXXI.pdf> (Accessed November 22, 2011).

86 *Doha Document for Peace in Darfur*, signed on July 14, 2011 by the Government of Sudan and the Liberation and Justice Movement, available at <http://unamid.unmissions.org/Portals/UNAMID/DDPD%20English.pdf> (Accessed November 22, 2011).

order to gain legitimacy from engaging in an AU-led process. However, it is far from clear that Sudan's engagement is underpinned by a genuine commitment to take steps towards the profound transformation that the implementation of the AUPD recommendations would entail. Equally, it is questionable whether the AU (and other relevant actors) have the necessary leverage to persuade the actors, in particular the GoS, to undertake the number of reforms needed. The implementation of measures that leave the power structures and root causes unaddressed would in this context not only fail to do justice to the AUPD's vision, it would also cast doubt on the AU's ability to end the crisis in Sudan identified by the body it had established.

13.4 The AUPD and AU Responses to International Crimes

13.4.1 *The AUPD as Model*

The AUPD's modus operandi bears the blueprint for a possible regional approach based on an integrated and coordinated vision of peace, justice and reconciliation pursued in a consultative process that supports national actors in agreeing on, and implementing workable solutions. It also demonstrates the role that the AU can play in fashioning regional solutions when addressing mass atrocities, impunity and a humanitarian and societal crisis in the context of conflict or fragile post-conflict societies. This consists of providing a framework for the process, in particular by setting up a credible and independent body with a mandate tailored to the exigencies of the situation. It also entails support and facilitation of the work of such body, national capacity building and taking measures with a view to ensuring effective implementation. The AU can in this context provide legitimacy and institutional oversight as well as technical expertise and support. In view of the politicized context in which implementation takes place, it is critical that the AU is prepared both to provide sustained support and to take vigorous action in case of non-cooperation. Based on the Sudan experience, it is important that the AU chooses AUPD-type interventions in future situations where there is reason to believe that the parties are genuinely committed to the process facilitated by the body concerned and actively cooperate in the implementation of any recommendations.

13.4.2 *The AUPD and Complementary Measures*

13.4.2.1 Framework for Justice and Reconciliation Interventions

The approach taken by the AU was largely ad-hoc and it has yet to develop a coherent framework for its role in conflict and post-conflict situations. The degree of flexibility and context-specificity inherent in this approach are useful. However, clearer guidance, in particular setting out specific modalities of implementation, will arguably need to be developed in the long run to ensure that any interventions contemplated reflect the AU's overall objectives and that impact is evaluated and lessons are learnt. This entails identifying transferable aspects of the AUPD's report, which could form the basis of AU approaches in other situations, such as the contextual construction of key concepts and emphasis on process as defining features.

13.4.2.2 Sustainability and Complementary Measures

The AUPD's engagement raises the question whether the AU can sustain such interventions, both in the case of Sudan and beyond, *i.e.* whether the AU has the financial means, structures and commitment to engage in what are resource and time-intensive processes, which may necessitate institutional reforms and resort to complementary approaches.

13.4.2.3 Capacity Building

Many if not most states witnessing instances of mass crimes face the twin challenge of weak capacity and limited political will to carry out effective investigations and prosecutions. The AU and African states arguably must address both aspects in order to develop a regional culture of accountability. There are many actors that can and have provided support in building capacity, including the UN, the ICC,[87] other organisations, states and civil society. However, it is clear that efforts have been insufficient to date and that a more coherent and sustained regional approach is needed, which the AU may develop through the establishment of permanent bodies and/or ad hoc mechanisms such as the AUPD. Where credible national systems are absent, AU-supported hybrid courts that combine national and regional expertise may play an important role as midwives for capable national institutions.[88] However, such an approach will need to be backed up by adequate resources and sustained commitment to the rule of law beyond the life-span of the court, in particular at the national level, in order to be effective. Establishing a body of experts tasked with supporting states on how best to prevent and to respond to international crimes, in particular by putting in place the requisite legal framework and strengthening institutional capacity

87 See on the notion of 'positive complementarity', Report of the Bureau on Stocktaking: Complementarity, 'Taking stock of the principle of complementarity: bridging the impunity gap', ICC-ASP/8/51 (March 18, 2010) paras 16-48; and W.W. Burke-White, '*Proactive Complementarity: The International Criminal Court and National Courts in the Rome System of International Justice*,' (Winter 2008) 49 HARVARD INTERNATIONAL LAW JOURNAL 1, 53-108.

88 The only hybrid court in Africa to date is the Special Court for Sierra Leone. The myriad questions raised by hybrid courts are examined in INTERNATIONALIZED CRIMINAL COURTS: SIERRA LEONE, EAST TIMOR, KOSOVO AND CAMBODIA (Cesaro P.R Romano, Andre Nollkaemper & Jann K. Kleffner eds., 2004).

to investigate and prosecute international crimes, would also constitute a significant addition to the AU's existing institutional structure.

13.4.3 *Proposals to Establish a Regional Criminal Court*

Proposals to empower the African Court of Justice and Human Rights (ACJHR) to 'try serious crimes of international concern such as genocide, crimes against humanity and war crimes, which would be complementary to national jurisdiction and processes for fighting impunity'[89] were being discussed by the AU at the time of writing.[90] Vesting the ACJHR with criminal jurisdiction would address a series of the conceptual and institutional obstacles addressed above, in particular if it has the mandate, power and resources to try those responsible for international crimes in situations such as Darfur. In such circumstances, the court could complement AUPD-style approaches. However, vesting the ACJHR with criminal jurisdiction may strain if not exceed the capacity of the existing system and, in the process, undermine the developing regional human rights regime. It would thus fail to provide an effective alternative and, worse, prove damaging to what is an important existing regional mechanism, not least for the prevention of international crimes. These concerns are genuine as the establishment of an effective criminal body requires considerable financial resources and institutional capacity to investigate and prosecute complex crimes.[91] The existing African human rights bodies already suffer from inadequate resources and capacity constraints and would be weakened further unless the AU were to dedicate significant resources to the investigation and prosecution of international crimes at the regional level. However, doing so would raise the question why the AU uses scarce resources for this purpose considering that there is already an international body vested with similar jurisdiction vis-à-vis a considerable number of African states. These factors do not appear conducive to having an effective regional court with criminal jurisdiction and need to be carefully considered and satisfactorily addressed. Proceeding

89 See African Union, Decision Assembly/Dec.213 (XII) (February 2009).

90 Three meetings of Government experts were held in 2011, resulting in an agreement on a draft statute of the ACHJR. After further consideration by the Ministers of Justice and the AU Executive Council, the draft will be put to the AU Assembly for formal adoption and signature, a process that was envisaged to take place in the course of 2012.

91 Amnesty International, *International Criminal Court: The Contribution Africa can make to the Review Conference*, AI-Index: AFR 01/017/2009 (October 2009); 'Implications of the African Court of Human and Peoples' Rights being empowered to try international crimes such as genocide, crimes against humanity and war crimes', An Opinion submitted by eight human rights organizations to the African Union on December 17, 2009, available at <www.soros.org/initiatives/justice/focus/international_justice/news/africa_20091217/africa_20091217.pdf> (Accessed November 22, 2011), argues that the word 'Court' refers to the ACJHR; Hon. Commissioner Bahame Tom Nyanduga, 'Reflections and Perspectives of the African Commission on Human and Peoples' Rights' Consultative Conference on International Criminal Justice' 5-6 (September 9-11, 2009).

with the proposed amendment irrespectively would in these circumstances threaten to become a licence for impunity rather than an important step towards combating it.[92]

13.4.4 Developments at the Sub-Regional Level

The sub-regional level can act as a critical site for the development of effective initiatives and responses. A smaller number of states with a shared or similar regional history and legal culture, which agree on relevant principles and establish adequate institutions, may be able to effectively build the capacity of member states and respond to mass crimes, thus lessening the need for, or scope of AU interventions. The Great Lakes Pact, which encompasses all current ICC situation states (except Libya and Cote D'Iuoire), including Sudan, and covers a region that has in recent years arguably experienced the worst conflicts and mass crimes in Africa, is an obvious example and critical test in this regard.[93] Its states parties have agreed on a number of principles and obligations, including the incorporation of international crimes in national laws, and their investigation and prosecution at the national level.[94] While there is limited evidence of its efficacy to date, and it may be criticized as simply adding a sub-regional layer without putting in place the necessary structures and measures to make it effective, the Great Lakes Pact carries the potential to develop a shared commitment and practice of justice and reconciliation in the sub-region.[95] However, the authoritarian nature and fragility of states and the resulting scope for conflict make political support at the regional and sub-regional level, such as by leading states, essential to establish the requisite culture and practice. The principle that the AU will not recognize any government that has come to power by way of a coup and will take measures to address resulting situations shows that a principled stance can have some effect even if it will not prevent violations altogether.[96]

---

92 Nyanduga, *supra* note 91 at 7. 'The extension of international criminal jurisdiction to the African Court must be a genuine framework for addressing impunity, fostering political accountability, and providing a different layer of a regional complement to the international criminal justice system. It should not be a rouse for shielding perpetrators of grave crimes against international criminal justice'.

93 Deirdre Clancy, *Lessons from a State of Flux: The International Justice Laboratory of the Great Lakes Pact, in* Oette, *supra* note 63 at 197-219.

94 Protocol on the Prevention and Punishment of the Crime of Genocide, War Crimes and Crimes against Humanity; Protocol on Judicial Cooperation and Protocol on the Prevention and Suppression of Sexual Violence against Women and Children, 2006.

95 International Refugee Rights Initiative, *In the Interests of Justice? Prospects and Challenges for International Justice in Africa* 45-47 (November 2008).

96 See in particular Art. 4(p) of the AU Constitutive Act. *See also* Khabele Matlosa, *The African Charter on Democracy, Elections and Governance: Declaration vs. Policy Practice*, 7, 8. (Centre for Policy Studies, Policy Brief No. 53, December 2008).

13.4.5 *The Role of Universal Jurisdiction*

Another important element in the development of a regional cultural of accountability is the exercise of universal jurisdiction and cooperation in criminal matters, particularly by way of extradition. Universal jurisdiction has been portrayed as an unfriendly act if not a neo-colonial tool against African politicians.[97] However, as the Habré case, the ICJ Arrest Warrants case and other instances have highlighted, universal jurisdiction often becomes prominent where there are no other avenues to hold someone accountable, *i.e.* where the alternative is impunity.[98] Rather than taking a purely defensive posture, strengthening universal jurisdiction at the regional level would send a clear signal that the AU promotes a culture of accountability and expects states to take the requisite steps domestically or face prosecution in other African states. This would be in line with states' obligation to extradite or prosecute that is stipulated in a number of international treaties.[99] The exercise of such jurisdiction in even a few cases could send a powerful message that impunity is not tolerated. The AU can play a role in lending technical support to states to adopt the requisite legislation, such as its current efforts to adopt a model law, as well as initiate and support efforts to strengthen cooperation in criminal matters in the region.[100] In turn, such an approach could reinforce efforts to strengthen national systems as set out in the AUPD report since it may provide states with an incentive to act themselves rather than see their nationals being prosecuted and tried in other states.

13.5 CONCLUSION: ASSESSMENT AND OUTLOOK

The current debate about international criminal justice in Africa constitutes a healthy opening, even if it appears to be partly motivated by attempts of those in power to evade accountability. The debate may be seen as a crucial, and perhaps inevitable, step in translating international criminal justice. However, as such, it will not be sufficient to rely on symbolic defensive measures that do not provide a foundation to inspire trust and gain legitimacy, be it internationally, regionally or locally. The challenge of developing an

97 *Supra* note 16.

98 See on the relationship between immunity and impunity in this regard the questionable approach taken in, *Case Concerning the Arrest Warrant of 11 April 2000 (Democratic Republic of the Congo v. Belgium)*, Judgment, I.C.J. Reports 2002, 3, paras. 60 and 61.

99 See for example Art. 5(2) of the UN Convention against Torture and other Cruel, Inhuman or Degrading Treatment or Punishment and the Articles related to grave breaches in the four Geneva Conventions of 1949 (Art. 50, 51, 130 and 147 of the First, Second, Third and Fourth Conventions) and Additional Protocol I of 1977 (Art. 11 and 85).

100 See in this regard African Union, 'Decision on the Meeting of African States Parties to the Rome Statute of the International Criminal Court', Doc. Assembly/AU/13 (XIII) (July 2009) para. 6.

effective regional approach is considerable, not least in light of the systemic difficulties that generally bedevil the use of criminal justice mechanisms in response to mass crimes.

The development of such a regional culture is predicated on a principled commitment to combating impunity and the putting in place of effective bodies and mechanisms. The AU plays a pivotal role in fashioning regional responses. It can provide a forum and establish mechanisms that seek to address challenges unique to the situation at hand, such as the AUPD. One of its most important roles at this stage is to foster a public debate about regional approaches to international crimes that includes civil society and others rather than simply reflect states' interests. Such a debate is vital to generate a shared sense of, and commitment to justice and accountability in the African context. At the institutional level, the AU can create a framework for processes, such as in relation to Darfur, by setting up bodies, facilitating their work, and acting upon their recommendations. However, there are limits to the role of the AU as a political body where there is a lack of political will and/or consensus. The AU's own capacity and limited resources are further constraints. In light of the often highly politicized and divisive nature of criminal proceedings, it will be important to focus equally on effective prevention and support for domestic, mixed and sub-regional processes aimed at establishing effective human rights protection and justice mechanisms with a view to deterring violations. In this context, addressing the responsibility of political leaders for international crimes will continue to pose a vexing challenge for a political body such as the AU.

The ICC retains an important role. It can contribute to the development of a regional culture of justice and reconciliation by being sensitive to context when interpreting complementarity and by engaging with national and regional bodies throughout when addressing international crimes in the region. For the AU, the current debates provide an opening to address conceptual and institutional concerns so as to make the ICC as legitimate and effective as possible in its response to situations in Africa. Positive responses to the work of the AUPD at the UN and the ICC level indicate that the AU is in a good position to do so where it demonstrates its own capacity to address international crimes in the region.[101]

Is Africa a laboratory of international criminal justice or a pioneer of contextual responses to international crimes? Posing the question in such stark dichotomy is misleading but captures the difference between being a passive object and an active subject in respect of the development of international criminal justice. There is no doubt that the bitter experiences of authoritarianism, conflict and international crimes, which date

101 See United Nations, 'Security Council Press Statement on Sudan', SC/9831, AFR/1925 (December 21, 2009) and ICC, 'Tenth Prosecutor's Statement to the United Nations Security Council on the situation in Darfur, the Sudan, pursuant to UNSCR 1593 (2005)' (December 4, 2009) paras 21, 22.

back to colonial times, make the question of how to combat impunity and prevent mass violations particularly pertinent in the African context. Taking a proactive approach in the debate and in relation to specific situations could well set a precedent for other regions and/or contribute to practices elsewhere. Criminal justice, be it national, regional or international, is invariably, at least to some degree, context specific. International criminal justice may have been considerably influenced by Western notions of criminal justice but this is by no means immutable. This is recognized in the complementarity principle whose relative openness makes it a site for the struggle of defining and 'appropriating' international criminal justice at the national and regional level. It is part of an ongoing dialectical process essential for the legitimacy of international criminal justice to fulfil its functions at the level where it matters most rather than being perceived as an abstract notion prone to being used as a tool of political power. The AUPD's role may yet prove to be pivotal in this process.

14 The Case for an African Criminal Court to Prosecute International Crimes Committed in Africa

Pacifique Manirakiza

14.1 Introduction

Africa has been ravaged by armed conflicts, dictatorships and/or political oppressive regimes for decades. During those situations, heinous crimes such as genocide, war crimes and crimes against humanity have been committed resulting in millions of victims. Among these victims, only a handful has seen some justice. This was possible essentially because the international community took a vigorous stance against the impunity of war criminals and genocidaires by creating judicial mechanisms to deal with it. For instance, in 1994, the United Nations Security Council created the International Criminal Tribunal for Rwanda in order to prosecute persons responsible for genocide, crimes against humanity and serious violations of international humanitarian law committed in Rwanda.[1] In 2002, the Special Court for Sierra Leone was set up in order to try persons who committed international crimes during the Sierra Leonean armed conflict.[2] But, as it is well known, international crimes have been committed almost everywhere in Africa. Therefore, it is practically impossible to have international *ad hoc* tribunals established in each case. The attention has therefore shifted to the nascent International Criminal Court (ICC)[3] as the appropriate mechanism to help fight impunity for international crimes committed in Africa. As the first permanent criminal court with a quasi-universal reach,[4] the ICC is sometimes presented as a panacea. However, it was never the intention of the Rome Statute drafters that the ICC should be the sole and unique response to international crimes. Indeed, the ICC has been tasked with the mandate to prosecute persons who bear the greatest responsibility for the perpetration of international crimes. Only a handful of suspected perpetrators

1 ICTR Statute, S.C. Res. 955, Art. 1, U.N. S.C.O.R., 49th Sess., 3453d mtg., U.N. Doc. S/RES/955 (November 8, 1994).

2 Agreement between the United Nations and the Government of Sierra Leone, S.C. Res. 1315, U.N. S.C.O.R., 4186th mtg, U.N. Doc. S/RES/1315 (August 14, 2000).

3 Rome Statute of the ICC, July 17, 1998, 2187 U.N.T.S. 90.

4 As of December 31, 2011; 120 States are parties to the ICC Statute, see International Criminal Court, available at: <www.icc-cpi.int/Menus/ASP/states+parties/> (Accessed December 31, 2011).

of international crimes can thus be effectively prosecuted. Moreover, for practical reasons, the ICC alone cannot fight impunity for the most serious crimes of international law given the magnitude of mass atrocities all over the world. This is why its statute requires, and in fact prioritizes the prosecution of international crimes by member States.[5] In so doing, the Rome Statute reaffirms pre-existing international norms that require individual States to investigate and prosecute perpetrators of international crimes before national courts.[6] In this way, the ICC acts as a complementary tool when States are either unable or unwilling to prosecute perpetrators of international crimes.[7]

So far in Africa, there has been no systematic use of States' courts to prosecute international crimes despite their primary responsibility. Some rather exceptional experiences such as Rwanda,[8] Ethiopia[9] and, to some extent, Democratic Republic of Congo (DRC)[10] and Uganda,[11] can be mentioned. In other African countries such as Burundi, Zimbabwe, Sudan, etc., impunity still rules. This hampers the development of and the establishment of the rule of law in most African countries.

---

5 ICC Statute, *supra* note 3; preamble, para. 6 and Art. 1.

6 Convention on the Prevention and Punishment of the Crime of Genocide, December 9, 1948, Art. 6; Convention (I) for the Amelioration of the Condition of the Wounded and Sick in Armed Forces in the Field, Geneva, August 12, 1949, Art. 49; Convention (II) for the Amelioration of the Condition of Wounded, Sick and Shipwrecked Members of Armed Forces at Sea; Geneva, August 12, 1949, Art. 50; Convention (III) relative to the Treatment of Prisoners of War, Geneva, August 12, 1949, Art. 129; Convention (IV) relative to the Protection of Civilian Persons in Time of War, Geneva, August 12, 1949, Art. 146.

7 ICC Statute, *supra* note 3 above, Art. 1 and Art. 17.

8 Organic Law No 8/96 of August 30, 1996 organising prosecutions of the crime of genocide or other crimes against humanity, committed from October 1, 1990, (1996) 17 Official Gazette of the Republic of Rwanda (September 1, 1996); Organic Law No 40/2000 of January 26, 2001 setting up "Gacaca Jurisdictions" and organising prosecutions offences constituting the crime of genocide or crimes against humanity, committed between October 1, 1990 and December 31, 1994, (2001) 14 Official Gazette of the Republic of Rwanda (July 15, 2001). This Law has been amended several times; the latest version dates back to March 2007: Organic Law No. 10/2007 of March 1, 2007 modifying and complementing Organic Law No. 16/2004 of June 19, 2004 establishing the organization, competence and functioning of Gacaca Courts charged with prosecuting and trying the perpetrators of the crime of genocide and other crimes against humanity, committed between October 1, 1990 and December 31, 1994 as modified and complemented to date, (2007) 5 Official Gazette of the Republic of Rwanda (March 1, 2007); William A. Schabas, *Genocide Trials and Gacaca Courts*, 3-4 International Criminal Justice 879 (2005).

9 Girmachew Alemu Aneme, *Apology and Trials: The case of the Red Terror trials in Ethiopia*, 6 African Human Rights Law Journal 64 (2006).

10 In the Democratic Republic of Congo, criminal prosecutions for international crimes are carried out before military courts, see *Loi N° 024/2002 du 18 novembre 2002 portant Code pénal militaire*, art. 161. For a brief summary of some cases already completed, see *Recommandations de l'atelier sur l'évaluation de la justice militaire comme mécanisme de répression des crimes internationaux*, International Centre for Transitional Justice. 12-14 (2009); *Military justice and human rights – An urgent need to complete reforms, A Discussion Paper*; AfriMAP & The Open Society Initiative for Southern Africa (2009).

11 The International Criminal Court Act, 2010, *Uganda Gazette* No 39, Vol. CIII, June 29, 2010. For a brief analysis of the Act, see Open Society Justice Initiative, *Putting Complementarity into Practice: Domestic Justice for International Crimes in DRC, Uganda, and Kenya*, at 59-61.

This chapter will argue that the establishment of a continental African Criminal Court (ACC) would significantly contribute to closing the impunity gap. I will demonstrate that an African Criminal Court will not only supplement but also contribute to legitimize, rather than compete with or jeopardize, the existing system of international criminal justice. For reasons of scope and space, the operational aspect of the proposed court and its relationship with other mechanisms, particularly the ICC, will be explored in a follow-up paper, as the main objective of this chapter is to make a case for a continental criminal court with jurisdiction on international crimes.

The chapter is divided into five main parts. Part 1 explores the contextual origin of the idea of a regional criminal court. Part 2 offers the justifications for such a judicial institution. Part 3 analyzes the legal basis for a future ACC. Part 4 addresses potential objections to an ACC and attempts to offer some counter-arguments. Part 5 concludes by reiterating that the ACC is a viable option for Africa and the whole international criminal justice system more broadly.

14.2 Contextual Origin of the Idea of an African Criminal Court

The idea of an ACC is not as old as was the ICC idea that goes back to the 1860s.[12] During the creation of the Organization of the African Unity (OAU) and its successor, the African Union (AU), only a court of justice was envisioned, with the mandate to settle states' disputes or to interpret regional legal instruments.[13] During the drafting process of the African Charter of Human and Peoples' Rights (ACHPR), no African criminal court was contemplated as a mechanism for the protection of human and peoples' rights. Only a human and peoples' rights commission[14] and later a human rights court have been envisaged.[15] One can infer from this inquiry that the non-reference to a criminal organ was probably due to the fact that, at the time of the adoption of these treaties, criminal matters were still strongly regarded as a domestic issue under the rather powerful principle of state sovereignty. Another factor that can explain the lack of a provision of an ACC in relevant instruments is that no other continent has set up a regional criminal court. So, there was nothing that could have directly inspired Africa to create its regional criminal court. If there were previous regional criminal courts, for example a European criminal court or an

12 The idea of an international criminal court was suggested by Gustav Monier, one of the founders of the Red Cross Movement, see William A, Schabas, an Introduction to the International Criminal Court 2 (2nd Ed., (2004)).

13 Art. 19 of the Protocol of the Court of Justice of the African Union (2003); see also Art. 28 of the Statute of the African Court of Justice and Human Rights (2008).

14 Art. 30 of the African Charter on Human and Peoples' Rights.

15 Protocol to the African Charter on Human and Peoples' Rights on the Establishment of an African Court on Human and Peoples' Rights (1998).

Inter-American criminal court, one would expect Africa to mimic these institutions, with more or less adaptation, as it has been done by the creation of most regional institutions, including the AU and its different organs and institutions.[16]

The idea of an ACC was considered for the first time during the drafting process of the legal instrument merging the African Court of Justice and the African Human Rights and Peoples' Rights Court.[17] At that time, the Committee of legal experts suggested a criminal division within the new envisioned court in order to deal with the egregious violations of human rights which amount to international crimes. Unfortunately, the idea was deemed premature and rejected outright by African political leaders without consideration on its merits. Curiously, the suggested idea didn't even get the attention of the African civil society fighting against the impunity of human rights violations. This can be explained by the fact that at that time, African civil society was actively campaigning for a strong and effective International Criminal Court through the Coalition for the International Criminal Court (CICC), an umbrella organization composed of more than 2,500 pro-ICC non-governmental organizations from 150 countries.[18]

Eventually, the idea resurfaced in 2006 when a Committee of Eminent African Jurists set up by the AU to consider options available for Hissène Habré's trial,[19] recommended that the future African court of justice and human rights be granted a criminal jurisdiction to deal with future possible Hissène Habré-related cases.[20] On the official and political level, the ACC idea received a formal acceptance at the AU Assembly of Heads of State and Government in early 2009. At its 12th Ordinary Session in February 2009, the Assembly adopted a decision by which it requested:

> [. . .] the Commission (of the African Union), in consultation with the African Commission on Human and Peoples' Rights, and the African Court on Human and Peoples' Rights, to examine the implications of the Court being empowered to try international crimes such as genocide, crimes against humanity and war crimes, and report thereon to the Assembly in 2010.[21]

16 For instance, the new name African Union has been inspired by the name change from Economic Community to European Union, see Belachew Gebrewold, *The Cynicism of African Solutions for African Problems*, 3 AFRICAN SECURITY 80, 82 (2010); the EU Parliament inspired the AU Parliament; the African Court of Human and Peoples' Rights has been created on the model of the European Court of Human Rights and the Inter-American Court of Human Rights, etc.

17 The decision to merge the two institutions was adopted in 2005. See Decision on the Merger of the African Court on Human and Peoples' Rights and the Court of Justice of the African Union, Doc. Assembly/AU/ Dec.83 (V).

18 For more information on the coalition and its work, available at: <www.iccnow.org/?mod=coalition> (Accessed September 17, 2009).

19 Decision on the Hissène Habré Case and the African Union, Doc. Assembly/AU/8 (VI)) Add. 9

20 *Rapport du Comité d'éminents juristes africains sur l'affaire Hissène Habré*, paras. 35 and 39.

21 Decision on the Implementation of the Assembly Decision on the Abuse of the Principle of Universal Jurisdiction, AU Doc. Assembly/AU/3 (XII) Assembly/AU/Dec. 213(XII), para. 9 (2009).

In the following sessions of the Assembly of Heads of State and Government, the same request was reaffirmed.[22] As of today, the matter is still active on the AU agenda. At the last Summit in June/July 2011 in Malabo, the AU Executive Council requested "the Commission in collaboration with AfCHPR to finalize the process of examining the implications of AfCHPR being empowered to try international crimes and report thereon to the Assembly, through the Executive Council in January 2012".[23] At the same Summit, the Assembly of Heads of State and Government also requested the Commission in collaboration with the Permanent Representatives' Committee "to actively pursue the implementation of the Assembly's Decisions on the African Court of Justice and Human and Peoples' Rights being empowered to try serious international crimes committed on African soil".[24]

At its fourteenth ordinary session, the African Court on Human and Peoples' Rights adopted a report on the implications of granting a criminal jurisdiction to the court so that it can effectively and directly contribute to the fight against impunity of international crimes.[25] According to the report, extending the court's jurisdiction to prosecute serious crimes will have implications on its internal structure as well as on its human and financial resources.[26] On its part, the African Commission on Human and Peoples' Rights, considered a draft paper[27] on extending the jurisdiction of the African court at its 46th session held in Banjul, The Gambia, in November 2009. Both the court and the commission did not object to the idea but expressed their concerns as to the financial and structural implications of empowering the court with a criminal jurisdiction on international crimes.

Nowadays, things are moving pretty fast. The assessment of the implications of extending a criminal jurisdiction on international crimes to the envisaged African Court of Justice and Human Rights along with drafting appropriate legal instrument were contracted out to the Pan African Lawyers Union (the PALU) by the AU Commission. The Consultant has already released its report which went through a series of validation meetings.[28]

22 Decision on the Meeting of African States Parties to the Rome Statute of the International Criminal Court (ICC), Doc.Assembly/AU/13(XIII), para. 5.
23 Decision on the Activity Report of the African Court on Human and Peoples' Rights, Doc.EX.CL/649(XIX), para. 7.
24 Decision on the Implementation of the Assembly Decisions on the International Criminal Court, Assembly/AU/ Dec.366(XVII), para. 8.
25 Report on paragraph nine (9) of the Assembly Decision –Assembly AU/DEC.213(XII) on the Abuse of the Principle of Universal Jurisdiction, hereinafter ACTHPR Report, African Court on Human and Peoples' Rights, Fourteenth Ordinary Session, Arusha, Tanzania, September 17-18, 2009.
26 *Ibid.* 6-9.
27 Exploring Possibilities for Exercise of International Criminal Jurisdiction by the African Court on Human and Peoples' Rights, ACHPR, November 2009 (on file with the author).
28 Report of the Study on the Implications of expanding the mandate of the African Court of Justice and Human Rights to try serious crimes of international concern, Doc.Legal/ACJHR-PAP/5(II) (2010).

It is important to note that this unprecedented move was accelerated by the African Union objection against the ICC 'intervention' in Africa and the exercise of universal jurisdiction by third States against Africans.[29] Since its inception, the ICC has particularly been active in Africa (Uganda, DRC, Central African Republic, Sudan, Kenya, Côte d'Ivoire and Libya). Although the ICC has been invited by different States (except Sudan and Libya) and despite the pivotal role that African States played in the process of creating the Court,[30] the ICC's focus on the African continent has attracted some resistance and resentments from the African Union. This was exacerbated by the indictment and the issuance of an arrest warrant against President al Bashir of Sudan.[31] Also, to some extent, the indictment of some Africans, notably Rwandans,[32] under the universal jurisdiction principle by some western courts provoked the African Union's outrage. According to the regional organization, the exercise of universal jurisdiction is abusive and unduly targets Africans, regardless of some international legal guarantees such as the regime of state officials' immunity.[33]

Those two situations – ICC intervention, especially the arrest warrant against President al Bashir, and the exercise of the principle of universal jurisdiction – were denounced by the African Union in the strongest terms.[34] Ultimately, for some African leaders, the whole system of international criminal justice is regarded as biased against Africa. Jean Ping, the AU Commission Chairman stated that 'there are double standards' in the ICC's manner of operating and that 'there seems to be some bullying against Africa'.[35] President Kagame of Rwanda stated that the ICC is made for Africans and poor countries.[36] Moreover, it was

29 AU Doc.Assembly/AU/3(XII)Assembly/AU/Dec.213(XII), *supra* note 17.

30 Dapo Akande, Charles Chernor Jalloh & Max du Plessis, *Assessing the African Union Concerns About Article 16 of the Rome Statute of the International Criminal Court*, 4 AFRICAN JOURNAL OF LEGAL STUDIES 5, 14 (2011); see also MAX DU PLESSIS, THE INTERNATIONAL CRIMINAL COURT THAT AFRICA WANTS 6-8 (2010).

31 *The Prosecutor v. Omar Hassan Ahmad Al Bashir (Omar Al Bashir)*, No. ICC-02/05-01/09 (March 4, 2009).

32 Spanish Judge Fernando Andreu Merelles issue an arrest warrant to 40 high ranking Rwandan officials, including President Kagame for war crimes and crimes against humanity, see *Rwanda/Espagne: L'enquête espagnole sur le Rwanda met le TPIR en difficulté*, Hirondelle news, available at: <http://fr.hirondellenews.com/content/view/1010/3> (Accessed February 3, 2008)

33 *Decision on the Abuse of the Principle of Universal Jurisdiction*, Doc. Assembly/AU/Dec. 243 (XIII) Rev.1, para. 6. For a critical view of this position, see Charles Chernor Jalloh, *Universal Jurisdiction, and Universal Prescription? A Preliminary Assessment of the African Union Perspective on Universal Jurisdiction*, 21 CRIMINAL LAW FORUM 11 (2010).

34 For instance, the Assembly of Heads of State and Government denounced the fact that "there has been blatant abuse of the Principle of Universal Jurisdiction particularly by some non-African States (...) [and] calls for immediate termination of all pending indictments"; Decision on the Abuse of the Principle of Universal Jurisdiction, Doc. Assembly/AU/11(XIII), para. 4.

35 AU Chief challenges ICC to arrest Sudanese President, July 23, 2010, available at: <http://sudaneseonline.org/cs/blogs/english/archive/2010/07/24/au-chief-challenges-icc-to-arrest-sudanese-president.aspx> (Accessed November 10, 2011).

36 President Wade: *La CPI donne l'impression d'être faite pour les Africains*, Jeune Afrique (March 5, 2009) ; D Kezio-Musoke, Kagame tells why he is against the ICC charging Bashir, available at: http://africanpress.me/2008/08/05/kagame-tells-why-he-is-against-icc-charging-bashir/ (Accessed November 10, 2011).

presented as a neocolonial and imperialistic tool in the hands of powerful nations against powerless states.[37] As a consequence of this perception, the African Union pursued every available legal and political option in order to have indictments against Africans repealed in the interest of peace or state sovereignty. Unfortunately, the efforts deployed proved unsuccessful. On one hand, the African request to obtain al Bashir's case deferral under Article 16 of the Rome Statute[38] was not acceded to by the UN Security Council.[39] Likewise, deferrals requested in the situations of Kenya and Libya were also unsuccessful. The AU subsequently decided that member States, including ICC State Parties, shall not cooperate with the ICC,[40] pursuant to the provisions of Article 98 of the Rome Statute relating to immunities, in the execution of the arrest warrants against Presidents Al Bashir[41] and Gaddafi[42]. Similarly, on the other hand, Rwandan cases are still pending before French[43] and Spanish[44] courts whereas the AU requested their suspension.[45]

Against this background, it is notable that the idea of an ACC is somewhat associated with frustration resulting from this tense relationship between Africa and the international criminal justice system as such. One can then understand the reason why the ACC idea has not been warmly welcomed outside the AU club. Instead, it provoked some fear and uneasiness among some international lawyers and members of civil society. For instance, eight influential[46] African NGOs submitted an opinion strongly

---

37 *Id.* But, Professors du Plessis and Gevers dismiss that argument. For them, the focus on Africa "is a reflection of other realities, including the sad preponderance of conflicts in Africa, the hostile political conditions and jurisdictional limitations that prevent the ICC from pursuing more deserving cases from other parts of the world (viz. Gaza), and the fact that four of the court's situations were self-referrals by the African states concerned". See Max du Plessis & Christopher Gevers, *Balancing Competing Obligations. The Rome Statute and AU Decisions*, ISS paper, 225 (2010) at 2.

38 Decision on the Report of the Second Meeting of States Parties to the Rome Statute on the International Criminal Court (ICC), Doc.Assembly/AU/Dec.270(XIV), para. 10.

39 UNSC, 63rd session, 5947th meeting, UN Doc. S/PV.5947, July 31, 2008, at 7-8. Professors Jalloh, Akande & Max du Plessis argue that African States members of the Security Council at that time lacked leadership on this issue since they did not author or sponsor a specific deferral draft resolution to be considered by the UNSC; see Jalloh, *supra* note 30, at 22.

40 For the (il)legality of that decision, see du Plessis & Gevers, *supra* note 37.

41 Decision on the Meeting of African States Parties to the Rome Statute of The ICC, Doc. Assembly/AU/Dec.245(XIII) Rev.1, para. 10.

42 Decision on the Implementation of the Assembly Decisions on the International Criminal Court, Assembly/AU/Dec.366(XVII), para. 6.

43 Vanessa Thalmann, *French Justice's Endeavours to Substitute for the ICTR*, 6 JOURNAL OF INTERNATIONAL CRIMINAL JUSTICE, 995 (2008).

44 Commentator, *The Spanish Indictment of High-ranking Rwandan Officials*, 6 JOURNAL OF INTERNATIONAL CRIMINAL JUSTICE, 1003 (2008).

45 Doc.Assembly/AU/11(XIII), ACTHPR Report, *supra* note 26, para. 4.

46 I label some NGOs as influential because most of them are umbrellas of national organizations and have also been granted an observer status within the AU. This is the case for the Coalition for an Effective African Court on Human and Peoples' Rights; the East African Law Society; The Pan-African Lawyers Union and the West African Bar Association.

opposing the idea[47] on the grounds of practical difficulties and the possible incompatibility of the structure with the objectives and purposes of the UN Charter.[48] This was rather strange because usually civil society salutes and welcomes every move towards accountability for human rights violations. In fact, one has to understand that civil society and the academia are interested in promoting the ICC,[49] an institution they fought for and which needs support in its infancy stages. For the civil society, a regional court would even diminish the voice and authority of Africa in the governance of the ICC.[50] So, instead of exploring the ACC idea, civil society and the academia have been busy searching for convincing legal and political means and ways to maintain African states' adherence and support to the ICC regime. For instance, professor du Plessis recommends that

> African ICC states parties should call for the AU to develop a plan to promote widespread ratification of the Rome Statute within and beyond Africa' and '[. . .] call for the AU to facilitate greater cooperation between the AU and the ICC by ensuring that the ICC-AU liaison office in Addis Ababa is established and that an agreement between the AU and the ICC on cooperation is finalized.[51]

On the ICC part, action has been taken. Since the negative reaction of the AU to the decision to indict President al Bashir, ICC officials have begun a diplomatic speed race and carried out an intensive outreach campaign in order to maintain confidence in the institution, by conveying a special message that the ICC is not solely targeting Africa. There is no single conference or official event on Africa and the international criminal justice system that has not been sponsored by the ICC or in which ICC officials or staffs have not participated.[52] Moreover, it is rightly argued that the ICC promotes African interests more than it does for any other continent or part of the world. For instance, one senior legal officer at the ICC, himself African, highlighted that

47 *Implications of the African Court of Human and Peoples' Rights Being Empowered to Try International Crimes Such as Genocide, Crimes against Humanity and War Crimes*; Opinion; hereinafter, Implications; available at: <www.africancourtcoalition.org/listDocuments.asp?page_id=27> (Accessed November 10, 2010).

48 *Id.* at 13.

49 See Statement by representatives of African civil society and the legal profession on the implications of the African Union's recent decisions on universal jurisdiction and the work of the International Criminal Court in Africa, Cape Town, May 11, 2009, available at: <www.issafrica.org/uploads/PRAUICC110509.PDF> (Accessed September 23, 2011).

50 *Implications, supra* note 47, at 22.

51 Akande *et al., supra* note 30, at 76.

52 At the an international conference on Africa and the future of international criminal justice held in the summer of 2010 at Wits University (South Africa), the Deputy Prosecutor and the President of the Appeals Chamber were present at the Conference.

> [n]o other continent has paid more dearly than Africa for the absence of legitimate institutions of law and accountability, resulting in a culture of impunity. Events in Rwanda were a grim reminder that such atrocities could be repeated anytime. This served to strengthen Africa's determination and commitment to the creation of a permanent, impartial, effective and independent judicial mechanism to try and punish the perpetrators of these types of crimes whenever they occur.[53]

The lack of interest and the reluctance of civil society and the academia to support the idea of an ACC have hampered a serious academic discussion on the issue. The ICC's active and intensive lobbying efforts also contributed to detract people from thinking outside the ICC box. In my view, the ACC is well warranted and there is a need for a serious academic discussion as to its merits and its feasibility. This chapter offers a modest contribution to this discussion.

14.3 JUSTIFICATIONS FOR AN AFRICAN CRIMINAL COURT

The nature and massive character of international crimes committed in Africa and the impunity resulting from the failure to prosecute the perpetrators call for imaginative and sometimes ambitious solutions. Individual states took important steps in this direction in order to hold accountable persons who committed horrendous crimes. Rwanda, for example, was creative by reviving a traditional judicial mechanism and tasking it with a mission to prosecute genocide and other crimes against humanity committed in Rwanda in 1994. South Africa was also imaginative with its Truth and Reconciliation Commission (TRC). At the regional level, if the AU wants to fulfill its mission and objectives outlined in the AU Constitutive Act and deliver on its promises, there is a real need for a mechanism equipped with the jurisdiction to prosecute individuals and possibly legal persons for the gravest crimes under international law and regional law.

14.3.1 Enhancing the Institutional Capacity to Fight Impunity

The international criminal justice rests on a twofold institutional system: international criminal courts and national criminal courts. National courts are at the frontline of the fight against the impunity of the most heinous international crimes. This is in accordance with principles of international law. Sovereign states where suspected perpetrators of

53 Phakiso Mochochoko, *Africa and the International Criminal Court, in* AFRICAN PERSPECTIVES ON INTERNATIONAL CRIMINAL JUSTICE 245 (Evelyn A. Ankumah & Edward K. Kwakwa eds., 2005).

international crimes are located or states on whose territories crimes were committed or whose nationals are victims or perpetrators have an inherent jurisdiction to prosecute such crimes.[54] If States are unable or unwilling[55] to do so, competent international courts can intervene to suppress international crimes. Hence, international courts act as a back-up for the domestic system.

Although the international justice system relies heavily on domestic and international courts, it is unrealistic to think that it can curb impunity. International courts have a limited jurisdictional mandate over the worst crimes of international law. Their reach is also constrained by limited resources.[56] Moreover, they can only prosecute a handful number of cases usually those involving high profile suspects with great responsibility.[57] For their part, national courts are no better. For various reasons, domestic courts are reluctant to prosecute such crimes, especially those committed by high ranking state officials. This has been the case in Rwanda (RPF genocide-related crimes) or in Uganda (UPDF crimes). Furthermore, domestic legal regimes lack appropriate legislation and expertise to adequately deal with the impunity of serious crimes committed in Africa. Only a handful number of African states have enacted genuine legislations implementing the ICC Statute.[58] Given this limited capacity and the flaws of the current international criminal justice system, impunity of numerous serious crimes reigns while numerous victims are left without any legal and credible way to see justice being rendered.

Some have argued that regional human rights courts and commissions can be appropriate tools to fight impunity.[59] This may be true to the extent that States comply with the rulings of regional bodies. In fact, one must keep in mind that current regional human rights bodies (African Commission and African Court) are charged with the determination of state

---

54 *United States v. Yunis*, District Court, DC, February 12th, 1988 82 ILR 347; 353 (1990).

55 Rome Statute of the ICC, *supra* note 3, Art. 17. It should be noted that ICC case law has added a third prong; that is, the inactivity of national courts, for the ICC's intervention despite the complementarity principle; see *Prosecutor v. Dyilo* ICC-01/04-01/06 (Decision on the Prosecutor's Application for a Warrant of Arrest, June 10, 2006); *Prosecutor v. Katanga and Chui* ICC-01/04-01/07 OA 8 (Judgment on the Appeal of Mr Germain Katanga against the Oral Decision of Trial Chamber II of June 12, 2009 on the Admissibility of the Case, September 25, 2009).

56 William W. Burke-White, *Proactive Complementarity: The International Criminal Court and National Courts in the Rome System of Justice*, 49 Harvard International Law Journal 53, 67 (2008).

57 In its 17 years of existence, the ICTR has completed 55 cases; 15 cases are still pending on appeal; 5 cases are in progress before trial chambers and one case is awaiting trial; available at: <www.unictr.org/Cases/tabid/204/Default.aspx> (Accessed on December 31, 2011).

58 South Africa (Implementation of the Rome Statute of the International Criminal Court Act 27 of 2002, Government Gazette 445, July 18, 2002, No. 23642), Kenya (The International Crimes Act, 2008), Senegal (*Loi* 2007-05 *du 12 fév 2007 modifiant le Code de procédure pénale relative à la mise en oeuvre du Traité instituant la Cour pénale internationale*).

59 Implications, *supra* note 46, at 4.

responsibility. If they were to function properly and effectively, they would at least mimic the inter-American system of human rights. The inter-American human rights mechanisms have developed

> [...] an impressive body of precedents regarding the obligation to investigate, prosecutes and punishes serious violations of the rights to life, to liberty and to physical integrity, especially when those violations are part of a widespread or systematic pattern.[60]

Although there's no equivalent from the African human rights mechanisms as of today, one can expect the African human rights court and commission to emphasize, at a certain time during their activities, on states' obligation to prosecute persons suspected of violating human rights. The systemic problem with these regional bodies is that they are not empowered with jurisdiction to prosecute individuals for human rights violations amounting to international crimes. They can of course play an important role in stigmatizing the need to end impunity but they rely on external institutions – national courts – to implement their findings. Thus, once a determination is made as to the state responsibility in human rights violations, one has again to count on states' courts to implement these findings related to the violation of international obligations. As it has been previously noted, compliance is not obvious[61] and states are not active in prosecuting international crimes suspects.

The inherent inability of the current institutional system provides a leeway to impunity. An ACC would then be an additional accountability mechanism. In this sense, the ACC would be a complementary tool to both national and international courts. It would act whenever there is no will or no capacity to act on the part of municipal courts and would definitely contribute to reduce the impunity comfort zone for perpetrators of international crimes. Therefore, contrary to what people may think, it is meant to supplement – not to supplant – domestic or international courts. It might provide 'a different layer of a regional complement to the international criminal justice System'.[62] This argument lines perfectly with the practice in the area of human rights in Africa. In this field, since most

60 Juan Mendez, *Regional Courts and Commissions,* Background Paper for Panel on Regional Organs of Protection, Consultative Conference on International Criminal Justice, 4 (2009).

61 According to Professor Frans Viljoen and Lirette Louw, state parties did comply fully and in timely fashion with the recommendations of the African Commission in only 14% of admissible communications; non-compliance was observed in 30% and partial compliance in 32%; see Frans Viljoen & Lirette Louw, *State Compliance with the Recommendations of the African Commission on Human and Peoples' Rights 1993-2004,* 101 AMERICAN JOURNAL OF INTERNATIONAL LAW 1, 5-6 (2007).

62 Bahame Tom Nyanduga, *Reflections and Perspectives of the African Commission on Human and Peoples' Rights,* Consultative Conference on International Criminal Justice, 6 (2009).

African States are part to different international human rights instruments, it has often been stressed that regional arrangements 'should be complementary to, rather than in competition with, the universal processes undertaken within the wider UN system'.[63] The same holds true in the area of international criminal law. The ACC would help the current international criminal justice system to effectively fulfill its mandate. Instead of competing with the ICC or domestic courts, the ACC would be part of a community of courts[64] acting in a decentralized system with the same goal: fighting against impunity.

14.3.2 An ACC is an Important Tool for the AU to Achieve its Main Objectives

In July 2000, at its thirty-sixth ordinary session held in Lomé (Togo), the Assembly of Heads of States and Government of the Organization of African Unity (OAU) adopted the Constitutive Act of the African Union (AU), a new institution replacing the OAU. The African Union was formally inaugurated in 2002. It is viewed as 'Africa's collective response to the phenomenon of globalization'[65] and also an adequate architecture to help Africans face the multiple problems that plague the continent. Therefore, the new organization is founded on key principles aimed at securing peace and stability as well as protecting African populations from the international crimes and armed conflicts.[66] To this effect, different organs have been instituted or reinforced within the AU. One can mention the creation of an African Standby Force, a Peace and Security Council, a Pan-African Parliament, the reinforcement of regional economic communities,[67] etc. This institution-building exercise aims at enhancing Africa's capacity to face regional problems by providing the AU with appropriate tools to achieve its objectives. A Common African Defence and Security Policy has been developed with the objective of ensuring collective responses to internal and external threats to Africa.[68] The existence of exceptional circumstances like the commission of international crimes has been identified and listed as an internal threat to common African security.[69] The AU has thus a responsibility to protect the victims of international crimes, especially when the responsible state is unable or unwilling to handle the situation

63 Tiyanjana Maluwa, *International Law Making in the Organization of the African Unity: An Overview*, 12 African Journal of International and Comparative Law 201, 202 (2000).

64 William W. Burke-White, *A Community of Courts: Towards a System of International Criminal Law Enforcement*, 24 Michigan Journal of International Law 1, 3 (2002).

65 Tiyanjana Maluwa, *The Constitutive Act of the African Union and Institution-Building in Postcolonial Africa*, 16 Leiden Journal of International Law 157, 160 (2003).

66 These core principles and others are found in Arts. 3 and 4 of the Constitutive Act.

67 Regional Economic Communities have been created pursuant to the 1991Abuja Treaty. But, they are now being tasked with security missions as demonstrated by ECOWAS' intervention in Liberia and SADC in Lesotho.

68 African Union, Solemn Declaration on a Common African Defence and Security Policy, Sirte (Libya), February 28, 2004 para. 13(a).

69 *Id.* para. 8(II)(e).

properly. In fact, the African Standby Force has been created for the purpose of, *inter alia*, military intervention inside AU member states facing genocide, crimes against humanity and war crimes or other exceptional circumstances.[70] No action of a judicial nature has been contemplated within the African Standby Force framework. Nevertheless, the latter can pave the way for judicial intervention. Once atrocities are stopped, an ACC can play an important role in prosecuting persons who jeopardized peace and security in Africa.

Finally, in order to maintain peace and security on the continent, it is important that the AU adopt a holistic approach which integrates justice as a fundamental pillar for a durable peace and stability. So far, no criminal justice initiative has been undertaken under the auspices of the AU. A recent development signals a selective and ad hoc action. For instance, the High-Level Panel on Darfur has recommended the creation of a hybrid court for Sudan.[71] While this is a praiseworthy shift, the AU cannot afford ad hoc judicial intervention in every African case. In order to fully accomplish its objectives as enshrined in the Constitutive Act, the AU needs an institution appropriate for regional action. The proposed ACC is a valuable means to that effect. According to Honorable Nyanduga, such an institution is feasible and it is a welcome development in the long run.[72]

14.4 Promoting a Regional Culture of Individual Criminal Accountability for Gross Violations of Human Rights and Strengthening the African Human Rights Protection Regime

The existing African human rights mechanisms are not competent to determine individual criminal responsibility for massive and gross violations of human rights. They can only ascertain state responsibility for these violations. Nevertheless, they can indirectly trigger individual responsibility when they recommend (African commission) or order (African court) states to investigate and subsequently prosecute persons responsible for human rights violations. However, they do not have control on state's follow-up action. Therefore, there is a high risk that persons responsible for human rights violations go unpunished since states are often inactive in prosecuting suspects. Moreover, there is no appropriate mechanism entitled to take action at a continental level in order to hold individuals accountable for their deeds.

The need to promote a regional culture of individual responsibility for gross human rights violations justifies the intervention of international criminal courts operating in or out of

70 Girmachew Alemu Aneme, *The African Standby Force: major issues under Mission Scenario Six*, 2 Political Perspectives Journal 1 (2008).

71 The Quest For Peace, Justice And Reconciliation: Report of The African Union High-Level Panel On Darfur (AUPD) (2009), AU Doc.PSC/AHG/2(CCVII); (hereinafter the Darfur Report), paras 246-254.

72 Nyanduga, *supra* note 61, at 5.

Africa. Some have even advocated for ICC regional trial chambers operating on the continent or in the state where crimes have been committed[73], with the participation of a number of locally recruited staff. This particular suggestion, which is legally based on Article 3 of the ICC Statute,[74] has some merit. For instance, regional ICC chambers can successfully address the serious criticism against the ICC as well as other international criminal courts that they administer a remote justice detached from the sight of the victims and the affected communities. This created a perception of a foreign justice with less deterrent effect. However, as regional trial chambers would be part of the ICC, they will suffer from the same limitations specific to the ICC: limited resources and hence a limited jurisdictional reach only over a small number of high profile perpetrators of international crimes. While their main contribution will be the visibility of justice, the impunity problem that needs to be tackled will remain unsolved. Also, since regional trial chambers are extensions of the ICC, the same African criticisms against the world court will not be addressed. The risk of a possible amplification of the imperialistic or neocolonialist argument is even higher since the ICC chambers will be prosecuting Africans at home, on the African soil. This is probably the reason why the AU is reluctant to accept an ICC regional bureau that ICC officials want to be based in Addis-Ababa,[75] the heart of the AU decision-making power.

A proper mechanism which, by its nature, is beyond imperialistic apprehensions and fears is needed. Creating an ACC is then timely. It would not only help to address those criticisms but it would also equip Africa with the required tools to establish a culture of individual criminal accountability for international crimes committed in Africa. The ACC will then strengthen the existing African human rights protection regime and will shield African States from a perceived undue judicial interference.

14.4.1 Prosecuting Serious Crimes of a Particular Resonance to Africa

The impunity that plagues Africa is related to serious crimes under international law, *i.e.* crimes against humanity, war crimes and genocide. These particular crimes are concerning to the humankind.[76] That is why the international community as a whole intervenes

73 Stuart Ford, *The Promise of Local or Regional ICC Trial Chambers: Incorporating the Benefits of the Hybrid Tribunals into the ICC*, (2010), available at: <http://ssrn.com/abstract=1605294> (Accessed April 23, 2010); William W. Burke-White, *Regionalization of International Criminal Law Enforcement: A Preliminary Exploration*, 38 Texas International Law Journal 729, 750-751 (2003).

74 Art. 3 of the Rome Statute provides for the possibility that "the Court may sit elsewhere, whenever it considers it desirable".

75 Decision on the Progress Report of the Commission on the Implementation of Decision Assembly/AU/DEC. 270(XIV) on the Second Ministerial Meeting on the Rome Statute of the International Criminal Court (ICC), Assembly of the African Union, Fifteenth Ordinary Session, Kampala, Uganda, July 25-27, 2010; Doc.Assembly/AU/10(XV), para. 8.

76 ICC Statute, *supra* note 3, Art. 2.

in order to protect some of its members who have been victimized by massive atrocities. Apart from these worst crimes, other types of crimes of a serious concern to Africa do not receive a particular attention at the international level. For instance, the practice of unconstitutional changes of government has hampered democracy in Africa to the extent that the AU adopted a treaty prohibiting, *inter alia*, illegal means of accessing or maintaining to power.[77] Other crimes particularly meaningful to Africa have not been prosecuted in international courts (ex: apartheid, slavery and colonization-related crimes). Moreover, crimes with major adverse political, economic, social or cultural consequences to Africa and Africans have been criminalized in regional conventions. This is the case for the unconstitutional change of government,[78] mercenarism,[79] corruption,[80] terrorism[81] and plunder of mineral resources.[82] Relevant treaties do not allude to an African criminal court that can carry out prosecutions of these crimes.[83] Following the international criminal law lines, the responsibility lies again with States' courts. According to most of the African treaties, States acting individually or in cooperation with others are expected to prosecute the said crimes.[84]

Nevertheless, when the AU Assembly of Heads of State and Government asked the AU Commission to study the implications of granting a criminal jurisdiction to the African Court of Human and Peoples' Rights, the Assembly identified in its resolution crimes *such as*[85] genocide, war crimes and crimes against humanity.[86] The use of the expression "*such as*" shows that the enumeration is not exhaustive. The above mentioned crimes of serious concern to Africa can then be included in the list of crimes constituting the material jurisdiction of the African criminal court. This regional institution would be an

77 The unconstitutional change of government is broadly defined so as to include, *inter alia*, any amendment or revision of the constitution or legal instruments, which is an infringement on the principles of democratic change of government; see African Charter on Democracy, Elections and Governance, adopted by the Eighth Ordinary Session of the Assembly, held in Addis Ababa, Ethiopia, January 30, 2007, Art. 23. Also, the AU Commission asked the Consultant on the extension of the criminal jurisdiction to the African court to consider the criminalization of the unconstitutional change of government in the statute of the ACC.

78 *Id.* Arts. 23 and 25(5).

79 Convention for the Elimination of Mercenarism in Africa, Libreville , Gabon, July 3, 1977.

80 African Union Convention on Preventing and Combating Corruption, AU 2nd Ordinary Session, Maputo, July 11, 2003.

81 Convention on the Prevention and Combating of Terrorism, Algiers, Algeria, July 14, 1999.

82 Protocol Against the Illegal Exploitation of Natural Resources, International Conference on the Great Lakes Region, November 30, 2006.

83 With the exception of the *African Charter on Democracy, Elections and Governance* which provides for that 'perpetrators of unconstitutional change of government may also be tried before the competent court of the Union', Art. 25 (5).

84 Terrorism Convention, *supra* note 80, Art. 8(4); Corruption Convention, *supra* note 79, Art. 13(c).

85 My emphasis.

86 Decision on the Implementation of the Assembly Decision on the Abuse of the Principle of Universal Jurisdiction, AU Doc.Assembly/AU/3(XII)Assembly/AU/Dec.213(XII), para. 9 (2009); Decision on the Abuse of the Principle of Universal Jurisdiction, Doc.EX.CL/606(XVII), para. 5 (2010).

appropriate enforcement mechanism for the relevant African treaties dealing with matters of African concern. Since international courts do not have jurisdiction over the specific crimes,[87] the ACC, along with municipal courts, can close the net over the impunity of their perpetrators.

A regional court is also well suited to address the transnational aspect of the criminality in Africa. In fact, modern criminality in Africa or elsewhere is not only national; it is transnational and has regional ramifications which go beyond the reach of some individual states. This aspect is well exemplified by the situation in the Great Lakes Region where government militaries and armed groups operate from one country to another in total impunity. For instance, Rwandan and Ugandan Defense forces have been operating in DRC, as well as the Ugandan Lord Resistance Army (LRA) and the rebels of the Forces démocratiques de libération du Rwanda (FDLR).[88] These conflicts' dynamics are rarely taken into consideration during the international prosecutions of crimes committed during the armed conflicts. Although international crimes are of great concern to the entire international community, their impact and ramifications are often very much felt in the region concerned. Therefore, regional institutions are well placed to tackle justice issues in an effective and efficient cultural sensitive manner. The ACC can then be a proper forum for addressing the transnational aspect of the massive criminality.

14.5 Spearheading African Contribution to the Development of International Criminal Law

It has been frequently argued that Africa is a recipient of, rather than a contributor to the development of international law.[89] To some extent, it rings true as far as international criminal law is concerned. The international criminal law applicable to the prosecutions of heinous crimes committed in Africa has always been created and developed in western cultures, especially since the Nuremberg trials. Of course African states have participated in and contributed to different forums where international criminal law norms are crafted.[90] But, fewer norms incorporate or, at least, allow the infusion of some African

87 International criminal courts prosecute war crimes, crimes against humanity and genocide, see for example ICC Statute, Art. 1; ICTR Statute, Art. 1; ICTY Statute, Art. 1; SCSL Statute, Art. 1. Crimes like terrorism, corruption, mercenarism, *coups d'Etats,* are not prosecutable per se unless they can be linked to one or more of the most core crimes under international law.

88 *Report of the Mapping Exercise documenting the most serious violations of human rights and international humanitarian law committed within the territory of the Democratic Republic of the Congo between March 1993 and June 2003* (August 2010), hereinafter Mapping Report, available at: <www.ohchr.org/Documents/Countries/ZR/DRC_MAPPING_REPORT_FINAL_EN.pdf> (Accessed January 8, 2012).

89 Peter A. Mutharika, *The Role of International Law in the Twenty-First Century: An African Perspective*, 18 Fordham International Law Journal 1706 (1994-1995); Maluwa, *supra* note 63, at 201.

90 For an African contribution to the establishment of the current ICC, see du Plessis, *supra* note 30.

spirit of justice. Since some time, Africa has been experiencing some forms of justice embedded and nurtured in African traditions and cultures. For instance, South Africa resorted to a Truth and Reconciliation Commission in order to hold accountable persons who committed apartheid related crimes and tackle some issues arising thereof. Rwanda has been very ingenious and revived the Gacaca, a traditional mechanism for disputes settlements, which has been used to prosecute genocidaires and criminals against humanity.[91] Acholi people in Uganda claim that they can use the traditional *Mato Oput* ceremonials in order to hold LRA members and other suspects accountable for their deeds during the never-ending Ugandan armed conflict.[92] The rationale behind the choice of these mechanisms is that in an African perspective, there is no genocidaire or war criminal by nature; genocidaires and war criminals are social products; that is why society as a whole has a say in tackling the genocide or war criminality situation. For that purpose, the mechanisms are in favor of peoples' participation in their proceedings with the aim of knowing why massive and systematic criminality occurred, restoring social harmony and fostering national reconciliation. Hence, the determination of the guilt is not the essential objective of the processes contrary to the classical and western methodology of determining individual criminal responsibility. As a consequence, in these national proceedings, thousands of cases are dealt with in a short period of time with minimal means.[93] This contrasts with the performance of international criminal courts with enormous financial and human resources.[94]

Though this development is very important for the fight against impunity, so far there has been no academic work to systematize the best practices from these different experiences so that they can inspire and be used by other transitional justice mechanisms, including a possible ACC. The ACC can contribute to systematize rules and principles for the operation of traditional and community justice mechanisms. As a purely African institution, it will have authority to do so, with the required sensitivity and expertise. The systematization and harmonization of the African approaches on transitional justice will be an

91 *Supra* note 4.

92 Kasaija Phillip Apuuli, *Amnesty and International Law: The Case of the Lord's Resistance Army Insurgents in Northern Uganda*, 5 AFRICAN JOURNAL ON CONFLICT RESOLUTION 33, 36 (2005). IRIN News, Acholi Leaders in The Hague to Meet ICC over LRA Probe (March 15, 2005); Bishop Baker Ochola, *Uganda: The Acholi Traditional Justice is Enough for Kony*, NEW VISION (August 28, 2006).

93 With a budget of only $40 million, the Gacaca courts have prosecuted over a million cases in 9 years, see Hirondelle News Agency Gacaca Official Closure Postponed Sine Die, of September 29, 2010 available at: <www.hirondellenews.com/content/view/13738/26> (Accessed September 30, 2010). See also Phil Clark, *Truth and Reconciliation at a Price*, 111 INTERNATIONAL JUSTICE TRIBUNE 2, 2 (2010).

94 With a budget of approximately $267 million (for the year 2008/2009), the ICTR has prosecuted a small number of cases in 15 years of its existence; *supra* note 48 above; see also Hirondelle News Agency, 1994 Genocide: Gacaca Trials Discharge One Million Cases So Far, of April 3, 2009, available at: <www.hirondellenews.com/content/view/12201/26> (Accessed November 25, 2011).

important contribution to the international criminal law. It will also enhance the credibility of the mechanisms so that their work could no longer be less regarded by classical criminal courts. During the process of systematization of the lessons learned from these processes, the ACC could also lay out the kind of relationship that criminal courts, either national, regional or international, would have with traditional or community mechanisms. Finally, I find it wise for criminal courts, including the ICC and the ACC, to show deference and refrain from exercising jurisdiction once credible traditional or community mechanisms have properly decided a case.

Once the systematization is accomplished, the ACC could also be guided by the systematized rules and principles. In its operation, the ACC should be able or have the courage to rely on African standards and initiatives. As Professor Murray pointed out speaking of the African Commission on Human and People's Rights (ACHPR) and the AU organs, 'not to do that will exacerbate the perception that the UN or European systems are in some way preferable'.[95] African perspectives and standards which, to the extent possible, should be consistent with international norms, are a fertile terrain for cross-fertilization and domestication of international criminal law. In fact, it is regrettable to see that most African bodies prefer to resort to international or western standards, because these ones are well developed and have been tested throughout the time. For instance, the ACHPR mirrors the European human rights mechanisms jurisprudential findings.[96] In so doing, African institutions reinforce and perpetuate the supremacy of the system which requires us to think in western terms and concentrate less on exploring and hence developing African standards. In this way, an important contextual element is missing and the solutions may be not well crafted.

This is very poignant in the area of international criminal justice where basic doctrines are of western origin. For example, the doctrine of superior responsibility was conceived in a well structured and organized western military and bureaucratic setting when it fits to think that a superior could be held responsible for the actions of his subordinates. In most African armed conflicts, this may not be the case. Problems can arise when principles and case-law have a poor sociological fit within the non-western societies to which they are to

95 Rachel Murray, *Women's Rights and the Organization of African Unity and African Union: The Protocol on the Rights of Women in Africa, in* INTERNATIONAL LAW: MODERN FEMINIST APPROACHES 253, 256 (Doris Buss & Ambreena Manji eds., 2005).

96 *Antoine Bissangou v. Republic of Congo*, Communication 253/2002, 40th Ordinary Session of the African Commission held in Banjul, The Gambia (November 15-29, 2006); *Article 19 v. The State of Eritrea*, Communication 275/2003, (Decided at the 41st Ordinary Session, May 2007), African Human Rights Law Reports 73 (ACHPR 2007); *Zimbabwe Human Rights NGO Forum v. Zimbabwe*, Communication 245/2002, (Decided at the 39th Ordinary Session of the African Commission 2006), African Human Rights Law Reports 128 (ACHPR 2006).

be applied.[97] Each norm and principle of international criminal law needs to be adapted to the culture, customs and practices of the affected communities. Otherwise, imposing western-based international norms on people of a different culture may be counter-productive. Africanizing international criminal norms lies with the mission of an ACC. There can be no imaginable institution that can do the job better than the ACC.

Now that the justifications for an ACC are provided, it is essential to explore its legal foundations.

14.6 Legal Basis for an African Criminal Court

The previous part of this book chapter has demonstrated that an African criminal court is worthwhile. This section explores the possible legal foundations for the creation and the operationalization of this institution.

14.6.1 *The Constitutive Act of the African Union and Other Regional Legal Instruments*

In 2000, the former Organization of African Unity metamorphosed in the African Union. Two fundamental principles are among the innovations of this transformation and are enshrined in the Constitutive Act of the new institution. Section 4(h) provides for an important 'right of the Union to intervene in a Member State pursuant to a decision of the Assembly in respect of grave circumstances, namely: war crimes, genocide and crimes against humanity'. Section 4(o) provides for the "respect for the sanctity of human life, condemnation and rejection of impunity (. . .)". These principles are interconnected. According to the first principle (Art. 4(h)), when mass atrocities erupt in a member state, the AU has a right to intervene and stop them.[98] This right to intervene provides for a legal framework to the new doctrine of the responsibility to protect, currently known under its acronym R2P.[99] This doctrine legitimizes some actions that may otherwise be characterized as violations of principles of international law protecting state sovereignty, namely the non-intervention principle and the prohibition of the use of force against a

97 Tim Kelsall, *International Criminal Justice and Non-Western Cultures, in* Oxford Transitional Justice Research, Debating International Justice in Africa, Otjr Collected Essays, 17 (2008-2010).

98 Soon after the entry into force of the Constitutive Act, Art. 4(h) was amended at the first extraordinary session of the Assembly of Heads of State and Government in order to add another ground for AU intervention, namely 'a serious threat to a legitimate order', upon the recommendation of the Peace and Security Council. For a critical analysis of these early amendments, see Evarist Baimu & Kathryn Sturman, *Amendment To The African Union's Right To Intervene,* 12 African Security Review 37 (2003).

99 Dan Kuwali, *The End of Humanitarian Intervention: Evaluation of the African Union's Right of Intervention,* 9 African Journal on Conflict Resolution 41, 43 (2009).

sovereign state, established under Article 2 of the UN Charter. According to Ben Kioko, Legal adviser to the AU,

> in providing for a right of intervention, the African Union has moved away from non-interference or non-intervention — which is a cardinal principle in both the United Nations Charter and the Constitutive Act of the African Union — to what could be referred to as the doctrine of "non-indifference".[100]

Although Article 4(h) of the AU Constitutive Act is 'one of the cornerstones for the vision of saving civilians from the scourges of armed conflicts in Africa',[101] it does not provide for a particular form of intervention, whether military or non military. However, it is to be expected that circumstances dictate the form of intervention. So far, laudable initiatives have been more or less successfully carried out in different countries. African peacekeeping missions have been sent to Burundi where they successfully helped in the reintegration of former belligerents in one army. Other peacekeeping missions are still underway in different parts of Africa like Somalia[102] and Sudan[103]. No judicial intervention has been carried out at the AU initiative in order to back-up peace agreements and uphold the sanctity of life and deter future crimes.[104] In order to uphold the AU commitment to eradicate impunity on the continent, a judicial intervention is well warranted in case of crimes against humanity, war crimes and genocide. In fact, empirical studies present justice as a pillar of a sustainable peace and stability.[105] Hence, criminal prosecutions against persons most responsible for heinous crimes committed during the atrocities, once these are successfully stopped or at the earliest possible, can contribute to deter future crimes and uphold the sanctity of life.

100 Ben Kioko, *The Right of Intervention Under the African Union's Constitutive Act: From Non-interference to Non-intervention,* 85 INTERNATIONAL REVIEW OF THE RED CROSS 807, 819 (2003).

101 Dan Kuwali, *Art. 4(h) + R2P: Towards a Doctrine of Persuasive, Prevention to End Mass Atrocity Crimes*, 3 INTERDISCIPLINARY JOURNAL OF HUMAN RIGHTS LAW 55 (2008-2009).

102 For the mandate and the activities of the African Union Mission in Somalia (AMISOM), available at: <www.africa-union.org/root/au/auc/departments/psc/amisom/amisom.htm> (Accessed December 22, 2011).

103 For the mandate and the activities of the African Union-United Nations Mission in Darfur (UNAMID), available at: <http://unamid.unmissions.org/> (Accessed December 22, 2011).

104 One can mention the exceptional case of Hissène Habré, former President of Chad who's being prosecuted in Senegal at the AU initiative; see for instance *Decision on the Hissene Habre Case*, Assembly of the African Union, Fifteenth Ordinary Session, Kampala, Uganda, July 25-27, 2010, Doc.Assembly/AU/11(XV).

105 Juan E. Mendez, *The Importance of Justice in Securing Peace*, Review Conference of the Rome Statute, ICC Doc.RC-ST-PJ-INF.3-ENG-30052010, Kampala, May 30, 2010, <www.icc-cpi.int/iccdocs/asp_docs/RC2010/Stocktaking/RC-ST-PJ-INF.3-ENG.pdf> (Accessed September 30, 2010); Priscilla Hayner, *Managing the Challenges of Integrating Justice Efforts and Peace Processes,* Review Conference of the Rome Statute, ICC Doc. RC-ST-PJ-INF.4-ENG-30052010, Kampala, May 30, 2010, <www.icc-cpi.int/iccdocs/asp_docs/RC2010/Stocktaking/RC-ST-PJ-INF.4-ENG.pdf> (Accessed September 30, 2010).

Other African legal instruments also demonstrate the resolve of the regional organization to condemn and combat international crimes. For instance, according to Article 58 of the *African Charter on Human and Peoples' Rights*, the African Commission has to act in case of massive or serious violations of human rights, which undoubtedly would comprise international crimes. In the African refugee law, persons suspected of international crimes or actions against the UN purposes are denied a refugee protection.[106] Likewise, women's rights law obliges states to consider certain acts of sexual violence directed against women in armed conflicts as international crimes and to bring the perpetrators to justice before a competent criminal jurisdiction.[107] Quite recently, Article 4(h) of the AU Constitutive Act has been reaffirmed in the *African Union Convention for the Protection and Assistance of Internally Displaced Persons in Africa.*[108] Moreover, the latter instrument requests states to criminalize arbitrary displacement amounting to war crimes, crimes against humanity and genocide[109] and to ensure individual responsibility or the accountability of non-State actors for those acts or complicity thereof.[110]

In order for the AU to keep up with its commitment to fight impunity, cement sustainable peace and stability and ensure a proper protection of African citizens in the long run, a continental-level criminal organ, such as the ACC, will be a valuable tool to discharge its responsibilities arising out of Article 4(h) and Article 4(o) of the AU Constitutive Act and other regional legal instruments. Given the nature of the heinous crimes and people who are involved – generally high ranking State officials – it is unrealistic to count on States' courts to do the job, especially in the aftermath of a repressive regime, a bloody ethnic or racial conflict. The ICC can help but it will not be able to deal with all possible cases.

14.6.2 *The Principle of Complementarity*

The principle of complementarity was adopted at the Rome conference on the creation of the International Criminal Court. According to paragraph 10 of the preamble and Article 1 of the Rome statute, the ICC is complementary to national courts.[111] In its original

106 Convention Governing the Specific Aspects of Refugee Problems in Africa (1969), adopted in Addis Ababa, September 10, 1969, Art. 1(5).

107 Protocol to the African Charter on Human and People's Rights on the Rights of Women in Africa, adopted in Maputo, 11 July 2003, Art. 11(3).

108 African Union Convention for the Protection and Assistance of Internally Displaced Persons in Africa (Kampala Convention), adopted in Kampala on 22 October 2009, Art. 8(1).

109 *Id.* Art. 4(6).

110 *Id.* Arts. 3(g) and 3(h).

111 This is a clear departure from the UN ad hoc tribunals' regime. The ICTR and the ICTY statutes provide for primacy of international courts over national courts of all states, see ICTY Statute, Art. 9(2), and Art. 8(2) of the ICTR Statute.

meaning, complementarity implies that the prosecution of international crimes lies primarily with states. In fact, national judicial institutions 'offer the best places to try these crimes, as they would serve as a deterrent to others and give victims an opportunity to participate and closely follow the proceedings at the national level'.[112] The international court intervenes as a backstop to national jurisdictions, only when states are, inactive, unable or unwilling to act against genocidaires, war criminals and criminals against humanity.[113] This is what some authors have termed passive complementarity.[114] The principle delicately balances the concept of an international criminal justice regime and the doctrine of state sovereignty.[115]

Nowadays, leading scholars, including ICC's Office of the Prosecutor (OTP), argue that the ICC should not act passively but more proactively in order to create a more active and cooperative relationship with States.[116] In one of the OTP's informal expert paper on complementarity, it has been suggested that the ICC should be

> [a]ctively encouraging non-territorial States to exercise jurisdiction. The guiding principle in doing so should be to actively encourage those States that provide the most promising prospect for an effective investigation and prosecution. The availability of and access to witnesses, the presence of the alleged perpetrator on a State's territory, and the independence and impartiality of the judiciary are important elements in determining that prospect.[117]

According to this passage, proactive complementarity can offer a legal framework for involving non-territorial states to exercise jurisdiction over ICC crimes using the principle of universal jurisdiction or the personality principle. In that case, ICC would not claim jurisdiction if a genuine action has been taken by non-territorial states. Although the birth of the complementarity principle is located within the Rome statute, it is important to note that it is not construed restrictively. Non-territorial states can invoke the ICC complementarity when they deal with international crimes.

---

112 Benson Olugbuo, *Positive Complementarity and the Fight against Impunity in Africa, in* PROSECUTING INTERNATIONAL CRIMES IN AFRICA 257(Chacha Murungu & Japhet Biegon eds., 2011).

113 *Supra* note 46.

114 Burke-White, *supra* note 56, at 53-108.

115 Jackson Nyamuya Maogoto, *The International Criminal Court goes to bat on African Terrain: A Snapshot of Jurisdictional Hurdles Posed by the Situation in Sudan and Uganda*, COMMENT, available at: <http://ssrn.com/abstract> (Accessed September 13, 2010) .

116 Prosecutorial Strategy 2009-2012, (2010) Office of the Prosecutor, para. 16-17; K.A. Marshall, *Prevention and Complementarity in the International Criminal Court: A Positive Approach,* 17 HUMAN RIGHTS BRIEF 21 (2010); Burke-White, *supra* note 56, at 68.

117 Informal Expert Paper: The Principle of Complementarity in Practice, ICC-OTP 2003, at para. 76.

Using the Rome Statute model, I think complementarity can indirectly offer a legal basis for the creation of a regional judicial institution. Up to now, international lawyers have insisted on and promoted domestic courts as the natural forum for prosecuting international crimes. According to one scholar, "[t]he lack of attention paid to regional opportunities for enforcing international criminal law is surprising in light of the trend toward new regionalism in the study of international relations and the growing number of other regional regimes enforcing other substantive areas of international law."[118] But, this is understandable given the current status and the central place of the principle of sovereignty according to which States have a primary responsibility in international law to ensure accountability for heinous crimes. However, the question of how they proceed is a policy choice and a matter of state sovereignty. Nothing in international law forbids them to act collectively and to cooperate among themselves and create bilateral or multilateral mechanisms complementary to municipal courts. Instead, international law does even encourage them to do so. For instance, the Rome Statute preamble affirms that the effective prosecution of the most serious crimes must be ensured by taking measures at the national level and by enhancing international cooperation.[119] According to Rule 161 identified in the *International Committee of the Red Cross (ICRC)* study on the customary rules of international humanitarian law, states must make every effort to cooperate, to the extent possible, with each other in order to facilitate the investigation of war crimes and the prosecution of the suspects.[120] In the 1973 *UN Principles of international cooperation in the detection, arrest, extradition and punishment of persons guilty of war crimes and crime against humanity*, it is also emphasized that "States shall co-operate with each other on a bilateral and multilateral basis with a view to halting and preventing war crimes and crimes against humanity, and shall take the domestic and international measures necessary for that purpose".[121]

International criminal law does not determine the form of state cooperation. Classical forms of cooperation in criminal matters include assisting a prosecuting state in securing the evidence, in arresting and transferring or extraditing the suspect, in protecting witnesses, etc. One can also think of a more institutionalized cooperation. In the African context, states can decide to get together and create a regional court for which they share the costs and to which they can contribute talent and expertise".

Therefore, through state cooperation, States can transfer or delegate their jurisdiction over international crimes to bilateral or multilateral institutions. International as well

118 Burke-White, *supra* note 73, at 730.

119 ICC Rome Statute, *supra* note 3, preamble, para. 4.

120 Jean-Marie Henckaerts & Louise Doswald-Beck, Customary International Humanitarian Law I (2005), Rule 161.

121 Principles of International Cooperation in the Detection, Arrest, Extradition and Punishment of Persons Guilty of War Crimes and Crime Against Humanity, GA, UN Doc. Res.3074(XXVIII) (1973), principle 3.

as regional mechanisms are conceived in order to complement the efforts of individual states. Accordingly, the principle of complementarity can serve as a legal foundation for the creation of the ACC. Indeed, a continental criminal court would supplement the ICC and national courts' efforts in combating impunity on the African continent.

14.6.3 Article 52(1) of the United Nations Charter

The United Nations Organization's main mission is the maintenance of global peace and security as well as the promotion and protection of human rights. It is well known that international crimes threaten and breach the international peace and security.[122] The UN system has resorted to criminal courts as means to maintain or restore international peace and security in the aftermath of mass atrocities such as genocide, ethnic cleansing, war crimes and crimes against humanity. This was the intention of the Security Council when it created the ad hoc international criminal tribunals for Rwanda and the former Yugoslavia.[123] Pursuant to Article 52(1) of the UN Charter, 'regional arrangements or agencies for dealing with such matters relatively to the maintenance of international peace' can be created at a regional level. However, some conditions are attached to the creation of regional arrangements or agencies: these institutions must be appropriate for regional action and not incompatible with the purposes and principles of the United Nations.[124] The meaning of 'regional arrangements or agencies' was not made clear. According to Boutros-Boutros Ghali, former UN Secretary General, this allows 'useful flexibility for undertakings by a group of States to deal with a matter appropriate for regional action which also could contribute to the maintenance of international peace and security'.[125] It is then suggested that regional agencies or arrangements will deal with matters covered by Chapters VI and VII of the UN Charter,[126] especially 'preventive diplomacy, peace-keeping, peacemaking and postconflict peace-building'.[127] Regional agencies are not relevant only in the absence of international institutions; they can be created in conjunction with international mechanisms in charge of the maintenance or the restoration of international peace and security.

---

122 ICC Statute, *supra* note 3, preamble, para. 3.

123 ICTY Statute, Art. 1, SC. Res.808, UN.S.C.O.R., 48th Session., 3175th mtg., UN. Doc. S/RES/808 (February 22, 1993); ICTR Statute, *supra* note 1 above.

124 United Nations Charter, Art. 52(2).

125 An Agenda for Peace Preventive Diplomacy, Peacemaking and Peace-keeping: Report of the Secretary-General pursuant to the statement adopted by the Summit Meeting of the Security Council on January 31, 1992, , U.N. Doc. A/47/277-S/24111, 17 June 1992, para. 61, (hereinafter the Agenda).

126 GOODRICH, M. LELAND & HAMBRO EDVARD, THE CHARTER OF THE UNITED NATIONS: COMMENTARY AND DOCUMENTS 183 (1946).

127 The Agenda, *supra* note 125, para. 64.

The ACC may be such a regional agency referred to in Article 52(1). It is appropriate for regional action against the pervasive phenomenon of impunity for international crimes in Africa. Also, since its material jurisdiction would comprise serious crimes with a particular resonance to Africa, these matters can well be dealt with in a regional context. The ACC is also compatible with the objectives of the UN. Like the ad hoc tribunals, the ACC would be an excellent means to reinforce the AU efforts to maintain peace, security and stability on the continent as previously referred to.[128]

In conclusion, the ACC has strong legal foundations. The main objections that this idea generates originate from elsewhere though they are not unsolvable.

14.7 Potential Objections and Counter-Objections to the ACC

The idea of creating an African criminal court has been met with mixed sentiments in Africa. Political actors in their majority are in favor of such an institution. Important segments of the African civil society strongly object to the idea.[129] The international community seems not to be prepared to accept it. In this last part, the main objections against the ACC are explored and some explanations and possibly some counter-objections are developed.

The first important objection against the ACC is linked to the general perception of poor performance or, at least, an unconvincing record of accomplishments of regional human rights institutions. Although some African regional institutions have been there for decades, their contribution towards the protection and promotion of human and peoples' rights is not very impressive. It is even poor if one compares their record of accomplishments to the magnitude of human rights violations.[130] For instance, the African Human and Peoples' Rights Court has one judgment[131] on its records in almost ten years of existence. For that reason, the idea of a new regional institution is not very attractive. But, I think one must take into consideration the youth of the African Union which can justify in part the failures or the poor record of performance of some of its organs. The AU itself, with its former mother organization the OAU, has gone through a lot of transformations

128 *Id.* at 15-16.

129 Implications, *supra* note 46.

130 George Mukundi Wachira, African Court on Human and Peoples' Rights: Ten Years on and Still No Justice 12-17 (2009).

131 *Michelot Yogogombaye v. Republic of Senegal*, application No. 001/2008. This decision was not even on the merits; the case failed the admissibility test as Senegal, the Defendant State has not yet signed a declaration, in conformity with Art. 34(6) of the Statute of the Court, allowing individuals or organizations to lodge complaints with the court.

132 Kioko, *supra* note 100, at 811.

of its organs, mandate and structures in order to face regional challenges and side effects of global phenomena such as financial crisis, globalization.[132] This was followed by an institution-building phase which culminated, three years ago, in the merger of the African Court of Justice and the African Court of Human and Peoples' Rights. The more the AU strengthens its organs and structures, the more effective and performing will they be. It will take some time for them to be fully functional.[133]

Setting up appropriate regional institutions will probably continue as new challenges arise. The ACC which is appropriate to face the African impunity problem will also encounter some organizational problems before it comes to fruition. A good performance of the ACC cannot easily be anticipated. It is a truism that institutions of this nature usually have start-up problems. It took years for the UN ad hoc tribunals to function properly and render judicial decisions.[134] The same holds true for the ICC. No single judgment has been handed down its ten years of existence.[135]

The second objection is the risk of political manipulation of the institution. AU has long been characterized as a trade union for Heads of State and Government[136] rather than a real pan African organization created in the interests of the African people. If this holds true, it would mean that ACC will protect and shield heads of state and governments from a potential criminal responsibility for their deeds or, at least get manipulated. In this sense, civil society and some authors fear that an ACC would create an African exceptionalism[137] by which leaders can avoid accountability.

The perception of a possible political manipulation of the court is supported by two factors. Firstly, a democratic and rule of law deficit in Africa: a retrospective look on Africa shows

133 Regional institutions are designated nascent communities because they are attempting to find their own solutions for their own problems at the regional level, see Gebrewold, *supra* note 16, at 84.

134 For a report examining some of the ICTY's early failures, see Expert Group, Report of the Expert Group to Conduct a Review of the Effective Operation and Functioning of the International Tribunal for the Former Yugoslavia and the International Criminal Tribunal for Rwanda, UN Doc.A/54/634 (November 22, 1999). For the ICTR, see J.E. Alvarez, *Crimes of States/Crimes of Hate: Lessons From Rwanda,* 24 Yale Journal of International Law 365, 414 (1999).

135 At the time of finalization of this chapter, deliberations are under way in the first case of *Prosecutor v. Thomas Dyilo Lubanga.*

136 The late President Nyerere of Tanzania once called the OAU a 'Talking Club of Heads of State'. See Tim Murithi, *Reflections on Leadership: From the OAU to the AU,* 2 Conflict Trends 9, 14 (2007); Prof. Reyntjens calls the AU a "Syndicate of Heads of State". See Filip Reyntjens, *The UN Report on Congo's Atrocities: The End of Impunity?* International Justice Tribune 114 (2010).

137 Implications, *supra* note 47; Comfort Ero, *Understanding Africa's Position on the International Criminal Court,* 11, 13 (2008–2010), available at: <www.fljs.org/uploads/documents/Justice_in_Africa.pdf> (Accessed November 25, 2011).

138 The Ibrahim Index Report (2010), available at: <www.moibrahimfoundation.org/en/section/the-ibrahim-index> (Accessed August 26, 2011).

that some countries' leaders are corrupt and non-democratic.[138] This in fact nourishes the reluctance to the ACC idea as conditions for delivering impartial justice on a continental level are not there yet. Secondly, the context in which the idea is being shaped. For Nyanduga, African Human and Peoples' Rights Commissioner, the decision to contemplate the creation of an ACC is a political backlash to what African Union considers as a selective justice.[139] I have already mentioned that African leaders rejected the idea of an ACC but decided to revisit it later when President al Bashir was formally indicted by the ICC for war crimes and crimes against humanity. Also, another troubling factor is that some presidents who are the most vocal on this issue like President Kagame, the late Gaddafi and others may be legitimate targets for international criminal justice. For instance, it is seriously alleged that former Rwandese Patriotic Army (RPA) and actual Rwandese Defence Forces (RDF) members, under the commanding authority of Paul Kagame, have committed war crimes, crimes against humanity and even genocide both in Rwanda[140] and in Democratic Republic of Congo.[141]

Nonetheless, political manipulation of judicial institutions is a reality within domestic political context, especially in transitional states. Being not embedded in these national political contexts, the ACC's manipulation will be minimized. In this sense, I echo Professor Burke-White who argues that 'regional courts, because of their relative separation from national politics, are significantly less likely to be captured by any particular nation or group within a nation'.[142] Moreover, one can found hope on the democratic progress that Africa has achieved in the last decades. Although there are still some irregularities in democratically organized elections or some attempts to resort to coups d'Etat, democratic change is taking place continent wide. This change will ultimately put in place responsible leaders with a sense of accountability, willing to have strong institutions sustaining the quest for a rule of law and accountability in Africa. One can mention the example of South African and Botswana leaders who distanced themselves from the quasi-unanimous AU

139 Nyanduga, *supra* note 62, at 5.

140 Robert Gersony, *Prospect of Early Repatriation of Rwandan Refugees Currently in Burundi, Tanzania and Zaire*; (hereinafter the Gersony Report). See also Summary of UNHCR Presentation before the Commission of Experts 4-7 (1994). Also, in a letter addressed to Ambassador John Negroponte, Kenneth Roth, Executive Director of Human Rights Watch, wrote: In 1994 soldiers of the Rwandan Patriotic Army killed thousands of civilians, in the process committing war crimes and crimes against humanity. See Letter from Kenneth Roth, Executive Director of Human Rights Watch, to US Ambassador John Negroponte of the United States (August 9, 2002).

141 Mapping Report, *supra* note 88, paras 22-32.

142 Burke-White, *supra* note 73, at 741.

143 In a letter dated July 8, 2009 to the ICC, Botswana assured the Court that "as a State Party to the Rome Statute of the ICC, Botswana will fully abide with its treaty obligations and will support the International Criminal Court in its endeavors to implement the provisions of the Rome Statute". See Letter from the Minister of Foreign Affairs and International Cooperation of the Republic of Botswana to Justice Sany-Hyun Song, President of the ICC (July 8, 2009). South Africa did support the resolution but retracted afterwards due to the pressure from civil society; see, for example, General Council of the Bar of South Africa Circular No 111/09, July 15, 2009.

decision requesting African member states not to cooperate with the ICC in the execution of the arrest warrant against Sudanese President Al Bashir.[143] At the same time, the AU High-Level Panel on Darfur did not endorse the Sudanese government position that its judiciary can handle Darfur-related cases.[144] Instead, the panel recommended a hybrid court be put in place in order to give credibility to transitional justice mechanisms.[145] These two examples of goodwill among some representatives of Africa's political elite lay solid foundations for an effective and independent ACC.The other promising factor for an independent court lies with the existence of an elite corps of African international criminal lawyers with relevant expertise in international criminal proceedings. Since the inception of the ad hoc tribunals, many African lawyers have been involved, at different levels, in the functioning of the international criminal justice system. Some have been acting as presidents of courts or chambers, judges, lead prosecutors, defence counsels, court registrars or deputy registrars, heads of different divisions or legal officers. This expertise acquired can easily be transferred to the ACC and strengthen its judicial capacity, its independence and impartiality. Finally, the African civil society is taking shape with demands for accountability, respect for human rights, good governance and good management. This can help alleviate the political pressure that can unduly be put on the ACC officials and staff in their daily duties. In fact, civil society is already actively and constructively involved in the work of other regional institutions. For instance, human rights NGOs constitute a valuable contributor to the work of the African Commission on Human and Peoples' Rights through shadow reporting or filing complaints before the Commission. One can hope that the same civil society can help the ACC take shape in different ways.

The third major objection relates to funding. Like any criminal court dealing with war crimes, genocide and crimes against humanity, the ACC will require substantial financial resources in order to successfully carry out its mission. The AU human rights court has a budget of about 8 million dollars a year.[146] Its extension to include a chamber with criminal jurisdiction would require probably a triple budget or more. This is a real challenge for the AU since most of the member states are not even contributing regularly to its budget.[147] We should also keep in mind the lingering case of Hissène Habré pending before Senegalese tribunals for years without decision on its merits, simply because the

144 Darfur Report, *supra* note 71, paras 228-245.

145 *Id.* paras 246-254.

146 African Union, Budget Execution Report, September 30, 2008, EX.CL/455 (XIV), Annex 1, at 9. The Court's annual budget was pegged at US$7,901,214.

147 Of the US$ 250.453.697 voted as the 2010 AU budget, US$111.763.676 has to be recovered from Member States, see *Décision sur le budget de l'Union Africaine pour l'exercice 2010*, AU Doc.Assembly/AU/13 (XIV), para. 1.

AU has not been able to mobilize the funds necessary for the prosecution of this case despite a constant reminder from Senegal – the prosecuting state – and the AU Assembly of Heads of State and Government.[148] If one case involving one man has been a headache for the AU, what about funding thousands of cases that the potential ACC would take on?

Although funding would be challenging, it will not be an unsolvable problem. By the way, the *Habré* case is not a good example. The problem for this prosecution lies within a lack political will from the prosecuting state. In my view, even the poorest African country can manage to prosecute one single case if a proper political will is present. This point can be reinforced by the fact that Rwanda, with its scarce financial resources, in any case poorer than Senegal, has been able to prosecute thousands of persons suspected of genocide and crimes against humanity in its national courts.[149] So, being not the poorest country in Africa, Senegal could successfully, even by itself, manage to fund the prosecution of Habré if the political will was there. Taking care of funding this case would be a Senegalese important contribution to the fight against impunity in Africa.

Hence, funding challenge for the ACC might be linked to a lack of political will. If it has a proper political support from the AU and its individual member states, the ACC may well be able to garner financial support. It may even get funding from other voluntary contributors. Civil society can also help fundraise its moneys given its good cause of reducing impunity. The international community should also support the ACC because it will help prosecute genocide, war crimes and crimes against humanity which are of serious concern to humanity since they attack its vital interests and values.[150] The ACC would then be an agent of the international community acting on its behalf to vindicate the rights of victims.

Finally, the suggested form of the regional court, a chamber, would be, as I argued elsewhere,[151] less costly than a full-fledged independent court. Its budget will be grafted to the budget of the African Court of Justice and Human Rights, which is an AU organ.

In conclusion, it is safe to say that these criticisms are not ACC-specific issues. They can be directed to existing African institutions created under the slogan of African solutions

148 *Decision on the Hissene Habre Case*, Assembly of the African Union, Fifteenth Ordinary Session, Kampala, Uganda, July 25-27, 2010, Doc.Assembly/AU/11(XV), para. 3: "[AU] REITERATES its appeal to all Member States to contribute to the budget of the trial and extend the necessary support to the Government of Senegal in the execution of the African Union mandate to prosecute and try Hissène Habré".

149 *Supra* note 93.

150 ANTONIO CASSESE, INTERNATIONAL CRIMINAL LAW 11-12 (2nd ed. 2008); GERHARD WERLE, PRINCIPLES OF INTERNATIONAL CRIMINAL LAW 57-61 (2005).

151 Pacifique Manirakiza, *L'Afrique et le système de justice pénale internationale*, 3 AFRICAN JOURNAL OF LEGAL STUDIES 21-52 (2009).

to African problems (ASAP). Moreover, the same objections are systemic to the whole international criminal justice system. They can and indeed have been formulated against international criminal tribunals such as the ICTR and the ICC. States, and more importantly the courts themselves, did manage to counter them more or less; that is why, African and international institutions facing the same challenges are already in place and are operating with some satisfactory results.

14.8 Conclusion

The magnitude of the massive and systematic atrocities committed in Africa and the practical incapacity of the existing mechanisms to deal with them require a closer look into other directions in order to find new ways and means to fight impunity arising thereof. It is against this background that this book chapter explored the possibility of an African Criminal Court. Although the ACC will undoubtedly face the same objections, concerns and difficulties like any other existing or future transitional justice institutions. I am convinced that it can offer a valuable contribution, in conjunction with other mechanisms, either national or supranational, to the legitimacy and the sustainability of the international criminal justice system. It is not incompatible with the ICC; similarly, national courts' will not be discharged from their primary responsibility to hear cases relating to international crimes.[152] I do not see the ACC as a panacea to the impunity problem in Africa but as an additional tool. For the time being, it is the missing link in the international criminal justice system.

Fears and apprehensions on a potential ACC are understandable, especially given the context in which the idea was resurrected by African leaders after they previously rejected it. However there some reasons for hope in an African sustainable court: conflicts are diminishing continental wide; an impressive African expertise in international criminal proceedings; a strong civil society is emerging with demands for accountability and respect for human rights; democratic changes are taking place in different countries and the awareness of Africans that the continent matters, that they have to take care of their destiny and not to look outside in the first place.

152 ACtHPR Report, *supra* note 25, para. 30.

15 Conclusion

Ensuring a Balanced Future for International Criminal Justice in Africa

Vincent O. Nmehielle

The debate about where international criminal justice stands in Africa is quite timely. The issues and questions raised in this book are relevant because Africa has been a center of international attention because of the numerous conflicts and gross human rights violations that have continually engulfed the continent since the independence of many African states from colonial rule. There has been a clear demonstration that issues of grave concerns remain in this regard. The experiences of dirty conflicts or wars in Sierra Leone, Liberia, Rwanda, Uganda, Burundi, the DRC, Somalia, Ivory Coast, Kenya and most recently Libya is unquestionably a cause for serious concern with regard to the search for accountability against those that engage in grave violations. Similarly, oppressive and repressive practices in a number of African states continue in a manner that echoes the observation of Alemika that:

> The chronic and worsening conditions of human rights in Africa have produced serious political, social and economic consequences. . . . The violations of political and civil rights by rulers often either include or result in the denial of the citizens of full participation in the formulation and implementation of vital policies affecting them and their society. Human rights violations, therefore, produce a vicious circle of repression, economic stagnation and regression, and political instability. The challenge therefore is how to break the vicious chain, set in motion and enliven the forces of liberation, social democracy, economic and scientific-technological advancement, and the enjoyment of the full range of human rights by everyone in every African nation.[1]

In this regard, statistics show that political instability and repressions in Africa have resulted in more than 30 active armed conflicts and produced more than half of all war-related deaths world-wide, as well as millions of refugees, returnees and other victims of

1 Etannibi E.O. Alemika, *Protection and Realisation of Human Rights in Africa, in* Perspectives on Human Rights 163 (Awa U. Kalu & Yemi Osinbajo eds., 1992).

forcible displacement.[2] Thus, the complexity of the situation is that gross human rights violations within African states produce consequences which run counter to the interests of sustained democracy and the rule of law. The Rwandan genocide is a very sad reminder of the gravest form of human rights violations in Africa, any semblance of which should never be allowed to occur again on the continent.[3] Yet the question remains whether the lessons of Rwanda ever resonated at all.

The establishment of international criminal justice mechanisms such as the ICTR and the SCSL on the African continent is arguably a demonstration of the international community's as well as Africa's rejection of impunity for atrocity crimes. The operation of these tribunals brought some measure of recognition to the need to end impunity for egregious violations of human rights. There is thus an expectation that these tribunals would have some impact on Africa, particularly the countries in which they were established. The impact that these tribunals have had on accountability for atrocity crimes in Africa, while still being assessed is very important in the evaluation of the future of international criminal justice in Africa. The ICTR was specifically established to deal with atrocity crimes that resulted from the Rwandan genocidal war of which the Tutsis and moderate Hutus were the victims while the Hutus were the alleged perpetrators. Thus, the tribunal was largely directed at the prosecution of the one side that apparently lost the war – former members and supporters of the Hutu-dominated government.

On the other hand, the SCSL though originally sought by President Tejan Kabbah as a court meant to "try and bring to credible justice those members of the Revolutionary United Front (RUF) and their accomplices responsible for committing crimes against the people of Sierra Leone and for taking of United Nations peacekeepers as hostages",[4] became a court that tried those that "bear the greatest responsibility for serious violations of international humanitarian law and Sierra Leonean law committed in the territory of Sierra Leone since November 30, 1996, including those leaders who, in committing such crimes, have threatened the establishment of and implementation of the peace process in Sierra Leone."[5] The way this mandate of the SCSL played out was that leaders of the Civil

2 The Secretary-General, *The Causes of Conflict and the Promotion of Durable Peace and Sustainable Development in Africa: Report of the Secretary General on the Work of the Organisation of African Unity, Reprinted* in 10 African Journal of International & Comparative Law 549 (1998). Also available at <www.un.org/ecosocdev/geninfo/afrec/sgreport/index.html>, (last accessed December 12, 2011).

3 The aftermath of the Rwanda genocide was the loss of approximately 800,000 lives. The ICTR was established pursuant to UNSC Resolution 955 of 1994 to prosecute the perpetrators of the genocide. For more information on the ICTR. See <www.ictr.org> (last accessed on November 25, 2011).

4 See Letter from President Tejan Kabbah of Sierra Leone, to Kofi Annan, UN Secretary-General requesting the establishment of the SCSL (12 June 2000), UN Doc. S/2000/786, (August 10, 2000).

5 Statute of the Special Court for Sierra Leone, Art. 1(1).

Defense Forces (CDF) that fought on the side of the government were also indicted along with members of the RUF and found guilty of war crimes and crimes against humanity.

Horovitz makes the point that the ICTR and the SCSL have had different and varying impacts or non-impacts, directly or indirectly in Rwanda and Sierra Leone, respectively (see chapter 2). This ranges from domestic prosecution or non-prosecution of other cases that, under the circumstances, the ICTR and the SCSL were incapable of dealing with, to normative impact on domestic law and principles; and judicial and legal capacity of nationals of Rwanda and Sierra Leone.

There is indeed no doubt that the ICTR and the SCSL may have impacted the two countries where they operated in ways that may have led to a greater appreciation of the rule of law and peaceful coexistence as Nmaju has alluded to (see chapter 3). One nagging question, however, remains relative to the future. The jury is still out on the extent these *ad hoc* tribunals have served as a deterrent to and contributed to the prevention of future commission of grave atrocity crimes in Rwanda, Sierra Leone, or anywhere else in Africa for that matter. Since Rwanda and Sierra Leone, there have been Liberia, Ivory Coast, the DRC, Kenya, Libya, among others. The real and true legacy of these tribunals would be when they help to prevent future commission of atrocity crimes in Africa. It is indeed doubtful that this needed legacy has been realized or will be realized as a result of the work of the ICTR and the SCSL because there is a danger of current and future domestic political and governance climates that reinvent the evils of the past.

It is this reinvention of the evils of the past, as replicated in different parts of the continent in the form of impunity for atrocity crimes – that continues to hunt the continent's future. But there is recognition that the continent cannot continue in this cycle of impunity – there have to be effective accountability measures to deal with the impunity associated with the atrocity crimes that these evils represent. The establishment of the ICC as a permanent court provided that opportunity and the massive support the court received from the African block raised the hopes of many that the continent is indeed turning a new leaf in finding a way to seriously address the lack of accountability for egregious violations of human rights on the continent – more so because the AU had outlawed impunity in its Constitutive Act.

Thus, the debate about the AU's objection to the ICC's work in Africa based on a perception, rightly or wrongly, that the court is targeting Africa becomes a very complicated one that appears to be framed in an either or manner. Contributions in this book make it clear that there is no alternative to ensuring the end of impunity for atrocity crimes in Africa because it is about the protection of helpless victims of gross human rights and humanitarian law abuse. It is also about African States Parties to the Rome Statute living up to the obligations they accepted when they joined the Rome Statute regime. On its part, the ICC should not operate in a manner that clearly gives the impression that Africa is the only place that violators and perpetrators of atrocity crimes exist, particularly because international criminal justice, to a large extent, is shaped by internal and international politics. Richardson demonstrates that that the AU's grievance relative to the work of the ICC in Africa must be evaluated from, among others, a perspective of equity in the global and international criminal law process (see chapter 4). This is important because of a need to strike a balance between ensuring justice and accountability and AU's ability to cater for peace in Africa, taking continental interests into account.

While no one can truly fault the call for Africa to submit to accountability measures, particularly those accepted under the Rome Statute regime, Nyawo suggests that the realities of the ICC's current emphasis on Africa evoke sentiments of colonial power relations in the face of historical colonial mass atrocities and injustice that were unaccounted for (see chapter 5). The dynamics of current power relations globally have serious impact on the future of international criminal justice in general and in Africa in particular. This is despite the clear fact that an international criminal justice mechanism such as the ICC is a creation of treaty and parties to the treaty are required to live up to their obligations under the treaty. On the other hand, the ICC is an institution that is unfortunately at the center of an unhealthy exercise of global power relations as a result of the central role given to the UNSC in the Rome Statute to refer cases to the ICC. It is this involvement of the UNSC that appears to complicate matters for the ICC in a number of the cases that it is dealing with in Africa. It is quite clear that whenever the UNSC is involved in taking any decision, that decision becomes complicated by global politics of interests and alliances, which would normally not favor Africa.

It is this high international politics of interests that is associated with international justice that Chuter is highly suspicious of relative to the ICC's role in Africa (see chapter 6). The point that is made is that the history of the implementation of international justice is riddled with power play and political insincerity. The surrender of Charles Taylor by Nigeria for trial at the SCSL due to pressure from the United States and the United Kingdom despite an understanding between these powers and the ECOWAS and the African Union to the contrary, if Taylor stepped down from power in Liberia and went into exile in Nigeria, is an example of power play in this regard. The impact and lesson of the Taylor surrender and trial are either a positive one – that no alleged perpetrator of atrocity crimes in Africa is protected no matter how highly placed, or a negative one – that accused African leaders would fight till the death against being 'humiliated' by any international justice mechanism, which they would perceive as an instrument of neo-colonial oppression. It is important to stress that something is not totally right with a system where some very powerful members of the international community that are not parties to the Rome Statute make decisions on situations to refer to the ICC including heads of states of non-party states. Because of the high level politics involved in this realm of international decision making, there is every likelihood that the system could be used to settle complex political and diplomatic scores. At the end of the day the international criminal justice accountability mechanisms that we are all rooting for becomes a victim of international politics.

It is in this light that the African Union's decision that its member states should not cooperate with the ICC because of the UNSC's handling of the Al-Bashir's indictment by refusing to attend to AU's deferral request under the Rome Statute, becomes a watershed decision that has serious implications for the future of international criminal justice accountability at the highest level in Africa. It is apparent that the AU's objections to the work of the ICC in Africa relate more to cases involving Heads of States as in Sudan and Libya where the AU had either played a role, or was prepared to play a role in resolving the conflicts. The AU's late deferral request in relation to the Kenya six indictment could be said to be only a reaction that was aggravated by the UNSC's lack of action on its earlier Al-Bashir deferral request rather than one that is based on the need to give any peaceful efforts it may have engaged in Kenya a chance. Accordingly, it is clear that the indictment of Laurent Gagbo, former President of Ivory Coast, on the other hand, did not attract, at least publicly, any serious objections from the AU probably because of Gagbo's rebuff of the AU's effort at resolving the conflict that resulted from his failure to relinquish power after losing the last presidential elections. This shows that there is need to recognize genuine efforts at ensuring accountability for atrocity crimes as well as efforts that explore peaceful resolution of the conflicts in Africa.[6]

It should not and it is not the case that the AU would shield any African leader from accountability for atrocity crimes, as doing so would undermine its normative principles. That is why the bold assertion by Dyani that the ICC is not targeting Africa (see chapter 7) speaks to the reality of the existence of gross human rights violations in Africa that must be redressed, hence the attraction of the ICC's attention to those violations. This effort at redressing these violations should ordinarily not wear the label of "targeting Africa."

6 The absence of a vociferous objection from the AU on the indictment, arrest and subsequent transfer of Laurent Gbagbo to stand trial in the ICC should not just be overlooked. There must be something to learn from it. Gbagbo's refusal to hand-over power after a democratic election was frowned at by the AU as a violation of its principled stance to recognize only democratic changes of government, which the elections that Gbagbo refused to respect represented. The fact that Gbagbo took further steps that resulted in a deadly conflict in which atrocity crimes were committed despite all AU peace overtures was enough for the AU to allow the ICC process to take its course.

In the course of the ICC pursuit of its mandate in Africa, however, the AU, as a regional organization must be allowed to explore the benefit that accrues from international law in furtherance of peace and stability of the continent, without being bullied. Thus, the question of immunity of heads of state under customary international law and the obligations of states in that regard that are protected by Article 98 of the Rome Statute, as argued by the African Union relative to the request to African States Parties to the Rome Statute to arrest and surrender Al-Bashir, should not be reduced to the view that the AU is shielding one of its own from accountability. It is as much a very serious political issue as it may be legal, which brings a lot of other interests and considerations into play.

The contributions in this volume have been emphatic on the need for the AU to play a proactive role in ensuring a credible future for accountability for atrocity crimes in Africa. The claim that Africa is being targeted by the ICC cannot be sustained for a very long time if no proactive action, not just on the part of the African States Parties to the Rome Statute, but also on the part of the AU as a regional body is taken. In this regard, Nmehielle emphasizes that the AU must play an active role in the implementation of the complementarity principle of the Rome Statute so that its member states can really take credible ownership of justice for atrocity crimes (see chapter 8). Credible domestic measures aimed at stamping out impunity for atrocity crimes are the bedrock of the Rome Statute. Africa cannot just continue to cry about being targeted without taking any meaningful action towards making domestic justice systems relevant and effective in dealing with impunity. The simple reason, as clearly articulated in the various contributions in this volume, is that the ICC is only a court of last resort that is not equipped to take over the role and place of domestic criminal systems.

We cannot overemphasize that the credibility of the domestic systems should not be in doubt. It is indeed in the interest of African States Parties to the Rome Statute that their domestic systems are not just in place but are equally credible within the reasonable standard expected in dealing with accountability for atrocity crimes provided for in the Rome Statute and under international humanitarian law. It is accepted that a number of African countries are not yet there. The AU should focus more on how its member states can meet this standard if it does not want to see more cases going to the ICC. The establishment by Uganda of the International Crimes Division of its High Court in the spirit of the Rome Statute's complementarity principle is a recent example of what is possible in taking credible ownership of justice and accountability for atrocity crimes. Even though Uganda's experience appears wobbly, or is a kind of "putting the cart before the horse", or seemingly an afterthought – an action taken after the Museveni government had already referred cases on its own to the ICC, as observed by Nalule and Odoi-Musoke (see chapter 9), it remains an important initiative that should over time result in the proper development of the domestic justice system in dealing with the kind of crimes created by the Rome Statute. Other African states must take such steps and the AU must be seen to be proactively promoting meaningful action in that direction.

An important recognition in this volume is that the idea of justice as represented by the ICC regime is not without limitations. While the ICC on its own cannot be "an obstacle to peace", it is also not necessarily "an instrument of peace" according to Clark (see chapter 10). It is therefore necessary that accountability mechanisms such as the ICC are not pitched against other notions of achieving peace in post-conflict societies. The workings of criminal prosecution and trials may not convey all about justice taking into account such considerations as cooperation of states, which is necessary for the effectiveness of an institution like the ICC; allegations of bias and selective justice, among others.

Above all, the Rome Statute regime, for whatever reasons, does not account for all notions of international criminal justice that may directly have an impact on Africa. The failure of this regime to recognize corporate criminal liability is a major limitation, which Colvin and Chella maintain poses a challenge to the credibility of international criminal justice measures that are undertaken in Africa (see chapter 11). The relevance of multinational corporate complicity in Africa's numerous conflicts, particularly those that are based on a struggle for natural resources is unquestionable. Granted that interested states, presumably backed by enormous corporate interests negotiated away corporate criminal liability during the Rome negotiations that gave birth to the ICC; it does not take away the increasingly important attention that is being paid to corporate complicity in international crimes in Africa. It is thus a new frontier on the future of international criminal justice in Africa. The fact that the AU is beginning to think of extending criminal responsibility for international crimes to corporate activities is instructive in this regard.[7]

That regional organizations like the AU are vital in discourses about justice and accountability in their component territories has been amply demonstrated in this volume. It is not unexpected that the involvement of regional organizations like the AU can be quite complex and must therefore involve a balanced consideration as Odo alluded to (see chapter 12). The challenge becomes how to ensure this critical balance without eroding either the need for a strong message on accountability for egregious human rights violations on the one hand and African regional efforts for peace and national reconciliation rather

7 Art. 46C of the Draft Statute of the African Court of Justice and Human and Peoples' Rights annexed to the Draft Protocol on Amendments to the Protocol on the Statute of the African Court of Justice and Human Rights (Legal/ACJHRPAP/4 (II) Rev. 2) clearly articulates corporate criminal liability in the AU new effort to have a regional criminal chamber to try international crimes.

than one-sided emphasis on criminal prosecution on the other. The AU's seeming objection to the work of the ICC on the continent has led to the question whether there is any African criminal justice alternative in dealing with impunity and ensuring justice. It is in this regard that Oette asserts that regional approaches like the African Union High-Level Panel on Darfur (AUPD) can go a long way to ameliorate "conceptual and institutional challenges" that face the implementation of international criminal justice in Africa (see chapter 13). For initiatives such as the AUPD to be successful, however, Oette is right that there has to be an implementable plan of action in this regard "as part of a broader regional approach that develops the legal and institutional framework needed to strengthen the capacity of national and regional bodies." The lack of a way forward since the release of the AUPD report that was well received by many is quite discouraging. The report elicited a strong expectation that the African Union would influence the deployment by Sudan of credible ways of dealing with and holding perpetrators of impunity in Darfur accountable.

Yet, as part of this question on an African international criminal justice alternative Manirakiza makes a case for the AU's call for an African criminal chamber within the structure of the African Court of Justice and Human Rights, which among other things, would enable the AU to achieve the objectives it set out for itself in its Constitutive Act (see chapter 14). As has been articulated, the move towards establishing an African criminal accountability mechanism stemmed from the AU's rejection of and protest against what it called "an abuse of the principle of universal jurisdiction"[8] on the one hand, and aggravated by the controversy that surrounded the indictment of President Al Bashir of Sudan by the ICC as well as the failure of the UNSC to act on the AU's deferral request under Article 16 of the Rome Statute on the other. While there may be nothing wrong on its own for a regional entity such as the AU to establish a regional criminal court, the question remains as to why there is need for this African alternative at this point in time after the AU rejected similar proposal during the discussions on the Protocol on the Merger of the African Court of Justice and Human Rights that was adopted in 2008.

There is no doubt that suspicions abound that the idea of an African criminal court or chamber at this time is an attempt by the AU to undermine the ICC – an institution that the AU has sharply disagreed with on its work in Africa. Yet those in support of this initiative like Manirakiza revel in the novelty of the idea – a regional mechanisms that makes a contribution to dealing with impunity for atrocity crimes from a regional perspective. When all is said and done, however, the innovativeness of this idea must be measured

8 See Decision on the Report of the Commission on the Abuse of the Principle of Universal Jurisdiction. Doc. Assembly/AU/14 (XI); Decision on the Implementation of the Assembly Decision on the Abuse of the Principle of Universal Jurisdiction, Assembly/AU/Dec.213(XII), Para. 4; and Decision on the Abuse of the Principle of Universal Jurisdiction, Assembly/AU/Dec.243(XIII) Rev.1.

against its expediency and whether or not it actually obstructs what the ICC stands for in ensuring criminal justice accountability in Africa.

The question regarding the future of international criminal justice in Africa will continue to remain relevant as clearly shown by the many issues that this volume has dealt with. The reality of continuing human rights violations and the commission of atrocity crimes across Africa, which attract accountability mechanisms such as the *ad hoc* tribunals and the ICC that in turn deploy their prosecutorial mandates in an effort to bring alleged perpetrators to justice are central. Thus, the coming into force of the Rome Statute and the wide African acceptance of the ICC as a permanent international criminal tribunal created a space for a lasting interaction between Africa and international criminal justice as a concept and as an ideal for dealing with impunity. However, the current ICC's near total focus on Africa for its investigations and indictments, which may rightly be because of the incessant or regular occurrence of atrocity crimes in the continent, continues to generate questions as to whether Africa is being targeted because it is the weakest link among other regional members of the international community. While this view may appear laughable, it is widely held among African leaders and political institutions, and even among some segments of civil society that are champions against impunity and egregious human rights violations on the continent. This leads to questioning the credibility of the ICC process in Africa, which stance will not take the promise of international criminal accountability for atrocity crimes in Africa to the height we all envisaged at the launch of the ICC.

However, because international justice does not only operate on purely legal considerations but also on high political considerations such as cooperation of states and interests of peace, in order for it to be effective, there is every need for a balance. The AU's objections to the work of the ICC in Africa is more of crying out against the lack of an existence of this balance and not because the AU actually supports impunity for atrocity crimes in Africa. The failure of the UNSC to act upon the AU deferral request in the Al Bashir situation was indeed unreasonable and only provided ammunition for the politicization of the work of the ICC in Africa, which is not in the interest of an effective international criminal justice implementation in the continent. While it is true the AU as a regional organization is not a party to the Rome Statute – but rather a sizeable portion of its member states, it must be accepted that the regional body has a stake on the implementation of international criminal justice in Africa and must therefore be engaged by both the ICC and other stakeholders on how to make it more effective. It is only reasonable to do so because, as things stand, the work of the ICC is relevant currently only because of Africa.

Finally, the AU on its part must seek not to obstruct the work of the ICC but must be seen to actualize the innovative principles of its Constitutive Act to tackle impunity and egregious violations of human rights in Africa. It can and should do this within the mechanism of the ICC that a majority of its member states have accepted. The complementarity principle enshrined in the Rome Statute presents a vital opportunity for the AU through its member states that are parties to the Rome regime to truly begin to address and tackle impunity and gross human rights abuse at the domestic level. Until and unless the AU takes a genuine interest in proactively pushing the realization and implementation of complementarity by African states generally, the future of international criminal justice in Africa will remain one where the ICC, an international criminal tribunal that is not equipped to be a court of primary jurisdiction will continue to comb the nooks and crannies of Africa to bring perpetrators of impunity for atrocity crimes to book. Because the AU may not be in favor of ICC looming large in its backyard in this way, the future will also continue to be subjected to the AU's and, by extension, larger African objections that will lead to the withholding of the vital cooperation that an international accountability mechanism like the ICC needs in order to function effectively. It is therefore in the interest of a credible international criminal justice system that it has a balanced future in Africa.

APPENDICES

Keynote Address by Mr. Adama Dieng, Assistant Secretary-General of the United Nations and Registrar of the International Criminal Tribunal for Rwanda

At the International Conference On Africa and the Future of International Criminal Justice

Organized By the Wits Programme in Law, Justice and Development in Africa School of Law, University of the Witwatersrand, Johannesburg, In Association with the Africa Interest Group of the American Society of International Law in Johannesburg, South Africa from 14-16 July 2010

It is with great honor that I have accepted the invitation of the Wits Programme in Law, Justice and Development in Africa to speak of the future of international criminal justice in Africa. As an African human rights activist during all my adult life and as the administrator of the UN Criminal Court operating in Africa, this topic is the *alpha* and *omega* of my life. It is therefore no surprise that I am always eager to speak about justice in Africa.

I also take particular pride to introduce this topic in the country of Nelson Mandela, the country that has shown that justice, when set on motion, even belatedly, can still bring about hope and smile in the face of its children; those very children that, not long ago, were deprived of the basic rights that a human being should enjoy. The scars of apartheid may be very long to suppress, and particularly so when many people did not have access to education, with the ensuing effect on their social and economic life. Still, when following the recent Football World Cup, a few years after the Rugby World Cup; when seeing this rainbow nation singing the same anthem, blowing the same vuvuzela, sticking together, having the same dream, the same fear, encouraging each other, I tell myself that my commitment to justice in Africa is really worth its while; I find motives to carry on in my resolve to fight injustice in Africa. And I am sure that what holds true for me in this regard equally applies to many other sons and daughters of Africa, and beyond them, to every human being interested in seeing justice prevail.

Africa is often at the forefront when we speak of international criminal justice. We owe this constant feature in the billboards to regular breaches of human rights, civil wars, with their corollaries in terms of violations of International Humanitarian Law (IHL). Despite genuine progress in rooting the democracy, our continent has been strife-ridden over the last half a century, following the independences. For a long time, the Cold War environment shielded many dictators from any accountability. The sacrosanct principle of sovereignty of States would not allow any interference.

As a result, despite the frenzy with which the rules of IHL were codified in the wake of the Second World War, very little was done to sanction their infringement. Many armed conflicts of different degrees of intensity have occurred between the early 1950s and late 1980s, with no proper action undertaken to bring those responsible to book. The criminals would often be those holding power, thus rendering futile any domestic prosecution, while the international community would also be powerless, given the prevailing doctrine in international relations.

The end of the Cold War in the late 1980s favored a paradigm shift. It was no longer satisfactory to have a cold and formal reading of the principle of non-interference in the internal affairs of a State. The world rediscovered that the brotherhood of human beings goes beyond borders; that basic rights, starting with the right to life, need to be preserved and fought for, wherever they are in jeopardy. This awakening translated into an unprecedented momentum in the development of the international criminal justice. The Security Council did not take long to set up two international tribunals, to tackle the grave breaches of IHL in the Balkans and in Rwanda. It did in two years what international lawyers in many quarters have been yearning for, for almost a century. When in September 1998, the International Criminal Tribunal for Rwanda (ICTR), passed the *Kambanda* and the *Akayesu* Judgements, the first ever decisions applying the 1948 Genocide Convention, dormant for fifty years, Koffi Annan, the then UN Secretary-General, could at last exhale a sigh of relief and exclaim: "*Le droit international pénal n'est plus muet*" [International Criminal Law is no longer dumb]. This was indeed a major breakthrough in the implementation of the IHL.

When the Security Council, acting under Chapter VII of the UN Charter, decided to set up the International Criminal Tribunal for the Former Yugoslavia (ICTY) in 1993 and the ICTR in 1994, it radically changed the landscape of international humanitarian law. Without wishing to make an exhaustive assessment of the achievements of the two ad hoc tribunals, it must be noted, all the same, especially in the case of Rwanda, that for the first time in the history of modern States, an entire government, its top army officers, its highest-ranking civil servants, its political party leaders, its clergy, its prominent figures, in short, its entire ruling class, have been prosecuted for acts of genocide and other violations of international humanitarian law. Their arrests and trials were made possible by an equally unprecedented international co-operation. About twenty countries across the globe have contributed to the arrest of suspects or accused persons and their transfer to the seat of the Tribunal in Arusha. More than fifty countries have facilitated the movement of witnesses, including irregular residents, thanks to original ad hoc arrangements. Such a co-operation from States has enabled the protection of witnesses, including, in some cases, their relocation with their families and the enforcement of sentences following conviction. An important body of jurisprudence has also been developed, setting out the legal ingredients of international crimes as Genocide, Crimes against humanity and war crimes. New international judicial standards for fair trial have also been developed by the ad hoc tribunals and are being carried forward by the International Criminal Court (ICC).

Today, one can safely say that the international criminal justice is a tangible reality with a globalized justice. This globalization derives from the notion of individual criminal responsibility. This requires that the rights of the individual as the subject of human rights be protected, which in turn obliges the individual to be answerable for his human rights violations.

The setting up of international ad hoc tribunals was just one aspect of the evolution in the international criminal justice system. We have also witnessed a development of the concept of "universal jurisdiction" whereby States can claim criminal jurisdiction, beyond their territories, over persons alleged to have committed universal crimes. And thirdly, a permanent international criminal court has been set up, with the International Criminal Court (ICC).

With the currently existing legal framework one could proudly conclude that we have come a long way. There is technically no longer any hiding place, any safe haven in the world where one could be beyond the reach of international criminal justice. When a particular domestic setting fails to take responsibility, an alternative domestic system should be able to take over by resort to universal jurisdiction. And if not, an international setting can fill the gap, including when there is no signed agreement, thanks to the concept of *jus cogens*. However, we must admit that it is one thing to have a complete set of laws readily available and practically workable and it is another thing to make those laws work, particularly in the international environment where consensus and cooperation are still key to any achievement. Fugitives have been escaping international justice while their location is well known. Some others do not even bother to hide, owing to the strong protection they enjoy. Other complex situations make it difficult to enforce the international criminal law.

In certain parts of Africa for example, the very existence of a State as a homogenous centre of authority and decision-making entity is not obvious. And alongside the total chaos in places like Somalia there are areas where the government lacks the requisite authority to ensure respect for the law throughout the territory, or is the very one that acts *ultra vires*.

The crusade against impunity is still plagued with inadequacies. In many dictatorships or countries experiencing internal conflict, the transition towards democracy and peace requires negotiation with those responsible for atrocious crimes. What do we do in such circumstances? Apparently, there is not only one way of guaranteeing efficiency at the same time as justice. Depending on the circumstances, peace may be the immediate objective to attain, while justice would be relegated to some distant future. Such is the case when crime perpetrators continue to wield, thanks to their weapons, immense negotiating power which cannot immediately be taken away from them by force. But, even in this kind of situation, actions taken by the international community, either through military interventions or through prosecution abroad, can always help to overcome difficulties. These setbacks should not detract us from this quest for justice. It is remarkable that in spite of its limits, the African Union has used all the available means and deployed a wealth of imagination to try to put an end to mass atrocities wherever they have been perpetrated. In this respect, it should be emphasized that it is after considerable political will that African countries spontaneously decided to send troops to the Somalia and Darfur quagmire, when even the United Nations was not clear on what to do.

By their massive adhesion to the ICC, African countries also gave themselves an option worthy of interest. With 44 African countries having signed the Rome Statute, it can be said that this is a major effort to bridge the impunity gap. However, the evolution in the development of international criminal justice is far from being straightforward. International criminal law being at the confluent between law and politics, some clashes between the two have the potential of wiping away decades of progress.

The judicial activism of some European investigative judges, targeting some African high figures, and the recent indictment by the ICC of the Sudanese President, sparked off a general outcry in Africa. The resulting political tough stance appears to presently call into question all the progress that has been made in the formulation of universal norms for the fight against impunity in the course of the just-ended decade. Strong protests have been made, denouncing what some have termed the judicial imperialism of the North. Moreover, some African countries at one point even threatened to send out letters notifying their withdrawal from the Rome Statute.

There may well be some truth regarding the position taken by African leaders, denouncing the unbalanced approach adopted by the ICC with respect to international crimes. There is no doubt that it was quite questionable for the Security Council to grant amnesty, under Article 16 of the ICC Statute, to American soldiers serving in the peacekeeping mission in the Balkans, simply because the American authorities had warned that they would withdraw their troops if it were otherwise. These troops were, of course, necessary.

But giving the impression that when you possess the necessary influence, you can avoid being brought to trial before the international court seriously undermines the credibility of the ICC. Moreover, this guarantee was, in any case, superfluous, given that even in case of alleged criminal conduct, the possibility that American soldiers could be brought to trial before the ICC was almost non-existent.

This said, we must, however, not forget that of the four countries in which the ICC is currently conducting proceedings, namely the DRC, the Central African Republic, Uganda and Sudan, three of them sought the intervention of the Court. This fact is inconsistent with the image of judicial imperialism that is being given to ICC interventions in Africa. Furthermore, it should be recalled that Africa was in the front line in the establishment of the ICC. As stakeholders of the institution, African countries must therefore work towards resolving any domestic disagreements relating to the Prosecutor's prosecution strategy, rather than trying to callously jeopardize the very existence of the ICC. The importance of ICC to Africa could naturally require the establishment of an equipped branch of the institution in Africa, in order not to lend credence to the criticism that Africans must not be tried in Europe, but in Africa, where they are alleged to have committed their crimes. But, even here, it should be noted that this issue can be raised and addressed within the framework of the ICC.

Setting up in the African Court on Human and Peoples' Rights a criminal branch dealing with international crimes would not necessarily translate into abandonment or a weakening of the ICC. It is quite natural for criminal courts to coexist and cohabit, including with concurrent jurisdiction. This could even be good for a further reduction of the impunity gap, provided of course, that the necessary synergy is worked out and the genuineness of the different actions be real.

But it would be a mistake to destroy the only universal instrument available to us today to fight impunity and which became a reality only after a struggle that spanned decades. We may well take issue with the selective prosecution policy of the ICC, but we cannot propose as an alternative the impunity for all, on grounds that the ICC has not systematically instituted proceedings for each possible international crime? Are we going to say that to avoid judicial imperialism of the North we prefer to put up with the impunity of our criminals? I do not have conclusive answers to these questions. However, I think that each of us should ponder them.

In the *Habré* case, the African Union deemed that it would not be appropriate to hold the trial outside Africa. It then proposed an alternative solution by giving Senegal the mandate to prosecute the former President of Chad, instead of handing him over to Belgium.

But, even then, African countries have failed to show the same zeal as to the mobilization of financial resources requested by Senegal to organize the envisaged trial, even though the African Union is still actively considering the issue. Ironically, the European countries, which have been accused of judicial imperialism, are being requested to make financial contributions to enable the holding of the trial in Senegal.

CONCLUSION

Enormous progress has been made in the setting up of international criminal justice and thus in the fight against impunity. The era during which the principle of State sovereignty constituted an insurmountable legal obstacle, prohibiting interference in the internal affairs of a country, is now a thing of the past. The obligation to interfere, each time and wherever serious human rights violations occur, is now an integral part of the universal values that we share. Naturally, Africa must show pride and firmness in order to be respected and treated as a full partner by all the other stakeholders involved in the management of world affairs. But our pride must not be misplaced. We must never confuse our priorities. When we proclaim that it is we, and we only, who have the responsibility to decide a given case, that we take the entire responsibility to institute proceedings, we must be equal to the task, as expected of us. Otherwise, the declarations we make will be nothing but empty noise. We must not forget that the progress recorded in the process of consolidating democracy and in the fight against impunity in Africa is not irreversible.

Any progress, no matter how it is handled, needs to be maintained, to avoid going backwards. There will always be issues of inconsistencies and of unequal treatment here and there imputed to the ICC, as well as other reasons to complain about the way in which the ICC itself or other international organizations will deal with issues concerning Africa. Each time that happens, we will always be at liberty to make known our preoccupations and our dissatisfaction, and to fight in order that the injustice is corrected. Yet these actions should never, and I repeat, never, cause us to throw away the compass which guides us as we move into an ever-growing democracy and justice.

Thank you for your kind attention.

Address by Mr. Andries Nel, MP, Deputy Minister of Justice & Constitutional Development of the Republic of South Africa on the Occasion of the International Conference on "Africa and the Future of International Criminal Justice" Held at the School of Law of the University of the Witwatersrand on 14 July 2010: Johannesburg

. . . Distinguished participants, Ladies and Gentlemen

Dumelang! Sawubona! Moleweni! Goeie More! Avuxeni! Ndi masiari! Good morning. Welcome to South Africa! Boa tarde. Sejam bem-vindos a Africa do Sul! Bonjour. Soyez les bienvenus a l'Afrique du Sud! In greeting and welcoming you I would like to convey the greetings and best wishes of the Minister of Justice and Constitutional Development, Minister Jeff Radebe, MP to this very important conference.

We would like to begin by reiterating the deep felt condolences expressed by President Jacob Zuma on behalf of the government and the people of South Africa to the government and the people of Uganda and, in particular, to the families and relatives of those who died in Kampala, Uganda on Sunday 11 July, and also to wish those who were injured a speedy recovery. The South African government condemns, in the strongest possible terms, these acts of terrorism aimed at maiming and hurting innocent people. We believe that, whatever reasons prompted the perpetrators of these deeds, it does not justify the killing of innocent people.

We would like to thank the Wits Programme in Law, Justice and Development in Africa and the Africa Interest Group of the American Society of International Law – both for organizing this important conference as well as for extending an invitation to the Minister of Justice and Constitutional Development to open it. The University of the Witwatersrand and its School of Law in particular, played an important role in the struggle against apartheid. Its alumni include: Nelson Mandela, Joe Slovo and George Bizos to name but a very few. This Conference brings together minds who are world-renowned in the field of International Criminal Justice and are well placed to contribute to a discussion on Africa and the future of international criminal justice. Indeed, as my comrade and friend, Mandla Nkomfe, argues in Umrabulo, the journal of the African National Congress, "African intellectuals played a leading role in the emancipation of Africa. WB Du Bois defined the basic question that would occupy the minds of the world as that of colour line. Against this backdrop, African intellectuals were inspired to mobilize for the liberation of the continent. By their actions and visions, they demonstrated that a new and better world is possible. This bold vision was undermined by the new post-independence African elite. He continues: "The confluence of political, economic and military factors (at the end of the last century) resulted in new possibilities for the rebirth of the continent. We have moved with speed to reorganize our political, economic and educational institutions. The African Union and the New Partnership for Africa's Development (NEPAD) have become beach-heads in an all-round struggle to rebuild our continent. We have stable political institutions and peace in most parts of the continent. Intellectuals have a critical role to play in ensuring that we do not go back to where we were forty years ago. "The performance of our political and economic leaders should be carefully monitored. As we do that, our intellectuals should be driven by a sense of progress and informed by the history of the continent. The challenge is not to romanticize the past to the extent of African nativism that glorifies reactionary ideas and our supposed unchanging nature – glorifying the past as if Africans have an innate and unchanging form. The contributions of the African continent to the development our world should be understood within the challenges posed by globalisation."

It is significant that this conference takes place only three days after the final whistle blew in what has generally been hailed as one of, if not the most successful FIFA World Cups, and the first to be held on the African Continent. On a lighter note, I recall that eight weeks ago, during the Review Conference of the Rome Statute in Kampala, I asked the President, the Prosecutor and the Deputy Prosecutor of the International Criminal Court whether they would be attending the 2010 FIFA World Cup in South Africa and whether they would be on standby to hear any cases involving manifestations of the crime of aggression on the football field. Fortunately, I am told that, in addition to being one of the most peaceful and crime-free competitions off the field, the 2010 FIFA World Cup had the distinction of being the most peaceful on the field, with the lowest number of yellow and red cards handed out.

No doubt participants in this conference will find time during some of its late night breakaway sessions to discuss certain of the refereeing decisions in the context of the ongoing debate regarding the relationship between peace and justice. It is also significant that this conference takes place four days before we celebrate the birthday of former President Nelson Mandela, an illustrious alumnus of the Wits School of Law, on 18 July. In celebrating his life and contribution, the people of South Africa and the world are called to contribute 67 minutes of their time in honour and emulation of his iconic example of 67 years of service to humanity. May his example as a committed lawyer, freedom fighter and statesperson guide us in the deliberations of this conference. In this regard, I would like to quote from his opening address at the 2nd Conference of African National Institutions for the Promotion and Protection of Human Rights in Durban on 1 July 1998, where he said that: "The third development referred to is the process which we hope will lead to the establishment of an International Criminal Court. We have sought to ensure that the ICC is guaranteed independence and bestowed with adequate powers. Our own continent has suffered enough horrors emanating from the inhumanity of human beings towards human beings. Who knows, many of these might not have occurred, or at least been minimized, had there been an effectively functioning International Criminal Court." Shortly after he delivered that address, South Africa became the 23rd state to ratify the Rome Statute on the International Criminal Court on 17 July 1998, almost exactly 12 years ago. And, on 16 August 2002, the Implementation of the Rome Statute of the International Criminal Court Act of 2002 (Act No 27 of 2002) commenced, thereby making the Rome Statute an integral part of our domestic law. It has, therefore, been a source of ongoing surprise to us that others find it surprising that we are committed, indeed obligated, to honour our undertakings to the ICC in terms of the Rome Statute, both by international law as well as our own domestic law. We hope that this annoyance will come to an end, and that our President will not be called upon to restate our position – which is, quite frankly, restating the obvious – every time curious persons examine the guest list of an international event hosted by South Africa.

At the time that the negotiations for the Rome Statute were taking place, South Africa was in the process of finalising its own democratic Constitution. Millions of South Africans suffered for generations the humiliation and human rights abuses associated with apartheid. It was, thus, gratifying that the crime of apartheid was criminalized in Article 7(2)(h) of the Rome Statute as a crime against humanity. Our support for the International Criminal Court is a principled one that reflects our commitment to the foundational values of our own Constitution as well as that of the African Union. The AU Constitutive Act affirms the sovereignty of the state as represented by the people and not just governments. It grants participation of African people in the activities of the Union and promises never again to be blind, deaf or mute to the evils of war crimes, genocide and crimes against humanity by granting powers to the Union to intervene in States where these crimes are committed.

It was no accident of history, therefore, that African States were amongst the most ardent proponents of the creation of the International Criminal Court during the negotiations leading to the adoption of the Rome Statute. It is also no accident that with 30 States Parties, Africa remains the biggest single regional block in the Assembly of 111 States Parties to the Rome Statute. It was, and continues to be the expectation of those thirty States that through, amongst others, the International Criminal Court, the AU principles of respect for democratic principles, human rights, the rule of law and good governance can be safeguarded and strengthened in the international sphere. In this regard, we must welcome the fact that, last week, from 7 to 9 July, 2010, Judge Sang-Hyun Song, President of the International Criminal Court (ICC), paid a two day visit to Addis Ababa, Ethiopia, the headquarters of the African Union, where he met with, amongst others, the Chairperson of the African Union Commission, H.E. Dr Jean Ping, who reiterated the African Union's commitment to end impunity. During the meeting Dr Ping and President Song agreed that the African Union and the ICC share the common value of ending impunity and bringing about lasting peace. They also agreed to work to facilitate the establishment of an ICC Liaison Office at the headquarters of the AU that would encourage dialogue and exchange of information for the mutual benefit of the two institutions. South Africa views the Rome Statute, and the International Criminal Court it created, not in isolation, but as an important element in a new system of international law and governance. This system is characterized by greater solidarity which, while remaining true to the principle of sovereignty, prioritizes the common good.

The foundations for this system of law are, of course, contained in the UN Charter and, in particular, the Purposes and Principles of the United Nations, namely to "maintain international peace and security" and to bring about peaceful solutions to conflict "in conformity with the principles of justice and international law." The importance of the International Criminal Court needs to be seen in the context of the need for the fundamental reform of the system of global governance. Last week, President Jacob Zuma, addressing the Investec Asset Management Global Investment Conference, Cape Town, said that, "We argue that the affairs of the world of today cannot continue to be managed by the existing institutions of global governance unless they undergo fundamental reform. We have further argued that the role and contribution of developing countries in global economic expansion must begin to be reflected in their voice, share-holding and representation in these international institutions. Our participation in the G20 cannot and must not be divorced from our participation in the multilateral institutions such as the United Nations and others. Our participation in the G20 adds to these international interfaces, as it provides real possibilities to advance our objectives in multi-lateral institutions such as the International Monetary Fund (IMF), World Bank and the World Trade Organisation (WTO)." In this regard, and in relation to the International Criminal Court, former UN Secretary-General Kofi Annan, speaking during the opening session of the Review Conference of the Rome Statute in Kampala said: "And questions of credibility will persist so long as three of the five permanent members of the Security Council refuse to reconsider their position and join those who have taken the courageous step to become parties to the Statute. The same is valid for countries that aspire to permanent membership. Indeed, the problem is not limited to the Security Council. Six of the G20 have not ratified the Rome Statute. "The States Parties to this historic Statute must therefore pose the question", "What kind of leadership is this which would absolve the powerful from the rules they apply to the weak?" A laggard leadership is no excuse. "The States Parties to the Rome Statute are on the right side of history. You are in the majority. There are G20 and P5 countries among you. You can demand that those who claim the mantle of global leadership accept the duty of promoting global values."

Indeed our world is changing, and it is changing fast. These are times of globalization and interdependence, times that are giving rise to new configurations of global power relations. There is an urgent need for global governance and effective multilateral coordination that reflect these realities. Most major threats and challenges faced by our world can only be effectively combated and met on a global scale, including that of impunity. Just as with climate change or terrorism, there can be no exceptions or exemptions when it comes to setting up enforcement regimes. Let us proceed in the spirit that led to the creation of the United Nations in 1944 when we pledged to create a system of global governance founded on the coordinated work of universal institutions working in harmony. A strong and independent ICC working together with other institutions of global governance will further the goal of a peaceful and just world order.

The Review Conference of the Rome Statute that was held in Kampala, Uganda was the first opportunity to amend the Rome Statute and to review the direction and impact of the Court. As you all may know by now, the Conference adopted a resolution by which it amended the Rome Statute to include a definition of the crime of aggression and the conditions under which the Court could exercise jurisdiction with respect to the crime. The actual exercise of jurisdiction is subject to a decision to be taken after 1 January 2017. Most African States Parties favoured the inclusion of the crime of aggression without these qualifications. The Review Conference also provided the opportunity to stock of the international criminal justice in the areas of: the impact of the Rome Statute system on victims and affected communities; peace and justice; and cooperation and complementarity. South Africa and Denmark were the so-called "focal points" for the stocktaking on complementarity. It is important to remind ourselves that the International Criminal Court is based on the principle of complementarity. The ICC only operates when a State that has jurisdiction is genuinely unable or unwilling to carry out investigations and prosecutions. Underlying the Rome Statute is the understanding that justice, like charity, should begin at home. However, the reality is that many States Parties face real challenges in this regard. In this context South Africa and Denmark advanced the notion of "positive complementarity", *i.e.* the need actively to assist each other to strengthen national jurisdictions effectively to investigate and prosecute these crimes. We hope that this conference will have the opportunity to reflect on this matter and to give guidance. It is clear that international criminal justice has come to a critical juncture in its development. Its future direction is in our hands. Let Africa, once again, be a leading force in steering its direction.

Before I conclude I would like to address the issue of xenophobia and violence against foreign nationals. The South African Government takes any threats of violence against foreign nationals seriously and we have reiterated that no such attacks will be tolerated. This is a message that has been articulated consistently by the leadership of our society in all sectors and spheres: political, civic, religious, labour and business. Last week Government announced a strategy to act in partnership with various organs of civil society to proactively curb and avert the threat of violence against foreign nationals. This strategy includes the extension of the 2010 FIFA World Cup National Joint Committee and the swift policing and justice approach that was witnessed during the World Cup. Law enforcement agencies will not hesitate to act speedily and decisively against anyone found to perpetrate or to incite violent acts against foreign nationals. Other key elements of this strategy include the proactive facilitation of a societal dialogue as well as reinforcing civic education in society and within the law enforcement agencies. This has taken place at various areas around the country comprising of police, churches, community policing fora and NGOs. Communities need to blow the whistle against any criminals that masquerade behind xenophobia. In short, to use the language of football, we have given notice that any manifestation of violence against foreign nationals will be given a massive red card and also that the entire justice, crime prevention and security cluster is ready to ensure that the instigators and perpetrators of such violence are banned from future matches. We wish you a successful conference and express our confidence in your collective ability to contribute to defining a clear vision of the kind of society we wish to become and to play an active role in the realization of that vision: A better Africa in a better World.

I thank you. Nkosi kakhulu. Baie dankie. Ngiyabonga. Ke a leboga. Inkomu. Ndi a livhuwa. Muito obrigado. Merci beaucoup.

Address by Professor Jeanne M. Woods Henry F. Bonura, Jr. Distinguished Professor of Law Loyola College of Law, New Orleans

I am deeply honored to be here, making an intervention at this very timely – one might even call it historic – conference. The last time I was in Johannesburg was 1997, when I was monitoring the Truth and Reconciliation Commission[9] as a representative of the International Association of Democratic Lawyers. It was winter, cold and rainy. I will never forget the very first witness in the very first session I observed. The hearing was held in a bare community center in Gauteng. As the witness began her testimony, I was vaguely aware that the events she described were personally familiar to me. As she continued, I recognized the names and the places; it was a South African commando raid in Gaborone, Botswana, in June 1985.[10] The young woman who was testifying was Busi, the little girl who had been shot in the thigh trying to escape as her grandfather, Mkulu, was murdered.

I was in Gaborone to document South African destabilization of the Frontline States for the United Nations Council for Namibia. Ironically I was almost a victim of that raid myself – I was to interview one of the targets that night – only my ride had not shown up – so I was not in the house when commandos shot into closets, under beds, killing everything that breathed. The realization that I was actually a part – even a remote part – of the tragic story being retold in that cold room was terrifying.

So you can understand that I was not anxious to return to Johannesburg. But thanks to the organizing committee, and especially Vincent Nmehielle, I have had the privilege of walking through this campus among all of these young black faces, smiling from ear to ear. And I am really glad to be back.

9 The Truth and Reconciliation Commission (TRC) was a quasi-judicial body created in South Africa after the abolition of apartheid. Individuals who were victims of human rights violations were allowed to give statements about their experiences. Perpetrators of violence could also testify and request amnesty from prosecution. The speaker served as an international monitor of the South African Truth and Reconciliation Commission from June 2-23, 1997.

10 For a description see Jeanne M. Woods, *Reconciling Reconciliation*, 3 University of Carlifornia Los Angeles Journal of International Law & Foreign Affairs 81, 113 (1998).

I would like to use this opportunity to posit not a definitive position on the weighty matters before this conference, but to pose questions for the body to consider. Our theme essentially calls into question many of the truisms associated with the project of building an international criminal justice regime. Such an inquiry is urgent in light of the momentum that the international criminal justice project has gained since the creation of the Yugoslav and Rwandan Tribunal, the International Criminal Court and the Special Court for Sierra Leone and the ratification of the Rome Treaty creating the International Criminal Court. The problem is whether the project of universal impartial justice is even conceivable in a hegemonic world order undergoing a neoliberal globalization process. Arguably, such a project would not have been undertaken without globalization. And yet, do we even agree on what kind of justice we are asking for? Is it retributive or restorative? Should it be compatible with or irreconcilable with peacemaking? Which approaches will further the goal of human dignity? And – most importantly – who gets to decide?

It is noteworthy that we are meeting here in South Africa, a mere sixteen years after the negotiated end of a centuries-old system of racial oppression – a system that in its legally entrenched, constitutionalized form, was declared a crime against humanity by the international community.[11] Yet there has been scant discussion here of the process that ultimately ended apartheid – a process that included internationally brokered negotiations and constitutionally-entrenched amnesties for politically motivated crimes,[12] amnesties promoted by the United Nations itself.

Thus, a system of institutionalized forced labor, forced removals, denationalization, disenfranchisement, torture, massacres, disappearances, impoverishment, international terrorism and assassinations, and military destabilization, was ended in a process that resulted

11 Apartheid Convention, G.A. Res. 3068 (XXVIII) at 75, U.N. Doc. A/9233 (November 30, 1973).

12 *AZAPO v. President of South Africa*, 1996 (4) SOUTH AFRICAN LAW REVIEW 671 (CC). The families of anti-apartheid activists Steve Biko, Griffiths Mxenge and Fabian Ribeiro argued that the Commission's power to grant amnesty deprived them and an entire class of victims from their right to recover damages from those who committed gross atrocities against their loved ones. The Court ruled that the national unity and reconciliation provision in the Interim Constitution contemplated amnesty in its "most comprehensive and generous meaning." *Id.* at 698. The Interim Constitution provided that "in order to advance such reconciliation and reconstruction, amnesty shall be granted in respect of acts, omissions and offenses associated with political objectives and committed in the course of the conflicts of the past." The Court pointed out that according to the language in the epilogue of the Interim Constitution, "Parliament not only has the authority . . . to make a law providing for amnesty to be granted . . . but . . . is in fact obliged to do so." *Id.* at 683. The Court stated that the Act was established as a means to encourage truth-telling and to "create [. . .] the emotional and structural climate essential for [South Africa's] reconciliation and reconstruction." *Id.* at 684. The Court added that "but for a mechanism providing for amnesty the 'bridge' itself might never have been erected . . . the terms of the transition required not only the agreement of those victimized by abuse but also those threatened by the transition to a "democratic society based on freedom and equality."" *Id.* at 685.

in only token prosecutions. And it has been hailed as a "miracle."[13] And it has been hailed as a "miracle."[14]

Justice in South Africa was defined as "truth": full disclosure of the relevant facts. Truth was enlisted as part of the state-building process in a country whose stability was deemed critical to global capital.

While South Africa's sovereignty was protected, however, sovereignty in other states undergoing civil wars has been superseded by international mechanisms. We should not be under the illusion that such mechanisms are apolitical. These institutions are established in the context of political compromise, where neither opposing side in a civil war has won an outright military and where key figures of the old regime share power, as F.W. DeKlerk did in South Africa. What then, can be the role of human rights discourse where glaring disparities of power and wealth persist after political transformation? Can the discourse be deemed fair and impartial? Even the groundbreaking post-WWII Tribunals that launched the international criminal justice project were tainted by racism, as the Allies refused to persecute Italian forces for war crimes committed against civilian populations in Ethiopia, including widespread use of mustard gas.[15]

Prosecutions were not pursued in Namibia or Zimbabwe, other white minority settler regimes, nor in Mozambique, Angola, or Guinea-Bissau, former Portuguese colonies liberated in the post-post colonial period. So while I must say that I was, and remain, highly critical of the TRC process in South Africa,[16] shouldn't we at least be asking ourselves whether there are any lessons to be learned from this model for the rest of Africa?

While African states were the most supportive bloc for the establishment of an International Criminal Court, much controversy has been generated by the prosecutor's exclusive focus on conflicts in African countries. True, some of these were technically self-referrals, but in a civil war context, is not a "self-referral" outcome-determinative, or at a minimum victors' justice? And what are the long-term implications for Africa of the empowerment

13 Truth and Reconciliation Commission Final Report, Volume 1, p. 5, South Africa (1998). See also David Everatt, Policy Brief: *Yet Another Transition? Urbanisation, Class Formation and the End of the National Liberation Struggle in South Africa*, 1, available at <www.pdf.usaid.gov/pdf_docs/PNACL306.pdf>.

14 Truth and Reconciliation Commission Final Report, Volume 1, p. 5, South Africa (1998). See also, Everatt, *supra* note 5, at 1.

15 Richard Pankhurst, *Italian Fascist War Crimes in Ethiopia: A History of their Discussion from the League of Nations to the United Nations* (1936-1949), 6 NORTHEAST AFRICAN STUDIES 83, 84 (1999), citing A. Gingold Duprey, *De l'invasion à la libération de l'Ethiopie*, Paris (1955), 340, 365-6, 572, 596, 627, 630-1, 647-52. Available at <http://muse.jhu.edu/journals/northeast_african_studies/v006/6.1pankhurst.html>.

16 See Woods, *supra* note 2 at 81.

of a permanent judicial criminal mechanism in the political context of neo-liberal globalization? Africa has been the subject of two prior globalizations: the trans-Atlantic slave trade from the 15th-19th centuries, and the global economic expansion dating from approximately 1870-1914 – the first Scramble for Africa. Neo-liberal globalization means the following:

- The further erosion of the already emaciated states' power to protect and provide for the welfare of their people. State authority has been forcibly transferred to
    1. International financial institutions and their most powerful Member States;
    2. Transnational corporations;
    3. International investors and banks;
    4. A variety of non-state actors, including private contractors, international NGOs, rebel groups, militias, and mercenaries.
- Neo-liberal globalization means a new Scramble for Africa's wealth and resources. This involves traditional booty such as diamonds and gold, old and new strategic and economic minerals. The Scramble has recently been intensified by the discovery of oil and gas deposits across the Continent, fueling conflicts of incredible brutality.[17]
- Globalization means for Africa a process of economic and political destabilization that invites foreign military intervention under the guise of the failed state doctrine, the war on terror, and, perhaps, enforcement of the arrest warrants of the International Criminal Court.

Is the Nuremberg paradigm of individual accountability the only, or the best, route to post-conflict justice? To what extent does the liberal paradigm of individual responsibility – whether under a reconciliation or prosecution model – obscure systemic, structural crimes like apartheid, occupation, colonialism, or the neo-liberal global trade regime? Indeed, might it be said that the Rome Statute itself reflects a form of victors' justice in the crimes it chose to codify?

Why isn't production of weapons of mass destruction, including nuclear weapons, a crime against humanity under the Statute? What about arms trafficking to conflict areas? Trade in conflict minerals? Recruitment of former child soldiers by private contractors? Is the ICC's legitimacy, and hence its efficacy, irreparably undermined as long as nationals of powerful States remain off-limits to the Court's jurisdiction, while the elite, undemocratic, and highly politicized Security Council can haul in non-parties to the Rome Statute?

---

17 Africa Policy Institute Background Paper, *The 21st Century Global Scramble for Africa and the Recession: Implications for Africa's Security and Democratic Crisis*, available at <www.africapi.org/.../BACKGROUND%20PAPER%20SCRAMBLE%20FOR%20AFRICA>.

Although the U.S. is not a party to the Rome Statute, the Legal Advisor to the United States Department of State led a delegation to the ICC Review Conference in Kampala. Reportedly the Obama Administration is considering a request from Prosecutor Luis Ocampo to deploy AFRICOM – the U.S. military command for Africa – to "assist" in the enforcement of ICC warrants.[18] As Harold Koh reportedly stated, the U.S., while still unwilling to become a party to the Rome Treaty, would cooperate with the ICC when it is in the interest of the U.S. to do so.[19] AFRICOM's genesis can be traced to a December 2000 CIA report in which analysts speculated about the future supply of African oil. In his May 2001 Report on U.S. energy policy, former Vice-President Richard Cheney highlighted the new significance of African oil for U.S. markets.[20] Eight months later, the Institute for Advanced Strategic and Political Studies (IASPS), a neoconservative think-tank based in Israel,[21] held a symposium in Washington, D.C. entitled "African Oil: A Priority for U.S. National Security and African Development." Speakers included U.S. diplomatic and intelligence officials, members of Congress, and energy industry executives. The symposium spawned a working group, the African Oil Policy Initiative Group (AOPIG), which issued recommendations for U.S. policy.

Asserting a convergence of U.S. energy security interests and African economic development goals, the Group proposed an "historic, strategic alignment with West Africa," with the Gulf of Guinea emerging as a "vital U.S. interest." The goal is a U.S.-West Africa relationship defined by: 1) a focus on U.S. military engagement in sub-Saharan Africa; 2) large scale U.S. capital investment in regional oil and gas infrastructure projects; 3) creation of a U.S.-Africa free trade agreement; and 4) conditioning debt forgiveness upon free market reforms in critical sectors.[22]

In 2002, the Bush Administration's National Security Strategy, in which the doctrine of preemptive military action was announced, asserted that Africa's "disease, war, and desperate poverty" threatens a U.S. strategic priority: "combating global terror."[23] A senior

18 Samar Al-Bulushi & Adam Branch, AFRICOM and the ICC: Enforcing International Justice in Africa? PAMBAZUKA NEWS, Issue 483, posted May 27, 2010, available at <http://pambazuka.org/en/category/features/64752>.

19 Harold H. Koh and Stephen J. Rapp. *US Engagement with the International Criminal Court and the outcome of the Recently Concluded Review Conference*, US Department of State, June 15, 2010. Available at <www.state.gov/s/wci/us_releases/remarks/143178.htm>.

20 National Energy Policy Report, Office of Vice President Richard Cheney, May 16, 2001.

21 According to the website of the IASPS, its mission is to save Western society from the "convergence of Western Elites and Islam." See <www.iasps.org/mission.php>, (last accessed September 28, 2007).

22 Report of the African Oil Initiative Policy Group, at 18. <www.iasps.org/strategic/africanwhitepaper.pdf> (last accessed November 10, 2007).

23 The National Security Strategy of the United States of America (2002) p. 7, available at <www.whitehouse.gov/nsc/nssall.html> (last accessed November 10, 2007).

Defense Department official reportedly commented in 2003 that "a key mission for U.S. forces (in Africa) would be to ensure that Nigeria's oil fields . . . are secure."[24] In 2004 a Congressionally-appointed panel proposed a "conceptual shift to a strategic view of Africa."[25] The Administration's 2006 National Security Strategy identifies Africa as "a high priority" and – in a resurrection of the doctrine of *terra nullius* – "recognizes that [U.S.] security depends upon . . . strengthening fragile and failing states and bring[ing] ungoverned areas under the control of effective democracies."[26] In February 2007, President Bush announced the formation of AFRICOM,[27] a new unified combatant command to "protect U.S. national security objectives in Africa and its surrounding waters,"[28] and to promote "peace . . . development, health, education, democracy, and economic growth in Africa."[29] Will AFRICOM further peace and justice in Africa? Far-away proceedings in The Hague, or an expensive show-trial in Sierra-Leone? Is impunity the only alternative?

If Africa is ever to determine its own destiny, Africa must build its own institutions, tailored to its own history and realities, as slow and as painful a process as this might be. There are some efforts underway under the authority of the African Union, ECOWAS, and other fledgling institutions. These institutions and independent entities must be strengthened. Moreover, vigorous conflict resolution will require the legal and political empowerment of minority sub-State groups so that they have a stake in peace. Some of these measures might include:

- Equitable resource distribution;
- Reconsideration of the Cairo Declaration;
- Consideration of the value of international legal personality for sub-State groups subject to their willingness to lay down arms;
- Experimenting with various forms of autonomy;
- Elevation of respect for language and other cultural rights.

---

24 Greg Jaffe, "In Massive Shift, U.S. is Planning to Cut Size of Military in Germany", WALL STREET JOURNAL, June 10, 2003.

25 Walter H. Kansteiner III and J. Stephen Morrison, *Rising U.S. Stakes in Africa: Seven Proposals to Strengthen U.S.-Africa Policy*, May 2004, available at <www.allafrica.com/sustainable/resources/view/00010230.pdf> (last accessed November 10, 2007).

26 The National Security Strategy of the United States of America (2006) p. 37, available at <www. whitehouse. gov/nsc/nss/2006/> (last accessed November 10, 2007).

27 The White House Office of the Press Secretary, "President Bush Creates a Department of Defense Unified Combatant Command for Africa", February 6, 2007.

28 CONGRESSIONAL RESEARCH SERVICE, AFRICA COMMAND: U.S. STRATEGIC INTERESTS AND THE ROLE OF THE U.S. MILITARY IN AFRICA (SUMMARY), July 6, 2007.

29 White House Press Statement, *supra* note 30.

At the same time, Africa's friends in the West must continue to fight for the right of Africa to control and use its own resources for the well-being and advancement of her people, and for the building of Afro-centric institutions that use Africa's rich history and traditions to solve Africa's problems.

Thank you.

Index

B

J

O

P

Q

R